Mott current ed,
GRL
12/2013

D1257047

United States Presidential Primary Elections

2000–2004

United States Presidential Primary Elections

2000–2004

A Handbook of Election Statistics

RHODES COOK

CQ PRESS

A Division of Congressional Quarterly Inc.
Washington, D.C.

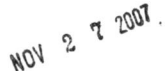
CQ Press
1255 22nd Street, NW, Suite 400
Washington, DC 20037

Phone: 202-729-1900; toll-free, 1-866-4CQ-PRESS (1-866-427-7737)

Web: www.cqpress.com

Cover design: Karen Rasmussen, Archeographics

⊗ The paper used in this publication exceeds the requirements of the American National Standard for Information Sciences—Permanence of Paper for Printed Library Materials, ANSI Z39.48-1992.

Printed and bound in the United States of America

10 09 08 07 06   1 2 3 4 5

The Library of Congress CIP data is available under
Library of Congress Control Number 2006051826.

ISBN 10: 0-87289-328-6
ISBN 13: 978-0-87289-328-6

CONTENTS

Preface   vii

Introduction   1
  Growth of Presidential
    Primaries   9
  Presidential Primary
    Winners by State   11
  National Primary Maps and
    Vote Summaries   15

Alabama   38
Alaska   49
Arizona   51
Arkansas   55
California   66
Colorado   76
Connecticut   81
Delaware   90
Florida   93
Georgia   102
Hawaii   117
Idaho   119
Illinois   126
Indiana   137
Iowa   146
Kansas   152
Kentucky   154
Louisiana   168
Maine   177
Maryland   185
Massachusetts   191

Michigan   202
Minnesota   207
Mississippi   210
Missouri   219
Montana   233
Nebraska   241
Nevada   249
New Hampshire   252
New Jersey   263
New Mexico   269
New York   274
North Carolina   282
North Dakota   290
Ohio   292
Oklahoma   301
Oregon   311
Pennsylvania   318
Rhode Island   327
South Carolina   336
South Dakota   341
Tennessee   348
Texas   358
Utah   385
Vermont   390
Virginia   399
Washington   407
West Virginia   412
Wisconsin   419
Wyoming   430
District of Columbia   432

PREFACE

United States Presidential Primary Elections, 2000–2004 is the second volume in a series presenting the official, county-by-county results for all contested Democratic and Republican presidential primary elections since 1968. The first volume, published in 2000, covered primary elections from 1968 through 1996.

Presidential primaries have been a part of the nominating process since the early twentieth century, but for more than a half century, they were comparatively few in number and played only an advisory role in the process. That began to change in 1968, a transition year in presidential politics that marked the last hurrah for the era of the convention as the decisive stage of the nominating process and the launch of the current period in which millions of voters in the myriad primary states decide their party's nominees.

The number of primaries grew rapidly after 1968, producing a new dynamic in presidential nominating politics requiring that candidates compete in and win them. Without exception, nominations over the last generation have been decided by primaries.

The layout of this book closely follows the first volume's. The introduction explains the evolution of the presidential nominating process to its present form. Particular emphasis is paid to more recent years, during which voters in early-voting states became kingmakers. At the end of the introduction, summary tables list the Democratic and Republican primary winners by state since 1976. These are followed by a one-page overview of each Democratic and Republican presidential nominating contest since 1968 that features a national map illustrating the primary winners in each state, a synopsis of the campaign, and a box of nationwide vote data for the leading candidates.

The heart of the book is an arrangement of the presidential primary results alphabetically by state. Each state's section begins with a brief essay that highlights the recent history of its presidential nominating process. References to various counties illustrate the political geography and internal voting patterns of the state and provide context to the county-by-county vote tables that follow. A table summarizing the state's presidential primary results since 1968 accompanies the essay. It cites the turnout for each Democratic and Republican primary along with the vote share for all candidates who received at least 5 percent of their party's primary vote. Each state section also includes a map showing counties and major population centers.

Following this overview material are year-by-year tables of presidential primary returns, broken down by county in every state except Massachusetts and by major cities and towns in all the New England states, including Massachusetts. For much of New England, more emphasis is placed on results from cities and towns than counties.

Democratic results are listed first for each year; Republican results follow. Included in the county tables are all candidates who won at least 5 percent of the primary vote—a change from 10 percent in the first volume—as well as those who received less than 5 percent but were the only other candidate on the ballot. The names of candidates are listed in alphabetical order.

United States Presidential Primary Elections, 2000–2004 includes roughly 150 county tables for 43 states. Only Alaska,

Hawaii, Iowa, Kansas, Minnesota, Nevada, North Dakota, and Wyoming did not hold a presidential primary in 2000 or 2004. Iowa Republicans, however, compile their caucus results like a primary vote, and the results for 2000 (when there was an active contest for the GOP nomination) are included because of the importance of Iowa in the nominating process.

Presidential primaries come in various forms. Most states have presidential preference primaries, which produce a direct vote for candidates. A few states, however, focus on the election of delegates and do not hold a direct vote for the candidates themselves. Most presidential primaries elect or allocate delegates, the coin of the realm in the nominating process, but some do not, acting instead as nonbinding "beauty contests" that measure the popularity of candidates without electing delegates.

Tables are included for every presidential primary in 2000 and 2004, with the exception of those for which no major candidates appeared on the ballot (such as the 2000 Michigan Democratic primary, which pitted Lyndon H. LaRouche Jr. against an "Uncommitted" line) or primaries in which a candidate ran unopposed and, at most, a small number of scattered write-ins were the only other votes cast. This was a common occurrence in the 2004 Republican primaries, as President George W. Bush cruised to renomination without significant opposition.

The county tables are based on official returns from the states, although the numbers in a few tables do not add up to the certified totals. In the case of discrepancies, both sets of totals are listed at the end of the table. The numbers certified by the state are used in other summary tables unless they are clearly erroneous. Individual county votes are reported as certified, even in the few cases where the results may appear suspect.

Like the first volume published a half dozen years ago, this book was a labor of love. As with any book this size, it was also labor. It would not have been possible without the assistance of state election boards across the country, who were invariably helpful in providing needed material.

Thanks also are in order to the staff at CQ Press, particularly development editor David Arthur, who with persistence and good humor pushed this project to completion. As always, a special debt of gratitude is owed my wife, Memrie McKay-Cook, whose support and forbearance continue not only to be deeply appreciated but vitally important to the completion of major projects such as this.

Rhodes Cook

United States Presidential Primary Elections

2000–2004

INTRODUCTION

The national conventions may be the culmination of the presidential nominating process, but it is in the presidential primaries months earlier where the Democratic and Republican nominations are actually decided.

At least that has been the case now for several decades, since the Democrats' tumultuous convention in Chicago in 1968 encouraged both parties—but the Democrats in particular—to look for ways to open the presidential nominating process to greater grass-roots participation.

The result was an explosive growth in presidential primaries—from 15 in 1968, to 36 in 1980, to more than 40 in 1996 and 2000. The number of primaries in 2004 dropped slightly to 38, including the District of Columbia, but they were still the preferred method of delegate selection in nearly three-fourths of the states.

As the number of primaries grew, power in the nominating process quickly shifted from party kingmakers at the national conventions to voters in the primary states. And it has stayed that way.

Long gone are the days when candidates could win their party's nomination without entering the primaries. No Democratic or Republican nominee has done so since Hubert Humphrey in 1968.

And long gone are the days when candidates could be nominated without first proving broad-based popularity among millions of their party's primary voters. Since Democrat George McGovern in 1972, every major-party nominee has been their party's highest vote-getter in the primaries.

In the process, the once climactic conventions have become little more than giant pep rallies, ratifying the choices of Democratic and Republican primary voters made months earlier.

Front-Loaded Process

In recent years, the nominations have been settled earlier and earlier, as more and more states have moved their primaries forward to dates near the beginning of the election year in a bid to heighten their influence (a process that is known as "front-loading.")

In 1968, only the New Hampshire primary was held before the end of March. In 1980, 10 states held primaries so early. By 1988, the number surpassed 20, and by 2004, two dozen primaries had been held by the ides of March.

The result in recent years has been an increasingly truncated nominating process, with the meaningful portion growing shorter and shorter. Early votes in Iowa and New Hampshire have tended to winnow the field to a handful of candidates. Then, after a short period of unpredictability, one candidate has scored a knockout in the glut of March primaries, with their victory ratified by a string of votes at the end of the nominating process.

That is what happened in 1992. The first five Democratic primaries that year produced four different winners. But Bill Clinton broke from the pack with a sweep of the early March primaries in his native South and ended up winning all but two of the primaries that followed.

The story was similar on the Republican side in 2000. George W. Bush struggled through a series of primary contests scattered across the opening weeks of the nominating process, losing almost as many as he won. But once the calendar flipped

Primary Wins Bring Convention Success

No candidate since Hubert Humphrey in 1968 has won the nomination of a major party without first entering its presidential primaries. And no candidate since George McGovern in 1972 has won the Democratic or Republican nomination without being the top vote-getter in his party's primaries; Humphrey won more votes in the Democratic primaries that year.

The chart below compares each nominee's share of his party's primary vote with the share of the delegate votes he won on the first ballot at his party's convention; not since 1952 has a convention taken more than one ballot to settle a presidential nomination. An asterisk (*) indicates an incumbent president.

	DEMOCRATS			REPUBLICANS		
Election Year	Nominee	% of Primary Vote	% of Convention Vote	Nominee	% of Primary Vote	% of Convention Vote
1968	Hubert Humphrey	2	67	Richard Nixon	38	52
1972	George McGovern	25	57	Richard Nixon*	92	99.9
1976	Jimmy Carter	39	74	Gerald Ford*	53	53
1980	Jimmy Carter*	51	64	Ronald Reagan	61	97
1984	Walter Mondale	38	56	Ronald Reagan*	99	99.9
1988	Michael Dukakis	43	69	George Bush	68	100
1992	Bill Clinton	52	79	George Bush*	72	99
1996	Bill Clinton*	89	99.7	Bob Dole	59	97
2000	Al Gore	76	100	George W. Bush	63	100
2004	John Kerry	61	98	George W. Bush*	98	100

to March and the primaries began to be held in large clusters, Bush's advantages of widespread party support, a large campaign chest, and high name recognition kicked in. Bush lost a handful of New England primaries in early March to his principal rival, John McCain. But Bush won everywhere else and drove McCain from the race before the middle of March.

In 2004, the Democratic nomination was determined at an even faster pace. John Kerry scored clear-cut victories in Iowa and New Hampshire, then cruised to nomination with barely a bump. He won seven of the nine primaries that took place in February, and eight of the nine primaries held on the first Tuesday of March (a nationwide votefest that has become known as "Super Tuesday"). By that evening, his last major rival for the Democratic nomination, John Edwards, had conceded.

Neither party has had an elongated tug-of-war since 1984, when Walter Mondale and Gary Hart battled for the Democratic nomination into the final week of the primary season. And neither party has had a nominating contest that was even vaguely competitive by the time of its national convention since the 1976 Republican race between President Gerald R. Ford and Ronald Reagan.

Starting Points

Even though much of the primary calendar has changed dramatically over the last few decades, the accepted starting points have remained Iowa and New Hampshire (even though other states have occasionally voted before them), with Iowa voting first and new Hampshire eight days later.

Both states have made their early events into cottage industries, but the candidates and the media have helped make them so. More than ever, Iowa and New Hampshire are about the only places left where candidates have some control over their destinies. They can woo voters one-on-one, whether in bowling alleys, coffee shops, or the frequent gatherings in neighborhood living rooms.

For if there is one thing that has become certain in recent years, once this opening round of voting is over, there is a frenetic burst of tarmac-to-tarmac campaigning heavily dependent on media advertising.

Occasionally, candidates have tried to skip Iowa or New Hampshire, or both, and launch their campaigns on terrain more to their choosing. But that streak of independence has not been beneficial for the candidate that tries it. Even skipping Iowa and starting in New Hampshire can be risky. McCain pulled it off in 2000, with a victory in New Hampshire after bypassing Iowa. But the Arizona senator is a rarity in making such a selective strategy succeed.

With one exception, every presidential nominee since 1976 has won either Iowa or New Hampshire, and finished no lower than third in the other. The exception was Clinton in 1992, who did not seriously contest Iowa in deference to the home-state appeal of Sen. Tom Harkin and finished second in New Hampshire behind former senator Paul Tsongas of neighboring Massachusetts.

The two states illustrate the two different types of delegate-selection processes that states basically have to choose from.

Iowa is a caucus. New Hampshire is a primary. Primaries require voters only to cast a ballot, an exercise that usually takes just a few minutes. The deliberative nature of a neighborhood caucus, though, often requires the commitment of an afternoon or evening.

There is an additional option of delegate selection in the form of a party-run primary. It is run by the state Democratic or Republican party, rather than state election officials, and follows the same form as a primary, but usually with fewer polling places and shorter hours. In some states, party officials call such an event a primary; in others, a caucus, even though it is not an Iowa-style deliberative affair at all. In 2004, Democrats had four party-run primaries. Those in South Carolina and Utah were called primaries by the state Democratic leadership. Those in Michigan and New Mexico were termed caucuses.

A Small Slice of the Electorate

Voter turnout is usually much higher in a primary than a caucus, but even in primaries the turnout is much lower than a general election. In New Hampshire, for instance, where interest in the presidential primary is probably greater than any other state, less than 300,000 voters turned out in January 2004 for the presidential primary, while more than 675,000 cast ballots in the presidential election that fall.

The disparity is much greater in many other states. When both parties last held competitive nominating contests in the same year (2000), barely 31 million votes were cast in the presidential primaries—roughly 17 million on the Republican side, 14 million on the Democratic. Activity in the handful of states that held caucuses involved several hundred thousand more voters. And better than 2 million voters (mainly in California and Washington) cast ballots outside the Democratic and Republican primaries.

By comparison, more than 105 million voters turned out for the November general election that year, roughly three times the number that took part in the nominating process. In 2004, the disparity between general election and primary participation was even greater, more in the order of 5 to 1, as the November vote went way up (to more than 122 million) while the primary vote went way down (to barely 24 million) with the absence of a competitive contest for the Republican nomination.

Rules governing voter participation play a role in the comparatively low turnouts for the nominating process. Every

Presidential Primary Turnouts Since 1968

From the inception of presidential primaries in 1912 through 1968, there were never more than 20 primaries in one year. But since then, the number of presidential primaries has grown steadily to the point that since 1988 at least 36 states plus the District of Columbia have held them each election.

The most votes cast in the presidential primaries came in 1988 when turnout exceeded 35 million. Nearly 23 million voters participated in the Democratic presidential primaries in 1988, the most for one party in any election before or since. The Republican high was in 2000, when more than 17 million ballots were cast in the GOP primaries.

Through much of the first half of the twentieth century, starting with the contest between former president Theodore Roosevelt and President William Howard Taft in 1912, more votes were cast in Republican presidential primaries than Democratic. But that has not been the case since then. Republicans had a higher turnout only three times—in 1952, when Dwight D. Eisenhower and Robert Taft had a vigorous contest for the GOP nomination; in 1996, when President Bill Clinton ran virtually unopposed for the Democratic nomination; and in 2000, when George W. Bush and John McCain aroused considerable voter interest in their battle for the Republican nomination.

Year	Number of States Holding Primaries	Democratic Vote	Republican Vote	Total Vote
1968	14 and D.C.	7,535,069	4,473,551	12,008,620
1972	20 and D.C.	15,993,965	6,188,281	22,182,246
1976	26 and D.C.	16,052,652	10,374,125	26,426,777
1980	35 and D.C.	18,747,825	12,690,451	31,438,276
1984	29 and D.C.	18,009,192	6,575,651	24,584,843
1988	36 and D.C.	22,961,936	12,165,115	35,127,051
1992	38 and D.C.	20,239,385	12,696,547	32,935,932
1996	41 and D.C.	10,947,364	13,991,649	24,939,013
2000	42 and D.C.	14,048,951	17,157,075	31,206,026
2004	37 and D.C.	16,182,439	7,940,331	24,122,770

Note: The number of primary states is those in which at least one of the major parties held a primary that allowed a direct vote for presidential candidates or produced an aggregated statewide vote for delegates. The vote tally does not include the 1996 and 2000 New York Republican primaries for the election of delegates only.

The Electorate: Primaries and General

It is often said that Republican primary voters are more conservative and that Democratic primary voters are more liberal than the electorate as a whole.

If true, it is due to the basic fact that only a fraction of those who participate in the November general election participate in the presidential nominating process. That was particularly true in 2004, when the number of votes cast in the Democratic and Republican presidential primaries was the lowest since 1972, when there were barely half as many primaries as 2004.

Following is a comparison of the vote in presidential primaries with those in general elections since 1968.

The number of primaries includes those where at least one of the major parties featured a vote for presidential candidates, or there was an aggregated statewide vote for delegates. The total number includes the District of Columbia.

The total primary vote includes both Democratic and Republican primaries. Not included is the voter turnout for primaries for delegates only such as that held by New York Republicans in 1996 and 2000 or for nonprimary states where caucuses were held. The latter usually does not produce more than several hundred thousand votes for both parties combined in an election year.

Year	Presidential Primaries	Voter Turnout		Primary Vote as Percent of General Election Vote
		Primaries	General Election	
1968	15	12,008,620	73,211,875	16.4
1972	21	22,182,246	77,718,554	28.5
1976	27	26,426,777	81,555,889	32.4
1980	36	31,438,276	86,515,221	36.3
1984	30	24,584,843	92,652,842	26.5
1988	37	35,127,051	91,594,809	38.4
1992	39	32,935,932	104,425,014	31.5
1996	42	24,939,013	96,277,872	25.9
2000	43	31,206,026	105,396,627	29.6
2004	38	24,122,770	122,295,345	19.7

primary is not as open as a general election, where any registered voter can participate. A number of states limit participation to registered Democratic and Republican voters. Some others allow independents to participate, but list them on the voting rolls afterward as members of the party in which they cast their primary ballot.

Still, the vast majority of registered voters across the country can participate in a presidential primary or caucus if they want. The fact that more do not has generated the conventional wisdom that the nominating process is dominated by ideological activists—liberals on the Democratic side, conservatives on the Republican.

That is debatable in the primaries, where the winners in recent years have been from the mainstreams of both parties. An ideological bent is more evident in the low-turnout world of the caucuses, where a small cadre of dedicated voters can dominate the outcome.

When religious broadcaster Pat Robertson tried for the Republican presidential nomination in 1988, for instance, he won first-round caucus voting in three states and finished second in three others, including Iowa. But Robertson did not come close that year to winning a presidential primary. Similarly, the anti–Iraq war candidacy of Dennis Kucinich in 2004 barely registered a blip in the Democratic primaries. But in the caucuses, the Ohio congressman's passionate band of supporters

was able to wield more influence, surpassing 25 percent of the vote in both Alaska and Hawaii, and reaching double digits percentage-wise in a number of other caucus states.

Primary Clues

It has been a matter of debate within the political community whether the current primary-dominated nominating process is better than the old system, in which party leaders controlled the selection process.

But it is a fact that the increased number of primaries helps provide valuable clues about the vote-getting potential of candidates in the general election. Nominees that have exhibited broad-based appeal among the diverse array of primary voters in the winter and spring have gone on to be quite competitive in the fall, while those nominees who have struggled through the primaries showing limited appeal among one or two of their party's major constituency groups have usually been buried under landslides in November.

A less reliable indicator of what will happen in the fall is the number of votes cast in each party's primaries. In every year but three from 1952 through 2004—1952, 1996, and 2000 being the exceptions—more ballots were cast in Democratic than Republican primaries. In part, it was due to the simple fact that through much of this period, Democrats outnumbered Republicans.

But it also reflected the fact that the Democratic primaries drew more voter interest because they often exhibited more conflict between competing constituencies within the party. That kind of political drama and angst was good for primary turnout, but not for the party's chances in the fall elections, as Republicans won most of the presidential contests in this period.

One Election: Two Systems

The quadrennial process of electing a president has two distinct parts—the nominating process and the general election. The latter is straightforward: a one-day nationwide vote on the first Tuesday after the first Monday in November between the Democratic and Republican nominees and any independent and third-party candidates that have met the various state ballot requirements. All registered voters may participate in the general election and the winner is the candidate that wins a majority of the state electoral votes.

By contrast, the presidential nominating process can seem like Alice in Wonderland. Primaries and caucuses are scattered across the calendar from January to June, culminating with party conventions in the summer. A nomination is won by a candidate attaining a majority of delegates, an honor which is formally bestowed at the conventions but in recent years has informally occurred months earlier during the primary season.

Size is less important in determining a state's importance in the nominating process than its tradition and place on the calendar. Hence, the quadrennial starring roles for Iowa and New Hampshire, and the bit parts frequently handed out to California, Texas, and New York.

States have different ground rules in the nominating process. Some have caucuses, many more have primaries. Most primaries allocate a state's delegates, but in a few cases primaries may be nonbinding "beauty contests." And rules on voter participation can vary from state to state.

The parties themselves also have different playing fields. Democrats require states to distribute delegates among the candidates in proportion to their vote, statewide and in congressional districts, with 15 percent required to win a share. Republicans allow a variety of allocation systems, including winner-take-all, where the top vote-getter in a state is awarded all the delegates.

Democrats reserve nearly 20 percent of their delegate seats for high-level party and elected officials (such as Democratic governors, members of Congress, and members of the party's national committee), who are free agents and do not have to declare a presidential preference.

Then, there is the business of campaign financing. In the wake of the Watergate scandal, a system of public financing was instituted in 1976. Participation is optional for candidates in the nominating process. Those who opt to take part must raise much of their money in small chunks and have it matched by federal funds up to a certain amount in exchange for acceptance of spending limits.

Over the years, most candidates have participated in the system, although recently it has begun to show cracks. Bush in 2000 and both Bush and Kerry in 2004 conspicuously did not participate and spent as much as they could raise before their party's convention. In 2004, that was approximately $250 million apiece. The fund raising by the Bush and Kerry camps during the long nominating period became so competitive that Kerry considered delaying his formal acceptance of the Democratic nomination beyond his party's late July convention. Since the convention is considered the end of each party's nominating period, and the Republican convention did not begin until late August, the unusual move would have allowed Kerry to continue to match Bush in raising and spending money before the stricter general election rules on public financing kicked in. Ultimately, though, Kerry rejected the idea.

An Evolutionary Process

If there is a basic difference between the nominating process and the general election, it is that the latter is generally static in form while the former is constantly changing.

During the early years of the Republic, presidential nominations were decided by party caucuses in Congress (derided by their critics as "King Caucus"). At the dawn of the Jacksonian era in the 1830s, though, the nominating role shifted to national conventions, a broader-based venue where party leaders from around the country held sway.

In the early twentieth century, presidential primaries appeared on the scene, adding a new element of grass-roots democracy and voter input. But for the next half century, the primaries were relatively few in number and played a limited advisory role. Nominations continued to be decided in the party conventions.

Yet after World War II, as the society became more mobile and media oriented, and once-powerful party organizations began to lose their clout, more presidential aspirants saw the primaries as a way to generate popular support that might overcome the resistance of party leaders. Both Dwight D. Eisenhower in 1952 and John F. Kennedy in 1960 scored a string of primary victories that demonstrated their vote-getting appeal and made their nominations possible.

The conventions continued to reign supreme through the 1960s, although 1968 proved to be a watershed year in the evolution of the nominating process. Eugene McCarthy and Robert F. Kennedy used the handful of Democratic primaries that spring to protest the war in Vietnam, with the two senators together taking more than two-thirds of the party's primary vote and driving President Lyndon B. Johnson from the race.

History might have been different if Kennedy had not been gunned down after his victory in the California primary in June. But without Kennedy on the scene, the party's embattled leadership was able to maintain a tenuous control of the

Presidential Primaries: A Brief History

1912: The first presidential primaries are held in 13 states. Most votes are cast in the Republican contests, nine of them won by former president Theodore Roosevelt. But President William Howard Taft retains control of the party machinery and wins renomination at the GOP convention. In his annual message the following year, President Woodrow Wilson includes a call for the overhaul of the nominating process so primaries across the country would determine each party's presidential nominee.

1916: The number of presidential primaries grows to twenty, before declining once the Progressive era is over. It the largest number of primaries until the 1970s.

1924: Democrats nominate John W. Davis on the one-hundred-third ballot to culminate the longest convention ever held. In what was normal for the period, Davis had not competed in any of the presidential primaries.

1944: Wendell Willkie, the GOP's dark-horse nominee in 1940, tries to mount a comeback in 1944 in the Republican presidential primaries. Willkie's distant fourth-place finish in Wisconsin, though, dashes his presidential ambitions.

1948: New York governor Thomas E. Dewey and former Minnesota governor Harold E. Stassen go head-to-head in the Oregon GOP primary, the high point of which is a coast-to-coast radio debate on the question of whether the Communist Party should be outlawed in the United States. Dewey wins the primary over Stassen by barely 10,000 votes and goes on to win the Republican nomination.

1952: Former general Dwight D. Eisenhower uses the Republican presidential primaries to demonstrate his broad vote-getting appeal to party leaders. Eisenhower wins the newly important, first-in-the-nation New Hampshire primary over Ohio senator Robert A. Taft and goes on to win the GOP nomination. Sen. Estes Kefauver of Tennessee also follows the primary route on the Democratic side. But Illinois governor Adlai E. Stevenson wins the Democratic nomination on the third ballot, the last time that any major-party convention takes more than a single roll call to decide its presidential nomination.

1960: Sen. John F. Kennedy of Massachusetts enters the Democratic primaries to show his electability. Kennedy scores a pivotal primary victory in heavily Protestant West Virginia that demonstrates his Catholicism is not a disqualifying liability.

1968: Vice President Hubert H. Humphrey becomes the last presidential candidate to win a major party nomination without entering the presidential primaries. Humphrey is nominated at a tumultuous Democratic convention in Chicago, where delegates approve a review of the party's nominating rules that would ensure a more open process in the future.

1972: Democratic rules reforms encourage more grass-roots participation in the presidential nominating process, with a growth in primaries one result. Sen. George McGovern of South Dakota, who headed the party's rules commission for a time, mounts a long-shot, anti–Vietnam War candidacy that wins the Democratic nomination. McGovern, though, is the last nominee of either party not to win at least a plurality of his party's primary vote.

1976: The presidential nominating process continues to evolve quickly. For the first time, a majority of states hold presidential primaries. For the first time, public money is made available to candidates through a system of matching federal funds. And for the first time, Democrats ban statewide winner-take-all primaries, used for years in California. (Republicans continue to allow winner-take-all contests.)

1980: After winning some attention but no victories, Rep. John B. Anderson of Illinois quits the Republican primaries, bolts the party, and runs as an independent presidential candidate in the fall campaign. He follows in the footsteps of Theodore Roosevelt, who after losing the Republican nomination in 1912, left the GOP to run on the Progressive Party ticket.

1984: Democrats create a large new category of delegates for party and elected officials that prove to be a key component in former vice president Walter F. Mondale's successful bid for the Democratic nomination. The new category comes to be known as "superdelegates."

1988: Super Tuesday is at its zenith. All the Southern states except South Carolina hold primaries on the second Tuesday in March. Vice President George Bush sweeps the Republican voting and essentially wraps up the GOP nomination. The Democratic results are more muddled. Rev. Jesse Jackson, Sen. Al Gore of Tennessee, and the eventual nominee, Massachusetts governor Michael S. Dukakis, all win primaries in the South.

1996: For the first time, the number of states holding presidential primaries breaks forty, more than two-thirds of which are held before the end of March.

Seeking to unclog the "front-loaded" primary calendar, the Republican convention approves awarding bonus delegates in 2000 to states that vote after the ides of March.

2000: George W. Bush becomes the first presidential candidate to decline public financing and go on and win his party's nomination. Bush spends roughly $100 million, a record up to that time.

2004: Both presidential nominees, Democrat John Kerry and Republican George W. Bush, turn down public funds and spend roughly $250 million each, much of it in the late spring and summer when the general election phase of the campaign was essentially under way. Technically, the nominating phase was longer than ever. For the first time, both Iowa and New Hampshire held their events in January. And for the first time, a major party convention spilled over into September, with the Republican gathering in New York concluding on Sept. 2.

convention that August in Chicago, nominating Vice President Humphrey, who had not competed in any primary state.

But Humphrey's nomination came at a price. For the first time in several generations, the legitimacy of the convention itself was thrown into question. And as an outgrowth, a series of Democratic rules review commissions began to overhaul the presidential nominating process to encourage much greater grass-roots participation.

Change Comes Rapidly

The immediate result was a dramatic increase in presidential primaries that enhanced the chances of long-shot outsiders, such as George McGovern and Jimmy Carter, who captured the Democratic nomination in 1972 and 1976, respectively.

In the 1970s, the primary season started slowly, giving little-known candidates the time to raise money and momentum after doing well in the early events. Most of the primaries then were held in May and June.

But the layout of the nominating process has been less favorable to dark horses since then. In the 1980s, Democrats reinserted party and elected officials into the process, creating a new category of automatic delegate seats for them that have come to be known as "superdelegates."

And states began to move their events forward on the calendar in a bid to increase their influence. Democrats sought to put a brake on the calendar sprawl toward New Year's Day by instituting the "window," which prohibited any of the party's primaries or caucuses from being held before early March, with the exception of Iowa, New Hampshire, and for a time, Maine.

With the creation of that early March firewall, many states parked their primary in March—gradually at first, but then in tidal wave proportions in 1988, with the creation of a full-scale primary vote across the South on the second Tuesday in March that came to be known as "Super Tuesday."

The event did not have the effect that its Democratic sponsors had hoped for, in terms of steering the nomination toward a centrist son of the South, such as then-senator Al Gore of Tennessee. And in the 1990s, the early March Southern primary lost some of its members.

But the concept of early regional primaries took hold elsewhere. In 1996, all of New England except New Hampshire voted on the first Tuesday in March. Six Southern states, led by Texas and Florida, voted on the second Tuesday. Four states in the industrial Midwest—Illinois, Michigan, Ohio, and Wisconsin—voted on the third Tuesday in March. And California anchored a three-state Western primary on the fourth Tuesday.

There continued to be regional groupings in March 2000. But the dominant event that year was a "national sampler" of sorts on the first Tuesday in March—an array of roughly a dozen primaries and caucuses scattered across the country—anchored by New York on one coast and California on the other. The cross-country votefest (the new Super Tuesday) continued to be a feature of the nominating process in 2004.

The upshot has been both a shorter and earlier nominating season in which only well-financed and well-known candidates have been able to effectively compete.

But it is a process that increasingly has drawn the ire of leaders in both parties. And for a while, the Republicans appeared as concerned as the Democrats about the need to change it.

When they were regularly winning the White House in the 1970s and 1980s, the GOP showed little interest in tinkering with the nominating process. But once they began to lose presidential elections in the 1990s, many Republicans began to decry the "front-loaded" primary calendar that produced nominees within a few weeks of voting.

At their convention in San Diego in 1996, Republicans approved a rules change designed to help spread out the calendar, by offering states bonus delegates the later they held their primary or caucus. It did not get many takers, though, in 2000 and was rescinded.

Republicans, though, came close in 2000 to adopting one of the most significant overhauls of the nominating process in a generation. A task force headed by former Republican National

Committee (RNC) chairman Bill Brock, recommended that the whole primary calendar be revamped, so that small states would vote first and large states would vote last. That way, the reasoning went, primaries would be spread out from March to June and more voters would be given a meaningful voice, as it would be mathematically impossible for a candidate to acquire a majority of delegates before most, if not all, of the states had voted.

The idea, called the "Delaware Plan" because of its state of origin, was not embraced with open arms by larger states, who feared a loss of influence if made to vote at the end of the primary season. With the prospect of a bitter fight on the convention floor, the plan was sacrificed by the Bush campaign on the altar of party harmony.

Once the Republicans regained the White House that fall, interest in reforming the nominating process slipped back exclusively to the Democrats. They tweaked their primary calendar in 2004 by moving forward their window a month to match the Republicans. The Democrats allowed states to hold their primaries or caucuses in February immediately after Iowa and New Hampshire voted in January. Seventeen states and the District of Columbia leaped in to fill the February void.

After 2004, Democrats tinkered with their calendar again to create more variety in the opening round of voting in January. In August 2006, party officials picked Nevada to hold a caucus in mid-January 2008 between Iowa and New Hampshire, and South Carolina to hold a primary in late January that year after New Hampshire.

Over the years, however, both parties have discovered there is a limited amount of change that they can accomplish on their own and that wholesale reform requires joint action. Rarely, though, are the two parties on the same page when it comes to that. But that does not stop the nominating process from continuing to evolve, so the ground rules of each campaign are different—sometimes, significantly different—than the one before.

GROWTH OF PRESIDENTIAL PRIMARIES . . . MORE AND MORE, EARLIER AND EARLIER

The Primaries: A Front-Loaded Process

Over the years, there have been more and more states holding primaries earlier and earlier in the presidential election year. The result is that a nominating system that once featured primaries sprinkled across the spring is now front-loaded with the bulk of the primaries held during the winter months of January, February and March.

Following is a list of primaries held in each month of every nominating season from 1968 through 2004. Primaries included are those in the 50 states and the District of Columbia in which at least one of the parties permitted a direct vote for presidential candidates, or there was an aggregated statewide vote for delegates.

	1968	1972	1976	1980	1984	1988	1992	1996	2000	2004
January	0	0	0	0	0	0	0	0	0	2
February	0	0	1	1	1	2	2	5	7	9
March	1	3	5	9	8	20	15	24	20	14
April	3	3	2	4	3	3	5	1	2	1
May	7	11	13	13	11	7	10	8	9	7
June	4	4	6	9	7	5	7	4	5	5
TOTAL	15	21	27	36	30	37	39	42	43	38

1968

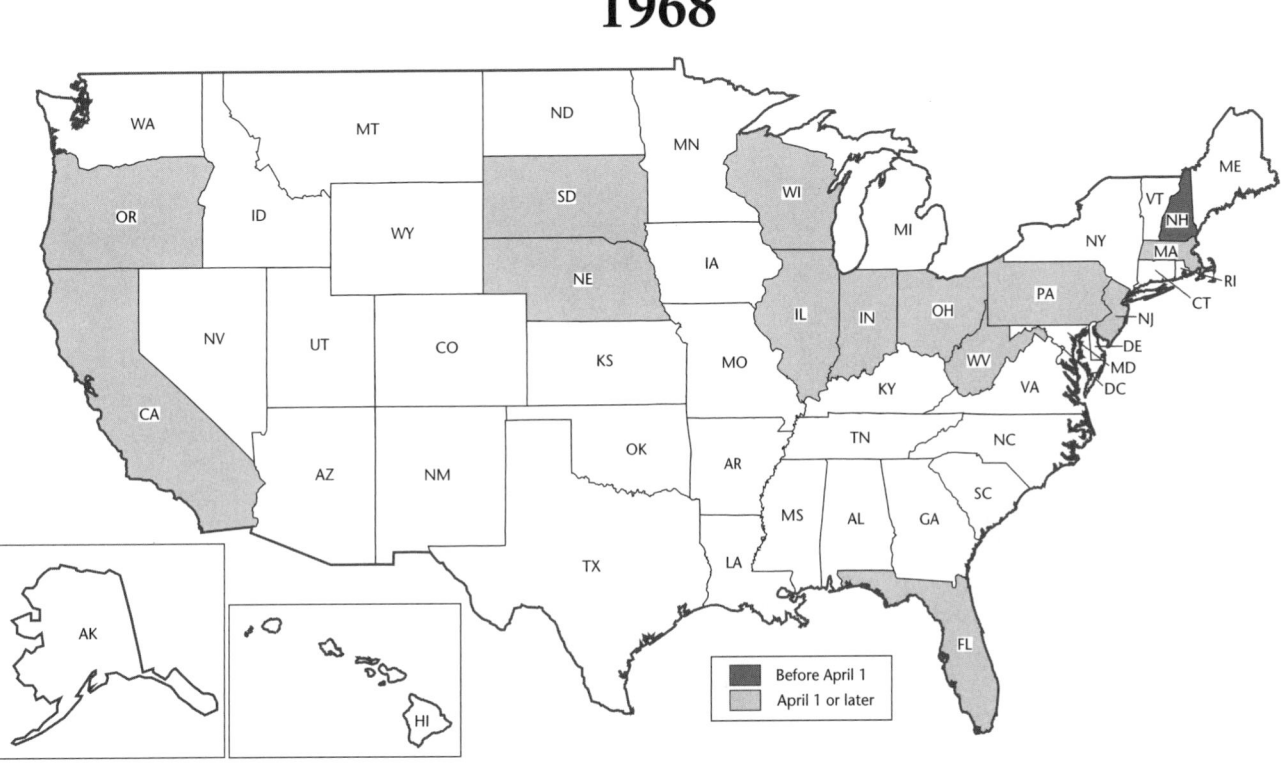

GROWTH OF PRESIDENTIAL PRIMARIES . . . MORE AND MORE, EARLIER AND EARLIER

1980

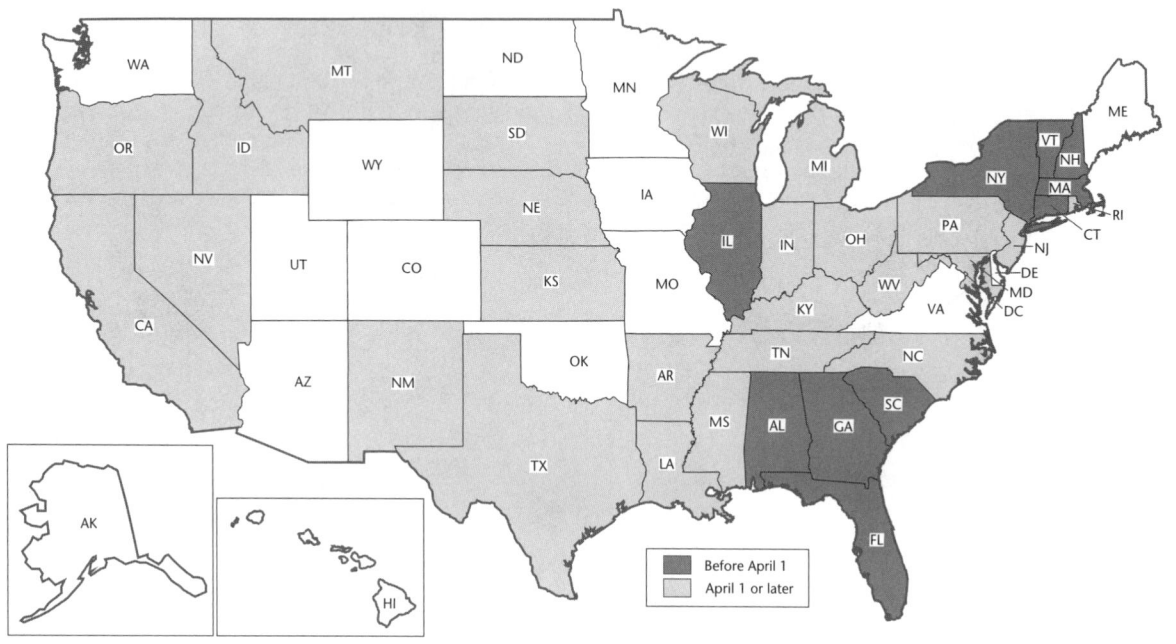

2004

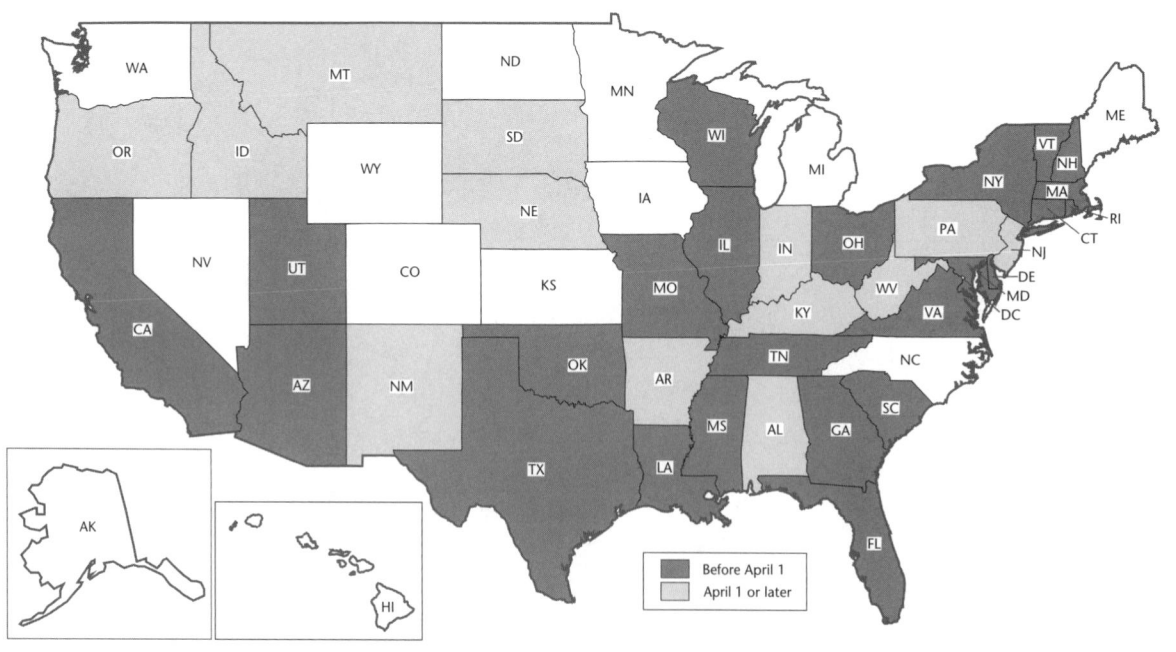

DEMOCRATIC PRESIDENTIAL PRIMARY WINNERS

1976–2004

NOMINEE	1976 Carter	%	1980 Carter	%	1984 Mondale	%	1988 Dukakis	%	1992 Clinton	%	1996 Clinton	%	2000 Gore	%	2004 Kerry	%
EAST															
Connecticut			E. Kennedy	47%	Hart	53%	Dukakis	58%	Brown	37%			Gore	55%	Kerry	58%
Delaware											Clinton	90%	Gore	57%	Kerry	50%
District of Col.	Carter	32%	E. Kennedy	62%	J. Jackson	67%	J. Jackson	80%	Clinton	74%	Clinton	98%	Gore	96%	Dean	43%
Maine											Clinton	88%	Gore	54%		
Maryland	Brown	48%	Carter	47%	Mondale	42%	Dukakis	46%	Tsongas	41%	Clinton	84%	Gore	67%	Kerry	60%
Massachusetts	H. Jackson	22%	E. Kennedy	65%	Hart	39%	Dukakis	59%	Tsongas	66%	Clinton	87%	Gore	60%	Kerry	72%
New Hampshire	Carter	28%	Carter	47%	Hart	37%	Dukakis	36%	Tsongas	33%	Clinton	84%	Gore	50%	Kerry	38%
New Jersey	Carter	58%	E. Kennedy	56%	Mondale	45%	Dukakis	63%	Clinton	62%	Clinton	95%	Gore	95%	Kerry	92%
New York			E. Kennedy	59%	Mondale	45%	Dukakis	51%	Clinton	41%			Gore	66%	Kerry	61%
Pennsylvania	Carter	37%	E. Kennedy	46%	Mondale	45%	Dukakis	66%	Clinton	57%	Clinton	92%	Gore	74%	Kerry	74%
Rhode Island	Unpledged	32%	E. Kennedy	68%	Hart	45%	Dukakis	70%	Tsongas	53%	Clinton	89%	Gore	57%	Kerry	71%
Vermont	Carter	42%	Carter	73%	Hart	70%	Dukakis	56%			Clinton	97%	Gore	54%	Dean	54%
West Virginia	Byrd	89%	Carter	62%	Mondale	54%	Dukakis	75%	Clinton	74%	Clinton	87%	Gore	72%	Kerry	69%
MIDWEST															
Illinois	Carter	48%	Carter	65%	Mondale	40%	Simon	42%	Clinton	52%	Clinton	96%	Gore	84%	Kerry	72%
Indiana	Carter	68%	Carter	68%	Hart	42%	Dukakis	70%	Clinton	63%	Clinton	100%	Gore	75%	Kerry	73%
Iowa																
Kansas			Carter	57%					Clinton	51%						
Michigan	Carter	43%	Uncom.	46%					Clinton	51%	Uncom.	87%	Uncom.	71%		
Minnesota									Clinton	31%						
Missouri							Gephardt	58%					Gore	65%	Kerry	51%
Nebraska	Church	38%	Carter	47%	Hart	58%	Dukakis	63%	Clinton	46%	Clinton	87%	Gore	70%	Kerry	73%
North Dakota					Hart	85%	Dukakis	85%	Perot	29%	Riemers	41%				
Ohio	Carter	52%	Carter	51%	Hart	42%	Dukakis	63%	Clinton	61%	Clinton	92%	Gore	74%	Kerry	52%
South Dakota	Carter	41%	E. Kennedy	49%	Hart	51%	Gephardt	44%	Kerrey	40%					Kerry	82%
Wisconsin	Carter	37%	Carter	56%	Hart	44%	Dukakis	48%	Clinton	37%	Clinton	98%	Gore	89%	Kerry	40%

DEMOCRATIC PRESIDENTIAL PRIMARY WINNERS

1976–2004

NOMINEE	1976 Carter	%	1980 Carter	%	1984 Mondale	%	1988 Dukakis	%	1992 Clinton	%	1996 Clinton	%	2000 Gore	%	2004 Kerry	%
SOUTH																
Alabama			Carter	82%	Mondale	35%	J. Jackson	44%	Clinton	68%	Clinton	81%	Gore	77%	Kerry	75%
Arkansas	Carter	63%	Carter	60%			Gore	37%	Clinton	68%	Clinton	79%	Gore	78%	Kerry	67%
Florida	Carter	35%	Carter	61%	Hart	39%	Dukakis	41%	Clinton	51%			Gore	82%	Kerry	77%
Georgia	Carter	83%	Carter	88%	Mondale	30%	J. Jackson	40%	Clinton	57%	Clinton	100%	Gore	84%	Kerry	47%
Kentucky	Carter	59%	Carter	67%			Gore	46%	Clinton	56%	Clinton	77%	Gore	71%	Kerry	60%
Louisiana			Carter	56%	J. Jackson	43%	J. Jackson	35%	Clinton	69%	Clinton	81%	Gore	73%	Kerry	70%
Mississippi							J. Jackson	45%	Clinton	73%	Clinton	92%	Gore	90%	Kerry	78%
North Carolina	Carter	54%	Carter	70%	Mondale	36%	Gore	35%	Clinton	64%	Clinton	81%	Gore	70%		
Oklahoma							Gore	41%	Clinton	70%	Clinton	76%	Gore	69%	Clark	30%
South Carolina									Clinton	63%					Edwards	45%
Tennessee	Carter	78%	Carter	75%	Mondale	41%	Gore	72%	Clinton	67%	Clinton	89%	Gore	92%	Kerry	41%
Texas			Carter	56%			Dukakis	33%	Clinton	66%	Clinton	86%	Gore	80%	Kerry	67%
Virginia							J. Jackson	45%							Kerry	52%
WEST																
Alaska																
Arizona													Gore	78%	Kerry	43%
California	Brown	59%	E. Kennedy	45%	Hart	39%	Dukakis	61%	Clinton	47%	Clinton	93%	Gore	81%	Kerry	64%
Colorado									Brown	29%	Clinton	89%	Gore	71%		
Hawaii																
Idaho	Church	79%	Carter	62%	Hart	58%	Dukakis	73%	Clinton	49%	Clinton	88%	Gore	76%	Kerry	82%
Montana	Church	59%	Carter	51%	No Pref.	83%	Dukakis	69%	Clinton	47%	Clinton	90%	Gore	78%	Kerry	68%
Nevada	Brown	53%	Carter	38%												
New Mexico			E. Kennedy	46%	Hart	47%	Dukakis	61%	Clinton	53%	Clinton	90%	Gore	75%		
Oregon	Church	34%	Carter	57%	Hart	58%	Dukakis	57%	Clinton	45%	Clinton	95%	Gore	85%	Kerry	79%
Utah													Gore	80%	Kerry	55%
Washington									Clinton	42%	Clinton	99%	Gore	68%		
Wyoming																

Note: The percentage in each state (and the District of Columbia) represents the winning candidate's share of his party's primary vote. A blank indicates that either no primary was held or there was not a direct vote for presidential candidates, as was the case in the New York Republican primary in 1996 and 2000.

REPUBLICAN PRESIDENTIAL PRIMARY WINNERS

1976–2004

NOMINEE	1976 Ford	%	1980 Reagan	%	1984 Reagan	%	1988 Bush	%	1992 Bush	%	1996 Dole	%	2000 Bush	%	2004 Bush	%
EAST																
Connecticut			Bush	39%			Bush	71%	Bush	67%	Dole	54%	McCain	49%		
Delaware											Forbes	33%	Bush	51%		
District of Col.			Bush	66%	Reagan	100%	Bush	88%	Bush	81%	Dole	76%	Bush	73%		
Maine											Dole	46%	Bush	51%		
Maryland	Ford	58%	Reagan	48%	Reagan	100%	Bush	53%	Bush	70%	Dole	53%	Bush	56%	Bush	100%
Massachusetts	Ford	61%	Bush	31%	Reagan	89%	Bush	59%	Bush	66%	Dole	48%	McCain	65%	Bush	89%
New Hampshire	Ford	49%	Reagan	50%	Reagan	86%	Bush	38%	Bush	53%	Buchanan	27%	McCain	49%	Bush	80%
New Jersey	Ford	100%	Reagan	81%	Reagan	100%	Bush	100%	Bush	78%	Dole	82%	Bush	84%	Bush	100%
New York																
Pennsylvania	Ford	92%	Bush	50%	Reagan	99%	Bush	79%	Bush	77%	Dole	64%	Bush	72%	Bush	100%
Rhode Island	Ford	65%	Reagan	72%	Reagan	91%	Bush	65%	Bush	63%	Dole	64%	McCain	60%	Bush	85%
Vermont	Ford	84%	Reagan	30%	Reagan	99%	Bush	49%			Dole	40%	McCain	60%	Bush	97%
West Virginia	Ford	57%	Reagan	84%	Reagan	92%	Bush	77%	Bush	81%	Dole	69%	Bush	80%	Bush	100%
MIDWEST																
Illinois	Ford	59%	Reagan	48%	Reagan	100%	Bush	55%	Bush	76%	Dole	65%	Bush	67%	Bush	100%
Indiana	Reagan	51%	Reagan	74%	Reagan	100%	Bush	80%	Bush	80%	Dole	71%	Bush	81%	Bush	100%
Iowa																
Kansas			Reagan	63%					Bush	62%						
Michigan	Ford	65%	Bush	57%					Bush	67%	Dole	51%	McCain	51%		
Minnesota									Bush	64%						
Missouri							Bush	42%					Bush	58%	Bush	95%
Nebraska	Reagan	54%	Reagan	76%	Reagan	100%	Bush	68%	Bush	81%	Dole	76%	Bush	78%	Bush	100%
North Dakota					Reagan	100%	Bush	94%	Bush	83%	Dole	42%				
Ohio	Ford	55%	Reagan	81%	Reagan	100%	Bush	81%	Bush	83%	Dole	67%	Bush	58%	Bush	100%
South Dakota	Reagan	51%	Reagan	82%			Dole	55%	Bush	69%	Dole	45%	Bush	78%		
Wisconsin	Ford	55%	Reagan	40%	Reagan	95%	Bush	82%	Bush	76%	Dole	52%	Bush	69%	Bush	99%

REPUBLICAN PRESIDENTIAL PRIMARY WINNERS

1976–2004

NOMINEE	1976 Ford	%	1980 Reagan	%	1984 Reagan	%	1988 Bush	%	1992 Bush	%	1996 Dole	%	2000 Bush	%	2004 Bush	%
SOUTH															
Alabama			Reagan	70%			Bush	65%	Bush	74%	Dole	76%	Bush	84%	Bush	93%
Arkansas	Reagan	63%					Bush	47%	Bush	87%	Dole	76%	Bush	80%	Bush	97%
Florida	Ford	53%	Reagan	56%	Reagan	100%	Bush	62%	Bush	68%	Dole	57%	Bush	74%		
Georgia	Reagan	68%	Reagan	73%	Reagan	100%	Bush	54%	Bush	64%	Dole	41%	Bush	67%	Bush	100%
Kentucky	Ford	51%	Reagan	82%			Bush	59%	Bush	75%	Dole	74%	Bush	83%	Bush	93%
Louisiana			Reagan	75%	Reagan	90%	Bush	58%	Bush	62%	Dole	48%	Bush	84%	Bush	96%
Mississippi			Reagan	89%			Bush	66%	Bush	72%	Dole	60%	Bush	88%		
North Carolina	Reagan	52%	Reagan	68%			Bush	45%	Bush	71%	Dole	71%	Bush	79%		
Oklahoma							Bush	37%	Bush	70%	Dole	59%	Bush	79%	Bush	90%
South Carolina			Reagan	55%			Bush	49%	Bush	67%	Dole	45%	Bush	53%		
Tennessee	Ford	50%	Reagan	74%	Reagan	91%	Bush	60%	Bush	73%	Dole	51%	Bush	77%	Bush	95%
Texas			Reagan	51%	Reagan	97%	Bush	64%	Bush	70%	Dole	56%	Bush	88%	Bush	92%
Virginia							Bush	54%					Bush	53%		
WEST															
Alaska																
Arizona											Forbes	33%	McCain	60%		
California	Reagan	65%	Reagan	80%	Reagan	100%	Bush	83%	Bush	74%	Dole	66%	Bush	61%	Bush	100%
Colorado									Bush	68%	Dole	44%	Bush	65%		
Hawaii																
Idaho	Reagan	74%	Reagan	83%	Reagan	92%	Bush	81%	Bush	63%	Dole	62%	Bush	73%	Bush	89%
Montana	Reagan	63%	Reagan	87%	Reagan	92%	Bush	73%	Bush	72%	Dole	61%	Bush	78%	Bush	94%
Nevada	Reagan	66%	Reagan	83%							Dole	52%				
New Mexico			Reagan	64%	Reagan	95%	Bush	78%	Bush	64%	Dole	76%	Bush	83%	Bush	100%
Oregon	Ford	50%	Reagan	54%	Reagan	98%	Bush	73%	Bush	67%	Dole	51%	Bush	84%	Bush	95%
Utah													Bush	63%		
Washington									Bush	67%	Dole	63%	Bush	58%		
Wyoming																

Note: The percentage in each state (and the District of Columbia) represents the winning candidate's share of his party's primary vote. A blank indicates that either no primary was held or there was not a direct vote for presidential candidates, as was the case in the New York Republican primary in 1996 and 2000.

NATIONAL PRIMARY MAPS
AND VOTE SUMMARIES, 1968–2004

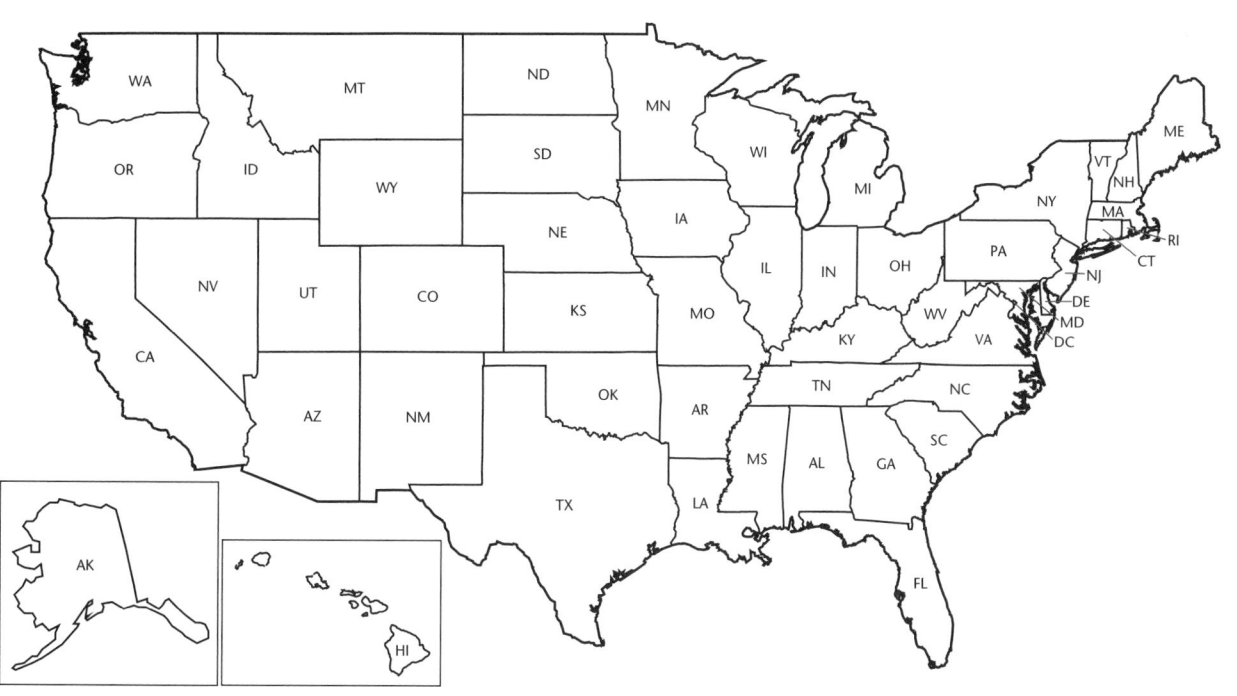

1968	Democratic Primaries	16	1988	Democratic Primaries	26
	Republican Primaries	17		Republican Primaries	27
1972	Democratic Primaries	18	1992	Democratic Primaries	28
	Republican Primaries	19		Republican Primaries	29
1976	Democratic Primaries	20	1996	Democratic Primaries	30
	Republican Primaries	21		Republican Primaries	31
1980	Democratic Primaries	22	2000	Democratic Primaries	32
	Republican Primaries	23		Republican Primaries	33
1984	Democratic Primaries	24	2004	Democratic Primaries	34
	Republican Primaries	25		Republican Primaries	35

1968 DEMOCRATIC PRIMARIES

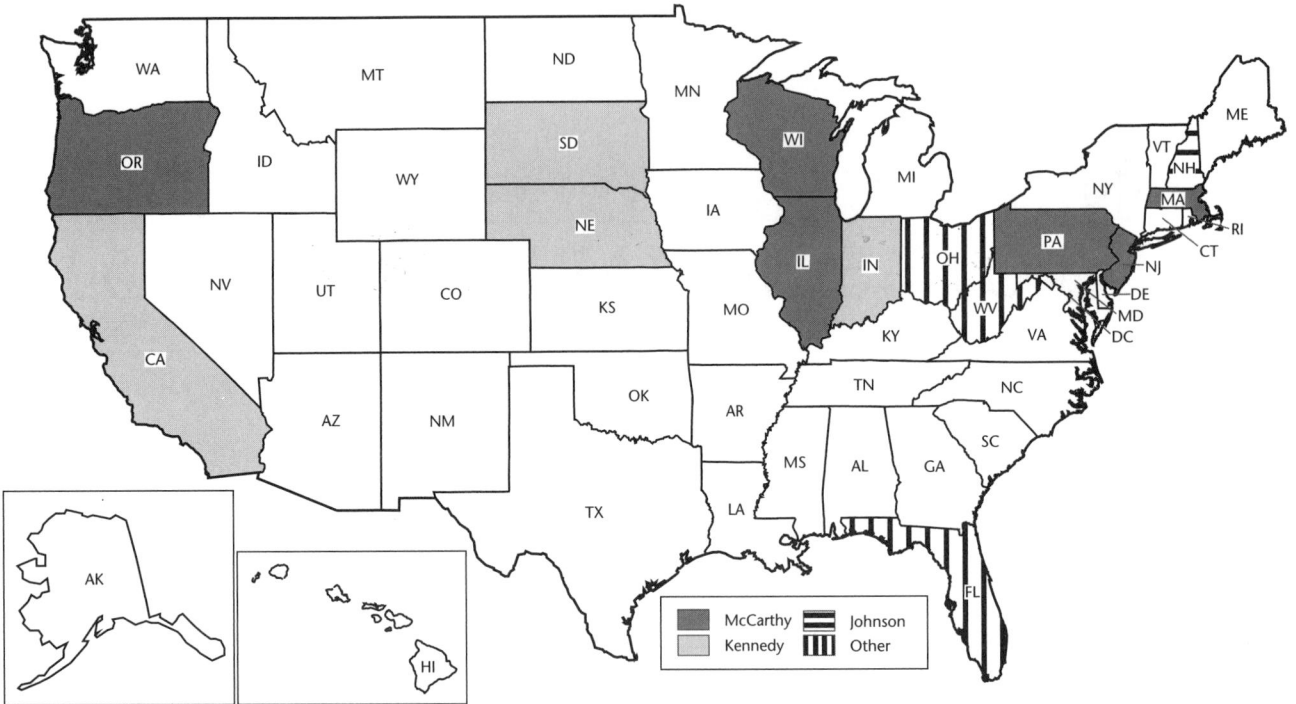

McCarthy | Johnson
Kennedy | Other

There were only a few presidential primaries in 1968. But nearly every one of them had significance, with the first-in-the-nation primary in New Hampshire March 12 setting the tone.

President Lyndon Johnson won on an organized write-in vote, but with less than a majority, while Minnesota Sen. Eugene McCarthy's grass-roots effort, focused around opposition to the Vietnam War, exceeded all expectations.

On March 16, New York Sen. Robert Kennedy entered the race. On March 31, the embattled president left it. Beginning in Wisconsin April 2, McCarthy registered a series of primary victories before he and Kennedy went head-to-head for the first time May 7 in Indiana.

Kennedy won Indiana, and beat McCarthy in three of four other primaries down the stretch, culminating with a victory in California June 4. But after claiming victory that night in Los Angeles, Kennedy was shot and died less than two days later.

Vice President Hubert Humphrey, who had not run in the primaries, was subsequently nominated that August at a tumultuous Democratic convention in Chicago. He was the last nominee of either major party to win its nomination without having first competed in the primaries.

	Total Vote	Percentage	Primary States Won
Eugene McCarthy (Minn.)	2,914,933	38.7	6
Robert Kennedy (N.Y.)	2,304,542	30.6	4
Lyndon Johnson (Texas)*	383,048	5.1	1
Others	1,932,546	25.6	3
TOTAL	7,535,069		

Note: In this chart and those that follow, all candidates are listed that drew at least 5 percent of their party's nationwide primary vote and were on the ballot in more than one state. The vote for "Others" includes other candidates, miscellaneous write-ins, and any derivation of "Uncommitted" that appeared on the primary ballots. An asterisk (*) indicates an incumbent president. Each candidate's home state is in parentheses. The source for vote data is Congressional Quarterly's *America at the Polls 1960–1996* and *Guide to U.S. Elections*. Results from the primary in the District of Columbia are included in the vote totals, but not territories such as Puerto Rico. The primary winners are shaded on the maps.

1968 REPUBLICAN PRIMARIES

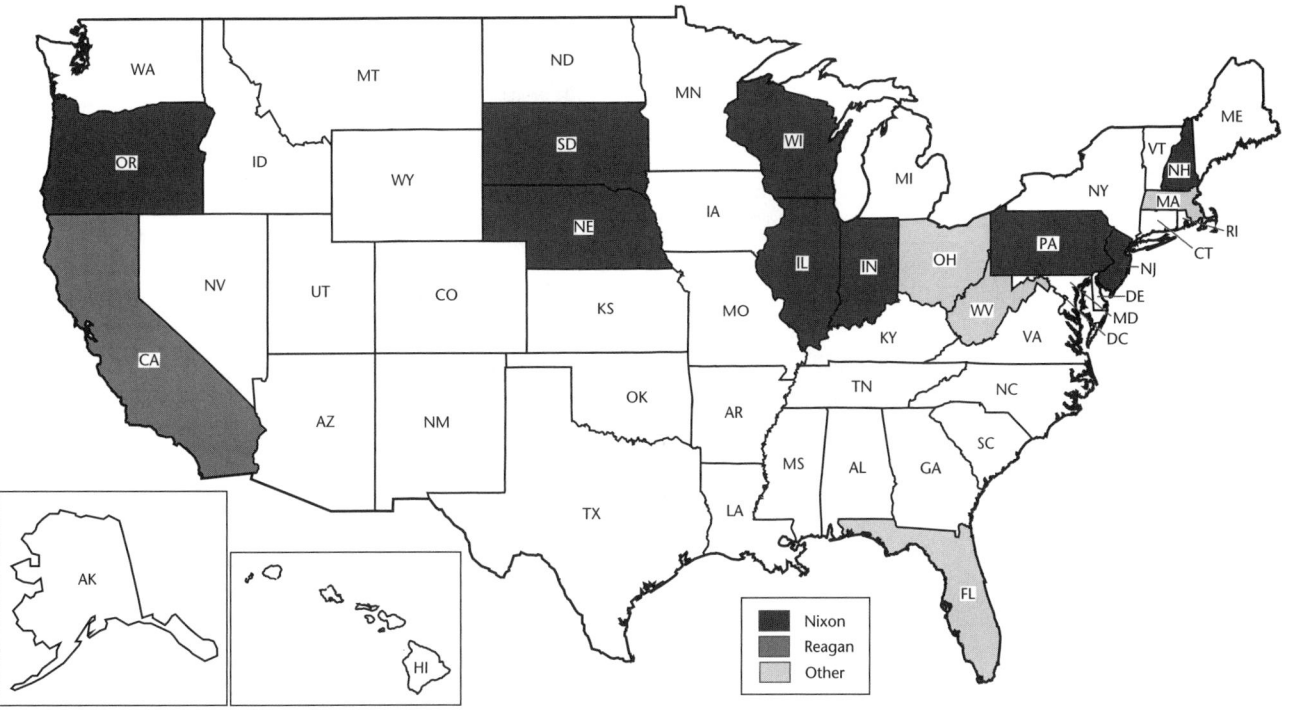

Unlike the Democrats, the Republican primaries in 1968 were like marking time before the August convention. Michigan Gov. George Romney dropped out of the race before the primaries began. New York Gov. Nelson Rockefeller entered too late to compete. And California Gov. Ronald Reagan did not formally announce his candidacy until the eve of the convention, although he was on several primary ballots in the spring, including California, where he ran as an unopposed favorite son.

Elsewhere, former Vice President Richard Nixon was virtually unopposed during the primary season. The only primaries he did not win were those he was not on the ballot. Still, Nixon did not have the nomination locked up when the convention in Miami Beach began. But the ideological gulf between the more liberal Rockefeller and the more conservative Reagan made it difficult for them to agree on a common strategy to stop Nixon, who ultimately prevailed on the first ballot.

	Total Vote	Percentage	Primary States Won
Ronald Reagan (Calif.)	1,696,270	37.9	1
Richard Nixon (N.Y.)	1,679,443	37.5	9
Others	1,097,838	24.5	4
TOTAL	4,473,551		

Note: Richard Nixon lived in New York during the 1968 campaign, although his political career is more associated with California.

1972 DEMOCRATIC PRIMARIES

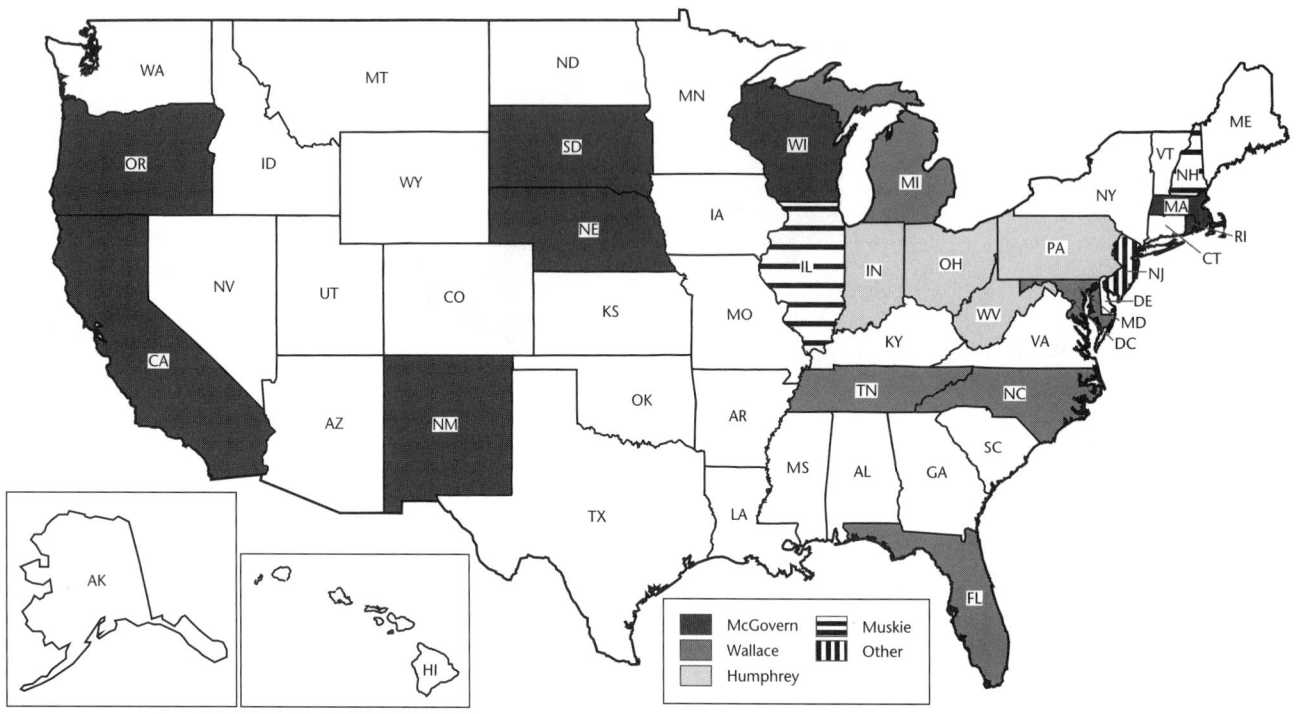

The presidential campaign of 1972 began a new era of nominating politics, where there were more primaries and candidates had to compete in them. Sen. George McGovern of South Dakota was the immediate beneficiary of the new system, mounting a long-shot candidacy that ultimately won the Democratic nomination.

McGovern had some of the same advantages that Eugene McCarthy had in 1968—an issue (opposition to the Vietnam War) and an army of volunteers. And McGovern burst onto the scene in much the same way that McCarthy had, with a stronger-than-expected showing in New Hampshire against a front-runner (Sen. Edmund Muskie from neighboring Maine) who did not do as well as expected.

McGovern carefully picked his way from there to the Democratic nomination, gaining momentum by winning high-profile primary states with progressive traditions, such as Wisconsin, Nebraska, Oregon and California. But he fared poorly in several regions that augured poorly for his chances that fall. He lost all the major industrial states—Pennsylvania and Ohio to former Vice President Hubert Humphrey, and Michigan to Alabama Gov. George Wallace. And he was a nonfactor in the Southern primaries, where Wallace dominated.

Altogether, McGovern received fewer primary votes than Humphrey, and not many more than Wallace. Since McGovern, every major-party nominee has first emerged from the primaries as his party's top vote-getter.

	Total Vote	Percentage	Primary States Won
Hubert Humphrey (Minn.)	4,121,372	25.8	4
George McGovern (S.D.)	4,053,451	25.3	8
George Wallace (Ala.)	3,755,424	23.5	5
Edmund Muskie (Maine)	1,840,217	11.5	2
Others	2,223,501	13.9	1
TOTAL	15,993,965		

1972 REPUBLICAN PRIMARIES

One point that has become clear during the modern era of presidential primaries is that sitting presidents that face little or no opposition for renomination are in great shape to win another term in the fall. On the other hand, every recent president that has struggled through his party's primaries has lost in November.

The first example of the upside of this dynamic was Richard Nixon. He faced minimal opposition for renomination in 1972 from a pair of little-known congressmen—Paul McCloskey of California, who mounted an anti-war challenge, and John Ashbrook of Ohio, who claimed that Nixon was too liberal for the GOP.

The contest was over quickly, as Nixon beat both easily in New Hampshire. Late in the spring, McCloskey did win a delegate in the New Mexico primary; it was the only vote cast against Nixon's renomination at the Republican convention that August.

	Total Vote	Percentage	Primary States Won
Richard Nixon (Calif.)*	5,378,704	86.9	18
John Ashbrook (Ohio)	311,543	5.0	0
Others	498,034	8.0	2
TOTAL	6,188,281		

1976 DEMOCRATIC PRIMARIES

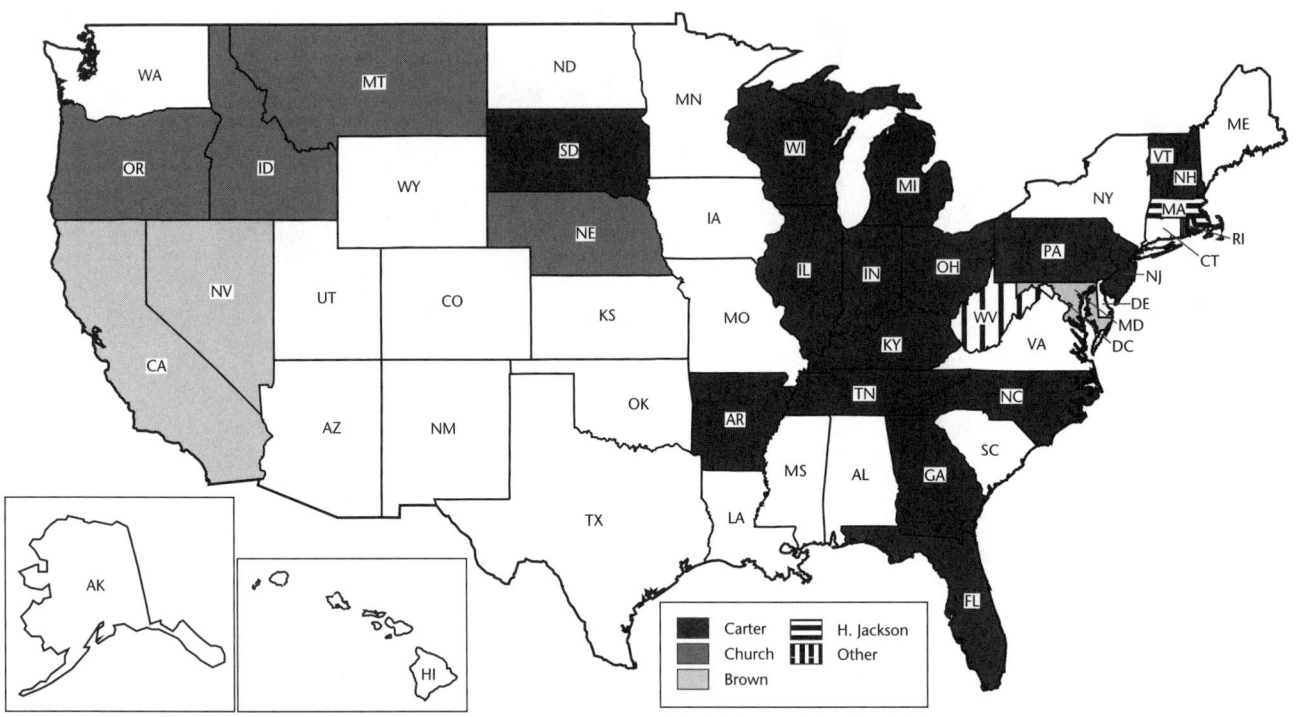

For the second straight election, a dark-horse candidate won the Democratic nomination. But unlike George McGovern four years earlier, former Georgia Gov. Jimmy Carter broke fast from the gate.

Carter established himself as a national candidate with victory in the New Hampshire primary, dispatched George Wallace in their home region with primary triumphs in Florida and North Carolina, eliminated Washington Sen. Henry Jackson in a key industrial state contest in Pennsylvania, and outpolled Rep. Morris Udall of Arizona at every turn, to the point that Udall became known as "Second Place Mo."

Carter lost some late primaries to two late entries from the West—California Gov. Jerry Brown and Sen. Frank Church of Idaho. But by then, Carter was comfortably ahead in the delegate count.

	Total Vote	Percentage	Primary States Won
Jimmy Carter (Ga.)	6,235,609	38.8	16
Jerry Brown (Calif.)	2,449,374	15.3	3
George Wallace (Ala.)	1,995,388	12.4	0
Morris Udall (Ariz.)	1,611,754	10.0	0
Henry Jackson (Wash.)	1,134,375	7.1	1
Frank Church (Idaho)	830,818	5.2	4
Others	1,795,334	11.2	2
TOTAL	16,052,652		

1976 REPUBLICAN PRIMARIES

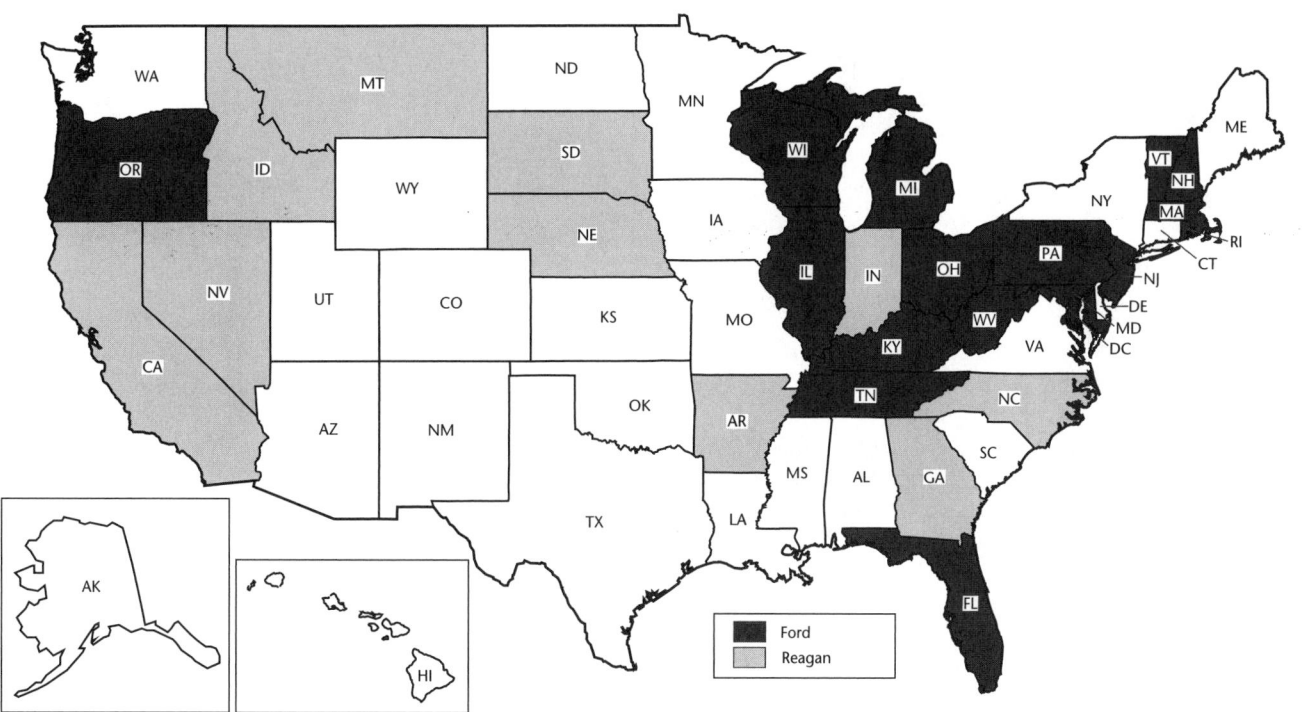

| Ford |
| Reagan |

Since presidential primaries were instituted in the early twentieth century, no president who wanted another term has been denied his party's nomination. But in 1976, Gerald Ford found himself more closely challenged in the Republican primaries than any sitting president since William Howard Taft in 1912.

In former California Gov. Ronald Reagan, Ford had a challenger with both strong appeal to the burgeoning conservative wing of the Republican Party and a base in the nation's largest state. The closeness of the challenge was evident from the start, as Ford defeated Reagan by just 1 percentage point in New Hampshire. Ford followed with a string of primary

victories that nearly knocked Reagan out of the race. But Reagan steadied himself with a late March victory in North Carolina.

As the primaries unfolded, Ford dominated in the Northeast and major states of the industrial Frost Belt. Reagan had the upper hand in much of the South and West. The only primary state that Ford was able to carry west of the Mississippi River was Oregon.

But Ford prevailed, in large part because he able to pick off some states in the South, including Florida, while Reagan was unable to deeply penetrate Ford's base in the major states of the Frost Belt.

	Total Vote	Percentage	Primary States Won
Gerald Ford (Mich.)*	5,529,899	53.3	16
Ronald Reagan (Calif.)	4,758,325	45.9	10
Others	85,901	0.8	0
TOTAL	10,374,125		

1980 DEMOCRATIC PRIMARIES

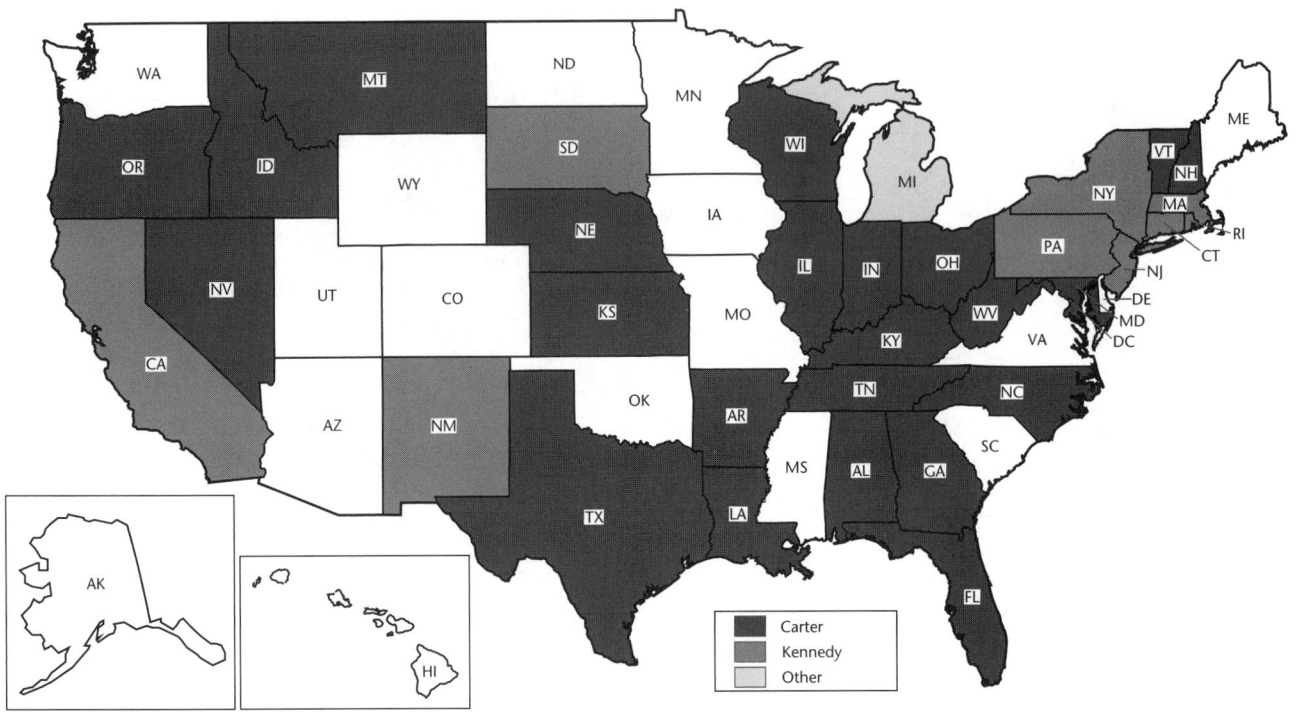

Carter
Kennedy
Other

The Democrats had an intra-party brawl of their own in 1980 between an incumbent president (Jimmy Carter) and a well-regarded challenger (Sen. Edward Kennedy of Massachusetts) from the liberal wing of the party. Some polls taken in 1979 showed Kennedy ahead. But a series of events, including the Iranian hostage crisis, shifted sentiment to Carter before the primaries even began.

Carter got off to a fast start, with victories in New Hampshire, Illinois and across the South that removed any suspense about who would win the nomination. But as the primaries

proceeded, Kennedy was able to fashion a bicoastal coalition that gave strong hints of Carter's vulnerability in the general election to come. Kennedy won primaries in New York, Pennsylvania and New Jersey on the East Coast and California on the West.

Yet there was also clear evidence that many Democratic voters would have preferred another choice beyond Carter and Kennedy, as more than 1 million votes were cast in the Democratic primaries for ballot lines that indicated "No preference."

	Total Vote	Percentage	Primary States Won
Jimmy Carter (Ga.)*	9,593,335	51.2	23
Edward Kennedy (Mass.)	6,963,625	37.1	9
Others	2,190,865	11.7	1
TOTAL	18,747,825		

1980 REPUBLICAN PRIMARIES

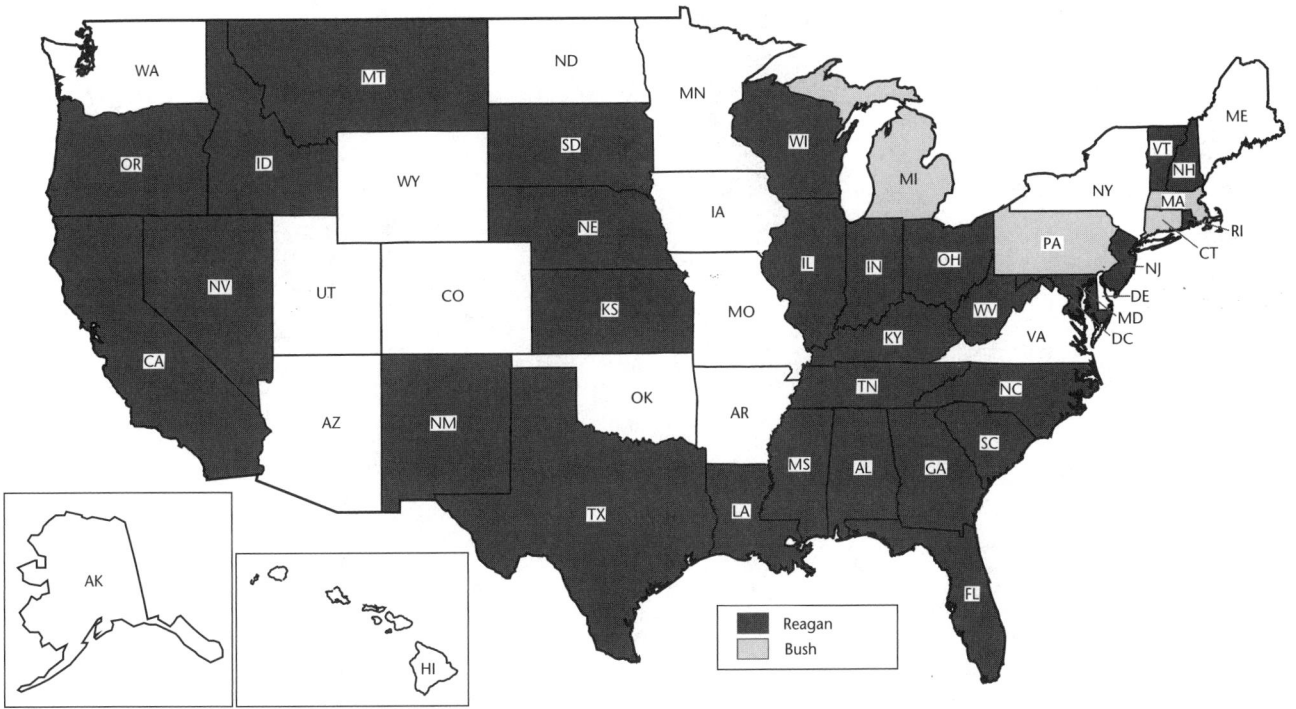

			Reagan
			Bush

Ronald Reagan's strong showing in the 1976 Republican primaries made him the front-runner for the GOP nomination in 1980. But he got off to a stumbling start, losing the Iowa caucuses to dark-horse challenger, George Bush, who courted the state in a way that Reagan had not.

Bush claimed that he had "Big Mo" after the Iowa vote, but Reagan quickly reestablished his hegemony with a decisive victory in New Hampshire. Bush managed several primary wins in his native New England, and Rep. John Anderson of Illinois briefly was a factor in the race with near-misses in early March voting in Massachusetts and Vermont.

But after losing to Reagan in Illinois and Wisconsin, Anderson quit the Republican race in April in favor of an independent presidential bid. Meanwhile, Bush had fallen far behind after a string of Reagan primary victories in the South and Midwest. But Bush hung around, winning late primaries in Pennsylvania and Michigan that ultimately led to his choice as Reagan's running mate.

	Total Vote	Percentage	Primary States Won
Ronald Reagan (Calif.)	7,709,793	60.8	29
George Bush (Texas)	2,958,093	23.3	4
John Anderson (Ill.)	1,572,174	12.4	0
Others	450,391	3.5	0
TOTAL	12,690,451		

1984 DEMOCRATIC PRIMARIES

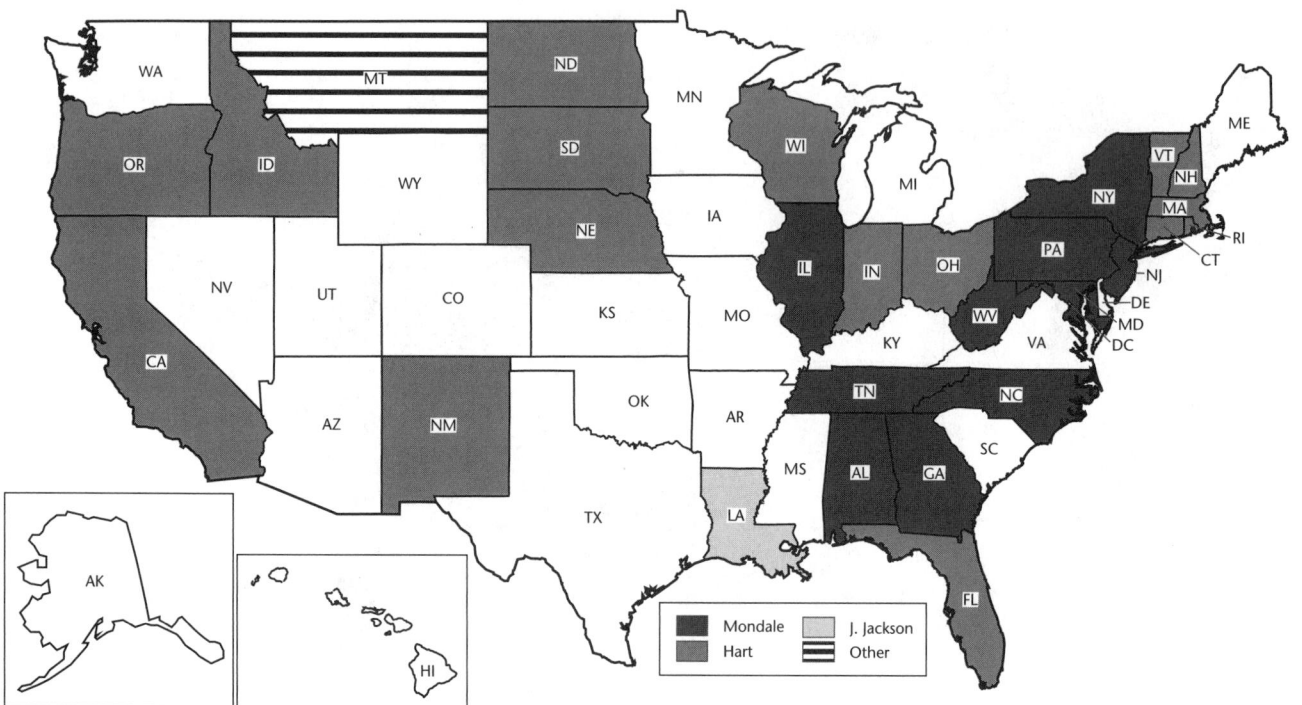

Former Vice President Walter Mondale entered the 1984 Democratic primaries with an array of endorsements from Democratic-related interest groups, including the AFL-CIO. But while the early support tended to serve Mondale well in his head-to-head maneuvering against Ohio Sen. John Glenn, it left Mondale open to an anti-establishment challenge from Sen. Gary Hart.

Hart, who had been campaign manager of George McGovern's 1972 presidential campaign, broke fast from the gate. His second-place finish in the Iowa caucuses put him in contention in New Hampshire, where an upset victory produced two weeks worth of momentum that left Mondale on the ropes. Only by winning Georgia and Alabama on Super Tuesday (March 13) was Mondale able to stabilize his campaign.

Mondale victories in the industrial states of Illinois, New York and Pennsylvania followed. But he could not shake Hart, as the senator from Colorado posted a succession of primary triumphs in the Midwest and West. On the final big day of primary voting in early June, Hart won California while Mondale took New Jersey, giving the former vice president just enough delegates to claim the nomination.

Although the Rev. Jesse Jackson won primaries only in Louisiana (and the District of Columbia), he was a factor throughout the primary season. Jackson ran well across the South and in urban centers of the Frost Belt by tapping the minority vote.

	Total Vote	Percentage	Primary States Won
Walter Mondale (Minn.)	6,811,214	37.8	10
Gary Hart (Colo.)	6,503,968	36.1	16
Jesse Jackson (Ill.)	3,282,380	18.2	1
Others	1,411,630	7.8	1
TOTAL	18,009,192		

1984 REPUBLICAN PRIMARIES

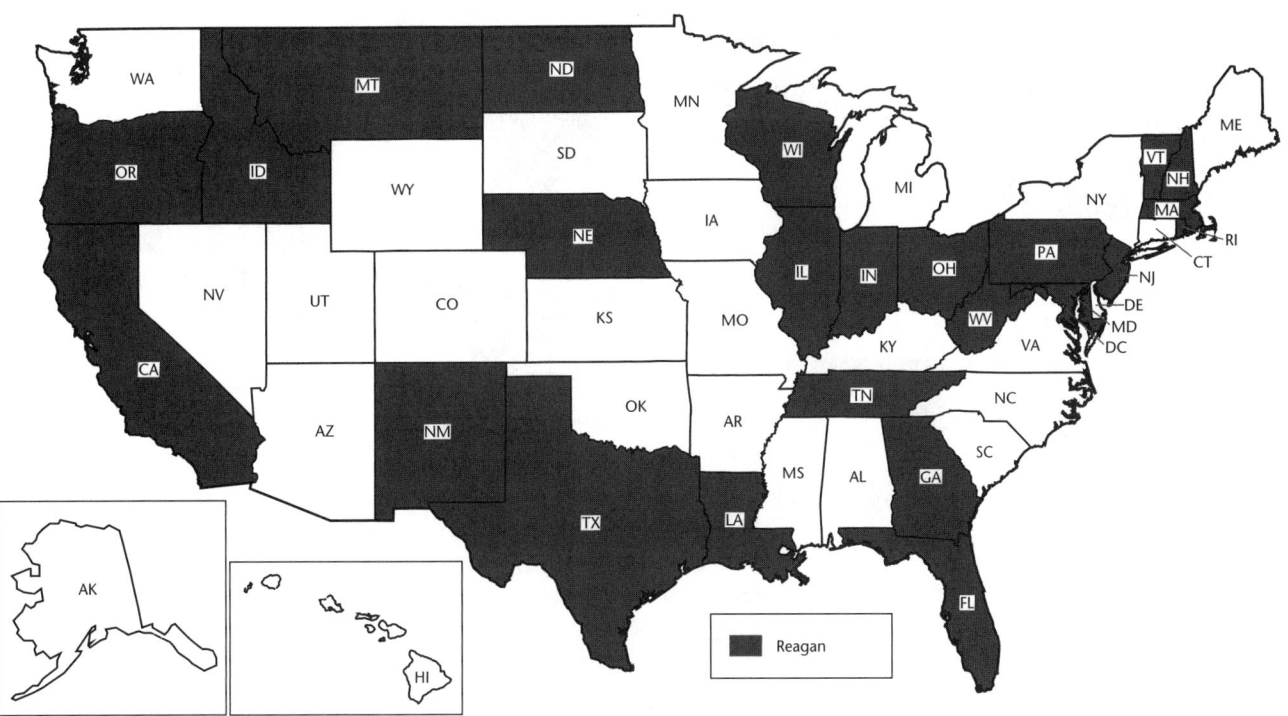

The 1984 GOP nominating process was more notable for what did not happen than what did. After two straight elections in which incumbent presidents faced serious primary challenges within their own party, President Ronald Reagan cruised to renomination over token opposition in 1984. It proved to be the precursor of an easy reelection victory for Reagan that fall.

	Total Vote	Percentage	Primary States Won
Ronald Reagan (Calif.)*	6,484,987	98.6	24
Others	90,664	1.4	0
TOTAL	6,575,651		

1988 DEMOCRATIC PRIMARIES

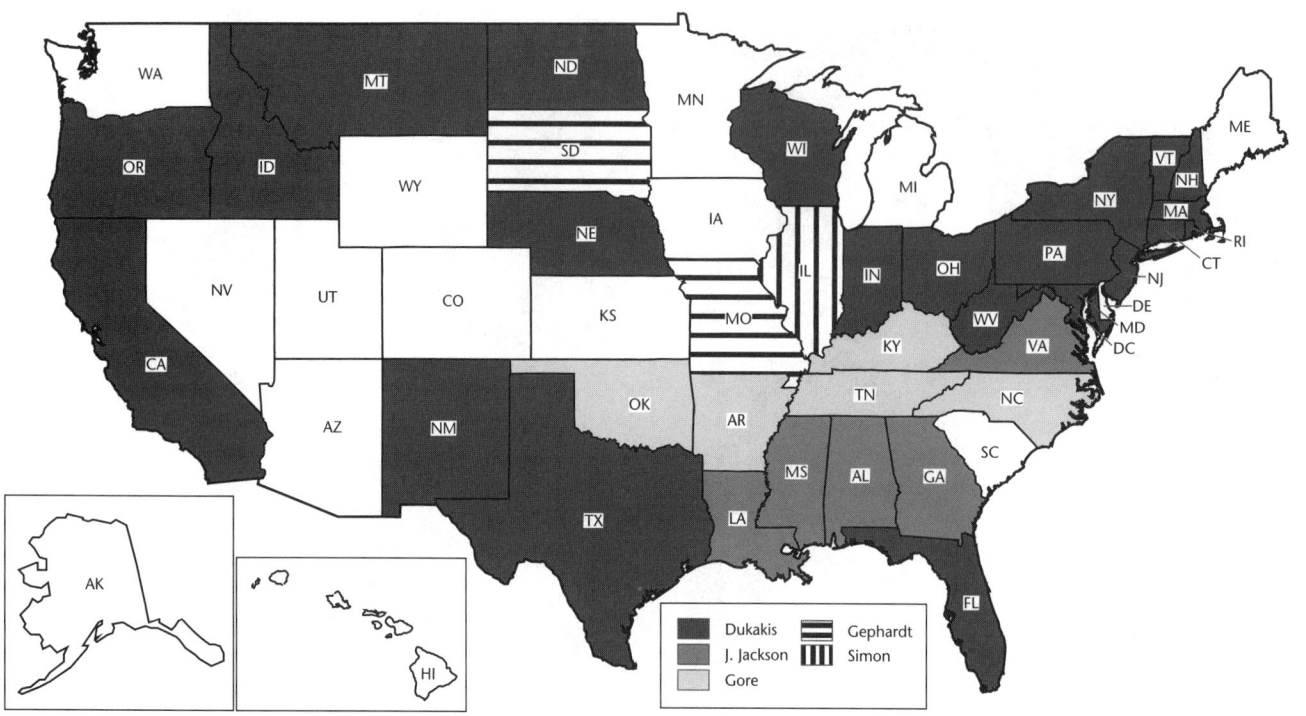

Dukakis
J. Jackson
Gore
Gephardt
Simon

The Democratic nominating process was slow to take shape in 1988. Rep. Richard Gephardt of Missouri won the lead-off caucuses in neighboring Iowa. Gov. Michael Dukakis of Massachusetts won the first-in-the-nation primary in neighboring New Hampshire.

The huge Super Tuesday vote across Dixie in early March was a wash. Dukakis won the two big states on the fringes, Texas and Florida. Jesse Jackson swept five states from the Deep South to Virginia. Sen. Al Gore of Tennessee won five states across the middle of the South from North Carolina to Oklahoma. And Gephardt won his home state of Missouri. The Democratic race got even more convoluted the following week when Sen. Paul Simon won the primary in his home state of Illinois.

But as fast as one could say "brokered convention," the situation began to clear. Gephardt dropped out, and Dukakis began to win decisively across the industrial Frost Belt, with April victories in Wisconsin and New York sending Simon and Gore to the sidelines and relegating Jackson to also-ran status. In the three months of primary voting after Super Tuesday, Jackson could win only in Puerto Rico and the District of Columbia.

	Total Vote	Percentage	Primary States Won
Michael Dukakis (Mass.)	9,817,185	42.8	22
Jesse Jackson (Ill.)	6,685,699	29.1	5
Al Gore (Tenn.)	3,134,516	13.7	5
Richard Gephardt (Mo.)	1,388,356	6.0	2
Others	1,936,180	8.4	1
TOTAL	22,961,936		

1988 REPUBLICAN PRIMARIES

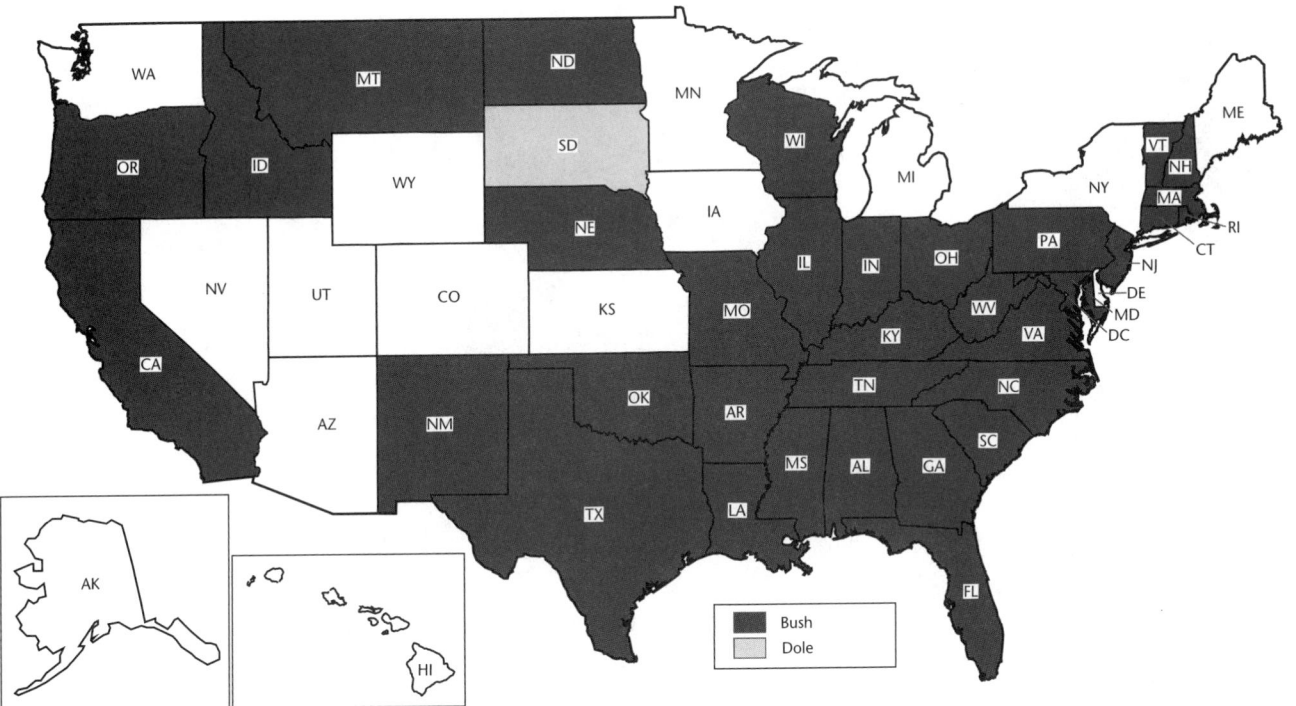

Bush
Dole

Like the Democrats in 1988, the Republicans began the year with a crowded field. But unlike the Democrats, the Republican picture cleared quickly.

Vice President George Bush could muster only a third-place finish in the first big event of the year, the Iowa precinct caucuses, where he trailed both Kansas Sen. Bob Dole and religious broadcaster Pat Robertson. But Bush rebounded quickly, beating Dole by nearly 10 percentage points in New Hampshire.

From there, Bush's momentum snowballed. A pivotal victory in the early March primary in South Carolina opened the door to a Bush sweep of the Super Tuesday GOP voting three days later, in which all of the remaining Southern states participated.

The results sent New York Rep. Jack Kemp to the sidelines. A week later, Bush's decisive win in Illinois drove Dole out of the race as well. Robertson lingered on, but was a factor only in a handful of caucus states where his small, but dedicated, cadre of supporters had gained a toehold.

In the end, Bush won every Republican primary but one, that a February event in South Dakota that he had essentially conceded to Dole.

	Total Vote	Percentage	Primary States Won
George Bush (Texas)	8,254,654	67.9	34
Bob Dole (Kan.)	2,333,268	19.2	1
Pat Robertson (Va.)	1,097,442	9.0	0
Others	479,751	3.9	0
TOTAL	12,165,115		

1992 DEMOCRATIC PRIMARIES

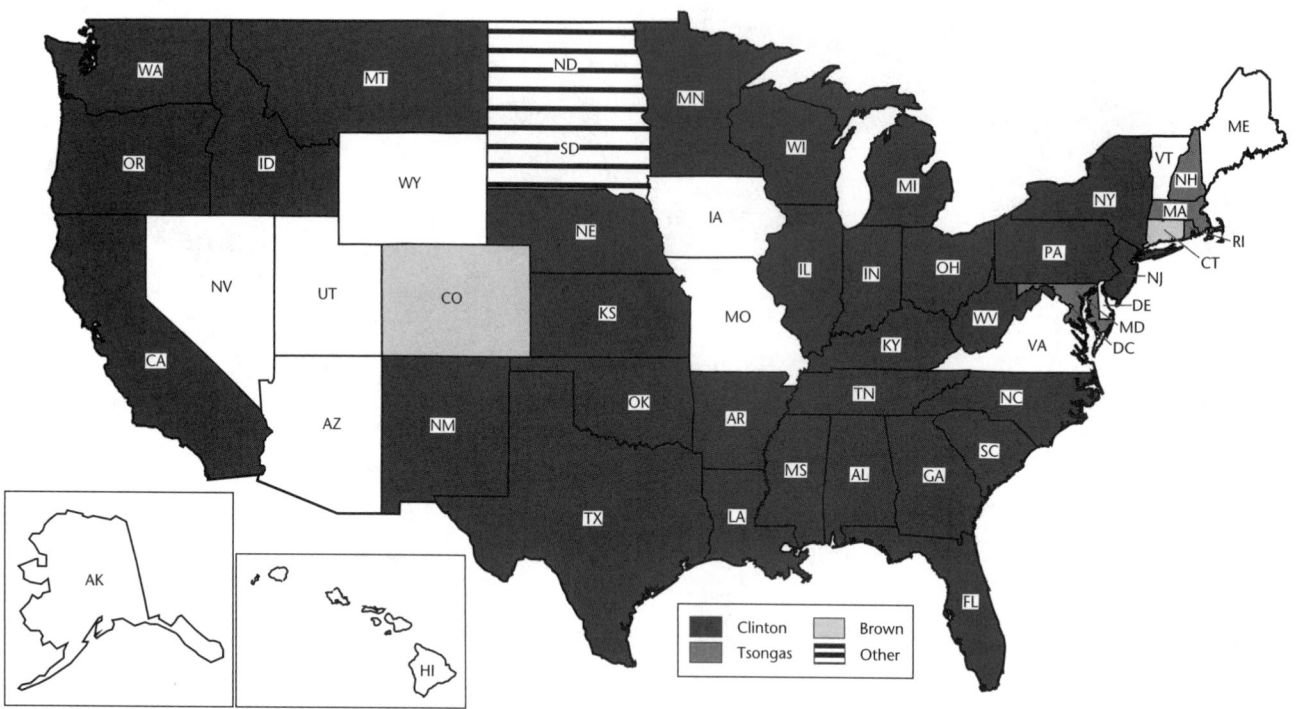

	Clinton
	Tsongas

	Brown
	Other

The 1992 Democratic presidential nominating contest had two phases. The first, pre-primary phase, focused on whether New York Gov. Mario Cuomo would run. He decided not to.

With Cuomo out of the race, Arkansas Gov. Bill Clinton was well positioned for the second phase, the primaries themselves. But it began for Clinton on a tenuous note. Hit with charges of womanizing and draft evasion (during the Vietnam War), Clinton did well to survive with a second-place finish in the New Hampshire primary behind former Sen. Paul Tsongas of neighboring Massachusetts.

But survival was enough. Clinton's home region, the South, was the first region to vote en masse and Clinton dominated the early March primaries there. Big victories followed for Clinton in mid-March in Illinois and Michigan that drove Tsongas from the race. Former California Gov. Jerry Brown briefly established himself as a challenger to Clinton with a late March victory in Connecticut. But Clinton swept all the primaries that followed, including a pivotal early April primary in New York that left his route clear to the nomination.

Clinton ended up with 52 percent of the vote in the primaries, the highest vote share for any Democratic nominee since 1956.

	Total Vote	Percentage	Primary States Won
Bill Clinton (Ark.)	10,482,411	51.8	30
Jerry Brown (Calif.)	4,071,232	20.1	2
Paul Tsongas (Mass.)	3,656,010	18.1	4
Others	2,029,732	10.0	2
TOTAL	20,239,385		

1992 REPUBLICAN PRIMARIES

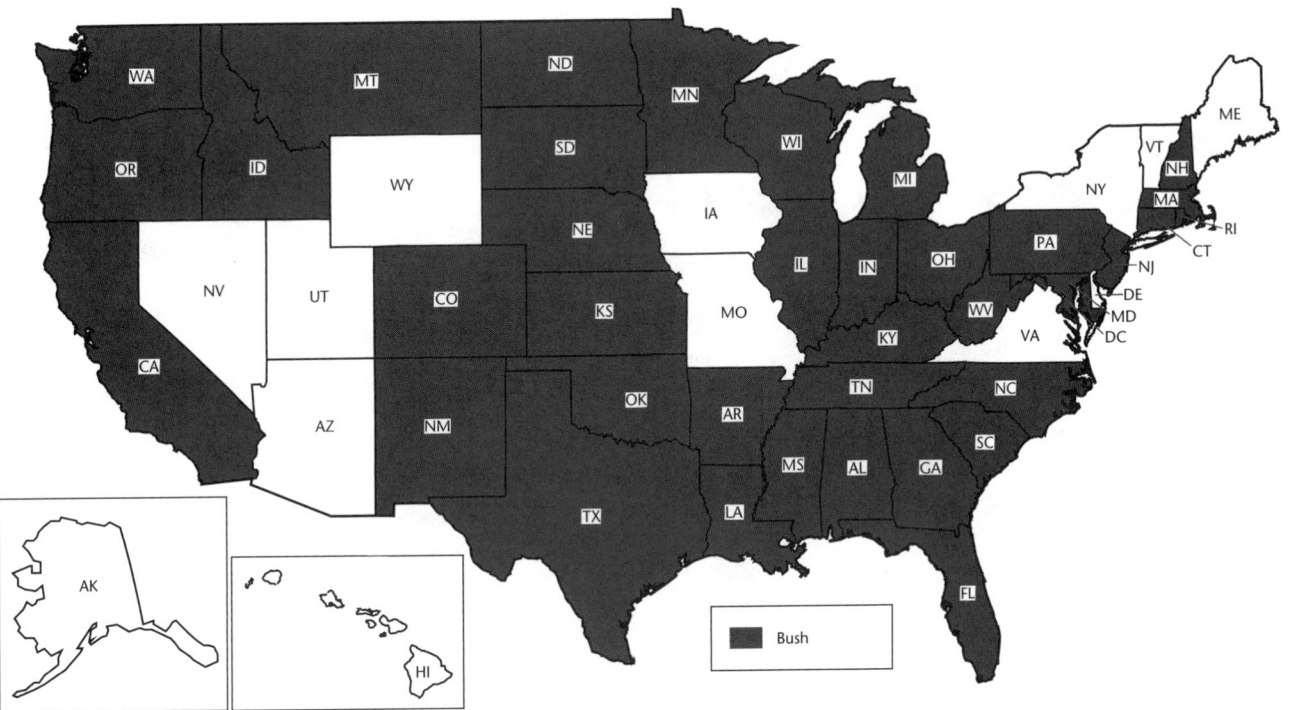

Bush

For the third time since 1976, an incumbent president struggled through his party's primaries and ended up a loser at the ballot box in the fall.

In reality, President George Bush was not as closely contested during the Republican primaries in 1992 as Gerald Ford had been in 1976 or Jimmy Carter in the Democratic primaries of 1980. But both Ford and Carter faced more serious challengers than Bush, who was opposed by television commentator Pat Buchanan.

Buchanan came no closer to beating Bush than his 37 percent share of the primary vote in the first-in-the-nation primary in New Hampshire. But Buchanan hung around, sounding a vocal challenge to Bush administration foreign and economic policy and serving as an outlet for anti-Bush protest votes throughout the primary season. Louisiana's David Duke briefly vied with Buchanan for that mantle, but failed to win more than 10 percent of the vote in any Republican primary except Mississippi.

	Total Vote	Percentage	Primary States Won
George Bush (Texas)*	9,199,463	72.5	37
Pat Buchanan (Va.)	2,899,488	22.8	0
Others	597,596	4.7	0
TOTAL	12,696,547		

1996 DEMOCRATIC PRIMARIES

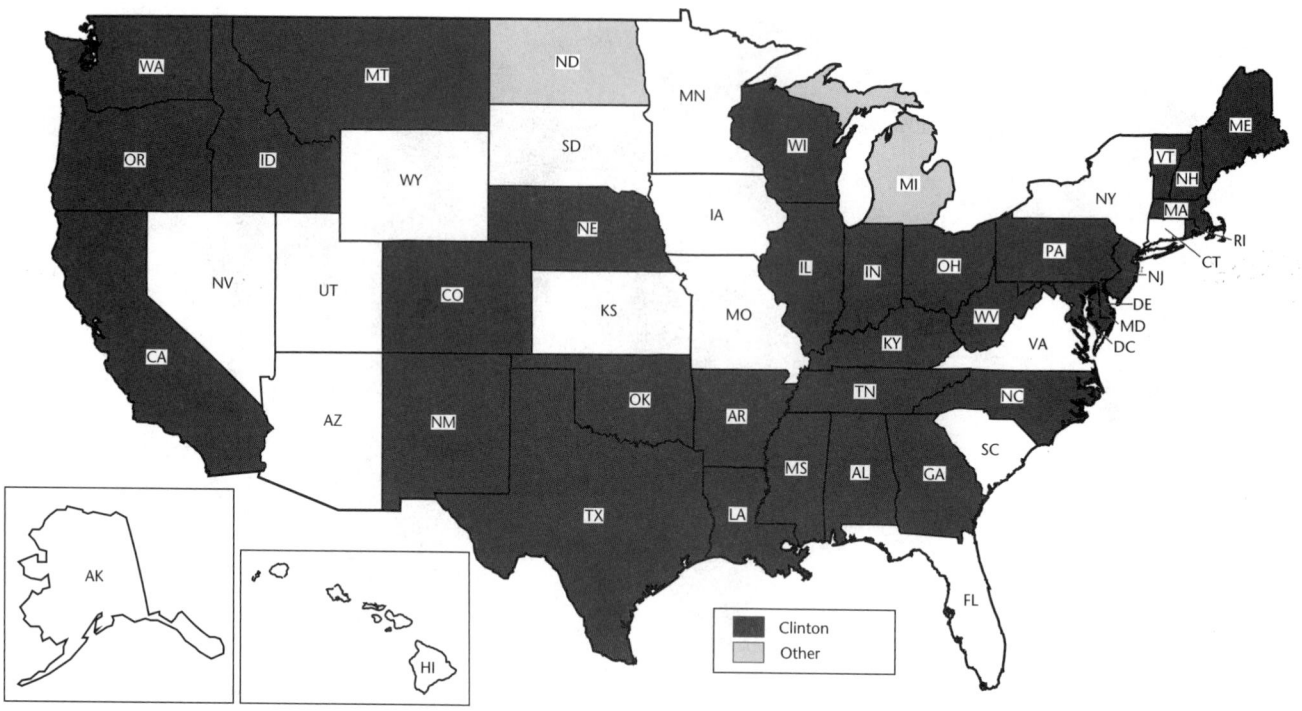

Clinton
Other

By the time the 1996 Democratic presidential primaries were to begin, President Bill Clinton had already won, as no more than token opposition filed against him. Clinton's most persistent challenge came from perennial presidential aspirant Lyndon LaRouche, but it was opposition the incumbent could safely ignore.

Clinton won easily in every primary that he was on the ballot. And when all the votes were tallied, he had made the best primary showing of any Democratic president since Franklin D. Roosevelt in 1936. That year, FDR took 93 percent of the Democratic primary ballots.

	Total Vote	Percentage	Primary States Won
Bill Clinton (Ark.)*	9,694,499	88.6	32
Lyndon LaRouche (Va.)	596,422	5.4	0
Others	656,443	6.0	2
TOTAL	10,947,364		

1996 REPUBLICAN PRIMARIES

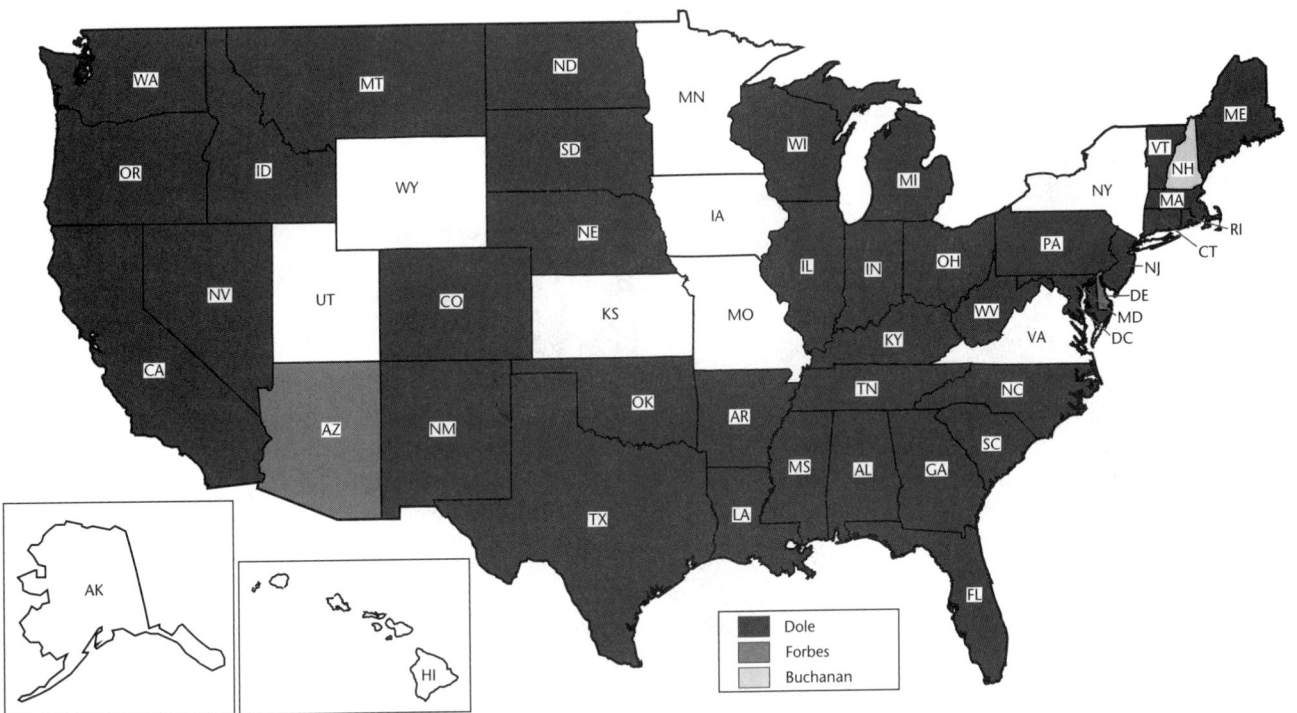

Dole
Forbes
Buchanan

Once former Gen. Colin Powell decided not to seek the Republican nomination in 1996, Bob Dole was the clear front-runner. But he had to survive a turbulent month of February before establishing his hegemony in the myriad primaries that filled the month of March.

Dole basically played ".500 ball" in the opening round of events in February. He won the Iowa caucuses by a small margin, narrowly lost New Hampshire to Pat Buchanan, lost primaries in Delaware and Arizona to Steve Forbes, and won primaries in North and South Dakota.

But once the calendar flipped to March and there was a staccato of primaries on multiple fronts, Dole's considerable assets paid off—a hefty campaign chest, support from much

of the Republican establishment and a broad acceptability to GOP voters.

Starting with his pivotal victory in South Carolina March 2, Dole did not lose another primary. He swept all eight primaries on March 5 (including all of New England outside New Hampshire), a New York delegate-selection event on March 7, all seven primaries on March 12 (most in the South), four contests in the industrial Midwest on March 19, and three Western primaries, anchored by California, on March 26. By the end of the month, Dole had won all the delegates he needed to assure himself the Republican nomination.

It marked a reversal of fortune for Dole, who had not won a primary *after* February when he ran in 1988.

	Total Vote	Percentage	Primary States Won
Bob Dole (Kan.)	8,191,239	58.5	37
Pat Buchanan (Va.)	3,020,746	21.6	1
Steve Forbes (N.J.)	1,424,898	10.2	2
Others	1,354,766	9.7	0
TOTAL	13,991,649		

2000 DEMOCRATIC PRIMARIES

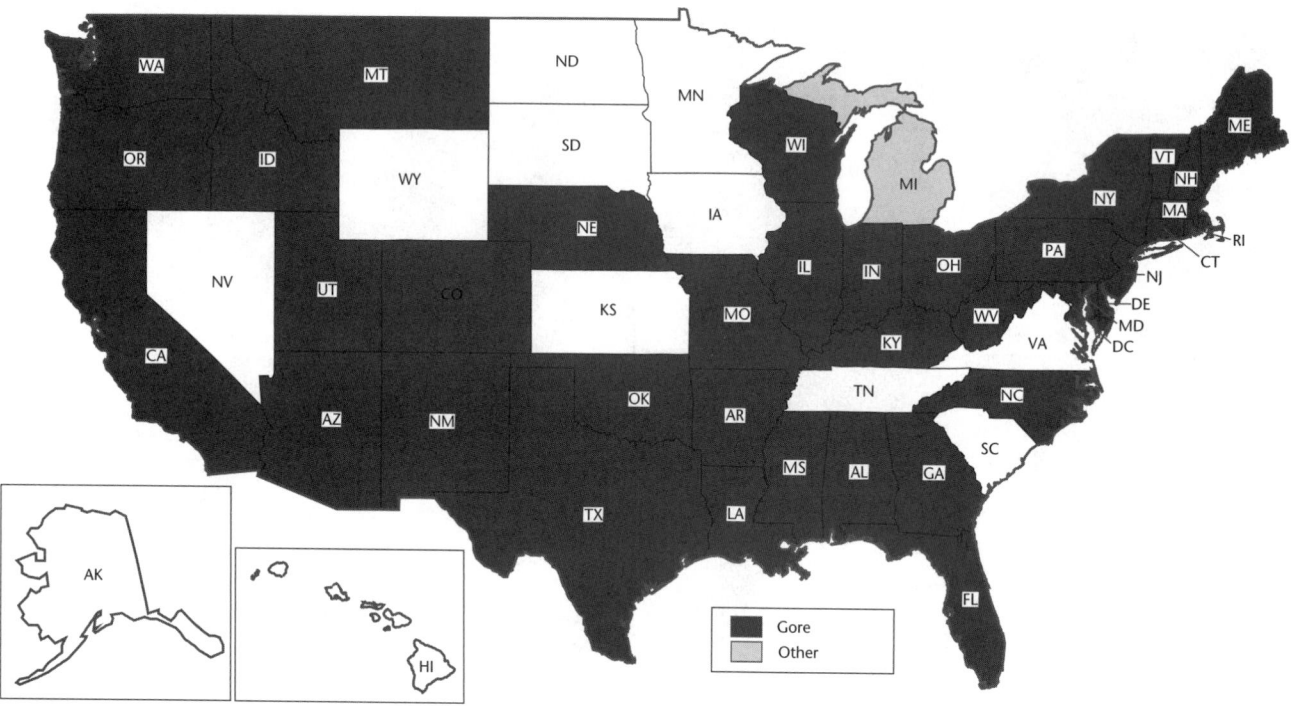

Vice President Al Gore won every Democratic presidential primary he contested. But the shift of barely 3,000 votes in New Hampshire from Gore to Bill Bradley would have given the former New Jersey senator victory in the first-in-the-nation primary and altered the dynamic of the race that followed.

As it was, New Hampshire was Bradley's last best opportunity to make the Democratic race competitive following a decisive loss to Gore the previous week in the Iowa caucuses. But with the lively GOP race between George W. Bush and John McCain drawing the lion's share of attention, Bradley was unable to make a successful late appeal for the votes of New Hampshire's independent voters. They could vote in either party's primary in the Granite State but went in droves for McCain.

Democratic rules at the time prevented any other delegate-selection events from being held before the first Tuesday in March, when a plethora of primaries and caucuses were held from Maine to Hawaii. Brandishing momentum as well as support from the party establishment and key interest groups, Gore won them all.

Bradley was beaten badly in the major battleground states that day, garnering only one-third of the Democratic primary vote in New York, one-quarter of the vote in Ohio, and less than 20 percent in California. He reached even 40 percent of the vote in only a handful of New England primaries. Shortly thereafter, he quit the race, conceding the Democratic nomination to Gore.

	Total Vote	Percentage	Primary States Won
Al Gore (Tenn.)	10,628,410	75.7	38
Bill Bradley (N.J.)	2,798,286	19.9	0
Other	622,255	4.4	1
TOTAL	14,048,951		

2000 REPUBLICAN PRIMARIES

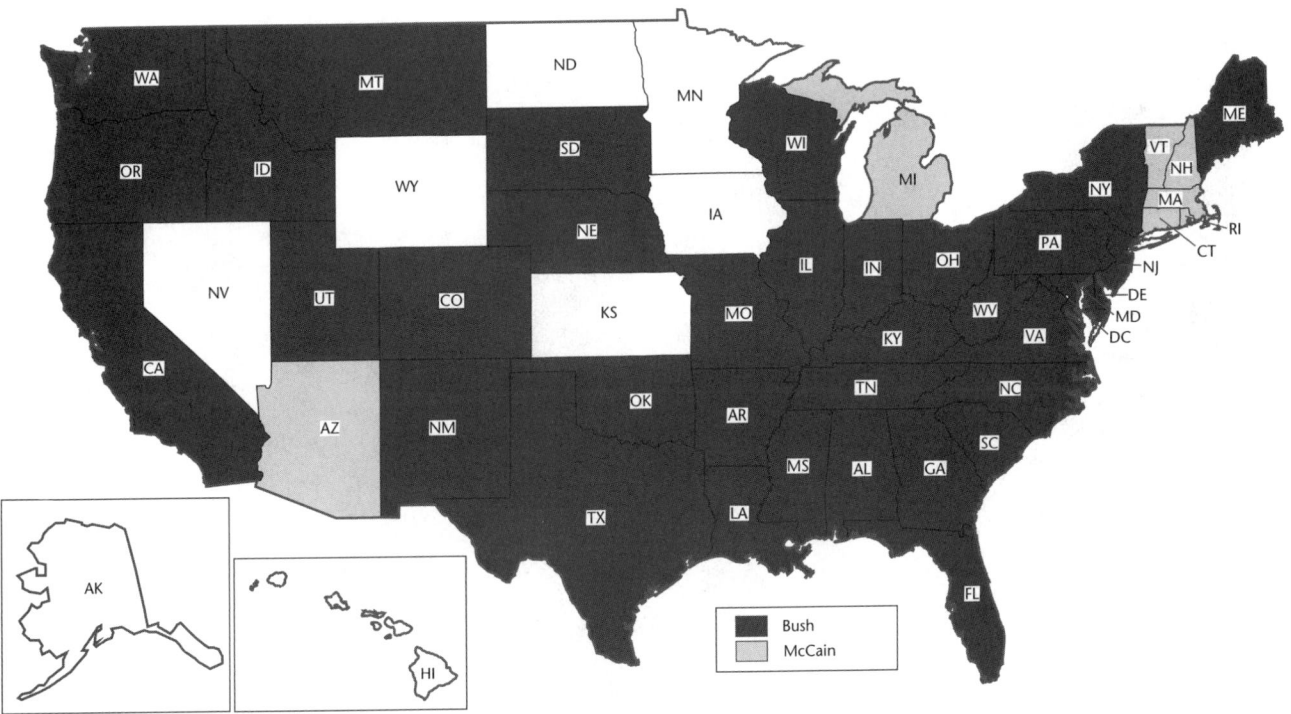

From the beginning, Texas governor George W. Bush was the odds-on favorite to win the Republican presidential nomination. The son of the nation's 41st president, he had the support of much of the party establishment—including virtually all of his fellow GOP governors—as well as a campaign chest that ultimately reached upwards of $100 million. It was far larger than any of his rivals and a record for any presidential nominating campaign up to that time.

But any thoughts of a quick coronation were dashed by the maverick challenge of Sen. John McCain of Arizona, who boasted an intriguing resume (as a former prisoner-of-war in Vietnam) and an issue, campaign finance reform, that made his candidacy particularly appealing to moderate Republicans and independent voters.

McCain skipped the Iowa caucuses to focus on campaigning in New Hampshire, where he stunned Bush with an 18 percentage point victory. Through the month of February, Bush and

McCain traded primary victories. Bush won in Delaware and South Carolina. McCain followed with wins in Michigan and his home state of Arizona. Bush responded with triumphs in Virginia and Washington. At the end of the month, the two were neck and neck in the overall primary vote count, with Bush amassing less than 3,000 votes more than McCain of the nearly 3.6 million cast to that point.

Republican primaries had unfolded at the rate of one or two per week through February. But once the calendar flipped to March, Bush's superior organization and funding placed him in position to dominate the vast cross-country action scheduled on the first Tuesday of the month. McCain continued to run well in New England that day, but Bush won everywhere else—including California, New York, and Ohio. Without a major victory to point to and Bush's home region, the South, coming up, McCain quit the race.

	Total Vote	Percentage	Primary States Won
George W. Bush (Texas)	10,844,401	63.2	35
John McCain (Ariz.)	5,118,788	29.8	7
Alan Keyes (Md.)	914,569	5.3	0
Other	279,317	1.6	0
TOTAL	17,157,075		

2004 DEMOCRATIC PRIMARIES

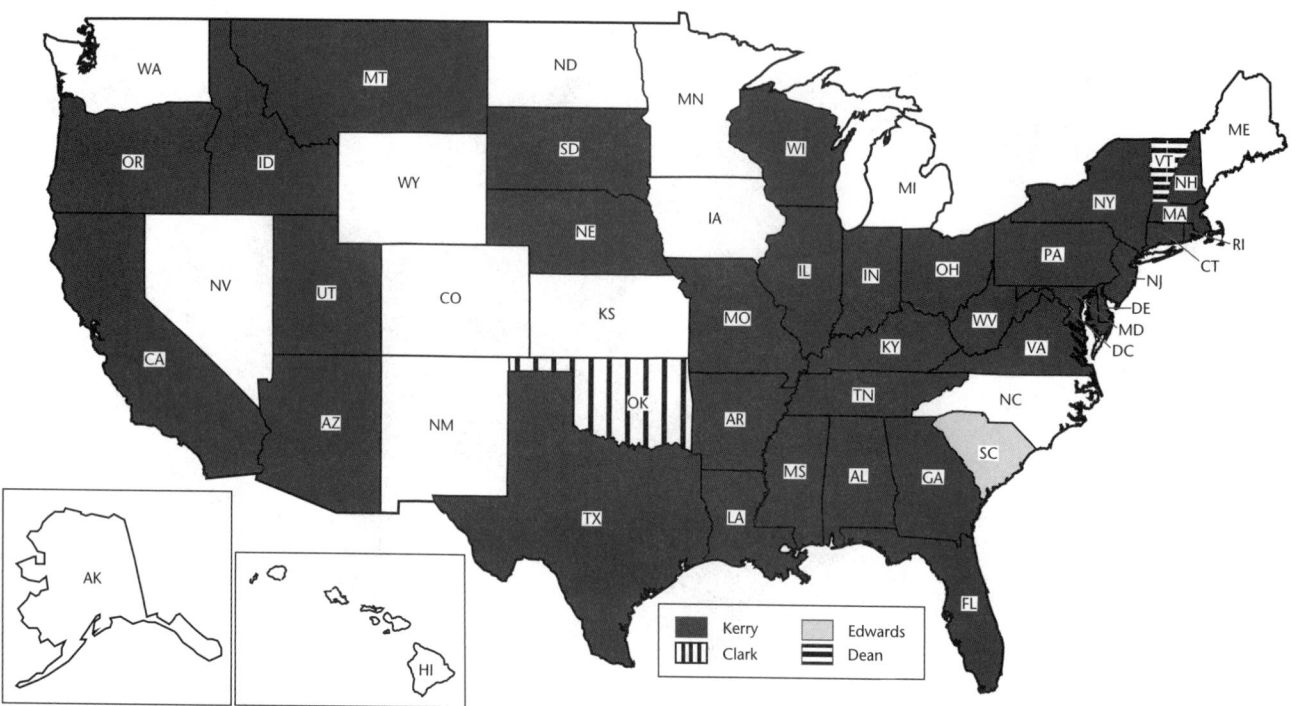

Kerry
Clark
Edwards
Dean

Probably the most competitive stage of the 2004 Democratic presidential nominating process took place in the year before the primaries were held. Over the course of 2003, the field of candidates jockeyed for position, with the lead in the public opinion polls for the Democratic nomination changing hands several times.

Two of the best known contenders–Sen. Joe Lieberman of Connecticut, the party's vice presidential candidate in 2000, and former House minority leader Richard Gephardt of Missouri—vied for the lead in the Gallup Poll through the spring and summer months of 2003. Retired general Wesley Clark of Arkansas vaulted to the fore once he entered the race in September, but was quickly displaced by former Vermont governor Howard Dean. The former Vermont governor's strong opposition to the Iraq war and success at using the Internet as a staple of organizing and fund raising made him a political sensation in the closing months of the year.

Yet once the voting actually began in early 2004, it was a different pair of candidates that prospered. One, Sen. John Kerry of Massachusetts, a decorated Vietnam War veteran, boasted a favorable resume for a wartime election, and enjoyed access to a personal fortune that he tapped before the primaries. The other, Sen. John Edwards of North Carolina, tied a compelling theme of "two Americas" with a prowess for raising money. Kerry handily won the nomination; Edwards, his last major rival standing, ended up as Kerry's vice presidential running mate.

Any drama during the primary season itself was doused quickly. Kerry won both of the critical leadoff contests in January–defeating Edwards by 6 percentage points in the Iowa caucuses and Dean by a dozen points in the first-in-the-nation New Hampshire primary. With momentum, Kerry was virtually unbeatable after that, sweeping seven of the nine primaries in February, and eight of the nine primaries on Super Tuesday (the first Tuesday in March). That night, his final rival of consequence, Edwards, quit the race.

	Total Vote	Percentage	Primary States Won
John Kerry (Mass.)	9,870,082	61.0	33
John Edwards (N.C.)	3,135,373	19.4	1
Howard Dean (Vt.)	894,524	5.5	1
Others	2,282,460	14.1	1
TOTAL	16,182,439		

2004 REPUBLICAN PRIMARIES

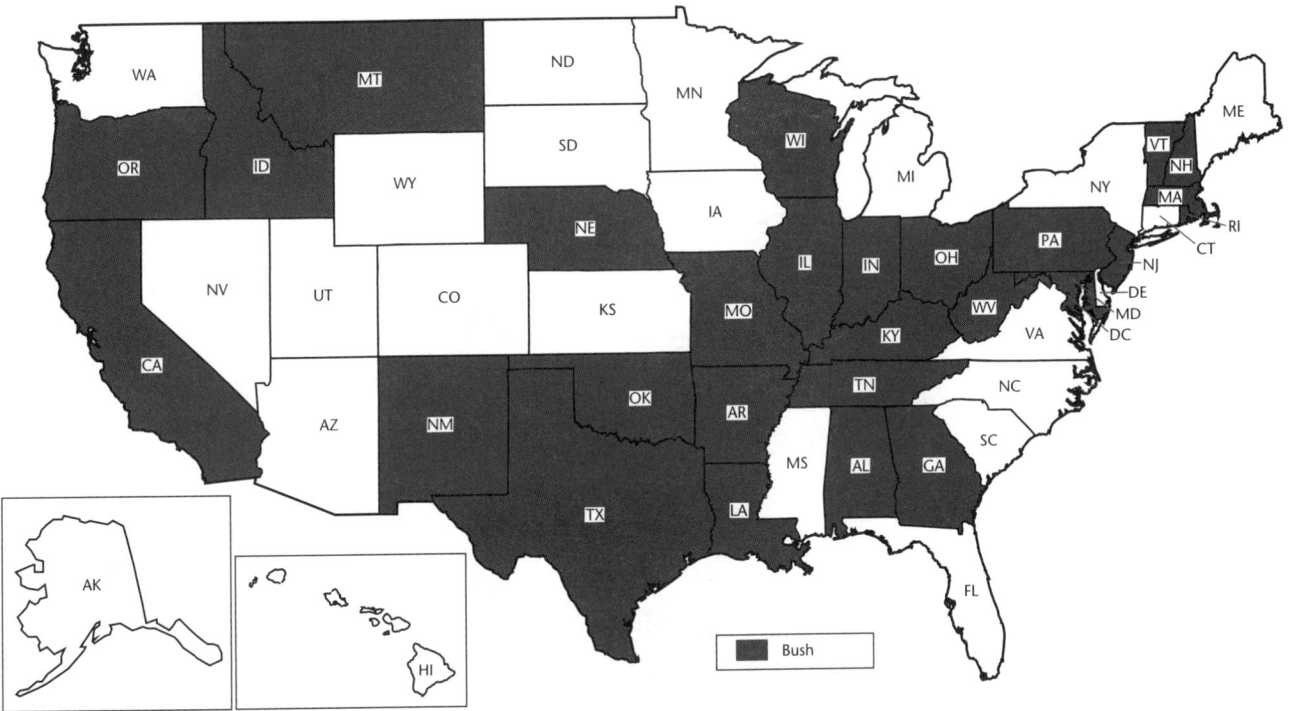

Bush

Arguably, the first term of George W. Bush was the most polarizing of any modern president. The launching of the Iraq war in the wake of the 9/11 terror attacks on the United States led a series of controversial decisions by Bush, which left many Democrats fuming at his assertive style of leadership and many Republicans hailing him as a candidate for Mount Rushmore. The result in 2004 was a clear path to renomination for the incumbent but a close fight for reelection in the fall.

Bush rolled up 98 percent of the Republican primary vote, the second-highest percentage by any candidate of either party since the proliferation of presidential primaries began in 1972.

(Ronald Reagan, with 99 percent of the GOP primary vote in 1984, is tops.)

With Bush facing token opposition at most, the number of Republican primaries fell to 27 in 2004, the lowest number since 1984. Still, the absence of competition did not prevent Bush from raising and spending roughly $250 million during the nominating season, roughly the same amount as Kerry. It marked the first time since the public financing of presidential campaigns was initiated in 1976 that both the Democratic and Republican nominees did not accept public financing.

	Total Vote	Percentage	Primary States Won
George W. Bush (Texas)	7,784,653	98.0	27
Others	155,678	2.0	0
TOTAL	7,940,331		

2000–2004
PRESIDENTIAL PRIMARY
RETURNS BY STATE

ALABAMA

By joining with Florida and Georgia to hold a presidential primary in early March 1980, Alabama helped form the embryo of the Southern regional vote that had developed by 1988 into "Super Tuesday." But Alabama voters never turned out in large numbers for the March primary, certainly when compared to the state's midterm gubernatorial primary. In the 1990s, the presidential primary was returned to June, when party nominations for Congress are also settled. And there it has stayed, too late to make any difference at all in recent presidential nominating contests.

Those that did vote in Alabama's Democratic presidential primaries in the 1980s disproportionately represented the liberal wing of the party. They handed Walter Mondale a critical victory in 1984 and gave Jesse Jackson a clear-cut primary win in 1988.

Mondale, rocked in early 1984 by an upset loss to Gary Hart in New Hampshire, regained his footing with a narrow victory

in Georgia and a decisive triumph the same day in Alabama. With support from organized labor Mondale rode to a large lead in Alabama's major industrial centers–Birmingham, Gadsden, Anniston, and the Quad Cities of the Tennessee River Valley.

But Mondale also relied on the support of blacks. Exit polls showed him splitting the white vote almost evenly with Hart and John Glenn. But with help from Birmingham Mayor Richard Arrington Jr. and other black leaders, Mondale picked off an estimated one-third to one-half of the black vote. Jackson won virtually all the rest.

The Democratic primary vote was more racially polarized in 1988. Blacks cast about one-third of the ballots, and Jackson won nearly all of them. Al Gore of neighboring Tennessee took a majority of the white vote, enabling him to finish a reasonably close second.

The racial pattern of the primary vote was visible on the map. Except for a pocket of white-majority counties near the Florida

Recent Alabama Primary Results

Alabama held its first presidential primary in 1928 to select delegates, but did not include a direct vote for presidential candidates until 1980.

Year	DEMOCRATS			REPUBLICANS		
	Turnout	Candidates	%	Turnout	Candidates	%
2004 (June 1)	218,574	JOHN KERRY	75	201,487	GEORGE W. BUSH*	93
		Uncommitted	17		Uncommitted	7
2000 (June 6)	278,527	AL GORE	77	203,079	GEORGE W. BUSH	84
		Uncommitted	17		Alan Keyes	12
		Lyndon LaRouche	6			
1996 (June 4)	302,038	BILL CLINTON*	81	211,933	BOB DOLE	76
		Uncommitted	15		Pat Buchanan	16
					Uncommitted	5
1992 (June 2)	450,899	BILL CLINTON	68	165,121	GEORGE BUSH*	74
		Uncommitted	20		Uncommitted	18
		Jerry Brown	7		Pat Buchanan	8
1988 (March 8)	405,642	JESSE JACKSON	44	213,561	GEORGE BUSH	65
		Al Gore	37		Bob Dole	16
		Michael Dukakis	8		Pat Robertson	14
		Richard Gephardt	7			
1984 (March 13)	428,283	WALTER MONDALE	35		No Primary	
		John Glenn	21			
		Gary Hart	21			
		Jesse Jackson	20			
1980 (March 11)	237,464	JIMMY CARTER*	82	211,353	RONALD REAGAN	70
		Edward Kennedy	13		George Bush	26

Note: All candidates are listed that drew at least 5 percent of their party's primary vote. The names of winning candidates are capitalized. An asterisk (*) indicates an incumbent president.

panhandle, Jackson swept every county in the southern half of the state. In the rural black-majority counties, his margins were huge. He won by nearly 40-to-1 in Macon County (Tuskegee), which had a population 85 percent black in the 2000 Census.

Meanwhile, Gore swept virtually every county in Alabama's hilly and overwhelmingly white northern half. Jackson won statewide by 25,000 votes by virtue of his urban strength. Of the state's five most populous counties, he carried four, losing only Madison (Huntsville), along the Tennessee border, to Gore.

Whether balloting in March or June, Republican primary voters have overwhelmingly endorsed the front-runner: Ronald Reagan in 1980, George Bush in 1988 and 1992, Bob Dole in 1996, and George W. Bush in 2000. In 2004, when Bush was president and ran essentially unopposed for renomination, he rolled up more than 90 percent of the Republican primary vote against an "Uncommitted" option on the ballot. Uncommitted reached 10 percent in only three counties, including Lee (the home of Auburn University) and Winston (a small county in northwest Alabama that has been loyally Republican since Reconstruction).

Yet sometimes it takes an election or two for even establishment candidates to make good in Alabama. Dole was beaten badly by the elder Bush in the 1988 primary. Bush was swamped by Reagan in 1980. Bush's loss that time was not from lack of effort. His TV ads featured an endorsement from

former Vietnam prisoner of war Jeremiah Denton (who was on his way to election to the Senate that fall). And Bush's state campaign manager, who was also the national president of the Bass Anglers Sportsman Society, sought to organize Alabama fishermen for Bush. The effort, though, did not land many voters.

Conservative Christian activists have had only modest success in Republican presidential primaries in spite of Alabama's location in the midst of the Bible Belt. Evangelist Pat Robertson drew just 14 percent of the vote in the 1988 GOP primary. Alan Keyes, who drew much of his support from conservative Christians, polled 12 percent against George W. Bush in 2000. In addition, the 2006 Republican gubernatorial primary was won handily by incumbent Bob Riley over the former chief justice of the state Supreme Court, Roy Moore, who had lost his position when he refused to remove a monument of the Ten Commandments from his court building. Riley's margin of victory over Moore was 2 to 1.

Since the mid-1990s, Republicans have held both of Alabama's Senate seats and a majority of the House delegation, which has been reflected in a more geographically diverse Republican primary electorate. For years, it was centered on the state's major metropolitan areas. More than half the vote in the 1996 GOP presidential primary was cast in four counties–Jefferson (Birmingham), Madison, Mobile, and Shelby (a suburban county outside Birmingham). In 2004, those same four counties cast barely one-third of the Republican primary vote.

But in recent years, the presidential primary turnout for both parties has been comparatively small. In 2004, barely 400,000 votes were cast in the presidential primaries, almost evenly split between the two parties. In 2006, with competitive gubernatorial contests on both sides, the combined primary turnout exceeded 900,000, again almost evenly divided between the two parties.

ALABAMA DEMOCRATIC PRIMARY

2000

County	Total Vote	Gore	LaRouche	Uncommitted	Winner	Percentage of Total Vote		
						Gore	LaRouche	Uncommitted
AUTAUGA	1,519	1,312	66	141	Gore	86.4%	4.3%	9.3%
BALDWIN	1,946	1,696	64	186	Gore	87.2%	3.3%	9.6%
BARBOUR	3,786	2,651	303	832	Gore	70.0%	8.0%	22.0%
BIBB	2,162	1,533	154	475	Gore	70.9%	7.1%	22.0%
BLOUNT	3,293	2,229	251	813	Gore	67.7%	7.6%	24.7%
BULLOCK	1,798	1,593	82	123	Gore	88.6%	4.6%	6.8%
BUTLER	3,144	2,195	235	714	Gore	69.8%	7.5%	22.7%
CALHOUN	2,827	2,293	124	410	Gore	81.1%	4.4%	14.5%
CHAMBERS	2,838	2,220	172	446	Gore	78.2%	6.1%	15.7%
CHEROKEE	3,337	2,319	192	826	Gore	69.5%	5.8%	24.8%
CHILTON	2,869	2,271	115	483	Gore	79.2%	4.0%	16.8%
CHOCTAW	2,870	2,182	156	532	Gore	76.0%	5.4%	18.5%
CLARKE	3,493	2,445	262	786	Gore	70.0%	7.5%	22.5%
CLAY	1,856	1,218	176	462	Gore	65.6%	9.5%	24.9%
CLEBURNE	2,738	1,567	247	924	Gore	57.2%	9.0%	33.7%
COFFEE	3,456	2,402	226	828	Gore	69.5%	6.5%	24.0%
COLBERT	7,778	5,471	491	1,816	Gore	70.3%	6.3%	23.3%
CONECUH	2,833	2,006	223	604	Gore	70.8%	7.9%	21.3%
COOSA	2,165	1,456	157	552	Gore	67.3%	7.3%	25.5%
COVINGTON	3,728	2,316	350	1,062	Gore	62.1%	9.4%	28.5%
CRENSHAW	1,961	1,283	165	513	Gore	65.4%	8.4%	26.2%
CULLMAN	5,798	4,195	372	1,231	Gore	72.4%	6.4%	21.2%
DALE	2,065	1,474	175	416	Gore	71.4%	8.5%	20.1%
DALLAS	10,101	7,440	755	1,906	Gore	73.7%	7.5%	18.9%
DE KALB	1,218	1,076	36	106	Gore	88.3%	3.0%	8.7%
ELMORE	2,333	1,865	116	352	Gore	79.9%	5.0%	15.1%
ESCAMBIA	3,999	2,433	339	1,227	Gore	60.8%	8.5%	30.7%
ETOWAH	4,347	3,759	112	476	Gore	86.5%	2.6%	11.0%
FAYETTE	3,557	2,297	313	947	Gore	64.6%	8.8%	26.6%
FRANKLIN	7,271	4,836	535	1,900	Gore	66.5%	7.4%	26.1%
GENEVA	1,065	798	70	197	Gore	74.9%	6.6%	18.5%
GREENE	2,702	2,411	205	86	Gore	89.2%	7.6%	3.2%
HALE	4,146	3,326	168	652	Gore	80.2%	4.1%	15.7%
HENRY	2,017	1,356	186	475	Gore	67.2%	9.2%	23.5%
HOUSTON	3,776	2,549	271	956	Gore	67.5%	7.2%	25.3%
JACKSON	5,733	4,382	259	1,092	Gore	76.4%	4.5%	19.0%
JEFFERSON	23,256	21,495	417	1,344	Gore	92.4%	1.8%	5.8%
LAMAR	3,754	2,260	225	1,269	Gore	60.2%	6.0%	33.8%
LAUDERDALE	6,030	4,454	364	1,212	Gore	73.9%	6.0%	20.1%
LAWRENCE	10,054	7,464	605	1,985	Gore	74.2%	6.0%	19.7%
LEE	2,485	2,308	56	121	Gore	92.9%	2.3%	4.9%
LIMESTONE	959	853	32	74	Gore	88.9%	3.3%	7.7%
LOWNDES	3,249	2,732	199	318	Gore	84.1%	6.1%	9.8%
MACON	3,529	3,221	130	178	Gore	91.3%	3.7%	5.0%
MADISON	7,434	6,274	244	916	Gore	84.4%	3.3%	12.3%

ALABAMA DEMOCRATIC PRIMARY

2000

County	Total Vote	Gore	LaRouche	Uncommitted	Winner	Percentage of Total Vote		
						Gore	LaRouche	Uncommitted
MARENGO	4,045	2,894	302	849	Gore	71.5%	7.5%	21.0%
MARION	3,131	2,168	176	787	Gore	69.2%	5.6%	25.1%
MARSHALL	1,981	1,625	78	278	Gore	82.0%	3.9%	14.0%
MOBILE	11,633	10,866	217	550	Gore	93.4%	1.9%	4.7%
MONROE	1,784	1,374	100	310	Gore	77.0%	5.6%	17.4%
MONTGOMERY	7,023	6,446	236	341	Gore	91.8%	3.4%	4.9%
MORGAN	4,539	3,517	308	714	Gore	77.5%	6.8%	15.7%
PERRY	3,578	2,951	175	452	Gore	82.5%	4.9%	12.6%
PICKENS	4,351	2,945	308	1,098	Gore	67.7%	7.1%	25.2%
PIKE	2,243	1,843	111	289	Gore	82.2%	4.9%	12.9%
RANDOLPH	3,331	2,130	272	929	Gore	63.9%	8.2%	27.9%
RUSSELL	4,317	3,148	238	931	Gore	72.9%	5.5%	21.6%
ST. CLAIR	1,035	884	39	112	Gore	85.4%	3.8%	10.8%
SHELBY	1,701	1,550	38	113	Gore	91.1%	2.2%	6.6%
SUMTER	2,348	2,148	62	138	Gore	91.5%	2.6%	5.9%
TALLADEGA	2,242	1,791	85	366	Gore	79.9%	3.8%	16.3%
TALLAPOOSA	6,538	4,016	604	1,918	Gore	61.4%	9.2%	29.3%
TUSCALOOSA	6,039	5,225	215	599	Gore	86.5%	3.6%	9.9%
WALKER	11,272	7,387	751	3,134	Gore	65.5%	6.7%	27.8%
WASHINGTON	4,580	2,971	390	1,219	Gore	64.9%	8.5%	26.6%
WILCOX	3,446	2,777	216	453	Gore	80.6%	6.3%	13.1%
WINSTON	271	230	12	29	Gore	84.9%	4.4%	10.7%
TOTAL	274,703	210,802	15,328	48,573	Gore	76.7%	5.6%	17.7%
Certified Totals	278,527	214,541	15,465	48,521	Gore	77.0%	5.6%	17.4%

ALABAMA REPUBLICAN PRIMARY

2000

County	Total Vote	G.W. Bush	Keyes	Uncommitted	Winner	Percentage of Total Vote		
						G.W. Bush	Keyes	Uncommitted
AUTAUGA	6,137	5,190	538	409	G.W. Bush	84.6%	8.8%	6.7%
BALDWIN	15,055	12,828	1,340	887	G.W. Bush	85.2%	8.9%	5.9%
BARBOUR	179	148	29	2	G.W. Bush	82.7%	16.2%	1.1%
BIBB	494	429	54	11	G.W. Bush	86.8%	10.9%	2.2%
BLOUNT	2,501	2,146	276	79	G.W. Bush	85.8%	11.0%	3.2%
BULLOCK	22	22	0	0	G.W. Bush	100.0%	0.0%	0.0%
BUTLER	312	288	21	3	G.W. Bush	92.3%	6.7%	1.0%
CALHOUN	3,250	2,725	387	138	G.W. Bush	83.8%	11.9%	4.2%
CHAMBERS	457	394	48	15	G.W. Bush	86.2%	10.5%	3.3%
CHEROKEE	181	143	31	7	G.W. Bush	79.0%	17.1%	3.9%
CHILTON	3,589	3,231	243	115	G.W. Bush	90.0%	6.8%	3.2%
CHOCTAW	120	111	8	1	G.W. Bush	92.5%	6.7%	0.8%
CLARKE	373	333	31	9	G.W. Bush	89.3%	8.3%	2.4%
CLAY	332	294	22	16	G.W. Bush	88.6%	6.6%	4.8%
CLEBURNE	96	76	16	4	G.W. Bush	79.2%	16.7%	4.2%
COFFEE	1,535	1,351	131	53	G.W. Bush	88.0%	8.5%	3.5%
COLBERT	1,011	798	192	21	G.W. Bush	78.9%	19.0%	2.1%
CONECUH	63	54	6	3	G.W. Bush	85.7%	9.5%	4.8%
COOSA	141	123	15	3	G.W. Bush	87.2%	10.6%	2.1%
COVINGTON	927	813	89	25	G.W. Bush	87.7%	9.6%	2.7%
CRENSHAW	102	95	5	2	G.W. Bush	93.1%	4.9%	2.0%
CULLMAN	3,636	3,141	395	100	G.W. Bush	86.4%	10.9%	2.8%
DALE	1,595	1,349	165	81	G.W. Bush	84.6%	10.3%	5.1%
DALLAS	166	146	15	5	G.W. Bush	88.0%	9.0%	3.0%
DE KALB	1,737	1,510	180	47	G.W. Bush	86.9%	10.4%	2.7%
ELMORE	7,946	6,889	677	380	G.W. Bush	86.7%	8.5%	4.8%
ESCAMBIA	251	221	26	4	G.W. Bush	88.0%	10.4%	1.6%
ETOWAH	5,921	4,856	763	302	G.W. Bush	82.0%	12.9%	5.1%
FAYETTE	175	149	18	8	G.W. Bush	85.1%	10.3%	4.6%
FRANKLIN	106	86	18	2	G.W. Bush	81.1%	17.0%	1.9%
GENEVA	2,581	2,183	178	220	G.W. Bush	84.6%	6.9%	8.5%
GREENE	147	130	8	9	G.W. Bush	88.4%	5.4%	6.1%
HALE	49	42	6	1	G.W. Bush	85.7%	12.2%	2.0%
HENRY	187	167	20	0	G.W. Bush	89.3%	10.7%	0.0%
HOUSTON	4,597	4,082	367	148	G.W. Bush	88.8%	8.0%	3.2%
JACKSON	596	495	86	15	G.W. Bush	83.1%	14.4%	2.5%
JEFFERSON	38,726	32,689	4,399	1,638	G.W. Bush	84.4%	11.4%	4.2%
LAMAR	96	87	5	4	G.W. Bush	90.6%	5.2%	4.2%
LAUDERDALE	2,346	1,811	462	73	G.W. Bush	77.2%	19.7%	3.1%
LAWRENCE	237	189	43	5	G.W. Bush	79.7%	18.1%	2.1%
LEE	7,181	5,736	941	504	G.W. Bush	79.9%	13.1%	7.0%
LIMESTONE	1,660	1,213	411	36	G.W. Bush	73.1%	24.8%	2.2%
LOWNDES	58	53	5	0	G.W. Bush	91.4%	8.6%	0.0%
MACON	93	74	18	1	G.W. Bush	79.6%	19.4%	1.1%
MADISON	11,342	8,174	2,734	434	G.W. Bush	72.1%	24.1%	3.8%

ALABAMA REPUBLICAN PRIMARY

2000

County	Total Vote	G.W. Bush	Keyes	Uncommitted	Winner	Percentage of Total Vote		
						G.W. Bush	Keyes	Uncommitted
MARENGO	168	156	10	2	G.W. Bush	92.9%	6.0%	1.2%
MARION	634	568	53	13	G.W. Bush	89.6%	8.4%	2.1%
MARSHALL	2,370	1,936	364	70	G.W. Bush	81.7%	15.4%	3.0%
MOBILE	23,822	20,979	2,032	811	G.W. Bush	88.1%	8.5%	3.4%
MONROE	598	542	50	6	G.W. Bush	90.6%	8.4%	1.0%
MONTGOMERY	8,665	7,396	1,045	224	G.W. Bush	85.4%	12.1%	2.6%
MORGAN	4,287	3,427	755	105	G.W. Bush	79.9%	17.6%	2.4%
PERRY	50	42	6	2	G.W. Bush	84.0%	12.0%	4.0%
PICKENS	89	73	15	1	G.W. Bush	82.0%	16.9%	1.1%
PIKE	1,424	1,322	64	38	G.W. Bush	92.8%	4.5%	2.7%
RANDOLPH	186	160	21	5	G.W. Bush	86.0%	11.3%	2.7%
RUSSELL	414	372	33	9	G.W. Bush	89.9%	8.0%	2.2%
ST. CLAIR	3,980	3,423	415	142	G.W. Bush	86.0%	10.4%	3.6%
SHELBY	12,019	9,896	1,654	469	G.W. Bush	82.3%	13.8%	3.9%
SUMTER	174	159	11	4	G.W. Bush	91.4%	6.3%	2.3%
TALLADEGA	2,311	2,013	211	87	G.W. Bush	87.1%	9.1%	3.8%
TALLAPOOSA	563	482	62	19	G.W. Bush	85.6%	11.0%	3.4%
TUSCALOOSA	6,555	5,574	721	260	G.W. Bush	85.0%	11.0%	4.0%
WALKER	1,361	1,169	135	57	G.W. Bush	85.9%	9.9%	4.2%
WASHINGTON	101	83	14	4	G.W. Bush	82.2%	13.9%	4.0%
WILCOX	34	29	5	0	G.W. Bush	85.3%	14.7%	0.0%
WINSTON	4,968	4,212	296	460	G.W. Bush	84.8%	6.0%	9.3%
TOTAL	203,079	171,077	23,394	8,608	G.W. Bush	84.2%	11.5%	4.2%

ALABAMA DEMOCRATIC PRIMARY

2004

County	Total Vote	Kerry	Uncommitted	Other	Winner	Percentage of Total Vote		
						Kerry	Uncommitted	Other
AUTAUGA	769	654	68	47	Kerry	85.0%	8.8%	6.1%
BALDWIN	1,829	1,605	123	101	Kerry	87.8%	6.7%	5.5%
BARBOUR	3,442	2,103	951	388	Kerry	61.1%	27.6%	11.3%
BIBB	1,184	833	243	108	Kerry	70.4%	20.5%	9.1%
BLOUNT	743	611	85	47	Kerry	82.2%	11.4%	6.3%
BULLOCK	2,218	1,753	255	210	Kerry	79.0%	11.5%	9.5%
BUTLER	2,679	1,790	619	270	Kerry	66.8%	23.1%	10.1%
CALHOUN	2,303	1,977	221	105	Kerry	85.8%	9.6%	4.6%
CHAMBERS	1,486	1,133	219	134	Kerry	76.2%	14.7%	9.0%
CHEROKEE	2,990	1,767	970	253	Kerry	59.1%	32.4%	8.5%
CHILTON	586	469	80	37	Kerry	80.0%	13.7%	6.3%
CHOCTAW	3,221	2,271	695	255	Kerry	70.5%	21.6%	7.9%
CLARKE	3,095	2,247	574	274	Kerry	72.6%	18.5%	8.9%
CLAY	2,238	1,352	647	239	Kerry	60.4%	28.9%	10.7%
CLEBURNE	517	360	106	51	Kerry	69.6%	20.5%	9.9%
COFFEE	1,781	1,341	346	94	Kerry	75.3%	19.4%	5.3%
COLBERT	6,061	4,374	1,272	415	Kerry	72.2%	21.0%	6.8%
CONECUH	2,718	1,861	636	221	Kerry	68.5%	23.4%	8.1%
COOSA	1,621	1,024	426	171	Kerry	63.2%	26.3%	10.5%
COVINGTON	3,255	1,762	1,121	372	Kerry	54.1%	34.4%	11.4%
CRENSHAW	749	531	149	69	Kerry	70.9%	19.9%	9.2%
CULLMAN	4,460	3,087	936	437	Kerry	69.2%	21.0%	9.8%
DALE	505	433	46	26	Kerry	85.7%	9.1%	5.1%
DALLAS	9,741	7,291	1,576	874	Kerry	74.8%	16.2%	9.0%
DE KALB	1,004	867	90	47	Kerry	86.4%	9.0%	4.7%
ELMORE	1,716	1,490	139	87	Kerry	86.8%	8.1%	5.1%
ESCAMBIA	2,626	1,428	878	320	Kerry	54.4%	33.4%	12.2%
ETOWAH	3,341	2,510	622	209	Kerry	75.1%	18.6%	6.3%
FAYETTE	1,986	1,215	573	198	Kerry	61.2%	28.9%	10.0%
FRANKLIN	3,973	2,643	990	340	Kerry	66.5%	24.9%	8.6%
GENEVA	152	127	14	11	Kerry	83.6%	9.2%	7.2%
GREENE	2,335	2,062	152	121	Kerry	88.3%	6.5%	5.2%
HALE	3,202	2,518	449	235	Kerry	78.6%	14.0%	7.3%
HENRY	1,817	1,158	441	218	Kerry	63.7%	24.3%	12.0%
HOUSTON	1,761	1,286	367	108	Kerry	73.0%	20.8%	6.1%
JACKSON	6,476	4,389	1,627	460	Kerry	67.8%	25.1%	7.1%
JEFFERSON	20,160	18,490	1,031	639	Kerry	91.7%	5.1%	3.2%
LAMAR	2,654	1,423	992	239	Kerry	53.6%	37.4%	9.0%
LAUDERDALE	9,167	6,089	2,170	908	Kerry	66.4%	23.7%	9.9%
LAWRENCE	2,970	2,168	568	234	Kerry	73.0%	19.1%	7.9%
LEE	1,397	1,220	77	100	Kerry	87.3%	5.5%	7.2%
LIMESTONE	5,128	3,182	1,443	503	Kerry	62.1%	28.1%	9.8%
LOWNDES	1,732	1,418	131	183	Kerry	81.9%	7.6%	10.6%
MACON	3,453	3,006	233	214	Kerry	87.1%	6.7%	6.2%
MADISON	8,141	6,652	829	660	Kerry	81.7%	10.2%	8.1%

ALABAMA DEMOCRATIC PRIMARY

2004

County	Total Vote	Kerry	Uncommitted	Other	Winner	Percentage of Total Vote		
						Kerry	Uncommitted	Other
MARENGO	4,386	3,153	809	424	Kerry	71.9%	18.4%	9.7%
MARION	3,022	1,741	986	295	Kerry	57.6%	32.6%	9.8%
MARSHALL	2,860	2,136	500	224	Kerry	74.7%	17.5%	7.8%
MOBILE	7,307	6,799	289	219	Kerry	93.0%	4.0%	3.0%
MONROE	3,171	2,038	784	349	Kerry	64.3%	24.7%	11.0%
MONTGOMERY	5,511	5,055	256	200	Kerry	91.7%	4.6%	3.6%
MORGAN	3,475	2,844	431	200	Kerry	81.8%	12.4%	5.8%
PERRY	3,248	2,761	296	191	Kerry	85.0%	9.1%	5.9%
PICKENS	2,961	1,828	808	325	Kerry	61.7%	27.3%	11.0%
PIKE	1,945	1,545	275	125	Kerry	79.4%	14.1%	6.4%
RANDOLPH	2,088	1,343	525	220	Kerry	64.3%	25.1%	10.5%
RUSSELL	3,595	2,683	670	242	Kerry	74.6%	18.6%	6.7%
ST. CLAIR	796	685	69	42	Kerry	86.1%	8.7%	5.3%
SHELBY	1,474	1,302	109	63	Kerry	88.3%	7.4%	4.3%
SUMTER	3,078	2,600	332	146	Kerry	84.5%	10.8%	4.7%
TALLADEGA	1,964	1,633	226	105	Kerry	83.1%	11.5%	5.3%
TALLAPOOSA	3,131	1,962	791	378	Kerry	62.7%	25.3%	12.1%
TUSCALOOSA	5,718	5,003	463	252	Kerry	87.5%	8.1%	4.4%
WALKER	7,380	4,611	2,163	606	Kerry	62.5%	29.3%	8.2%
WASHINGTON	3,071	1,902	892	277	Kerry	61.9%	29.0%	9.0%
WILCOX	2,808	2,251	349	208	Kerry	80.2%	12.4%	7.4%
WINSTON	203	176	20	7	Kerry	86.7%	9.9%	3.4%
TOTAL	218,574	164,021	38,223	16,330	Kerry	75.0%	17.5%	7.5%

Note: Other vote was 9,076 Dennis J. Kucinich; 7,254 Lyndon H. LaRouche Jr.

ALABAMA REPUBLICAN PRIMARY

2004

| County | Total Vote | G.W. Bush | Uncommitted | Winner | Percentage of Total Vote | |
					G.W. Bush	Uncommitted
AUTAUGA	4,935	4,598	337	G.W. Bush	93.2%	6.8%
BALDWIN	12,845	11,830	1,015	G.W. Bush	92.1%	7.9%
BARBOUR	284	272	12	G.W. Bush	95.8%	4.2%
BIBB	740	704	36	G.W. Bush	95.1%	4.9%
BLOUNT	3,914	3,617	297	G.W. Bush	92.4%	7.6%
BULLOCK	34	31	3	G.W. Bush	91.2%	8.8%
BUTLER	428	415	13	G.W. Bush	97.0%	3.0%
CALHOUN	4,632	4,275	357	G.W. Bush	92.3%	7.7%
CHAMBERS	677	657	20	G.W. Bush	97.0%	3.0%
CHEROKEE	175	170	5	G.W. Bush	97.1%	2.9%
CHILTON	2,259	2,187	72	G.W. Bush	96.8%	3.2%
CHOCTAW	37	36	1	G.W. Bush	97.3%	2.7%
CLARKE	489	482	7	G.W. Bush	98.6%	1.4%
CLAY	448	417	31	G.W. Bush	93.1%	6.9%
CLEBURNE	394	382	12	G.W. Bush	97.0%	3.0%
COFFEE	3,039	2,878	161	G.W. Bush	94.7%	5.3%
COLBERT	1,009	973	36	G.W. Bush	96.4%	3.6%
CONECUH	89	82	7	G.W. Bush	92.1%	7.9%
COOSA	206	192	14	G.W. Bush	93.2%	6.8%
COVINGTON	937	913	24	G.W. Bush	97.4%	2.6%
CRENSHAW	397	386	11	G.W. Bush	97.2%	2.8%
CULLMAN	4,648	4,425	223	G.W. Bush	95.2%	4.8%
DALE	4,412	3,987	425	G.W. Bush	90.4%	9.6%
DALLAS	297	284	13	G.W. Bush	95.6%	4.4%
DE KALB	1,655	1,567	88	G.W. Bush	94.7%	5.3%
ELMORE	7,587	7,081	506	G.W. Bush	93.3%	6.7%
ESCAMBIA	410	403	7	G.W. Bush	98.3%	1.7%
ETOWAH	3,183	3,031	152	G.W. Bush	95.2%	4.8%
FAYETTE	462	437	25	G.W. Bush	94.6%	5.4%
FRANKLIN	229	219	10	G.W. Bush	95.6%	4.4%
GENEVA	2,934	2,641	293	G.W. Bush	90.0%	10.0%
GREENE	27	26	1	G.W. Bush	96.3%	3.7%
HALE	143	138	5	G.W. Bush	96.5%	3.5%
HENRY	377	363	14	G.W. Bush	96.3%	3.7%
HOUSTON	6,299	5,960	339	G.W. Bush	94.6%	5.4%
JACKSON	354	337	17	G.W. Bush	95.2%	4.8%
JEFFERSON	29,964	27,617	2,347	G.W. Bush	92.2%	7.8%
LAMAR	64	63	1	G.W. Bush	98.4%	1.6%
LAUDERDALE	1,747	1,672	75	G.W. Bush	95.7%	4.3%
LAWRENCE	435	413	22	G.W. Bush	94.9%	5.1%
LEE	6,362	5,588	774	G.W. Bush	87.8%	12.2%
LIMESTONE	1,849	1,748	101	G.W. Bush	94.5%	5.5%
LOWNDES	228	220	8	G.W. Bush	96.5%	3.5%
MACON	133	122	11	G.W. Bush	91.7%	8.3%
MADISON	11,858	10,760	1,098	G.W. Bush	90.7%	9.3%

ALABAMA REPUBLICAN PRIMARY

2004

County	Total Vote	G.W. Bush	Uncommitted	Winner	Percentage of Total Vote	
					G.W. Bush	Uncommitted
MARENGO	88	88	0	G.W. Bush	100.0%	0.0%
MARION	546	528	18	G.W. Bush	96.7%	3.3%
MARSHALL	3,906	3,687	219	G.W. Bush	94.4%	5.6%
MOBILE	15,299	14,397	902	G.W. Bush	94.1%	5.9%
MONROE	418	402	16	G.W. Bush	96.2%	3.8%
MONTGOMERY	8,516	7,909	607	G.W. Bush	92.9%	7.1%
MORGAN	7,592	6,931	661	G.W. Bush	91.3%	8.7%
PERRY	86	80	6	G.W. Bush	93.0%	7.0%
PICKENS	288	281	7	G.W. Bush	97.6%	2.4%
PIKE	1,737	1,642	95	G.W. Bush	94.5%	5.5%
RANDOLPH	291	271	20	G.W. Bush	93.1%	6.9%
RUSSELL	601	576	25	G.W. Bush	95.8%	4.2%
ST. CLAIR	5,779	5,385	394	G.W. Bush	93.2%	6.8%
SHELBY	15,071	14,005	1,066	G.W. Bush	92.9%	7.1%
SUMTER	69	68	1	G.W. Bush	98.6%	1.4%
TALLADEGA	2,866	2,691	175	G.W. Bush	93.9%	6.1%
TALLAPOOSA	1,330	1,255	75	G.W. Bush	94.4%	5.6%
TUSCALOOSA	7,437	6,844	593	G.W. Bush	92.0%	8.0%
WALKER	1,708	1,648	60	G.W. Bush	96.5%	3.5%
WASHINGTON	146	144	2	G.W. Bush	98.6%	1.4%
WILCOX	85	80	5	G.W. Bush	94.1%	5.9%
WINSTON	4,003	3,527	476	G.W. Bush	88.1%	11.9%
TOTAL	201,487	187,038	14,449	G.W. Bush	92.8%	7.2%

ALASKA

Alaska is one of the few states in the country that has never held a presidential primary, although it dabbled with one during its territorial days in 1956 that produced victories for the eventual nominees, Adlai Stevenson on the Democratic side and President Dwight Eisenhower on the Republican.

While Alaska has not held a presidential primary since then, the state's Republicans have sought ways to offset the state's small delegate prize and remote location. In 1996 and 2000, the answer was late January precinct caucuses accompanied by a statewide straw poll. In 1996, the timing made Alaska the first event of the nominating season, ahead of both Iowa and New Hampshire, and it attracted more than 9,000 caucus participants, far more than the usual number.

The top two vote-getters in Alaska, Pat Buchanan, with 33 percent, and Steve Forbes, with 31 percent, both made campaign forays to the nation's frigid northern frontier. Front-runner, Bob Dole, though, did not, and finished third in the straw vote with 17 percent, in spite of endorsements from much of the state Republican hierarchy.

In 2000, Alaska Republicans shared the leadoff spot with Iowa and turnout for the non-binding straw vote was down to barely 4,300. But the result was even closer than four years earlier, as George W. Bush defeated Forbes by a margin of five votes, 1,571-to-1,566. Voting on the Internet was allowed for voters living in the largely vacant northern and western frontiers of Alaska, as well as for Alaska Republicans living in Washington, D.C. Ultimately, only 35 votes were cast electronically, but they provided Bush with his margin of victory, as he received 23 of the votes cast on the Internet to four for Forbes.

In votes cast on traditional paper ballots, Forbes had a 14-vote edge.

In recent elections, the Democrats have launched their caucus process after their party's presidential nomination has been decided. In 2004, that left an opening for the liberal wing of the Alaska Democratic Party to flex their muscles in support of the anti-Iraq war candidacy of Rep. Dennis J. Kucinich of Ohio. Kucinich paid a visit to Alaska on the eve of the late March caucuses and was rewarded with 26 percent of the state convention delegates (compared to 48 percent for the nominee in waiting, John Kerry). It was Kucinich's second-best showing of the 2004 nominating season, exceeded only by his 31 percent share in the Hawaii caucuses.

The ability to surprise has always been a part of the Alaska delegate-selection process. In 1988, it was the only state in the country to buck the political mainstream and give first-round caucus victories to the two preachers who were running, Democrat Jesse Jackson and Republican Pat Robertson.

Robertson's success reflected the rise of social conservatives within the Alaska GOP. But they have not always been so powerful. In 1964, Alaska Republicans broke with the rest of the West to give most of their delegates to Pennsylvania governor William Scranton, rather than Arizona's Barry Goldwater. And in 1976, Alaska had one of the few Republican delegations from the West that supported President Gerald Ford, rather than Ronald Reagan.

Meanwhile, Alaska Democrats have often had a penchant for taking their time in deciding whom to support. In much of the last quarter century, the winner of the Democratic mass meetings has been "Uncommitted."

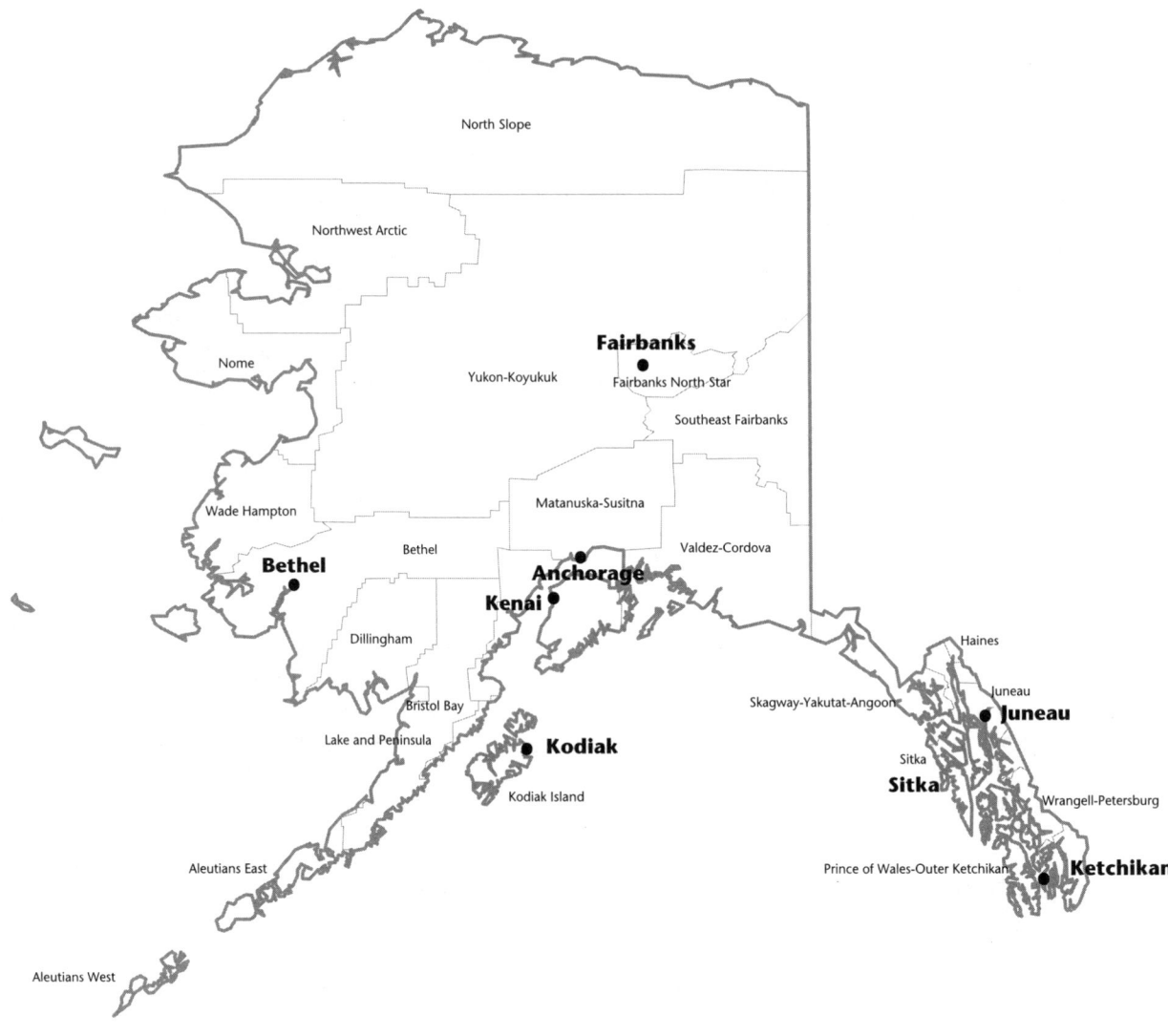

North Slope

Northwest Arctic

Nome

Yukon-Koyukuk

Fairbanks
Fairbanks North Star

Southeast Fairbanks

Wade Hampton

Bethel

Matanuska-Susitna

Valdez-Cordova

Bethel

Anchorage

Kenai

Dillingham

Haines

Juneau

Skagway-Yakutat-Angoon

Juneau

Bristol Bay

Sitka

Lake and Peninsula

Kodiak

Sitka

Kodiak Island

Wrangell-Petersburg

Aleutians East

Prince of Wales-Outer Ketchikan

Ketchikan

Aleutians West

Adak Station

ARIZONA

Every dozen years since 1964, Arizona has fielded a presidential candidate–Republican Barry Goldwater in 1964, Democrat Morris Udall in 1976, Democrat Bruce Babbitt in 1988, and Republican John McCain in 2000.

What Arizona did not have until 1996 was a presidential primary. And that it has one at all is due in no small part to McCain, who lobbied hard for the creation of the February event. Traveling in Asia when the legislation was being debated, he reportedly made a call from Hanoi to a wavering state legislator.

That first primary did not go as McCain had hoped. As national chairman of Texas senator Phil Gramm's presidential campaign, McCain saw his candidate drop out of the race before Arizona even voted.

But McCain had better luck with his own presidential candidacy four years later, winning his home state's primary in what was arguably his best day in the 2000 primary season. McCain not only swamped the eventual nominee, George W. Bush, in Arizona, but also defeated him handily in the Republican primary the same late February day in Michigan. As it was, McCain defeated Bush in all 15 counties in Arizona, 14 of them by majorities that ranged up to 68 percent of the vote in Pima County (Tucson).

With President Bush virtually unopposed for renomination in 2004, Arizona Republicans did not hold a presidential primary. But Arizona Democrats did, with an event scheduled on the first Tuesday in February, one week after New Hampshire. However, it was just one of six primaries held across the country that day, and in Arizona the result mainly illustrated the considerable momentum that John Kerry had gained with his January victories in Iowa and New Hampshire. Kerry swept every Arizona county except tiny Greenlee on the New Mexico border, which was won by the primary runner-up, Wesley Clark.

Altogether, the bulk of the Democratic vote was cast in just two counties, with nearly half the ballots from populous Maricopa County (Phoenix) and fully one quarter from Pima County. In the Republican primary four years earlier, the dominance of Maricopa County was even greater, as it provided nearly 60 percent of the GOP primary ballots.

From its beginning, Arizona's presidential primary proved a success–attracting candidates to Arizona and voters to the polls.

Steve Forbes mounted a lavish media campaign in 1996 that accented his flat tax proposal and outsider image. Pat Buchanan and Bob Dole seemed at times to engage in a battle of photo opportunities. Dole was photographed visiting Goldwater, his most famous Arizona supporter. Buchanan cultivated a frontier image, culminating with a visit to the O.K. Corral in Tombstone where he dressed in cowboy garb.

Buchanan came into Arizona fresh from an upset victory over Dole in New Hampshire. And the state's decision to save

Recent Arizona Primary Results

Arizona held its first presidential primary in 1996. The Democratic primaries in 1996 and 2000 were conducted by the party.

Year	DEMOCRATS			REPUBLICANS		
	Turnout	Candidates	%	Turnout	Candidates	%
2004 (Feb. 3)	238,942	JOHN KERRY	43		No Primary	
		Wesley Clark	26			
		Howard Dean	14			
		John Edwards	7			
		Joe Lieberman	7			
2000 (Feb. 22 Reps.; March 11 Dems.)	86,762	AL GORE	78	322,669	JOHN McCAIN	60
		Bill Bradley	19		George W. Bush	36
1996 (Feb. 27 Reps.; March 9 Dems.)	12,884	BILL CLINTON*	95	347,482	STEVE FORBES	33
					Bob Dole	30
					Pat Buchanan	28
					Lamar Alexander	7

Note: All candidates are listed that drew at least 5 percent of their party's primary vote. The names of winning candidates are capitalized. An asterisk (*) indicates an incumbent president.

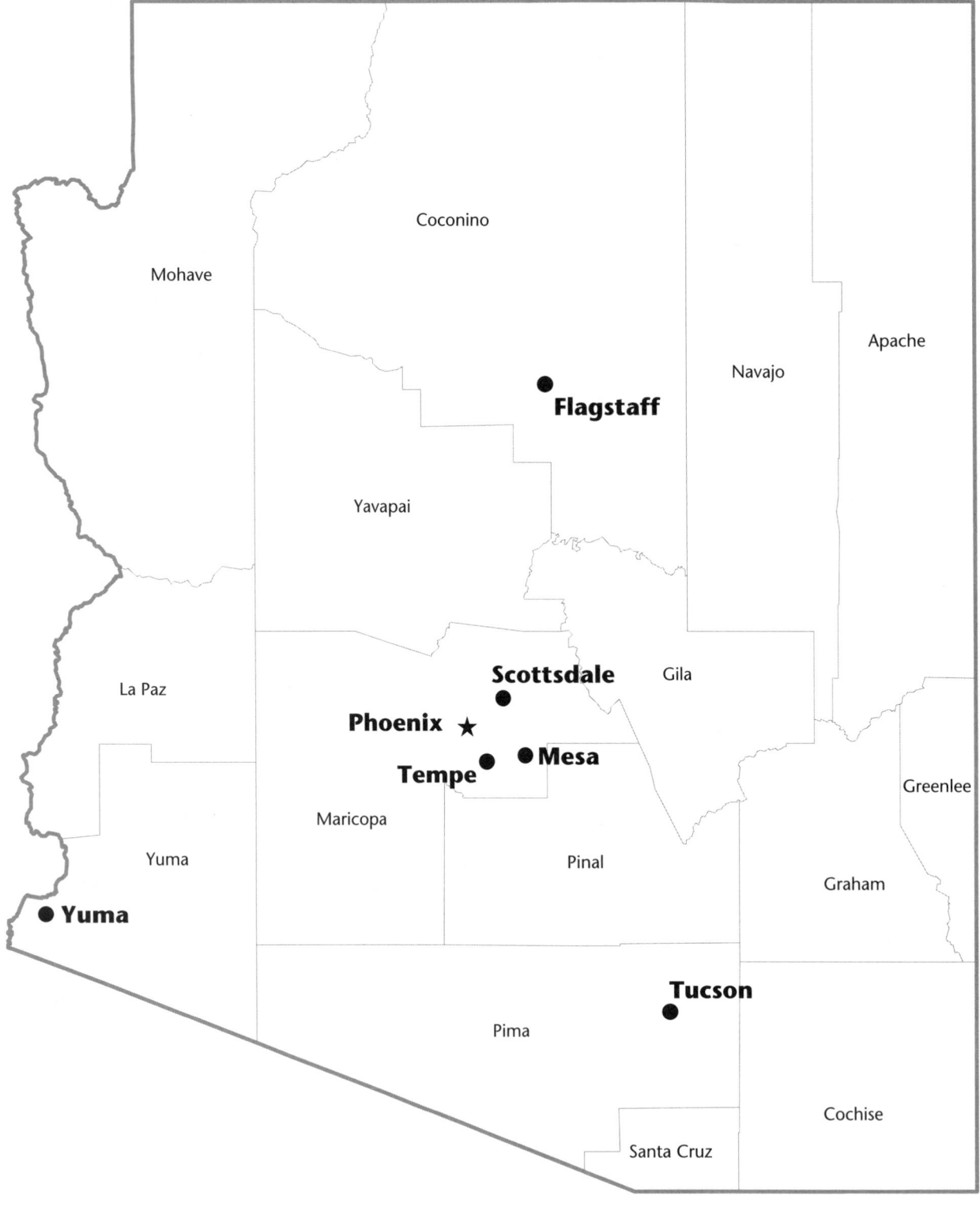

Mohave

Coconino

Apache

Navajo

● Flagstaff

Yavapai

La Paz

● Scottsdale

Gila

Phoenix ★

● Mesa

Tempe ●

Greenlee

Maricopa

Yuma

Pinal

Graham

● Yuma

● Tucson

Pima

Cochise

Santa Cruz

money by opening barely one-quarter of the usual polling places seemed to favor Buchanan and his energetic cadre of supporters.

Yet the turnout was larger than expected. More Republican ballots were cast in Maricopa County (Phoenix) alone (roughly 215,000) than had been cast the previous week in the entire state of New Hampshire. Maricopa was one of only two counties that Forbes won statewide, but he carried it decisively enough to win the state by more than 10,000 votes over Dole.

Buchanan finished a close third by winning much of rural Arizona, including the two major Native American counties, Apache and Navajo. But his tough stance on immigration did not serve him well in voting along the Mexican border. Dole carried three of the four counties that border Mexico, including populous Pima.

According to exit polling, Dole had the edge among Arizona's large contingent of voters age 60 and older (which cast more than four out of every ten GOP primary ballots). Buchanan showed a narrow lead among middle-aged voters. But neither could overcome the consistency of Forbes, who took about one-third of the Arizona primary ballots among all age groups and both sexes. Yet for Forbes, it was his second and last victory of the 1996 primary season.

Arizona Democrats expressed interest in joining the Republicans on their February primary date. But with national Democratic rules prior to 2004 preventing states from establishing primaries so early, they had to content themselves with a small, party-run vote at a limited number of polling places around the state.

Turnout for the Democratic event was comparatively light. The contest in 2000 drew less than 90,000 voters – slightly more than one quarter of the turnout for the Republican presidential primary the same year. But the party-run nature of the event allowed for Arizona Democrats to be creative in its operation, and they used it as a laboratory to experiment with Internet voting. Concerns were raised that the "digital divide" might work to the disadvantage of the state's large minority population of Hispanics, Native Americans, and blacks. But a number of Internet voting sites were established in communities with limited Internet access, as were some additional polling places.

Altogether, voters were given three options of voting in the 2000 Democratic primary—by paper ballot, by mail, or on the Internet. Ultimately, nearly half the votes were cast on the Internet, nearly 40 percent by mail, and the rest by traditional paper ballots at polling places.

Off-site Internet voting was allowed over a four-day span from March 7 through March 10, creating an unusual situation where Bill Bradley received votes while both an active and inactive candidate. Bradley withdrew from the Democratic contest on March 9. Polling places, where paper and Internet ballots could be cast, were open only on March 11.

Arizona's sizable minority presence has given the Democratic voting a liberal hue, with the result that three of the four winners from 1980 to 1992 were Massachusetts Democrats.

Many of the Southern Democrats who have fared well nationally have had less success in Arizona. Bill Clinton lost the party-run primary to Paul Tsongas in 1992 by 5 percentage points. Meanwhile, Al Gore drew a total of 5 percent of the vote in 1988, hitting double digits only in a few rural counties. Clinton and Gore, though, both did better as incumbents. President Clinton won the party-run Democratic primary in Arizona in 1996 with 95 percent of the vote. Four years later, Vice President Gore won with 78 percent.

ARIZONA DEMOCRATIC PRIMARY

2000

| Region | Total Vote | Bradley | Gore | Other | Winner | Percentage of Total Vote | | |
						Bradley	Gore	Other
REGION 1	18,278	3,422	14,001	855	Gore	18.7%	76.6%	4.7%
REGION 2	16,600	3,569	12,578	453	Gore	21.5%	75.8%	2.7%
REGION 3	20,444	3,372	16,445	627	Gore	16.5%	80.4%	3.1%
REGION 4	14,625	2,669	11,504	452	Gore	18.2%	78.7%	3.1%
REGION 5	16,815	3,351	13,054	410	Gore	19.9%	77.6%	2.4%
TOTAL	86,762	16,383	67,582	2,797	Gore	18.9%	77.9%	3.2%

Note: Other vote was 1,439 No Preference; 1,358 Heather Harder. The primary was conducted by the Arizona Democratic Party, which tallied the vote by regions rather than by county. The regions were described as follows: Region 1 - Pima County; Region 2 - Rural Counties (all except Maricopa and Pima); Region 3 - Maricopa West; Region 4 - Maricopa Central; Region 5 - Maricopa East.

ARIZONA REPUBLICAN PRIMARY

2000

County	Total Vote	G.W. Bush	McCain	Other	Winner	Percentage of Total Vote		
						G.W. Bush	McCain	Other
APACHE	1,714	561	1,030	123	McCain	32.7%	60.1%	7.2%
COCHISE	7,734	2,596	4,795	343	McCain	33.6%	62.0%	4.4%
COCONINO	6,198	1,980	3,940	278	McCain	31.9%	63.6%	4.5%
GILA	3,942	1,327	2,351	264	McCain	33.7%	59.6%	6.7%
GRAHAM	1,768	743	851	174	McCain	42.0%	48.1%	9.8%
GREENLEE	298	120	153	25	McCain	40.3%	51.3%	8.4%
LA PAZ	1,083	451	592	40	McCain	41.6%	54.7%	3.7%
MARICOPA	186,872	70,792	107,828	8,252	McCain	37.9%	57.7%	4.4%
MOHAVE	11,464	3,885	7,153	426	McCain	33.9%	62.4%	3.7%
NAVAJO	4,728	1,620	2,752	356	McCain	34.3%	58.2%	7.5%
PIMA	61,951	17,772	42,200	1,979	McCain	28.7%	68.1%	3.2%
PINAL	7,727	2,813	4,610	304	McCain	36.4%	59.7%	3.9%
SANTA CRUZ	1,034	286	693	55	McCain	27.7%	67.0%	5.3%
YAVAPAI	19,657	7,272	11,425	960	McCain	37.0%	58.1%	4.9%
YUMA	6,499	2,897	3,335	267	McCain	44.6%	51.3%	4.1%
TOTAL	322,669	115,115	193,708	13,846	McCain	35.7%	60.0%	4.3%

Note: Other vote was 11,500 Alan Keyes; 1,211 Steve Forbes; 637 Orrin G. Hatch; 239 John R. McGrath; 177 Gary Bauer; 54 James T. Zanon; 28 Chuck See.

ARIZONA DEMOCRATIC PRIMARY

2004

County	Total Vote	Clark	Dean	Edwards	Kerry	Lieberman	Other	Winner	Percentage of Total Vote					
									Clark	Dean	Edwards	Kerry	Lieberman	Other
APACHE	4,512	877	494	208	1,651	923	359	Kerry	19.4%	10.9%	4.6%	36.6%	20.5%	8.0%
COCHISE	6,663	2,153	1,161	376	2,484	288	201	Kerry	32.3%	17.4%	5.6%	37.3%	4.3%	3.0%
COCONINO	7,039	2,175	1,104	436	2,358	455	511	Kerry	30.9%	15.7%	6.2%	33.5%	6.5%	7.3%
GILA	3,261	1,045	305	234	1,332	232	113	Kerry	32.0%	9.4%	7.2%	40.8%	7.1%	3.5%
GRAHAM	1,365	447	108	71	567	122	50	Kerry	32.7%	7.9%	5.2%	41.5%	8.9%	3.7%
GREENLEE	756	294	60	50	283	41	28	Clark	38.9%	7.9%	6.6%	37.4%	5.4%	3.7%
LA PAZ	684	209	68	41	292	54	20	Kerry	30.6%	9.9%	6.0%	42.7%	7.9%	2.9%
MARICOPA	117,323	31,191	15,202	8,921	51,154	7,984	2,871	Kerry	26.6%	13.0%	7.6%	43.6%	6.8%	2.4%
MOHAVE	5,883	1,584	579	502	2,808	296	114	Kerry	26.9%	9.8%	8.5%	47.7%	5.0%	1.9%
NAVAJO	4,377	1,203	419	255	1,488	661	351	Kerry	27.5%	9.6%	5.8%	34.0%	15.1%	8.0%
PIMA	62,061	15,593	10,858	3,608	26,605	3,140	2,257	Kerry	25.1%	17.5%	5.8%	42.9%	5.1%	3.6%
PINAL	8,617	2,816	905	523	3,643	505	225	Kerry	32.7%	10.5%	6.1%	42.3%	5.9%	2.6%
SANTA CRUZ	1,529	364	267	86	637	136	39	Kerry	23.8%	17.5%	5.6%	41.7%	8.9%	2.6%
YAVAPAI	9,529	2,333	1,198	815	4,267	471	445	Kerry	24.5%	12.6%	8.6%	44.8%	4.9%	4.7%
YUMA	5,343	972	827	470	2,240	598	236	Kerry	18.2%	15.5%	8.8%	41.9%	11.2%	4.4%
TOTAL	238,942	63,256	33,555	16,596	101,809	15,906	7,820	Kerry	26.5%	14.0%	6.9%	42.6%	6.7%	3.3%

Note: Other vote was 3,896 Dennis J. Kucinich; 1,177 Al Sharpton; 755 Richard A. Gephardt; 325 Carol Moseley Braun; 295 Lyndon H. LaRouche Jr.; 257 Dianne Barker; 233 Bill Wyatt; 225 Keith Brand; 208 Fern Penna; 136 William Barchilon; 119 Huda Muhammad; 117 Evelyn L. Vitullo; 77 Ray Caplette.

ARKANSAS

Bill Clinton may be Arkansas' most famous politician ever. But at times, the state's Democrats gave him little more than a passing grade.

Running for his fifth (and last) term as governor in 1990, Clinton was renominated with a lackluster 55 percent of the primary vote. In the state's presidential primary two years later, he took a more impressive 68 percent. Still, his home-state percentage was less than the share of the vote he won in six other primaries in 1992. And in 1996, running essentially unopposed for renomination, his 79 percent share in Arkansas was his third-lowest percentage in any Democratic primary in the country.

To know him may not have been to love him, particularly to a significant swath of Arkansas Democrats. But Clinton's presidential primary victories in the 1990s reflected the coalition he had put together to dominate the state for more than a decade. He won by large margins in the Little Rock area, the heavily black counties of rural eastern Arkansas, and rural white-majority counties such as Hempstead (Hope), where he was born.

Meanwhile, Republicans have had a slow time constructing a base in Arkansas, even after Clinton's departure from the state's political scene saw the GOP win a string of gubernatorial victories. Although it is now a staple of Arkansas politics, the presidential primary has been of little help in their party-building efforts. Before 1996, each party conducted its own, with Republicans lacking enough workers in some counties to open more than one polling place. The frequent result: minimal

Recent Arkansas Primary Results

Arkansas held its first presidential primary in 1976.

	DEMOCRATS			REPUBLICANS		
Year	Turnout	Candidates	%	Turnout	Candidates	%
2004 (May 18)	266,848	JOHN KERRY	67	38,363	GEORGE W. BUSH*	97
		Uncommitted	23			
		Dennis Kucinich	5			
		Lyndon LaRouche	5			
2000 (May 23)	246,900	AL GORE	78	44,573	GEORGE W. BUSH	80
		Lyndon LaRouche	22		Alan Keyes	20
1996 (May 21)	300,389	BILL CLINTON*	79	42,814	BOB DOLE	76
		Uncommitted	10		Pat Buchanan	24
		Lyndon LaRouche	7			
1992 (May 26)	502,617	BILL CLINTON	68	52,141	GEORGE BUSH*	87
		Uncommitted	18		Pat Buchanan	13
		Jerry Brown	11			
1988 (March 8)	497,544	AL GORE	37	68,305	GEORGE BUSH	47
		Michael Dukakis	19		Bob Dole	26
		Jesse Jackson	17		Pat Robertson	19
		Richard Gephardt	12		Jack Kemp	5
		Uncommitted	7			
1984	—	NO PRIMARY		—	No Primary	
1980 (May 27)	448,290	JIMMY CARTER*	60	—	No Primary	
		Uncommitted	18			
		Edward Kennedy	18			
1976 (May 25)	501,800	JIMMY CARTER	63	32,541	RONALD REAGAN	63
		George Wallace	17		Gerald Ford*	35
		Uncommitted	11			
		Morris Udall	8			

Note: All candidates are listed that drew at least 5 percent of their party's primary vote. The names of winning candidates are capitalized. An asterisk (*) indicates an incumbent president.

interest in the GOP contest, to the point that in 1992, just one vote was cast in the Republican presidential primary in all of Lee County (it was for Pat Buchanan).

Even with the state operating the primary since 1996, the ratio of Democratic to Republican primary ballots has never been less than five to one. And in 2004, when President George W. Bush was paired against an "Uncommitted" line, no Republican presidential primary vote was even recorded in nearly two dozen counties. In a number of others, the vote for Uncommitted was apparently not tallied. In Benton County, in Arkansas' northwest corner, the vote was Bush 8,120, Uncommitted 0. And in a half dozen other counties, Bush won more than a 1,000 votes while no votes were recorded for Uncommitted.

The largest concentration of GOP primary voters is in the historically Republican Ozarks in the northwest quadrant of the state. George Bush handily won the region in the party's most competitive primary in 1988. Pat Robertson showed strength in eastern and southern Arkansas, where Republican turnout was light, and his cadre of supporters, though small, was enough to carry 19 counties.

On the Democratic side that year, Al Gore won in dominating fashion, leaving little more than beachheads for Michael Dukakis, Jesse Jackson, and Richard Gephardt.

Gephardt and Dukakis each won a handful of counties in northern Arkansas near the Missouri border, an area loaded with retirees. Jackson carried a cluster of counties with a significant black population, most of them hugging the west bank of the Mississippi River. Gore won the rest of the state.

No presidential primaries before or since then have been so compelling for either party. With the exception of 1984 (when

Arkansas did not hold a presidential primary) and 1988, when it joined the vast majority of other Southern states in early March, the presidential primary has been held in late May, usually far too late on the nominating calendar to make a difference.

Ronald Reagan swamped President Gerald Ford in Republican voting in 1976, as Reagan did in many other parts of the South. But in 1980, Arkansas Republicans did not conduct a presidential primary at all. Instead, they positioned themselves on the calendar between Iowa and New Hampshire with a controversial caucus process that was open only to local party officials. GOP candidates that year were encouraged to fill vacant party positions with their supporters.

Former Texas governor John Connally made the most lavish effort, at one point hosting likely caucus participants at an Ozarks resort. But his effort did not pay off. Connally took only one delegate, a conspicuous failure in his expensive, but short-lived, presidential campaign.

ARKANSAS DEMOCRATIC PRIMARY
2000

County	Total Vote	Gore	LaRouche	Winner	Percentage of Total Vote	
					Gore	LaRouche
ARKANSAS	0	0	0			
ASHLEY	4,650	3,547	1,103	Gore	76.3%	23.7%
BAXTER	601	534	67	Gore	88.9%	11.1%
BENTON	1,248	1,144	104	Gore	91.7%	8.3%
BOONE	3,513	2,588	925	Gore	73.7%	26.3%
BRADLEY	2,269	1,719	550	Gore	75.8%	24.2%
CALHOUN	1,875	1,352	523	Gore	72.1%	27.9%
CARROLL	1,309	927	382	Gore	70.8%	29.2%
CHICOT	2,262	1,876	386	Gore	82.9%	17.1%
CLARK	4,491	3,737	754	Gore	83.2%	16.8%
CLAY	2,819	2,360	459	Gore	83.7%	16.3%
CLEBURNE	5,143	3,561	1,582	Gore	69.2%	30.8%
CLEVELAND	1,807	1,309	498	Gore	72.4%	27.6%
COLUMBIA	3,742	2,874	868	Gore	76.8%	23.2%
CONWAY	4,102	3,096	1,006	Gore	75.5%	24.5%
CRAIGHEAD	7,897	6,483	1,414	Gore	82.1%	17.9%
CRAWFORD	2,145	1,628	517	Gore	75.9%	24.1%
CRITTENDEN	3,083	2,688	395	Gore	87.2%	12.8%
CROSS	2,980	2,333	647	Gore	78.3%	21.7%
DALLAS	2,694	2,007	687	Gore	74.5%	25.5%
DESHA	1,000	871	129	Gore	87.1%	12.9%
DREW	3,248	2,490	758	Gore	76.7%	23.3%
FAULKNER	5,229	4,107	1,122	Gore	78.5%	21.5%
FRANKLIN	2,898	2,076	822	Gore	71.6%	28.4%
FULTON	997	797	200	Gore	79.9%	20.1%
GARLAND	8,233	6,331	1,902	Gore	76.9%	23.1%
GRANT	3,355	2,390	965	Gore	71.2%	28.8%
GREENE	7,381	5,800	1,581	Gore	78.6%	21.4%
HEMPSTEAD	3,327	2,686	641	Gore	80.7%	19.3%
HOT SPRING	5,457	4,196	1,261	Gore	76.9%	23.1%
HOWARD	2,378	1,868	510	Gore	78.6%	21.4%
INDEPENDENCE	6,183	4,609	1,574	Gore	74.5%	25.5%
IZARD	1,217	959	258	Gore	78.8%	21.2%
JACKSON	1,682	1,422	260	Gore	84.5%	15.5%
JEFFERSON	8,248	7,176	1,072	Gore	87.0%	13.0%
JOHNSON	2,990	2,235	755	Gore	74.7%	25.3%
LAFAYETTE	2,384	1,846	538	Gore	77.4%	22.6%
LAWRENCE	1,870	1,531	339	Gore	81.9%	18.1%
LEE	2,798	2,281	517	Gore	81.5%	18.5%
LINCOLN	1,992	1,513	479	Gore	76.0%	24.0%
LITTLE RIVER	3,606	2,802	804	Gore	77.7%	22.3%
LOGAN	3,967	2,892	1,075	Gore	72.9%	27.1%
LONOKE	4,813	3,508	1,305	Gore	72.9%	27.1%
MADISON	2,530	1,648	882	Gore	65.1%	34.9%
MARION	1,247	853	394	Gore	68.4%	31.6%

ARKANSAS DEMOCRATIC PRIMARY

2000

County	Total Vote	Gore	LaRouche	Winner	Percentage of Total Vote	
					Gore	LaRouche
MILLER	4,486	3,298	1,188	Gore	73.5%	26.5%
MISSISSIPPI	4,842	4,105	737	Gore	84.8%	15.2%
MONROE	1,724	1,331	393	Gore	77.2%	22.8%
MONTGOMERY	1,321	918	403	Gore	69.5%	30.5%
NEVADA	2,084	1,593	491	Gore	76.4%	23.6%
NEWTON	129	103	26	Gore	79.8%	20.2%
OUACHITA	5,709	4,471	1,238	Gore	78.3%	21.7%
PERRY	1,921	1,408	513	Gore	73.3%	26.7%
PHILLIPS	7,122	6,123	999	Gore	86.0%	14.0%
PIKE	1,076	832	244	Gore	77.3%	22.7%
POINSETT	2,712	2,254	458	Gore	83.1%	16.9%
POLK	1,534	1,003	531	Gore	65.4%	34.6%
POPE	3,279	2,457	822	Gore	74.9%	25.1%
PRAIRIE	1,516	1,091	425	Gore	72.0%	28.0%
PULASKI	15,468	13,772	1,696	Gore	89.0%	11.0%
RANDOLPH	2,561	2,003	558	Gore	78.2%	21.8%
ST. FRANCIS	4,457	3,583	874	Gore	80.4%	19.6%
SALINE	4,423	3,473	950	Gore	78.5%	21.5%
SCOTT	1,825	1,182	643	Gore	64.8%	35.2%
SEARCY	153	134	19	Gore	87.6%	12.4%
SEBASTIAN	1,509	1,316	193	Gore	87.2%	12.8%
SEVIER	1,612	1,290	322	Gore	80.0%	20.0%
SHARP	2,703	1,967	736	Gore	72.8%	27.2%
STONE	2,978	1,993	985	Gore	66.9%	33.1%
UNION	1,873	1,501	372	Gore	80.1%	19.9%
VAN BUREN	3,474	2,574	900	Gore	74.1%	25.9%
WASHINGTON	8,280	6,686	1,594	Gore	80.7%	19.3%
WHITE	2,851	2,267	584	Gore	79.5%	20.5%
WOODRUFF	2,204	1,844	360	Gore	83.7%	16.3%
YELL	3,414	2,528	886	Gore	74.0%	26.0%
TOTAL	246,900	193,750	53,150	Gore	78.5%	21.5%

Note: No vote reported from Arkansas County.

ARKANSAS REPUBLICAN PRIMARY

2000

| County | Total Vote | G.W. Bush | Keyes | Winner | Percentage of Total Vote | |
					G.W. Bush	Keyes
ARKANSAS	0	0	0			
ASHLEY	67	60	7	G.W. Bush	89.6%	10.4%
BAXTER	745	619	126	G.W. Bush	83.1%	16.9%
BENTON	13,634	10,337	3,297	G.W. Bush	75.8%	24.2%
BOONE	321	265	56	G.W. Bush	82.6%	17.4%
BRADLEY	27	26	1	G.W. Bush	96.3%	3.7%
CALHOUN	6	5	1	G.W. Bush	83.3%	16.7%
CARROLL	741	616	125	G.W. Bush	83.1%	16.9%
CHICOT	12	12	0	G.W. Bush	100.0%	0.0%
CLARK	101	82	19	G.W. Bush	81.2%	18.8%
CLAY	65	57	8	G.W. Bush	87.7%	12.3%
CLEBURNE	468	421	47	G.W. Bush	90.0%	10.0%
CLEVELAND	40	39	1	G.W. Bush	97.5%	2.5%
COLUMBIA	167	141	26	G.W. Bush	84.4%	15.6%
CONWAY	79	69	10	G.W. Bush	87.3%	12.7%
CRAIGHEAD	838	744	94	G.W. Bush	88.8%	11.2%
CRAWFORD	1,148	892	256	G.W. Bush	77.7%	22.3%
CRITTENDEN	189	173	16	G.W. Bush	91.5%	8.5%
CROSS	25	21	4	G.W. Bush	84.0%	16.0%
DALLAS	6	5	1	G.W. Bush	83.3%	16.7%
DESHA	41	34	7	G.W. Bush	82.9%	17.1%
DREW	81	73	8	G.W. Bush	90.1%	9.9%
FAULKNER	2,035	1,673	362	G.W. Bush	82.2%	17.8%
FRANKLIN	124	101	23	G.W. Bush	81.5%	18.5%
FULTON	150	130	20	G.W. Bush	86.7%	13.3%
GARLAND	1,071	930	141	G.W. Bush	86.8%	13.2%
GRANT	59	52	7	G.W. Bush	88.1%	11.9%
GREENE	122	107	15	G.W. Bush	87.7%	12.3%
HEMPSTEAD	83	75	8	G.W. Bush	90.4%	9.6%
HOT SPRING	44	32	12	G.W. Bush	72.7%	27.3%
HOWARD	21	21	0	G.W. Bush	100.0%	0.0%
INDEPENDENCE	140	114	26	G.W. Bush	81.4%	18.6%
IZARD	182	146	36	G.W. Bush	80.2%	19.8%
JACKSON	87	80	7	G.W. Bush	92.0%	8.0%
JEFFERSON	448	394	54	G.W. Bush	87.9%	12.1%
JOHNSON	141	115	26	G.W. Bush	81.6%	18.4%
LAFAYETTE	21	16	5	G.W. Bush	76.2%	23.8%
LAWRENCE	89	76	13	G.W. Bush	85.4%	14.6%
LEE	24	20	4	G.W. Bush	83.3%	16.7%
LINCOLN	19	19	0	G.W. Bush	100.0%	0.0%
LITTLE RIVER	22	19	3	G.W. Bush	86.4%	13.6%
LOGAN	279	249	30	G.W. Bush	89.2%	10.8%
LONOKE	645	541	104	G.W. Bush	83.9%	16.1%
MADISON	136	104	32	G.W. Bush	76.5%	23.5%
MARION	174	127	47	G.W. Bush	73.0%	27.0%

ARKANSAS REPUBLICAN PRIMARY

2000

County	Total Vote	G.W. Bush	Keyes	Winner	Percentage of Total Vote	
					G.W. Bush	Keyes
MILLER	229	208	21	G.W. Bush	90.8%	9.2%
MISSISSIPPI	180	156	24	G.W. Bush	86.7%	13.3%
MONROE	10	10	0	G.W. Bush	100.0%	0.0%
MONTGOMERY	193	157	36	G.W. Bush	81.3%	18.7%
NEVADA	28	24	4	G.W. Bush	85.7%	14.3%
NEWTON	129	109	20	G.W. Bush	84.5%	15.5%
OUACHITA	67	56	11	G.W. Bush	83.6%	16.4%
PERRY	89	79	10	G.W. Bush	88.8%	11.2%
PHILLIPS	27	24	3	G.W. Bush	88.9%	11.1%
PIKE	55	49	6	G.W. Bush	89.1%	10.9%
POINSETT	121	107	14	G.W. Bush	88.4%	11.6%
POLK	167	136	31	G.W. Bush	81.4%	18.6%
POPE	598	517	81	G.W. Bush	86.5%	13.5%
PRAIRIE	41	36	5	G.W. Bush	87.8%	12.2%
PULASKI	6,600	5,498	1,102	G.W. Bush	83.3%	16.7%
RANDOLPH	145	116	29	G.W. Bush	80.0%	20.0%
ST. FRANCIS	6	6	0	G.W. Bush	100.0%	0.0%
SALINE	1,419	1,207	212	G.W. Bush	85.1%	14.9%
SCOTT	48	38	10	G.W. Bush	79.2%	20.8%
SEARCY	1,343	1,133	210	G.W. Bush	84.4%	15.6%
SEBASTIAN	1,466	1,112	354	G.W. Bush	75.9%	24.1%
SEVIER	62	51	11	G.W. Bush	82.3%	17.7%
SHARP	265	210	55	G.W. Bush	79.2%	20.8%
STONE	50	11	39	Keyes	22.0%	78.0%
UNION	1,037	900	137	G.W. Bush	86.8%	13.2%
VAN BUREN	355	316	39	G.W. Bush	89.0%	11.0%
WASHINGTON	3,938	2,833	1,105	G.W. Bush	71.9%	28.1%
WHITE	908	759	149	G.W. Bush	83.6%	16.4%
WOODRUFF	11	10	1	G.W. Bush	90.9%	9.1%
YELL	69	59	10	G.W. Bush	85.5%	14.5%
TOTAL	44,573	35,759	8,814	G.W. Bush	80.2%	19.8%

Note: No vote was reported from Arkansas County.

ARKANSAS DEMOCRATIC PRIMARY

2004

County	Total Vote	Kerry	Kucinich	LaRouche	Uncommitted	Winner	Percentage of Total Vote			
							Kerry	Kucinich	LaRouche	Uncommitted
ARKANSAS	1,956	1,277	130	104	445	Kerry	65.3%	6.6%	5.3%	22.8%
ASHLEY	4,245	2,451	172	188	1,434	Kerry	57.7%	4.1%	4.4%	33.8%
BAXTER	905	767	41	9	88	Kerry	84.8%	4.5%	1.0%	9.7%
BENTON	2,723	2,423	62	23	215	Kerry	89.0%	2.3%	0.8%	7.9%
BOONE	927	802	71	54	0	Kerry	86.5%	7.7%	5.8%	0.0%
BRADLEY	3,025	1,757	111	101	1,056	Kerry	58.1%	3.7%	3.3%	34.9%
CALHOUN	1,464	829	62	53	520	Kerry	56.6%	4.2%	3.6%	35.5%
CARROLL	1,791	1,258	102	54	377	Kerry	70.2%	5.7%	3.0%	21.0%
CHICOT	2,206	1,419	75	96	616	Kerry	64.3%	3.4%	4.4%	27.9%
CLARK	3,139	2,336	149	109	545	Kerry	74.4%	4.7%	3.5%	17.4%
CLAY	1,843	1,364	43	41	395	Kerry	74.0%	2.3%	2.2%	21.4%
CLEBURNE	2,436	1,650	128	87	571	Kerry	67.7%	5.3%	3.6%	23.4%
CLEVELAND	1,797	1,072	84	97	544	Kerry	59.7%	4.7%	5.4%	30.3%
COLUMBIA	3,104	1,724	172	241	967	Kerry	55.5%	5.5%	7.8%	31.2%
CONWAY	1,657	1,224	106	92	235	Kerry	73.9%	6.4%	5.6%	14.2%
CRAIGHEAD	11,727	7,594	539	495	3,099	Kerry	64.8%	4.6%	4.2%	26.4%
CRAWFORD	5,322	2,983	258	228	1,853	Kerry	56.1%	4.8%	4.3%	34.8%
CRITTENDEN	3,032	2,200	131	108	593	Kerry	72.6%	4.3%	3.6%	19.6%
CROSS	3,857	2,147	145	175	1,390	Kerry	55.7%	3.8%	4.5%	36.0%
DALLAS	1,583	1,033	68	57	425	Kerry	65.3%	4.3%	3.6%	26.8%
DESHA	1,704	1,258	110	112	224	Kerry	73.8%	6.5%	6.6%	13.1%
DREW	3,406	2,008	164	160	1,074	Kerry	59.0%	4.8%	4.7%	31.5%
FAULKNER	3,171	2,313	261	306	291	Kerry	72.9%	8.2%	9.6%	9.2%
FRANKLIN	4,351	3,123	621	607	0	Kerry	71.8%	14.3%	14.0%	0.0%
FULTON	2,883	1,727	133	75	948	Kerry	59.9%	4.6%	2.6%	32.9%
GARLAND	10,271	6,387	518	514	2,852	Kerry	62.2%	5.0%	5.0%	27.8%
GRANT	2,694	1,537	136	99	922	Kerry	57.1%	5.0%	3.7%	34.2%
GREENE	6,393	4,051	198	211	1,933	Kerry	63.4%	3.1%	3.3%	30.2%
HEMPSTEAD	2,926	1,799	88	95	944	Kerry	61.5%	3.0%	3.2%	32.3%
HOT SPRING	5,035	3,908	493	634	0	Kerry	77.6%	9.8%	12.6%	0.0%
HOWARD	2,318	1,316	68	72	862	Kerry	56.8%	2.9%	3.1%	37.2%
INDEPENDENCE	6,056	4,528	738	790	0	Kerry	74.8%	12.2%	13.0%	0.0%
IZARD	2,791	1,784	137	107	763	Kerry	63.9%	4.9%	3.8%	27.3%
JACKSON	3,338	2,301	93	112	832	Kerry	68.9%	2.8%	3.4%	24.9%
JEFFERSON	8,580	6,339	612	859	770	Kerry	73.9%	7.1%	10.0%	9.0%
JOHNSON	1,903	1,385	50	53	415	Kerry	72.8%	2.6%	2.8%	21.8%
LAFAYETTE	670	516	38	20	96	Kerry	77.0%	5.7%	3.0%	14.3%
LAWRENCE	4,148	2,679	162	135	1,172	Kerry	64.6%	3.9%	3.3%	28.3%
LEE	3,214	2,002	169	129	914	Kerry	62.3%	5.3%	4.0%	28.4%
LINCOLN	2,583	1,483	108	114	878	Kerry	57.4%	4.2%	4.4%	34.0%
LITTLE RIVER	2,806	1,591	92	69	1,054	Kerry	56.7%	3.3%	2.5%	37.6%
LOGAN	3,878	2,267	162	164	1,285	Kerry	58.5%	4.2%	4.2%	33.1%
LONOKE	3,999	2,498	197	223	1,081	Kerry	62.5%	4.9%	5.6%	27.0%
MADISON	2,824	1,605	160	149	910	Kerry	56.8%	5.7%	5.3%	32.2%
MARION	2,187	1,271	184	188	544	Kerry	58.1%	8.4%	8.6%	24.9%

ARKANSAS DEMOCRATIC PRIMARY

2004

County	Total Vote	Kerry	Kucinich	LaRouche	Uncommitted	Winner	Percentage of Total Vote			
							Kerry	Kucinich	LaRouche	Uncommitted
MILLER	4,678	2,612	200	150	1,716	Kerry	55.8%	4.3%	3.2%	36.7%
MISSISSIPPI	3,128	2,390	377	361	0	Kerry	76.4%	12.1%	11.5%	0.0%
MONROE	2,629	1,679	69	98	783	Kerry	63.9%	2.6%	3.7%	29.8%
MONTGOMERY	969	582	62	52	273	Kerry	60.1%	6.4%	5.4%	28.2%
NEVADA	862	666	90	106	0	Kerry	77.3%	10.4%	12.3%	0.0%
NEWTON	597	457	50	13	77	Kerry	76.5%	8.4%	2.2%	12.9%
OUACHITA	2,628	1,745	128	193	562	Kerry	66.4%	4.9%	7.3%	21.4%
PERRY	2,161	1,334	175	133	519	Kerry	61.7%	8.1%	6.2%	24.0%
PHILLIPS	5,663	3,561	296	280	1,526	Kerry	62.9%	5.2%	4.9%	26.9%
PIKE	1,986	1,170	64	86	666	Kerry	58.9%	3.2%	4.3%	33.5%
POINSETT	2,718	1,810	103	91	714	Kerry	66.6%	3.8%	3.3%	26.3%
POLK	3,411	1,645	197	202	1,367	Kerry	48.2%	5.8%	5.9%	40.1%
POPE	5,359	2,974	227	241	1,917	Kerry	55.5%	4.2%	4.5%	35.8%
PRAIRIE	1,987	1,200	84	96	607	Kerry	60.4%	4.2%	4.8%	30.5%
PULASKI	27,488	22,054	1,157	956	3,321	Kerry	80.2%	4.2%	3.5%	12.1%
RANDOLPH	3,154	2,075	84	124	871	Kerry	65.8%	2.7%	3.9%	27.6%
ST. FRANCIS	4,802	3,145	172	162	1,323	Kerry	65.5%	3.6%	3.4%	27.6%
SALINE	5,099	3,473	233	273	1,120	Kerry	68.1%	4.6%	5.4%	22.0%
SCOTT	2,346	1,180	134	143	889	Kerry	50.3%	5.7%	6.1%	37.9%
SEARCY	213	190	10	12	1	Kerry	89.2%	4.7%	5.6%	0.5%
SEBASTIAN	3,586	2,916	115	66	489	Kerry	81.3%	3.2%	1.8%	13.6%
SEVIER	799	578	26	30	165	Kerry	72.3%	3.3%	3.8%	20.7%
SHARP	3,691	2,103	177	165	1,246	Kerry	57.0%	4.8%	4.5%	33.8%
STONE	2,916	1,557	171	136	1,052	Kerry	53.4%	5.9%	4.7%	36.1%
UNION	3,640	1,977	229	348	1,086	Kerry	54.3%	6.3%	9.6%	29.8%
VAN BUREN	1,367	1,022	55	44	246	Kerry	74.8%	4.0%	3.2%	18.0%
WASHINGTON	7,016	5,272	425	196	1,123	Kerry	75.1%	6.1%	2.8%	16.0%
WHITE	4,121	3,037	141	156	787	Kerry	73.7%	3.4%	3.8%	19.1%
WOODRUFF	2,024	1,436	65	82	441	Kerry	70.9%	3.2%	4.1%	21.8%
YELL	2,942	1,928	109	124	781	Kerry	65.5%	3.7%	4.2%	26.5%
TOTAL	266,848	177,754	13,766	13,528	61,800	Kerry	66.6%	5.2%	5.1%	23.2%

ARKANSAS REPUBLICAN PRIMARY

2004

County	Total Vote	G.W. Bush	Uncommitted	Winner	Percentage of Total Vote	
					G.W. Bush	Uncommitted
ARKANSAS	416	416	0	G.W. Bush	100.0%	0.0%
ASHLEY	129	129	0	G.W. Bush	100.0%	0.0%
BAXTER	3,088	3,088	0	G.W. Bush	100.0%	0.0%
BENTON	8,120	8,120	0	G.W. Bush	100.0%	0.0%
BOONE	0	0	0			
BRADLEY	34	34	0	G.W. Bush	100.0%	0.0%
CALHOUN	0	0	0			
CARROLL	1,173	1,173	0	G.W. Bush	100.0%	0.0%
CHICOT	41	41	0	G.W. Bush	100.0%	0.0%
CLARK	193	186	7	G.W. Bush	96.4%	3.6%
CLAY	49	49	0	G.W. Bush	100.0%	0.0%
CLEBURNE	0	0	0			
CLEVELAND	0	0	0			
COLUMBIA	291	291	0	G.W. Bush	100.0%	0.0%
CONWAY	192	192	0	G.W. Bush	100.0%	0.0%
CRAIGHEAD	830	790	40	G.W. Bush	95.2%	4.8%
CRAWFORD	0	0	0			
CRITTENDEN	287	287	0	G.W. Bush	100.0%	0.0%
CROSS	15	15	0	G.W. Bush	100.0%	0.0%
DALLAS	0	0	0			
DESHA	78	78	0	G.W. Bush	100.0%	0.0%
DREW	118	118	0	G.W. Bush	100.0%	0.0%
FAULKNER	1,482	1,482	0	G.W. Bush	100.0%	0.0%
FRANKLIN	0	0	0			
FULTON	0	0	0			
GARLAND	1,663	1,663	0	G.W. Bush	100.0%	0.0%
GRANT	0	0	0			
GREENE	0	0	0			
HEMPSTEAD	106	106	0	G.W. Bush	100.0%	0.0%
HOT SPRING	150	150	0	G.W. Bush	100.0%	0.0%
HOWARD	42	42	0	G.W. Bush	100.0%	0.0%
INDEPENDENCE	453	453	0	G.W. Bush	100.0%	0.0%
IZARD	0	0	0			
JACKSON	0	0	0			
JEFFERSON	631	595	36	G.W. Bush	94.3%	5.7%
JOHNSON	424	384	40	G.W. Bush	90.6%	9.4%
LAFAYETTE	147	138	9	G.W. Bush	93.9%	6.1%
LAWRENCE	92	92	0	G.W. Bush	100.0%	0.0%
LEE	0	0	0			
LINCOLN	13	13	0	G.W. Bush	100.0%	0.0%
LITTLE RIVER	23	23	0	G.W. Bush	100.0%	0.0%
LOGAN	162	162	0	G.W. Bush	100.0%	0.0%
LONOKE	0	0	0			
MADISON	204	204	0	G.W. Bush	100.0%	0.0%
MARION	118	118	0	G.W. Bush	100.0%	0.0%

ARKANSAS REPUBLICAN PRIMARY

2004

County	Total Vote	G.W. Bush	Uncommitted	Winner	Percentage of Total Vote	
					G.W. Bush	Uncommitted
MILLER	0	0	0			
MISSISSIPPI	131	131	0	G.W. Bush	100.0%	0.0%
MONROE	6	6	0	G.W. Bush	100.0%	0.0%
MONTGOMERY	144	144	0	G.W. Bush	100.0%	0.0%
NEVADA	16	16	0	G.W. Bush	100.0%	0.0%
NEWTON	0	0	0			
OUACHITA	176	168	8	G.W. Bush	95.5%	4.5%
PERRY	113	113	0	G.W. Bush	100.0%	0.0%
PHILLIPS	21	21	0	G.W. Bush	100.0%	0.0%
PIKE	57	57	0	G.W. Bush	100.0%	0.0%
POINSETT	0	0	0	G.W. Bush		
POLK	212	212	0	G.W. Bush	100.0%	0.0%
POPE	1,100	1,100	0	G.W. Bush	100.0%	0.0%
PRAIRIE	49	48	1	G.W. Bush	98.0%	2.0%
PULASKI	9,285	8,808	477	G.W. Bush	94.9%	5.1%
RANDOLPH	84	84	0	G.W. Bush	100.0%	0.0%
ST. FRANCIS	0	0	0			
SALINE	1,328	1,328	0	G.W. Bush	100.0%	0.0%
SCOTT	5	4	1	G.W. Bush	80.0%	20.0%
SEARCY	0	0	0			
SEBASTIAN	0	0	0			
SEVIER	159	145	14	G.W. Bush	91.2%	8.8%
SHARP	0	0	0			
STONE	0	0	0			
UNION	784	758	26	G.W. Bush	96.7%	3.3%
VAN BUREN	366	341	25	G.W. Bush	93.2%	6.8%
WASHINGTON	0	0	0			
WHITE	3,461	3,016	445	G.W. Bush	87.1%	12.9%
WOODRUFF	10	10	0	G.W. Bush	100.0%	0.0%
YELL	92	92	0	G.W. Bush	100.0%	0.0%
TOTAL	38,363	37,234	1,129	G.W. Bush	97.1%	2.9%

Note: No vote was reported in 23 counties.

CALIFORNIA

Hubert Humphrey once called California "the Super Bowl of the primaries." But during the last quarter century, the nation's most populous state has been anything but that. The proliferation of primaries that increased the clout of Iowa and New Hampshire at the beginning of the calendar reduced California's significance at the end, or in recent years, the middle.

A generation ago, California's late-inning position often lent drama to the proceedings in one party or the other. The state's 1964 primary was critical for the Republicans; the 1968 and 1972 events offered high drama for the Democrats.

But for a quarter century after that, the California primary receded to the status of epilogue. In 1976, it was a mere formality, thanks to the home-state candidacies of then governor Jerry Brown and former governor Ronald Reagan. And through the rest of the twentieth century, California voted long after the nominees in both parties were all but certain.

Recent California Primary Results

California held its first presidential primary in 1912.

Year	Turnout	DEMOCRATS Candidates	%	Turnout	REPUBLICANS Candidates	%
2004 (March 2)	3,107,629	JOHN KERRY	64	2,216,351	GEORGE W. BUSH*	100
		John Edwards	20			
2000 (March 7)	2,654,114	AL GORE	81	2,847,921	GEORGE W. BUSH	61
		Bill Bradley	18		John McCain	35
1996 (March 26)	2,523,062	BILL CLINTON*	93	2,452,312	BOB DOLE	66
		Lyndon LaRouche	7		Pat Buchanan	18
					Steve Forbes	7
1992 (June 2)	2,863,609	BILL CLINTON	47	2,156,464	GEORGE BUSH*	74
		Jerry Brown	40		Pat Buchanan	26
		Paul Tsongas	7			
1988 (June 7)	3,138,734	MICHAEL DUKAKIS	61	2,240,387	GEORGE BUSH	83
		Jesse Jackson	35		Bob Dole	13
1984 (June 5)	2,970,903	GARY HART	39	1,874,975	RONALD REAGAN*	100
		Walter Mondale	35			
		Jesse Jackson	18			
1980 (June 3)	3,363,969	EDWARD KENNEDY	45	2,564,072	RONALD REAGAN	80
		Jimmy Carter*	38		John Anderson	14
		Unpledged	11			
1976 (June 8)	3,409,701	JERRY BROWN	59	2,450,511	RONALD REAGAN	65
		Jimmy Carter	20		Gerald Ford*	35
		Frank Church	7			
		Morris Udall	5			
1972 (June 6)	3,564,518	GEORGE McGOVERN	44	2,283,922	RICHARD NIXON*	90
		Hubert Humphrey	39		John Ashbrook	10
		George Wallace#	8			
1968 (June 4)	3,181,753	ROBERT KENNEDY	46	1,525,091	RONALD REAGAN	100
		Eugene McCarthy	42			
		Unpledged	12			

Note: All candidates are listed that drew at least 5 percent of their party's primary vote. The names of winning candidates are capitalized. An asterisk (*) indicates an incumbent president. A pound sign (#) indicates a write-in candidate. There was no direct vote for candidates in the 1984 Democratic primary; results are based on the vote for delegates. In 2000, there was also an unaffiliated ballot that listed candidates from all parties. A total of 2,082,124 votes were cast in this non-binding, all-party primary, with the leaders as follows: John McCain (R), 38 percent; Al Gore (D), 22 percent; and George W. Bush (R), 21 percent.

Finally willing to seek an earlier and more advantageous spot on the primary calendar, California officials moved their primary to late March in 1996, then to early March in 2000. In the latter year, turnout kicked up—a product of the earlier primary date and the unusual "blanket" nature of the primary in 2000 that encouraged broader participation. Only the votes of registered Democrats and Republicans counted for delegate-selection purposes, and they overwhelmingly favored the party front-runners, Democrat Al Gore and Republican George W. Bush, respectively.

But voters that did not participate in one of the party primaries could take another nonbinding ballot that listed candidates of all parties. Roughly 2 million voters did so, with the plurality voting for Republican John McCain. In the separate party primaries, Gore and Bush swept every county in the state. But when the "beauty contest" vote was factored in, it produced an electoral map with a very different look – showing Gore on top in the traditional Democratic strongholds of Los Angeles County and the San Francisco Bay area, Bush ahead in the Southern California suburbs and much of the state's interior, and McCain the candidate of choice in San Diego County.

But in 2004, California officials dispensed with the beauty contest vote, and the party primaries proved of little appeal in luring voters to the polls. President Bush ran unopposed in the Republican primary and Democratic front-runner John Kerry encountered little opposition in his party's primary. Kerry's only significant rival at the time, John Edwards, conceded California to Kerry long before the primary was held as Edwards focused his efforts on states such as Georgia and Ohio that voted the same day. In the end, Kerry handily won every county in California, but in a Democratic primary where fewer ballots were cast than in 1968.

In its heyday, the California primary was hospitable to political outsiders willing to take on their national party establishment. Two of the Kennedy brothers–Robert and Edward–won the Democratic primary; so did George McGovern and Gary Hart. Barry Goldwater won the 1964 Republican primary, a pivotal triumph for him and for conservative insurgents attempting to take over the party.

California voters have also been willing to support the presidential ambitions of their governors, giving Democrat Brown and Republican Reagan one-sided primary victories (Brown in 1976; Reagan each time he was on the primary ballot from 1968 through 1984). In national terms, both Brown and Reagan were also outsiders when they launched their presidential campaigns.

With the notable exception of 2000, voter interest in the presidential primary has declined as its stature diminished.

Yet even with turnout for the presidential primary at a low ebb, more than twice as many ballots were cast in California in 2004 than any other state, both in the Democratic and Republican primaries.

In much of the Sun Belt, population growth has been synonymous with Republican growth. But not in California, where the population has taken on a rainbow hue, with a large influx of Hispanics and Asians. Since the 1930s, Democrats have been able to maintain a wide voter registration edge.

Historically, California elections often have pitted the state's north against its south. But that has become an unfair contest, with most of the population growth concentrated in the south. Roughly 40 percent of the vote in any California primary, Democratic or Republican, is cast in just three southern counties: Los Angeles, Orange, and San Diego.

For more than four decades, Southern California's GOP has had a distinctly conservative cast. In the pivotal 1964 primary, Nelson Rockefeller swept the San Francisco Bay area and built up a big lead in the north. But Goldwater more than offset that in Southern California to win the primary, 52 to 48 percent.

The tenor of Southern California Republicanism had not changed that much by 1976, as Reagan swept Los Angeles, Orange, and San Diego counties with at least two-thirds of the vote. President Gerald Ford carried just two counties, San Francisco and its affluent suburban neighbor, Marin.

Democratic primary results sometime follow the same north-south variation. Both McGovern in 1972 and Hart in 1984 fashioned their victories in Northern California, particularly in the Bay area, which includes the high-tech "Silicon Valley." Both lost Los Angeles County, the anchor of Southern California.

Yet in the 1988 Democratic primary between Michael Dukakis and Jesse Jackson, there was evidence of another fault-line developing between the coastal counties and those inland. Jackson ran relatively well in many of the coastal counties where most liberal Democrats are found. But Dukakis dominated in the more conservative counties to the east across the Coast Range and swamped Jackson statewide.

Some of the same dynamics were present in the Democratic primary four years later. Brown carried many of the environmentally conscious coastal counties in the Bay area and north, the usual starting point for any liberal candidate running in California. But Brown fell short statewide, in part because he lost several counties in the Bay area, including Alameda (which includes Oakland, where Brown was subsequently elected mayor).

CALIFORNIA DEMOCRATIC PRIMARY

2000

County	Total Vote	Bradley	Gore	LaRouche	Winner	Percentage of Total Vote Bradley	Gore	LaRouche
ALAMEDA	164,611	39,922	123,871	818	Gore	24.3%	75.3%	0.5%
ALPINE	115	30	85	0	Gore	26.1%	73.9%	0.0%
AMADOR	3,448	657	2,774	17	Gore	19.1%	80.5%	0.5%
BUTTE	16,071	3,804	12,169	98	Gore	23.7%	75.7%	0.6%
CALAVERAS	3,775	734	3,005	36	Gore	19.4%	79.6%	1.0%
COLUSA	1,101	192	891	18	Gore	17.4%	80.9%	1.6%
CONTRA COSTA	107,693	22,614	84,761	318	Gore	21.0%	78.7%	0.3%
DEL NORTE	1,783	381	1,386	16	Gore	21.4%	77.7%	0.9%
EL DORADO	12,119	2,709	9,338	72	Gore	22.4%	77.1%	0.6%
FRESNO	49,865	6,909	42,782	174	Gore	13.9%	85.8%	0.3%
GLENN	1,513	333	1,143	37	Gore	22.0%	75.5%	2.4%
HUMBOLDT	11,704	3,266	8,398	40	Gore	27.9%	71.8%	0.3%
IMPERIAL	7,813	677	6,953	183	Gore	8.7%	89.0%	2.3%
INYO	1,313	275	1,027	11	Gore	20.9%	78.2%	0.8%
KERN	30,274	4,022	25,904	348	Gore	13.3%	85.6%	1.1%
KINGS	6,010	702	5,254	54	Gore	11.7%	87.4%	0.9%
LAKE	6,209	961	5,215	33	Gore	15.5%	84.0%	0.5%
LASSEN	1,759	438	1,287	34	Gore	24.9%	73.2%	1.9%
LOS ANGELES	773,059	107,941	659,800	5,318	Gore	14.0%	85.3%	0.7%
MADERA	6,277	1,074	5,156	47	Gore	17.1%	82.1%	0.7%
MARIN	36,785	12,172	24,560	53	Gore	33.1%	66.8%	0.1%
MARIPOSA	1,484	355	1,120	9	Gore	23.9%	75.5%	0.6%
MENDOCINO	8,547	2,183	6,308	56	Gore	25.5%	73.8%	0.7%
MERCED	12,616	1,703	10,850	63	Gore	13.5%	86.0%	0.5%
MODOC	605	179	420	6	Gore	29.6%	69.4%	1.0%
MONO	681	150	527	4	Gore	22.0%	77.4%	0.6%
MONTEREY	30,703	5,217	25,247	239	Gore	17.0%	82.2%	0.8%
NAPA	14,066	3,156	10,800	110	Gore	22.4%	76.8%	0.8%
NEVADA	8,383	2,149	6,197	37	Gore	25.6%	73.9%	0.4%
ORANGE	155,591	27,762	127,063	766	Gore	17.8%	81.7%	0.5%
PLACER	19,680	3,962	15,625	93	Gore	20.1%	79.4%	0.5%
PLUMAS	1,989	529	1,443	17	Gore	26.6%	72.5%	0.9%
RIVERSIDE	85,222	12,523	72,152	547	Gore	14.7%	84.7%	0.6%
SACRAMENTO	112,447	20,828	90,888	731	Gore	18.5%	80.8%	0.7%
SAN BENITO	4,276	619	3,618	39	Gore	14.5%	84.6%	0.9%
SAN BERNARDINO	90,389	11,843	77,319	1,227	Gore	13.1%	85.5%	1.4%
SAN DIEGO	165,820	26,446	138,063	1,311	Gore	15.9%	83.3%	0.8%
SAN FRANCISCO	106,216	28,471	77,604	141	Gore	26.8%	73.1%	0.1%
SAN JOAQUIN	38,884	5,989	32,698	197	Gore	15.4%	84.1%	0.5%
SAN LUIS OBISPO	20,284	4,772	15,445	67	Gore	23.5%	76.1%	0.3%
SAN MATEO	76,917	17,630	59,107	180	Gore	22.9%	76.8%	0.2%
SANTA BARBARA	33,176	7,549	25,546	81	Gore	22.8%	77.0%	0.2%
SANTA CLARA	142,679	32,144	109,802	733	Gore	22.5%	77.0%	0.5%
SANTA CRUZ	32,122	8,901	23,088	133	Gore	27.7%	71.9%	0.4%
SHASTA	10,758	2,529	8,145	84	Gore	23.5%	75.7%	0.8%

CALIFORNIA DEMOCRATIC PRIMARY

2000

County	Total Vote	Bradley	Gore	LaRouche	Winner	Percentage of Total Vote		
						Bradley	Gore	LaRouche
SIERRA	312	82	228	2	Gore	26.3%	73.1%	0.6%
SISKIYOU	3,408	1,018	2,339	51	Gore	29.9%	68.6%	1.5%
SOLANO	34,711	5,475	29,007	229	Gore	15.8%	83.6%	0.7%
SONOMA	61,191	14,424	46,516	251	Gore	23.6%	76.0%	0.4%
STANISLAUS	29,155	4,016	24,869	270	Gore	13.8%	85.3%	0.9%
SUTTER	4,666	876	3,752	38	Gore	18.8%	80.4%	0.8%
TEHAMA	3,901	822	3,028	51	Gore	21.1%	77.6%	1.3%
TRINITY	1,044	311	723	10	Gore	29.8%	69.3%	1.0%
TULARE	16,962	2,407	14,432	123	Gore	14.2%	85.1%	0.7%
TUOLUMNE	5,183	1,088	4,065	30	Gore	21.0%	78.4%	0.6%
VENTURA	55,321	9,952	45,234	135	Gore	18.0%	81.8%	0.2%
YOLO	18,235	4,428	13,709	98	Gore	24.3%	75.2%	0.5%
YUBA	3,193	581	2,585	27	Gore	18.2%	81.0%	0.8%
TOTAL	2,654,114	482,882	2,155,321	15,911	Gore	18.2%	81.2%	0.6%

CALIFORNIA REPUBLICAN PRIMARY

2000

County	Total Vote	G.W. Bush	McCain	Other	Winner	Percentage of Total Vote		
						G.W. Bush	McCain	Other
ALAMEDA	71,529	39,677	28,794	3,058	G.W. Bush	55.5%	40.3%	4.3%
ALPINE	212	117	79	16	G.W. Bush	55.2%	37.3%	7.5%
AMADOR	5,885	3,657	1,952	276	G.W. Bush	62.1%	33.2%	4.7%
BUTTE	29,557	18,984	8,953	1,620	G.W. Bush	64.2%	30.3%	5.5%
CALAVERAS	7,006	4,272	2,341	393	G.W. Bush	61.0%	33.4%	5.6%
COLUSA	2,262	1,566	580	116	G.W. Bush	69.2%	25.6%	5.1%
CONTRA COSTA	93,898	53,259	37,135	3,504	G.W. Bush	56.7%	39.5%	3.7%
DEL NORTE	2,813	1,703	904	206	G.W. Bush	60.5%	32.1%	7.3%
EL DORADO	27,482	16,819	9,096	1,567	G.W. Bush	61.2%	33.1%	5.7%
FRESNO	73,949	53,207	17,026	3,716	G.W. Bush	72.0%	23.0%	5.0%
GLENN	3,601	2,551	916	134	G.W. Bush	70.8%	25.4%	3.7%
HUMBOLDT	14,049	8,863	4,717	469	G.W. Bush	63.1%	33.6%	3.3%
IMPERIAL	7,370	5,072	2,016	282	G.W. Bush	68.8%	27.4%	3.8%
INYO	3,172	1,902	1,127	143	G.W. Bush	60.0%	35.5%	4.5%
KERN	68,820	46,391	19,058	3,371	G.W. Bush	67.4%	27.7%	4.9%

CALIFORNIA REPUBLICAN PRIMARY

2000

County	Total Vote	G.W. Bush	McCain	Other	Winner	Percentage of Total Vote		
						G.W. Bush	McCain	Other
KINGS	9,207	6,355	2,392	460	G.W. Bush	69.0%	26.0%	5.0%
LAKE	6,102	3,242	2,583	277	G.W. Bush	53.1%	42.3%	4.5%
LASSEN	3,762	2,293	1,225	244	G.W. Bush	61.0%	32.6%	6.5%
LOS ANGELES	510,170	308,878	179,297	21,995	G.W. Bush	60.5%	35.1%	4.3%
MADERA	12,726	8,902	3,117	707	G.W. Bush	70.0%	24.5%	5.6%
MARIN	23,670	11,549	11,409	712	G.W. Bush	48.8%	48.2%	3.0%
MARIPOSA	3,247	2,071	916	260	G.W. Bush	63.8%	28.2%	8.0%
MENDOCINO	7,782	4,216	3,206	360	G.W. Bush	54.2%	41.2%	4.6%
MERCED	13,594	9,440	3,393	761	G.W. Bush	69.4%	25.0%	5.6%
MODOC	1,652	1,088	481	83	G.W. Bush	65.9%	29.1%	5.0%
MONO	1,570	868	602	100	G.W. Bush	55.3%	38.3%	6.4%
MONTEREY	28,448	16,349	10,601	1,498	G.W. Bush	57.5%	37.3%	5.3%
NAPA	13,963	7,582	5,788	593	G.W. Bush	54.3%	41.5%	4.2%
NEVADA	17,928	11,278	5,726	924	G.W. Bush	62.9%	31.9%	5.2%
ORANGE	359,986	225,099	115,968	18,919	G.W. Bush	62.5%	32.2%	5.3%
PLACER	44,226	27,416	14,462	2,348	G.W. Bush	62.0%	32.7%	5.3%
PLUMAS	3,803	2,250	1,334	219	G.W. Bush	59.2%	35.1%	5.8%
RIVERSIDE	148,650	91,167	50,422	7,061	G.W. Bush	61.3%	33.9%	4.8%
SACRAMENTO	124,824	77,993	40,042	6,789	G.W. Bush	62.5%	32.1%	5.4%
SAN BENITO	4,598	2,784	1,656	158	G.W. Bush	60.5%	36.0%	3.4%
SAN BERNARDINO	132,291	84,081	41,573	6,637	G.W. Bush	63.6%	31.4%	5.0%
SAN DIEGO	297,483	165,006	118,968	13,509	G.W. Bush	55.5%	40.0%	4.5%
SAN FRANCISCO	25,877	13,089	12,037	751	G.W. Bush	50.6%	46.5%	2.9%
SAN JOAQUIN	51,116	34,567	14,078	2,471	G.W. Bush	67.6%	27.5%	4.8%
SAN LUIS OBISPO	38,409	23,743	12,836	1,830	G.W. Bush	61.8%	33.4%	4.8%
SAN MATEO	50,830	26,984	22,228	1,618	G.W. Bush	53.1%	43.7%	3.2%
SANTA BARBARA	46,350	28,918	15,568	1,864	G.W. Bush	62.4%	33.6%	4.0%
SANTA CLARA	117,864	63,866	49,323	4,675	G.W. Bush	54.2%	41.8%	4.0%
SANTA CRUZ	20,323	10,216	8,764	1,343	G.W. Bush	50.3%	43.1%	6.6%
SHASTA	25,254	17,557	6,437	1,260	G.W. Bush	69.5%	25.5%	5.0%
SIERRA	694	422	230	42	G.W. Bush	60.8%	33.1%	6.1%
SISKIYOU	6,680	4,018	2,153	509	G.W. Bush	60.1%	32.2%	7.6%
SOLANO	29,109	17,329	10,215	1,565	G.W. Bush	59.5%	35.1%	5.4%
SONOMA	45,296	23,121	20,040	2,135	G.W. Bush	51.0%	44.2%	4.7%
STANISLAUS	39,242	26,700	10,206	2,336	G.W. Bush	68.0%	26.0%	6.0%
SUTTER	11,347	7,763	2,941	643	G.W. Bush	68.4%	25.9%	5.7%
TEHAMA	7,604	4,854	2,418	332	G.W. Bush	63.8%	31.8%	4.4%
TRINITY	1,966	1,110	754	102	G.W. Bush	56.5%	38.4%	5.2%
TULARE	32,848	23,861	7,611	1,376	G.W. Bush	72.6%	23.2%	4.2%
TUOLUMNE	8,715	5,474	2,773	468	G.W. Bush	62.8%	31.8%	5.4%
VENTURA	86,587	50,942	31,470	4,175	G.W. Bush	58.8%	36.3%	4.8%
YOLO	14,886	8,778	5,333	775	G.W. Bush	59.0%	35.8%	5.2%
YUBA	5,637	3,903	1,436	298	G.W. Bush	69.2%	25.5%	5.3%
TOTAL	2,847,921	1,725,162	988,706	134,053	G.W. Bush	60.6%	34.7%	4.7%

Note: Other vote was 112,747 Alan Keyes; 8,449 Steve Forbes; 6,860 Gary Bauer; 5,997 Orrin G. Hatch.

CALIFORNIA ALL-PARTY PRIMARY

2000

County	Total Vote	Bradley	G.W. Bush	Gore	McCain	Other	Winner	Percentage of Total Vote Bradley	G.W. Bush	Gore	McCain	Other
ALAMEDA	328,960	50,441	52,544	145,075	56,998	23,902	Gore	15.3%	16.0%	44.1%	17.3%	7.3%
ALPINE	499	49	147	122	142	39	G.W. Bush	9.8%	29.5%	24.4%	28.5%	7.8%
AMADOR	13,034	853	4,520	3,226	3,771	664	G.W. Bush	6.5%	34.7%	24.8%	28.9%	5.1%
BUTTE	63,321	4,976	23,030	14,560	16,451	4,304	G.W. Bush	7.9%	36.4%	23.0%	26.0%	6.8%
CALAVERAS	15,379	1,027	5,334	3,628	4,310	1,080	G.W. Bush	6.7%	34.7%	23.6%	28.0%	7.0%
COLUSA	4,632	233	1,987	1,061	1,098	253	G.W. Bush	5.0%	42.9%	22.9%	23.7%	5.5%
CONTRA COSTA	272,126	29,650	65,780	100,919	63,668	12,109	Gore	10.9%	24.2%	37.1%	23.4%	4.4%
DEL NORTE	6,826	492	2,294	1,687	1,805	548	G.W. Bush	7.2%	33.6%	24.7%	26.4%	8.0%
EL DORADO	55,391	3,649	20,228	11,631	16,365	3,518	G.W. Bush	6.6%	36.5%	21.0%	29.5%	6.4%
FRESNO	162,923	8,536	66,080	49,231	31,148	7,928	G.W. Bush	5.2%	40.6%	30.2%	19.1%	4.9%
GLENN	7,170	412	3,232	1,318	1,835	373	G.W. Bush	5.7%	45.1%	18.4%	25.6%	5.2%
HUMBOLDT	41,254	4,194	11,645	10,336	10,272	4,807	G.W. Bush	10.2%	28.2%	25.1%	24.9%	11.7%
IMPERIAL	21,078	842	7,308	8,257	3,718	953	Gore	4.0%	34.7%	39.2%	17.6%	4.5%
INYO	6,294	403	2,317	1,258	1,955	361	G.W. Bush	6.4%	36.8%	20.0%	31.1%	5.7%
KERN	133,114	5,171	57,446	30,357	33,344	6,796	G.W. Bush	3.9%	43.2%	22.8%	25.0%	5.1%
KINGS	20,867	911	8,252	6,235	4,432	1,037	G.W. Bush	4.4%	39.5%	29.9%	21.2%	5.0%
LAKE	17,338	1,255	4,175	6,188	4,725	995	Gore	7.2%	24.1%	35.7%	27.3%	5.7%
LASSEN	8,424	548	3,151	1,531	2,609	585	G.W. Bush	6.5%	37.4%	18.2%	31.0%	6.9%
LOS ANGELES	1,748,419	141,606	405,177	779,432	336,947	85,257	Gore	8.1%	23.2%	44.6%	19.3%	4.9%
MADERA	25,639	1,365	11,174	6,129	5,468	1,503	G.W. Bush	5.3%	43.6%	23.9%	21.3%	5.9%
MARIN	87,650	15,861	14,339	30,055	22,050	5,345	Gore	18.1%	16.4%	34.3%	25.2%	6.1%
MARIPOSA	6,739	472	2,534	1,365	1,769	599	G.W. Bush	7.0%	37.6%	20.3%	26.3%	8.9%
MENDOCINO	26,078	2,760	5,608	7,713	6,625	3,372	Gore	10.6%	21.5%	29.6%	25.4%	12.9%
MERCED	36,323	2,095	12,846	12,464	7,105	1,813	G.W. Bush	5.8%	35.4%	34.3%	19.6%	5.0%
MODOC	3,459	237	1,498	511	994	219	G.W. Bush	6.9%	43.3%	14.8%	28.7%	6.3%
MONO	3,356	231	1,072	705	1,074	274	McCain	6.9%	31.9%	21.0%	32.0%	8.2%
MONTEREY	81,852	6,888	21,150	29,970	19,034	4,810	Gore	8.4%	25.8%	36.6%	23.3%	5.9%
NAPA	39,265	4,220	9,510	13,053	10,367	2,115	Gore	10.7%	24.2%	33.2%	26.4%	5.4%
NEVADA	36,988	2,949	13,303	7,882	10,202	2,652	G.W. Bush	8.0%	36.0%	21.3%	27.6%	7.2%
ORANGE	712,334	42,751	270,470	171,371	187,555	40,187	G.W. Bush	6.0%	38.0%	24.1%	26.3%	5.6%
PLACER	87,382	5,501	32,609	19,211	25,045	5,016	G.W. Bush	6.3%	37.3%	22.0%	28.7%	5.7%
PLUMAS	8,568	688	2,956	1,691	2,640	593	G.W. Bush	8.0%	34.5%	19.7%	30.8%	6.9%
RIVERSIDE	313,223	17,658	109,639	90,212	80,588	15,126	G.W. Bush	5.6%	35.0%	28.8%	25.7%	4.8%
SACRAMENTO	326,395	26,679	96,957	106,505	77,329	18,925	Gore	8.2%	29.7%	32.6%	23.7%	5.8%
SAN BENITO	12,241	824	3,544	4,447	2,856	570	Gore	6.7%	29.0%	36.3%	23.3%	4.7%
SAN BERNARDINO	302,210	16,574	104,227	93,752	70,171	17,486	G.W. Bush	5.5%	34.5%	31.0%	23.2%	5.8%
SAN DIEGO	665,230	37,078	205,321	176,293	210,529	36,009	McCain	5.6%	30.9%	26.5%	31.6%	5.4%
SAN FRANCISCO	199,827	36,727	19,885	96,271	29,741	17,203	Gore	18.4%	10.0%	48.2%	14.9%	8.6%
SAN JOAQUIN	120,465	7,870	43,234	38,621	25,198	5,542	G.W. Bush	6.5%	35.9%	32.1%	20.9%	4.6%
SAN LUIS OBISPO	83,239	6,742	28,631	19,431	23,219	5,216	G.W. Bush	8.1%	34.4%	23.3%	27.9%	6.3%
SAN MATEO	178,211	23,348	35,216	71,693	40,594	7,360	Gore	13.1%	19.8%	40.2%	22.8%	4.1%
SANTA BARBARA	114,573	10,552	36,259	32,047	29,205	6,510	G.W. Bush	9.2%	31.6%	28.0%	25.5%	5.7%
SANTA CLARA	363,297	42,814	81,400	136,062	85,022	17,999	Gore	11.8%	22.4%	37.5%	23.4%	5.0%
SANTA CRUZ	78,471	11,618	12,999	27,901	17,986	7,967	Gore	14.8%	16.6%	35.6%	22.9%	10.2%
SHASTA	50,809	3,326	22,124	9,600	12,743	3,016	G.W. Bush	6.5%	43.5%	18.9%	25.1%	5.9%

CALIFORNIA ALL-PARTY PRIMARY

2000

County	Total Vote	Bradley	G.W. Bush	Gore	McCain	Other	Winner	Percentage of Total Vote				
								Bradley	G.W. Bush	Gore	McCain	Other
SIERRA	1,633	116	589	294	513	121	G.W. Bush	7.1%	36.1%	18.0%	31.4%	7.4%
SISKIYOU	15,453	1,290	5,375	2,781	4,660	1,347	G.W. Bush	8.3%	34.8%	18.0%	30.2%	8.7%
SOLANO	88,580	7,045	22,832	34,055	20,041	4,607	Gore	8.0%	25.8%	38.4%	22.6%	5.2%
SONOMA	152,808	18,549	29,181	56,006	37,657	11,415	Gore	12.1%	19.1%	36.7%	24.6%	7.5%
STANISLAUS	93,615	5,206	34,235	29,164	19,669	5,341	G.W. Bush	5.6%	36.6%	31.2%	21.0%	5.7%
SUTTER	21,073	1,121	9,365	4,502	4,930	1,155	G.W. Bush	5.3%	44.4%	21.4%	23.4%	5.5%
TEHAMA	16,765	1,059	6,429	3,552	4,869	856	G.W. Bush	6.3%	38.3%	21.2%	29.0%	5.1%
TRINITY	4,853	426	1,516	899	1,626	386	McCain	8.8%	31.2%	18.5%	33.5%	8.0%
TULARE	66,083	3,006	29,982	16,705	13,417	2,973	G.W. Bush	4.5%	45.4%	25.3%	20.3%	4.5%
TUOLUMNE	19,315	1,411	6,745	4,767	5,241	1,151	G.W. Bush	7.3%	34.9%	24.7%	27.1%	6.0%
VENTURA	196,484	13,905	62,520	56,965	52,969	10,125	G.W. Bush	7.1%	31.8%	29.0%	27.0%	5.2%
YOLO	47,593	5,712	11,385	16,149	11,430	2,917	Gore	12.0%	23.9%	33.9%	24.0%	6.1%
YUBA	12,593	732	5,160	3,104	2,846	751	G.W. Bush	5.8%	41.0%	24.6%	22.6%	6.0%
TOTAL	7,627,721	642,654	2,168,466	2,609,950	1,780,570	426,081	Gore	8.4%	28.4%	34.2%	23.3%	5.6%

Note: The 2000 presidential primary vote in California was counted in two ways - first, by party for delegate-selection purposes; then, in terms of all votes, including those cast by registered third party and independent voters, as well as registered Democrats and Republicans who preferred a choice for president outside their own party. The combined results from these various counts produced a nonbinding overall vote that is presented in this table. Other vote was 170,442 Alan Keyes (R); 112,345 Ralph Nader (Green); 20,825 Harry Browne (Libertarian); 19,419 Lyndon H. LaRouche Jr. (D); 15,311 Donald Trump (Reform); 14,484 Steve Forbes (R); 10,529 Gary Bauer (R); 9,390 George D. Weber (Reform); 9,202 Orrin G. Hatch (R); 8,979 Howard Phillips (American Independent); 6,714 Joel Kovel (Green); 5,891 John Hagelin (Natural Law); 4,879 Robert Bowman (Reform); 4,009 Kip Lee (Libertarian); 3,165 L. Neil Smith (Libertarian); 3,158 John B. Anderson (Reform); 2,984 Larry Hines (Libertarian); 2,487 Dave Lynn Hollist (Libertarian); 1,837 Charles Collins (Reform); 15 Joel Gary Neuberg (Reform write-in); 5 Joe Schriner (R write-in); 4 Odessa Lightfoot (D write-in); 4 David S. Rosenbaum (R write-in); 2 Mark Greenstein (D write-in); 1 Kent P. Mesplay (Green write-in).

CALIFORNIA DEMOCRATIC PRIMARY

2004

County	Total Vote	Edwards	Kerry	Other	Winner	Percentage of Total Vote		
						Edwards	Kerry	Other
ALAMEDA	201,617	33,502	127,586	40,529	Kerry	16.6%	63.3%	20.1%
ALPINE	198	42	124	32	Kerry	21.2%	62.6%	16.2%
AMADOR	4,704	1,188	2,921	595	Kerry	25.3%	62.1%	12.6%
BUTTE	22,080	4,952	13,627	3,501	Kerry	22.4%	61.7%	15.9%
CALAVERAS	5,776	1,410	3,474	892	Kerry	24.4%	60.1%	15.4%
COLUSA	1,334	336	794	204	Kerry	25.2%	59.5%	15.3%
CONTRA COSTA	130,983	25,450	87,044	18,489	Kerry	19.4%	66.5%	14.1%
DEL NORTE	2,389	529	1,506	354	Kerry	22.1%	63.0%	14.8%
EL DORADO	17,625	4,361	10,725	2,539	Kerry	24.7%	60.9%	14.4%
FRESNO	56,719	14,930	34,932	6,857	Kerry	26.3%	61.6%	12.1%
GLENN	2,094	529	1,230	335	Kerry	25.3%	58.7%	16.0%
HUMBOLDT	25,138	5,133	13,755	6,250	Kerry	20.4%	54.7%	24.9%
IMPERIAL	8,584	1,593	5,278	1,713	Kerry	18.6%	61.5%	20.0%
INYO	2,063	456	1,250	357	Kerry	22.1%	60.6%	17.3%
KERN	39,972	8,684	25,213	6,075	Kerry	21.7%	63.1%	15.2%
KINGS	6,736	1,616	4,280	840	Kerry	24.0%	63.5%	12.5%
LAKE	7,761	1,713	4,835	1,213	Kerry	22.1%	62.3%	15.6%
LASSEN	2,410	654	1,408	348	Kerry	27.1%	58.4%	14.4%
LOS ANGELES	742,234	139,215	486,781	116,238	Kerry	18.8%	65.6%	15.7%
MADERA	8,462	2,049	5,178	1,235	Kerry	24.2%	61.2%	14.6%
MARIN	51,003	8,821	32,357	9,825	Kerry	17.3%	63.4%	19.3%
MARIPOSA	2,093	535	1,207	351	Kerry	25.6%	57.7%	16.8%
MENDOCINO	14,384	3,094	7,721	3,569	Kerry	21.5%	53.7%	24.8%
MERCED	14,187	3,090	9,173	1,924	Kerry	21.8%	64.7%	13.6%
MODOC	991	288	532	171	Kerry	29.1%	53.7%	17.3%
MONO	1,247	308	730	209	Kerry	24.7%	58.5%	16.8%
MONTEREY	34,211	5,752	23,561	4,898	Kerry	16.8%	68.9%	14.3%
NAPA	17,656	3,423	11,967	2,266	Kerry	19.4%	67.8%	12.8%
NEVADA	13,547	2,948	7,747	2,852	Kerry	21.8%	57.2%	21.1%
ORANGE	178,755	39,242	115,058	24,455	Kerry	22.0%	64.4%	13.7%
PLACER	31,732	7,307	20,581	3,844	Kerry	23.0%	64.9%	12.1%
PLUMAS	2,760	705	1,641	414	Kerry	25.5%	59.5%	15.0%
RIVERSIDE	100,941	20,126	67,194	13,621	Kerry	19.9%	66.6%	13.5%
SACRAMENTO	130,700	27,396	84,789	18,515	Kerry	21.0%	64.9%	14.2%
SAN BENITO	5,876	1,112	3,843	921	Kerry	18.9%	65.4%	15.7%
SAN BERNARDINO	95,267	18,624	62,798	13,845	Kerry	19.5%	65.9%	14.5%
SAN DIEGO	241,193	50,665	157,299	33,229	Kerry	21.0%	65.2%	13.8%
SAN FRANCISCO	135,795	23,406	80,701	31,688	Kerry	17.2%	59.4%	23.3%
SAN JOAQUIN	44,873	8,882	29,980	6,011	Kerry	19.8%	66.8%	13.4%
SAN LUIS OBISPO	30,256	6,651	18,613	4,992	Kerry	22.0%	61.5%	16.5%
SAN MATEO	92,176	18,419	61,005	12,752	Kerry	20.0%	66.2%	13.8%
SANTA BARBARA	44,933	8,305	28,903	7,725	Kerry	18.5%	64.3%	17.2%
SANTA CLARA	173,169	33,297	117,424	22,448	Kerry	19.2%	67.8%	13.0%
SANTA CRUZ	46,855	8,459	25,903	12,493	Kerry	18.1%	55.3%	26.7%
SHASTA	15,381	3,900	9,124	2,357	Kerry	25.4%	59.3%	15.3%

CALIFORNIA DEMOCRATIC PRIMARY

2004

County	Total Vote	Edwards	Kerry	Other	Winner	Percentage of Total Vote		
						Edwards	Kerry	Other
SIERRA	490	134	273	83	Kerry	27.3%	55.7%	16.9%
SISKIYOU	5,202	1,353	2,722	1,127	Kerry	26.0%	52.3%	21.7%
SOLANO	40,648	7,762	27,487	5,399	Kerry	19.1%	67.6%	13.3%
SONOMA	84,595	15,610	52,541	16,444	Kerry	18.5%	62.1%	19.4%
STANISLAUS	33,632	7,917	21,285	4,430	Kerry	23.5%	63.3%	13.2%
SUTTER	5,594	1,475	3,332	787	Kerry	26.4%	59.6%	14.1%
TEHAMA	5,319	1,370	3,168	781	Kerry	25.8%	59.6%	14.7%
TRINITY	1,843	491	1,014	338	Kerry	26.6%	55.0%	18.3%
TULARE	19,803	4,585	12,660	2,558	Kerry	23.2%	63.9%	12.9%
TUOLUMNE	6,818	1,706	4,155	957	Kerry	25.0%	60.9%	14.0%
VENTURA	67,149	13,145	45,072	8,932	Kerry	19.6%	67.1%	13.3%
YOLO	23,883	4,917	14,782	4,184	Kerry	20.6%	61.9%	17.5%
YUBA	3,793	879	2,256	658	Kerry	23.2%	59.5%	17.3%
TOTAL	3,107,629	614,441	2,002,539	490,649	Kerry	19.8%	64.4%	15.8%

Note: Registered Democratic and unaffiliated voters could participate in the Democratic primary. Their votes were tallied separately and as a combined total. The combined total is presented in this table. Other vote was 144,954 Dennis J. Kucinich; 130,892 Howard Dean; 59,326 Al Sharpton; 52,780 Joseph I. Lieberman; 51,084 Wesley Clark; 24,501 Carol Moseley Braun; 19,139 Richard A. Gephardt; 7,953 Lyndon H. LaRouche Jr.; 6 Katarina Dunmar (write-in); 4 James Alexander-Pace (write-in); 4 John Nigro Jr. (write-in); 3 David Giacomuzzi (write-in); 3 Fern Penna (write-in).

COLORADO

Colorado was late to join the national movement to presidential primaries, not holding its first until 1992. And after a brief three-time experiment with the primary, the state was quick to return to its traditional low-turnout caucus process in 2004.

Colorado's initial decision to hold a presidential primary was due in no small part to the contentious caucus process that Democrats went through in 1988.

The precinct caucuses in 1988 were held in early April, just as Jesse Jackson's candidacy was peaking. The critical Wisconsin primary was to be held the next day. When Colorado Democratic officials seemed slow in tallying the caucus results, Jackson cried foul. He accused the state party chairman, a supporter of Michael Dukakis, of delaying the count so that Colorado would not influence Wisconsin.

State party officials countered that they were tabulating the votes from the nearly 3,000 precinct caucuses more quickly than they usually did. But they were clearly caught off-guard by the clamor of both Jackson and the national media for quicker returns. When the results were finally in, Dukakis had won (as sample precincts had indicated from the beginning), but the whole episode helped fuel momentum for a state-operated presidential primary.

When the first primary was held four years later, Jackson and Dukakis were gone from the scene, but the race on the Democratic side was as closely contested as it had been in 1988.

The early March date that Colorado voted was at a time when all of the candidates were looking for traction. And when the nearly quarter million Democratic primary votes were cast, less than 8,000 separated the top three finishers. Jerry Brown emerged the winner, one of only two primaries he was to win in 1992; the other was Connecticut.

Brown won with a pro-environment, anti-establishment appeal that swept Colorado's liberal "granola belt," which extends westward from Denver through the college town of Boulder and skiing communities on the Western Slope, such as Aspen (Pitkin County), Vail (Eagle), and Telluride (San Miguel). Denver and Boulder counties, in particular, had a disproportionate influence on the outcome, together casting 30 percent of the Democratic primary ballots.

Bill Clinton finished a close second that year by winning the farm counties of the High Plains, ranching counties of the Western Slope, Hispanic counties of southern Colorado, and blue-collar strongholds such as Pueblo and Adams counties (the latter in the Denver suburbs). Paul Tsongas ran a close third by carrying the more upscale suburban counties of Arapahoe and Douglas, as well as El Paso County (Colorado Springs).

None of the Republican presidential primaries have been nearly as compelling as the inaugural Democratic contest in 1992, as each GOP primary has given a boost to the front-runner.

Recent Colorado Primary Results

Colorado held its first presidential primary in 1992.

| Year | DEMOCRATS | | | REPUBLICANS | | |
	Turnout	Candidates	%	Turnout	Candidates	%
2004		No Primary			No Primary	
2000 (March 10)	88,678	AL GORE	71	180,638	GEORGE W. BUSH	65
		Bill Bradley	23		John McCain	27
					Alan Keyes	7
1996 (March 5)	54,527	BILL CLINTON*	89	247,930	BOB DOLE	44
		Lyndon LaRouche	11		Pat Buchanan	22
					Steve Forbes	21
					Lamar Alexander	10
1992 (March 3)	239,643	JERRY BROWN	29	195,690	GEORGE BUSH*	68
		Bill Clinton	27		Pat Buchanan	30
		Paul Tsongas	26			
		Bob Kerrey	12			

Note: All candidates are listed who drew at least 5 percent of their party's primary vote. The names of winning candidates are capitalized. An asterisk (*) indicates an incumbent president.

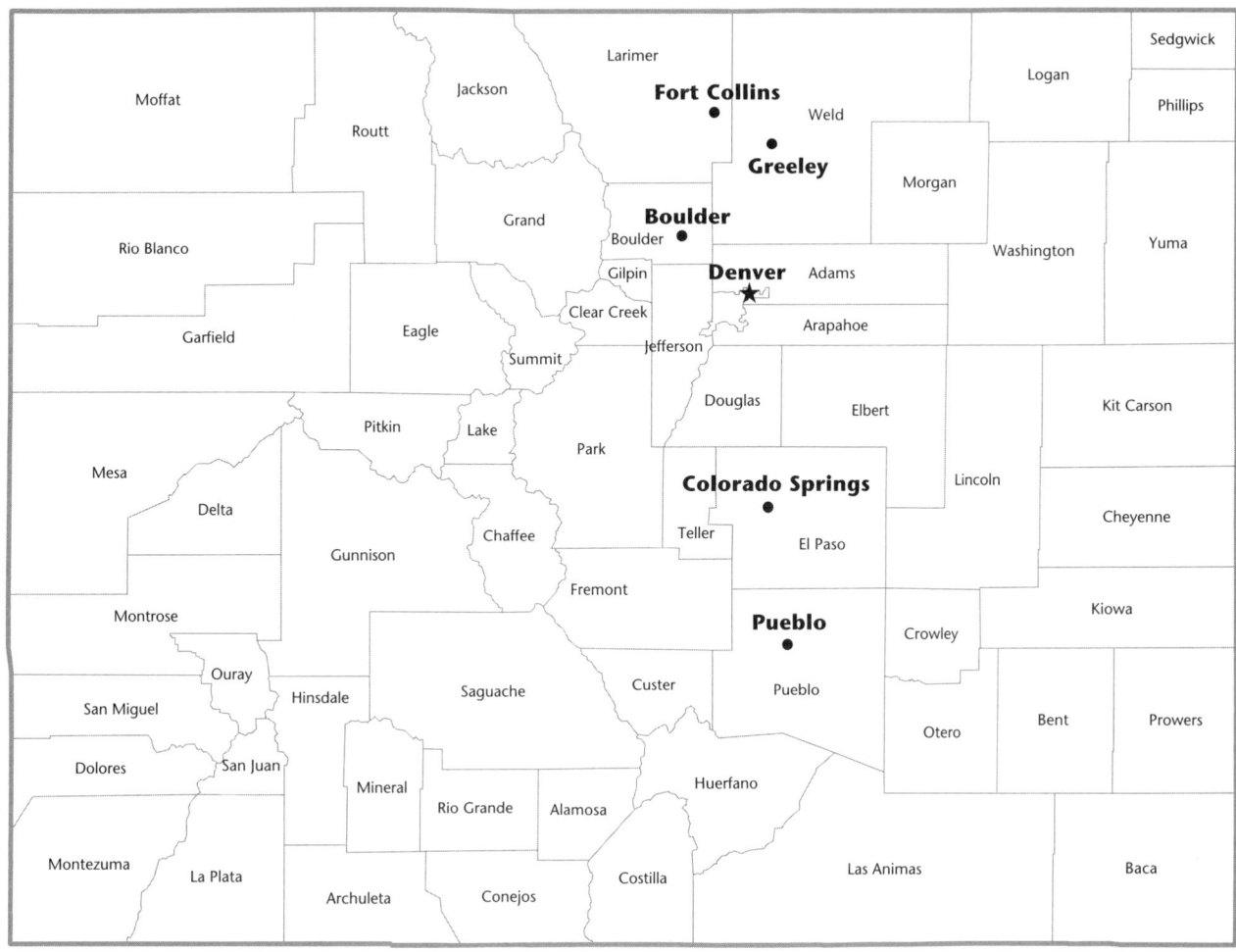

President George Bush swept all 63 counties in winning the Republican primary in 1992. His lone challenger, Pat Buchanan, reached 40 percent only in tiny Gilpin County, high in the mountains west of Denver.

Bob Dole won Colorado's Republican primary in 1996 almost as convincingly. He garnered more votes than his two nearest rivals combined, Buchanan and Steve Forbes, and carried every county except small, predominantly Hispanic Costilla, along Colorado's southern border. It went for Forbes.

In 2000, both the Democratic and Republican primaries were held after the nominations in each party had been settled. Even though he had left the race, Republican John McCain established beachheads of a sort in many of the mountain counties of the granola belt, where he consistently pulled at least one-third of the vote against the erstwhile GOP nominee, George W. Bush.

The bulk of both parties' voters can be found in a strip less than 200 miles long along the Front Range of the Rocky Mountains. Democrats traditionally tend to be strongest at the two ends–Boulder, Adams, and Denver counties on the north

and Pueblo on the south. Republicans tend to be stronger in between: in the affluent suburbs of Arapahoe and Jefferson counties near Denver, and just to the south in El Paso County, with its large representation of military and Christian conservatives.

No part of Colorado, though, whether the populous Front Range or more rural reaches, played much of a role in either party's caucuses in 2004. The only semblance of competition was on the Democratic side. But even there, Colorado's return to April precinct caucuses meant for a low turnout and minimal interest. An estimated 12,000 voters participated, roughly 5 percent the number that had voted in the Democrats' first presidential primary in 1992.

As expected, the cadre of caucus-goers gave John Kerry (by then, the party's 2004 nominee in waiting) a big victory. Kerry won 61 percent of the county convention delegates, compared to 22 percent for "Uncommitted" and 13 percent for Dennis Kucinich. In a sign of hesitation about the Kerry candidacy, however, the Uncommitted option prevailed in a dozen counties, including two of the larger Democratic strongholds, Adams and Pueblo.

COLORADO DEMOCRATIC PRIMARY

2000

County	Total Vote	Bradley	Gore	Other	Winner	Percentage of Total Vote		
						Bradley	Gore	Other
ADAMS	4,005	614	3,187	204	Gore	15.3%	79.6%	5.1%
ALAMOSA	441	71	342	28	Gore	16.1%	77.6%	6.3%
ARAPAHOE	8,867	1,691	6,839	337	Gore	19.1%	77.1%	3.8%
ARCHULETA	120	21	85	14	Gore	17.5%	70.8%	11.7%
BACA	237	58	142	37	Gore	24.5%	59.9%	15.6%
BENT	170	34	115	21	Gore	20.0%	67.6%	12.4%
BOULDER	4,914	1,434	3,301	179	Gore	29.2%	67.2%	3.6%
CHAFFEE	326	64	245	17	Gore	19.6%	75.2%	5.2%
CHEYENNE	44	6	34	4	Gore	13.6%	77.3%	9.1%
CLEAR CREEK	157	43	102	12	Gore	27.4%	65.0%	7.6%
CONEJOS	241	31	202	8	Gore	12.9%	83.8%	3.3%
COSTILLA	249	31	216	2	Gore	12.4%	86.7%	0.8%
CROWLEY	112	24	86	2	Gore	21.4%	76.8%	1.8%
CUSTER	91	23	62	6	Gore	25.3%	68.1%	6.6%
DELTA	702	164	463	75	Gore	23.4%	66.0%	10.7%
DENVER	17,445	3,919	12,992	534	Gore	22.5%	74.5%	3.1%
DOLORES	88	32	34	22	Gore	36.4%	38.6%	25.0%
DOUGLAS	1,889	461	1,342	86	Gore	24.4%	71.0%	4.6%
EAGLE	276	57	200	19	Gore	20.7%	72.5%	6.9%
ELBERT	134	32	99	3	Gore	23.9%	73.9%	2.2%
EL PASO	5,135	1,134	3,684	317	Gore	22.1%	71.7%	6.2%
FREMONT	484	110	341	33	Gore	22.7%	70.5%	6.8%
GARFIELD	478	127	328	23	Gore	26.6%	68.6%	4.8%
GILPIN	70	23	41	6	Gore	32.9%	58.6%	8.6%
GRAND	129	34	86	9	Gore	26.4%	66.7%	7.0%
GUNNISON	262	76	164	22	Gore	29.0%	62.6%	8.4%
HINSDALE	39	10	25	4	Gore	25.6%	64.1%	10.3%
HUERFANO	437	105	311	21	Gore	24.0%	71.2%	4.8%
JACKSON	36	15	18	3	Gore	41.7%	50.0%	8.3%
JEFFERSON	23,368	6,504	15,472	1,392	Gore	27.8%	66.2%	6.0%
KIOWA	40	13	25	2	Gore	32.5%	62.5%	5.0%
KIT CARSON	133	22	100	11	Gore	16.5%	75.2%	8.3%
LAKE	243	66	152	25	Gore	27.2%	62.6%	10.3%
LA PLATA	468	145	291	32	Gore	31.0%	62.2%	6.8%
LARIMER	2,956	726	2,082	148	Gore	24.6%	70.4%	5.0%
LAS ANIMAS	932	125	749	58	Gore	13.4%	80.4%	6.2%
LINCOLN	104	28	66	10	Gore	26.9%	63.5%	9.6%
LOGAN	364	72	265	27	Gore	19.8%	72.8%	7.4%
MESA	3,594	774	2,513	307	Gore	21.5%	69.9%	8.5%
MINERAL	32	9	19	4	Gore	28.1%	59.4%	12.5%
MOFFAT	190	59	117	14	Gore	31.1%	61.6%	7.4%
MONTEZUMA	422	104	272	46	Gore	24.6%	64.5%	10.9%
MONTROSE	433	106	288	39	Gore	24.5%	66.5%	9.0%
MORGAN	346	57	268	21	Gore	16.5%	77.5%	6.1%
OTERO	346	51	270	25	Gore	14.7%	78.0%	7.2%

COLORADO DEMOCRATIC PRIMARY

2000

County	Total Vote	Bradley	Gore	Other	Winner	Percentage of Total Vote		
						Bradley	Gore	Other
OURAY	55	17	37	1	Gore	30.9%	67.3%	1.8%
PARK	196	30	154	12	Gore	15.3%	78.6%	6.1%
PHILLIPS	102	16	77	9	Gore	15.7%	75.5%	8.8%
PITKIN	256	86	162	8	Gore	33.6%	63.3%	3.1%
PROWERS	165	27	121	17	Gore	16.4%	73.3%	10.3%
PUEBLO	2,908	414	2,348	146	Gore	14.2%	80.7%	5.0%
RIO BLANCO	119	28	75	16	Gore	23.5%	63.0%	13.4%
RIO GRANDE	322	55	237	30	Gore	17.1%	73.6%	9.3%
ROUTT	266	73	170	23	Gore	27.4%	63.9%	8.6%
SAGUACHE	146	20	110	16	Gore	13.7%	75.3%	11.0%
SAN JUAN	23	6	17	0	Gore	26.1%	73.9%	0.0%
SAN MIGUEL	106	35	63	8	Gore	33.0%	59.4%	7.5%
SEDGWICK	87	16	61	10	Gore	18.4%	70.1%	11.5%
SUMMIT	203	63	129	11	Gore	31.0%	63.5%	5.4%
TELLER	265	59	180	26	Gore	22.3%	67.9%	9.8%
WASHINGTON	80	12	57	11	Gore	15.0%	71.3%	13.8%
WELD	1,611	329	1,170	112	Gore	20.4%	72.6%	7.0%
YUMA	219	56	146	17	Gore	25.6%	66.7%	7.8%
TOTAL	88,678	20,647	63,349	4,682	Gore	23.3%	71.4%	5.3%

Note: Other vote was 3,864 Non-committed; 818 Lyndon H. LaRouche Jr.

COLORADO REPUBLICAN PRIMARY

2000

County	Total Vote	G.W. Bush	Keyes	McCain	Other	Winner	Percentage of Total Vote			
							G.W. Bush	Keyes	McCain	Other
ADAMS	5,617	3,885	451	1,199	82	G.W. Bush	69.2%	8.0%	21.3%	1.5%
ALAMOSA	612	378	37	174	23	G.W. Bush	61.8%	6.0%	28.4%	3.8%
ARAPAHOE	22,127	14,588	1,257	5,984	298	G.W. Bush	65.9%	5.7%	27.0%	1.3%
ARCHULETA	625	406	49	168	2	G.W. Bush	65.0%	7.8%	26.9%	0.3%
BACA	429	340	28	53	8	G.W. Bush	79.3%	6.5%	12.4%	1.9%
BENT	193	147	13	30	3	G.W. Bush	76.2%	6.7%	15.5%	1.6%
BOULDER	8,027	4,812	679	2,454	82	G.W. Bush	59.9%	8.5%	30.6%	1.0%
CHAFFEE	802	522	41	230	9	G.W. Bush	65.1%	5.1%	28.7%	1.1%
CHEYENNE	223	172	10	39	2	G.W. Bush	77.1%	4.5%	17.5%	0.9%
CLEAR CREEK	420	233	23	154	10	G.W. Bush	55.5%	5.5%	36.7%	2.4%
CONEJOS	249	195	1	37	16	G.W. Bush	78.3%	0.4%	14.9%	6.4%
COSTILLA	70	48	3	18	1	G.W. Bush	68.6%	4.3%	25.7%	1.4%
CROWLEY	212	150	16	42	4	G.W. Bush	70.8%	7.5%	19.8%	1.9%
CUSTER	410	287	31	81	11	G.W. Bush	70.0%	7.6%	19.8%	2.7%
DELTA	2,319	1,601	198	485	35	G.W. Bush	69.0%	8.5%	20.9%	1.5%

COLORADO REPUBLICAN PRIMARY

2000

County	Total Vote	G.W. Bush	Keyes	McCain	Other	Winner	Percentage of Total Vote			
							G.W. Bush	Keyes	McCain	Other
DENVER	13,174	7,742	704	4,515	213	G.W. Bush	58.8%	5.3%	34.3%	1.6%
DOLORES	125	82	12	31	0	G.W. Bush	65.6%	9.6%	24.8%	0.0%
DOUGLAS	9,851	6,756	563	2,440	92	G.W. Bush	68.6%	5.7%	24.8%	0.9%
EAGLE	621	369	23	219	10	G.W. Bush	59.4%	3.7%	35.3%	1.6%
ELBERT	931	672	79	161	19	G.W. Bush	72.2%	8.5%	17.3%	2.0%
EL PASO	25,017	17,175	2,532	5,040	270	G.W. Bush	68.7%	10.1%	20.1%	1.1%
FREMONT	1,609	1,150	103	336	20	G.W. Bush	71.5%	6.4%	20.9%	1.2%
GARFIELD	1,287	786	86	394	21	G.W. Bush	61.1%	6.7%	30.6%	1.6%
GILPIN	155	84	14	56	1	G.W. Bush	54.2%	9.0%	36.1%	0.6%
GRAND	574	330	34	202	8	G.W. Bush	57.5%	5.9%	35.2%	1.4%
GUNNISON	487	284	29	167	7	G.W. Bush	58.3%	6.0%	34.3%	1.4%
HINSDALE	129	76	3	49	1	G.W. Bush	58.9%	2.3%	38.0%	0.8%
HUERFANO	221	143	21	55	2	G.W. Bush	64.7%	9.5%	24.9%	0.9%
JACKSON	210	138	4	65	3	G.W. Bush	65.7%	1.9%	31.0%	1.4%
JEFFERSON	40,305	23,232	1,846	14,336	891	G.W. Bush	57.6%	4.6%	35.6%	2.2%
KIOWA	129	106	6	15	2	G.W. Bush	82.2%	4.7%	11.6%	1.6%
KIT CARSON	463	331	27	93	12	G.W. Bush	71.5%	5.8%	20.1%	2.6%
LAKE	160	108	8	41	3	G.W. Bush	67.5%	5.0%	25.6%	1.9%
LA PLATA	1,259	771	97	368	23	G.W. Bush	61.2%	7.7%	29.2%	1.8%
LARIMER	10,323	6,671	1,003	2,539	110	G.W. Bush	64.6%	9.7%	24.6%	1.1%
LAS ANIMAS	410	303	26	74	7	G.W. Bush	73.9%	6.3%	18.0%	1.7%
LINCOLN	400	295	19	80	6	G.W. Bush	73.8%	4.8%	20.0%	1.5%
LOGAN	963	725	39	187	12	G.W. Bush	75.3%	4.0%	19.4%	1.2%
MESA	9,422	6,612	479	2,067	264	G.W. Bush	70.2%	5.1%	21.9%	2.8%
MINERAL	22	13	1	8	0	G.W. Bush	59.1%	4.5%	36.4%	0.0%
MOFFAT	688	428	43	201	16	G.W. Bush	62.2%	6.3%	29.2%	2.3%
MONTEZUMA	1,036	689	73	260	14	G.W. Bush	66.5%	7.0%	25.1%	1.4%
MONTROSE	1,595	1,102	119	338	36	G.W. Bush	69.1%	7.5%	21.2%	2.3%
MORGAN	978	788	29	151	10	G.W. Bush	80.6%	3.0%	15.4%	1.0%
OTERO	662	506	33	112	11	G.W. Bush	76.4%	5.0%	16.9%	1.7%
OURAY	360	227	10	119	4	G.W. Bush	63.1%	2.8%	33.1%	1.1%
PARK	686	462	44	170	10	G.W. Bush	67.3%	6.4%	24.8%	1.5%
PHILLIPS	331	256	12	54	9	G.W. Bush	77.3%	3.6%	16.3%	2.7%
PITKIN	370	191	13	161	5	G.W. Bush	51.6%	3.5%	43.5%	1.4%
PROWERS	405	307	25	71	2	G.W. Bush	75.8%	6.2%	17.5%	0.5%
PUEBLO	2,820	2,195	161	432	32	G.W. Bush	77.8%	5.7%	15.3%	1.1%
RIO BLANCO	529	315	24	178	12	G.W. Bush	59.5%	4.5%	33.6%	2.3%
RIO GRANDE	639	435	51	141	12	G.W. Bush	68.1%	8.0%	22.1%	1.9%
ROUTT	614	330	27	245	12	G.W. Bush	53.7%	4.4%	39.9%	2.0%
SAGUACHE	183	116	12	46	9	G.W. Bush	63.4%	6.6%	25.1%	4.9%
SAN JUAN	26	14	1	10	1	G.W. Bush	53.8%	3.8%	38.5%	3.8%
SAN MIGUEL	152	98	5	45	4	G.W. Bush	64.5%	3.3%	29.6%	2.6%
SEDGWICK	197	148	4	42	3	G.W. Bush	75.1%	2.0%	21.3%	1.5%
SUMMIT	536	307	19	207	3	G.W. Bush	57.3%	3.5%	38.6%	0.6%
TELLER	1,260	852	136	259	13	G.W. Bush	67.6%	10.8%	20.6%	1.0%
WASHINGTON	491	388	18	78	7	G.W. Bush	79.0%	3.7%	15.9%	1.4%
WELD	4,961	3,586	392	915	68	G.W. Bush	72.3%	7.9%	18.4%	1.4%
YUMA	537	419	20	87	11	G.W. Bush	78.0%	3.7%	16.2%	2.0%
TOTAL	180,638	116,877	11,866	49,008	2,887	G.W. Bush	64.7%	6.6%	27.1%	1.6%

Note: Other vote was 1,197 Steve Forbes; 1,187 Gary Bauer; 503 Orrin G. Hatch.

CONNECTICUT

For years, Connecticut was the home base of the Bush family. George W. Bush was born in New Haven and graduated from Yale University. His father, George Bush, was raised in Greenwich and was educated at Yale. His father, Prescott Bush, won election from Connecticut to the U.S. Senate in 1952 and served two terms.

George Bush won the state's Republican presidential primary three times and carried Connecticut in the 1988 presidential election. George W., though, never carried the state in two successful runs for the White House. He came closest in the 2000 Republican primary, when he lost to John McCain by barely 4,000 votes out of nearly 180,000 cast.

Bush had two big assets in his battle with McCain: the support of Connecticut's Republican governor, John Rowland, and primary rules that limited participation to registered Republicans. But New England, with its moderate brand of Republicanism, was McCain's natural base. He carried five of eight

counties, including all four that fronted the Atlantic Ocean, and won places such as Greenwich and New Haven that are near and dear to the Bush family.

The Bush-McCain contest was the most hotly contested Republican primary in Connecticut since 1980, when George Bush, Ronald Reagan, and John Anderson were all able to find toeholds.

Bush fashioned his 39 percent to 34 percent victory over Reagan in Connecticut's traditional Republican strongholds, the upper-crust suburbs near New York City and the Yankee towns and villages on the north and east sides of the state.

Reagan nearly offset all that by combining the votes of conservative activists and blue-collar workers in industrial cities such as Bridgeport, Norwalk, Waterbury, and New Britain. But to Bush's advantage, more Republican primary votes were cast in suburban Greenwich alone than in any of the state's larger urban centers. Meanwhile, Anderson took 22 percent of the

Recent Connecticut Primary Results

Connecticut held its first presidential primary in 1980.

	DEMOCRATS				REPUBLICANS		
Year	Turnout	Candidates	%	Turnout	Candidates	%
2004 (March 2)	130,023	JOHN KERRY John Edwards Joe Lieberman	58 24 5	—	No Primary	
2000 (March 7)	177,301	AL GORE Bill Bradley	55 42	178,985	JOHN McCAIN George W. Bush	49 46
1996 (March 5)	—	No Primary		130,418	BOB DOLE Steve Forbes Pat Buchanan Lamar Alexander	54 20 15 5
1992 (March 24)	173,119	JERRY BROWN Bill Clinton Paul Tsongas	37 36 20	99,473	GEORGE BUSH* Pat Buchanan Uncommitted	67 22 9
1988 (March 29)	241,395	MICHAEL DUKAKIS Jesse Jackson Al Gore	58 28 8	104,171	GEORGE BUSH Bob Dole	71 20
1984 (March 27)	220,842	GARY HART Walter Mondale Jesse Jackson	53 29 12	—	No Primary	
1980 (March 25)	210,275	EDWARD KENNEDY Jimmy Carter*	47 41	182,284	GEORGE BUSH Ronald Reagan John Anderson	39 34 22

Note: All candidates are listed that drew at least 5 percent of their party's primary vote. The names of winning candidates are capitalized. An asterisk (*) indicates an incumbent president.

primary vote by carrying communities with large academic institutions, such as New Haven (Yale) and Mansfield (the University of Connecticut).

Bush had a much easier time in 1988 and 1992. Dole withdrew from the race on the day of the Connecticut voting in late March 1988, while Pat Robertson could muster just 3 percent of the vote, his weakest showing of the primary season.

Pat Buchanan did better four years later by tapping into Connecticut's sudden economic discomfort. He took more than 35 percent of the vote in Waterbury, a figure that he almost matched in 1996. But in the latter year, Buchanan finished third in the statewide primary vote behind both Dole and Steve Forbes, who ran best in upscale suburbs such as Greenwich and New Canaan.

Connecticut's most competitive presidential primary of the 1990s took place on the Democratic side, where Jerry Brown slowed Bill Clinton's bandwagon in 1992 just as it had been picking up steam with a sweep of the Super Tuesday South and St. Patrick's Day voting in Illinois and Michigan. Brown won in Connecticut by fewer than 3,000 votes out of 170,000 cast.

But the result, at least temporarily, reopened doubts about the strength of Clinton's candidacy.

Several factors worked to Brown's benefit in Connecticut: a one-on-one shot against Clinton (Paul Tsongas had withdrawn from the race less than a week earlier); a geographically compact electorate, much of which Brown could reach with a media blitz on Hartford television; and low turnout, particularly in the cities where Clinton had hoped to tap the sizable minority vote.

The Democratic base in Connecticut is more urban than the Republican. Still, no Connecticut city dominates the political landscape. The largest are Bridgeport, Hartford, and New Haven, and none of the three holds more than 5 percent of the state population.

Hartford, the state capital, is roughly 40 percent black. Jesse Jackson carried the city in 1984 and 1988, adding victories in Bridgeport and New Haven (both more than 25 percent black) in the latter campaign.

But Jackson was unable to make headway elsewhere in the state, where Gary Hart marched to victory in 1984 and Michael

Dukakis did the same four years later. Dukakis benefited from Al Gore's decision to forgo the all-out effort in Connecticut that might have produced a more competitive three-way contest. (Gore took just 8 percent of the Democratic primary vote in 1988.)

Gore was much more successful in 2000. As the choice of the Democratic Party establishment, he defeated Bill Bradley in Connecticut by more than a dozen percentage points. Bradley carried many of the well-heeled suburbs near New York, including Greenwich and Darien, but little else. The former profes-sional basketball star was even beaten decisively in Bristol, the longtime home of ESPN (the nationwide cable sports network).

Gore's 2000 Democratic running-mate, Joe Lieberman, probably would have won his home state in the party's 2004 primary if he had still been a candidate at the time it voted. As it was, his campaign had folded weeks earlier. But Lieberman's name remained on the primary ballot, and he polled 5 percent statewide, ranging from 3 percent or less in many of the affluent suburbs along the New York border to 15 percent or more in cities such as Bridgeport and Hartford.

CONNECTICUT DEMOCRATIC PRIMARY

2000

County	Total Vote	Bradley	Gore	Uncommitted	Winner	Percentage of Total Vote		
						Bradley	Gore	Uncommitted
FAIRFIELD	39,564	17,134	21,427	1,003	Gore	43.3%	54.2%	2.5%
HARTFORD	57,709	21,433	34,266	2,010	Gore	37.1%	59.4%	3.5%
LITCHFIELD	7,339	3,677	3,448	214	Bradley	50.1%	47.0%	2.9%
MIDDLESEX	8,800	3,873	4,702	225	Gore	44.0%	53.4%	2.6%
NEW HAVEN	42,006	17,608	23,150	1,248	Gore	41.9%	55.1%	3.0%
NEW LONDON	10,740	4,853	5,540	347	Gore	45.2%	51.6%	3.2%
TOLLAND	6,348	2,939	3,208	201	Gore	46.3%	50.5%	3.2%
WINDHAM	4,795	2,072	2,571	152	Gore	43.2%	53.6%	3.2%
TOTAL	177,301	73,589	98,312	5,400	Gore	41.5%	55.4%	3.0%

City/Town	Total Vote	Bradley	Gore	Uncommitted	Winner	Percentage of Total Vote		
						Bradley	Gore	Uncommitted
ANSONIA	814	308	485	21	Gore	37.8%	59.6%	2.6%
BLOOMFIELD	1,970	572	1,369	29	Gore	29.0%	69.5%	1.5%
BRANFORD	1,590	826	733	31	Bradley	51.9%	46.1%	1.9%
BRIDGEPORT	6,596	1,820	4,445	331	Gore	27.6%	67.4%	5.0%
BRISTOL	3,126	1,100	1,934	92	Gore	35.2%	61.9%	2.9%
CHESHIRE	1,128	579	534	15	Bradley	51.3%	47.3%	1.3%
DANBURY	2,589	1,040	1,411	138	Gore	40.2%	54.5%	5.3%
DARIEN	736	427	303	6	Bradley	58.0%	41.2%	0.8%
EAST HARTFORD	3,330	1,090	2,119	121	Gore	32.7%	63.6%	3.6%
EAST HAVEN	958	321	613	24	Gore	33.5%	64.0%	2.5%
ENFIELD	2,414	883	1,435	96	Gore	36.6%	59.4%	4.0%
FAIRFIELD	2,613	1,389	1,175	49	Bradley	53.2%	45.0%	1.9%
FARMINGTON	1,182	540	606	36	Gore	45.7%	51.3%	3.0%
GLASTONBURY	2,124	1,107	966	51	Bradley	52.1%	45.5%	2.4%
GREENWICH	2,466	1,296	1,144	26	Bradley	52.6%	46.4%	1.1%
GROTON	1,039	466	556	17	Gore	44.9%	53.5%	1.6%
GUILFORD	1,221	638	566	17	Bradley	52.3%	46.4%	1.4%
HAMDEN	3,918	1,584	2,273	61	Gore	40.4%	58.0%	1.6%
HARTFORD	8,233	1,560	6,230	443	Gore	18.9%	75.7%	5.4%
MANCHESTER	2,815	1,213	1,512	90	Gore	43.1%	53.7%	3.2%
MANSFIELD	1,180	574	580	26	Gore	48.6%	49.2%	2.2%
MERIDEN	1,914	682	1,156	76	Gore	35.6%	60.4%	4.0%
MIDDLETOWN	3,112	1,217	1,829	66	Gore	39.1%	58.8%	2.1%
MILFORD	1,955	865	1,052	38	Gore	44.2%	53.8%	1.9%
NAUGATUCK	1,127	537	553	37	Gore	47.6%	49.1%	3.3%
NEW BRITAIN	4,790	1,412	3,232	146	Gore	29.5%	67.5%	3.0%
NEW CANAAN	710	383	318	9	Bradley	53.9%	44.8%	1.3%
NEW HAVEN	7,790	2,556	4,898	336	Gore	32.8%	62.9%	4.3%
NEW LONDON	894	378	497	19	Gore	42.3%	55.6%	2.1%
NEW MILFORD	821	415	385	21	Bradley	50.5%	46.9%	2.6%

CONNECTICUT DEMOCRATIC PRIMARY

2000

City/Town	Total Vote	Bradley	Gore	Uncommitted	Winner	Percentage of Total Vote		
						Bradley	Gore	Uncommitted
NEWINGTON	3,832	1,492	2,134	206	Gore	38.9%	55.7%	5.4%
NEWTOWN	1,013	518	473	22	Bradley	51.1%	46.7%	2.2%
NORTH HAVEN	819	364	432	23	Gore	44.4%	52.7%	2.8%
NORWALK	3,007	1,232	1,743	32	Gore	41.0%	58.0%	1.1%
NORWICH	1,788	724	1,016	48	Gore	40.5%	56.8%	2.7%
RIDGEFIELD	1,064	594	454	16	Bradley	55.8%	42.7%	1.5%
SHELTON	1,207	568	595	44	Gore	47.1%	49.3%	3.6%
SIMSBURY	1,366	782	559	25	Bradley	57.2%	40.9%	1.8%
SOUTH WINDSOR	1,648	713	892	43	Gore	43.3%	54.1%	2.6%
SOUTHINGTON	1,728	685	1,006	37	Gore	39.6%	58.2%	2.1%
STAMFORD	7,996	3,020	4,807	169	Gore	37.8%	60.1%	2.1%
STRATFORD	1,992	876	1,069	47	Gore	44.0%	53.7%	2.4%
TORRINGTON	1,298	609	654	35	Gore	46.9%	50.4%	2.7%
TRUMBULL	1,136	603	520	13	Bradley	53.1%	45.8%	1.1%
VERNON	1,123	480	614	29	Gore	42.7%	54.7%	2.6%
WALLINGFORD	1,572	645	897	30	Gore	41.0%	57.1%	1.9%
WATERBURY	4,336	2,034	2,128	174	Gore	46.9%	49.1%	4.0%
WATERTOWN	671	346	304	21	Bradley	51.6%	45.3%	3.1%
WEST HARTFORD	5,950	2,886	2,968	96	Gore	48.5%	49.9%	1.6%
WEST HAVEN	6,705	2,768	3,692	245	Gore	41.3%	55.1%	3.7%
WESTPORT	2,081	1,037	1,030	14	Bradley	49.8%	49.5%	0.7%
WETHERSFIELD	2,486	1,028	1,377	81	Gore	41.4%	55.4%	3.3%
WINDHAM	1,085	461	621	3	Gore	42.5%	57.2%	0.3%
WINDSOR	2,617	874	1,605	138	Gore	33.4%	61.3%	5.3%

Note: The cities and towns included are basically those with a population of at least 20,000 in the 2000 Census plus a few other selected communities.

CONNECTICUT REPUBLICAN PRIMARY

2000

County	Total Vote	G.W. Bush	McCain	Other	Winner	Percentage of Total Vote		
						G.W. Bush	McCain	Other
FAIRFIELD	56,377	24,965	28,946	2,466	McCain	44.3%	51.3%	4.4%
HARTFORD	42,300	21,512	18,736	2,052	G.W. Bush	50.9%	44.3%	4.9%
LITCHFIELD	13,322	6,394	6,144	784	G.W. Bush	48.0%	46.1%	5.9%
MIDDLESEX	9,447	4,103	4,883	461	McCain	43.4%	51.7%	4.9%
NEW HAVEN	33,013	15,550	15,617	1,846	McCain	47.1%	47.3%	5.6%
NEW LONDON	12,624	4,770	7,241	613	McCain	37.8%	57.4%	4.9%
TOLLAND	6,928	3,340	3,203	385	G.W. Bush	48.2%	46.2%	5.6%
WINDHAM	4,974	2,247	2,406	321	McCain	45.2%	48.4%	6.5%
TOTAL	178,985	82,881	87,176	8,928	McCain	46.3%	48.7%	5.0%

Note: Other vote was 5,913 Alan Keyes; 1,242 Steve Forbes; 1,222 Uncommitted; 373 Gary Bauer; 178 Orrin G. Hatch.

City/Town	Total Vote	G.W. Bush	McCain	Other	Winner	Percentage of Total Vote		
						G.W. Bush	McCain	Other
ANSONIA	536	269	228	39	G.W. Bush	50.2%	42.5%	7.3%
BLOOMFIELD	794	373	372	49	G.W. Bush	47.0%	46.9%	6.2%
BRANFORD	1,130	469	605	56	McCain	41.5%	53.5%	5.0%
BRIDGEPORT	1,350	632	645	73	McCain	46.8%	47.8%	5.4%
BRISTOL	2,081	1,068	833	180	G.W. Bush	51.3%	40.0%	8.6%
CHESHIRE	2,011	948	969	94	McCain	47.1%	48.2%	4.7%
DANBURY	1,934	902	911	121	McCain	46.6%	47.1%	6.3%
DARIEN	3,044	1,355	1,606	83	McCain	44.5%	52.8%	2.7%
EAST HARTFORD	1,278	682	527	69	G.W. Bush	53.4%	41.2%	5.4%
EAST HAVEN	639	306	302	31	G.W. Bush	47.9%	47.3%	4.9%
ENFIELD	1,891	1,026	758	107	G.W. Bush	54.3%	40.1%	5.7%
FAIRFIELD	4,790	1,914	2,708	168	McCain	40.0%	56.5%	3.5%
FARMINGTON	1,874	955	840	79	G.W. Bush	51.0%	44.8%	4.2%
GLASTONBURY	3,073	1,465	1,515	93	McCain	47.7%	49.3%	3.0%
GREENWICH	6,926	3,205	3,438	283	McCain	46.3%	49.6%	4.1%
GROTON	1,611	694	853	64	McCain	43.1%	52.9%	4.0%
GUILFORD	1,622	649	917	56	McCain	40.0%	56.5%	3.5%
HAMDEN	2,441	1,105	1,211	125	McCain	45.3%	49.6%	5.1%
HARTFORD	751	394	268	89	G.W. Bush	52.5%	35.7%	11.9%
MANCHESTER	2,736	1,376	1,207	153	G.W. Bush	50.3%	44.1%	5.6%
MANSFIELD	583	243	309	31	McCain	41.7%	53.0%	5.3%
MERIDEN	1,496	757	633	106	G.W. Bush	50.6%	42.3%	7.1%
MIDDLETOWN	1,412	688	633	91	G.W. Bush	48.7%	44.8%	6.4%
MILFORD	2,804	1,177	1,459	168	McCain	42.0%	52.0%	6.0%
NAUGATUCK	1,025	519	440	66	G.W. Bush	50.6%	42.9%	6.4%
NEW BRITAIN	1,641	859	666	116	G.W. Bush	52.3%	40.6%	7.1%
NEW CANAAN	2,867	1,343	1,434	90	McCain	46.8%	50.0%	3.1%
NEW HAVEN	955	415	459	81	McCain	43.5%	48.1%	8.5%
NEW LONDON	496	173	297	26	McCain	34.9%	59.9%	5.2%
NEW MILFORD	1,693	762	821	110	McCain	45.0%	48.5%	6.5%

CONNECTICUT REPUBLICAN PRIMARY

2000

City/Town	Total Vote	G.W. Bush	McCain	Other	Winner	Percentage of Total Vote		
						G.W. Bush	McCain	Other
NEWINGTON	1,524	776	668	80	G.W. Bush	50.9%	43.8%	5.2%
NEWTOWN	1,887	817	981	89	McCain	43.3%	52.0%	4.7%
NORTH HAVEN	1,682	746	854	82	McCain	44.4%	50.8%	4.9%
NORWALK	3,728	1,666	1,781	281	McCain	44.7%	47.8%	7.5%
NORWICH	960	327	562	71	McCain	34.1%	58.5%	7.4%
RIDGEFIELD	2,877	1,167	1,610	100	McCain	40.6%	56.0%	3.5%
SHELTON	2,387	1,117	1,141	129	McCain	46.8%	47.8%	5.4%
SIMSBURY	2,761	1,365	1,302	94	G.W. Bush	49.4%	47.2%	3.4%
SOUTH WINDSOR	1,600	800	730	70	G.W. Bush	50.0%	45.6%	4.4%
SOUTHINGTON	2,032	1,051	893	88	G.W. Bush	51.7%	43.9%	4.3%
STAMFORD	6,259	2,877	3,079	303	McCain	46.0%	49.2%	4.8%
STRATFORD	2,168	967	1,099	102	McCain	44.6%	50.7%	4.7%
TORRINGTON	1,559	794	680	85	G.W. Bush	50.9%	43.6%	5.5%
TRUMBULL	2,374	1,086	1,192	96	McCain	45.7%	50.2%	4.0%
VERNON	1,322	661	568	93	G.W. Bush	50.0%	43.0%	7.0%
WALLINGFORD	1,695	835	769	91	G.W. Bush	49.3%	45.4%	5.4%
WATERBURY	2,500	1,319	937	244	G.W. Bush	52.8%	37.5%	9.8%
WATERTOWN	1,270	699	483	88	G.W. Bush	55.0%	38.0%	6.9%
WEST HARTFORD	4,329	2,187	1,982	160	G.W. Bush	50.5%	45.8%	3.7%
WEST HAVEN	1,174	544	532	98	G.W. Bush	46.3%	45.3%	8.3%
WESTPORT	2,720	1,029	1,584	107	McCain	37.8%	58.2%	3.9%
WETHERSFIELD	1,934	1,000	855	79	G.W. Bush	51.7%	44.2%	4.1%
WINDHAM	582	273	271	38	G.W. Bush	46.9%	46.6%	6.5%
WINDSOR	1,369	707	600	62	G.W. Bush	51.6%	43.8%	4.5%

Note: The cities and towns included are basically those with a population of at least 20,000 in the 2000 Census plus a few other selected communities.

CONNECTICUT DEMOCRATIC PRIMARY

2004

County	Total Vote	Edwards	Kerry	Lieberman	Other	Winner	Percentage of Total Vote			
							Edwards	Kerry	Lieberman	Other
FAIRFIELD	30,718	6,135	18,961	1,666	3,956	Kerry	20.0%	61.7%	5.4%	12.9%
HARTFORD	38,634	9,185	22,185	2,205	5,059	Kerry	23.8%	57.4%	5.7%	13.1%
LITCHFIELD	5,915	1,576	3,568	131	640	Kerry	26.6%	60.3%	2.2%	10.8%
MIDDLESEX	6,490	1,782	3,771	113	824	Kerry	27.5%	58.1%	1.7%	12.7%
NEW HAVEN	31,623	7,882	17,358	2,211	4,172	Kerry	24.9%	54.9%	7.0%	13.2%
NEW LONDON	7,861	1,943	4,895	199	824	Kerry	24.7%	62.3%	2.5%	10.5%
TOLLAND	5,152	1,452	2,886	92	722	Kerry	28.2%	56.0%	1.8%	14.0%
WINDHAM	3,630	889	2,236	88	417	Kerry	24.5%	61.6%	2.4%	11.5%
TOTAL	130,023	30,844	75,860	6,705	16,614	Kerry	23.7%	58.3%	5.2%	12.8%

Note: Other vote was 5,166 Howard Dean; 4,133 Dennis J. Kucinich; 3,312 Al Sharpton; 1,546 Wesley Clark; 1,467 Lyndon H. LaRouche Jr.; 990 Uncommitted.

City/Town	Total Vote	Edwards	Kerry	Lieberman	Other	Winner	Percentage of Total Vote			
							Edwards	Kerry	Lieberman	Other
ANSONIA	410	107	256	11	36	Kerry	26.1%	62.4%	2.7%	8.8%
BLOOMFIELD	2,334	390	1,543	74	327	Kerry	16.7%	66.1%	3.2%	14.0%
BRANFORD	1,185	285	713	28	159	Kerry	24.1%	60.2%	2.4%	13.4%
BRIDGEPORT	4,417	541	1,833	872	1,171	Kerry	12.2%	41.5%	19.7%	26.5%
BRISTOL	1,761	478	1,059	65	159	Kerry	27.1%	60.1%	3.7%	9.0%
CHESHIRE	841	199	540	17	85	Kerry	23.7%	64.2%	2.0%	10.1%
DANBURY	2,241	586	1,381	79	195	Kerry	26.1%	61.6%	3.5%	8.7%
DARIEN	565	107	393	13	52	Kerry	18.9%	69.6%	2.3%	9.2%
EAST HARTFORD	1,633	434	962	69	168	Kerry	26.6%	58.9%	4.2%	10.3%
EAST HAVEN	442	121	250	26	45	Kerry	27.4%	56.6%	5.9%	10.2%
ENFIELD	1,393	384	852	33	124	Kerry	27.6%	61.2%	2.4%	8.9%
FAIRFIELD	1,820	397	1,195	38	190	Kerry	21.8%	65.7%	2.1%	10.4%
FARMINGTON	941	244	569	18	110	Kerry	25.9%	60.5%	1.9%	11.7%
GLASTONBURY	1,591	396	968	41	186	Kerry	24.9%	60.8%	2.6%	11.7%
GREENWICH	1,875	362	1,281	54	178	Kerry	19.3%	68.3%	2.9%	9.5%
GROTON	910	186	603	21	100	Kerry	20.4%	66.3%	2.3%	11.0%
GUILFORD	1,149	218	763	16	152	Kerry	19.0%	66.4%	1.4%	13.2%
HAMDEN	3,583	770	2,137	138	538	Kerry	21.5%	59.6%	3.9%	15.0%
HARTFORD	4,900	659	2,175	791	1,275	Kerry	13.4%	44.4%	16.1%	26.0%
MANCHESTER	1,844	483	1,100	53	208	Kerry	26.2%	59.7%	2.9%	11.3%
MANSFIELD	1,087	235	635	12	205	Kerry	21.6%	58.4%	1.1%	18.9%
MERIDEN	1,409	347	855	51	156	Kerry	24.6%	60.7%	3.6%	11.1%
MIDDLETOWN	1,821	471	1,012	38	300	Kerry	25.9%	55.6%	2.1%	16.5%
MILFORD	1,203	314	740	29	120	Kerry	26.1%	61.5%	2.4%	10.0%
NAUGATUCK	691	234	399	17	41	Kerry	33.9%	57.7%	2.5%	5.9%
NEW BRITAIN	4,751	1,116	2,266	625	744	Kerry	23.5%	47.7%	13.2%	15.7%
NEW CANAAN	675	162	455	7	51	Kerry	24.0%	67.4%	1.0%	7.6%
NEW HAVEN	6,797	1,266	3,496	562	1,473	Kerry	18.6%	51.4%	8.3%	21.7%
NEW LONDON	660	140	412	12	96	Kerry	21.2%	62.4%	1.8%	14.5%
NEW MILFORD	761	200	469	21	71	Kerry	26.3%	61.6%	2.8%	9.3%

CONNECTICUT DEMOCRATIC PRIMARY

2004

City/Town	Total Vote	Edwards	Kerry	Lieberman	Other	Winner	Percentage of Total Vote			
							Edwards	Kerry	Lieberman	Other
NEWINGTON	1,522	440	914	44	124	Kerry	28.9%	60.1%	2.9%	8.1%
NEWTOWN	953	223	634	12	84	Kerry	23.4%	66.5%	1.3%	8.8%
NORTH HAVEN	636	134	405	8	89	Kerry	21.1%	63.7%	1.3%	14.0%
NORWALK	2,343	452	1,493	59	339	Kerry	19.3%	63.7%	2.5%	14.5%
NORWICH	1,178	308	706	49	115	Kerry	26.1%	59.9%	4.2%	9.8%
RIDGEFIELD	919	179	628	23	89	Kerry	19.5%	68.3%	2.5%	9.7%
SHELTON	977	242	614	40	81	Kerry	24.8%	62.8%	4.1%	8.3%
SIMSBURY	936	232	583	16	105	Kerry	24.8%	62.3%	1.7%	11.2%
SOUTH WINDSOR	1,048	324	609	31	84	Kerry	30.9%	58.1%	3.0%	8.0%
SOUTHINGTON	1,235	348	775	25	87	Kerry	28.2%	62.8%	2.0%	7.0%
STAMFORD	6,216	1,356	3,814	317	729	Kerry	21.8%	61.4%	5.1%	11.7%
STRATFORD	975	211	605	23	136	Kerry	21.6%	62.1%	2.4%	13.9%
TORRINGTON	691	232	399	22	38	Kerry	33.6%	57.7%	3.2%	5.5%
TRUMBULL	863	202	556	20	85	Kerry	23.4%	64.4%	2.3%	9.8%
VERNON	798	238	451	11	98	Kerry	29.8%	56.5%	1.4%	12.3%
WALLINGFORD	1,098	263	702	35	98	Kerry	24.0%	63.9%	3.2%	8.9%
WATERBURY	1,751	554	910	63	224	Kerry	31.6%	52.0%	3.6%	12.8%
WATERTOWN	454	146	246	11	51	Kerry	32.2%	54.2%	2.4%	11.2%
WEST HARTFORD	4,363	973	2,797	105	488	Kerry	22.3%	64.1%	2.4%	11.2%
WEST HAVEN	5,670	1,931	2,168	1,065	506	Kerry	34.1%	38.2%	18.8%	8.9%
WESTPORT	2,105	347	1,536	30	192	Kerry	16.5%	73.0%	1.4%	9.1%
WETHERSFIELD	1,403	353	896	36	118	Kerry	25.2%	63.9%	2.6%	8.4%
WINDHAM	759	185	430	30	114	Kerry	24.4%	56.7%	4.0%	15.0%
WINDSOR	1,416	330	830	45	211	Kerry	23.3%	58.6%	3.2%	14.9%

Note: The cities and towns included are basically those with a population of at least 20,000 in the 2000 Census plus a few other selected communities.

DELAWARE

Delaware never held a presidential primary before 1996. But when it did, it aimed high, setting a date just four days after New Hampshire's first-in-the-nation primary.

That created conflict for Delaware on two fronts–with the national Democratic Party, which at the time forbid states other than Iowa and New Hampshire from voting before March–and with New Hampshire, which had a state statute requiring a seven-day hiatus between its primary and any that follow.

New Hampshire's displeasure with Delaware's chutzpah had its effect. In deference to the Granite State and its political importance, most of the Republican candidates scaled back their Delaware campaigning. One who did not was Steve Forbes, who campaigned around the state by bus and ran his usual media blitz.

Forbes, though, did not have a clear track to victory. His main rivals were on the Delaware ballot. And Bob Dole had the backing of several big-name Delaware Republicans, including Sen. William V. Roth Jr., who endorsed Dole three days before the primary. But Dole did not come to the state to receive the endorsement. He accepted it by phone while traveling on his campaign plane.

Meanwhile, Forbes's assiduous personal attention to the state probably provided him with the margin of victory, as he defeated Dole by barely 5 percentage points.

Four years later, Delaware Republicans held their primary one week after New Hampshire. George W. Bush participated in the event and won, scoring a low-profile, but badly needed victory just a week after he had been routed by John McCain in New Hampshire. McCain did not campaign in Delaware, however, enabling Bush to register his first victory of the 2000 primary season by a comfortable margin.

Delaware Democrats have yet to hold a presidential primary of political consequence. President Bill Clinton easily won the party's initial contest in 1996 with 90 percent of the vote after initial uncertainty about whether he would even be on the ballot. At first, Clinton opted not to run and there was talk of fielding the state's venerable former governor, Elbert N. Carvel (1949–1953, 1961–1965), as a favorite son.

But Delaware officials took matters into their own hands by putting Clinton on the ballot, along with those major GOP presidential contenders who also did not file for fear of upsetting voters in New Hampshire. After talk among national Democratic officials of penalizing Delaware for its forwardness, they backed away from the threat to deprive the state's Democrats of some of their delegates.

Delaware's Democratic primary in 2000 was a nonbinding affair held four days after New Hampshire. With the wind at his back after victories in Iowa and New Hampshire, Al Gore

Recent Delaware Primary Results

Delaware held its first presidential primary in 1996. The Republican primary in 2000 was conducted by the state party.

| Year | DEMOCRATS | | | REPUBLICANS | | |
	Turnout	Candidates	%	Turnout	Candidates	%
2004 (Feb. 3)	33,291	JOHN KERRY	50	—	No Primary	
		Joe Lieberman	11			
		John Edwards	11			
		Howard Dean	10			
		Wesley Clark	10			
		Al Sharpton	6			
2000 (Feb. 5 Dems.; Feb. 8 Reps.)	11,141	AL GORE	57	30,060	GEORGE W. BUSH	51
		Bill Bradley	40		John McCain	25
					Steve Forbes	20
1996 (Feb. 24)	10,740	BILL CLINTON*	90	32,773	STEVE FORBES	33
		Lyndon LaRouche	10		Bob Dole	27
					Pat Buchanan	19
					Lamar Alexander	13
					Alan Keyes	5

Note: All candidates are listed that drew at least 5 percent of their party's primary vote. The names of winning candidates are capitalized. An asterisk (*) indicates an incumbent president.

won the primary handily. The state's early February primary in 2004 did elect delegates. But the result was similar to four years earlier, as front-runner John Kerry rolled up a majority of the vote in Delaware against a still-crowded Democratic field. Joe Lieberman sought to jump-start his faltering candidacy with a concentrated effort in Delaware, but finished a very distant second with 11 percent of the vote. Meanwhile, Al Sharpton found a toehold of sorts in the majority-black city of Wilmington, where he ran second to Kerry with 16 percent.

In terms of political geography, Delaware is divided into two parts by the Chesapeake and Delaware Canal, which slices across the northern quarter of the state. The portion north of the canal comprises the heart of populous New Castle County, with Wilmington and its suburbs. It is part of the busy Northeast Corridor. Below the canal, the state is rural and lightly settled; its values, attitude, and voting behavior are similar to those of the border South.

Bush ran best in the southern portion of Delaware in the 2000 Republican primary, a precursor of his critical victory in South Carolina less than two weeks later. But elections in Delaware tend to be won or lost in New Castle County, which has cast a clear majority of the vote in every presidential primary that Delaware has held.

DELAWARE DEMOCRATIC PRIMARY

2000

County	Total Vote	Bradley	Gore	LaRouche	Winner	Percentage of Total Vote		
						Bradley	Gore	LaRouche
KENT	1,486	559	905	22	Gore	37.6%	60.9%	1.5%
NEW CASTLE	7,461	3,009	4,208	244	Gore	40.3%	56.4%	3.3%
SUSSEX	2,194	908	1,264	22	Gore	41.4%	57.6%	1.0%
TOTAL	11,141	4,476	6,377	288	Gore	40.2%	57.2%	2.6%

DELAWARE REPUBLICAN PRIMARY

2000

County	Total Vote	G.W. Bush	Forbes	McCain	Other	Winner	Percentage of Total Vote			
							G.W. Bush	Forbes	McCain	Other
KENT	4,666	2,568	965	955	178	G.W. Bush	55.0%	20.7%	20.5%	3.8%
NEW CASTLE	17,935	8,876	3,245	4,956	858	G.W. Bush	49.5%	18.1%	27.6%	4.8%
SUSSEX	7,459	3,806	1,673	1,727	253	G.W. Bush	51.0%	22.4%	23.2%	3.4%
TOTAL	30,060	15,250	5,883	7,638	1,289	G.W. Bush	50.7%	19.6%	25.4%	4.3%

Note: Other vote was 1,148 Alan Keyes; 120 Gary Bauer; 21 Orrin G. Hatch.

DELAWARE DEMOCRATIC PRIMARY

2004

County	Total Vote	Clark	Dean	Edwards	Kerry	Lieberman	Sharpton	Other	Winner	Percentage of Total Vote						
										Clark	Dean	Edwards	Kerry	Lieberman	Sharpton	Other
KENT	3,717	357	312	474	1,802	538	165	69	Kerry	9.6%	8.4%	12.8%	48.5%	14.5%	4.4%	1.9%
NEW CASTLE	23,160	2,378	2,577	2,224	11,483	2,450	1,625	423	Kerry	10.3%	11.1%	9.6%	49.6%	10.6%	7.0%	1.8%
SUSSEX	6,414	430	573	976	3,502	718	98	117	Kerry	6.7%	8.9%	15.2%	54.6%	11.2%	1.5%	1.8%
TOTAL	33,291	3,165	3,462	3,674	16,787	3,706	1,888	609	Kerry	9.5%	10.4%	11.0%	50.4%	11.1%	5.7%	1.8%

Note: Other vote was 344 Dennis J. Kucinich; 187 Richard A. Gephardt; 78 Lyndon H. LaRouche Jr.

FLORIDA

In recent years, vote-rich Florida has become one of the prime battleground states in the November presidential balloting, reaching its zenith of importance in the 2000 cliffhanger that made Florida the center of the political universe for weeks afterwards. Yet at the same time, the state's once influential role in the nominating process has largely evaporated. By the time the Florida primary was held in 2000, the principal challengers to Democrat Al Gore and Republican George W. Bush had already quit the race. The story was similar in 2004, with the Republicans not even bothering to hold a presidential primary.

The insignificance of recent Florida primaries stands in sharp contrast to its history-making past, for in the beginning, there was Florida. The state enacted the nation's first presidential primary law in 1901. But it was not until 1972, when Florida

Recent Florida Primary Results

Florida held its first presidential primary in 1928 that recorded a vote for candidates.

	DEMOCRATS			REPUBLICANS		
Year	Turnout	Candidates	%	Turnout	Candidates	%
2004 (March 9)	753,762	JOHN KERRY John Edwards	77 10	—	No Primary	
2000 (March 14)	551,995	AL GORE Bill Bradley	82 18	699,503	GEORGE W. BUSH John McCain	74 20
1996 (March 12)	—	No Primary		898,516	BOB DOLE Steve Forbes Pat Buchanan	57 20 18
1992 (March 10)	1,123,857	BILL CLINTON Paul Tsongas Jerry Brown	51 35 12	893,463	GEORGE BUSH* Pat Buchanan	68 32
1988 (March 8)	1,273,298	MICHAEL DUKAKIS Jesse Jackson Richard Gephardt Al Gore Undecided	41 20 14 13 6	901,222	GEORGE BUSH Bob Dole Pat Robertson	62 21 11
1984 (March 13)	1,182,190	GARY HART Walter Mondale Jesse Jackson John Glenn	39 33 12 11	344,150	RONALD REAGAN*	100
1980 (March 11)	1,098,003	JIMMY CARTER* Edward Kennedy No Preference	61 23 10	614,995	RONALD REAGAN George Bush John Anderson	56 30 9
1976 (March 9)	1,300,330	JIMMY CARTER George Wallace Henry Jackson	35 31 24	609,819	GERALD FORD* Ronald Reagan	53 47
1972 (March 14)	1,264,554	GEORGE WALLACE Hubert Humphrey Henry Jackson Edmund Muskie John Lindsay George McGovern	42 19 13 9 7 6	414,207	RICHARD NIXON* John Ashbrook	87 9
1968 (May 28)	512,357	GEORGE SMATHERS Eugene McCarthy No Preference	46 29 25	51,509	NO PREFERENCE	100

Note: All candidates are listed that drew at least 5 percent of their party's primary vote. The names of winning candidates are capitalized. An asterisk (*) indicates an incumbent president.

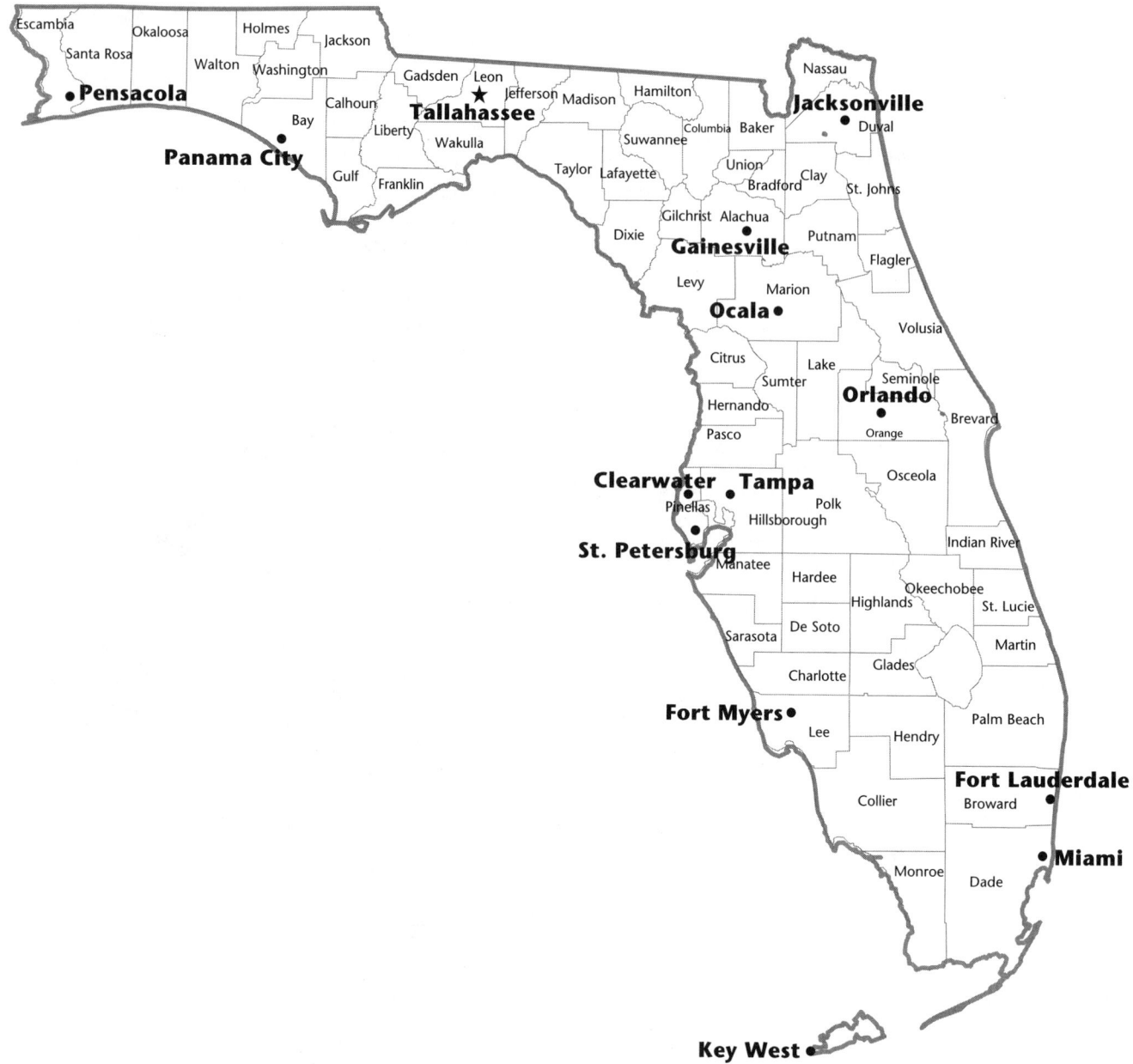

officials began scheduling the primary on the second Tuesday in March that the Sunshine State became an important stop for White House aspirants looking for something other than rest and recreation. In the decades that followed, Florida was joined on its early March date by a number of other Southern states, creating a regional cornerstone for a nationwide flurry of voting that became known as "Super Tuesday." As one of the most populous states in the country, Florida—along with Texas—tended to dominate the event.

In its heyday in the 1970s and 1980s, the combined Democratic and Republican primary vote in Florida was often in the vicinity of 2 million, with the Democrats having the larger number. In 2000, though, the combined turnout for the Florida presidential primary was down to one and a quarter million, with more ballots cast on the Republican side.

From 1976 through 1988, the candidates who won the first-in-the-nation primary in New Hampshire also won in Florida. But what had been a one-week interval between the two primaries in the early 1970s had grown to three weeks in the 1990s, a length of time in which the momentum from the New Hampshire primary could largely dissipate. In 1996, Granite State winner Pat Buchanan ran third in Florida's GOP primary with less than one-third the vote of the victorious Bob Dole. Four years earlier, New Hampshire winner Paul Tsongas was beaten by Bill Clinton in Democratic voting in Florida

Arkansas native Clinton was one in a long line of Southern Democrats to run well in Florida's presidential primary. Sen. George A. Smathers won as a favorite-son candidate in 1968. Alabama's George Wallace capitalized on strong antibusing sentiment to overwhelm a large Democratic field in 1972. Georgia's Jimmy Carter scored critical primary victories in Florida in 1976 and 1980, beating Wallace and Edward Kennedy, respectively.

But Southerners do not always win Florida's Democratic primary. That was conspicuously the case in 1988, when Tennessee's Al Gore ran far behind Massachusetts governor Michael Dukakis—a result that underscored the fact that while Florida is one of the South's political kingpins, much of the state is not of the South. The result, noted Sen. Henry Jackson of Washington, a two-time Democratic presidential aspirant, is that Florida's political geography is basically inverted. "Northern Florida is Southern and southern Florida is Northern," he once said.

While Democrats in south Florida have tended to be more liberal than in the rest of the state, there are limits to how far left they will go. To many, Henry Jackson was the ideal candidate—moderately liberal on economic and social issues, conservative on defense, and strongly supportive of Israel. Dubbed the "king of the condos," Jackson won south Florida in the 1976 Democratic primary, although he had trouble establishing a toe-hold elsewhere in the state. Meanwhile, zealously anti-Castro Cubans became a major force in Republican politics in south Florida, especially Dade County (Miami).

The other end of Florida is quite different. Northern Florida has long resembled its Southern neighbors in both geography and attitude. For years the area from the panhandle east to Jacksonville was "Wallace country"; it was the backbone of the former Alabama governor's successful 1972 primary campaign and his unsuccessful 1976 effort. Gore ran well across northern Florida in his first try for the Democratic presidential nomination in 1988, carrying more than a dozen counties, including those with Panama City and Pensacola. But Gore finished fourth statewide because he ran poorly in the other, more populous portions of the state.

In between the two ends of the state is central Florida, which includes the GOP's historic base in the retirement communities along the Gulf Coast. It is in central Florida where many primary battles are decided. That includes the Ford-Reagan contest of 1976, which not only had ideological overtones but was by far the most competitive presidential primary that Florida Republicans have ever held. Reagan won north and south Florida, but still lost because of Ford's strength in central Florida, especially along the Gulf Coast.

Although Florida Republicans are approaching parity with the long-dominant Democrats in voter registration, the burgeoning size of the GOP has not resulted in increased competition in the party's presidential primary. Only the Ford-Reagan contest was decided by a margin of less than 25 percentage points.

FLORIDA DEMOCRATIC PRIMARY

2000

County	Total Vote	Bradley	Gore	Winner	Percentage of Total Vote	
					Bradley	Gore
ALACHUA	13,339	2,994	10,345	Gore	22.4%	77.6%
BAKER	945	389	556	Gore	41.2%	58.8%
BAY	3,119	999	2,120	Gore	32.0%	68.0%
BRADFORD	1,135	372	763	Gore	32.8%	67.2%
BREVARD	14,671	2,987	11,684	Gore	20.4%	79.6%
BROWARD	91,680	11,893	79,787	Gore	13.0%	87.0%
CALHOUN	666	237	429	Gore	35.6%	64.4%
CHARLOTTE	4,325	687	3,638	Gore	15.9%	84.1%
CITRUS	4,817	1,085	3,732	Gore	22.5%	77.5%
CLAY	2,485	655	1,830	Gore	26.4%	73.6%
COLLIER	4,909	1,107	3,802	Gore	22.6%	77.4%
COLUMBIA	2,176	658	1,518	Gore	30.2%	69.8%
DESOTO	919	278	641	Gore	30.3%	69.7%
DIXIE	613	195	418	Gore	31.8%	68.2%
DUVAL	27,063	6,065	20,998	Gore	22.4%	77.6%
ESCAMBIA	8,600	2,266	6,334	Gore	26.3%	73.7%
FLAGLER	2,692	449	2,243	Gore	16.7%	83.3%
FRANKLIN	489	149	340	Gore	30.5%	69.5%
GADSDEN	3,187	395	2,792	Gore	12.4%	87.6%
GILCHRIST	694	228	466	Gore	32.9%	67.1%
GLADES	483	146	337	Gore	30.2%	69.8%
GULF	1,106	401	705	Gore	36.3%	63.7%
HAMILTON	575	150	425	Gore	26.1%	73.9%
HARDEE	846	282	564	Gore	33.3%	66.7%
HENDRY	864	269	595	Gore	31.1%	68.9%
HERNANDO	4,781	928	3,853	Gore	19.4%	80.6%
HIGHLANDS	2,718	551	2,167	Gore	20.3%	79.7%
HILLSBOROUGH	27,097	5,806	21,291	Gore	21.4%	78.6%
HOLMES	654	314	340	Gore	48.0%	52.0%
INDIAN RIVER	2,695	531	2,164	Gore	19.7%	80.3%
JACKSON	2,071	585	1,486	Gore	28.2%	71.8%
JEFFERSON	1,127	231	896	Gore	20.5%	79.5%
LAFAYETTE	342	152	190	Gore	44.4%	55.6%
LAKE	4,866	859	4,007	Gore	17.7%	82.3%
LEE	22,929	5,119	17,810	Gore	22.3%	77.7%
LEON	15,367	2,604	12,763	Gore	16.9%	83.1%
LEVY	1,639	421	1,218	Gore	25.7%	74.3%
LIBERTY	506	184	322	Gore	36.4%	63.6%
MADISON	1,269	351	918	Gore	27.7%	72.3%
MANATEE	7,094	1,275	5,819	Gore	18.0%	82.0%
MARION	8,165	1,484	6,681	Gore	18.2%	81.8%
MARTIN	3,188	592	2,596	Gore	18.6%	81.4%
MIAMI-DADE	44,181	4,222	39,959	Gore	9.6%	90.4%
MONROE	3,165	873	2,292	Gore	27.6%	72.4%
NASSAU	1,612	519	1,093	Gore	32.2%	67.8%

FLORIDA DEMOCRATIC PRIMARY

2000

County	Total Vote	Bradley	Gore	Winner	Percentage of Total Vote	
					Bradley	Gore
OKALOOSA	3,346	1,073	2,273	Gore	32.1%	67.9%
OKEECHOBEE	794	189	605	Gore	23.8%	76.2%
ORANGE	34,855	5,741	29,114	Gore	16.5%	83.5%
OSCEOLA	3,188	624	2,564	Gore	19.6%	80.4%
PALM BEACH	55,091	7,593	47,498	Gore	13.8%	86.2%
PASCO	10,012	1,939	8,073	Gore	19.4%	80.6%
PINELLAS	30,688	5,992	24,696	Gore	19.5%	80.5%
POLK	14,221	2,913	11,308	Gore	20.5%	79.5%
PUTNAM	2,823	706	2,117	Gore	25.0%	75.0%
ST. JOHNS	3,259	786	2,473	Gore	24.1%	75.9%
ST. LUCIE	6,639	1,103	5,536	Gore	16.6%	83.4%
SANTA ROSA	2,147	746	1,401	Gore	34.7%	65.3%
SARASOTA	12,365	2,367	9,998	Gore	19.1%	80.9%
SEMINOLE	4,947	909	4,038	Gore	18.4%	81.6%
SUMTER	1,419	292	1,127	Gore	20.6%	79.4%
SUWANNEE	1,524	546	978	Gore	35.8%	64.2%
TAYLOR	1,154	317	837	Gore	27.5%	72.5%
UNION	408	149	259	Gore	36.5%	63.5%
VOLUSIA	11,806	2,183	9,623	Gore	18.5%	81.5%
WAKULLA	1,269	363	906	Gore	28.6%	71.4%
WALTON	1,420	524	896	Gore	36.9%	63.1%
WASHINGTON	677	267	410	Gore	39.4%	60.6%
Federal Absentees	79	18	61	Gore	22.8%	77.2%
TOTAL	551,995	100,277	451,718	Gore	18.2%	81.8%

FLORIDA REPUBLICAN PRIMARY

2000

County	Total Vote	G.W. Bush	McCain	Other	Winner	Percentage of Total Vote		
						G.W. Bush	McCain	Other
ALACHUA	6,978	4,735	1,544	699	G.W. Bush	67.9%	22.1%	10.0%
BAKER	273	236	26	11	G.W. Bush	86.4%	9.5%	4.0%
BAY	4,360	3,253	846	261	G.W. Bush	74.6%	19.4%	6.0%
BRADFORD	492	415	40	37	G.W. Bush	84.3%	8.1%	7.5%
BREVARD	28,260	19,703	6,334	2,223	G.W. Bush	69.7%	22.4%	7.9%
BROWARD	51,097	35,436	11,777	3,884	G.W. Bush	69.4%	23.0%	7.6%
CALHOUN	107	78	22	7	G.W. Bush	72.9%	20.6%	6.5%
CHARLOTTE	10,606	7,872	2,155	579	G.W. Bush	74.2%	20.3%	5.5%
CITRUS	7,611	5,194	1,776	641	G.W. Bush	68.2%	23.3%	8.4%
CLAY	9,262	7,455	1,347	460	G.W. Bush	80.5%	14.5%	5.0%
COLLIER	21,423	16,411	3,992	1,020	G.W. Bush	76.6%	18.6%	4.8%
COLUMBIA	1,311	1,050	152	109	G.W. Bush	80.1%	11.6%	8.3%
DESOTO	531	425	69	37	G.W. Bush	80.0%	13.0%	7.0%
DIXIE	98	80	14	4	G.W. Bush	81.6%	14.3%	4.1%
DUVAL	25,118	20,861	2,661	1,596	G.W. Bush	83.1%	10.6%	6.4%
ESCAMBIA	15,686	10,275	3,484	1,927	G.W. Bush	65.5%	22.2%	12.3%
FLAGLER	3,674	2,405	1,109	160	G.W. Bush	65.5%	30.2%	4.4%
FRANKLIN	198	153	36	9	G.W. Bush	77.3%	18.2%	4.5%
GADSDEN	412	291	72	49	G.W. Bush	70.6%	17.5%	11.9%
GILCHRIST	295	214	37	44	G.W. Bush	72.5%	12.5%	14.9%
GLADES	218	180	28	10	G.W. Bush	82.6%	12.8%	4.6%
GULF	284	226	44	14	G.W. Bush	79.6%	15.5%	4.9%
HAMILTON	99	76	14	9	G.W. Bush	76.8%	14.1%	9.1%
HARDEE	332	270	46	16	G.W. Bush	81.3%	13.9%	4.8%
HENDRY	554	436	82	36	G.W. Bush	78.7%	14.8%	6.5%
HERNANDO	7,761	5,660	1,694	407	G.W. Bush	72.9%	21.8%	5.2%
HIGHLANDS	5,536	4,384	882	270	G.W. Bush	79.2%	15.9%	4.9%
HILLSBOROUGH	33,148	25,253	5,835	2,060	G.W. Bush	76.2%	17.6%	6.2%
HOLMES	129	107	12	10	G.W. Bush	82.9%	9.3%	7.8%
INDIAN RIVER	8,152	5,921	1,739	492	G.W. Bush	72.6%	21.3%	6.0%
JACKSON	598	447	93	58	G.W. Bush	74.7%	15.6%	9.7%
JEFFERSON	286	213	52	21	G.W. Bush	74.5%	18.2%	7.3%
LAFAYETTE	57	43	9	5	G.W. Bush	75.4%	15.8%	8.8%
LAKE	12,915	9,848	2,272	795	G.W. Bush	76.3%	17.6%	6.2%
LEE	51,081	36,962	11,439	2,680	G.W. Bush	72.4%	22.4%	5.2%
LEON	8,852	6,054	2,030	768	G.W. Bush	68.4%	22.9%	8.7%
LEVY	1,015	735	187	93	G.W. Bush	72.4%	18.4%	9.2%
LIBERTY	30	23	3	4	G.W. Bush	76.7%	10.0%	13.3%
MADISON	243	172	39	32	G.W. Bush	70.8%	16.0%	13.2%
MANATEE	16,073	11,794	3,220	1,059	G.W. Bush	73.4%	20.0%	6.6%
MARION	13,426	10,217	2,296	913	G.W. Bush	76.1%	17.1%	6.8%
MARTIN	11,677	7,733	3,329	615	G.W. Bush	66.2%	28.5%	5.3%
MIAMI-DADE	53,793	48,018	4,247	1,528	G.W. Bush	89.3%	7.9%	2.8%
MONROE	4,466	3,015	1,166	285	G.W. Bush	67.5%	26.1%	6.4%
NASSAU	2,369	1,934	284	151	G.W. Bush	81.6%	12.0%	6.4%

FLORIDA REPUBLICAN PRIMARY

2000

County	Total Vote	G.W. Bush	McCain	Other	Winner	Percentage of Total Vote		
						G.W. Bush	McCain	Other
OKALOOSA	13,482	8,996	3,390	1,096	G.W. Bush	66.7%	25.1%	8.1%
OKEECHOBEE	571	430	109	32	G.W. Bush	75.3%	19.1%	5.6%
ORANGE	41,266	31,740	6,845	2,681	G.W. Bush	76.9%	16.6%	6.5%
OSCEOLA	4,766	3,745	704	317	G.W. Bush	78.6%	14.8%	6.7%
PALM BEACH	42,609	28,048	11,803	2,758	G.W. Bush	65.8%	27.7%	6.5%
PASCO	15,263	11,279	3,134	850	G.W. Bush	73.9%	20.5%	5.6%
PINELLAS	50,724	35,864	11,772	3,088	G.W. Bush	70.7%	23.2%	6.1%
POLK	19,714	15,498	3,154	1,062	G.W. Bush	78.6%	16.0%	5.4%
PUTNAM	1,722	1,395	200	127	G.W. Bush	81.0%	11.6%	7.4%
ST. JOHNS	8,099	6,268	1,371	460	G.W. Bush	77.4%	16.9%	5.7%
ST. LUCIE	9,540	6,984	2,072	484	G.W. Bush	73.2%	21.7%	5.1%
SANTA ROSA	6,744	4,749	1,289	706	G.W. Bush	70.4%	19.1%	10.5%
SARASOTA	27,703	18,327	7,767	1,609	G.W. Bush	66.2%	28.0%	5.8%
SEMINOLE	13,427	10,463	2,020	944	G.W. Bush	77.9%	15.0%	7.0%
SUMTER	2,154	1,700	332	122	G.W. Bush	78.9%	15.4%	5.7%
SUWANNEE	798	628	101	69	G.W. Bush	78.7%	12.7%	8.6%
TAYLOR	260	185	43	32	G.W. Bush	71.2%	16.5%	12.3%
UNION	101	79	7	15	G.W. Bush	78.2%	6.9%	14.9%
VOLUSIA	17,255	11,910	4,330	1,015	G.W. Bush	69.0%	25.1%	5.9%
WAKULLA	422	270	105	47	G.W. Bush	64.0%	24.9%	11.1%
WALTON	1,554	1,158	263	133	G.W. Bush	74.5%	16.9%	8.6%
WASHINGTON	257	182	51	24	G.W. Bush	70.8%	19.8%	9.3%
Federal Absentees	186	102	68	16	G.W. Bush	54.8%	36.6%	8.6%
TOTAL	699,503	516,263	139,465	43,775	G.W. Bush	73.8%	19.9%	6.3%

Note: Other vote was 32,354 Alan Keyes; 6,553 Steve Forbes; 3,496 Gary Bauer; 1,372 Orrin G. Hatch.

FLORIDA DEMOCRATIC PRIMARY

2004

County	Total Vote	Edwards	Kerry	Other	Winner	Percentage of Total Vote		
						Edwards	Kerry	Other
ALACHUA	17,509	2,043	11,671	3,795	Kerry	11.7%	66.7%	21.7%
BAKER	754	130	481	143	Kerry	17.2%	63.8%	19.0%
BAY	9,967	2,363	5,756	1,848	Kerry	23.7%	57.8%	18.5%
BRADFORD	1,048	163	678	207	Kerry	15.6%	64.7%	19.8%
BREVARD	17,605	2,080	13,607	1,918	Kerry	11.8%	77.3%	10.9%
BROWARD	90,036	6,043	72,834	11,159	Kerry	6.7%	80.9%	12.4%
CALHOUN	755	139	475	141	Kerry	18.4%	62.9%	18.7%
CHARLOTTE	8,713	877	7,247	589	Kerry	10.1%	83.2%	6.8%
CITRUS	8,186	1,007	6,582	597	Kerry	12.3%	80.4%	7.3%
CLAY	3,022	421	2,167	434	Kerry	13.9%	71.7%	14.4%
COLLIER	7,542	785	6,134	623	Kerry	10.4%	81.3%	8.3%
COLUMBIA	2,396	358	1,628	410	Kerry	14.9%	67.9%	17.1%
DESOTO	907	120	687	100	Kerry	13.2%	75.7%	11.0%
DIXIE	533	87	335	111	Kerry	16.3%	62.9%	20.8%
DUVAL	30,980	3,529	22,640	4,811	Kerry	11.4%	73.1%	15.5%
ESCAMBIA	21,128	3,505	13,773	3,850	Kerry	16.6%	65.2%	18.2%
FLAGLER	3,924	331	3,190	403	Kerry	8.4%	81.3%	10.3%
FRANKLIN	722	132	467	123	Kerry	18.3%	64.7%	17.0%
GADSDEN	4,853	426	3,597	830	Kerry	8.8%	74.1%	17.1%
GILCHRIST	869	166	551	152	Kerry	19.1%	63.4%	17.5%
GLADES	587	91	421	75	Kerry	15.5%	71.7%	12.8%
GULF	700	129	453	118	Kerry	18.4%	64.7%	16.9%
HAMILTON	711	121	465	125	Kerry	17.0%	65.4%	17.6%
HARDEE	911	157	581	173	Kerry	17.2%	63.8%	19.0%
HENDRY	979	149	664	166	Kerry	15.2%	67.8%	17.0%
HERNANDO	12,993	1,206	10,443	1,344	Kerry	9.3%	80.4%	10.3%
HIGHLANDS	3,481	367	2,796	318	Kerry	10.5%	80.3%	9.1%
HILLSBOROUGH	38,315	3,608	28,981	5,726	Kerry	9.4%	75.6%	14.9%
HOLMES	665	211	313	141	Kerry	31.7%	47.1%	21.2%
INDIAN RIVER	4,354	447	3,384	523	Kerry	10.3%	77.7%	12.0%
JACKSON	3,003	459	2,067	477	Kerry	15.3%	68.8%	15.9%
JEFFERSON	1,007	118	729	160	Kerry	11.7%	72.4%	15.9%
LAFAYETTE	573	170	266	137	Kerry	29.7%	46.4%	23.9%
LAKE	9,525	1,107	7,528	890	Kerry	11.6%	79.0%	9.3%
LEE	17,111	1,741	13,963	1,407	Kerry	10.2%	81.6%	8.2%
LEON	21,021	2,740	14,952	3,329	Kerry	13.0%	71.1%	15.8%
LEVY	2,186	354	1,479	353	Kerry	16.2%	67.7%	16.1%
LIBERTY	293	66	174	53	Kerry	22.5%	59.4%	18.1%
MADISON	1,037	188	646	203	Kerry	18.1%	62.3%	19.6%
MANATEE	19,364	1,948	15,277	2,139	Kerry	10.1%	78.9%	11.0%
MARION	13,857	1,554	11,130	1,173	Kerry	11.2%	80.3%	8.5%
MARTIN	3,534	336	2,891	307	Kerry	9.5%	81.8%	8.7%
MIAMI-DADE	56,909	3,684	45,713	7,512	Kerry	6.5%	80.3%	13.2%
MONROE	5,908	774	4,213	921	Kerry	13.1%	71.3%	15.6%
NASSAU	2,016	340	1,393	283	Kerry	16.9%	69.1%	14.0%

FLORIDA DEMOCRATIC PRIMARY

2004

County	Total Vote	Edwards	Kerry	Other	Winner	Percentage of Total Vote		
						Edwards	Kerry	Other
OKALOOSA	3,528	584	2,424	520	Kerry	16.6%	68.7%	14.7%
OKEECHOBEE	1,066	146	819	101	Kerry	13.7%	76.8%	9.5%
ORANGE	36,442	4,462	26,320	5,660	Kerry	12.2%	72.2%	15.5%
OSCEOLA	8,474	1,087	6,320	1,067	Kerry	12.8%	74.6%	12.6%
PALM BEACH	77,030	4,327	65,692	7,011	Kerry	5.6%	85.3%	9.1%
PASCO	31,325	3,458	23,805	4,062	Kerry	11.0%	76.0%	13.0%
PINELLAS	45,273	3,652	35,355	6,266	Kerry	8.1%	78.1%	13.8%
POLK	28,664	3,698	21,306	3,660	Kerry	12.9%	74.3%	12.8%
PUTNAM	2,986	465	2,086	435	Kerry	15.6%	69.9%	14.6%
ST. JOHNS	5,408	637	4,106	665	Kerry	11.8%	75.9%	12.3%
ST. LUCIE	8,414	913	6,761	740	Kerry	10.9%	80.4%	8.8%
SANTA ROSA	2,544	386	1,853	305	Kerry	15.2%	72.8%	12.0%
SARASOTA	14,418	1,019	11,793	1,606	Kerry	7.1%	81.8%	11.1%
SEMINOLE	7,029	816	5,368	845	Kerry	11.6%	76.4%	12.0%
SUMTER	2,602	272	2,027	303	Kerry	10.5%	77.9%	11.6%
SUWANNEE	1,493	317	926	250	Kerry	21.2%	62.0%	16.7%
TAYLOR	1,218	266	770	182	Kerry	21.8%	63.2%	14.9%
UNION	430	83	269	78	Kerry	19.3%	62.6%	18.1%
VOLUSIA	18,899	1,581	15,660	1,658	Kerry	8.4%	82.9%	8.8%
WAKULLA	1,658	326	1,079	253	Kerry	19.7%	65.1%	15.3%
WALTON	1,435	237	964	234	Kerry	16.5%	67.2%	16.3%
WASHINGTON	937	201	547	189	Kerry	21.5%	58.4%	20.2%
TOTAL	753,762	75,703	581,672	96,387	Kerry	10.0%	77.2%	12.8%

Note: Other vote was 21,031 Al Sharpton; 20,834 Howard Dean; 17,198 Dennis J. Kucinich; 14,287 Joseph I. Lieberman; 10,226 Wesley Clark; 6,789 Carol Moseley Braun; 6,022 Richard A. Gephardt.

GEORGIA

Through some shrewd scheduling, Georgia has made its presidential primary more significant in recent years than many states that are much larger. Georgia's primary in 1976 was held in May. In 1980, it was moved to the second Tuesday in March, and in 1992 to the first Tuesday in March. In the process, it became the first Southern state to vote in 1992 and the second in 1996. And while several Southern states voted before Georgia in 2004, it provided North Carolina's John Edwards the venue to mount a last stand against John Kerry on "Super Tuesday" (the cross-country votefest recently held on the first Tuesday in March).

Edwards lost the Georgia primary to Kerry, 47 to 41 percent. But he showed a vote-getting appeal that complemented Kerry's, and no doubt enhanced his prospects to be named

Kerry's vice presidential running mate. Kerry ran well among blacks and "yellow dog" Democrats in the Georgia primary, while Edwards made inroads among conservative white voters that have tilted the region to the Republicans.

In the Atlanta suburbs, for instance, Kerry swamped Edwards in black-majority DeKalb County by nearly 25 percentage points. But in predominantly white Cobb County, which Bush won handily over Gore in the fall of 2000, Edwards prevailed narrowly. A similar dynamic was evident in rural Georgia. In racially mixed Sumter County, which includes former president Carter's hometown of Plains, Edwards and Kerry ran almost even. But in Towns County, an almost unanimously white enclave in mountainous northern Georgia that was the home of Sen. Zell Miller (the head of "Democrats for

Georgia Primary Results

Georgia held its first presidential primary in 1932, but none between then and 1976.

| Year | DEMOCRATS | | | REPUBLICANS | | |
	Turnout	Candidates	%	Turnout	Candidates	%
2004 (March 2)	626,813	JOHN KERRY	47	161,374	GEORGE W. BUSH*	100
		John Edwards	41			
		Al Sharpton	6			
2000 (March 7)	284,431	AL GORE	84	643,188	GEORGE W. BUSH	67
		Bill Bradley	16		John McCain	28
1996 (March 5)	95,103	BILL CLINTON*	100	559,067	BOB DOLE	41
					Pat Buchanan	29
					Lamar Alexander	14
					Steve Forbes	13
1992 (March 3)	454,631	BILL CLINTON	57	453,990	GEORGE BUSH*	64
		Paul Tsongas	24		Pat Buchanan	36
		Jerry Brown	8			
1988 (March 8)	622,752	JESSE JACKSON	40	400,928	GEORGE BUSH	54
		Al Gore	32		Bob Dole	24
		Michael Dukakis	16		Pat Robertson	16
		Richard Gephardt	7		Jack Kemp	6
1984 (March 13)	684,541	WALTER MONDALE	30	50,793	RONALD REAGAN*	100
		Gary Hart	27			
		Jesse Jackson	21			
		John Glenn	18			
1980 (March 11)	384,780	JIMMY CARTER*	88	200,171	RONALD REAGAN	73
		Edward Kennedy	8		George Bush	13
					John Anderson	8
1976 (May 4)	502,471	JIMMY CARTER	83	188,472	RONALD REAGAN	68
		George Wallace	11		Gerald Ford*	32

Note: All candidates are listed who drew at least 5 percent of their party's primary vote. The names of winning candidates are capitalized. An asterisk (*) indicates an incumbent president.

Bush" in 2004), Edwards defeated Kerry by fully 20 percentage points.

But calendar position has not been Georgia's only asset in attracting attention for its presidential primary. Unlike many Southern states that have a handful of medium-sized cities, Georgia boasts one large metropolitan area, Atlanta, that is one of the nation's leading transportation and communications centers.

The outcome of Georgia's first two presidential primaries of the last half century was quite predictable. Native-son Jimmy Carter swept the 1976 and 1980 Democratic primaries with more than 80 percent of the vote, while Ronald Reagan won the first two Republican primaries almost as decisively.

Georgia's primary was first of national import in 1984. As much as any state in the country, Georgia scuttled the presidential hopes of Gary Hart and put Walter Mondale back in the driver's seat for the Democratic nomination. After his devastating loss in New Hampshire, Mondale needed to slow Hart's momentum by scoring at least two primary wins in the trio of Southern states that voted then in early March.

Mondale barely did that–carrying Alabama easily and Georgia narrowly.

In 1992, Georgia was again on center stage, giving Bill Clinton his first win of the primary season. Touting his Southern roots and support from much of the state party establishment, Clinton swept all parts of Georgia–from black-majority counties to those with a military orientation. Paul Tsongas ran reasonably close to Clinton in the Atlanta area, where voters from all parts of the country are plentiful. But outside metropolitan Atlanta, it was no contest. The only Georgia county that Tsongas won was the academic enclave of Clarke County, home of the University of Georgia at Athens.

Clinton's broad-based victory in 1992 was a sharp contrast to the Democratic primary four years earlier, which featured Jesse Jackson and Clinton's eventual running mate, Al Gore. The northern third of the state, which borders Tennessee, generally preferred Gore. Jackson carried the rural counties of the "black belt" and nearly all of the state's population centers, including Fulton County (Atlanta), which enabled him to win the primary.

Georgia's Republican primary did not draw much national interest until Pat Buchanan mounted his anti-establishment campaigns against President George Bush in 1992 and Bob Dole in 1996.

The contest between Bush and Buchanan was intense, as Georgia provided the first big test for the two after Buchanan had shocked the president in New Hampshire by drawing nearly 40 percent of the vote. Bush took advantage of the trappings of the presidency by flying *Air Force One* to major population centers around the state. Buchanan filled the role of irreverent challenger, barnstorming rural Georgia in a bus dubbed "Asphalt One." Buchanan ended up carrying 15 counties outside the Atlanta area, but Bush won the primary decisively by garnering roughly two-thirds of the vote in metropolitan Atlanta.

Buchanan returned to Georgia in 1996 with high hopes, having beaten Dole in the New Hampshire primary two weeks earlier. But the results were not much better for him than in 1992. Buchanan won more than 70 counties this time, but they were mainly in rural areas of Georgia where turnout was low for the GOP primary. Like Bush four years earlier, Dole ran well in the leading population centers, including metropolitan Atlanta, to win the statewide vote by a comfortable margin.

Both the Democratic and Republican primaries in 2000 were very one-sided, as Al Gore and George W. Bush registered their highest vote shares of the contested phase of the nominating season in Georgia.

More noteworthy was the voter turnout. For the first time in the state's history, a contested Republican primary for president drew more voters than a contested primary on the Democratic side. It proved a precursor of sorts of GOP success in Georgia in the early years of the new millennium.

GEORGIA DEMOCRATIC PRIMARY

2000

County	Total Vote	Bradley	Gore	Winner	Percentage of Total Vote Bradley	Gore
APPLING	790	173	617	Gore	21.9%	78.1%
ATKINSON	207	40	167	Gore	19.3%	80.7%
BACON	188	58	130	Gore	30.9%	69.1%
BAKER	175	35	140	Gore	20.0%	80.0%
BALDWIN	2,627	438	2,189	Gore	16.7%	83.3%
BANKS	395	88	307	Gore	22.3%	77.7%
BARROW	934	154	780	Gore	16.5%	83.5%
BARTOW	1,787	266	1,521	Gore	14.9%	85.1%
BEN HILL	902	176	726	Gore	19.5%	80.5%
BERRIEN	411	67	344	Gore	16.3%	83.7%
BIBB	6,892	895	5,997	Gore	13.0%	87.0%
BLECKLEY	308	66	242	Gore	21.4%	78.6%
BRANTLEY	337	81	256	Gore	24.0%	76.0%
BROOKS	587	107	480	Gore	18.2%	81.8%
BRYAN	405	77	328	Gore	19.0%	81.0%
BULLOCH	1,087	218	869	Gore	20.1%	79.9%
BURKE	989	111	878	Gore	11.2%	88.8%
BUTTS	690	103	587	Gore	14.9%	85.1%
CALHOUN	305	33	272	Gore	10.8%	89.2%
CAMDEN	955	200	755	Gore	20.9%	79.1%
CANDLER	289	50	239	Gore	17.3%	82.7%
CARROLL	2,831	500	2,331	Gore	17.7%	82.3%
CATOOSA	1,510	219	1,291	Gore	14.5%	85.5%
CHARLTON	235	51	184	Gore	21.7%	78.3%
CHATHAM	8,424	1,327	7,097	Gore	15.8%	84.2%
CHATTAHOOCHEE	133	22	111	Gore	16.5%	83.5%
CHATTOOGA	677	102	575	Gore	15.1%	84.9%
CHEROKEE	3,070	662	2,408	Gore	21.6%	78.4%
CLARKE	4,143	1,001	3,142	Gore	24.2%	75.8%
CLAY	276	51	225	Gore	18.5%	81.5%
CLAYTON	8,907	888	8,019	Gore	10.0%	90.0%
CLINCH	141	26	115	Gore	18.4%	81.6%
COBB	17,231	3,284	13,947	Gore	19.1%	80.9%
COFFEE	670	142	528	Gore	21.2%	78.8%
COLQUITT	1,039	172	867	Gore	16.6%	83.4%
COLUMBIA	1,736	390	1,346	Gore	22.5%	77.5%
COOK	478	74	404	Gore	15.5%	84.5%
COWETA	2,440	366	2,074	Gore	15.0%	85.0%
CRAWFORD	384	66	318	Gore	17.2%	82.8%
CRISP	502	95	407	Gore	18.9%	81.1%
DADE	351	72	279	Gore	20.5%	79.5%
DAWSON	629	119	510	Gore	18.9%	81.1%
DECATUR	795	120	675	Gore	15.1%	84.9%
DE KALB	38,723	6,002	32,721	Gore	15.5%	84.5%
DODGE	597	100	497	Gore	16.8%	83.2%

GEORGIA DEMOCRATIC PRIMARY

2000

County	Total Vote	Bradley	Gore	Winner	Percentage of Total Vote	
					Bradley	Gore
DOOLY	471	85	386	Gore	18.0%	82.0%
DOUGHERTY	4,590	497	4,093	Gore	10.8%	89.2%
DOUGLAS	2,550	366	2,184	Gore	14.4%	85.6%
EARLY	450	56	394	Gore	12.4%	87.6%
ECHOLS	40	4	36	Gore	10.0%	90.0%
EFFINGHAM	576	107	469	Gore	18.6%	81.4%
ELBERT	677	97	580	Gore	14.3%	85.7%
EMANUEL	612	111	501	Gore	18.1%	81.9%
EVANS	231	48	183	Gore	20.8%	79.2%
FANNIN	1,328	164	1,164	Gore	12.3%	87.7%
FAYETTE	2,632	534	2,098	Gore	20.3%	79.7%
FLOYD	3,145	468	2,677	Gore	14.9%	85.1%
FORSYTH	1,828	424	1,404	Gore	23.2%	76.8%
FRANKLIN	781	166	615	Gore	21.3%	78.7%
FULTON	38,138	5,517	32,621	Gore	14.5%	85.5%
GILMER	569	69	500	Gore	12.1%	87.9%
GLASCOCK	249	53	196	Gore	21.3%	78.7%
GLYNN	1,747	351	1,396	Gore	20.1%	79.9%
GORDON	1,174	156	1,018	Gore	13.3%	86.7%
GRADY	1,573	320	1,253	Gore	20.3%	79.7%
GREENE	772	88	684	Gore	11.4%	88.6%
GWINNETT	11,076	2,253	8,823	Gore	20.3%	79.7%
HABERSHAM	893	199	694	Gore	22.3%	77.7%
HALL	2,968	674	2,294	Gore	22.7%	77.3%
HANCOCK	745	94	651	Gore	12.6%	87.4%
HARALSON	1,008	184	824	Gore	18.3%	81.7%
HARRIS	749	119	630	Gore	15.9%	84.1%
HART	785	145	640	Gore	18.5%	81.5%
HEARD	383	50	333	Gore	13.1%	86.9%
HENRY	2,774	391	2,383	Gore	14.1%	85.9%
HOUSTON	3,428	607	2,821	Gore	17.7%	82.3%
IRWIN	307	53	254	Gore	17.3%	82.7%
JACKSON	1,079	183	896	Gore	17.0%	83.0%
JASPER	516	86	430	Gore	16.7%	83.3%
JEFF DAVIS	378	81	297	Gore	21.4%	78.6%
JEFFERSON	764	144	620	Gore	18.8%	81.2%
JENKINS	273	49	224	Gore	17.9%	82.1%
JOHNSON	319	65	254	Gore	20.4%	79.6%
JONES	846	133	713	Gore	15.7%	84.3%
LAMAR	888	114	774	Gore	12.8%	87.2%
LANIER	166	26	140	Gore	15.7%	84.3%
LAURENS	1,727	269	1,458	Gore	15.6%	84.4%
LEE	523	87	436	Gore	16.6%	83.4%
LIBERTY	990	140	850	Gore	14.1%	85.9%
LINCOLN	332	34	298	Gore	10.2%	89.8%

GEORGIA DEMOCRATIC PRIMARY

2000

County	Total Vote	Bradley	Gore	Winner	Percentage of Total Vote	
					Bradley	Gore
LONG	162	34	128	Gore	21.0%	79.0%
LOWNDES	2,104	326	1,778	Gore	15.5%	84.5%
LUMPKIN	568	133	435	Gore	23.4%	76.6%
MCDUFFIE	747	107	640	Gore	14.3%	85.7%
MCINTOSH	778	140	638	Gore	18.0%	82.0%
MACON	642	94	548	Gore	14.6%	85.4%
MADISON	510	109	401	Gore	21.4%	78.6%
MARION	227	43	184	Gore	18.9%	81.1%
MERIWETHER	1,159	134	1,025	Gore	11.6%	88.4%
MILLER	129	23	106	Gore	17.8%	82.2%
MITCHELL	904	101	803	Gore	11.2%	88.8%
MONROE	815	111	704	Gore	13.6%	86.4%
MONTGOMERY	221	37	184	Gore	16.7%	83.3%
MORGAN	838	141	697	Gore	16.8%	83.2%
MURRAY	1,681	374	1,307	Gore	22.2%	77.8%
MUSCOGEE	8,431	830	7,601	Gore	9.8%	90.2%
NEWTON	1,964	295	1,669	Gore	15.0%	85.0%
OCONEE	847	203	644	Gore	24.0%	76.0%
OGLETHORPE	414	78	336	Gore	18.8%	81.2%
PAULDING	1,271	197	1,074	Gore	15.5%	84.5%
PEACH	1,203	152	1,051	Gore	12.6%	87.4%
PICKENS	515	77	438	Gore	15.0%	85.0%
PIERCE	368	76	292	Gore	20.7%	79.3%
PIKE	562	79	483	Gore	14.1%	85.9%
POLK	2,113	342	1,771	Gore	16.2%	83.8%
PULASKI	358	58	300	Gore	16.2%	83.8%
PUTNAM	968	194	774	Gore	20.0%	80.0%
QUITMAN	399	96	303	Gore	24.1%	75.9%
RABUN	630	129	501	Gore	20.5%	79.5%
RANDOLPH	430	53	377	Gore	12.3%	87.7%
RICHMOND	6,211	782	5,429	Gore	12.6%	87.4%
ROCKDALE	1,909	329	1,580	Gore	17.2%	82.8%
SCHLEY	110	19	91	Gore	17.3%	82.7%
SCREVEN	665	118	547	Gore	17.7%	82.3%
SEMINOLE	491	93	398	Gore	18.9%	81.1%
SPALDING	1,676	225	1,451	Gore	13.4%	86.6%
STEPHENS	973	190	783	Gore	19.5%	80.5%
STEWART	328	48	280	Gore	14.6%	85.4%
SUMTER	1,059	172	887	Gore	16.2%	83.8%
TALBOT	418	64	354	Gore	15.3%	84.7%
TALIAFERRO	181	19	162	Gore	10.5%	89.5%
TATTNALL	419	85	334	Gore	20.3%	79.7%
TAYLOR	522	75	447	Gore	14.4%	85.6%
TELFAIR	456	68	388	Gore	14.9%	85.1%
TERRELL	559	88	471	Gore	15.7%	84.3%

GEORGIA DEMOCRATIC PRIMARY

2000

County	Total Vote	Bradley	Gore	Winner	Percentage of Total Vote Bradley	Gore
THOMAS	1,214	157	1,057	Gore	12.9%	87.1%
TIFT	825	148	677	Gore	17.9%	82.1%
TOOMBS	544	99	445	Gore	18.2%	81.8%
TOWNS	804	190	614	Gore	23.6%	76.4%
TREUTLEN	231	44	187	Gore	19.0%	81.0%
TROUP	1,610	211	1,399	Gore	13.1%	86.9%
TURNER	230	45	185	Gore	19.6%	80.4%
TWIGGS	533	67	466	Gore	12.6%	87.4%
UNION	784	196	588	Gore	25.0%	75.0%
UPSON	996	141	855	Gore	14.2%	85.8%
WALKER	1,568	249	1,319	Gore	15.9%	84.1%
WALTON	1,386	200	1,186	Gore	14.4%	85.6%
WARE	2,731	555	2,176	Gore	20.3%	79.7%
WARREN	352	58	294	Gore	16.5%	83.5%
WASHINGTON	1,655	320	1,335	Gore	19.3%	80.7%
WAYNE	1,026	242	784	Gore	23.6%	76.4%
WEBSTER	136	25	111	Gore	18.4%	81.6%
WHEELER	160	26	134	Gore	16.3%	83.8%
WHITE	617	134	483	Gore	21.7%	78.3%
WHITFIELD	1,771	280	1,491	Gore	15.8%	84.2%
WILCOX	247	37	210	Gore	15.0%	85.0%
WILKES	682	122	560	Gore	17.9%	82.1%
WILKINSON	539	90	449	Gore	16.7%	83.3%
WORTH	623	110	513	Gore	17.7%	82.3%
TOTAL	284,431	46,035	238,396	Gore	16.2%	83.8%

GEORGIA REPUBLICAN PRIMARY

2000

County	Total Vote	G.W. Bush	McCain	Other	Winner	Percentage of Total Vote		
						G.W. Bush	McCain	Other
APPLING	1,520	1,098	334	88	G.W. Bush	72.2%	22.0%	5.8%
ATKINSON	299	225	57	17	G.W. Bush	75.3%	19.1%	5.7%
BACON	499	366	110	23	G.W. Bush	73.3%	22.0%	4.6%
BAKER	175	143	28	4	G.W. Bush	81.7%	16.0%	2.3%
BALDWIN	3,528	2,351	1,050	127	G.W. Bush	66.6%	29.8%	3.6%
BANKS	1,130	810	270	50	G.W. Bush	71.7%	23.9%	4.4%
BARROW	3,187	2,259	758	170	G.W. Bush	70.9%	23.8%	5.3%
BARTOW	5,539	3,914	1,246	379	G.W. Bush	70.7%	22.5%	6.8%
BEN HILL	913	669	213	31	G.W. Bush	73.3%	23.3%	3.4%
BERRIEN	757	553	172	32	G.W. Bush	73.1%	22.7%	4.2%
BIBB	11,223	8,202	2,584	437	G.W. Bush	73.1%	23.0%	3.9%
BLECKLEY	810	500	276	34	G.W. Bush	61.7%	34.1%	4.2%
BRANTLEY	747	521	187	39	G.W. Bush	69.7%	25.0%	5.2%
BROOKS	806	587	176	43	G.W. Bush	72.8%	21.8%	5.3%
BRYAN	1,887	1,283	537	67	G.W. Bush	68.0%	28.5%	3.6%
BULLOCH	3,872	2,311	1,431	130	G.W. Bush	59.7%	37.0%	3.4%
BURKE	1,431	948	397	86	G.W. Bush	66.2%	27.7%	6.0%
BUTTS	1,212	870	280	62	G.W. Bush	71.8%	23.1%	5.1%
CALHOUN	212	150	54	8	G.W. Bush	70.8%	25.5%	3.8%
CAMDEN	2,118	1,428	621	69	G.W. Bush	67.4%	29.3%	3.3%
CANDLER	645	402	227	16	G.W. Bush	62.3%	35.2%	2.5%
CARROLL	7,949	5,611	1,996	342	G.W. Bush	70.6%	25.1%	4.3%
CATOOSA	4,512	3,186	1,027	299	G.W. Bush	70.6%	22.8%	6.6%
CHARLTON	490	365	97	28	G.W. Bush	74.5%	19.8%	5.7%
CHATHAM	20,151	13,087	6,454	610	G.W. Bush	64.9%	32.0%	3.0%
CHATTAHOOCHEE	170	113	47	10	G.W. Bush	66.5%	27.6%	5.9%
CHATTOOGA	1,074	733	285	56	G.W. Bush	68.2%	26.5%	5.2%
CHEROKEE	18,769	12,849	4,594	1,326	G.W. Bush	68.5%	24.5%	7.1%
CLARKE	6,086	3,446	2,287	353	G.W. Bush	56.6%	37.6%	5.8%
CLAY	196	129	64	3	G.W. Bush	65.8%	32.7%	1.5%
CLAYTON	10,345	6,918	2,790	637	G.W. Bush	66.9%	27.0%	6.2%
CLINCH	230	159	62	9	G.W. Bush	69.1%	27.0%	3.9%
COBB	70,034	45,870	19,927	4,237	G.W. Bush	65.5%	28.5%	6.0%
COFFEE	1,334	962	291	81	G.W. Bush	72.1%	21.8%	6.1%
COLQUITT	2,092	1,513	472	107	G.W. Bush	72.3%	22.6%	5.1%
COLUMBIA	13,065	8,999	3,212	854	G.W. Bush	68.9%	24.6%	6.5%
COOK	700	527	153	20	G.W. Bush	75.3%	21.9%	2.9%
COWETA	9,797	6,708	2,356	733	G.W. Bush	68.5%	24.0%	7.5%
CRAWFORD	737	530	172	35	G.W. Bush	71.9%	23.3%	4.7%
CRISP	945	686	225	34	G.W. Bush	72.6%	23.8%	3.6%
DADE	1,117	733	287	97	G.W. Bush	65.6%	25.7%	8.7%
DAWSON	2,111	1,518	519	74	G.W. Bush	71.9%	24.6%	3.5%
DECATUR	1,090	821	228	41	G.W. Bush	75.3%	20.9%	3.8%
DE KALB	37,099	19,982	15,085	2,032	G.W. Bush	53.9%	40.7%	5.5%
DODGE	1,043	732	273	38	G.W. Bush	70.2%	26.2%	3.6%

GEORGIA REPUBLICAN PRIMARY

2000

| County | Total Vote | G.W. Bush | McCain | Other | Winner | Percentage of Total Vote | | |
						G.W. Bush	McCain	Other
DOOLY	495	372	105	18	G.W. Bush	75.2%	21.2%	3.6%
DOUGHERTY	5,248	4,003	1,118	127	G.W. Bush	76.3%	21.3%	2.4%
DOUGLAS	8,518	6,018	1,977	523	G.W. Bush	70.7%	23.2%	6.1%
EARLY	670	499	140	31	G.W. Bush	74.5%	20.9%	4.6%
ECHOLS	87	66	16	5	G.W. Bush	75.9%	18.4%	5.7%
EFFINGHAM	2,773	1,808	843	122	G.W. Bush	65.2%	30.4%	4.4%
ELBERT	1,341	872	398	71	G.W. Bush	65.0%	29.7%	5.3%
EMANUEL	1,149	706	410	33	G.W. Bush	61.4%	35.7%	2.9%
EVANS	622	393	189	40	G.W. Bush	63.2%	30.4%	6.4%
FANNIN	3,619	2,486	1,015	118	G.W. Bush	68.7%	28.0%	3.3%
FAYETTE	15,043	9,893	4,278	872	G.W. Bush	65.8%	28.4%	5.8%
FLOYD	6,777	4,657	1,749	371	G.W. Bush	68.7%	25.8%	5.5%
FORSYTH	12,978	9,027	3,231	720	G.W. Bush	69.6%	24.9%	5.5%
FRANKLIN	1,527	964	494	69	G.W. Bush	63.1%	32.4%	4.5%
FULTON	52,184	30,642	19,228	2,314	G.W. Bush	58.7%	36.8%	4.4%
GILMER	2,165	1,462	577	126	G.W. Bush	67.5%	26.7%	5.8%
GLASCOCK	599	417	171	11	G.W. Bush	69.6%	28.5%	1.8%
GLYNN	6,731	4,734	1,801	196	G.W. Bush	70.3%	26.8%	2.9%
GORDON	2,962	2,117	669	176	G.W. Bush	71.5%	22.6%	5.9%
GRADY	1,755	1,269	419	67	G.W. Bush	72.3%	23.9%	3.8%
GREENE	1,377	1,002	340	35	G.W. Bush	72.8%	24.7%	2.5%
GWINNETT	57,453	38,906	15,321	3,226	G.W. Bush	67.7%	26.7%	5.6%
HABERSHAM	2,936	2,000	768	168	G.W. Bush	68.1%	26.2%	5.7%
HALL	11,866	8,368	2,784	714	G.W. Bush	70.5%	23.5%	6.0%
HANCOCK	187	122	58	7	G.W. Bush	65.2%	31.0%	3.7%
HARALSON	1,937	1,410	435	92	G.W. Bush	72.8%	22.5%	4.7%
HARRIS	2,317	1,651	560	106	G.W. Bush	71.3%	24.2%	4.6%
HART	1,908	1,141	705	62	G.W. Bush	59.8%	36.9%	3.2%
HEARD	712	522	173	17	G.W. Bush	73.3%	24.3%	2.4%
HENRY	11,221	7,739	2,519	963	G.W. Bush	69.0%	22.4%	8.6%
HOUSTON	9,797	6,522	2,690	585	G.W. Bush	66.6%	27.5%	6.0%
IRWIN	532	410	103	19	G.W. Bush	77.1%	19.4%	3.6%
JACKSON	3,223	2,388	673	162	G.W. Bush	74.1%	20.9%	5.0%
JASPER	973	713	215	45	G.W. Bush	73.3%	22.1%	4.6%
JEFF DAVIS	704	506	164	34	G.W. Bush	71.9%	23.3%	4.8%
JEFFERSON	1,019	703	265	51	G.W. Bush	69.0%	26.0%	5.0%
JENKINS	401	265	120	16	G.W. Bush	66.1%	29.9%	4.0%
JOHNSON	578	419	135	24	G.W. Bush	72.5%	23.4%	4.2%
JONES	1,902	1,369	465	68	G.W. Bush	72.0%	24.4%	3.6%
LAMAR	1,344	953	328	63	G.W. Bush	70.9%	24.4%	4.7%
LANIER	237	164	66	7	G.W. Bush	69.2%	27.8%	3.0%
LAURENS	2,862	1,967	756	139	G.W. Bush	68.7%	26.4%	4.9%
LEE	1,929	1,476	396	57	G.W. Bush	76.5%	20.5%	3.0%
LIBERTY	1,821	1,102	665	54	G.W. Bush	60.5%	36.5%	3.0%
LINCOLN	768	480	261	27	G.W. Bush	62.5%	34.0%	3.5%

GEORGIA REPUBLICAN PRIMARY

2000

County	Total Vote	G.W. Bush	McCain	Other	Winner	Percentage of Total Vote		
						G.W. Bush	McCain	Other
LONG	343	222	99	22	G.W. Bush	64.7%	28.9%	6.4%
LOWNDES	4,755	3,280	1,252	223	G.W. Bush	69.0%	26.3%	4.7%
LUMPKIN	1,509	974	470	65	G.W. Bush	64.5%	31.1%	4.3%
MCDUFFIE	1,777	1,216	492	69	G.W. Bush	68.4%	27.7%	3.9%
MCINTOSH	907	544	340	23	G.W. Bush	60.0%	37.5%	2.5%
MACON	520	354	139	27	G.W. Bush	68.1%	26.7%	5.2%
MADISON	2,075	1,486	476	113	G.W. Bush	71.6%	22.9%	5.4%
MARION	327	249	64	14	G.W. Bush	76.1%	19.6%	4.3%
MERIWETHER	1,046	998	35	13	G.W. Bush	95.4%	3.3%	1.2%
MILLER	218	168	46	4	G.W. Bush	77.1%	21.1%	1.8%
MITCHELL	869	633	212	24	G.W. Bush	72.8%	24.4%	2.8%
MONROE	1,928	1,452	397	79	G.W. Bush	75.3%	20.6%	4.1%
MONTGOMERY	493	322	157	14	G.W. Bush	65.3%	31.8%	2.8%
MORGAN	1,508	1,090	352	66	G.W. Bush	72.3%	23.3%	4.4%
MURRAY	2,032	1,456	480	96	G.W. Bush	71.7%	23.6%	4.7%
MUSCOGEE	12,096	8,724	3,015	357	G.W. Bush	72.1%	24.9%	3.0%
NEWTON	5,448	3,774	1,399	275	G.W. Bush	69.3%	25.7%	5.0%
OCONEE	3,753	2,495	1,038	220	G.W. Bush	66.5%	27.7%	5.9%
OGLETHORPE	1,199	797	337	65	G.W. Bush	66.5%	28.1%	5.4%
PAULDING	6,117	4,429	1,256	432	G.W. Bush	72.4%	20.5%	7.1%
PEACH	1,582	1,106	395	81	G.W. Bush	69.9%	25.0%	5.1%
PICKENS	2,168	1,509	553	106	G.W. Bush	69.6%	25.5%	4.9%
PIERCE	1,085	807	228	50	G.W. Bush	74.4%	21.0%	4.6%
PIKE	1,404	1,025	290	89	G.W. Bush	73.0%	20.7%	6.3%
POLK	2,931	2,088	705	138	G.W. Bush	71.2%	24.1%	4.7%
PULASKI	565	360	177	28	G.W. Bush	63.7%	31.3%	5.0%
PUTNAM	1,768	1,226	499	43	G.W. Bush	69.3%	28.2%	2.4%
QUITMAN	171	128	36	7	G.W. Bush	74.9%	21.1%	4.1%
RABUN	1,810	1,107	619	84	G.W. Bush	61.2%	34.2%	4.6%
RANDOLPH	296	222	65	9	G.W. Bush	75.0%	22.0%	3.0%
RICHMOND	13,455	8,956	3,614	885	G.W. Bush	66.6%	26.9%	6.6%
ROCKDALE	7,798	5,364	2,023	411	G.W. Bush	68.8%	25.9%	5.3%
SCHLEY	262	177	65	20	G.W. Bush	67.6%	24.8%	7.6%
SCREVEN	1,139	740	376	23	G.W. Bush	65.0%	33.0%	2.0%
SEMINOLE	636	464	162	10	G.W. Bush	73.0%	25.5%	1.6%
SPALDING	4,360	3,173	958	229	G.W. Bush	72.8%	22.0%	5.3%
STEPHENS	2,263	1,472	605	186	G.W. Bush	65.0%	26.7%	8.2%
STEWART	220	156	59	5	G.W. Bush	70.9%	26.8%	2.3%
SUMTER	1,516	1,058	389	69	G.W. Bush	69.8%	25.7%	4.6%
TALBOT	342	231	92	19	G.W. Bush	67.5%	26.9%	5.6%
TALIAFERRO	114	71	38	5	G.W. Bush	62.3%	33.3%	4.4%
TATTNALL	1,198	783	368	47	G.W. Bush	65.4%	30.7%	3.9%
TAYLOR	664	495	146	23	G.W. Bush	74.5%	22.0%	3.5%
TELFAIR	496	357	118	21	G.W. Bush	72.0%	23.8%	4.2%
TERRELL	681	540	110	31	G.W. Bush	79.3%	16.2%	4.6%

GEORGIA REPUBLICAN PRIMARY

2000

County	Total Vote	G.W. Bush	McCain	Other	Winner	Percentage of Total Vote		
						G.W. Bush	McCain	Other
THOMAS	2,499	1,871	493	135	G.W. Bush	74.9%	19.7%	5.4%
TIFT	2,351	1,820	441	90	G.W. Bush	77.4%	18.8%	3.8%
TOOMBS	1,723	1,153	460	110	G.W. Bush	66.9%	26.7%	6.4%
TOWNS	1,375	914	417	44	G.W. Bush	66.5%	30.3%	3.2%
TREUTLEN	328	202	112	14	G.W. Bush	61.6%	34.1%	4.3%
TROUP	4,159	3,130	853	176	G.W. Bush	75.3%	20.5%	4.2%
TURNER	372	289	64	19	G.W. Bush	77.7%	17.2%	5.1%
TWIGGS	570	419	131	20	G.W. Bush	73.5%	23.0%	3.5%
UNION	1,824	1,132	610	82	G.W. Bush	62.1%	33.4%	4.5%
UPSON	1,884	1,367	443	74	G.W. Bush	72.6%	23.5%	3.9%
WALKER	4,093	2,864	954	275	G.W. Bush	70.0%	23.3%	6.7%
WALTON	5,391	3,928	1,213	250	G.W. Bush	72.9%	22.5%	4.6%
WARE	3,007	2,159	716	132	G.W. Bush	71.8%	23.8%	4.4%
WARREN	416	285	114	17	G.W. Bush	68.5%	27.4%	4.1%
WASHINGTON	1,660	1,171	420	69	G.W. Bush	70.5%	25.3%	4.2%
WAYNE	1,950	1,233	626	91	G.W. Bush	63.2%	32.1%	4.7%
WEBSTER	113	82	27	4	G.W. Bush	72.6%	23.9%	3.5%
WHEELER	146	108	34	4	G.W. Bush	74.0%	23.3%	2.7%
WHITE	1,934	1,290	557	87	G.W. Bush	66.7%	28.8%	4.5%
WHITFIELD	5,561	4,064	1,185	312	G.W. Bush	73.1%	21.3%	5.6%
WILCOX	332	239	75	18	G.W. Bush	72.0%	22.6%	5.4%
WILKES	948	642	271	35	G.W. Bush	67.7%	28.6%	3.7%
WILKINSON	565	393	146	26	G.W. Bush	69.6%	25.8%	4.6%
WORTH	1,250	977	234	39	G.W. Bush	78.2%	18.7%	3.1%
TOTAL	643,188	430,480	179,046	33,662	G.W. Bush	66.9%	27.8%	5.2%

Note: Other vote was 29,640 Alan Keyes; 1,962 Gary Bauer; 1,647 Steve Forbes; 413 Orrin G. Hatch.

GEORGIA DEMOCRATIC PRIMARY

2004

County	Total Vote	Edwards	Kerry	Sharpton	Other	Winner	Percentage of Total Vote			
							Edwards	Kerry	Sharpton	Other
APPLING	1,143	539	463	48	93	Edwards	47.2%	40.5%	4.2%	8.1%
ATKINSON	293	144	118	15	16	Edwards	49.1%	40.3%	5.1%	5.5%
BACON	483	309	134	16	24	Edwards	64.0%	27.7%	3.3%	5.0%
BAKER	419	152	215	12	40	Kerry	36.3%	51.3%	2.9%	9.5%
BALDWIN	3,638	1,417	1,837	149	235	Kerry	38.9%	50.5%	4.1%	6.5%
BANKS	1,275	796	366	27	86	Edwards	62.4%	28.7%	2.1%	6.7%
BARROW	2,217	1,160	823	118	116	Edwards	52.3%	37.1%	5.3%	5.2%
BARTOW	4,436	2,392	1,684	171	189	Edwards	53.9%	38.0%	3.9%	4.3%
BEN HILL	1,100	533	458	40	69	Edwards	48.5%	41.6%	3.6%	6.3%
BERRIEN	899	512	319	12	56	Edwards	57.0%	35.5%	1.3%	6.2%
BIBB	15,484	6,454	7,458	850	722	Kerry	41.7%	48.2%	5.5%	4.7%
BLECKLEY	727	421	250	16	40	Edwards	57.9%	34.4%	2.2%	5.5%
BRANTLEY	637	344	217	17	59	Edwards	54.0%	34.1%	2.7%	9.3%
BROOKS	1,053	444	495	43	71	Kerry	42.2%	47.0%	4.1%	6.7%
BRYAN	1,216	666	430	58	62	Edwards	54.8%	35.4%	4.8%	5.1%
BULLOCH	2,814	1,388	1,180	93	153	Edwards	49.3%	41.9%	3.3%	5.4%
BURKE	1,940	616	991	186	147	Kerry	31.8%	51.1%	9.6%	7.6%
BUTTS	1,532	720	652	71	89	Edwards	47.0%	42.6%	4.6%	5.8%
CALHOUN	546	174	313	24	35	Kerry	31.9%	57.3%	4.4%	6.4%
CAMDEN	1,331	489	665	71	106	Kerry	36.7%	50.0%	5.3%	8.0%
CANDLER	537	257	231	19	30	Edwards	47.9%	43.0%	3.5%	5.6%
CARROLL	5,875	3,029	2,252	237	357	Edwards	51.6%	38.3%	4.0%	6.1%
CATOOSA	2,559	1,330	1,032	42	155	Edwards	52.0%	40.3%	1.6%	6.1%
CHARLTON	428	200	168	19	41	Edwards	46.7%	39.3%	4.4%	9.6%
CHATHAM	18,976	7,471	9,448	1,081	976	Kerry	39.4%	49.8%	5.7%	5.1%
CHATTAHOOCHEE	243	93	116	18	16	Kerry	38.3%	47.7%	7.4%	6.6%
CHATTOOGA	1,759	938	687	35	99	Edwards	53.3%	39.1%	2.0%	5.6%
CHEROKEE	7,994	4,400	2,575	452	567	Edwards	55.0%	32.2%	5.7%	7.1%
CLARKE	9,923	4,137	4,701	359	726	Kerry	41.7%	47.4%	3.6%	7.3%
CLAY	331	140	156	8	27	Kerry	42.3%	47.1%	2.4%	8.2%
CLAYTON	21,140	6,515	11,758	2,019	848	Kerry	30.8%	55.6%	9.6%	4.0%
CLINCH	236	122	72	21	21	Edwards	51.7%	30.5%	8.9%	8.9%
COBB	45,964	20,423	19,842	3,150	2,549	Edwards	44.4%	43.2%	6.9%	5.5%
COFFEE	1,362	641	587	59	75	Edwards	47.1%	43.1%	4.3%	5.5%
COLQUITT	2,019	1,100	757	50	112	Edwards	54.5%	37.5%	2.5%	5.5%
COLUMBIA	5,182	2,327	2,115	486	254	Edwards	44.9%	40.8%	9.4%	4.9%
COOK	862	400	381	25	56	Edwards	46.4%	44.2%	2.9%	6.5%
COWETA	7,018	3,477	2,705	397	439	Edwards	49.5%	38.5%	5.7%	6.3%
CRAWFORD	741	360	301	39	41	Edwards	48.6%	40.6%	5.3%	5.5%
CRISP	1,120	553	441	59	67	Edwards	49.4%	39.4%	5.3%	6.0%
DADE	691	351	279	9	52	Edwards	50.8%	40.4%	1.3%	7.5%
DAWSON	1,184	696	364	47	77	Edwards	58.8%	30.7%	4.0%	6.5%
DECATUR	1,642	629	819	73	121	Kerry	38.3%	49.9%	4.4%	7.4%
DE KALB	87,007	27,079	47,836	7,166	4,926	Kerry	31.1%	55.0%	8.2%	5.7%
DODGE	1,296	751	429	39	77	Edwards	57.9%	33.1%	3.0%	5.9%

GEORGIA DEMOCRATIC PRIMARY

2004

County	Total Vote	Edwards	Kerry	Sharpton	Other	Winner	Percentage of Total Vote			
							Edwards	Kerry	Sharpton	Other
DOOLY	908	419	395	36	58	Edwards	46.1%	43.5%	4.0%	6.4%
DOUGHERTY	9,742	3,623	5,089	641	389	Kerry	37.2%	52.2%	6.6%	4.0%
DOUGLAS	6,858	2,908	2,989	577	384	Kerry	42.4%	43.6%	8.4%	5.6%
EARLY	745	328	336	29	52	Kerry	44.0%	45.1%	3.9%	7.0%
ECHOLS	143	90	40	4	9	Edwards	62.9%	28.0%	2.8%	6.3%
EFFINGHAM	2,017	1,171	667	58	121	Edwards	58.1%	33.1%	2.9%	6.0%
ELBERT	1,545	858	555	48	84	Edwards	55.5%	35.9%	3.1%	5.4%
EMANUEL	1,384	625	595	73	91	Edwards	45.2%	43.0%	5.3%	6.6%
EVANS	608	293	260	26	29	Edwards	48.2%	42.8%	4.3%	4.8%
FANNIN	1,280	645	558	25	52	Edwards	50.4%	43.6%	2.0%	4.1%
FAYETTE	8,319	3,957	3,366	575	421	Edwards	47.6%	40.5%	6.9%	5.1%
FLOYD	5,707	2,972	2,207	192	336	Edwards	52.1%	38.7%	3.4%	5.9%
FORSYTH	6,232	3,618	1,797	371	446	Edwards	58.1%	28.8%	6.0%	7.2%
FRANKLIN	1,611	1,015	457	40	99	Edwards	63.0%	28.4%	2.5%	6.1%
FULTON	78,282	23,359	44,780	6,239	3,904	Kerry	29.8%	57.2%	8.0%	5.0%
GILMER	1,559	924	528	38	69	Edwards	59.3%	33.9%	2.4%	4.4%
GLASCOCK	135	66	44	14	11	Edwards	48.9%	32.6%	10.4%	8.1%
GLYNN	3,699	1,547	1,731	174	247	Kerry	41.8%	46.8%	4.7%	6.7%
GORDON	2,517	1,360	946	66	145	Edwards	54.0%	37.6%	2.6%	5.8%
GRADY	1,654	813	656	51	134	Edwards	49.2%	39.7%	3.1%	8.1%
GREENE	1,775	795	728	135	117	Edwards	44.8%	41.0%	7.6%	6.6%
GWINNETT	33,724	15,569	13,981	2,191	1,983	Edwards	46.2%	41.5%	6.5%	5.9%
HABERSHAM	2,247	1,354	678	88	127	Edwards	60.3%	30.2%	3.9%	5.7%
HALL	8,135	4,591	2,690	346	508	Edwards	56.4%	33.1%	4.3%	6.2%
HANCOCK	995	242	607	81	65	Kerry	24.3%	61.0%	8.1%	6.5%
HARALSON	1,741	1,031	553	58	99	Edwards	59.2%	31.8%	3.3%	5.7%
HARRIS	1,738	876	715	62	85	Edwards	50.4%	41.1%	3.6%	4.9%
HART	2,215	1,334	713	50	118	Edwards	60.2%	32.2%	2.3%	5.3%
HEARD	846	424	332	38	52	Edwards	50.1%	39.2%	4.5%	6.1%
HENRY	11,513	5,044	4,974	817	678	Edwards	43.8%	43.2%	7.1%	5.9%
HOUSTON	6,802	3,094	3,124	294	290	Kerry	45.5%	45.9%	4.3%	4.3%
IRWIN	655	376	219	25	35	Edwards	57.4%	33.4%	3.8%	5.3%
JACKSON	2,431	1,354	834	94	149	Edwards	55.7%	34.3%	3.9%	6.1%
JASPER	919	439	376	46	58	Edwards	47.8%	40.9%	5.0%	6.3%
JEFF DAVIS	777	360	333	25	59	Edwards	46.3%	42.9%	3.2%	7.6%
JEFFERSON	1,424	477	729	123	95	Kerry	33.5%	51.2%	8.6%	6.7%
JENKINS	658	272	308	35	43	Kerry	41.3%	46.8%	5.3%	6.5%
JOHNSON	532	270	202	19	41	Edwards	50.8%	38.0%	3.6%	7.7%
JONES	2,226	1,076	933	84	133	Edwards	48.3%	41.9%	3.8%	6.0%
LAMAR	1,434	642	650	78	64	Kerry	44.8%	45.3%	5.4%	4.5%
LANIER	331	157	137	12	25	Edwards	47.4%	41.4%	3.6%	7.6%
LAURENS	3,520	1,657	1,502	124	237	Edwards	47.1%	42.7%	3.5%	6.7%
LEE	1,292	762	428	42	60	Edwards	59.0%	33.1%	3.3%	4.6%
LIBERTY	2,125	802	1,079	138	106	Kerry	37.7%	50.8%	6.5%	5.0%
LINCOLN	804	317	363	72	52	Kerry	39.4%	45.1%	9.0%	6.5%

GEORGIA DEMOCRATIC PRIMARY

2004

County	Total Vote	Edwards	Kerry	Sharpton	Other	Winner	Percentage of Total Vote			
							Edwards	Kerry	Sharpton	Other
LONG	443	218	167	25	33	Edwards	49.2%	37.7%	5.6%	7.4%
LOWNDES	4,503	1,828	2,211	226	238	Kerry	40.6%	49.1%	5.0%	5.3%
LUMPKIN	1,568	899	498	49	122	Edwards	57.3%	31.8%	3.1%	7.8%
MCDUFFIE	1,286	444	580	171	91	Kerry	34.5%	45.1%	13.3%	7.1%
MCINTOSH	998	400	460	55	83	Kerry	40.1%	46.1%	5.5%	8.3%
MACON	1,149	411	596	73	69	Kerry	35.8%	51.9%	6.4%	6.0%
MADISON	1,506	805	558	36	107	Edwards	53.5%	37.1%	2.4%	7.1%
MARION	539	233	250	14	42	Kerry	43.2%	46.4%	2.6%	7.8%
MERIWETHER	1,994	841	964	74	115	Kerry	42.2%	48.3%	3.7%	5.8%
MILLER	305	161	118	6	20	Edwards	52.8%	38.7%	2.0%	6.6%
MITCHELL	1,733	694	878	72	89	Kerry	40.0%	50.7%	4.2%	5.1%
MONROE	1,789	890	748	71	80	Edwards	49.7%	41.8%	4.0%	4.5%
MONTGOMERY	520	287	177	23	33	Edwards	55.2%	34.0%	4.4%	6.3%
MORGAN	1,594	754	695	57	88	Edwards	47.3%	43.6%	3.6%	5.5%
MURRAY	1,485	789	567	23	106	Edwards	53.1%	38.2%	1.5%	7.1%
MUSCOGEE	12,547	4,496	6,930	562	559	Kerry	35.8%	55.2%	4.5%	4.5%
NEWTON	5,101	2,243	2,282	316	260	Kerry	44.0%	44.7%	6.2%	5.1%
OCONEE	2,429	1,313	907	70	139	Edwards	54.1%	37.3%	2.9%	5.7%
OGLETHORPE	1,127	546	464	41	76	Edwards	48.4%	41.2%	3.6%	6.7%
PAULDING	4,791	2,334	1,845	318	294	Edwards	48.7%	38.5%	6.6%	6.1%
PEACH	1,759	666	910	105	78	Kerry	37.9%	51.7%	6.0%	4.4%
PICKENS	1,493	840	522	60	71	Edwards	56.3%	35.0%	4.0%	4.8%
PIERCE	617	296	257	15	49	Edwards	48.0%	41.7%	2.4%	7.9%
PIKE	1,116	555	425	59	77	Edwards	49.7%	38.1%	5.3%	6.9%
POLK	3,620	1,997	1,275	113	235	Edwards	55.2%	35.2%	3.1%	6.5%
PULASKI	544	285	224	13	22	Edwards	52.4%	41.2%	2.4%	4.0%
PUTNAM	1,690	781	740	63	106	Edwards	46.2%	43.8%	3.7%	6.3%
QUITMAN	195	64	96	11	24	Kerry	32.8%	49.2%	5.6%	12.3%
RABUN	1,399	858	429	25	87	Edwards	61.3%	30.7%	1.8%	6.2%
RANDOLPH	657	242	335	25	55	Kerry	36.8%	51.0%	3.8%	8.4%
RICHMOND	14,191	4,388	7,686	1,437	680	Kerry	30.9%	54.2%	10.1%	4.8%
ROCKDALE	5,534	2,360	2,514	398	262	Kerry	42.6%	45.4%	7.2%	4.7%
SCHLEY	218	115	84	5	14	Edwards	52.8%	38.5%	2.3%	6.4%
SCREVEN	1,157	481	556	57	63	Kerry	41.6%	48.1%	4.9%	5.4%
SEMINOLE	688	294	318	30	46	Kerry	42.7%	46.2%	4.4%	6.7%
SPALDING	3,573	1,575	1,613	191	194	Kerry	44.1%	45.1%	5.3%	5.4%
STEPHENS	1,912	1,216	550	51	95	Edwards	63.6%	28.8%	2.7%	5.0%
STEWART	479	180	251	14	34	Kerry	37.6%	52.4%	2.9%	7.1%
SUMTER	1,976	897	895	77	107	Edwards	45.4%	45.3%	3.9%	5.4%
TALBOT	750	283	374	39	54	Kerry	37.7%	49.9%	5.2%	7.2%
TALIAFERRO	207	59	109	26	13	Kerry	28.5%	52.7%	12.6%	6.3%
TATTNALL	995	485	391	57	62	Edwards	48.7%	39.3%	5.7%	6.2%
TAYLOR	670	342	254	34	40	Edwards	51.0%	37.9%	5.1%	6.0%
TELFAIR	677	300	296	29	52	Edwards	44.3%	43.7%	4.3%	7.7%
TERRELL	737	283	368	34	52	Kerry	38.4%	49.9%	4.6%	7.1%

GEORGIA DEMOCRATIC PRIMARY

2004

County	Total Vote	Edwards	Kerry	Sharpton	Other	Winner	Percentage of Total Vote			
							Edwards	Kerry	Sharpton	Other
THOMAS	2,351	887	1,166	107	191	Kerry	37.7%	49.6%	4.6%	8.1%
TIFT	1,646	853	642	55	96	Edwards	51.8%	39.0%	3.3%	5.8%
TOOMBS	1,232	677	429	55	71	Edwards	55.0%	34.8%	4.5%	5.8%
TOWNS	927	528	331	17	51	Edwards	57.0%	35.7%	1.8%	5.5%
TREUTLEN	448	198	203	17	30	Kerry	44.2%	45.3%	3.8%	6.7%
TROUP	3,495	1,517	1,647	162	169	Kerry	43.4%	47.1%	4.6%	4.8%
TURNER	492	253	187	23	29	Edwards	51.4%	38.0%	4.7%	5.9%
TWIGGS	963	349	478	82	54	Kerry	36.2%	49.6%	8.5%	5.6%
UNION	2,055	1,245	645	62	103	Edwards	60.6%	31.4%	3.0%	5.0%
UPSON	1,981	931	866	86	98	Edwards	47.0%	43.7%	4.3%	4.9%
WALKER	3,124	1,547	1,270	52	255	Edwards	49.5%	40.7%	1.7%	8.2%
WALTON	3,447	1,719	1,342	179	207	Edwards	49.9%	38.9%	5.2%	6.0%
WARE	1,746	715	789	117	125	Kerry	41.0%	45.2%	6.7%	7.2%
WARREN	581	193	284	59	45	Kerry	33.2%	48.9%	10.2%	7.7%
WASHINGTON	1,941	770	925	105	141	Kerry	39.7%	47.7%	5.4%	7.3%
WAYNE	1,738	906	627	61	144	Edwards	52.1%	36.1%	3.5%	8.3%
WEBSTER	226	98	104	12	12	Kerry	43.4%	46.0%	5.3%	5.3%
WHEELER	296	118	148	13	17	Kerry	39.9%	50.0%	4.4%	5.7%
WHITE	1,979	1,126	640	71	142	Edwards	56.9%	32.3%	3.6%	7.2%
WHITFIELD	3,109	1,604	1,252	79	174	Edwards	51.6%	40.3%	2.5%	5.6%
WILCOX	392	203	150	10	29	Edwards	51.8%	38.3%	2.6%	7.4%
WILKES	1,070	426	522	79	43	Kerry	39.8%	48.8%	7.4%	4.0%
WILKINSON	963	396	491	31	45	Kerry	41.1%	51.0%	3.2%	4.7%
WORTH	1,274	704	456	45	69	Edwards	55.3%	35.8%	3.5%	5.4%
TOTAL	626,813	259,386	293,265	39,129	35,033	Kerry	41.4%	46.8%	6.2%	5.6%

Note: Other vote was 11,322 Howard Dean; 7,701 Dennis J. Kucinich; 5,666 Joseph I. Lieberman; 4,247 Wesley Clark; 3,747 Carol Moseley Braun; 2,350 Richard A. Gephardt.

HAWAII

If it were simply a matter of the candidates' personal preference, Hawaii most likely would be glutted with presidential aspirants canvassing its beaches for the state's late-winter caucuses. But the small size of the delegate harvest and the absence of a presidential primary to attract some media attention has kept Hawaii a distant sideshow in the presidential nominating process.

Long-shot candidates, though, have seen the low-turnout Hawaii caucuses as an appealing venue to make a strong showing on the cheap. The latest to make an effort was Dennis Kucinich, who made two trips to Hawaii in advance of the late February Democratic caucuses in 2004. The effort paid off for the Ohio congressman in his best showing of the primary season. Kucinich drew 31 percent of the 4,073 votes cast, second to John Kerry's 47 percent, and carried the island of Maui. Kucinich's performance earned him eight delegate votes, nearly one-fifth of the 43 that were cast for him at the Democratic national convention in Boston.

Hawaii Republicans sought to make a splash in 1988 by scheduling their precinct caucuses in late January—before even Iowa had spoken. And for much of 1987, Bob Dole looked like the best bet to win the early event. He was the choice of the moderate element dominant within the Hawaii GOP.

But in the month preceding the caucuses, the party was inundated with new registrants, most wanting to vote for evangelist Pat Robertson. The number of card-carrying Republicans swelled from barely 11,000 to more than 18,000. State GOP officials were stunned by the unexpected influx. First, they postponed the caucuses indefinitely. Then, with Robertson denouncing "banana republic" politics, the vote was rescheduled for a week after the original date.

When the caucuses were finally held in early February, an estimated 4,000 to 5,000 Republicans showed up and voted overwhelmingly for Robertson delegates to the June state convention. His candidacy had collapsed by the time the state convention was held, but his supporters pushed through a platform that emphasized the conservative "family values" that he had espoused in his campaign.

Robertson's control of the state GOP, though, proved temporary. Party regulars regained the upper hand in 1992 and the state party issued no platform at all.

For most of the state's history, Hawaii—with its rainbow-hued electorate—has not harbored any affection for ideological activism on either end of the political spectrum. Hawaii Republicans gave President Gerald Ford all but one of their delegates in 1976 and were slow to embrace Ronald Reagan in 1980. Even as opposition to Reagan was crumbling nationally in the spring of 1980, the state party selected a predominantly uncommitted delegation to send to the national convention in Detroit.

Democratic caucus voters in Hawaii have traditionally followed the wishes of the party leadership. Typical was the situation in 1988. The multiracial nature of Hawaii's political landscape seemed tailor-made for Jesse Jackson. But less than a week before the early March caucuses, then-governor John Waihee III endorsed his gubernatorial colleague, Michael Dukakis. A stream of endorsements for Dukakis followed from lesser Democratic elected officials on the islands. And when the caucuses were held, Dukakis won easily with 55 percent of the nearly 5,000 votes cast.

Four years later the result was similar. Waihee threw his support to another gubernatorial colleague, Bill Clinton, who also won a majority of the Democratic caucus vote. In 2000, Hawaii Democrats provided an exclamation point to Al Gore's "Super Tuesday" sweep of Bill Bradley. Gore won 80 percent of the Democratic caucus vote in Hawaii. But with Bradley's candidacy already on the wane, turnout fell below 1,500.

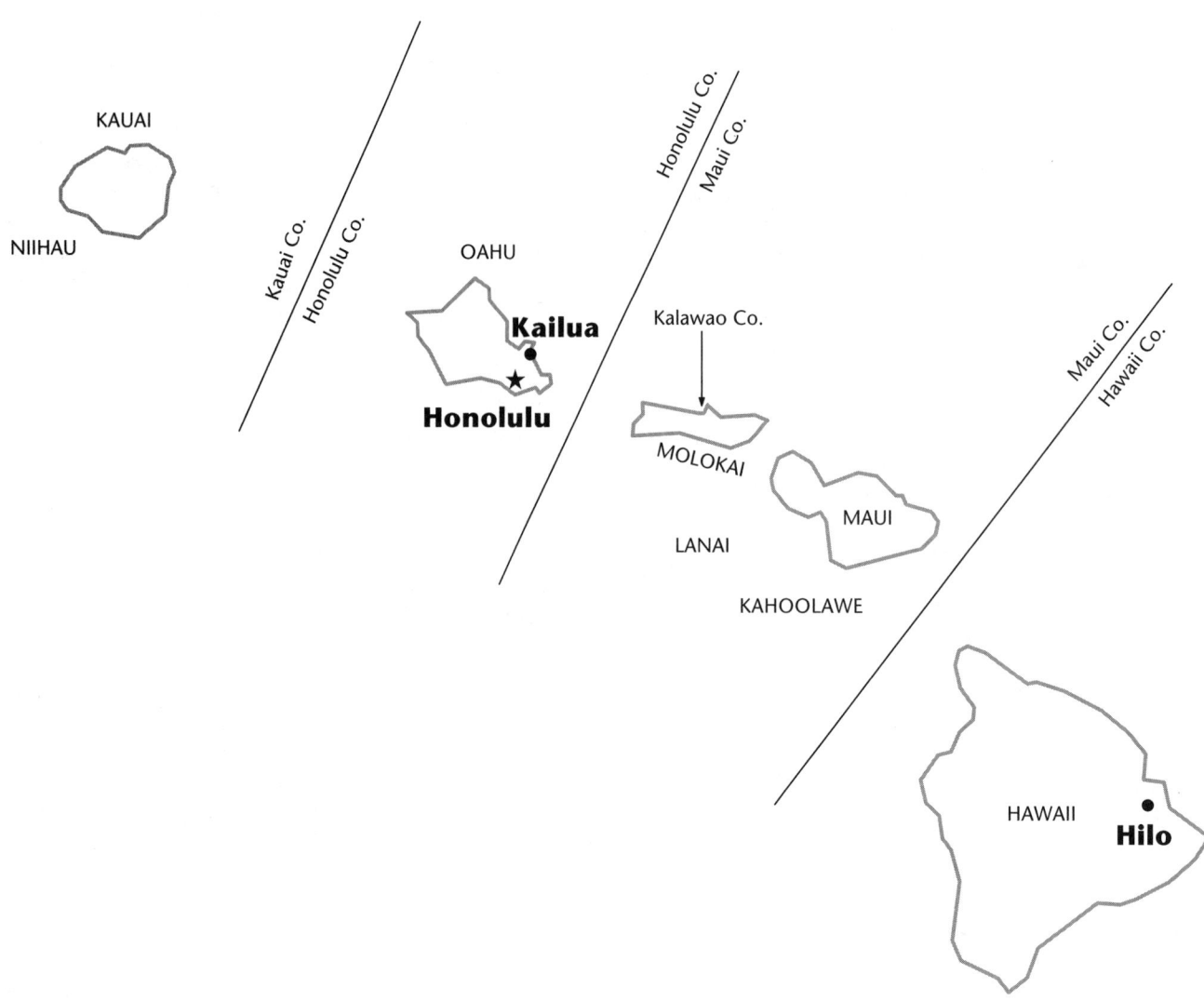

KAUAI

NIIHAU

Kauai Co.

Honolulu Co.

Honolulu Co.

Maui Co.

OAHU

Kailua

Honolulu

Kalawao Co.

MOLOKAI

LANAI

MAUI

KAHOOLAWE

Maui Co.

Hawaii Co.

HAWAII

Hilo

IDAHO

Idaho has held a presidential primary for more than a quarter century, but never has it been competitive. None of the Democratic or Republican contests have been decided by less than 20 percentage points. And only once did an Idaho primary winner draw less than a majority of the vote. That was in 1992 when Democrat Bill Clinton took 49 percent, in the process losing resort-oriented Blaine County (Sun Valley) to a line designated "None of the Names Shown."

The lack of action in the Idaho primary is due largely to the fact that the state votes late in the primary season, well after the field has been winnowed. To play some role in the nominating process, Idaho Democrats in recent years have held both a primary and a caucus. The caucus process that begins in late February or early March has been to select delegates, while Democrats use the May primary as a "beauty contest" to reflect broader popular sentiment.

The low-turnout caucuses tend to be influenced by liberal elements within the Democratic Party. In 1992, for instance, Clinton ran a distant fourth in the caucus vote of roughly 3,000 Democrats. The winner was Sen. Tom Harkin of Iowa, who ran as an unapologetic New Deal liberal.

In 2000, when turnout for the caucuses was roughly half as large as it was in 1992, Bill Bradley took one-third of the state convention delegates elected in the first round of caucus voting—his best showing in any caucus state outside Iowa. In the process, Bradley carried several rural Idaho counties, among them liberal Blaine County.

In 2004, interest in the caucuses spiked, with nearly 5,000 Idaho Democrats turning out to give a majority to the

Recent Idaho Primary Results

Idaho held its first presidential primary in 1976.

Year	DEMOCRATS			REPUBLICANS		
	Turnout	Candidates	%	Turnout	Candidates	%
2004 (May 25)	31,485	JOHN KERRY	82	123,808	GEORGE W. BUSH*	89
		"None"	8		"None"	10
2000 (May 23)	35,688	AL GORE	76	158,446	GEORGE W. BUSH	73
		"None"	16		Alan Keyes	19
		Lyndon LaRouche	8		"None"	7
1996 (May 28)	40,228	BILL CLINTON*	88	118,715	BOB DOLE	62
		"None"	12		Pat Buchanan	22
					"None"	10
					Alan Keyes	5
1992 (May 26)	55,124	BILL CLINTON	49	115,502	GEORGE BUSH*	63
		"None"	29		"None"	23
		Jerry Brown	17		Pat Buchanan	13
1988 (May 24)	51,370	MICHAEL DUKAKIS	73	68,275	GEORGE BUSH	81
		Jesse Jackson	16		"None"	10
					Pat Robertson	9
1984 (May 22)	54,722	GARY HART	58	105,687	RONALD REAGAN*	92
		Walter Mondale	30		"None"	8
		Jesse Jackson	6			
1980 (May 27)	50,482	JIMMY CARTER*	62	134,879	RONALD REAGAN	83
		Edward Kennedy	22		John Anderson	10
		"None"	12			
1976 (May 25)	74,405	FRANK CHURCH	79	89,793	RONALD REAGAN	74
		Jimmy Carter	12		Gerald Ford*	25

Note: All candidates are listed that drew at least 5 percent of their party's primary vote. The names of winning candidates are capitalized. An asterisk (*) indicates an incumbent president.

high-flying front-runner, John Kerry. For decades his wife, Teresa Heinz Kerry, had owned a vacation home in the Sun Valley area.

Idaho Republicans have stuck with the primary as their principal method of delegate selection. The backbone of GOP strength is the farm and ranch country of southeast Idaho, a heavily Mormon area that ranks among the most conservative in the country. In his 1976 primary victory over President Gerald Ford, Ronald Reagan carried a number of counties in the region with more than 80 percent of the vote.

Moderate Republicans are more apt to be found in the Boise area. In the 1980 GOP primary, John Anderson drew nearly one out of every five ballots in Ada County (Boise), even though he had already bolted the party to mount his independent presidential campaign. Reagan, though, still won handily in the Boise area, as he did statewide.

But Idaho voters are far from a rubber stamp. Nearly 40 percent of those who participated in the 1992 and 1996 Republican primaries withheld their votes from the presumptive nominees, George Bush and Bob Dole, respectively. And in 2004, fully 10 percent of Republican primary votes opted for the "None of the Names Shown" line rather than vote for President George W. Bush. Support for "None" reached double digits percentage-wise in more than a dozen counties and surpassed 30 percent in one of them, Latah, which includes the University of Idaho at Moscow.

Boundary

Bonner

Coeur d'Alene
●

Kootenai

Benewah

Shoshone

Moscow ● Latah

Clearwater

Nez Perce

Lewiston ●

Lewis

Idaho

Adams

Valley

Lemhi

Washington

Custer

Clark

Fremont

Payette

Jefferson

Madison

Gem

Boise

Teton

Canyon

Butte

● **Idaho Falls**

★

Boise

Elmore

Camas

Blaine

Bingham

Bonneville

Ada

● **Pocatello**

Gooding

Lincoln

Caribou

Jerome

Minidoka

Power

Bannock

Owyhee

● **Twin Falls**

Cassia

Oneida

Bear Lake

Twin Falls

Franklin

IDAHO DEMOCRATIC PRIMARY

2000

County	Total Vote	Gore	LaRouche	"None"	Winner	Percentage of Total Vote		
						Gore	LaRouche	"None"
ADA	7,720	6,701	300	719	Gore	86.8%	3.9%	9.3%
ADAMS	84	63	11	10	Gore	75.0%	13.1%	11.9%
BANNOCK	4,811	3,413	565	833	Gore	70.9%	11.7%	17.3%
BEAR LAKE	51	43	8	0	Gore	84.3%	15.7%	0.0%
BENEWAH	293	226	57	10	Gore	77.1%	19.5%	3.4%
BINGHAM	611	459	51	101	Gore	75.1%	8.3%	16.5%
BLAINE	1,424	1,030	69	325	Gore	72.3%	4.8%	22.8%
BOISE	130	108	13	9	Gore	83.1%	10.0%	6.9%
BONNER	839	684	53	102	Gore	81.5%	6.3%	12.2%
BONNEVILLE	1,586	1,247	108	231	Gore	78.6%	6.8%	14.6%
BOUNDARY	227	187	20	20	Gore	82.4%	8.8%	8.8%
BUTTE	64	43	13	8	Gore	67.2%	20.3%	12.5%
CAMAS	11	7	4	0	Gore	63.6%	36.4%	0.0%
CANYON	1,990	1,595	146	249	Gore	80.2%	7.3%	12.5%
CARIBOU	111	94	16	1	Gore	84.7%	14.4%	0.9%
CASSIA	214	152	30	32	Gore	71.0%	14.0%	15.0%
CLARK	5	3	2	0	Gore	60.0%	40.0%	0.0%
CLEARWATER	547	283	69	195	Gore	51.7%	12.6%	35.6%
CUSTER	112	68	26	18	Gore	60.7%	23.2%	16.1%
ELMORE	347	305	22	20	Gore	87.9%	6.3%	5.8%
FRANKLIN	106	54	21	31	Gore	50.9%	19.8%	29.2%
FREMONT	207	138	26	43	Gore	66.7%	12.6%	20.8%
GEM	257	202	20	35	Gore	78.6%	7.8%	13.6%
GOODING	212	181	13	18	Gore	85.4%	6.1%	8.5%
IDAHO	411	297	86	28	Gore	72.3%	20.9%	6.8%
JEFFERSON	215	158	28	29	Gore	73.5%	13.0%	13.5%
JEROME	143	124	8	11	Gore	86.7%	5.6%	7.7%
KOOTENAI	2,483	2,169	68	246	Gore	87.4%	2.7%	9.9%
LATAH	1,921	1,418	124	379	Gore	73.8%	6.5%	19.7%
LEMHI	88	73	10	5	Gore	83.0%	11.4%	5.7%
LEWIS	158	114	25	19	Gore	72.2%	15.8%	12.0%
LINCOLN	76	70	6	0	Gore	92.1%	7.9%	0.0%
MADISON	405	263	45	97	Gore	64.9%	11.1%	24.0%
MINIDOKA	220	157	20	43	Gore	71.4%	9.1%	19.5%
NEZ PERCE	2,714	1,631	300	783	Gore	60.1%	11.1%	28.9%
ONEIDA	76	58	7	11	Gore	76.3%	9.2%	14.5%
OWYHEE	106	84	19	3	Gore	79.2%	17.9%	2.8%
PAYETTE	481	318	56	107	Gore	66.1%	11.6%	22.2%
POWER	212	174	19	19	Gore	82.1%	9.0%	9.0%
SHOSHONE	2,337	1,302	234	801	Gore	55.7%	10.0%	34.3%
TETON	307	226	70	11	Gore	73.6%	22.8%	3.6%
TWIN FALLS	781	669	52	60	Gore	85.7%	6.7%	7.7%
VALLEY	148	128	8	12	Gore	86.5%	5.4%	8.1%
WASHINGTON	447	306	93	48	Gore	68.5%	20.8%	10.7%
TOTAL	35,688	27,025	2,941	5,722	Gore	75.7%	8.2%	16.0%

IDAHO REPUBLICAN PRIMARY

2000

County	Total Vote	G.W. Bush	Keyes	"None"	Winner	Percentage of Total Vote		
						G.W. Bush	Keyes	"None"
ADA	37,194	26,127	7,572	3,495	G.W. Bush	70.2%	20.4%	9.4%
ADAMS	951	752	146	53	G.W. Bush	79.1%	15.4%	5.6%
BANNOCK	4,771	3,741	883	147	G.W. Bush	78.4%	18.5%	3.1%
BEAR LAKE	1,791	1,486	233	72	G.W. Bush	83.0%	13.0%	4.0%
BENEWAH	1,028	680	342	6	G.W. Bush	66.1%	33.3%	0.6%
BINGHAM	6,609	4,957	1,018	634	G.W. Bush	75.0%	15.4%	9.6%
BLAINE	523	439	66	18	G.W. Bush	83.9%	12.6%	3.4%
BOISE	1,663	1,238	303	122	G.W. Bush	74.4%	18.2%	7.3%
BONNER	5,424	3,594	1,142	688	G.W. Bush	66.3%	21.1%	12.7%
BONNEVILLE	10,334	7,214	2,333	787	G.W. Bush	69.8%	22.6%	7.6%
BOUNDARY	1,547	1,072	397	78	G.W. Bush	69.3%	25.7%	5.0%
BUTTE	593	439	117	37	G.W. Bush	74.0%	19.7%	6.2%
CAMAS	298	209	52	37	G.W. Bush	70.1%	17.4%	12.4%
CANYON	15,652	11,756	2,868	1,028	G.W. Bush	75.1%	18.3%	6.6%
CARIBOU	1,097	934	156	7	G.W. Bush	85.1%	14.2%	0.6%
CASSIA	3,871	3,229	416	226	G.W. Bush	83.4%	10.7%	5.8%
CLARK	262	220	32	10	G.W. Bush	84.0%	12.2%	3.8%
CLEARWATER	951	741	120	90	G.W. Bush	77.9%	12.6%	9.5%
CUSTER	1,374	1,115	192	67	G.W. Bush	81.1%	14.0%	4.9%
ELMORE	2,180	1,666	306	208	G.W. Bush	76.4%	14.0%	9.5%
FRANKLIN	1,886	1,540	216	130	G.W. Bush	81.7%	11.5%	6.9%
FREMONT	2,441	1,866	428	147	G.W. Bush	76.4%	17.5%	6.0%
GEM	2,977	2,268	437	272	G.W. Bush	76.2%	14.7%	9.1%
GOODING	1,809	1,345	294	170	G.W. Bush	74.4%	16.3%	9.4%
IDAHO	3,575	2,794	675	106	G.W. Bush	78.2%	18.9%	3.0%
JEFFERSON	2,697	2,071	534	92	G.W. Bush	76.8%	19.8%	3.4%
JEROME	2,250	1,733	371	146	G.W. Bush	77.0%	16.5%	6.5%
KOOTENAI	13,217	7,956	4,133	1,128	G.W. Bush	60.2%	31.3%	8.5%
LATAH	2,476	1,846	386	244	G.W. Bush	74.6%	15.6%	9.9%
LEMHI	1,879	1,496	241	142	G.W. Bush	79.6%	12.8%	7.6%
LEWIS	646	543	83	20	G.W. Bush	84.1%	12.8%	3.1%
LINCOLN	681	562	119	0	G.W. Bush	82.5%	17.5%	0.0%
MADISON	3,711	2,994	534	183	G.W. Bush	80.7%	14.4%	4.9%
MINIDOKA	1,920	1,492	302	126	G.W. Bush	77.7%	15.7%	6.6%
NEZ PERCE	2,610	2,226	231	153	G.W. Bush	85.3%	8.9%	5.9%
ONEIDA	989	775	142	72	G.W. Bush	78.4%	14.4%	7.3%
OWYHEE	1,532	1,321	203	8	G.W. Bush	86.2%	13.3%	0.5%
PAYETTE	2,260	1,727	342	191	G.W. Bush	76.4%	15.1%	8.5%
POWER	560	476	70	14	G.W. Bush	85.0%	12.5%	2.5%
SHOSHONE	586	403	151	32	G.W. Bush	68.8%	25.8%	5.5%
TETON	642	499	110	33	G.W. Bush	77.7%	17.1%	5.1%
TWIN FALLS	5,526	4,181	1,044	301	G.W. Bush	75.7%	18.9%	5.4%
VALLEY	1,930	1,445	250	235	G.W. Bush	74.9%	13.0%	12.2%
WASHINGTON	1,533	1,217	273	43	G.W. Bush	79.4%	17.8%	2.8%
TOTAL	158,446	116,385	30,263	11,798	G.W. Bush	73.5%	19.1%	7.4%

IDAHO DEMOCRATIC PRIMARY

2004

County	Total Vote	Kerry	Kucinich	"None"	Other	Winner	Percentage of Total Vote Kerry	Kucinich	"None"	Other
ADA	7,510	6,359	475	415	261	Kerry	84.7%	6.3%	5.5%	3.5%
ADAMS	72	64	5	0	3	Kerry	88.9%	6.9%	0.0%	4.2%
BANNOCK	2,623	2,255	105	137	126	Kerry	86.0%	4.0%	5.2%	4.8%
BEAR LAKE	67	62	1	1	3	Kerry	92.5%	1.5%	1.5%	4.5%
BENEWAH	544	392	28	67	57	Kerry	72.1%	5.1%	12.3%	10.5%
BINGHAM	479	376	22	53	28	Kerry	78.5%	4.6%	11.1%	5.8%
BLAINE	2,063	1,771	80	140	72	Kerry	85.8%	3.9%	6.8%	3.5%
BOISE	115	98	6	1	10	Kerry	85.2%	5.2%	0.9%	8.7%
BONNER	1,818	1,412	152	157	97	Kerry	77.7%	8.4%	8.6%	5.3%
BONNEVILLE	893	711	33	87	62	Kerry	79.6%	3.7%	9.7%	6.9%
BOUNDARY	188	163	21	0	4	Kerry	86.7%	11.2%	0.0%	2.1%
BUTTE	66	52	4	2	8	Kerry	78.8%	6.1%	3.0%	12.1%
CAMAS	51	24	1	7	19	Kerry	47.1%	2.0%	13.7%	37.3%
CANYON	1,578	1,308	52	137	81	Kerry	82.9%	3.3%	8.7%	5.1%
CARIBOU	113	97	4	0	12	Kerry	85.8%	3.5%	0.0%	10.6%
CASSIA	163	123	11	14	15	Kerry	75.5%	6.7%	8.6%	9.2%
CLARK	10	6	0	3	1	Kerry	60.0%	0.0%	30.0%	10.0%
CLEARWATER	581	418	22	103	38	Kerry	71.9%	3.8%	17.7%	6.5%
CUSTER	104	89	7	1	7	Kerry	85.6%	6.7%	1.0%	6.7%
ELMORE	304	260	14	14	16	Kerry	85.5%	4.6%	4.6%	5.3%
FRANKLIN	60	39	2	12	7	Kerry	65.0%	3.3%	20.0%	11.7%
FREMONT	89	73	4	6	6	Kerry	82.0%	4.5%	6.7%	6.7%
GEM	249	212	12	12	13	Kerry	85.1%	4.8%	4.8%	5.2%
GOODING	208	185	5	12	6	Kerry	88.9%	2.4%	5.8%	2.9%
IDAHO	626	529	32	11	54	Kerry	84.5%	5.1%	1.8%	8.6%
JEFFERSON	138	109	5	9	15	Kerry	79.0%	3.6%	6.5%	10.9%
JEROME	186	169	9	1	7	Kerry	90.9%	4.8%	0.5%	3.8%
KOOTENAI	2,326	2,107	77	82	60	Kerry	90.6%	3.3%	3.5%	2.6%
LATAH	1,185	979	121	44	41	Kerry	82.6%	10.2%	3.7%	3.5%
LEMHI	98	74	10	5	9	Kerry	75.5%	10.2%	5.1%	9.2%
LEWIS	182	159	6	8	9	Kerry	87.4%	3.3%	4.4%	4.9%
LINCOLN	102	94	3	0	5	Kerry	92.2%	2.9%	0.0%	4.9%
MADISON	71	55	6	2	8	Kerry	77.5%	8.5%	2.8%	11.3%
MINIDOKA	224	182	13	18	11	Kerry	81.3%	5.8%	8.0%	4.9%
NEZ PERCE	2,361	1,936	64	265	96	Kerry	82.0%	2.7%	11.2%	4.1%
ONEIDA	48	44	2	0	2	Kerry	91.7%	4.2%	0.0%	4.2%
OWYHEE	102	92	4	2	4	Kerry	90.2%	3.9%	2.0%	3.9%
PAYETTE	287	241	6	29	11	Kerry	84.0%	2.1%	10.1%	3.8%
POWER	158	130	4	12	12	Kerry	82.3%	2.5%	7.6%	7.6%
SHOSHONE	2,160	1,358	84	573	145	Kerry	62.9%	3.9%	26.5%	6.7%
TETON	244	214	12	0	18	Kerry	87.7%	4.9%	0.0%	7.4%
TWIN FALLS	688	590	28	28	42	Kerry	85.8%	4.1%	4.1%	6.1%
VALLEY	157	137	12	5	3	Kerry	87.3%	7.6%	3.2%	1.9%
WASHINGTON	194	173	4	4	13	Kerry	89.2%	2.1%	2.1%	6.7%
TOTAL	31,485	25,921	1,568	2,479	1,517	Kerry	82.3%	5.0%	7.9%	4.8%

Note: Other vote was 927 Al Sharpton; 590 Lyndon H. LaRouche Jr.

IDAHO REPUBLICAN PRIMARY

2004

County	Total Vote	G.W. Bush	"None"	Other	Winner	Percentage of Total Vote		
						G.W. Bush	"None"	Other
ADA	15,946	13,679	2,267	0	G.W. Bush	85.8%	14.2%	0.0%
ADAMS	535	516	19	0	G.W. Bush	96.4%	3.6%	0.0%
BANNOCK	3,183	3,008	175	0	G.W. Bush	94.5%	5.5%	0.0%
BEAR LAKE	1,906	1,862	44	0	G.W. Bush	97.7%	2.3%	0.0%
BENEWAH	721	695	26	0	G.W. Bush	96.4%	3.6%	0.0%
BINGHAM	5,868	5,260	608	0	G.W. Bush	89.6%	10.4%	0.0%
BLAINE	1,025	900	125	0	G.W. Bush	87.8%	12.2%	0.0%
BOISE	639	624	14	1	G.W. Bush	97.7%	2.2%	0.2%
BONNER	3,065	2,658	407	0	G.W. Bush	86.7%	13.3%	0.0%
BONNEVILLE	6,136	5,614	522	0	G.W. Bush	91.5%	8.5%	0.0%
BOUNDARY	1,700	1,636	63	1	G.W. Bush	96.2%	3.7%	0.1%
BUTTE	241	230	11	0	G.W. Bush	95.4%	4.6%	0.0%
CAMAS	163	158	5	0	G.W. Bush	96.9%	3.1%	0.0%
CANYON	14,599	12,815	1,784	0	G.W. Bush	87.8%	12.2%	0.0%
CARIBOU	709	707	2	0	G.W. Bush	99.7%	0.3%	0.0%
CASSIA	2,663	2,565	98	0	G.W. Bush	96.3%	3.7%	0.0%
CLARK	190	176	14	0	G.W. Bush	92.6%	7.4%	0.0%
CLEARWATER	782	721	61	0	G.W. Bush	92.2%	7.8%	0.0%
CUSTER	821	811	10	0	G.W. Bush	98.8%	1.2%	0.0%
ELMORE	1,998	1,721	277	0	G.W. Bush	86.1%	13.9%	0.0%
FRANKLIN	3,381	3,179	202	0	G.W. Bush	94.0%	6.0%	0.0%
FREMONT	3,021	2,797	224	0	G.W. Bush	92.6%	7.4%	0.0%
GEM	2,790	2,421	369	0	G.W. Bush	86.8%	13.2%	0.0%
GOODING	1,534	1,352	182	0	G.W. Bush	88.1%	11.9%	0.0%
IDAHO	3,481	3,394	87	0	G.W. Bush	97.5%	2.5%	0.0%
JEFFERSON	2,138	2,044	91	3	G.W. Bush	95.6%	4.3%	0.1%
JEROME	2,447	2,204	243	0	G.W. Bush	90.1%	9.9%	0.0%
KOOTENAI	10,206	8,715	1,491	0	G.W. Bush	85.4%	14.6%	0.0%
LATAH	3,467	2,399	1,068	0	G.W. Bush	69.2%	30.8%	0.0%
LEMHI	1,275	1,169	106	0	G.W. Bush	91.7%	8.3%	0.0%
LEWIS	610	574	36	0	G.W. Bush	94.1%	5.9%	0.0%
LINCOLN	737	715	22	0	G.W. Bush	97.0%	3.0%	0.0%
MADISON	4,775	4,491	284	0	G.W. Bush	94.1%	5.9%	0.0%
MINIDOKA	1,951	1,774	177	0	G.W. Bush	90.9%	9.1%	0.0%
NEZ PERCE	2,673	2,419	254	0	G.W. Bush	90.5%	9.5%	0.0%
ONEIDA	692	649	41	2	G.W. Bush	93.8%	5.9%	0.3%
OWYHEE	1,267	1,230	37	0	G.W. Bush	97.1%	2.9%	0.0%
PAYETTE	2,947	2,602	345	0	G.W. Bush	88.3%	11.7%	0.0%
POWER	944	836	101	7	G.W. Bush	88.6%	10.7%	0.7%
SHOSHONE	489	458	31	0	G.W. Bush	93.7%	6.3%	0.0%
TETON	806	797	9	0	G.W. Bush	98.9%	1.1%	0.0%
TWIN FALLS	6,351	5,697	654	0	G.W. Bush	89.7%	10.3%	0.0%
VALLEY	1,721	1,348	372	1	G.W. Bush	78.3%	21.6%	0.1%
WASHINGTON	1,215	1,180	35	0	G.W. Bush	97.1%	2.9%	0.0%
TOTAL	123,808	110,800	12,993	15	G.W. Bush	89.5%	10.5%	0.0%

Note: Other vote was 15 Nancy Warrick (write-in).

ILLINOIS

For years, the Illinois primary stood alone as a gateway to the later primaries in the industrial Frost Belt. But no more. Once near the beginning of the presidential nominating process, Illinois' mid-March vote is now closer to the end. And in recent years, it has actually voted after the conclusion of the competitive stage of the primary season.

Yet Illinois still offers a rich harvest of delegates plus the reputation it has earned as a harbinger of things to come. Every Republican presidential nominee since 1976 and seven of the last eight Democratic nominees have first won the Illinois preference primary.

When candidates come to Illinois, there is no guesswork as to where they go. Democrats head to Chicago—nearly 40 percent black, more than 25 percent Hispanic (in 2000)—and the source of more than one-third of the party's statewide primary vote.

Republicans go to the suburban "collar" counties that surround Chicago on the north, south, and west, before campaigning in the small cities, towns, and farm country downstate.

The collar counties, paced by Du Page and Lake, are among the most affluent in the country. Loaded with white-collar professionals, they tend to prefer more moderate Republican

Recent Illinois Primary Results

Illinois held its first presidential primary in 1912.

Year	DEMOCRATS			REPUBLICANS		
	Turnout	Candidates	%	Turnout	Candidates	%
2004 (March 16)	1,217,515	JOHN KERRY	72	583,575	GEORGE W. BUSH*	100
		John Edwards	11			
2000 (March 21)	809,667	AL GORE	84	736,921	GEORGE W. BUSH	67
		Bill Bradley	14		John McCain	22
					Alan Keyes	9
1996 (March 19)	800,676	BILL CLINTON*	96	818,364	BOB DOLE	65
					Pat Buchanan	23
1992 (March 17)	1,504,130	BILL CLINTON	52	831,140	GEORGE BUSH*	76
		Paul Tsongas	26		Pat Buchanan	22
		Jerry Brown	15			
1988 (March 15)	1,500,930	PAUL SIMON	42	858,637	GEORGE BUSH	55
		Jesse Jackson	32		Bob Dole	36
		Michael Dukakis	16		Pat Robertson	7
		Al Gore	5			
1984 (March 20)	1,659,425	WALTER MONDALE	40	595,078	RONALD REAGAN*	100
		Gary Hart	35			
		Jesse Jackson	21			
1980 (March 18)	1,201,067	JIMMY CARTER*	65	1,130,081	RONALD REAGAN	48
		Edward Kennedy	30		John Anderson	37
					George Bush	11
1976 (March 16)	1,311,914	JIMMY CARTER	48	775,893	GERALD FORD*	59
		George Wallace	28		Ronald Reagan	40
		Sargent Shriver	16			
		Fred Harris	8			
1972 (March 21)	1,225,144	EDMUND MUSKIE	63	33,569	RICHARD NIXON* #	97
		Eugene McCarthy	36			
1968 (June 11)	12,038	EUGENE McCARTHY#	39	22,403	RICHARD NIXON#	78
		Edward Kennedy#	34		Nelson Rockefeller#	10
		Hubert Humphrey#	17		Ronald Reagan#	7

Note: All candidates are listed that drew at least 5 percent of their party's primary vote. The names of winning candidates are capitalized. An asterisk (*) indicates an incumbent president. A pound sign (#) indicates a write-in candidate.

candidates than do GOP voters in rural Illinois. In 1980, native-son John Anderson won Cook (which includes Chicago) and Lake counties and ran virtually even with Ronald Reagan in Du Page. In 2000, John McCain's aborted presidential campaign drew 25 to 30 percent of the Republican primary vote in many of the "collar" counties, making the Chicago suburbs his prime Illinois beachhead.

Downstate, there is a more conservative brand of Republicanism that Reagan knew intimately. He was born in Tampico in the northwest part of the state and grew up in nearby Dixon.

Reagan's Illinois roots were not much help in his 1976 challenge to President Gerald Ford, as Ford easily swept the state. But in 1980, downstate Republicans found Reagan preferable to Anderson, which pushed the former California governor to a comfortable victory statewide and Anderson toward an independent presidential bid.

In 1980, Illinois was still near the beginning of the primary calendar. Not so in 1988. Then, the Republican presidential contest essentially ended in Illinois. Bob Dole had considered dropping out of the race after winning zero states on Super Tuesday. But he chose instead to plunge on into Illinois the next week, hoping that support from farm areas would revive his candidacy and raise fresh doubts about George Bush.

It was not to be. Dole carried a few rural counties but did not come close to the breakthrough he needed in the mother lode: Chicago's Republican suburbs.

Meanwhile, Alan Keyes scored no breakthroughs at all in Illinois in his two presidential runs, taking 4 percent and 9 percent of the Republican primary vote in 1996 and 2000, respectively. Yet that did not deter Illinois GOP officials in 2004 from picking Keyes, a longtime Maryland native, as their stand-in Senate candidate after the primary winner stepped down. Keyes' socially conservative candidacy, however, was a disaster, as he lost to Democrat Barack Obama by a margin of more than 2 million votes.

The Illinois Democratic primary for president has rarely produced much drama. For years, Democratic presidential politics in Illinois was neat and tidy. Chicago Mayor Richard J. Daley controlled the bulk of the delegation and took it to the national convention uncommitted. Since Daley's death in 1976, the party's Democratic nominating process within the state has often been less orderly. But more than once the Democratic primary has provided a big win for the early front-runner at a critical point in the process.

President Jimmy Carter's 1980 demolition of Edward Kennedy (the margin was more than 2 to 1) essentially removed Kennedy as a realistic threat to Carter's renomination. In 1984, Walter Mondale's 5 percentage point victory over Gary Hart brought Mondale back from the verge of elimination and marked Hart's last chance to land a knockout blow. In 1992, Bill Clinton so thoroughly dominated the mid-March primaries in Illinois and Michigan that his major rival, Paul Tsongas, quit the race shortly thereafter.

Presidential primaries since then have been spectacularly one-sided. But turnout for the Democratic contest in 2004 still surpassed 1.2 million, the third-highest number of votes cast in a Democratic presidential primary that year after California and Ohio. Yet it was not the already decided presidential contest that drew voters to the polls but spirited races for other offices on the Illinois ballot, including the open Senate seat that was ultimately won by Obama.

ILLINOIS DEMOCRATIC PRIMARY

2000

County	Total Vote	Bradley	Gore	LaRouche	Winner	Percentage of Total Vote		
						Bradley	Gore	LaRouche
ADAMS	1,833	279	1,536	18	Gore	15.2%	83.8%	1.0%
ALEXANDER	1,934	315	1,550	69	Gore	16.3%	80.1%	3.6%
BOND	921	161	748	12	Gore	17.5%	81.2%	1.3%
BOONE	809	99	698	12	Gore	12.2%	86.3%	1.5%
BROWN	376	67	306	3	Gore	17.8%	81.4%	0.8%
BUREAU	2,474	411	2,031	32	Gore	16.6%	82.1%	1.3%
CALHOUN	737	117	608	12	Gore	15.9%	82.5%	1.6%
CARROLL	478	78	395	5	Gore	16.3%	82.6%	1.0%
CASS	923	114	799	10	Gore	12.4%	86.6%	1.1%
CHAMPAIGN	11,171	2,142	8,929	100	Gore	19.2%	79.9%	0.9%
CHRISTIAN	4,154	767	3,298	89	Gore	18.5%	79.4%	2.1%
CLARK	554	70	477	7	Gore	12.6%	86.1%	1.3%
CLAY	803	111	675	17	Gore	13.8%	84.1%	2.1%
CLINTON	936	113	812	11	Gore	12.1%	86.8%	1.2%
COLES	1,777	236	1,522	19	Gore	13.3%	85.6%	1.1%
COOK	494,319	65,634	421,606	7,079	Gore	13.3%	85.3%	1.4%
CRAWFORD	813	107	691	15	Gore	13.2%	85.0%	1.8%
CUMBERLAND	864	151	697	16	Gore	17.5%	80.7%	1.9%
DE KALB	2,424	377	2,029	18	Gore	15.6%	83.7%	0.7%
DE WITT	642	77	557	8	Gore	12.0%	86.8%	1.2%
DOUGLAS	1,473	226	1,234	13	Gore	15.3%	83.8%	0.9%
DU PAGE	26,437	4,198	21,998	241	Gore	15.9%	83.2%	0.9%
EDGAR	773	109	647	17	Gore	14.1%	83.7%	2.2%
EDWARDS	247	41	202	4	Gore	16.6%	81.8%	1.6%
EFFINGHAM	2,563	624	1,881	58	Gore	24.3%	73.4%	2.3%
FAYETTE	1,763	255	1,466	42	Gore	14.5%	83.2%	2.4%
FORD	380	53	323	4	Gore	13.9%	85.0%	1.1%
FRANKLIN	8,916	1,881	6,866	169	Gore	21.1%	77.0%	1.9%
FULTON	5,099	844	4,168	87	Gore	16.6%	81.7%	1.7%
GALLATIN	2,121	462	1,593	66	Gore	21.8%	75.1%	3.1%
GREENE	668	95	559	14	Gore	14.2%	83.7%	2.1%
GRUNDY	1,413	210	1,181	22	Gore	14.9%	83.6%	1.6%
HAMILTON	1,327	265	1,037	25	Gore	20.0%	78.1%	1.9%
HANCOCK	805	139	658	8	Gore	17.3%	81.7%	1.0%
HARDIN	832	128	680	24	Gore	15.4%	81.7%	2.9%
HENDERSON	389	53	333	3	Gore	13.6%	85.6%	0.8%
HENRY	2,137	283	1,825	29	Gore	13.2%	85.4%	1.4%
IROQUOIS	775	118	643	14	Gore	15.2%	83.0%	1.8%
JACKSON	2,329	436	1,862	31	Gore	18.7%	79.9%	1.3%
JASPER	572	102	464	6	Gore	17.8%	81.1%	1.0%
JEFFERSON	2,217	412	1,753	52	Gore	18.6%	79.1%	2.3%
JERSEY	1,098	181	902	15	Gore	16.5%	82.1%	1.4%
JO DAVIESS	683	117	555	11	Gore	17.1%	81.3%	1.6%
JOHNSON	735	106	619	10	Gore	14.4%	84.2%	1.4%
KANE	8,894	1,227	7,564	103	Gore	13.8%	85.0%	1.2%

ILLINOIS DEMOCRATIC PRIMARY

2000

County	Total Vote	Bradley	Gore	LaRouche	Winner	Percentage of Total Vote		
						Bradley	Gore	LaRouche
KANKAKEE	3,265	409	2,813	43	Gore	12.5%	86.2%	1.3%
KENDALL	918	93	813	12	Gore	10.1%	88.6%	1.3%
KNOX	1,502	209	1,271	22	Gore	13.9%	84.6%	1.5%
LAKE	16,847	2,432	14,248	167	Gore	14.4%	84.6%	1.0%
LA SALLE	7,014	1,184	5,755	75	Gore	16.9%	82.1%	1.1%
LAWRENCE	1,234	178	1,038	18	Gore	14.4%	84.1%	1.5%
LEE	1,748	285	1,440	23	Gore	16.3%	82.4%	1.3%
LIVINGSTON	850	108	724	18	Gore	12.7%	85.2%	2.1%
LOGAN	650	78	564	8	Gore	12.0%	86.8%	1.2%
MCDONOUGH	1,169	170	989	10	Gore	14.5%	84.6%	0.9%
MCHENRY	6,127	906	5,173	48	Gore	14.8%	84.4%	0.8%
MCLEAN	6,082	846	5,204	32	Gore	13.9%	85.6%	0.5%
MACON	5,726	608	5,064	54	Gore	10.6%	88.4%	0.9%
MACOUPIN	4,084	657	3,363	64	Gore	16.1%	82.3%	1.6%
MADISON	20,332	4,198	15,716	418	Gore	20.6%	77.3%	2.1%
MARION	2,059	285	1,751	23	Gore	13.8%	85.0%	1.1%
MARSHALL	423	55	361	7	Gore	13.0%	85.3%	1.7%
MASON	772	108	654	10	Gore	14.0%	84.7%	1.3%
MASSAC	1,554	220	1,304	30	Gore	14.2%	83.9%	1.9%
MENARD	419	45	372	2	Gore	10.7%	88.8%	0.5%
MERCER	1,594	281	1,286	27	Gore	17.6%	80.7%	1.7%
MONROE	486	94	387	5	Gore	19.3%	79.6%	1.0%
MONTGOMERY	3,929	728	3,126	75	Gore	18.5%	79.6%	1.9%
MORGAN	834	90	737	7	Gore	10.8%	88.4%	0.8%
MOULTRIE	780	87	685	8	Gore	11.2%	87.8%	1.0%
OGLE	1,916	262	1,630	24	Gore	13.7%	85.1%	1.3%
PEORIA	8,766	1,133	7,554	79	Gore	12.9%	86.2%	0.9%
PERRY	1,415	206	1,192	17	Gore	14.6%	84.2%	1.2%
PIATT	836	112	711	13	Gore	13.4%	85.0%	1.6%
PIKE	2,002	522	1,425	55	Gore	26.1%	71.2%	2.7%
POPE	572	116	441	15	Gore	20.3%	77.1%	2.6%
PULASKI	455	57	387	11	Gore	12.5%	85.1%	2.4%
PUTNAM	1,457	297	1,117	43	Gore	20.4%	76.7%	3.0%
RANDOLPH	3,188	637	2,487	64	Gore	20.0%	78.0%	2.0%
RICHLAND	526	104	417	5	Gore	19.8%	79.3%	1.0%
ROCK ISLAND	11,078	1,757	9,186	135	Gore	15.9%	82.9%	1.2%
ST. CLAIR	16,734	1,876	14,655	203	Gore	11.2%	87.6%	1.2%
SALINE	3,359	607	2,697	55	Gore	18.1%	80.3%	1.6%
SANGAMON	6,708	735	5,918	55	Gore	11.0%	88.2%	0.8%
SCHUYLER	301	36	259	6	Gore	12.0%	86.0%	2.0%
SCOTT	189	25	161	3	Gore	13.2%	85.2%	1.6%
SHELBY	2,273	364	1,869	40	Gore	16.0%	82.2%	1.8%
STARK	179	22	153	4	Gore	12.3%	85.5%	2.2%
STEPHENSON	1,389	210	1,163	16	Gore	15.1%	83.7%	1.2%
TAZEWELL	5,336	677	4,596	63	Gore	12.7%	86.1%	1.2%

ILLINOIS DEMOCRATIC PRIMARY

2000

County	Total Vote	Bradley	Gore	LaRouche	Winner	Percentage of Total Vote		
						Bradley	Gore	LaRouche
UNION	3,846	801	2,943	102	Gore	20.8%	76.5%	2.7%
VERMILION	5,640	780	4,794	66	Gore	13.8%	85.0%	1.2%
WABASH	627	124	493	10	Gore	19.8%	78.6%	1.6%
WARREN	351	48	301	2	Gore	13.7%	85.8%	0.6%
WASHINGTON	433	56	372	5	Gore	12.9%	85.9%	1.2%
WAYNE	517	83	421	13	Gore	16.1%	81.4%	2.5%
WHITE	1,832	427	1,358	47	Gore	23.3%	74.1%	2.6%
WHITESIDE	1,894	278	1,602	14	Gore	14.7%	84.6%	0.7%
WILL	16,885	2,257	14,446	182	Gore	13.4%	85.6%	1.1%
WILLIAMSON	6,245	1,264	4,840	141	Gore	20.2%	77.5%	2.3%
WINNEBAGO	7,901	983	6,827	91	Gore	12.4%	86.4%	1.2%
WOODFORD	831	119	702	10	Gore	14.3%	84.5%	1.2%
TOTAL	809,667	115,320	682,932	11,415	Gore	14.2%	84.3%	1.4%

ILLINOIS REPUBLICAN PRIMARY

2000

County	Total Vote	G.W. Bush	Keyes	McCain	Other	Winner	Percentage of Total Vote			
							G.W. Bush	Keyes	McCain	Other
ADAMS	4,430	3,431	380	545	74	G.W. Bush	77.4%	8.6%	12.3%	1.7%
ALEXANDER	229	194	9	18	8	G.W. Bush	84.7%	3.9%	7.9%	3.5%
BOND	1,566	1,214	115	197	40	G.W. Bush	77.5%	7.3%	12.6%	2.6%
BOONE	4,207	2,755	405	962	85	G.W. Bush	65.5%	9.6%	22.9%	2.0%
BROWN	676	553	33	80	10	G.W. Bush	81.8%	4.9%	11.8%	1.5%
BUREAU	3,478	2,523	235	596	124	G.W. Bush	72.5%	6.8%	17.1%	3.6%
CALHOUN	322	254	15	50	3	G.W. Bush	78.9%	4.7%	15.5%	0.9%
CARROLL	2,558	1,742	170	542	104	G.W. Bush	68.1%	6.6%	21.2%	4.1%
CASS	958	775	55	120	8	G.W. Bush	80.9%	5.7%	12.5%	0.8%
CHAMPAIGN	20,444	13,362	2,934	3,760	388	G.W. Bush	65.4%	14.4%	18.4%	1.9%
CHRISTIAN	1,416	1,109	102	188	17	G.W. Bush	78.3%	7.2%	13.3%	1.2%
CLARK	966	755	64	131	16	G.W. Bush	78.2%	6.6%	13.6%	1.7%
CLAY	1,064	824	86	134	20	G.W. Bush	77.4%	8.1%	12.6%	1.9%
CLINTON	2,468	1,897	136	392	43	G.W. Bush	76.9%	5.5%	15.9%	1.7%
COLES	2,960	2,071	293	528	68	G.W. Bush	70.0%	9.9%	17.8%	2.3%
COOK	140,279	92,423	12,659	32,246	2,951	G.W. Bush	65.9%	9.0%	23.0%	2.1%
CRAWFORD	1,454	1,114	85	234	21	G.W. Bush	76.6%	5.8%	16.1%	1.4%
CUMBERLAND	1,032	777	70	162	23	G.W. Bush	75.3%	6.8%	15.7%	2.2%
DE KALB	6,974	4,518	635	1,668	153	G.W. Bush	64.8%	9.1%	23.9%	2.2%
DE WITT	1,936	1,170	209	502	55	G.W. Bush	60.4%	10.8%	25.9%	2.8%

ILLINOIS REPUBLICAN PRIMARY

2000

County	Total Vote	G.W. Bush	Keyes	McCain	Other	Winner	Percentage of Total Vote			
							G.W. Bush	Keyes	McCain	Other
DOUGLAS	2,885	2,189	229	431	36	G.W. Bush	75.9%	7.9%	14.9%	1.2%
DU PAGE	92,737	58,529	9,022	23,503	1,683	G.W. Bush	63.1%	9.7%	25.3%	1.8%
EDGAR	2,030	1,543	122	315	50	G.W. Bush	76.0%	6.0%	15.5%	2.5%
EDWARDS	1,271	962	65	206	38	G.W. Bush	75.7%	5.1%	16.2%	3.0%
EFFINGHAM	2,918	2,193	257	384	84	G.W. Bush	75.2%	8.8%	13.2%	2.9%
FAYETTE	1,995	1,614	109	248	24	G.W. Bush	80.9%	5.5%	12.4%	1.2%
FORD	3,187	2,237	283	594	73	G.W. Bush	70.2%	8.9%	18.6%	2.3%
FRANKLIN	1,795	1,442	120	204	29	G.W. Bush	80.3%	6.7%	11.4%	1.6%
FULTON	2,142	1,637	123	337	45	G.W. Bush	76.4%	5.7%	15.7%	2.1%
GALLATIN	330	273	21	29	7	G.W. Bush	82.7%	6.4%	8.8%	2.1%
GREENE	777	628	31	108	10	G.W. Bush	80.8%	4.0%	13.9%	1.3%
GRUNDY	2,841	2,042	227	512	60	G.W. Bush	71.9%	8.0%	18.0%	2.1%
HAMILTON	699	557	55	75	12	G.W. Bush	79.7%	7.9%	10.7%	1.7%
HANCOCK	1,906	1,326	199	337	44	G.W. Bush	69.6%	10.4%	17.7%	2.3%
HARDIN	1,155	936	25	172	22	G.W. Bush	81.0%	2.2%	14.9%	1.9%
HENDERSON	661	492	52	91	26	G.W. Bush	74.4%	7.9%	13.8%	3.9%
HENRY	4,131	2,955	403	620	153	G.W. Bush	71.5%	9.8%	15.0%	3.7%
IROQUOIS	5,172	3,743	366	942	121	G.W. Bush	72.4%	7.1%	18.2%	2.3%
JACKSON	2,131	1,568	192	335	36	G.W. Bush	73.6%	9.0%	15.7%	1.7%
JASPER	524	432	38	48	6	G.W. Bush	82.4%	7.3%	9.2%	1.1%
JEFFERSON	1,770	1,433	118	187	32	G.W. Bush	81.0%	6.7%	10.6%	1.8%
JERSEY	1,567	1,166	111	262	28	G.W. Bush	74.4%	7.1%	16.7%	1.8%
JO DAVIESS	3,304	2,066	297	797	144	G.W. Bush	62.5%	9.0%	24.1%	4.4%
JOHNSON	1,970	1,498	78	340	54	G.W. Bush	76.0%	4.0%	17.3%	2.7%
KANE	38,940	23,607	3,748	10,772	813	G.W. Bush	60.6%	9.6%	27.7%	2.1%
KANKAKEE	7,024	4,919	612	1,356	137	G.W. Bush	70.0%	8.7%	19.3%	2.0%
KENDALL	7,220	4,628	594	1,834	164	G.W. Bush	64.1%	8.2%	25.4%	2.3%
KNOX	3,984	2,770	317	800	97	G.W. Bush	69.5%	8.0%	20.1%	2.4%
LAKE	59,238	36,225	4,731	16,893	1,389	G.W. Bush	61.2%	8.0%	28.5%	2.3%
LA SALLE	7,381	4,978	730	1,519	154	G.W. Bush	67.4%	9.9%	20.6%	2.1%
LAWRENCE	1,629	1,266	88	240	35	G.W. Bush	77.7%	5.4%	14.7%	2.1%
LEE	3,755	2,746	304	620	85	G.W. Bush	73.1%	8.1%	16.5%	2.3%
LIVINGSTON	4,926	3,564	283	983	96	G.W. Bush	72.4%	5.7%	20.0%	1.9%
LOGAN	6,322	4,416	400	1,333	173	G.W. Bush	69.9%	6.3%	21.1%	2.7%
MCDONOUGH	4,176	2,811	283	983	99	G.W. Bush	67.3%	6.8%	23.5%	2.4%
MCHENRY	34,971	22,613	2,872	8,747	739	G.W. Bush	64.7%	8.2%	25.0%	2.1%
MCLEAN	21,122	15,081	1,433	4,267	341	G.W. Bush	71.4%	6.8%	20.2%	1.6%
MACON	6,313	4,451	873	895	94	G.W. Bush	70.5%	13.8%	14.2%	1.5%
MACOUPIN	2,807	2,224	176	355	52	G.W. Bush	79.2%	6.3%	12.6%	1.9%
MADISON	6,981	5,100	801	941	139	G.W. Bush	73.1%	11.5%	13.5%	2.0%
MARION	1,840	1,401	135	275	29	G.W. Bush	76.1%	7.3%	14.9%	1.6%
MARSHALL	1,295	880	98	295	22	G.W. Bush	68.0%	7.6%	22.8%	1.7%
MASON	1,031	805	69	143	14	G.W. Bush	78.1%	6.7%	13.9%	1.4%
MASSAC	2,185	1,811	82	220	72	G.W. Bush	82.9%	3.8%	10.1%	3.3%
MENARD	1,862	1,447	103	292	20	G.W. Bush	77.7%	5.5%	15.7%	1.1%

ILLINOIS REPUBLICAN PRIMARY

2000

County	Total Vote	G.W. Bush	Keyes	McCain	Other	Winner	Percentage of Total Vote			
							G.W. Bush	Keyes	McCain	Other
MERCER	1,758	1,236	195	259	68	G.W. Bush	70.3%	11.1%	14.7%	3.9%
MONROE	1,153	867	102	160	24	G.W. Bush	75.2%	8.8%	13.9%	2.1%
MONTGOMERY	2,063	1,590	128	302	43	G.W. Bush	77.1%	6.2%	14.6%	2.1%
MORGAN	2,002	1,467	163	345	27	G.W. Bush	73.3%	8.1%	17.2%	1.3%
MOULTRIE	1,354	945	106	267	36	G.W. Bush	69.8%	7.8%	19.7%	2.7%
OGLE	8,112	5,535	695	1,700	182	G.W. Bush	68.2%	8.6%	21.0%	2.2%
PEORIA	13,468	9,672	1,054	2,504	238	G.W. Bush	71.8%	7.8%	18.6%	1.8%
PERRY	1,838	1,424	95	290	29	G.W. Bush	77.5%	5.2%	15.8%	1.6%
PIATT	1,977	1,344	262	328	43	G.W. Bush	68.0%	13.3%	16.6%	2.2%
PIKE	1,302	1,022	86	169	25	G.W. Bush	78.5%	6.6%	13.0%	1.9%
POPE	505	425	14	58	8	G.W. Bush	84.2%	2.8%	11.5%	1.6%
PULASKI	565	477	20	60	8	G.W. Bush	84.4%	3.5%	10.6%	1.4%
PUTNAM	455	337	39	71	8	G.W. Bush	74.1%	8.6%	15.6%	1.8%
RANDOLPH	1,032	807	79	133	13	G.W. Bush	78.2%	7.7%	12.9%	1.3%
RICHLAND	811	547	106	142	16	G.W. Bush	67.4%	13.1%	17.5%	2.0%
ROCK ISLAND	8,371	5,812	899	1,305	355	G.W. Bush	69.4%	10.7%	15.6%	4.2%
ST. CLAIR	6,143	4,593	570	886	94	G.W. Bush	74.8%	9.3%	14.4%	1.5%
SALINE	2,029	1,618	94	276	41	G.W. Bush	79.7%	4.6%	13.6%	2.0%
SANGAMON	17,522	13,454	1,114	2,736	218	G.W. Bush	76.8%	6.4%	15.6%	1.2%
SCHUYLER	1,475	1,063	85	297	30	G.W. Bush	72.1%	5.8%	20.1%	2.0%
SCOTT	408	330	13	60	5	G.W. Bush	80.9%	3.2%	14.7%	1.2%
SHELBY	2,038	1,570	207	222	39	G.W. Bush	77.0%	10.2%	10.9%	1.9%
STARK	1,263	872	79	271	41	G.W. Bush	69.0%	6.3%	21.5%	3.2%
STEPHENSON	6,169	3,916	567	1,515	171	G.W. Bush	63.5%	9.2%	24.6%	2.8%
TAZEWELL	9,955	7,215	974	1,556	210	G.W. Bush	72.5%	9.8%	15.6%	2.1%
UNION	1,470	1,212	81	158	19	G.W. Bush	82.4%	5.5%	10.7%	1.3%
VERMILION	6,616	4,960	611	887	158	G.W. Bush	75.0%	9.2%	13.4%	2.4%
WABASH	1,200	930	86	162	22	G.W. Bush	77.5%	7.2%	13.5%	1.8%
WARREN	1,758	1,269	126	319	44	G.W. Bush	72.2%	7.2%	18.1%	2.5%
WASHINGTON	901	690	52	145	14	G.W. Bush	76.6%	5.8%	16.1%	1.6%
WAYNE	1,421	1,170	88	129	34	G.W. Bush	82.3%	6.2%	9.1%	2.4%
WHITE	954	821	43	80	10	G.W. Bush	86.1%	4.5%	8.4%	1.0%
WHITESIDE	3,434	2,476	323	549	86	G.W. Bush	72.1%	9.4%	16.0%	2.5%
WILL	31,070	21,331	2,714	6,409	616	G.W. Bush	68.7%	8.7%	20.6%	2.0%
WILLIAMSON	2,887	2,255	264	299	69	G.W. Bush	78.1%	9.1%	10.4%	2.4%
WINNEBAGO	22,804	13,611	3,602	5,120	471	G.W. Bush	59.7%	15.8%	22.5%	2.1%
WOODFORD	4,321	3,157	365	704	95	G.W. Bush	73.1%	8.4%	16.3%	2.2%
TOTAL	736,921	496,685	66,066	158,768	15,402	G.W. Bush	67.4%	9.0%	21.5%	2.1%

Note: Other vote was 10,334 Steve Forbes; 5,068 Gary Bauer.

ILLINOIS DEMOCRATIC PRIMARY

2004

County	Total Vote	Edwards	Kerry	Other	Winner	Percentage of Total Vote		
						Edwards	Kerry	Other
ADAMS	4,945	665	3,888	392	Kerry	13.4%	78.6%	7.9%
ALEXANDER	1,372	203	911	258	Kerry	14.8%	66.4%	18.8%
BOND	1,005	176	735	94	Kerry	17.5%	73.1%	9.4%
BOONE	2,797	352	2,111	334	Kerry	12.6%	75.5%	11.9%
BROWN	304	57	217	30	Kerry	18.8%	71.4%	9.9%
BUREAU	2,978	441	2,171	366	Kerry	14.8%	72.9%	12.3%
CALHOUN	586	83	476	27	Kerry	14.2%	81.2%	4.6%
CARROLL	861	135	638	88	Kerry	15.7%	74.1%	10.2%
CASS	1,177	184	848	145	Kerry	15.6%	72.0%	12.3%
CHAMPAIGN	11,619	1,249	7,338	3,032	Kerry	10.7%	63.2%	26.1%
CHRISTIAN	4,368	798	2,963	607	Kerry	18.3%	67.8%	13.9%
CLARK	899	161	623	115	Kerry	17.9%	69.3%	12.8%
CLAY	1,436	279	902	255	Kerry	19.4%	62.8%	17.8%
CLINTON	1,330	187	1,040	103	Kerry	14.1%	78.2%	7.7%
COLES	2,400	359	1,759	282	Kerry	15.0%	73.3%	11.8%
COOK	700,148	64,916	492,441	142,791	Kerry	9.3%	70.3%	20.4%
CRAWFORD	969	167	686	116	Kerry	17.2%	70.8%	12.0%
CUMBERLAND	1,008	204	678	126	Kerry	20.2%	67.3%	12.5%
DE KALB	5,290	615	3,856	819	Kerry	11.6%	72.9%	15.5%
DE WITT	1,511	240	1,089	182	Kerry	15.9%	72.1%	12.0%
DOUGLAS	856	166	614	76	Kerry	19.4%	71.7%	8.9%
DU PAGE	62,624	6,645	47,962	8,017	Kerry	10.6%	76.6%	12.8%
EDGAR	853	155	584	114	Kerry	18.2%	68.5%	13.4%
EDWARDS	268	49	198	21	Kerry	18.3%	73.9%	7.8%
EFFINGHAM	2,853	586	1,823	444	Kerry	20.5%	63.9%	15.6%
FAYETTE	1,504	241	1,122	141	Kerry	16.0%	74.6%	9.4%
FORD	436	54	326	56	Kerry	12.4%	74.8%	12.8%
FRANKLIN	6,681	1,138	4,624	919	Kerry	17.0%	69.2%	13.8%
FULTON	6,379	910	4,553	916	Kerry	14.3%	71.4%	14.4%
GALLATIN	1,678	306	1,098	274	Kerry	18.2%	65.4%	16.3%
GREENE	1,658	318	1,126	214	Kerry	19.2%	67.9%	12.9%
GRUNDY	2,961	349	2,311	301	Kerry	11.8%	78.0%	10.2%
HAMILTON	1,587	302	1,107	178	Kerry	19.0%	69.8%	11.2%
HANCOCK	1,041	195	738	108	Kerry	18.7%	70.9%	10.4%
HARDIN	706	108	498	100	Kerry	15.3%	70.5%	14.2%
HENDERSON	442	61	340	41	Kerry	13.8%	76.9%	9.3%
HENRY	2,772	415	2,102	255	Kerry	15.0%	75.8%	9.2%
IROQUOIS	975	141	724	110	Kerry	14.5%	74.3%	11.3%
JACKSON	6,376	1,034	4,276	1,066	Kerry	16.2%	67.1%	16.7%
JASPER	865	152	603	110	Kerry	17.6%	69.7%	12.7%
JEFFERSON	2,706	485	1,926	295	Kerry	17.9%	71.2%	10.9%
JERSEY	1,318	196	999	123	Kerry	14.9%	75.8%	9.3%
JO DAVIESS	1,322	173	1,001	148	Kerry	13.1%	75.7%	11.2%
JOHNSON	1,048	170	775	103	Kerry	16.2%	74.0%	9.8%
KANE	21,582	2,402	16,112	3,068	Kerry	11.1%	74.7%	14.2%

ILLINOIS DEMOCRATIC PRIMARY

2004

County	Total Vote	Edwards	Kerry	Other	Winner	Percentage of Total Vote		
						Edwards	Kerry	Other
KANKAKEE	6,543	760	4,681	1,102	Kerry	11.6%	71.5%	16.8%
KENDALL	3,170	377	2,404	389	Kerry	11.9%	75.8%	12.3%
KNOX	3,845	560	2,790	495	Kerry	14.6%	72.6%	12.9%
LAKE	45,743	4,454	35,285	6,004	Kerry	9.7%	77.1%	13.1%
LA SALLE	7,813	942	6,066	805	Kerry	12.1%	77.6%	10.3%
LAWRENCE	831	128	583	120	Kerry	15.4%	70.2%	14.4%
LEE	1,804	214	1,357	233	Kerry	11.9%	75.2%	12.9%
LIVINGSTON	1,752	240	1,296	216	Kerry	13.7%	74.0%	12.3%
LOGAN	1,130	156	815	159	Kerry	13.8%	72.1%	14.1%
MCDONOUGH	1,676	253	1,221	202	Kerry	15.1%	72.9%	12.1%
MCHENRY	17,580	2,237	13,325	2,018	Kerry	12.7%	75.8%	11.5%
MCLEAN	8,192	1,145	5,733	1,314	Kerry	14.0%	70.0%	16.0%
MACON	10,075	1,285	7,402	1,388	Kerry	12.8%	73.5%	13.8%
MACOUPIN	6,937	1,101	4,986	850	Kerry	15.9%	71.9%	12.3%
MADISON	21,448	3,077	16,151	2,220	Kerry	14.3%	75.3%	10.4%
MARION	4,041	635	2,910	496	Kerry	15.7%	72.0%	12.3%
MARSHALL	779	104	587	88	Kerry	13.4%	75.4%	11.3%
MASON	2,036	345	1,391	300	Kerry	16.9%	68.3%	14.7%
MASSAC	981	108	776	97	Kerry	11.0%	79.1%	9.9%
MENARD	603	94	428	81	Kerry	15.6%	71.0%	13.4%
MERCER	2,006	379	1,418	209	Kerry	18.9%	70.7%	10.4%
MONROE	1,286	197	993	96	Kerry	15.3%	77.2%	7.5%
MONTGOMERY	2,771	435	2,057	279	Kerry	15.7%	74.2%	10.1%
MORGAN	1,333	181	995	157	Kerry	13.6%	74.6%	11.8%
MOULTRIE	966	174	681	111	Kerry	18.0%	70.5%	11.5%
OGLE	2,435	378	1,740	317	Kerry	15.5%	71.5%	13.0%
PEORIA	13,744	1,501	10,386	1,857	Kerry	10.9%	75.6%	13.5%
PERRY	2,685	440	1,972	273	Kerry	16.4%	73.4%	10.2%
PIATT	1,020	185	702	133	Kerry	18.1%	68.8%	13.0%
PIKE	1,262	192	970	100	Kerry	15.2%	76.9%	7.9%
POPE	533	73	382	78	Kerry	13.7%	71.7%	14.6%
PULASKI	587	103	383	101	Kerry	17.5%	65.2%	17.2%
PUTNAM	1,138	202	775	161	Kerry	17.8%	68.1%	14.1%
RANDOLPH	4,195	738	2,975	482	Kerry	17.6%	70.9%	11.5%
RICHLAND	1,145	189	786	170	Kerry	16.5%	68.6%	14.8%
ROCK ISLAND	15,508	2,426	11,322	1,760	Kerry	15.6%	73.0%	11.3%
ST. CLAIR	24,028	2,757	17,873	3,398	Kerry	11.5%	74.4%	14.1%
SALINE	4,052	704	2,697	651	Kerry	17.4%	66.6%	16.1%
SANGAMON	12,749	1,620	9,219	1,910	Kerry	12.7%	72.3%	15.0%
SCHUYLER	441	51	343	47	Kerry	11.6%	77.8%	10.7%
SCOTT	367	62	268	37	Kerry	16.9%	73.0%	10.1%
SHELBY	2,475	457	1,664	354	Kerry	18.5%	67.2%	14.3%
STARK	295	37	226	32	Kerry	12.5%	76.6%	10.8%
STEPHENSON	2,727	417	1,988	322	Kerry	15.3%	72.9%	11.8%
TAZEWELL	8,132	1,086	6,085	961	Kerry	13.4%	74.8%	11.8%

ILLINOIS DEMOCRATIC PRIMARY

2004

County	Total Vote	Edwards	Kerry	Other	Winner	Percentage of Total Vote		
						Edwards	Kerry	Other
UNION	4,051	873	2,593	585	Kerry	21.6%	64.0%	14.4%
VERMILION	3,994	521	2,965	508	Kerry	13.0%	74.2%	12.7%
WABASH	1,119	237	679	203	Kerry	21.2%	60.7%	18.1%
WARREN	1,044	188	751	105	Kerry	18.0%	71.9%	10.1%
WASHINGTON	1,421	219	1,038	164	Kerry	15.4%	73.0%	11.5%
WAYNE	923	154	651	118	Kerry	16.7%	70.5%	12.8%
WHITE	1,467	245	1,037	185	Kerry	16.7%	70.7%	12.6%
WHITESIDE	3,058	414	2,342	302	Kerry	13.5%	76.6%	9.9%
WILL	39,257	4,286	29,434	5,537	Kerry	10.9%	75.0%	14.1%
WILLIAMSON	4,304	797	2,992	515	Kerry	18.5%	69.5%	12.0%
WINNEBAGO	21,845	2,386	15,541	3,918	Kerry	10.9%	71.1%	17.9%
WOODFORD	1,679	225	1,208	246	Kerry	13.4%	71.9%	14.7%
TOTAL	1,217,515	131,966	873,230	212,319	Kerry	10.8%	71.7%	17.4%

Note: Other vote was 53,249 Carol Moseley Braun; 47,343 Howard Dean; 36,123 Al Sharpton; 28,083 Dennis J. Kucinich; 24,354 Joseph I. Lieberman; 19,304 Wesley Clark; 3,863 Lyndon H. LaRouche Jr.

INDIANA

What the West Virginia primary did for John F. Kennedy in 1960, Indiana's did for his brother Robert eight years later, providing a high-profile victory on uncertain political terrain.

Indiana has a more conservative political milieu than many of its larger Midwestern neighbors, which made it a dramatic launching pad for Robert Kennedy's ill-fated, but memorable, presidential campaign. Kennedy crossed and crisscrossed the state, wooing minority voters in the inner cities (where he quoted Aeschylus on the night of the assassination of Martin Luther King) and white voters in the small towns that dot the state. For a time, Kennedy rode on a photogenic campaign train that followed the route of the old Wabash Cannonball.

And on primary day, he rolled to a clear-cut victory over both Eugene McCarthy and Roger Branigin, the state's governor and favorite-son presidential candidate. Kennedy swept most of the major population centers as well as much of rural Indiana, giving the first indication in 1968 of his broad-based voter appeal.

Recent Indiana Primary Results

Indiana held its first presidential primary in 1916.

Year	DEMOCRATS			REPUBLICANS		
	Turnout	Candidates	%	Turnout	Candidates	%
2004 (May 4)	317,211	JOHN KERRY	73	469,528	GEORGE W. BUSH*	100
		John Edwards	11			
		Howard Dean	7			
		Wesley Clark	5			
2000 (May 2)	294,977	AL GORE	75	406,664	GEORGE W. BUSH	81
		Bill Bradley	22		John McCain	19
1996 (May 7)	329,462	BILL CLINTON*	100	516,514	BOB DOLE	71
					Pat Buchanan	19
					Steve Forbes	10
1992 (May 5)	476,849	BILL CLINTON	63	467,615	GEORGE BUSH*	80
		Jerry Brown	21		Pat Buchanan	20
		Paul Tsongas	12			
1988 (May 3)	645,708	MICHAEL DUKAKIS	70	437,655	GEORGE BUSH	80
		Jesse Jackson	22		Bob Dole	10
					Pat Robertson	7
1984 (May 8)	716,955	GARY HART	42	428,559	RONALD REAGAN*	100
		Walter Mondale	41			
		Jesse Jackson	14			
1980 (May 6)	589,441	JIMMY CARTER*	68	568,313	RONALD REAGAN	74
		Edward Kennedy	32		George Bush	16
					John Anderson	10
1976 (May 4)	614,389	JIMMY CARTER	68	631,292	RONALD REAGAN	51
		George Wallace	15		Gerald Ford*	49
		Henry Jackson	12			
		Ellen McCormack	5			
1972 (May 2)	751,458	HUBERT HUMPHREY	47	417,069	RICHARD NIXON*	100
		George Wallace	41			
		Edmund Muskie	12			
1968 (May 7)	776,513	ROBERT KENNEDY	42	508,362	RICHARD NIXON	100
		Roger Branigin	31			
		Eugene McCarthy	27			

Note: All candidates are listed that drew at least 5 percent of their party's primary vote. The names of winning candidates are capitalized. An asterisk (*) indicates an incumbent president.

No Indiana primary since then has captured such national attention, although the Hoosier State has an unmistakable history of backing political outsiders that some of its larger Midwestern neighbors would not. George Wallace ran well in the Democratic primary in 1964 and 1972. Ronald Reagan won the 1976 GOP vote, his only primary victory over President Gerald Ford in a Frost Belt state east of the Great Plains. And in the 1984 Democratic contest, Gary Hart edged Walter Mondale, the favorite almost everywhere else in the industrial Frost Belt.

Coupled with his victory the same day in Ohio, Hart's win in Indiana revived his faltering campaign. But it was by the narrowest of margins, barely 6,000 votes out of more than 700,000 cast. Basically, Hart won rural Indiana while Mondale had the edge in the urban centers. Jesse Jackson, though, won Marion County (Indianapolis) and sliced away enough of the vote in other major population centers to enable Hart to prevail statewide.

The 1976 Republican contest was nearly as close. Ford carried the southwest and northeast portions of Indiana, including traditional industrial counties such as Allen (Fort Wayne) and St. Joseph (South Bend) near his home state of Michigan. Reagan drew much of his strength from vocal and influential conservatives concentrated in the Indianapolis area and several industrial centers nearby.

The Indiana GOP, though, has not been noted for pursuing ideological crusades. And when Pat Buchanan ran in 1992 and 1996, he could not break 20 percent either time.

Still, Indiana has been a reliably Republican state in the fall presidential voting, and Democrat Bill Clinton was unable to carry its electoral votes in either of his presidential victories in the 1990s. But in 1992, Indiana gave him his largest share of the primary vote (63 percent) in any non-Southern state except West Virginia. Clinton won decisively in every Indiana county but Monroe, home of Indiana University in Bloomington, where he edged Jerry Brown by just 2 percentage points.

Since Branigin's run in 1968, Indiana voters have not had a home-state candidate to vote for in their presidential primary. Sen. Birch Bayh sought the Democratic presidential nomination in 1976, while former vice president Dan Quayle pursued the 2000 Republican nomination. But neither Hoosier was still a candidate when Indiana voted and their names did not appear on the primary ballot.

INDIANA DEMOCRATIC PRIMARY

2000

County	Total Vote	Bradley	Gore	LaRouche	Winner	Percentage of Total Vote		
						Bradley	Gore	LaRouche
ADAMS	1,764	490	1,217	57	Gore	27.8%	69.0%	3.2%
ALLEN	7,285	1,649	5,469	167	Gore	22.6%	75.1%	2.3%
BARTHOLOMEW	2,379	483	1,855	41	Gore	20.3%	78.0%	1.7%
BENTON	313	61	243	9	Gore	19.5%	77.6%	2.9%
BLACKFORD	666	138	517	11	Gore	20.7%	77.6%	1.7%
BOONE	805	207	581	17	Gore	25.7%	72.2%	2.1%
BROWN	1,147	263	850	34	Gore	22.9%	74.1%	3.0%
CARROLL	905	170	714	21	Gore	18.8%	78.9%	2.3%
CASS	1,926	531	1,331	64	Gore	27.6%	69.1%	3.3%
CLARK	10,012	2,315	7,340	357	Gore	23.1%	73.3%	3.6%
CLAY	3,062	846	2,071	145	Gore	27.6%	67.6%	4.7%
CLINTON	972	199	745	28	Gore	20.5%	76.6%	2.9%
CRAWFORD	1,369	281	1,042	46	Gore	20.5%	76.1%	3.4%
DAVIESS	1,273	286	959	28	Gore	22.5%	75.3%	2.2%
DEARBORN	1,887	297	1,556	34	Gore	15.7%	82.5%	1.8%
DECATUR	679	129	523	27	Gore	19.0%	77.0%	4.0%
DE KALB	1,302	278	1,002	22	Gore	21.4%	77.0%	1.7%
DELAWARE	9,212	1,800	7,167	245	Gore	19.5%	77.8%	2.7%
DUBOIS	3,457	927	2,465	65	Gore	26.8%	71.3%	1.9%
ELKHART	2,893	577	2,251	65	Gore	19.9%	77.8%	2.2%
FAYETTE	1,548	326	1,171	51	Gore	21.1%	75.6%	3.3%
FLOYD	5,009	983	3,895	131	Gore	19.6%	77.8%	2.6%
FOUNTAIN	713	129	567	17	Gore	18.1%	79.5%	2.4%
FRANKLIN	937	196	722	19	Gore	20.9%	77.1%	2.0%
FULTON	724	147	566	11	Gore	20.3%	78.2%	1.5%
GIBSON	4,189	1,101	2,917	171	Gore	26.3%	69.6%	4.1%
GRANT	3,215	670	2,442	103	Gore	20.8%	76.0%	3.2%
GREENE	2,675	665	1,917	93	Gore	24.9%	71.7%	3.5%
HAMILTON	1,811	378	1,403	30	Gore	20.9%	77.5%	1.7%
HANCOCK	1,216	260	928	28	Gore	21.4%	76.3%	2.3%
HARRISON	4,578	1,088	3,238	252	Gore	23.8%	70.7%	5.5%
HENDRICKS	1,757	372	1,344	41	Gore	21.2%	76.5%	2.3%
HENRY	2,635	503	2,074	58	Gore	19.1%	78.7%	2.2%
HOWARD	4,102	852	3,153	97	Gore	20.8%	76.9%	2.4%
HUNTINGTON	1,032	237	769	26	Gore	23.0%	74.5%	2.5%
JACKSON	3,576	928	2,567	81	Gore	26.0%	71.8%	2.3%
JASPER	771	155	602	14	Gore	20.1%	78.1%	1.8%
JAY	1,779	358	1,363	58	Gore	20.1%	76.6%	3.3%
JEFFERSON	1,898	390	1,458	50	Gore	20.5%	76.8%	2.6%
JENNINGS	1,559	334	1,186	39	Gore	21.4%	76.1%	2.5%
JOHNSON	1,675	357	1,279	39	Gore	21.3%	76.4%	2.3%
KNOX	4,581	1,298	3,104	179	Gore	28.3%	67.8%	3.9%
KOSCIUSKO	1,012	232	737	43	Gore	22.9%	72.8%	4.2%
LAGRANGE	927	207	703	17	Gore	22.3%	75.8%	1.8%
LAKE	37,212	6,461	29,293	1,458	Gore	17.4%	78.7%	3.9%
LA PORTE	8,053	1,714	6,094	245	Gore	21.3%	75.7%	3.0%
LAWRENCE	1,139	202	906	31	Gore	17.7%	79.5%	2.7%
MADISON	10,331	1,982	8,091	258	Gore	19.2%	78.3%	2.5%
MARION	31,572	8,045	22,517	1,010	Gore	25.5%	71.3%	3.2%
MARSHALL	972	208	747	17	Gore	21.4%	76.9%	1.7%

INDIANA DEMOCRATIC PRIMARY

2000

County	Total Vote	Bradley	Gore	LaRouche	Winner	Percentage of Total Vote		
						Bradley	Gore	LaRouche
MARTIN	1,649	461	1,124	64	Gore	28.0%	68.2%	3.9%
MIAMI	1,072	314	707	51	Gore	29.3%	66.0%	4.8%
MONROE	4,739	1,077	3,606	56	Gore	22.7%	76.1%	1.2%
MONTGOMERY	863	165	681	17	Gore	19.1%	78.9%	2.0%
MORGAN	1,382	299	1,046	37	Gore	21.6%	75.7%	2.7%
NEWTON	840	173	612	55	Gore	20.6%	72.9%	6.5%
NOBLE	1,229	292	905	32	Gore	23.8%	73.6%	2.6%
OHIO	346	62	273	11	Gore	17.9%	78.9%	3.2%
ORANGE	1,116	188	893	35	Gore	16.8%	80.0%	3.1%
OWEN	1,170	266	869	35	Gore	22.7%	74.3%	3.0%
PARKE	989	186	775	28	Gore	18.8%	78.4%	2.8%
PERRY	1,629	360	1,221	48	Gore	22.1%	75.0%	2.9%
PIKE	2,215	604	1,514	97	Gore	27.3%	68.4%	4.4%
PORTER	4,420	871	3,434	115	Gore	19.7%	77.7%	2.6%
POSEY	2,898	737	2,054	107	Gore	25.4%	70.9%	3.7%
PULASKI	768	182	576	10	Gore	23.7%	75.0%	1.3%
PUTNAM	985	226	728	31	Gore	22.9%	73.9%	3.1%
RANDOLPH	1,298	245	1,004	49	Gore	18.9%	77.3%	3.8%
RIPLEY	1,145	247	869	29	Gore	21.6%	75.9%	2.5%
RUSH	646	135	486	25	Gore	20.9%	75.2%	3.9%
ST. JOSEPH	12,994	2,789	9,715	490	Gore	21.5%	74.8%	3.8%
SCOTT	3,191	665	2,403	123	Gore	20.8%	75.3%	3.9%
SHELBY	1,681	339	1,314	28	Gore	20.2%	78.2%	1.7%
SPENCER	1,384	259	1,085	40	Gore	18.7%	78.4%	2.9%
STARKE	1,907	462	1,396	49	Gore	24.2%	73.2%	2.6%
STEUBEN	546	90	443	13	Gore	16.5%	81.1%	2.4%
SULLIVAN	2,932	750	2,056	126	Gore	25.6%	70.1%	4.3%
SWITZERLAND	1,296	321	916	59	Gore	24.8%	70.7%	4.6%
TIPPECANOE	3,915	751	3,089	75	Gore	19.2%	78.9%	1.9%
TIPTON	915	220	675	20	Gore	24.0%	73.8%	2.2%
UNION	283	57	219	7	Gore	20.1%	77.4%	2.5%
VANDERBURGH	9,773	1,973	7,529	271	Gore	20.2%	77.0%	2.8%
VERMILLION	2,487	641	1,728	118	Gore	25.8%	69.5%	4.7%
VIGO	10,470	2,410	7,708	352	Gore	23.0%	73.6%	3.4%
WABASH	928	181	724	23	Gore	19.5%	78.0%	2.5%
WARREN	383	76	298	9	Gore	19.8%	77.8%	2.3%
WARRICK	4,694	1,167	3,375	152	Gore	24.9%	71.9%	3.2%
WASHINGTON	1,767	358	1,359	50	Gore	20.3%	76.9%	2.8%
WAYNE	2,583	384	2,132	67	Gore	14.9%	82.5%	2.6%
WELLS	820	197	599	24	Gore	24.0%	73.0%	2.9%
WHITE	952	196	740	16	Gore	20.6%	77.7%	1.7%
WHITLEY	1,171	258	873	40	Gore	22.0%	74.6%	3.4%
TOTAL	294,977	64,339	221,404	9,234	Gore	21.8%	75.1%	3.1%
Certified Totals	293,172	64,339	219,604	9,229	Gore	21.9%	74.9%	3.1%

Note: The certified statewide totals for Sullivan County were 750 Bradley; 256 Gore; 121 LaRouche. County election officials reported the totals listed for Sullivan County in this chart.

INDIANA REPUBLICAN PRIMARY

2000

| County | Total Vote | G.W. Bush | McCain | Winner | Percentage of Total Vote | |
					G.W. Bush	McCain
ADAMS	2,466	2,132	334	G.W. Bush	86.5%	13.5%
ALLEN	20,090	16,411	3,679	G.W. Bush	81.7%	18.3%
BARTHOLOMEW	5,263	4,374	889	G.W. Bush	83.1%	16.9%
BENTON	1,428	1,068	360	G.W. Bush	74.8%	25.2%
BLACKFORD	658	560	98	G.W. Bush	85.1%	14.9%
BOONE	6,908	5,453	1,455	G.W. Bush	78.9%	21.1%
BROWN	1,294	1,061	233	G.W. Bush	82.0%	18.0%
CARROLL	2,638	2,010	628	G.W. Bush	76.2%	23.8%
CASS	4,074	3,237	837	G.W. Bush	79.5%	20.5%
CLARK	2,431	2,177	254	G.W. Bush	89.6%	10.4%
CLAY	2,634	2,141	493	G.W. Bush	81.3%	18.7%
CLINTON	3,448	2,734	714	G.W. Bush	79.3%	20.7%
CRAWFORD	675	598	77	G.W. Bush	88.6%	11.4%
DAVIESS	3,776	3,082	694	G.W. Bush	81.6%	18.4%
DEARBORN	2,636	2,141	495	G.W. Bush	81.2%	18.8%
DECATUR	2,367	1,948	419	G.W. Bush	82.3%	17.7%
DE KALB	3,974	3,243	731	G.W. Bush	81.6%	18.4%
DELAWARE	8,801	6,950	1,851	G.W. Bush	79.0%	21.0%
DUBOIS	1,400	1,235	165	G.W. Bush	88.2%	11.8%
ELKHART	13,478	10,591	2,887	G.W. Bush	78.6%	21.4%
FAYETTE	1,607	1,329	278	G.W. Bush	82.7%	17.3%
FLOYD	2,855	2,452	403	G.W. Bush	85.9%	14.1%
FOUNTAIN	1,892	1,476	416	G.W. Bush	78.0%	22.0%
FRANKLIN	1,437	1,198	239	G.W. Bush	83.4%	16.6%
FULTON	1,991	1,571	420	G.W. Bush	78.9%	21.1%
GIBSON	1,084	934	150	G.W. Bush	86.2%	13.8%
GRANT	6,589	5,538	1,051	G.W. Bush	84.0%	16.0%
GREENE	2,662	2,256	406	G.W. Bush	84.7%	15.3%
HAMILTON	17,891	14,780	3,111	G.W. Bush	82.6%	17.4%
HANCOCK	6,267	5,100	1,167	G.W. Bush	81.4%	18.6%
HARRISON	1,726	1,495	231	G.W. Bush	86.6%	13.4%
HENDRICKS	13,397	10,804	2,593	G.W. Bush	80.6%	19.4%
HENRY	5,131	4,162	969	G.W. Bush	81.1%	18.9%
HOWARD	6,732	5,664	1,068	G.W. Bush	84.1%	15.9%
HUNTINGTON	3,905	3,209	696	G.W. Bush	82.2%	17.8%
JACKSON	2,091	1,824	267	G.W. Bush	87.2%	12.8%
JASPER	2,974	2,442	532	G.W. Bush	82.1%	17.9%
JAY	2,691	2,140	551	G.W. Bush	79.5%	20.5%
JEFFERSON	1,323	1,126	197	G.W. Bush	85.1%	14.9%
JENNINGS	2,375	1,978	397	G.W. Bush	83.3%	16.7%
JOHNSON	9,475	7,647	1,828	G.W. Bush	80.7%	19.3%
KNOX	2,380	2,023	357	G.W. Bush	85.0%	15.0%
KOSCIUSKO	6,406	5,241	1,165	G.W. Bush	81.8%	18.2%
LAGRANGE	2,543	2,043	500	G.W. Bush	80.3%	19.7%
LAKE	7,978	6,483	1,495	G.W. Bush	81.3%	18.7%

INDIANA REPUBLICAN PRIMARY

2000

County	Total Vote	G.W. Bush	McCain	Winner	Percentage of Total Vote G.W. Bush	McCain
LA PORTE	5,455	4,185	1,270	G.W. Bush	76.7%	23.3%
LAWRENCE	4,409	3,625	784	G.W. Bush	82.2%	17.8%
MADISON	9,773	8,129	1,644	G.W. Bush	83.2%	16.8%
MARION	51,215	42,433	8,782	G.W. Bush	82.9%	17.1%
MARSHALL	3,090	2,416	674	G.W. Bush	78.2%	21.8%
MARTIN	649	572	77	G.W. Bush	88.1%	11.9%
MIAMI	3,343	2,737	606	G.W. Bush	81.9%	18.1%
MONROE	6,279	5,210	1,069	G.W. Bush	83.0%	17.0%
MONTGOMERY	6,074	4,563	1,511	G.W. Bush	75.1%	24.9%
MORGAN	8,022	6,482	1,540	G.W. Bush	80.8%	19.2%
NEWTON	1,933	1,502	431	G.W. Bush	77.7%	22.3%
NOBLE	2,997	2,418	579	G.W. Bush	80.7%	19.3%
OHIO	253	208	45	G.W. Bush	82.2%	17.8%
ORANGE	3,435	2,814	621	G.W. Bush	81.9%	18.1%
OWEN	1,545	1,257	288	G.W. Bush	81.4%	18.6%
PARKE	1,707	1,375	332	G.W. Bush	80.6%	19.4%
PERRY	436	383	53	G.W. Bush	87.8%	12.2%
PIKE	1,021	880	141	G.W. Bush	86.2%	13.8%
PORTER	5,893	4,564	1,329	G.W. Bush	77.4%	22.6%
POSEY	886	746	140	G.W. Bush	84.2%	15.8%
PULASKI	1,482	1,191	291	G.W. Bush	80.4%	19.6%
PUTNAM	2,754	2,184	570	G.W. Bush	79.3%	20.7%
RANDOLPH	3,261	2,568	693	G.W. Bush	78.7%	21.3%
RIPLEY	1,995	1,655	340	G.W. Bush	83.0%	17.0%
RUSH	2,585	2,029	556	G.W. Bush	78.5%	21.5%
ST. JOSEPH	8,449	6,624	1,825	G.W. Bush	78.4%	21.6%
SCOTT	654	572	82	G.W. Bush	87.5%	12.5%
SHELBY	3,751	3,101	650	G.W. Bush	82.7%	17.3%
SPENCER	876	765	111	G.W. Bush	87.3%	12.7%
STARKE	1,071	903	168	G.W. Bush	84.3%	15.7%
STEUBEN	3,119	2,341	778	G.W. Bush	75.1%	24.9%
SULLIVAN	903	742	161	G.W. Bush	82.2%	17.8%
SWITZERLAND	502	421	81	G.W. Bush	83.9%	16.1%
TIPPECANOE	13,378	9,726	3,652	G.W. Bush	72.7%	27.3%
TIPTON	2,397	1,993	404	G.W. Bush	83.1%	16.9%
UNION	802	649	153	G.W. Bush	80.9%	19.1%
VANDERBURGH	5,444	4,720	724	G.W. Bush	86.7%	13.3%
VERMILLION	533	419	114	G.W. Bush	78.6%	21.4%
VIGO	4,306	3,566	740	G.W. Bush	82.8%	17.2%
WABASH	2,894	2,356	538	G.W. Bush	81.4%	18.6%
WARREN	1,186	902	284	G.W. Bush	76.1%	23.9%
WARRICK	2,272	1,888	384	G.W. Bush	83.1%	16.9%
WASHINGTON	2,032	1,693	339	G.W. Bush	83.3%	16.7%
WAYNE	7,448	5,937	1,511	G.W. Bush	79.7%	20.3%
WELLS	2,624	2,188	436	G.W. Bush	83.4%	16.6%
WHITE	2,333	1,763	570	G.W. Bush	75.6%	24.4%
WHITLEY	3,357	2,639	718	G.W. Bush	78.6%	21.4%
TOTAL	406,664	330,095	76,569	G.W. Bush	81.2%	18.8%

INDIANA DEMOCRATIC PRIMARY

2004

County	Total Vote	Clark	Dean	Edwards	Kerry	Other	Winner	Percentage of Total Vote				
								Clark	Dean	Edwards	Kerry	Other
ADAMS	1,153	56	99	138	822	38	Kerry	4.9%	8.6%	12.0%	71.3%	3.3%
ALLEN	8,657	550	624	937	6,242	304	Kerry	6.4%	7.2%	10.8%	72.1%	3.5%
BARTHOLOMEW	3,812	243	259	451	2,770	89	Kerry	6.4%	6.8%	11.8%	72.7%	2.3%
BENTON	256	8	23	35	189	1	Kerry	3.1%	9.0%	13.7%	73.8%	0.4%
BLACKFORD	983	68	79	129	689	18	Kerry	6.9%	8.0%	13.1%	70.1%	1.8%
BOONE	828	73	53	106	575	21	Kerry	8.8%	6.4%	12.8%	69.4%	2.5%
BROWN	1,270	69	87	145	909	60	Kerry	5.4%	6.9%	11.4%	71.6%	4.7%
CARROLL	799	43	60	94	592	10	Kerry	5.4%	7.5%	11.8%	74.1%	1.3%
CASS	1,713	106	141	229	1,178	59	Kerry	6.2%	8.2%	13.4%	68.8%	3.4%
CLARK	9,347	585	764	1,220	6,414	364	Kerry	6.3%	8.2%	13.1%	68.6%	3.9%
CLAY	1,990	134	153	312	1,337	54	Kerry	6.7%	7.7%	15.7%	67.2%	2.7%
CLINTON	1,115	72	74	147	794	28	Kerry	6.5%	6.6%	13.2%	71.2%	2.5%
CRAWFORD	1,323	77	102	127	969	48	Kerry	5.8%	7.7%	9.6%	73.2%	3.6%
DAVIESS	941	73	86	125	632	25	Kerry	7.8%	9.1%	13.3%	67.2%	2.7%
DEARBORN	1,354	60	87	171	1,007	29	Kerry	4.4%	6.4%	12.6%	74.4%	2.1%
DECATUR	645	45	49	80	455	16	Kerry	7.0%	7.6%	12.4%	70.5%	2.5%
DE KALB	1,147	59	67	128	858	35	Kerry	5.1%	5.8%	11.2%	74.8%	3.1%
DELAWARE	10,318	630	747	1,285	7,303	353	Kerry	6.1%	7.2%	12.5%	70.8%	3.4%
DUBOIS	4,210	281	437	554	2,794	144	Kerry	6.7%	10.4%	13.2%	66.4%	3.4%
ELKHART	3,465	130	247	317	2,629	142	Kerry	3.8%	7.1%	9.1%	75.9%	4.1%
FAYETTE	1,712	102	123	251	1,197	39	Kerry	6.0%	7.2%	14.7%	69.9%	2.3%
FLOYD	4,277	224	247	509	3,164	133	Kerry	5.2%	5.8%	11.9%	74.0%	3.1%
FOUNTAIN	701	30	52	83	523	13	Kerry	4.3%	7.4%	11.8%	74.6%	1.9%
FRANKLIN	1,185	85	93	183	780	44	Kerry	7.2%	7.8%	15.4%	65.8%	3.7%
FULTON	612	27	56	82	436	11	Kerry	4.4%	9.2%	13.4%	71.2%	1.8%
GIBSON	3,201	210	249	442	2,186	114	Kerry	6.6%	7.8%	13.8%	68.3%	3.6%
GRANT	3,099	198	310	427	2,079	85	Kerry	6.4%	10.0%	13.8%	67.1%	2.7%
GREENE	2,385	266	178	309	1,562	70	Kerry	11.2%	7.5%	13.0%	65.5%	2.9%
HAMILTON	3,860	226	232	389	2,905	108	Kerry	5.9%	6.0%	10.1%	75.3%	2.8%
HANCOCK	1,334	76	81	157	992	28	Kerry	5.7%	6.1%	11.8%	74.4%	2.1%
HARRISON	3,801	226	296	574	2,515	190	Kerry	5.9%	7.8%	15.1%	66.2%	5.0%
HENDRICKS	2,273	177	143	277	1,615	61	Kerry	7.8%	6.3%	12.2%	71.1%	2.7%
HENRY	2,896	177	175	380	2,076	88	Kerry	6.1%	6.0%	13.1%	71.7%	3.0%
HOWARD	3,984	198	287	495	2,886	118	Kerry	5.0%	7.2%	12.4%	72.4%	3.0%
HUNTINGTON	951	69	73	112	663	34	Kerry	7.3%	7.7%	11.8%	69.7%	3.6%
JACKSON	2,381	148	170	320	1,676	67	Kerry	6.2%	7.1%	13.4%	70.4%	2.8%
JASPER	761	43	51	72	580	15	Kerry	5.7%	6.7%	9.5%	76.2%	2.0%
JAY	1,149	67	80	121	854	27	Kerry	5.8%	7.0%	10.5%	74.3%	2.3%
JEFFERSON	2,173	140	146	264	1,561	62	Kerry	6.4%	6.7%	12.1%	71.8%	2.9%
JENNINGS	1,750	120	142	206	1,217	65	Kerry	6.9%	8.1%	11.8%	69.5%	3.7%
JOHNSON	2,437	135	155	293	1,756	98	Kerry	5.5%	6.4%	12.0%	72.1%	4.0%
KNOX	4,063	349	348	584	2,658	124	Kerry	8.6%	8.6%	14.4%	65.4%	3.1%
KOSCIUSKO	998	58	74	142	680	44	Kerry	5.8%	7.4%	14.2%	68.1%	4.4%
LAGRANGE	560	17	47	74	405	17	Kerry	3.0%	8.4%	13.2%	72.3%	3.0%
LAKE	44,854	2,547	2,489	4,114	33,479	2,225	Kerry	5.7%	5.5%	9.2%	74.6%	5.0%

INDIANA DEMOCRATIC PRIMARY

2004

County	Total Vote	Clark	Dean	Edwards	Kerry	Other	Winner	Percentage of Total Vote				
								Clark	Dean	Edwards	Kerry	Other
LA PORTE	7,394	361	588	765	5,414	266	Kerry	4.9%	8.0%	10.3%	73.2%	3.6%
LAWRENCE	1,352	96	88	146	984	38	Kerry	7.1%	6.5%	10.8%	72.8%	2.8%
MADISON	9,271	501	703	1,101	6,729	237	Kerry	5.4%	7.6%	11.9%	72.6%	2.6%
MARION	39,646	1,501	2,021	2,775	32,388	961	Kerry	3.8%	5.1%	7.0%	81.7%	2.4%
MARSHALL	1,195	82	91	136	854	32	Kerry	6.9%	7.6%	11.4%	71.5%	2.7%
MARTIN	2,063	157	212	328	1,250	116	Kerry	7.6%	10.3%	15.9%	60.6%	5.6%
MIAMI	1,234	84	101	164	851	34	Kerry	6.8%	8.2%	13.3%	69.0%	2.8%
MONROE	5,986	236	520	485	4,164	581	Kerry	3.9%	8.7%	8.1%	69.6%	9.7%
MONTGOMERY	893	59	72	98	642	22	Kerry	6.6%	8.1%	11.0%	71.9%	2.5%
MORGAN	1,346	101	113	156	931	45	Kerry	7.5%	8.4%	11.6%	69.2%	3.3%
NEWTON	672	40	55	79	470	28	Kerry	6.0%	8.2%	11.8%	69.9%	4.2%
NOBLE	1,280	60	69	194	928	29	Kerry	4.7%	5.4%	15.2%	72.5%	2.3%
OHIO	270	9	12	23	221	5	Kerry	3.3%	4.4%	8.5%	81.9%	1.9%
ORANGE	1,306	76	106	170	905	49	Kerry	5.8%	8.1%	13.0%	69.3%	3.8%
OWEN	1,308	79	77	166	915	71	Kerry	6.0%	5.9%	12.7%	70.0%	5.4%
PARKE	1,031	56	75	117	767	16	Kerry	5.4%	7.3%	11.3%	74.4%	1.6%
PERRY	2,664	170	204	324	1,890	76	Kerry	6.4%	7.7%	12.2%	70.9%	2.9%
PIKE	1,596	104	109	238	1,087	58	Kerry	6.5%	6.8%	14.9%	68.1%	3.6%
PORTER	5,909	217	365	604	4,486	237	Kerry	3.7%	6.2%	10.2%	75.9%	4.0%
POSEY	2,349	199	233	340	1,478	99	Kerry	8.5%	9.9%	14.5%	62.9%	4.2%
PULASKI	795	40	62	99	579	15	Kerry	5.0%	7.8%	12.5%	72.8%	1.9%
PUTNAM	1,052	108	76	119	730	19	Kerry	10.3%	7.2%	11.3%	69.4%	1.8%
RANDOLPH	1,144	56	87	129	841	31	Kerry	4.9%	7.6%	11.3%	73.5%	2.7%
RIPLEY	1,261	61	67	191	907	35	Kerry	4.8%	5.3%	15.1%	71.9%	2.8%
RUSH	500	35	41	79	336	9	Kerry	7.0%	8.2%	15.8%	67.2%	1.8%
ST. JOSEPH	15,841	430	789	1,654	12,254	714	Kerry	2.7%	5.0%	10.4%	77.4%	4.5%
SCOTT	3,062	189	174	401	2,177	121	Kerry	6.2%	5.7%	13.1%	71.1%	4.0%
SHELBY	1,349	112	97	200	910	30	Kerry	8.3%	7.2%	14.8%	67.5%	2.2%
SPENCER	1,011	54	73	153	711	20	Kerry	5.3%	7.2%	15.1%	70.3%	2.0%
STARKE	1,769	113	119	209	1,269	59	Kerry	6.4%	6.7%	11.8%	71.7%	3.3%
STEUBEN	698	23	44	65	548	18	Kerry	3.3%	6.3%	9.3%	78.5%	2.6%
SULLIVAN	2,920	225	250	390	1,969	86	Kerry	7.7%	8.6%	13.4%	67.4%	2.9%
SWITZERLAND	1,012	50	69	120	729	44	Kerry	4.9%	6.8%	11.9%	72.0%	4.3%
TIPPECANOE	4,095	156	283	458	3,020	178	Kerry	3.8%	6.9%	11.2%	73.7%	4.3%
TIPTON	827	50	63	165	530	19	Kerry	6.0%	7.6%	20.0%	64.1%	2.3%
UNION	321	21	17	30	241	12	Kerry	6.5%	5.3%	9.3%	75.1%	3.7%
VANDERBURGH	8,814	487	628	1,112	6,275	312	Kerry	5.5%	7.1%	12.6%	71.2%	3.5%
VERMILLION	2,802	190	222	373	1,896	121	Kerry	6.8%	7.9%	13.3%	67.7%	4.3%
VIGO	14,518	941	1,113	2,200	9,593	671	Kerry	6.5%	7.7%	15.2%	66.1%	4.6%
WABASH	927	60	64	112	654	37	Kerry	6.5%	6.9%	12.1%	70.6%	4.0%
WARREN	291	24	12	29	220	6	Kerry	8.2%	4.1%	10.0%	75.6%	2.1%
WARRICK	3,514	213	290	482	2,446	83	Kerry	6.1%	8.3%	13.7%	69.6%	2.4%
WASHINGTON	1,592	87	118	219	1,130	38	Kerry	5.5%	7.4%	13.8%	71.0%	2.4%
WAYNE	2,823	98	167	299	2,129	130	Kerry	3.5%	5.9%	10.6%	75.4%	4.6%
WELLS	779	47	68	114	538	12	Kerry	6.0%	8.7%	14.6%	69.1%	1.5%
WHITE	1,093	57	73	122	816	25	Kerry	5.2%	6.7%	11.2%	74.7%	2.3%
WHITLEY	913	45	67	128	642	31	Kerry	4.9%	7.3%	14.0%	70.3%	3.4%
TOTAL	317,211	17,437	21,482	35,651	231,047	11,594	Kerry	5.5%	6.8%	11.2%	72.8%	3.7%

Note: Other vote was 7,003 Dennis J. Kucinich; 4,591 Lyndon H. LaRouche Jr.

IOWA

Probably the most indelible image from the 2004 presidential nominating season was "the Scream"—Howard Dean's impromptu pep talk to his supporters after a disappointing showing in the Iowa caucuses that on television looked like a desperate, over-the-top rant. Whatever it was, though, it was understandable, given the recent importance of Iowa as the state that votes first and sets the tone for the host of primaries that follow.

For all its importance, Iowa is a relative newcomer to the national spotlight. It stepped into the nation's political consciousness on a snowy January night in 1972, when George McGovern ran unexpectedly close to Edmund Muskie in the Democratic precinct caucus voting. While the results drew only a smidgen of attention in the next day's newspapers, it was enough to lend credibility to McGovern's dark-horse candidacy.

McGovern spent only a day and a half campaigning in Iowa before he made his breakthrough in 1972. Now it is routine for every candidate to spend at least several weeks in the state, and for little-known dark-horse contenders to devote even more time than that.

Candidates who have tried to win Iowa by making only an occasional stop in the state do so at their peril. Ronald Reagan essentially bypassed Iowa in 1980 and lost the caucuses to George Bush, and then had to work overtime in New Hampshire to regain his position as the Republican front-runner.

Yet the thinking of Reagan's strategists was understandable. Front-runners, by and large, have little to gain in Iowa. At best, they survive.

That ability to flummox the experts has helped make the Iowa caucuses one of the most successful political inventions of recent times. And results are often not measured by who won and who lost, but who exceeded expectations and who did not. Sometimes, it has been the runner-up who enjoyed the big "Iowa bounce" and landed at the center of the national imagination.

McGovern was the first beneficiary of this momentum in 1972. Four years later, Iowa helped create the phenomenon of Jimmy Carter. Perhaps the quintessential Iowa bounce, though, was the one that surprised even its beneficiary, Gary Hart.

Walter Mondale came down from Minnesota to claim about half the 1984 Democratic caucus vote. But Hart got half the momentum with just 16 percent of the vote because he exceeded the modest expectations of the media (and because John Glenn and Alan Cranston fell miserably short by the same standard). A week later, Hart won New Hampshire.

For a time, Iowa was more successful at winnowing the field than serving as a harbinger of things to come. In 1988, the eventual nominees—Michael Dukakis and George Bush—both placed third in Iowa, while the two Iowa winners—Richard Gephardt and Bob Dole—were both out of the race by the end of March.

In 1992, Iowa Democrats rallied around their home-state senator, Tom Harkin, who was unable to gain traction elsewhere and also quit the race in March.

In 1996, Pat Buchanan got the Iowa bounce with a close second-place finish to Dole, but was unable to make the momentum extend beyond victory in New Hampshire.

Dole's winning vote share in Iowa fell by more than 10 percentage points from eight years earlier to 26 percent. Meanwhile, Buchanan nearly matched the 25 percent share that runner-up Pat Robertson had garnered in 1988.

But Buchanan's showing was not simply a reprise of Robertson's. Robertson carried 14 Iowa counties, mostly in the industrialized eastern half of the state and many in Democratic areas where the Republican caucuses offered a vacuum to be filled.

Buchanan carried 24 counties, mostly in rural southwest Iowa, where concern about the encroachment of big agricultural interests melded with social-issue conservatism. Dole, though, enjoyed broad-based success in 1996 that belied his modest winning percentage. Of Iowa's 99 counties, he carried 70. As in 1988, Dole ran best in the small towns and farm country of rural Iowa. He was weaker in the larger population centers, carrying Polk County (Des Moines) by just seven votes over Lamar Alexander, and Linn County (Cedar Rapids) by just three votes over Alan Keyes.

Still, Dole was able to make his victory go further than he had eight years earlier, when his failures in the rest of the country led to joking references to him as "the president of Iowa."

In 2000, both parties held competitive contests in the Hawkeye State for the first time since 1988. But unlike a dozen years earlier, the eventual nominees in 2000 won Iowa handily—George W. Bush on the Republican side, Al Gore on the Democratic.

What made the caucus results interesting was how their principal opponents dealt with the state. Republican John McCain skipped the caucuses in favor of a more intensive effort in New Hampshire, which he won. Meanwhile, Democrat Bill Bradley battled Gore head-to-head in Iowa, losing time, money, and momentum with a nearly 2-to-1 loss to the vice president that undoubtedly contributed to Bradley's narrow defeat in New Hampshire.

Recent Iowa Caucus Results

Iowa held its only presidential primary in 1916. Since 1972, its precinct caucuses have been a notable part of the political scene.

		DEMOCRATS			REPUBLICANS	
Year	Estimated Turnout	Candidates	%	Turnout	Candidates	%
2004 (Jan. 19)	124,331	JOHN KERRY	38	—	No Caucus Vote	
		John Edwards	32			
		Howard Dean	18			
		Richard Gephardt	11			
2000 (Jan. 24)	61,000	AL GORE	63	87,233	GEORGE W. BUSH	41
		Bill Bradley	35		Steve Forbes	30
					Alan Keyes	14
					Gary Bauer	9
1996 (Feb. 12)	50,000	BILL CLINTON*	100	96,451	BOB DOLE	26
					Pat Buchanan	23
					Lamar Alexander	18
					Steve Forbes	10
					Phil Gramm	9
					Alan Keyes	7
1992 (Feb. 10)	30,000	TOM HARKIN	76	—	No Caucus Vote	
		Uncommitted	12			
1988 (Feb. 8)	126,000	RICHARD GEPHARDT	31	108,838	BOB DOLE	37
		Paul Simon	27		Pat Robertson	25
		Michael Dukakis	22		George Bush	19
		Jesse Jackson	9		Jack Kemp	11
		Bruce Babbitt	6		Pierre du Pont	7
1984 (Feb. 20)	75,000	WALTER MONDALE	49	—	No Caucus Vote	
		Gary Hart	16			
		George McGovern	10			
		Uncommitted	9			
		Alan Cranston	7			
1980 (Jan. 21)	100,000	JIMMY CARTER*	59	106,051	GEORGE BUSH	32
		Edward Kennedy	31		Ronald Reagan	30
		Uncommitted	10		Howard Baker	15
					John Connally	9
					Phil Crane	7
1976 (Jan. 19)	38,500	UNCOMMITTED	39	20,000	GERALD FORD*	45
		Jimmy Carter	29		Ronald Reagan	43
		Birch Bayh	11		Undecided	11
		Fred Harris	9			
		Morris Udall	6			
1972 (Jan. 24)	20,000	UNCOMMITTED	36	—	No Caucus Vote	
		Edmund Muskie	36			
		George McGovern	23			

Note: Democratic turnouts are estimates. Republican results are from the straw vote held in conjunction with the precinct caucuses. Percentages for Democratic candidates are based on a weighted measurement compiled by the Iowa Democratic Party. The 1976 GOP results are based on returns from a sampling of precincts. All candidates are listed that drew at least 5 percent of their party's vote. The names of winning candidates are capitalized. An asterisk (*) indicates an incumbent president.

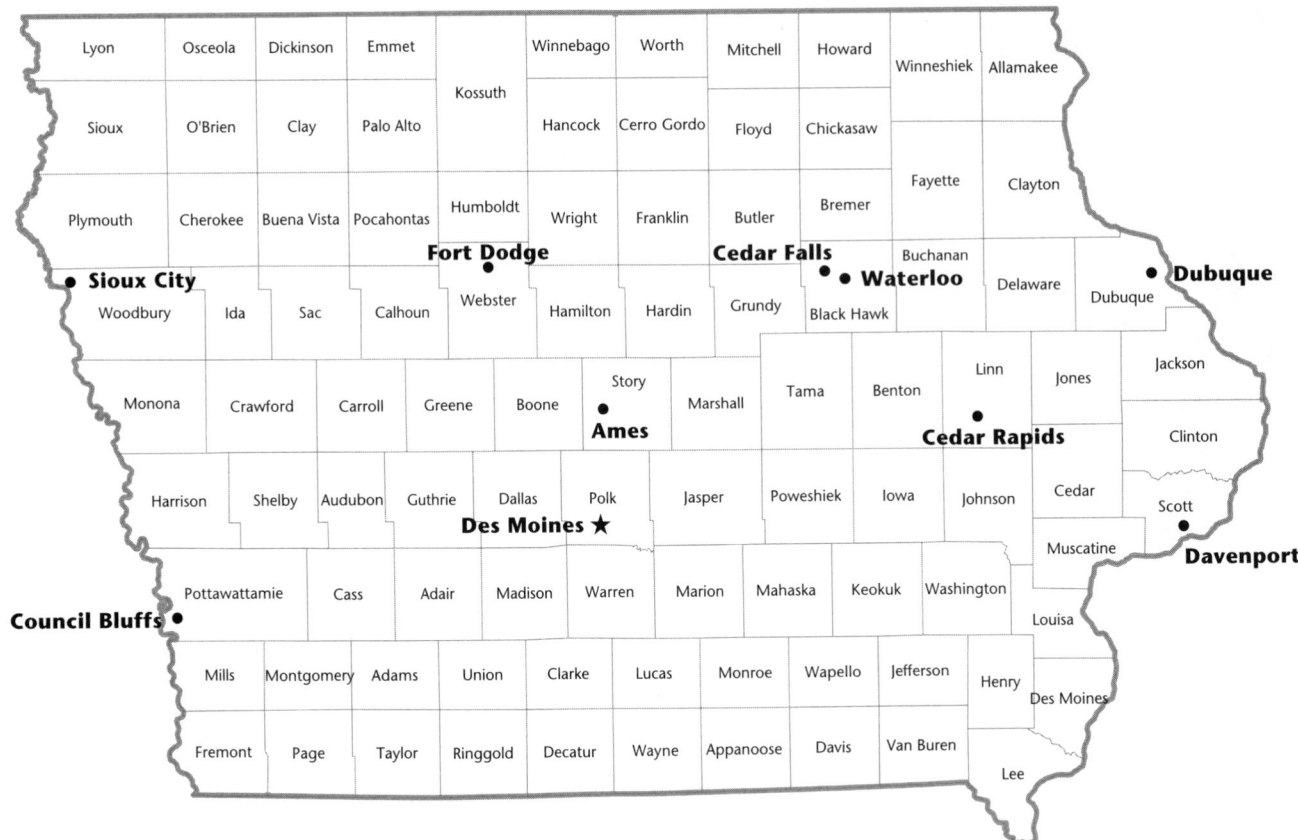

Bradley did carry Johnson County (Iowa City), a liberal, academically oriented enclave that includes the University of Iowa. But with the active support of organized labor and teachers, Gore won virtually everywhere else in the state.

In 2004, four Democrats approached the Iowa caucuses with a chance to win—John Kerry, John Edwards, Dean, and Gephardt. The latter two were considered to be best organized to get out their voters on caucus night. But Kerry and Edwards had the late momentum, which they rode to a one-two finish.

Kerry effectively tied into the strong anti-Iraq war sentiment among Iowa Democrats by evoking his Vietnam experience, replete with stump appearances by wartime comrades who became known as his "band of brothers." Edwards used his rural Carolina roots to connect with voters in small towns and farm communities across Iowa. Edwards also benefited from an endorsement from the state's largest newspaper, the *Des Moines Register*, which helped him carry populous Polk County. Kerry, though, swept most of the state's other major population centers.

Dean, the erstwhile front-runner for the Democratic nomination in late 2003, carried only two small counties and never recovered the momentum he once had. Gephardt, the 1988 Iowa winner, carried no counties and quit the race shortly thereafter.

IOWA REPUBLICAN CAUCUSES

2000

County	Total Vote	Bauer	G.W. Bush	Forbes	Hatch	Keyes	McCain	Winner	Percentage of Total Vote					
									Bauer	G.W. Bush	Forbes	Hatch	Keyes	McCain
ADAIR	274	10	138	78	2	32	14	G.W. Bush	3.6%	50.4%	28.5%	0.7%	11.7%	5.1%
ADAMS	149	12	74	36	2	19	6	G.W. Bush	8.1%	49.7%	24.2%	1.3%	12.8%	4.0%
ALLAMAKEE	453	26	200	82	4	122	19	G.W. Bush	5.7%	44.2%	18.1%	0.9%	26.9%	4.2%
APPANOOSE	466	31	219	159	5	29	23	G.W. Bush	6.7%	47.0%	34.1%	1.1%	6.2%	4.9%
AUDUBON	131	14	80	28	2	5	2	G.W. Bush	10.7%	61.1%	21.4%	1.5%	3.8%	1.5%
BENTON	676	56	256	187	5	155	17	G.W. Bush	8.3%	37.9%	27.7%	0.7%	22.9%	2.5%
BLACK HAWK	2,802	353	1,199	764	10	372	104	G.W. Bush	12.6%	42.8%	27.3%	0.4%	13.3%	3.7%
BOONE	879	118	297	309	10	124	21	Forbes	13.4%	33.8%	35.2%	1.1%	14.1%	2.4%
BREMER	600	49	271	174	6	75	25	G.W. Bush	8.2%	45.2%	29.0%	1.0%	12.5%	4.2%
BUCHANAN	491	87	172	155	1	62	14	G.W. Bush	17.7%	35.0%	31.6%	0.2%	12.6%	2.9%
BUENA VISTA	671	90	264	233	3	67	14	G.W. Bush	13.4%	39.3%	34.7%	0.4%	10.0%	2.1%
BUTLER	483	64	201	147	1	55	15	G.W. Bush	13.3%	41.6%	30.4%	0.2%	11.4%	3.1%
CALHOUN	326	15	129	134	3	34	11	Forbes	4.6%	39.6%	41.1%	0.9%	10.4%	3.4%
CARROLL	530	22	183	186	3	105	31	Forbes	4.2%	34.5%	35.1%	0.6%	19.8%	5.8%
CASS	632	47	321	157	5	70	32	G.W. Bush	7.4%	50.8%	24.8%	0.8%	11.1%	5.1%
CEDAR	549	90	221	162	8	55	13	G.W. Bush	16.4%	40.3%	29.5%	1.5%	10.0%	2.4%
CERRO GORDO	1,274	67	558	398	9	201	41	G.W. Bush	5.3%	43.8%	31.2%	0.7%	15.8%	3.2%
CHEROKEE	486	29	196	186	2	49	24	G.W. Bush	6.0%	40.3%	38.3%	0.4%	10.1%	4.9%
CHICKASAW	302	28	146	90	8	17	13	G.W. Bush	9.3%	48.3%	29.8%	2.6%	5.6%	4.3%
CLARKE	201	11	99	58	2	27	4	G.W. Bush	5.5%	49.3%	28.9%	1.0%	13.4%	2.0%
CLAY	702	75	284	247	7	58	31	G.W. Bush	10.7%	40.5%	35.2%	1.0%	8.3%	4.4%
CLAYTON	453	26	210	142	4	52	19	G.W. Bush	5.7%	46.4%	31.3%	0.9%	11.5%	4.2%
CLINTON	1,159	25	477	461	17	136	43	G.W. Bush	2.2%	41.2%	39.8%	1.5%	11.7%	3.7%
CRAWFORD	306	14	145	88	0	48	11	G.W. Bush	4.6%	47.4%	28.8%	0.0%	15.7%	3.6%
DALLAS	1,647	59	736	574	21	191	66	G.W. Bush	3.6%	44.7%	34.9%	1.3%	11.6%	4.0%
DAVIS	211	11	76	66	2	51	5	G.W. Bush	5.2%	36.0%	31.3%	0.9%	24.2%	2.4%
DECATUR	347	34	160	75	20	42	16	G.W. Bush	9.8%	46.1%	21.6%	5.8%	12.1%	4.6%
DELAWARE	464	18	186	164	3	82	11	G.W. Bush	3.9%	40.1%	35.3%	0.6%	17.7%	2.4%
DES MOINES	963	47	334	328	17	183	54	G.W. Bush	4.9%	34.7%	34.1%	1.8%	19.0%	5.6%
DICKINSON	371	42	161	106	2	35	25	G.W. Bush	11.3%	43.4%	28.6%	0.5%	9.4%	6.7%
DUBUQUE	1,588	141	542	541	19	299	46	G.W. Bush	8.9%	34.1%	34.1%	1.2%	18.8%	2.9%
EMMET	196	14	90	52	0	28	12	G.W. Bush	7.1%	45.9%	26.5%	0.0%	14.3%	6.1%
FAYETTE	668	56	286	210	9	80	27	G.W. Bush	8.4%	42.8%	31.4%	1.3%	12.0%	4.0%
FLOYD	339	31	136	113	1	40	18	G.W. Bush	9.1%	40.1%	33.3%	0.3%	11.8%	5.3%
FRANKLIN	418	13	206	130	9	42	18	G.W. Bush	3.1%	49.3%	31.1%	2.2%	10.0%	4.3%
FREMONT	193	8	116	44	0	14	11	G.W. Bush	4.1%	60.1%	22.8%	0.0%	7.3%	5.7%
GREENE	436	16	168	162	6	68	16	G.W. Bush	3.7%	38.5%	37.2%	1.4%	15.6%	3.7%
GRUNDY	461	31	216	146	2	61	5	G.W. Bush	6.7%	46.9%	31.7%	0.4%	13.2%	1.1%
GUTHRIE	404	8	173	170	1	34	18	G.W. Bush	2.0%	42.8%	42.1%	0.2%	8.4%	4.5%
HAMILTON	627	31	346	164	4	63	19	G.W. Bush	4.9%	55.2%	26.2%	0.6%	10.0%	3.0%
HANCOCK	308	26	126	94	3	54	5	G.W. Bush	8.4%	40.9%	30.5%	1.0%	17.5%	1.6%
HARDIN	773	30	239	397	1	80	26	Forbes	3.9%	30.9%	51.4%	0.1%	10.3%	3.4%
HARRISON	394	36	188	89	3	50	28	G.W. Bush	9.1%	47.7%	22.6%	0.8%	12.7%	7.1%
HENRY	489	18	195	164	6	83	23	G.W. Bush	3.7%	39.9%	33.5%	1.2%	17.0%	4.7%
HOWARD	243	15	115	71	5	29	8	G.W. Bush	6.2%	47.3%	29.2%	2.1%	11.9%	3.3%

IOWA REPUBLICAN CAUCUSES

2000

County	Total Vote	Bauer	G.W. Bush	Forbes	Hatch	Keyes	McCain	Winner	Percentage of Total Vote					
									Bauer	G.W. Bush	Forbes	Hatch	Keyes	McCain
HUMBOLDT	300	11	105	122	4	39	19	Forbes	3.7%	35.0%	40.7%	1.3%	13.0%	6.3%
IDA	241	17	59	139	1	16	9	Forbes	7.1%	24.5%	57.7%	0.4%	6.6%	3.7%
IOWA	440	24	153	150	0	94	19	G.W. Bush	5.5%	34.8%	34.1%	0.0%	21.4%	4.3%
JACKSON	339	13	170	99	3	44	10	G.W. Bush	3.8%	50.1%	29.2%	0.9%	13.0%	2.9%
JASPER	1,328	121	535	462	17	155	38	G.W. Bush	9.1%	40.3%	34.8%	1.3%	11.7%	2.9%
JEFFERSON	528	21	179	155	2	153	18	G.W. Bush	4.0%	33.9%	29.4%	0.4%	29.0%	3.4%
JOHNSON	2,408	96	1,013	491	75	458	275	G.W. Bush	4.0%	42.1%	20.4%	3.1%	19.0%	11.4%
JONES	471	14	203	169	2	69	14	G.W. Bush	3.0%	43.1%	35.9%	0.4%	14.6%	3.0%
KEOKUK	339	16	135	140	2	42	4	Forbes	4.7%	39.8%	41.3%	0.6%	12.4%	1.2%
KOSSUTH	456	46	175	136	4	79	16	G.W. Bush	10.1%	38.4%	29.8%	0.9%	17.3%	3.5%
LEE	472	20	207	144	4	61	36	G.W. Bush	4.2%	43.9%	30.5%	0.8%	12.9%	7.6%
LINN	5,072	361	1,995	1,380	46	960	330	G.W. Bush	7.1%	39.3%	27.2%	0.9%	18.9%	6.5%
LOUISA	286	11	121	106	0	37	11	G.W. Bush	3.8%	42.3%	37.1%	0.0%	12.9%	3.8%
LUCAS	286	37	105	103	3	34	4	G.W. Bush	12.9%	36.7%	36.0%	1.0%	11.9%	1.4%
LYON	438	191	147	36	2	47	15	Bauer	43.6%	33.6%	8.2%	0.5%	10.7%	3.4%
MADISON	495	37	183	178	6	80	11	G.W. Bush	7.5%	37.0%	36.0%	1.2%	16.2%	2.2%
MAHASKA	923	165	367	246	4	123	18	G.W. Bush	17.9%	39.8%	26.7%	0.4%	13.3%	2.0%
MARION	942	173	337	292	2	113	25	G.W. Bush	18.4%	35.8%	31.0%	0.2%	12.0%	2.7%
MARSHALL	1,633	72	704	540	8	253	56	G.W. Bush	4.4%	43.1%	33.1%	0.5%	15.5%	3.4%
MILLS	358	48	164	73	2	49	22	G.W. Bush	13.4%	45.8%	20.4%	0.6%	13.7%	6.1%
MITCHELL	290	21	127	99	2	30	11	G.W. Bush	7.2%	43.8%	34.1%	0.7%	10.3%	3.8%
MONONA	248	51	107	69	1	14	6	G.W. Bush	20.6%	43.1%	27.8%	0.4%	5.6%	2.4%
MONROE	197	12	77	88	0	14	6	Forbes	6.1%	39.1%	44.7%	0.0%	7.1%	3.0%
MONTGOMERY	374	12	223	76	5	37	21	G.W. Bush	3.2%	59.6%	20.3%	1.3%	9.9%	5.6%
MUSCATINE	1,052	68	436	333	10	136	69	G.W. Bush	6.5%	41.4%	31.7%	1.0%	12.9%	6.6%
O'BRIEN	667	196	182	166	4	99	20	Bauer	29.4%	27.3%	24.9%	0.6%	14.8%	3.0%
OSCEOLA	196	30	97	39	1	21	8	G.W. Bush	15.3%	49.5%	19.9%	0.5%	10.7%	4.1%
PAGE	383	26	180	74	0	78	25	G.W. Bush	6.8%	47.0%	19.3%	0.0%	20.4%	6.5%
PALO ALTO	273	19	117	81	6	46	4	G.W. Bush	7.0%	42.9%	29.7%	2.2%	16.8%	1.5%
PLYMOUTH	1,002	95	351	414	4	114	24	Forbes	9.5%	35.0%	41.3%	0.4%	11.4%	2.4%
POCAHONTAS	301	32	119	104	0	41	5	G.W. Bush	10.6%	39.5%	34.6%	0.0%	13.6%	1.7%
POLK	14,288	898	6,296	4,005	164	2,059	866	G.W. Bush	6.3%	44.1%	28.0%	1.1%	14.4%	6.1%
POTTAWATTAMIE	1,766	104	934	410	21	187	110	G.W. Bush	5.9%	52.9%	23.2%	1.2%	10.6%	6.2%
POWESHIEK	577	46	239	186	7	63	36	G.W. Bush	8.0%	41.4%	32.2%	1.2%	10.9%	6.2%
RINGGOLD	160	9	88	53	0	7	3	G.W. Bush	5.6%	55.0%	33.1%	0.0%	4.4%	1.9%
SAC	386	6	150	140	4	57	29	G.W. Bush	1.6%	38.9%	36.3%	1.0%	14.8%	7.5%
SCOTT	4,379	218	1,730	1,467	87	654	223	G.W. Bush	5.0%	39.5%	33.5%	2.0%	14.9%	5.1%
SHELBY	332	55	138	75	1	41	22	G.W. Bush	16.6%	41.6%	22.6%	0.3%	12.3%	6.6%
SIOUX	2,322	931	657	307	7	378	42	Bauer	40.1%	28.3%	13.2%	0.3%	16.3%	1.8%
STORY	3,300	300	1,346	883	45	463	263	G.W. Bush	9.1%	40.8%	26.8%	1.4%	14.0%	8.0%
TAMA	569	35	202	215	5	102	10	Forbes	6.2%	35.5%	37.8%	0.9%	17.9%	1.8%
TAYLOR	154	10	71	38	1	24	10	G.W. Bush	6.5%	46.1%	24.7%	0.6%	15.6%	6.5%
UNION	351	23	123	131	0	61	13	Forbes	6.6%	35.0%	37.3%	0.0%	17.4%	3.7%
VAN BUREN	314	15	118	115	4	48	14	G.W. Bush	4.8%	37.6%	36.6%	1.3%	15.3%	4.5%
WAPELLO	687	37	276	260	9	92	13	G.W. Bush	5.4%	40.2%	37.8%	1.3%	13.4%	1.9%

IOWA REPUBLICAN CAUCUSES

2000

County	Total Vote	Bauer	G.W. Bush	Forbes	Hatch	Keyes	McCain	Winner	Percentage of Total Vote					
									Bauer	G.W. Bush	Forbes	Hatch	Keyes	McCain
WARREN	1,463	103	579	496	13	221	51	G.W. Bush	7.0%	39.6%	33.9%	0.9%	15.1%	3.5%
WASHINGTON	482	29	152	173	3	106	19	Forbes	6.0%	31.5%	35.9%	0.6%	22.0%	3.9%
WAYNE	185	19	72	55	2	33	4	G.W. Bush	10.3%	38.9%	29.7%	1.1%	17.8%	2.2%
WEBSTER	913	65	342	402	5	77	22	Forbes	7.1%	37.5%	44.0%	0.5%	8.4%	2.4%
WINNEBAGO	407	60	140	154	2	35	16	Forbes	14.7%	34.4%	37.8%	0.5%	8.6%	3.9%
WINNESHIEK	538	32	258	139	3	62	44	G.W. Bush	5.9%	48.0%	25.8%	0.6%	11.5%	8.2%
WOODBURY	2,887	220	1,058	1,178	24	336	71	Forbes	7.6%	36.6%	40.8%	0.8%	11.6%	2.5%
WORTH	184	14	71	77	0	16	6	Forbes	7.6%	38.6%	41.8%	0.0%	8.7%	3.3%
WRIGHT	523	34	216	159	5	96	13	G.W. Bush	6.5%	41.3%	30.4%	1.0%	18.4%	2.5%
TOTAL	86,440	7,363	35,464	26,343	885	12,332	4,053	G.W. Bush	8.5%	41.0%	30.5%	1.0%	14.3%	4.7%
Final Total	87,233	7,444	35,787	26,595	893	12,430	4,084	G.W. Bush	8.5%	41.0%	30.5%	1.0%	14.2%	4.7%

Note: County returns were based on totals from 2,083 of Iowa's 2,131 precincts. The final totals were based on results from 2,104 precincts, but were not updated by county.

KANSAS

Kansas was the birthplace of several candidates who sought the White House in the late twentieth century. Gary Hart grew up in Ottawa in the eastern part of the state. Arlen Specter (who briefly pursued the 1996 Republican nomination) was born in Wichita.

But none made their mark in Kansas politics like Bob Dole, who was born, raised and sunk roots in the small town of Russell. And for nearly two decades, Kansas tried hard to boost Dole's presidential ambitions, although the results were not always as planned.

On Dole's first try for the White House in 1980, Kansas created its first-ever presidential primary. But his candidacy collapsed quickly, and he did not even enter his home-state primary that spring.

On Dole's second presidential run in 1988, Kansas Republicans got their licks in early with a pre–Super Tuesday caucus that Dole dominated. Pat Robertson tried to rally religious conservatives in parts of Kansas but failed to win a single delegate. Yet ultimately, Dole abandoned his candidacy before the convention, and all the Kansas delegates ended up voting for nominee George Bush.

In 1996, Kansas first scheduled a presidential primary, then canceled it, although the change did not threaten Dole's control of the delegation in the year that he finally won the Republican presidential nomination.

Not only were Kansas Republicans loyal to their longtime senator, but they sometimes looked askance at his presidential rivals, even when Dole was not on the ballot. President Bush won a comparatively modest 62 percent of the Kansas GOP primary vote in 1992, his second-lowest share of the primary season behind New Hampshire.

Republicans dominate the political scene in Kansas but they are not all of a like mind. Voters in small-town Kansas–the party's traditional backbone–do not always vote the same as those in the more affluent suburbs outside Kansas City.

The disparity between the two was noticeable in the 1980 GOP primary. Ronald Reagan won easily. But while he rolled up more than 70 percent of the vote in many rural counties, where "moral values" issues have increasingly come to define the political landscape, Reagan was held to a bare majority in suburban Johnson County, where both George Bush and John Anderson established toeholds.

The two Democratic presidential primaries in Kansas have been won by Southerners who were able to appeal to the state's rural nature. President Jimmy Carter trounced Edward Kennedy by 25 percentage points in 1980, although Carter's agricultural policy was not widely popular across the Plains and he lost a handful of farm counties to Kennedy.

Recent Kansas Primary Results

Kansas held its first presidential primary in 1980.

| Year | DEMOCRATS | | | REPUBLICANS | | |
	Turnout	Candidates	%	Turnout	Candidates	%
2004	—	No Primary		—	No Primary	
2000	—	No Primary		—	No Primary	
1996	—	No Primary		—	No Primary	
1992 (April 7)	160,251	BILL CLINTON	51	213,196	GEORGE BUSH*	62
		Paul Tsongas	15		"None"	17
		"None"	14		Pat Buchanan	15
		Jerry Brown	13			
1988	—	No Primary		—	No Primary	
1984	—	No Primary		—	No Primary	
1980 (April 1)	193,918	JIMMY CARTER*	57	285,398	RONALD REAGAN	63
		Edward Kennedy	32		John Anderson	18
					George Bush	13

Note: All candidates are listed that drew at least 5 percent of their party's primary vote. The names of winning candidates are capitalized. An asterisk (*) indicates an incumbent president.

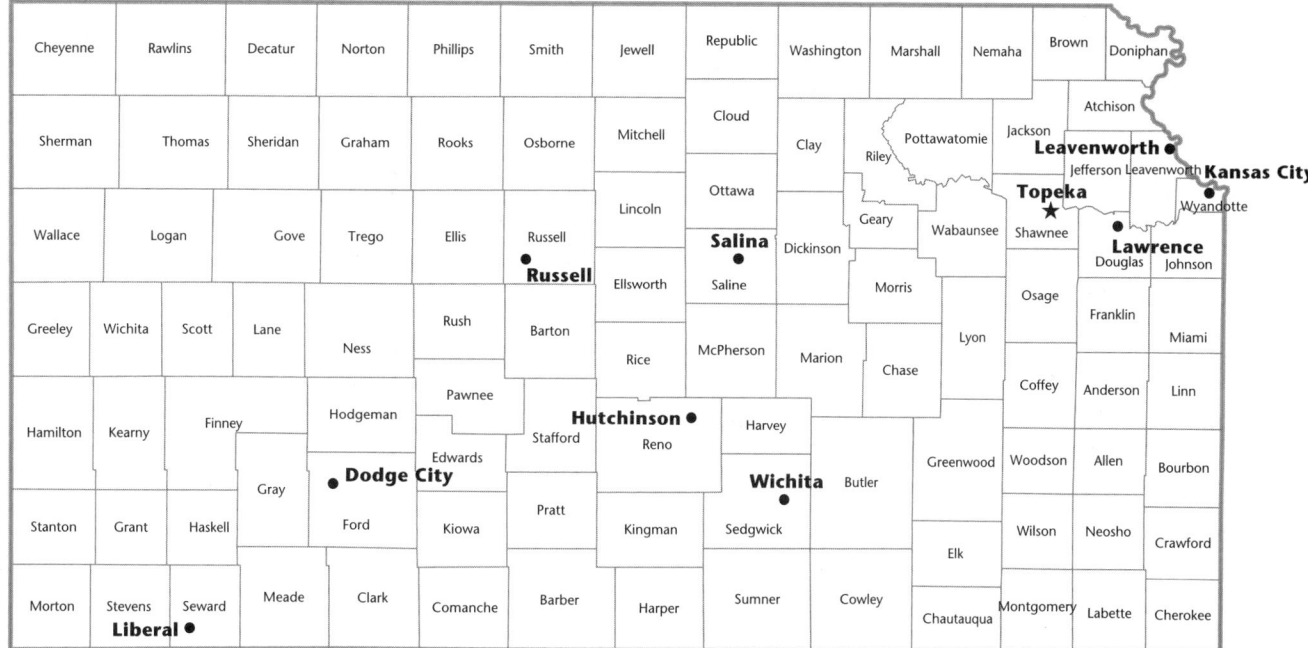

Twelve years later, Bill Clinton won a majority of the vote against a crowded Democratic field. Yet like Carter, Clinton did not win everywhere in Kansas. Rawlins County, in the far northwest corner of the state, opted for its local entry, Dean Beamgard, a longtime community activist and retired postmaster. The vote in Rawlins County: Beamgard, 174; Clinton, 89.

In the post-Dole era, Kansas has reverted to being a political backwater in the presidential nominating process. The state scheduled an early April primary in 2000, then repealed it as a cost-cutting measure. In 2004, Kansas Democrats launched a caucus process to elect delegates in mid-March, but even

that was too late to have any impact on the presidential race. According to an Associated Press tally, John Kerry had won the majority of national convention delegates required to secure his nomination about an hour before the Kansas caucuses were to begin.

As it was, Kerry swept the Kansas event easily, winning 72 percent of the delegates selected in the caucuses to 10 percent for Dennis Kucinich, who finished a distant second. An estimated 2,000 voters took part at 50 caucus sites around the state, a turnout that represented barely 1 percent of the number that participated in the state's first Democratic presidential primary in 1980.

154

KENTUCKY

Basketball and politics are two of the leading spectator sports in Kentucky, but the state's presidential primary has never drawn more than a collective yawn. That has been due in no small part to the fact that it has generally been held in late May, a time when recent nominating contests have been in the mop-up stage.

Since Kentucky held its first presidential primary in 1976, its only vote of significance came in the Republican contest that year between President Gerald Ford and Ronald Reagan. Out of nearly 135,000 votes cast, Ford won by barely 5,000—a narrow victory, but an important one in slowing the momentum that Reagan had built up earlier that month with a series of primary victories.

Reagan carried one stronghold of Kentucky Republicanism—the relatively affluent Louisville suburbs. Ford carried

the other—the state's mountainous southeastern corner. Many of the mountaineers are "New Deal Republicans"—joined in poverty with Democrats in nearby hills and hollows but separated from them politically by partisan divisions dating back to the Civil War.

The Democratic eastern end of Kentucky is similar to neighboring West Virginia. The region has a long union tradition and the voters have looked favorably on New Deal-style Democrats. It was the only part of Kentucky where Edward Kennedy ran reasonably close to President Jimmy Carter in Kennedy's landslide 1980 primary loss.

Across the state in the western panhandle is a different breed of Democrat. That area resembles the Deep South in its voting habits and contains the only Kentucky counties that supported George Wallace's 1968 third-party presidential bid.

Recent Kentucky Primary Results

Kentucky held its first presidential primary in 1976.

| Year | DEMOCRATS | | | REPUBLICANS | | |
	Turnout	Candidates	%	Turnout	Candidates	%
2004 (May 18)	229,916	JOHN KERRY	60	117,379	GEORGE W. BUSH*	93
		John Edwards	15		Uncommitted	7
		Uncommitted	9			
2000 (May 23)	220,279	AL GORE	71	91,323	GEORGE W. BUSH	83
		Bill Bradley	15		John McCain	6
		Uncommitted	12			
1996 (May 28)	276,019	BILL CLINTON*	77	103,839	BOB DOLE	74
		Uncommitted	16		Pat Buchanan	8
		Lyndon LaRouche	7			
1992 (May 26)	370,578	BILL CLINTON	56	101,119	GEORGE BUSH*	75
		Uncommitted	28		Uncommitted	25
		Jerry Brown	8			
1988 (March 8)	318,721	AL GORE	46	121,402	GEORGE BUSH	59
		Michael Dukakis	19		Bob Dole	23
		Jesse Jackson	16		Pat Robertson	11
		Richard Gephardt	9			
1984	—	No Primary		—	No Primary	
1980 (May 27)	240,331	JIMMY CARTER*	67	94,795	RONALD REAGAN	82
		Edward Kennedy	23		George Bush	7
		Uncommitted	8		John Anderson	5
1976 (May 25)	306,006	JIMMY CARTER	59	133,528	GERALD FORD*	51
		George Wallace	17		Ronald Reagan	47
		Morris Udall	11			
		Ellen McCormack	6			

Note: All candidates are listed that drew at least 5 percent of their party's primary vote. The names of winning candidates are capitalized. An asterisk (*) indicates an incumbent president.

Except for the initial Ford-Reagan GOP primary in 1976, every Kentucky primary for president—Democratic and Republican alike—has been decided by a margin of more than 25 percentage points. As a result, turnout has been driven less by the presidential contest than by other races on the primary ballot—frequently an array of local, state, and federal offices.

The winner of the Democratic primary has often been the candidate that the Democratic governor supported. (Between 1967 and 2003, Kentucky did not elect a Republican governor.)

In 1988, Gov. Wallace G. Wilkinson backed Al Gore, who won easily. In 1992, Gov. Brereton Jones backed Bill Clinton, who carried the Kentucky primary by an even larger vote.

As it was, Gore's winning 46 percent share in Kentucky was his highest percentage in any 1988 primary outside his home state of Tennessee. Gore had trouble shaking his two closest rivals, Michael Dukakis and Jesse Jackson, in Kentucky's two leading population centers, Jefferson (Louisville) and Fayette (Lexington) counties.

But moving south across the state toward the Tennessee border, Gore's vote share increased dramatically. In Monroe County, which lies about 30 miles north of his hometown of Carthage, Tenn., Gore won 95 percent of the votes cast.

As in much of the rest of the South, George Bush's victory in the 1988 Republican primary in Kentucky was notable for its completeness. He lost only one county, Ballard, a rural Democratic enclave bordering Illinois and Missouri that was carried by Bob Dole.

Bush swept every Kentucky county in the 1992 Republican primary, as did his son, George W., in the 2004 GOP contest. That year, the younger Bush's only competition came from an "Uncommitted" line, which reached double digits percentagewise in nine counties, including the one (Franklin) that contains the state capital of Frankfort.

KENTUCKY DEMOCRATIC PRIMARY

2000

County	Total Vote	Bradley	Gore	LaRouche	Uncommitted	Winner	Percentage of Total Vote			
							Bradley	Gore	LaRouche	Uncommitted
ADAIR	240	46	177	4	13	Gore	19.2%	73.8%	1.7%	5.4%
ALLEN	468	56	375	4	33	Gore	12.0%	80.1%	0.9%	7.1%
ANDERSON	1,300	243	858	52	147	Gore	18.7%	66.0%	4.0%	11.3%
BALLARD	502	53	367	8	74	Gore	10.6%	73.1%	1.6%	14.7%
BARREN	2,091	283	1,564	31	213	Gore	13.5%	74.8%	1.5%	10.2%
BATH	984	200	757	23	4	Gore	20.3%	76.9%	2.3%	0.4%
BELL	1,371	168	1,093	20	90	Gore	12.3%	79.7%	1.5%	6.6%
BOONE	1,887	378	1,145	67	297	Gore	20.0%	60.7%	3.6%	15.7%
BOURBON	1,826	337	1,161	47	281	Gore	18.5%	63.6%	2.6%	15.4%
BOYD	3,752	409	2,887	44	412	Gore	10.9%	76.9%	1.2%	11.0%
BOYLE	2,067	366	1,375	33	293	Gore	17.7%	66.5%	1.6%	14.2%
BRACKEN	240	37	153	8	42	Gore	15.4%	63.8%	3.3%	17.5%
BREATHITT	1,513	205	1,145	32	131	Gore	13.5%	75.7%	2.1%	8.7%
BRECKINRIDGE	661	123	520	18	0	Gore	18.6%	78.7%	2.7%	0.0%
BULLITT	3,645	552	2,430	103	560	Gore	15.1%	66.7%	2.8%	15.4%
BUTLER	182	19	151	1	11	Gore	10.4%	83.0%	0.5%	6.0%
CALDWELL	546	94	353	12	87	Gore	17.2%	64.7%	2.2%	15.9%
CALLOWAY	2,199	298	1,523	33	345	Gore	13.6%	69.3%	1.5%	15.7%
CAMPBELL	2,963	450	2,074	67	372	Gore	15.2%	70.0%	2.3%	12.6%
CARLISLE	324	41	228	8	47	Gore	12.7%	70.4%	2.5%	14.5%
CARROLL	1,812	241	1,223	40	308	Gore	13.3%	67.5%	2.2%	17.0%
CARTER	1,103	131	848	27	97	Gore	11.9%	76.9%	2.4%	8.8%
CASEY	159	22	119	3	15	Gore	13.8%	74.8%	1.9%	9.4%
CHRISTIAN	3,452	505	2,337	65	545	Gore	14.6%	67.7%	1.9%	15.8%
CLARK	3,074	524	2,022	75	453	Gore	17.0%	65.8%	2.4%	14.7%
CLAY	289	36	216	7	30	Gore	12.5%	74.7%	2.4%	10.4%
CLINTON	165	24	128	3	10	Gore	14.5%	77.6%	1.8%	6.1%
CRITTENDEN	606	107	422	13	64	Gore	17.7%	69.6%	2.1%	10.6%
CUMBERLAND	91	16	68	4	3	Gore	17.6%	74.7%	4.4%	3.3%
DAVIESS	7,129	1,133	4,856	148	992	Gore	15.9%	68.1%	2.1%	13.9%
EDMONSON	387	55	306	8	18	Gore	14.2%	79.1%	2.1%	4.7%
ELLIOTT	209	30	158	5	16	Gore	14.4%	75.6%	2.4%	7.7%
ESTILL	251	29	208	3	11	Gore	11.6%	82.9%	1.2%	4.4%
FAYETTE	11,224	1,904	7,969	265	1,086	Gore	17.0%	71.0%	2.4%	9.7%
FLEMING	465	83	316	11	55	Gore	17.8%	68.0%	2.4%	11.8%
FLOYD	8,608	1,230	6,391	141	846	Gore	14.3%	74.2%	1.6%	9.8%
FRANKLIN	9,137	1,515	6,214	204	1,204	Gore	16.6%	68.0%	2.2%	13.2%
FULTON	338	38	239	10	51	Gore	11.2%	70.7%	3.0%	15.1%
GALLATIN	257	32	173	10	42	Gore	12.5%	67.3%	3.9%	16.3%
GARRARD	332	42	252	7	31	Gore	12.7%	75.9%	2.1%	9.3%
GRANT	1,612	277	1,043	46	246	Gore	17.2%	64.7%	2.9%	15.3%
GRAVES	1,200	149	814	41	196	Gore	12.4%	67.8%	3.4%	16.3%
GRAYSON	526	65	422	6	33	Gore	12.4%	80.2%	1.1%	6.3%
GREEN	180	28	120	5	27	Gore	15.6%	66.7%	2.8%	15.0%
GREENUP	2,637	300	2,027	45	265	Gore	11.4%	76.9%	1.7%	10.0%

KENTUCKY DEMOCRATIC PRIMARY

2000

County	Total Vote	Bradley	Gore	LaRouche	Uncommitted	Winner	Percentage of Total Vote			
							Bradley	Gore	LaRouche	Uncommitted
HANCOCK	526	112	356	10	48	Gore	21.3%	67.7%	1.9%	9.1%
HARDIN	5,891	896	3,733	123	1,139	Gore	15.2%	63.4%	2.1%	19.3%
HARLAN	3,708	467	2,704	104	433	Gore	12.6%	72.9%	2.8%	11.7%
HARRISON	786	146	509	15	116	Gore	18.6%	64.8%	1.9%	14.8%
HART	1,463	264	1,018	28	153	Gore	18.0%	69.6%	1.9%	10.5%
HENDERSON	1,237	183	851	24	179	Gore	14.8%	68.8%	1.9%	14.5%
HENRY	832	148	525	28	131	Gore	17.8%	63.1%	3.4%	15.7%
HICKMAN	301	31	220	7	43	Gore	10.3%	73.1%	2.3%	14.3%
HOPKINS	1,798	341	1,081	46	330	Gore	19.0%	60.1%	2.6%	18.4%
JACKSON	81	9	65	3	4	Gore	11.1%	80.2%	3.7%	4.9%
JEFFERSON	40,383	4,785	30,778	963	3,857	Gore	11.8%	76.2%	2.4%	9.6%
JESSAMINE	2,227	414	1,409	54	350	Gore	18.6%	63.3%	2.4%	15.7%
JOHNSON	1,436	250	1,072	26	88	Gore	17.4%	74.7%	1.8%	6.1%
KENTON	3,938	642	2,543	111	642	Gore	16.3%	64.6%	2.8%	16.3%
KNOTT	4,299	597	3,152	91	459	Gore	13.9%	73.3%	2.1%	10.7%
KNOX	363	43	282	12	26	Gore	11.8%	77.7%	3.3%	7.2%
LARUE	618	112	393	22	91	Gore	18.1%	63.6%	3.6%	14.7%
LAUREL	533	65	419	16	33	Gore	12.2%	78.6%	3.0%	6.2%
LAWRENCE	696	90	546	14	46	Gore	12.9%	78.4%	2.0%	6.6%
LEE	205	29	151	2	23	Gore	14.1%	73.7%	1.0%	11.2%
LESLIE	123	11	100	3	9	Gore	8.9%	81.3%	2.4%	7.3%
LETCHER	2,908	462	2,159	58	229	Gore	15.9%	74.2%	2.0%	7.9%
LEWIS	460	48	376	5	31	Gore	10.4%	81.7%	1.1%	6.7%
LINCOLN	1,936	352	1,336	36	212	Gore	18.2%	69.0%	1.9%	11.0%
LIVINGSTON	478	47	351	8	72	Gore	9.8%	73.4%	1.7%	15.1%
LOGAN	1,568	199	1,153	28	188	Gore	12.7%	73.5%	1.8%	12.0%
LYON	1,454	144	1,096	20	194	Gore	9.9%	75.4%	1.4%	13.3%
MCCRACKEN	2,815	331	2,020	51	413	Gore	11.8%	71.8%	1.8%	14.7%
MCCREARY	163	19	124	6	14	Gore	11.7%	76.1%	3.7%	8.6%
MCLEAN	634	116	412	14	92	Gore	18.3%	65.0%	2.2%	14.5%
MADISON	1,623	260	1,179	43	141	Gore	16.0%	72.6%	2.6%	8.7%
MAGOFFIN	1,590	200	1,230	38	122	Gore	12.6%	77.4%	2.4%	7.7%
MARION	422	55	270	12	85	Gore	13.0%	64.0%	2.8%	20.1%
MARSHALL	2,551	309	1,799	57	386	Gore	12.1%	70.5%	2.2%	15.1%
MARTIN	265	44	197	5	19	Gore	16.6%	74.3%	1.9%	7.2%
MASON	451	70	296	9	76	Gore	15.5%	65.6%	2.0%	16.9%
MEADE	1,858	266	1,274	52	266	Gore	14.3%	68.6%	2.8%	14.3%
MENIFEE	329	57	219	14	39	Gore	17.3%	66.6%	4.3%	11.9%
MERCER	2,069	379	1,356	49	285	Gore	18.3%	65.5%	2.4%	13.8%
METCALFE	512	77	374	11	50	Gore	15.0%	73.0%	2.1%	9.8%
MONROE	174	11	134	2	27	Gore	6.3%	77.0%	1.1%	15.5%
MONTGOMERY	2,696	438	1,862	53	343	Gore	16.2%	69.1%	2.0%	12.7%
MORGAN	496	89	310	10	87	Gore	17.9%	62.5%	2.0%	17.5%
MUHLENBERG	900	99	728	13	60	Gore	11.0%	80.9%	1.4%	6.7%
NELSON	1,104	171	752	36	145	Gore	15.5%	68.1%	3.3%	13.1%

KENTUCKY DEMOCRATIC PRIMARY

2000

County	Total Vote	Bradley	Gore	LaRouche	Uncommitted	Winner	Percentage of Total Vote			
							Bradley	Gore	LaRouche	Uncommitted
NICHOLAS	1,002	200	613	47	142	Gore	20.0%	61.2%	4.7%	14.2%
OHIO	748	112	578	14	44	Gore	15.0%	77.3%	1.9%	5.9%
OLDHAM	1,203	234	770	47	152	Gore	19.5%	64.0%	3.9%	12.6%
OWEN	567	115	315	25	112	Gore	20.3%	55.6%	4.4%	19.8%
OWSLEY	88	28	54	3	3	Gore	31.8%	61.4%	3.4%	3.4%
PENDLETON	341	65	205	13	58	Gore	19.1%	60.1%	3.8%	17.0%
PERRY	3,177	485	2,321	61	310	Gore	15.3%	73.1%	1.9%	9.8%
PIKE	9,121	1,216	6,940	131	834	Gore	13.3%	76.1%	1.4%	9.1%
POWELL	1,616	251	1,168	40	157	Gore	15.5%	72.3%	2.5%	9.7%
PULASKI	939	121	712	22	84	Gore	12.9%	75.8%	2.3%	8.9%
ROBERTSON	137	29	71	5	32	Gore	21.2%	51.8%	3.6%	23.4%
ROCKCASTLE	156	17	126	2	11	Gore	10.9%	80.8%	1.3%	7.1%
ROWAN	631	77	491	7	56	Gore	12.2%	77.8%	1.1%	8.9%
RUSSELL	441	67	307	7	60	Gore	15.2%	69.6%	1.6%	13.6%
SCOTT	2,232	376	1,491	55	310	Gore	16.8%	66.8%	2.5%	13.9%
SHELBY	1,477	302	930	48	197	Gore	20.4%	63.0%	3.2%	13.3%
SIMPSON	987	139	718	15	115	Gore	14.1%	72.7%	1.5%	11.7%
SPENCER	420	90	266	13	51	Gore	21.4%	63.3%	3.1%	12.1%
TAYLOR	413	48	320	16	29	Gore	11.6%	77.5%	3.9%	7.0%
TODD	512	78	309	14	111	Gore	15.2%	60.4%	2.7%	21.7%
TRIGG	551	103	367	14	67	Gore	18.7%	66.6%	2.5%	12.2%
TRIMBLE	318	57	197	14	50	Gore	17.9%	61.9%	4.4%	15.7%
UNION	1,180	202	756	18	204	Gore	17.1%	64.1%	1.5%	17.3%
WARREN	1,714	233	1,205	41	235	Gore	13.6%	70.3%	2.4%	13.7%
WASHINGTON	312	57	191	17	47	Gore	18.3%	61.2%	5.4%	15.1%
WAYNE	273	31	223	3	16	Gore	11.4%	81.7%	1.1%	5.9%
WEBSTER	1,219	235	781	16	187	Gore	19.3%	64.1%	1.3%	15.3%
WHITLEY	586	64	452	10	60	Gore	10.9%	77.1%	1.7%	10.2%
WOLFE	440	58	314	16	52	Gore	13.2%	71.4%	3.6%	11.8%
WOODFORD	2,574	498	1,634	54	388	Gore	19.3%	63.5%	2.1%	15.1%
TOTAL	220,279	32,340	156,966	4,927	26,046	Gore	14.7%	71.3%	2.2%	11.8%

KENTUCKY REPUBLICAN PRIMARY

2000

County	Total Vote	G.W. Bush	McCain	Other	Winner	Percentage of Total Vote		
						G.W. Bush	McCain	Other
ADAIR	443	390	23	30	G.W. Bush	88.0%	5.2%	6.8%
ALLEN	511	436	21	54	G.W. Bush	85.3%	4.1%	10.6%
ANDERSON	227	199	7	21	G.W. Bush	87.7%	3.1%	9.3%
BALLARD	42	34	3	5	G.W. Bush	81.0%	7.1%	11.9%
BARREN	921	816	27	78	G.W. Bush	88.6%	2.9%	8.5%
BATH	45	43	0	2	G.W. Bush	95.6%	0.0%	4.4%
BELL	1,552	1,263	120	169	G.W. Bush	81.4%	7.7%	10.9%
BOONE	2,396	1,892	167	337	G.W. Bush	79.0%	7.0%	14.1%
BOURBON	192	161	16	15	G.W. Bush	83.9%	8.3%	7.8%
BOYD	2,033	1,610	186	237	G.W. Bush	79.2%	9.1%	11.7%
BOYLE	533	436	38	59	G.W. Bush	81.8%	7.1%	11.1%
BRACKEN	57	45	4	8	G.W. Bush	78.9%	7.0%	14.0%
BREATHITT	68	53	4	11	G.W. Bush	77.9%	5.9%	16.2%
BRECKINRIDGE	344	276	14	54	G.W. Bush	80.2%	4.1%	15.7%
BULLITT	822	666	51	105	G.W. Bush	81.0%	6.2%	12.8%
BUTLER	721	619	35	67	G.W. Bush	85.9%	4.9%	9.3%
CALDWELL	153	139	3	11	G.W. Bush	90.8%	2.0%	7.2%
CALLOWAY	366	293	24	49	G.W. Bush	80.1%	6.6%	13.4%
CAMPBELL	1,714	1,270	156	288	G.W. Bush	74.1%	9.1%	16.8%
CARLISLE	30	26	0	4	G.W. Bush	86.7%	0.0%	13.3%
CARROLL	94	86	3	5	G.W. Bush	91.5%	3.2%	5.3%
CARTER	474	377	47	50	G.W. Bush	79.5%	9.9%	10.5%
CASEY	395	337	17	41	G.W. Bush	85.3%	4.3%	10.4%
CHRISTIAN	626	529	22	75	G.W. Bush	84.5%	3.5%	12.0%
CLARK	410	326	35	49	G.W. Bush	79.5%	8.5%	12.0%
CLAY	2,004	1,610	126	268	G.W. Bush	80.3%	6.3%	13.4%
CLINTON	1,905	1,649	103	153	G.W. Bush	86.6%	5.4%	8.0%
CRITTENDEN	829	730	46	53	G.W. Bush	88.1%	5.5%	6.4%
CUMBERLAND	567	492	26	49	G.W. Bush	86.8%	4.6%	8.6%
DAVIESS	1,994	1,628	131	235	G.W. Bush	81.6%	6.6%	11.8%
EDMONSON	2,253	1,929	142	182	G.W. Bush	85.6%	6.3%	8.1%
ELLIOTT	10	9	0	1	G.W. Bush	90.0%	0.0%	10.0%
ESTILL	279	236	16	27	G.W. Bush	84.6%	5.7%	9.7%
FAYETTE	5,163	4,047	481	635	G.W. Bush	78.4%	9.3%	12.3%
FLEMING	148	129	6	13	G.W. Bush	87.2%	4.1%	8.8%
FLOYD	323	255	28	40	G.W. Bush	78.9%	8.7%	12.4%
FRANKLIN	833	659	58	116	G.W. Bush	79.1%	7.0%	13.9%
FULTON	40	35	2	3	G.W. Bush	87.5%	5.0%	7.5%
GALLATIN	54	47	4	3	G.W. Bush	87.0%	7.4%	5.6%
GARRARD	521	433	30	58	G.W. Bush	83.1%	5.8%	11.1%
GRANT	240	199	15	26	G.W. Bush	82.9%	6.3%	10.8%
GRAVES	183	155	2	26	G.W. Bush	84.7%	1.1%	14.2%
GRAYSON	547	480	25	42	G.W. Bush	87.8%	4.6%	7.7%
GREEN	488	445	11	32	G.W. Bush	91.2%	2.3%	6.6%
GREENUP	709	550	54	105	G.W. Bush	77.6%	7.6%	14.8%

KENTUCKY REPUBLICAN PRIMARY

2000

County	Total Vote	G.W. Bush	McCain	Other	Winner	Percentage of Total Vote		
						G.W. Bush	McCain	Other
HANCOCK	194	152	21	21	G.W. Bush	78.4%	10.8%	10.8%
HARDIN	2,094	1,765	141	188	G.W. Bush	84.3%	6.7%	9.0%
HARLAN	650	547	37	66	G.W. Bush	84.2%	5.7%	10.2%
HARRISON	117	100	5	12	G.W. Bush	85.5%	4.3%	10.3%
HART	279	239	19	21	G.W. Bush	85.7%	6.8%	7.5%
HENDERSON	236	198	12	26	G.W. Bush	83.9%	5.1%	11.0%
HENRY	119	104	5	10	G.W. Bush	87.4%	4.2%	8.4%
HICKMAN	34	34	0	0	G.W. Bush	100.0%	0.0%	0.0%
HOPKINS	300	243	15	42	G.W. Bush	81.0%	5.0%	14.0%
JACKSON	803	705	35	63	G.W. Bush	87.8%	4.4%	7.8%
JEFFERSON	13,741	11,525	774	1,442	G.W. Bush	83.9%	5.6%	10.5%
JESSAMINE	880	709	57	114	G.W. Bush	80.6%	6.5%	13.0%
JOHNSON	1,983	1,678	147	158	G.W. Bush	84.6%	7.4%	8.0%
KENTON	2,656	2,018	235	403	G.W. Bush	76.0%	8.8%	15.2%
KNOTT	77	33	3	41	Bauer	42.9%	3.9%	53.2%
KNOX	563	454	36	73	G.W. Bush	80.6%	6.4%	13.0%
LARUE	109	95	3	11	G.W. Bush	87.2%	2.8%	10.1%
LAUREL	1,181	991	74	116	G.W. Bush	83.9%	6.3%	9.8%
LAWRENCE	629	548	31	50	G.W. Bush	87.1%	4.9%	7.9%
LEE	219	177	7	35	G.W. Bush	80.8%	3.2%	16.0%
LESLIE	847	695	56	96	G.W. Bush	82.1%	6.6%	11.3%
LETCHER	527	427	43	57	G.W. Bush	81.0%	8.2%	10.8%
LEWIS	502	412	32	58	G.W. Bush	82.1%	6.4%	11.6%
LINCOLN	567	490	36	41	G.W. Bush	86.4%	6.3%	7.2%
LIVINGSTON	80	65	3	12	G.W. Bush	81.3%	3.8%	15.0%
LOGAN	299	264	6	29	G.W. Bush	88.3%	2.0%	9.7%
LYON	112	94	9	9	G.W. Bush	83.9%	8.0%	8.0%
MCCRACKEN	771	673	35	63	G.W. Bush	87.3%	4.5%	8.2%
MCCREARY	290	259	9	22	G.W. Bush	89.3%	3.1%	7.6%
MCLEAN	127	108	7	12	G.W. Bush	85.0%	5.5%	9.4%
MADISON	670	534	45	91	G.W. Bush	79.7%	6.7%	13.6%
MAGOFFIN	243	200	12	31	G.W. Bush	82.3%	4.9%	12.8%
MARION	36	31	2	3	G.W. Bush	86.1%	5.6%	8.3%
MARSHALL	355	308	10	37	G.W. Bush	86.8%	2.8%	10.4%
MARTIN	1,327	1,099	126	102	G.W. Bush	82.8%	9.5%	7.7%
MASON	131	111	5	15	G.W. Bush	84.7%	3.8%	11.5%
MEADE	297	244	15	38	G.W. Bush	82.2%	5.1%	12.8%
MENIFEE	47	35	5	7	G.W. Bush	74.5%	10.6%	14.9%
MERCER	398	321	23	54	G.W. Bush	80.7%	5.8%	13.6%
METCALFE	468	419	24	25	G.W. Bush	89.5%	5.1%	5.3%
MONROE	2,445	2,166	113	166	G.W. Bush	88.6%	4.6%	6.8%
MONTGOMERY	245	201	18	26	G.W. Bush	82.0%	7.3%	10.6%
MORGAN	64	54	7	3	G.W. Bush	84.4%	10.9%	4.7%
MUHLENBERG	229	202	12	15	G.W. Bush	88.2%	5.2%	6.6%
NELSON	230	174	18	38	G.W. Bush	75.7%	7.8%	16.5%

KENTUCKY REPUBLICAN PRIMARY

2000

County	Total Vote	G.W. Bush	McCain	Other	Winner	Percentage of Total Vote		
						G.W. Bush	McCain	Other
NICHOLAS	33	23	3	7	G.W. Bush	69.7%	9.1%	21.2%
OHIO	1,046	858	74	114	G.W. Bush	82.0%	7.1%	10.9%
OLDHAM	1,183	987	83	113	G.W. Bush	83.4%	7.0%	9.6%
OWEN	72	58	7	7	G.W. Bush	80.6%	9.7%	9.7%
OWSLEY	158	131	11	16	G.W. Bush	82.9%	7.0%	10.1%
PENDLETON	120	101	3	16	G.W. Bush	84.2%	2.5%	13.3%
PERRY	562	454	41	67	G.W. Bush	80.8%	7.3%	11.9%
PIKE	1,460	1,228	75	157	G.W. Bush	84.1%	5.1%	10.8%
POWELL	222	190	12	20	G.W. Bush	85.6%	5.4%	9.0%
PULASKI	3,771	3,255	227	289	G.W. Bush	86.3%	6.0%	7.7%
ROBERTSON	22	19	0	3	G.W. Bush	86.4%	0.0%	13.6%
ROCKCASTLE	536	467	31	38	G.W. Bush	87.1%	5.8%	7.1%
ROWAN	217	175	16	26	G.W. Bush	80.6%	7.4%	12.0%
RUSSELL	2,411	2,125	112	174	G.W. Bush	88.1%	4.6%	7.2%
SCOTT	523	425	25	73	G.W. Bush	81.3%	4.8%	14.0%
SHELBY	401	334	13	54	G.W. Bush	83.3%	3.2%	13.5%
SIMPSON	92	82	0	10	G.W. Bush	89.1%	0.0%	10.9%
SPENCER	125	105	4	16	G.W. Bush	84.0%	3.2%	12.8%
TAYLOR	376	307	17	52	G.W. Bush	81.6%	4.5%	13.8%
TODD	57	45	3	9	G.W. Bush	78.9%	5.3%	15.8%
TRIGG	143	122	8	13	G.W. Bush	85.3%	5.6%	9.1%
TRIMBLE	51	42	3	6	G.W. Bush	82.4%	5.9%	11.8%
UNION	52	41	4	7	G.W. Bush	78.8%	7.7%	13.5%
WARREN	692	553	37	102	G.W. Bush	79.9%	5.3%	14.7%
WASHINGTON	105	93	3	9	G.W. Bush	88.6%	2.9%	8.6%
WAYNE	839	733	46	60	G.W. Bush	87.4%	5.5%	7.2%
WEBSTER	51	40	4	7	G.W. Bush	78.4%	7.8%	13.7%
WHITLEY	3,026	2,411	223	392	G.W. Bush	79.7%	7.4%	13.0%
WOLFE	39	34	3	2	G.W. Bush	87.2%	7.7%	5.1%
WOODFORD	508	405	35	68	G.W. Bush	79.7%	6.9%	13.4%
TOTAL	91,323	75,783	5,780	9,760	G.W. Bush	83.0%	6.3%	10.7%

Note: Other vote was 4,337 Alan Keyes; 2,408 Gary Bauer; 1,829 Uncommitted; 1,186 Steve Forbes.

KENTUCKY DEMOCRATIC PRIMARY

2004

County	Total Vote	Edwards	Kerry	Uncommitted	Other	Winner	Percentage of Total Vote			
							Edwards	Kerry	Uncommitted	Other
ADAIR	387	69	236	25	57	Kerry	17.8%	61.0%	6.5%	14.7%
ALLEN	399	90	252	13	44	Kerry	22.6%	63.2%	3.3%	11.0%
ANDERSON	1,983	337	976	278	392	Kerry	17.0%	49.2%	14.0%	19.8%
BALLARD	930	135	552	116	127	Kerry	14.5%	59.4%	12.5%	13.7%
BARREN	1,228	212	773	80	163	Kerry	17.3%	62.9%	6.5%	13.3%
BATH	489	85	303	36	65	Kerry	17.4%	62.0%	7.4%	13.3%
BELL	930	149	642	40	99	Kerry	16.0%	69.0%	4.3%	10.6%
BOONE	2,337	429	1,229	312	367	Kerry	18.4%	52.6%	13.4%	15.7%
BOURBON	2,198	304	1,152	365	377	Kerry	13.8%	52.4%	16.6%	17.2%
BOYD	2,063	295	1,428	122	218	Kerry	14.3%	69.2%	5.9%	10.6%
BOYLE	2,025	301	1,160	217	347	Kerry	14.9%	57.3%	10.7%	17.1%
BRACKEN	332	68	171	28	65	Kerry	20.5%	51.5%	8.4%	19.6%
BREATHITT	1,136	174	750	61	151	Kerry	15.3%	66.0%	5.4%	13.3%
BRECKINRIDGE	1,082	162	684	74	162	Kerry	15.0%	63.2%	6.8%	15.0%
BULLITT	3,653	597	1,900	468	688	Kerry	16.3%	52.0%	12.8%	18.8%
BUTLER	209	37	146	10	16	Kerry	17.7%	69.9%	4.8%	7.7%
CALDWELL	685	147	353	82	103	Kerry	21.5%	51.5%	12.0%	15.0%
CALLOWAY	1,106	179	646	125	156	Kerry	16.2%	58.4%	11.3%	14.1%
CAMPBELL	3,610	505	2,190	364	551	Kerry	14.0%	60.7%	10.1%	15.3%
CARLISLE	508	88	290	58	72	Kerry	17.3%	57.1%	11.4%	14.2%
CARROLL	843	155	456	85	147	Kerry	18.4%	54.1%	10.1%	17.4%
CARTER	1,061	197	687	58	119	Kerry	18.6%	64.8%	5.5%	11.2%
CASEY	247	62	136	15	34	Kerry	25.1%	55.1%	6.1%	13.8%
CHRISTIAN	3,675	773	1,516	640	746	Kerry	21.0%	41.3%	17.4%	20.3%
CLARK	2,960	451	1,649	394	466	Kerry	15.2%	55.7%	13.3%	15.7%
CLAY	327	73	189	19	46	Kerry	22.3%	57.8%	5.8%	14.1%
CLINTON	173	27	123	4	19	Kerry	15.6%	71.1%	2.3%	11.0%
CRITTENDEN	362	56	240	26	40	Kerry	15.5%	66.3%	7.2%	11.0%
CUMBERLAND	118	21	76	4	17	Kerry	17.8%	64.4%	3.4%	14.4%
DAVIESS	8,294	1,204	4,580	1,173	1,337	Kerry	14.5%	55.2%	14.1%	16.1%
EDMONSON	255	42	169	12	32	Kerry	16.5%	66.3%	4.7%	12.5%
ELLIOTT	432	66	300	23	43	Kerry	15.3%	69.4%	5.3%	10.0%
ESTILL	434	76	287	15	56	Kerry	17.5%	66.1%	3.5%	12.9%
FAYETTE	14,401	1,792	8,443	1,100	3,066	Kerry	12.4%	58.6%	7.6%	21.3%
FLEMING	744	147	438	40	119	Kerry	19.8%	58.9%	5.4%	16.0%
FLOYD	6,776	890	4,562	508	816	Kerry	13.1%	67.3%	7.5%	12.0%
FRANKLIN	10,324	1,445	5,664	1,405	1,810	Kerry	14.0%	54.9%	13.6%	17.5%
FULTON	656	97	356	99	104	Kerry	14.8%	54.3%	15.1%	15.9%
GALLATIN	377	73	224	24	56	Kerry	19.4%	59.4%	6.4%	14.9%
GARRARD	434	76	276	43	39	Kerry	17.5%	63.6%	9.9%	9.0%
GRANT	872	178	444	94	156	Kerry	20.4%	50.9%	10.8%	17.9%
GRAVES	1,376	245	809	143	179	Kerry	17.8%	58.8%	10.4%	13.0%
GRAYSON	906	160	575	55	116	Kerry	17.7%	63.5%	6.1%	12.8%
GREEN	276	81	168	8	19	Kerry	29.3%	60.9%	2.9%	6.9%
GREENUP	1,706	255	1,199	87	165	Kerry	14.9%	70.3%	5.1%	9.7%

KENTUCKY DEMOCRATIC PRIMARY

2004

County	Total Vote	Edwards	Kerry	Uncommitted	Other	Winner	Percentage of Total Vote			
							Edwards	Kerry	Uncommitted	Other
HANCOCK	502	94	292	36	80	Kerry	18.7%	58.2%	7.2%	15.9%
HARDIN	4,308	797	2,310	514	687	Kerry	18.5%	53.6%	11.9%	15.9%
HARLAN	1,484	235	910	137	202	Kerry	15.8%	61.3%	9.2%	13.6%
HARRISON	1,056	164	600	113	179	Kerry	15.5%	56.8%	10.7%	17.0%
HART	817	183	446	64	124	Kerry	22.4%	54.6%	7.8%	15.2%
HENDERSON	1,750	281	1,007	197	265	Kerry	16.1%	57.5%	11.3%	15.1%
HENRY	1,558	285	801	207	265	Kerry	18.3%	51.4%	13.3%	17.0%
HICKMAN	490	70	269	70	81	Kerry	14.3%	54.9%	14.3%	16.5%
HOPKINS	1,923	429	950	217	327	Kerry	22.3%	49.4%	11.3%	17.0%
JACKSON	101	14	72	5	10	Kerry	13.9%	71.3%	5.0%	9.9%
JEFFERSON	50,951	4,767	34,290	3,326	8,568	Kerry	9.4%	67.3%	6.5%	16.8%
JESSAMINE	2,063	326	1,117	256	364	Kerry	15.8%	54.1%	12.4%	17.6%
JOHNSON	792	134	521	26	111	Kerry	16.9%	65.8%	3.3%	14.0%
KENTON	5,073	814	2,751	629	879	Kerry	16.0%	54.2%	12.4%	17.3%
KNOTT	3,884	455	2,588	333	508	Kerry	11.7%	66.6%	8.6%	13.1%
KNOX	482	85	315	16	66	Kerry	17.6%	65.4%	3.3%	13.7%
LARUE	715	134	372	83	126	Kerry	18.7%	52.0%	11.6%	17.6%
LAUREL	830	134	540	41	115	Kerry	16.1%	65.1%	4.9%	13.9%
LAWRENCE	1,163	189	784	69	121	Kerry	16.3%	67.4%	5.9%	10.4%
LEE	264	35	172	15	42	Kerry	13.3%	65.2%	5.7%	15.9%
LESLIE	142	12	95	7	28	Kerry	8.5%	66.9%	4.9%	19.7%
LETCHER	1,660	259	1,067	100	234	Kerry	15.6%	64.3%	6.0%	14.1%
LEWIS	253	47	168	15	23	Kerry	18.6%	66.4%	5.9%	9.1%
LINCOLN	720	134	438	35	113	Kerry	18.6%	60.8%	4.9%	15.7%
LIVINGSTON	580	77	369	65	69	Kerry	13.3%	63.6%	11.2%	11.9%
LOGAN	1,737	355	936	169	277	Kerry	20.4%	53.9%	9.7%	15.9%
LYON	1,470	181	840	236	213	Kerry	12.3%	57.1%	16.1%	14.5%
MCCRACKEN	3,678	499	2,223	369	587	Kerry	13.6%	60.4%	10.0%	16.0%
MCCREARY	252	66	136	13	37	Kerry	26.2%	54.0%	5.2%	14.7%
MCLEAN	404	63	258	29	54	Kerry	15.6%	63.9%	7.2%	13.4%
MADISON	2,618	378	1,564	195	481	Kerry	14.4%	59.7%	7.4%	18.4%
MAGOFFIN	1,007	164	735	33	75	Kerry	16.3%	73.0%	3.3%	7.4%
MARION	908	146	513	73	176	Kerry	16.1%	56.5%	8.0%	19.4%
MARSHALL	1,801	331	1,048	190	232	Kerry	18.4%	58.2%	10.5%	12.9%
MARTIN	168	24	120	5	19	Kerry	14.3%	71.4%	3.0%	11.3%
MASON	657	129	354	61	113	Kerry	19.6%	53.9%	9.3%	17.2%
MEADE	1,477	267	823	151	236	Kerry	18.1%	55.7%	10.2%	16.0%
MENIFEE	493	86	286	38	83	Kerry	17.4%	58.0%	7.7%	16.8%
MERCER	2,306	322	1,138	356	490	Kerry	14.0%	49.3%	15.4%	21.2%
METCALFE	385	79	237	19	50	Kerry	20.5%	61.6%	4.9%	13.0%
MONROE	142	30	95	5	12	Kerry	21.1%	66.9%	3.5%	8.5%
MONTGOMERY	1,198	209	722	102	165	Kerry	17.4%	60.3%	8.5%	13.8%
MORGAN	1,163	249	648	103	163	Kerry	21.4%	55.7%	8.9%	14.0%
MUHLENBERG	1,222	166	834	54	168	Kerry	13.6%	68.2%	4.4%	13.7%
NELSON	1,721	318	926	179	298	Kerry	18.5%	53.8%	10.4%	17.3%

KENTUCKY DEMOCRATIC PRIMARY

2004

County	Total Vote	Edwards	Kerry	Uncommitted	Other	Winner	Percentage of Total Vote			
							Edwards	Kerry	Uncommitted	Other
NICHOLAS	365	66	206	26	67	Kerry	18.1%	56.4%	7.1%	18.4%
OHIO	1,277	203	808	97	169	Kerry	15.9%	63.3%	7.6%	13.2%
OLDHAM	1,980	337	1,107	179	357	Kerry	17.0%	55.9%	9.0%	18.0%
OWEN	768	162	352	103	151	Kerry	21.1%	45.8%	13.4%	19.7%
OWSLEY	109	26	60	4	19	Kerry	23.9%	55.0%	3.7%	17.4%
PENDLETON	565	113	299	59	94	Kerry	20.0%	52.9%	10.4%	16.6%
PERRY	1,811	295	1,199	103	214	Kerry	16.3%	66.2%	5.7%	11.8%
PIKE	5,153	799	3,519	279	556	Kerry	15.5%	68.3%	5.4%	10.8%
POWELL	737	133	457	44	103	Kerry	18.0%	62.0%	6.0%	14.0%
PULASKI	1,323	232	841	83	167	Kerry	17.5%	63.6%	6.3%	12.6%
ROBERTSON	161	27	85	14	35	Kerry	16.8%	52.8%	8.7%	21.7%
ROCKCASTLE	199	25	137	9	28	Kerry	12.6%	68.8%	4.5%	14.1%
ROWAN	1,346	176	895	76	199	Kerry	13.1%	66.5%	5.6%	14.8%
RUSSELL	463	85	261	37	80	Kerry	18.4%	56.4%	8.0%	17.3%
SCOTT	1,774	242	1,034	203	295	Kerry	13.6%	58.3%	11.4%	16.6%
SHELBY	2,852	527	1,494	312	519	Kerry	18.5%	52.4%	10.9%	18.2%
SIMPSON	400	81	214	39	66	Kerry	20.3%	53.5%	9.8%	16.5%
SPENCER	839	153	403	113	170	Kerry	18.2%	48.0%	13.5%	20.3%
TAYLOR	679	109	432	46	92	Kerry	16.1%	63.6%	6.8%	13.5%
TODD	471	109	222	51	89	Kerry	23.1%	47.1%	10.8%	18.9%
TRIGG	926	209	436	121	160	Kerry	22.6%	47.1%	13.1%	17.3%
TRIMBLE	812	158	415	100	139	Kerry	19.5%	51.1%	12.3%	17.1%
UNION	561	89	312	90	70	Kerry	15.9%	55.6%	16.0%	12.5%
WARREN	5,003	904	2,704	527	868	Kerry	18.1%	54.0%	10.5%	17.3%
WASHINGTON	576	98	313	62	103	Kerry	17.0%	54.3%	10.8%	17.9%
WAYNE	479	115	286	15	63	Kerry	24.0%	59.7%	3.1%	13.2%
WEBSTER	724	123	426	67	108	Kerry	17.0%	58.8%	9.3%	14.9%
WHITLEY	532	90	354	24	64	Kerry	16.9%	66.5%	4.5%	12.0%
WOLFE	589	104	380	31	74	Kerry	17.7%	64.5%	5.3%	12.6%
WOODFORD	2,755	392	1,445	381	537	Kerry	14.2%	52.5%	13.8%	19.5%
TOTAL	229,916	33,403	138,175	21,199	37,139	Kerry	14.5%	60.1%	9.2%	16.2%

Note: Other vote was 11,062 Joseph I. Lieberman; 8,222 Howard Dean; 6,519 Wesley Clark; 5,022 Al Sharpton; 4,508 Dennis J. Kucinich; 1,806 Lyndon H. LaRouche Jr.

KENTUCKY REPUBLICAN PRIMARY

2004

County	Total Vote	G.W. Bush	Uncommitted	Winner	Percentage of Total Vote	
					G.W. Bush	Uncommitted
ADAIR	922	873	49	G.W. Bush	94.7%	5.3%
ALLEN	370	346	24	G.W. Bush	93.5%	6.5%
ANDERSON	585	559	26	G.W. Bush	95.6%	4.4%
BALLARD	48	45	3	G.W. Bush	93.8%	6.3%
BARREN	462	444	18	G.W. Bush	96.1%	3.9%
BATH	55	51	4	G.W. Bush	92.7%	7.3%
BELL	837	765	72	G.W. Bush	91.4%	8.6%
BOONE	6,080	5,727	353	G.W. Bush	94.2%	5.8%
BOURBON	278	255	23	G.W. Bush	91.7%	8.3%
BOYD	1,203	1,115	88	G.W. Bush	92.7%	7.3%
BOYLE	896	855	41	G.W. Bush	95.4%	4.6%
BRACKEN	109	107	2	G.W. Bush	98.2%	1.8%
BREATHITT	69	68	1	G.W. Bush	98.6%	1.4%
BRECKINRIDGE	851	797	54	G.W. Bush	93.7%	6.3%
BULLITT	992	943	49	G.W. Bush	95.1%	4.9%
BUTLER	760	709	51	G.W. Bush	93.3%	6.7%
CALDWELL	149	143	6	G.W. Bush	96.0%	4.0%
CALLOWAY	267	252	15	G.W. Bush	94.4%	5.6%
CAMPBELL	3,112	2,896	216	G.W. Bush	93.1%	6.9%
CARLISLE	38	38	0	G.W. Bush	100.0%	0.0%
CARROLL	73	69	4	G.W. Bush	94.5%	5.5%
CARTER	785	720	65	G.W. Bush	91.7%	8.3%
CASEY	1,115	1,054	61	G.W. Bush	94.5%	5.5%
CHRISTIAN	671	645	26	G.W. Bush	96.1%	3.9%
CLARK	1,163	1,092	71	G.W. Bush	93.9%	6.1%
CLAY	2,752	2,505	247	G.W. Bush	91.0%	9.0%
CLINTON	331	307	24	G.W. Bush	92.7%	7.3%
CRITTENDEN	206	195	11	G.W. Bush	94.7%	5.3%
CUMBERLAND	260	239	21	G.W. Bush	91.9%	8.1%
DAVIESS	2,845	2,607	238	G.W. Bush	91.6%	8.4%
EDMONSON	325	304	21	G.W. Bush	93.5%	6.5%
ELLIOTT	12	11	1	G.W. Bush	91.7%	8.3%
ESTILL	777	734	43	G.W. Bush	94.5%	5.5%
FAYETTE	8,702	7,914	788	G.W. Bush	90.9%	9.1%
FLEMING	261	247	14	G.W. Bush	94.6%	5.4%
FLOYD	300	279	21	G.W. Bush	93.0%	7.0%
FRANKLIN	1,365	1,225	140	G.W. Bush	89.7%	10.3%
FULTON	87	84	3	G.W. Bush	96.6%	3.4%
GALLATIN	115	109	6	G.W. Bush	94.8%	5.2%
GARRARD	667	621	46	G.W. Bush	93.1%	6.9%
GRANT	397	382	15	G.W. Bush	96.2%	3.8%
GRAVES	200	189	11	G.W. Bush	94.5%	5.5%
GRAYSON	1,937	1,815	122	G.W. Bush	93.7%	6.3%
GREEN	312	289	23	G.W. Bush	92.6%	7.4%
GREENUP	845	806	39	G.W. Bush	95.4%	4.6%

KENTUCKY REPUBLICAN PRIMARY

2004

County	Total Vote	G.W. Bush	Uncommitted	Winner	Percentage of Total Vote	
					G.W. Bush	Uncommitted
HANCOCK	249	231	18	G.W. Bush	92.8%	7.2%
HARDIN	1,769	1,653	116	G.W. Bush	93.4%	6.6%
HARLAN	532	497	35	G.W. Bush	93.4%	6.6%
HARRISON	320	297	23	G.W. Bush	92.8%	7.2%
HART	360	332	28	G.W. Bush	92.2%	7.8%
HENDERSON	226	210	16	G.W. Bush	92.9%	7.1%
HENRY	287	274	13	G.W. Bush	95.5%	4.5%
HICKMAN	38	36	2	G.W. Bush	94.7%	5.3%
HOPKINS	307	291	16	G.W. Bush	94.8%	5.2%
JACKSON	1,412	1,332	80	G.W. Bush	94.3%	5.7%
JEFFERSON	18,140	16,447	1,693	G.W. Bush	90.7%	9.3%
JESSAMINE	1,375	1,293	82	G.W. Bush	94.0%	6.0%
JOHNSON	818	724	94	G.W. Bush	88.5%	11.5%
KENTON	6,257	5,849	408	G.W. Bush	93.5%	6.5%
KNOTT	38	34	4	G.W. Bush	89.5%	10.5%
KNOX	779	712	67	G.W. Bush	91.4%	8.6%
LARUE	258	252	6	G.W. Bush	97.7%	2.3%
LAUREL	5,252	4,854	398	G.W. Bush	92.4%	7.6%
LAWRENCE	472	435	37	G.W. Bush	92.2%	7.8%
LEE	283	270	13	G.W. Bush	95.4%	4.6%
LESLIE	1,418	1,269	149	G.W. Bush	89.5%	10.5%
LETCHER	427	384	43	G.W. Bush	89.9%	10.1%
LEWIS	1,132	1,000	132	G.W. Bush	88.3%	11.7%
LINCOLN	402	385	17	G.W. Bush	95.8%	4.2%
LIVINGSTON	71	68	3	G.W. Bush	95.8%	4.2%
LOGAN	367	331	36	G.W. Bush	90.2%	9.8%
LYON	100	91	9	G.W. Bush	91.0%	9.0%
MCCRACKEN	935	874	61	G.W. Bush	93.5%	6.5%
MCCREARY	904	799	105	G.W. Bush	88.4%	11.6%
MCLEAN	91	83	8	G.W. Bush	91.2%	8.8%
MADISON	1,338	1,248	90	G.W. Bush	93.3%	6.7%
MAGOFFIN	248	248	0	G.W. Bush	100.0%	0.0%
MARION	95	90	5	G.W. Bush	94.7%	5.3%
MARSHALL	286	282	4	G.W. Bush	98.6%	1.4%
MARTIN	425	380	45	G.W. Bush	89.4%	10.6%
MASON	286	265	21	G.W. Bush	92.7%	7.3%
MEADE	542	518	24	G.W. Bush	95.6%	4.4%
MENIFEE	116	110	6	G.W. Bush	94.8%	5.2%
MERCER	730	684	46	G.W. Bush	93.7%	6.3%
METCALFE	160	155	5	G.W. Bush	96.9%	3.1%
MONROE	388	366	22	G.W. Bush	94.3%	5.7%
MONTGOMERY	260	244	16	G.W. Bush	93.8%	6.2%
MORGAN	63	60	3	G.W. Bush	95.2%	4.8%
MUHLENBERG	190	178	12	G.W. Bush	93.7%	6.3%
NELSON	678	648	30	G.W. Bush	95.6%	4.4%

KENTUCKY REPUBLICAN PRIMARY

2004

County	Total Vote	G.W. Bush	Uncommitted	Winner	Percentage of Total Vote	
					G.W. Bush	Uncommitted
NICHOLAS	53	48	5	G.W. Bush	90.6%	9.4%
OHIO	660	600	60	G.W. Bush	90.9%	9.1%
OLDHAM	2,113	1,976	137	G.W. Bush	93.5%	6.5%
OWEN	140	133	7	G.W. Bush	95.0%	5.0%
OWSLEY	367	345	22	G.W. Bush	94.0%	6.0%
PENDLETON	289	277	12	G.W. Bush	95.8%	4.2%
PERRY	477	451	26	G.W. Bush	94.5%	5.5%
PIKE	1,085	1,028	57	G.W. Bush	94.7%	5.3%
POWELL	289	285	4	G.W. Bush	98.6%	1.4%
PULASKI	4,842	4,537	305	G.W. Bush	93.7%	6.3%
ROBERTSON	27	27	0	G.W. Bush	100.0%	0.0%
ROCKCASTLE	667	618	49	G.W. Bush	92.7%	7.3%
ROWAN	369	337	32	G.W. Bush	91.3%	8.7%
RUSSELL	2,070	1,893	177	G.W. Bush	91.4%	8.6%
SCOTT	700	653	47	G.W. Bush	93.3%	6.7%
SHELBY	568	539	29	G.W. Bush	94.9%	5.1%
SIMPSON	60	58	2	G.W. Bush	96.7%	3.3%
SPENCER	229	222	7	G.W. Bush	96.9%	3.1%
TAYLOR	607	582	25	G.W. Bush	95.9%	4.1%
TODD	49	48	1	G.W. Bush	98.0%	2.0%
TRIGG	129	122	7	G.W. Bush	94.6%	5.4%
TRIMBLE	127	125	2	G.W. Bush	98.4%	1.6%
UNION	32	31	1	G.W. Bush	96.9%	3.1%
WARREN	1,920	1,799	121	G.W. Bush	93.7%	6.3%
WASHINGTON	171	160	11	G.W. Bush	93.6%	6.4%
WAYNE	1,274	1,170	104	G.W. Bush	91.8%	8.2%
WEBSTER	45	42	3	G.W. Bush	93.3%	6.7%
WHITLEY	1,897	1,627	270	G.W. Bush	85.8%	14.2%
WOLFE	55	54	1	G.W. Bush	98.2%	1.8%
WOODFORD	658	603	55	G.W. Bush	91.6%	8.4%
TOTAL	117,379	108,603	8,776	G.W. Bush	92.5%	7.5%

LOUISIANA

In recent years, Louisiana Republicans have been one of the more ambitious players challenging Iowa for the lead-off position on the presidential nominating calendar. The Bayou State GOP held delegate-selection caucuses in early February 1996, a week before the Iowa caucuses and had planned a similar event in 2000 before abandoning it.

Louisiana's caucuses in 1996 were sparsely attended (less than 25,000 of the roughly 500,000 registered Republicans at the time) and virtually ignored by most of the contenders. Bob Dole led a lobbying effort on Iowa's behalf, and most of the Republican candidates signed a letter urging Louisiana to stick with its March primary.

Ultimately, only Phil Gramm, Pat Buchanan, and Alan Keyes competed in Louisiana. Yet while the early event did not make the Bayou State a kingmaker, it did establish which candidate would anchor the right side of the GOP field.

The caucuses severely wounded Gramm, who had appeared to be a prohibitive favorite to win them. But Buchanan closed fast, and won 13 of the 21 delegates at stake in the district caucuses. Dole won the remaining Louisiana delegates that were at stake in the primary.

All and all, the experience was not out of character for Louisiana. While state and local politics are often colorful and absorbing, Louisiana voters have seemed less than enchanted with presidential nominating politics.

Cost-conscious state officials tried to kill the presidential primary in 1984, just four years after it was instituted. When a federal court intervened, then-governor Edwin Edwards encouraged voters to stay away from the polls. Many white Democrats took his advice, which helped Jesse Jackson score his only primary win that year outside the District of Columbia.

Recent Louisiana Primary Results

Louisiana held its first presidential primary in 1980.

Year	DEMOCRATS			REPUBLICANS		
	Turnout	Candidates	%	Turnout	Candidates	%
2004 (March 9)	161,653	JOHN KERRY	70	72,010	GEORGE W. BUSH*	96
		John Edwards	16			
2000 (March 14)	157,551	AL GORE	73	102,912	GEORGE W. BUSH	84
		Bill Bradley	20		John McCain	9
					Alan Keyes	6
1996 (March 12)	154,701	BILL CLINTON*	81	77,789	BOB DOLE	48
		Lyndon LaRouche	12		Pat Buchanan	33
		Elvena Lloyd-Duffie	8		Steve Forbes	13
1992 (March 10)	384,397	BILL CLINTON	69	135,109	GEORGE BUSH*	62
		Paul Tsongas	11		Pat Buchanan	27
		Jerry Brown	7		David Duke	9
1988 (March 8)	624,450	JESSE JACKSON	35	144,781	GEORGE BUSH	58
		Al Gore	28		Pat Robertson	18
		Michael Dukakis	15		Bob Dole	18
		Richard Gephardt	11		Jack Kemp	5
1984 (May 5)	318,810	JESSE JACKSON	43	16,687	RONALD REAGAN*	90
		Gary Hart	25		Uncommitted	10
		Walter Mondale	22			
		Uncommitted	6			
1980 (April 5)	358,741	JIMMY CARTER*	56	41,683	RONALD REAGAN	75
		Edward Kennedy	23		George Bush	19
		Uncommitted	12		Uncommitted	5

Note: All candidates are listed that drew at least 5 percent of their party's primary vote. The names of winning candidates are capitalized. An asterisk (*) indicates an incumbent president.

In 1988, Louisiana Democrats joined the Super Tuesday lineup and doubled their primary turnout to more than 600,000—by far the highest total for a presidential primary in the state before or since. But the result was the same: Jackson won again. In predominantly black New Orleans, Jackson took nearly two-thirds of the vote. Elsewhere, he and runner-up Al Gore ran about even. Jackson won the large population centers–including Caddo (Shreveport), East Baton Rouge (Baton Rouge), and Calcasieu (Lake Charles) parishes–as well as the largely black parishes on the Mississippi River.

Gore carried Winn Parish, birthplace of the legendary Huey Long, and much of the rest of Protestant northern Louisiana. And he won Lafayette Parish, the heart of Cajun country. But Gore had to share his base. Michael Dukakis carried New Orleans' major suburban parishes–Jefferson, St. Bernard, and St. Tammany.

The Republican primary in 1988 was not so close. George Bush outpolled runner-up Pat Robertson by a margin of more than 3 to 1. Dole ran second to Bush in the New Orleans area, but Robertson won three small parishes in southwestern Louisiana and finished second most everywhere else.

Bush was an easy winner again four years later. But the big story was the collapse of David Duke as a credible political force. The former Ku Klux Klan leader had frightened Louisiana's political establishment with unexpectedly strong runs for the Senate in 1990 and governor in 1991. But Duke's share in the 1992 GOP presidential primary was just 9 percent.

Pat Buchanan finished a distant second in the 1992 Republican primary. But he did better in 1996, as Buchanan's 33 percent share was his best in any Sun Belt primary that year. Buchanan carried more than two dozen parishes, about evenly divided between Protestant northern Louisiana and the Catholic Cajun country to the south.

In every election since 1988, Louisiana has held its presidential primary on the second Tuesday in March. Yet in 2000 and 2004, that was after the Democratic and Republican nominations had been settled. Each year, George W. Bush drew a higher share of the Republican primary vote than the Democratic "nominee in waiting" pulled on the Democratic side of the ballot. It turned out to be a precursor of Bush's general election victories in Louisiana each time.

LOUISIANA DEMOCRATIC PRIMARY

2000

Parish	Total Vote	Bradley	Gore	Other	Winner	Percentage of Total Vote		
						Bradley	Gore	Other
ACADIA	1,548	395	1,050	103	Gore	25.5%	67.8%	6.7%
ALLEN	858	171	596	91	Gore	19.9%	69.5%	10.6%
ASCENSION	2,716	531	2,029	156	Gore	19.6%	74.7%	5.7%
ASSUMPTION	657	128	473	56	Gore	19.5%	72.0%	8.5%
AVOYELLES	1,390	262	984	144	Gore	18.8%	70.8%	10.4%
BEAUREGARD	802	184	532	86	Gore	22.9%	66.3%	10.7%
BIENVILLE	2,727	620	1,787	320	Gore	22.7%	65.5%	11.7%
BOSSIER	1,691	358	1,168	165	Gore	21.2%	69.1%	9.8%
CADDO	7,638	1,653	5,455	530	Gore	21.6%	71.4%	6.9%
CALCASIEU	15,824	2,589	12,376	859	Gore	16.4%	78.2%	5.4%
CALDWELL	548	153	343	52	Gore	27.9%	62.6%	9.5%
CAMERON	282	70	187	25	Gore	24.8%	66.3%	8.9%
CATAHOULA	443	87	305	51	Gore	19.6%	68.8%	11.5%
CLAIBORNE	1,340	312	912	116	Gore	23.3%	68.1%	8.7%
CONCORDIA	1,625	305	1,152	168	Gore	18.8%	70.9%	10.3%
DE SOTO	835	167	595	73	Gore	20.0%	71.3%	8.7%
EAST BATON ROUGE	6,967	1,413	5,174	380	Gore	20.3%	74.3%	5.5%
EAST CARROLL	342	60	251	31	Gore	17.5%	73.4%	9.1%
EAST FELICIANA	1,155	265	808	82	Gore	22.9%	70.0%	7.1%
EVANGELINE	839	185	569	85	Gore	22.1%	67.8%	10.1%
FRANKLIN	621	151	417	53	Gore	24.3%	67.1%	8.5%
GRANT	520	160	288	72	Gore	30.8%	55.4%	13.8%
IBERIA	1,195	287	793	115	Gore	24.0%	66.4%	9.6%
IBERVILLE	794	143	588	63	Gore	18.0%	74.1%	7.9%
JACKSON	2,722	784	1,634	304	Gore	28.8%	60.0%	11.2%
JEFFERSON	14,403	3,521	9,968	914	Gore	24.4%	69.2%	6.3%
JEFFERSON DAVIS	1,106	287	732	87	Gore	25.9%	66.2%	7.9%
LAFAYETTE	3,607	954	2,318	335	Gore	26.4%	64.3%	9.3%
LAFOURCHE	2,380	480	1,678	222	Gore	20.2%	70.5%	9.3%
LA SALLE	509	140	272	97	Gore	27.5%	53.4%	19.1%
LINCOLN	1,653	431	1,078	144	Gore	26.1%	65.2%	8.7%
LIVINGSTON	1,148	260	737	151	Gore	22.6%	64.2%	13.2%
MADISON	587	99	449	39	Gore	16.9%	76.5%	6.6%
MOREHOUSE	1,580	294	1,151	135	Gore	18.6%	72.8%	8.5%
NATCHITOCHES	3,899	756	2,790	353	Gore	19.4%	71.6%	9.1%
ORLEANS	26,240	3,076	22,406	758	Gore	11.7%	85.4%	2.9%
OUACHITA	11,044	2,107	8,123	814	Gore	19.1%	73.6%	7.4%
PLAQUEMINES	656	138	481	37	Gore	21.0%	73.3%	5.6%
POINTE COUPEE	718	136	507	75	Gore	18.9%	70.6%	10.4%
RAPIDES	2,279	511	1,555	213	Gore	22.4%	68.2%	9.3%
RED RIVER	612	123	423	66	Gore	20.1%	69.1%	10.8%
RICHLAND	807	232	483	92	Gore	28.7%	59.9%	11.4%
SABINE	821	257	454	110	Gore	31.3%	55.3%	13.4%
ST. BERNARD	1,536	342	1,058	136	Gore	22.3%	68.9%	8.9%
ST. CHARLES	1,210	301	802	107	Gore	24.9%	66.3%	8.8%

LOUISIANA DEMOCRATIC PRIMARY

2000

Parish	Total Vote	Bradley	Gore	Other	Winner	Percentage of Total Vote		
						Bradley	Gore	Other
ST. HELENA	553	107	377	69	Gore	19.3%	68.2%	12.5%
ST. JAMES	1,134	231	820	83	Gore	20.4%	72.3%	7.3%
ST. JOHN THE BAPTIST	677	127	483	67	Gore	18.8%	71.3%	9.9%
ST. LANDRY	1,870	391	1,369	110	Gore	20.9%	73.2%	5.9%
ST. MARTIN	1,429	293	991	145	Gore	20.5%	69.3%	10.1%
ST. MARY	971	230	653	88	Gore	23.7%	67.3%	9.1%
ST. TAMMANY	3,088	802	2,056	230	Gore	26.0%	66.6%	7.4%
TANGIPAHOA	5,496	1,290	3,809	397	Gore	23.5%	69.3%	7.2%
TENSAS	465	69	360	36	Gore	14.8%	77.4%	7.7%
TERREBONNE	2,071	426	1,482	163	Gore	20.6%	71.6%	7.9%
UNION	768	176	506	86	Gore	22.9%	65.9%	11.2%
VERMILION	1,063	224	764	75	Gore	21.1%	71.9%	7.1%
VERNON	928	240	565	123	Gore	25.9%	60.9%	13.3%
WASHINGTON	1,518	319	946	253	Gore	21.0%	62.3%	16.7%
WEBSTER	866	194	602	70	Gore	22.4%	69.5%	8.1%
WEST BATON ROUGE	483	78	389	16	Gore	16.1%	80.5%	3.3%
WEST CARROLL	346	96	205	45	Gore	27.7%	59.2%	13.0%
WEST FELICIANA	334	56	250	28	Gore	16.8%	74.9%	8.4%
WINN	617	158	384	75	Gore	25.6%	62.2%	12.2%
TOTAL	157,551	31,385	114,942	11,224	Gore	19.9%	73.0%	7.1%

Note: Other vote was 6,127 Lyndon H. LaRouche Jr.; 5,097 Randy Crow.

LOUISIANA REPUBLICAN PRIMARY

2000

Parish	Total Vote	G.W. Bush	Keyes	McCain	Other	Winner	Percentage of Total Vote			
							G.W. Bush	Keyes	McCain	Other
ACADIA	922	751	86	67	18	G.W. Bush	81.5%	9.3%	7.3%	2.0%
ALLEN	288	242	13	28	5	G.W. Bush	84.0%	4.5%	9.7%	1.7%
ASCENSION	1,443	1,198	116	98	31	G.W. Bush	83.0%	8.0%	6.8%	2.1%
ASSUMPTION	191	136	10	21	24	G.W. Bush	71.2%	5.2%	11.0%	12.6%
AVOYELLES	400	306	19	52	23	G.W. Bush	76.5%	4.8%	13.0%	5.8%
BEAUREGARD	676	572	39	54	11	G.W. Bush	84.6%	5.8%	8.0%	1.6%
BIENVILLE	581	514	11	47	9	G.W. Bush	88.5%	1.9%	8.1%	1.5%
BOSSIER	2,007	1,723	76	186	22	G.W. Bush	85.8%	3.8%	9.3%	1.1%
CADDO	7,278	6,368	232	572	106	G.W. Bush	87.5%	3.2%	7.9%	1.5%
CALCASIEU	5,892	4,964	381	451	96	G.W. Bush	84.2%	6.5%	7.7%	1.6%
CALDWELL	309	251	29	25	4	G.W. Bush	81.2%	9.4%	8.1%	1.3%
CAMERON	68	58	7	3	0	G.W. Bush	85.3%	10.3%	4.4%	0.0%
CATAHOULA	135	114	7	8	6	G.W. Bush	84.4%	5.2%	5.9%	4.4%
CLAIBORNE	467	413	8	42	4	G.W. Bush	88.4%	1.7%	9.0%	0.9%
CONCORDIA	403	344	13	36	10	G.W. Bush	85.4%	3.2%	8.9%	2.5%
DE SOTO	360	320	13	22	5	G.W. Bush	88.9%	3.6%	6.1%	1.4%
EAST BATON ROUGE	9,765	8,422	585	629	129	G.W. Bush	86.2%	6.0%	6.4%	1.3%
EAST CARROLL	132	115	5	10	2	G.W. Bush	87.1%	3.8%	7.6%	1.5%
EAST FELICIANA	469	403	21	33	12	G.W. Bush	85.9%	4.5%	7.0%	2.6%
EVANGELINE	197	171	11	11	4	G.W. Bush	86.8%	5.6%	5.6%	2.0%

LOUISIANA REPUBLICAN PRIMARY

2000

Parish	Total Vote	G.W. Bush	Keyes	McCain	Other	Winner	Percentage of Total Vote			
							G.W. Bush	Keyes	McCain	Other
FRANKLIN	361	309	22	27	3	G.W. Bush	85.6%	6.1%	7.5%	0.8%
GRANT	304	254	16	23	11	G.W. Bush	83.6%	5.3%	7.6%	3.6%
IBERIA	1,240	1,068	74	83	15	G.W. Bush	86.1%	6.0%	6.7%	1.2%
IBERVILLE	274	229	17	16	12	G.W. Bush	83.6%	6.2%	5.8%	4.4%
JACKSON	869	726	40	89	14	G.W. Bush	83.5%	4.6%	10.2%	1.6%
JEFFERSON	15,400	12,630	869	1,636	265	G.W. Bush	82.0%	5.6%	10.6%	1.7%
JEFFERSON DAVIS	367	308	22	28	9	G.W. Bush	83.9%	6.0%	7.6%	2.5%
LAFAYETTE	4,715	3,913	412	291	99	G.W. Bush	83.0%	8.7%	6.2%	2.1%
LAFOURCHE	1,007	811	79	94	23	G.W. Bush	80.5%	7.8%	9.3%	2.3%
LA SALLE	261	230	13	17	1	G.W. Bush	88.1%	5.0%	6.5%	0.4%
LINCOLN	1,403	1,219	78	85	21	G.W. Bush	86.9%	5.6%	6.1%	1.5%
LIVINGSTON	1,405	1,190	106	98	11	G.W. Bush	84.7%	7.5%	7.0%	0.8%
MADISON	349	307	12	20	10	G.W. Bush	88.0%	3.4%	5.7%	2.9%
MOREHOUSE	815	696	39	72	8	G.W. Bush	85.4%	4.8%	8.8%	1.0%
NATCHITOCHES	1,270	1,058	53	134	25	G.W. Bush	83.3%	4.2%	10.6%	2.0%
ORLEANS	8,427	6,579	437	1,238	173	G.W. Bush	78.1%	5.2%	14.7%	2.1%
OUACHITA	6,835	5,799	299	615	122	G.W. Bush	84.8%	4.4%	9.0%	1.8%
PLAQUEMINES	400	331	26	37	6	G.W. Bush	82.8%	6.5%	9.3%	1.5%
POINTE COUPEE	381	320	19	39	3	G.W. Bush	84.0%	5.0%	10.2%	0.8%
RAPIDES	2,036	1,730	136	140	30	G.W. Bush	85.0%	6.7%	6.9%	1.5%
RED RIVER	272	250	1	20	1	G.W. Bush	91.9%	0.4%	7.4%	0.4%
RICHLAND	476	419	23	26	8	G.W. Bush	88.0%	4.8%	5.5%	1.7%
SABINE	491	439	20	26	6	G.W. Bush	89.4%	4.1%	5.3%	1.2%
ST. BERNARD	1,004	804	78	102	20	G.W. Bush	80.1%	7.8%	10.2%	2.0%
ST. CHARLES	1,260	1,037	95	102	26	G.W. Bush	82.3%	7.5%	8.1%	2.1%
ST. HELENA	215	158	9	12	36	G.W. Bush	73.5%	4.2%	5.6%	16.7%
ST. JAMES	179	143	18	15	3	G.W. Bush	79.9%	10.1%	8.4%	1.7%
ST. JOHN THE BAPTIST	441	359	40	31	11	G.W. Bush	81.4%	9.1%	7.0%	2.5%
ST. LANDRY	792	647	59	69	17	G.W. Bush	81.7%	7.4%	8.7%	2.1%
ST. MARTIN	565	474	36	44	11	G.W. Bush	83.9%	6.4%	7.8%	1.9%
ST. MARY	1,461	1,225	88	121	27	G.W. Bush	83.8%	6.0%	8.3%	1.8%
ST. TAMMANY	7,538	6,086	507	824	121	G.W. Bush	80.7%	6.7%	10.9%	1.6%
TANGIPAHOA	2,447	2,040	155	198	54	G.W. Bush	83.4%	6.3%	8.1%	2.2%
TENSAS	138	118	7	10	3	G.W. Bush	85.5%	5.1%	7.2%	2.2%
TERREBONNE	1,591	1,318	118	125	30	G.W. Bush	82.8%	7.4%	7.9%	1.9%
UNION	499	440	27	27	5	G.W. Bush	88.2%	5.4%	5.4%	1.0%
VERMILION	664	582	37	34	11	G.W. Bush	87.7%	5.6%	5.1%	1.7%
VERNON	578	492	29	48	9	G.W. Bush	85.1%	5.0%	8.3%	1.6%
WASHINGTON	703	616	38	42	7	G.W. Bush	87.6%	5.4%	6.0%	1.0%
WEBSTER	497	447	15	27	8	G.W. Bush	89.9%	3.0%	5.4%	1.6%
WEST BATON ROUGE	256	216	22	15	3	G.W. Bush	84.4%	8.6%	5.9%	1.2%
WEST CARROLL	299	263	10	21	5	G.W. Bush	88.0%	3.3%	7.0%	1.7%
WEST FELICIANA	185	153	10	19	3	G.W. Bush	82.7%	5.4%	10.3%	1.6%
WINN	259	220	7	30	2	G.W. Bush	84.9%	2.7%	11.6%	0.8%
TOTAL	102,912	86,038	5,900	9,165	1,809	G.W. Bush	83.6%	5.7%	8.9%	1.8%

Note: Other vote was 1,041 Steve Forbes; 768 Gary Bauer.

LOUISIANA DEMOCRATIC PRIMARY

2004

Parish	Total Vote	Edwards	Kerry	Other	Winner	Percentage of Total Vote		
						Edwards	Kerry	Other
ACADIA	1,772	396	1,105	271	Kerry	22.3%	62.4%	15.3%
ALLEN	646	96	446	104	Kerry	14.9%	69.0%	16.1%
ASCENSION	6,059	1,226	3,775	1,058	Kerry	20.2%	62.3%	17.5%
ASSUMPTION	646	88	495	63	Kerry	13.6%	76.6%	9.8%
AVOYELLES	1,013	136	756	121	Kerry	13.4%	74.6%	11.9%
BEAUREGARD	653	131	410	112	Kerry	20.1%	62.8%	17.2%
BIENVILLE	779	116	544	119	Kerry	14.9%	69.8%	15.3%
BOSSIER	1,295	252	878	165	Kerry	19.5%	67.8%	12.7%
CADDO	5,798	953	4,039	806	Kerry	16.4%	69.7%	13.9%
CALCASIEU	5,190	980	3,452	758	Kerry	18.9%	66.5%	14.6%
CALDWELL	789	200	458	131	Kerry	25.3%	58.0%	16.6%
CAMERON	620	148	388	84	Kerry	23.9%	62.6%	13.5%
CATAHOULA	1,110	250	660	200	Kerry	22.5%	59.5%	18.0%
CLAIBORNE	472	74	338	60	Kerry	15.7%	71.6%	12.7%
CONCORDIA	2,768	498	1,764	506	Kerry	18.0%	63.7%	18.3%
DE SOTO	858	131	609	118	Kerry	15.3%	71.0%	13.8%
EAST BATON ROUGE	8,884	1,438	6,129	1,317	Kerry	16.2%	69.0%	14.8%
EAST CARROLL	671	123	439	109	Kerry	18.3%	65.4%	16.2%
EAST FELICIANA	927	203	531	193	Kerry	21.9%	57.3%	20.8%
EVANGELINE	989	150	705	134	Kerry	15.2%	71.3%	13.5%
FRANKLIN	876	180	519	177	Kerry	20.5%	59.2%	20.2%
GRANT	474	117	269	88	Kerry	24.7%	56.8%	18.6%
IBERIA	1,120	187	769	164	Kerry	16.7%	68.7%	14.6%
IBERVILLE	671	107	467	97	Kerry	15.9%	69.6%	14.5%
JACKSON	1,099	222	741	136	Kerry	20.2%	67.4%	12.4%
JEFFERSON	13,820	2,135	9,725	1,960	Kerry	15.4%	70.4%	14.2%
JEFFERSON DAVIS	998	198	677	123	Kerry	19.8%	67.8%	12.3%
LAFAYETTE	4,369	918	2,759	692	Kerry	21.0%	63.1%	15.8%
LAFOURCHE	2,208	339	1,613	256	Kerry	15.4%	73.1%	11.6%
LA SALLE	321	86	183	52	Kerry	26.8%	57.0%	16.2%
LINCOLN	2,975	626	1,889	460	Kerry	21.0%	63.5%	15.5%
LIVINGSTON	1,344	291	872	181	Kerry	21.7%	64.9%	13.5%
MADISON	404	57	292	55	Kerry	14.1%	72.3%	13.6%
MOREHOUSE	648	97	467	84	Kerry	15.0%	72.1%	13.0%
NATCHITOCHES	4,817	966	2,923	928	Kerry	20.1%	60.7%	19.3%
ORLEANS	30,788	2,040	25,787	2,961	Kerry	6.6%	83.8%	9.6%
OUACHITA	9,244	1,363	6,588	1,293	Kerry	14.7%	71.3%	14.0%
PLAQUEMINES	1,065	181	715	169	Kerry	17.0%	67.1%	15.9%
POINTE COUPEE	577	83	420	74	Kerry	14.4%	72.8%	12.8%
RAPIDES	2,369	429	1,635	305	Kerry	18.1%	69.0%	12.9%
RED RIVER	375	67	251	57	Kerry	17.9%	66.9%	15.2%
RICHLAND	901	197	570	134	Kerry	21.9%	63.3%	14.9%
SABINE	713	166	409	138	Kerry	23.3%	57.4%	19.4%
ST. BERNARD	3,122	581	1,947	594	Kerry	18.6%	62.4%	19.0%
ST. CHARLES	877	119	650	108	Kerry	13.6%	74.1%	12.3%

LOUISIANA DEMOCRATIC PRIMARY

2004

Parish	Total Vote	Edwards	Kerry	Other	Winner	Percentage of Total Vote		
						Edwards	Kerry	Other
ST. HELENA	538	128	306	104	Kerry	23.8%	56.9%	19.3%
ST. JAMES	1,566	213	1,139	214	Kerry	13.6%	72.7%	13.7%
ST. JOHN THE BAPTIST	1,034	126	787	121	Kerry	12.2%	76.1%	11.7%
ST. LANDRY	3,344	523	2,313	508	Kerry	15.6%	69.2%	15.2%
ST. MARTIN	1,219	185	873	161	Kerry	15.2%	71.6%	13.2%
ST. MARY	821	121	595	105	Kerry	14.7%	72.5%	12.8%
ST. TAMMANY	4,651	851	3,044	756	Kerry	18.3%	65.4%	16.3%
TANGIPAHOA	8,655	2,334	4,796	1,525	Kerry	27.0%	55.4%	17.6%
TENSAS	274	38	203	33	Kerry	13.9%	74.1%	12.0%
TERREBONNE	3,509	583	2,529	397	Kerry	16.6%	72.1%	11.3%
UNION	499	97	317	85	Kerry	19.4%	63.5%	17.0%
VERMILION	1,018	172	707	139	Kerry	16.9%	69.4%	13.7%
VERNON	2,816	677	1,598	541	Kerry	24.0%	56.7%	19.2%
WASHINGTON	882	128	639	115	Kerry	14.5%	72.4%	13.0%
WEBSTER	1,372	300	876	196	Kerry	21.9%	63.8%	14.3%
WEST BATON ROUGE	399	69	270	60	Kerry	17.3%	67.7%	15.0%
WEST CARROLL	213	55	123	35	Kerry	25.8%	57.7%	16.4%
WEST FELICIANA	329	47	229	53	Kerry	14.3%	69.6%	16.1%
WINN	400	86	237	77	Kerry	21.5%	59.3%	19.3%
TOTAL	161,653	26,074	112,639	22,940	Kerry	16.1%	69.7%	14.2%

Note: Other vote was 7,948 Howard Dean; 7,091 Wesley Clark; 3,161 Bill McGaughey; 2,411 Dennis J. Kucinich; 2,329 Lyndon H. LaRouche Jr.

LOUISIANA REPUBLICAN PRIMARY

2004

Parish	Total Vote	G.W. Bush	Wyatt	Winner	Percentage of Total Vote	
					G.W. Bush	Wyatt
ACADIA	488	467	21	G.W. Bush	95.7%	4.3%
ALLEN	132	126	6	G.W. Bush	95.5%	4.5%
ASCENSION	2,565	2,492	73	G.W. Bush	97.2%	2.8%
ASSUMPTION	85	83	2	G.W. Bush	97.6%	2.4%
AVOYELLES	197	194	3	G.W. Bush	98.5%	1.5%
BEAUREGARD	363	351	12	G.W. Bush	96.7%	3.3%
BIENVILLE	171	169	2	G.W. Bush	98.8%	1.2%
BOSSIER	593	569	24	G.W. Bush	96.0%	4.0%
CADDO	3,933	3,788	145	G.W. Bush	96.3%	3.7%
CALCASIEU	2,392	2,323	69	G.W. Bush	97.1%	2.9%
CALDWELL	218	206	12	G.W. Bush	94.5%	5.5%
CAMERON	73	71	2	G.W. Bush	97.3%	2.7%
CATAHOULA	246	235	11	G.W. Bush	95.5%	4.5%
CLAIBORNE	116	111	5	G.W. Bush	95.7%	4.3%
CONCORDIA	789	771	18	G.W. Bush	97.7%	2.3%
DE SOTO	217	211	6	G.W. Bush	97.2%	2.8%
EAST BATON ROUGE	4,532	4,384	148	G.W. Bush	96.7%	3.3%
EAST CARROLL	169	166	3	G.W. Bush	98.2%	1.8%
EAST FELICIANA	323	314	9	G.W. Bush	97.2%	2.8%
EVANGELINE	138	128	10	G.W. Bush	92.8%	7.2%

LOUISIANA REPUBLICAN PRIMARY

2004

Parish	Total Vote	G.W. Bush	Wyatt	Winner	Percentage of Total Vote	
					G.W. Bush	Wyatt
FRANKLIN	435	424	11	G.W. Bush	97.5%	2.5%
GRANT	153	150	3	G.W. Bush	98.0%	2.0%
IBERIA	675	662	13	G.W. Bush	98.1%	1.9%
IBERVILLE	129	127	2	G.W. Bush	98.4%	1.6%
JACKSON	411	398	13	G.W. Bush	96.8%	3.2%
JEFFERSON	12,054	11,550	504	G.W. Bush	95.8%	4.2%
JEFFERSON DAVIS	410	403	7	G.W. Bush	98.3%	1.7%
LAFAYETTE	3,855	3,759	96	G.W. Bush	97.5%	2.5%
LAFOURCHE	575	553	22	G.W. Bush	96.2%	3.8%
LA SALLE	105	100	5	G.W. Bush	95.2%	4.8%
LINCOLN	2,010	1,966	44	G.W. Bush	97.8%	2.2%
LIVINGSTON	681	653	28	G.W. Bush	95.9%	4.1%
MADISON	191	185	6	G.W. Bush	96.9%	3.1%
MOREHOUSE	170	163	7	G.W. Bush	95.9%	4.1%
NATCHITOCHES	1,813	1,745	68	G.W. Bush	96.2%	3.8%
ORLEANS	5,930	5,463	467	G.W. Bush	92.1%	7.9%
OUACHITA	4,456	4,339	117	G.W. Bush	97.4%	2.6%
PLAQUEMINES	494	481	13	G.W. Bush	97.4%	2.6%
POINTE COUPEE	339	331	8	G.W. Bush	97.6%	2.4%
RAPIDES	995	961	34	G.W. Bush	96.6%	3.4%
RED RIVER	95	88	7	G.W. Bush	92.6%	7.4%
RICHLAND	445	433	12	G.W. Bush	97.3%	2.7%
SABINE	240	229	11	G.W. Bush	95.4%	4.6%
ST. BERNARD	1,329	1,258	71	G.W. Bush	94.7%	5.3%
ST. CHARLES	648	628	20	G.W. Bush	96.9%	3.1%
ST. HELENA	103	99	4	G.W. Bush	96.1%	3.9%
ST. JAMES	178	168	10	G.W. Bush	94.4%	5.6%
ST. JOHN THE BAPTIST	177	166	11	G.W. Bush	93.8%	6.2%
ST. LANDRY	527	498	29	G.W. Bush	94.5%	5.5%
ST. MARTIN	271	258	13	G.W. Bush	95.2%	4.8%
ST. MARY	573	564	9	G.W. Bush	98.4%	1.6%
ST. TAMMANY	6,019	5,761	258	G.W. Bush	95.7%	4.3%
TANGIPAHOA	3,163	3,016	147	G.W. Bush	95.4%	4.6%
TENSAS	53	49	4	G.W. Bush	92.5%	7.5%
TERREBONNE	1,751	1,695	56	G.W. Bush	96.8%	3.2%
UNION	312	306	6	G.W. Bush	98.1%	1.9%
VERMILION	205	197	8	G.W. Bush	96.1%	3.9%
VERNON	1,064	1,033	31	G.W. Bush	97.1%	2.9%
WASHINGTON	154	144	10	G.W. Bush	93.5%	6.5%
WEBSTER	703	676	27	G.W. Bush	96.2%	3.8%
WEST BATON ROUGE	110	107	3	G.W. Bush	97.3%	2.7%
WEST CARROLL	111	106	5	G.W. Bush	95.5%	4.5%
WEST FELICIANA	54	52	2	G.W. Bush	96.3%	3.7%
WINN	104	102	2	G.W. Bush	98.1%	1.9%
TOTAL	72,010	69,205	2,805	G.W. Bush	96.1%	3.9%

MAINE

The Bush family is identified with Kennebunkport in particular and Maine in general. The family ties, as well as the political networking that went with it, no doubt helped George W. Bush win the state's presidential primary in 2000—the only one in New England that he took from John McCain.

That "against the grain" quality underscored Maine's recent image as a place where political contrariness and individualism flourish. In the presidential elections of 1992 and 1996, Maine gave Ross Perot a higher percentage of the vote than any other state. In 1994 and 1998, Maine was the only state to elect an independent governor (Angus King). And in 1992, Maine gave Jerry Brown his first victory of the year, a narrow 1 percentage point victory over the New Hampshire primary winner and regional favorite son, Paul Tsongas.

Brown's victory broke a trend evident throughout the 1980s—that the winner in New Hampshire would also win the Maine vote several days later. In 1980, the double winner was President Jimmy Carter, whose New Hampshire and Maine victories put an early chill on Edward Kennedy in his New England backyard. In 1984, Gary Hart's stunning breakthrough win in New Hampshire yanked him from down-in-the-weeds status in Maine to a victorious 50 percent share of the caucus vote. In 1988, Michael Dukakis swept out of New Hampshire to win Maine's caucuses handily 12 days later.

Meanwhile, on the Republican side, Maine was long the personal preserve of George Bush. From his youth, he had vacationed at his family's seaside compound in Kennebunkport, establishing a personal relationship with Maine voters that helped launch him onto the presidential stage with an upset victory in a party-sponsored straw poll in late 1979. The following spring

he swept virtually all of Maine's delegates, even as his first bid for the White House was crumbling nationally.

Maine was also in Bush's corner when he successfully pursued the GOP presidential nomination in 1988 and 1992. Bob Dole won the state's first Republican presidential primary in 1996, although he drew a majority of the vote in only two counties. One of them, though, was Cumberland (Portland), the state's most populous. The primary runner-up, Pat Buchanan, could dent the 30 percent mark in only two counties, the largest of which was historically blue-collar and heavily Democratic Androscoggin (Lewiston).

In 2000, both the Democratic and Republican primaries were comparatively close. The winners, Al Gore and George W. Bush, respectively, each carried 12 of Maine's 16 counties.

Three of the four counties that Bush lost to McCain, as well as all four counties that Gore lost to Bill Bradley, were along the Atlantic coast, where voters are apt to be more liberal and environmentally conscious than in the interior of the state. Bradley carried Cumberland County and Maine's largest city (Portland). He also won the college town of Orono (home of the University of Maine) by one vote over Gore.

Although turnout on both the Democratic and Republican sides in 2000 was much higher than the first time the presidential primary was held in 1996, Maine returned to a lower-turnout caucus process to elect its delegates in 2004. Nearly 20,000 voters participated in the Democratic event, which was held just 12 days after John Kerry's break out victory in New Hampshire. Kerry drew major caucus-eve endorsements from Gov. John Baldacci and former senator George Mitchell, while Howard Dean and Dennis Kucinich also mounted major efforts

Maine Primary Results

Maine held its first presidential primary in 1996.

| Year | DEMOCRATS | | | REPUBLICANS | | |
	Turnout	Candidates	%	Turnout	Candidates	%
2004	—	No Primary	—		No Primary	
2000 (March 7)	64,279	AL GORE Bill Bradley	54 41	96,624	GEORGE W. BUSH John McCain	51 44
1996 (March 5)	27,027	BILL CLINTON* Uncommitted	88 9	67,280	BOB DOLE Pat Buchanan Steve Forbes Lamar Alexander	46 24 15 7

Note: All candidates are listed who drew at least 5 percent of their party's primary vote. The names of winning candidates are capitalized. An asterisk (*) indicates an incumbent president.

in Maine that culminated with late campaign swings through the state. Yet Dean and Kucinich split the anti-Kerry vote, enabling the Democratic front-runner to win comfortably. The tally by the state party showed Kerry winning 44 percent of the Maine caucus vote, with 28 percent for Dean and 16 percent for Kucinich.

MAINE DEMOCRATIC PRIMARY

2000

County	Total Vote	Bradley	Gore	Other	Winner	Percentage of Total Vote		
						Bradley	Gore	Other
ANDROSCOGGIN	5,195	1,717	3,209	269	Gore	33.1%	61.8%	5.2%
AROOSTOOK	4,096	939	2,774	383	Gore	22.9%	67.7%	9.4%
CUMBERLAND	17,092	8,466	8,156	470	Bradley	49.5%	47.7%	2.7%
FRANKLIN	1,071	405	621	45	Gore	37.8%	58.0%	4.2%
HANCOCK	2,540	1,293	1,149	98	Bradley	50.9%	45.2%	3.9%
KENNEBEC	5,463	2,044	3,160	259	Gore	37.4%	57.8%	4.7%
KNOX	2,085	1,078	954	53	Bradley	51.7%	45.8%	2.5%
LINCOLN	1,858	929	859	70	Bradley	50.0%	46.2%	3.8%
OXFORD	2,452	885	1,413	154	Gore	36.1%	57.6%	6.3%
PENOBSCOT	5,100	1,982	2,844	274	Gore	38.9%	55.8%	5.4%
PISCATAQUIS	750	239	445	66	Gore	31.9%	59.3%	8.8%
SAGADAHOC	1,866	868	909	89	Gore	46.5%	48.7%	4.8%
SOMERSET	1,998	623	1,247	128	Gore	31.2%	62.4%	6.4%
WALDO	1,746	786	855	105	Gore	45.0%	49.0%	6.0%
WASHINGTON	1,306	462	720	124	Gore	35.4%	55.1%	9.5%
YORK	9,661	3,804	5,410	447	Gore	39.4%	56.0%	4.6%
TOTAL	64,279	26,520	34,725	3,034	Gore	41.3%	54.0%	4.7%

Note: Other vote was 2,634 Uncommitted; 208 Lyndon H. LaRouche Jr.; 192 Richard Jan Epstein.

MAINE DEMOCRATIC PRIMARY

2000

City/Town	Total Vote	Bradley	Gore	Other	Winner	Percentage of Total Vote		
						Bradley	Gore	Other
AUBURN	1,141	392	695	54	Gore	34.4%	60.9%	4.7%
AUGUSTA	799	278	489	32	Gore	34.8%	61.2%	4.0%
BANGOR	1,178	508	635	35	Gore	43.1%	53.9%	3.0%
BATH	522	229	266	27	Gore	43.9%	51.0%	5.2%
BELFAST	346	183	152	11	Bradley	52.9%	43.9%	3.2%
BERWICK	219	74	134	11	Gore	33.8%	61.2%	5.0%
BIDDEFORD	1,185	412	720	53	Gore	34.8%	60.8%	4.5%
BREWER	344	130	201	13	Gore	37.8%	58.4%	3.8%
BRUNSWICK	1,344	674	639	31	Bradley	50.1%	47.5%	2.3%
BUXTON	436	182	221	33	Gore	41.7%	50.7%	7.6%
CAMDEN	508	278	229	1	Bradley	54.7%	45.1%	0.2%
CAPE ELIZABETH	847	480	353	14	Bradley	56.7%	41.7%	1.7%
CARIBOU	236	55	170	11	Gore	23.3%	72.0%	4.7%
CUMBERLAND TOWN	438	239	193	6	Bradley	54.6%	44.1%	1.4%
ELIOT	363	158	190	15	Gore	43.5%	52.3%	4.1%
ELLSWORTH	246	108	135	3	Gore	43.9%	54.9%	1.2%
FAIRFIELD	196	57	129	10	Gore	29.1%	65.8%	5.1%
FALMOUTH	725	423	292	10	Bradley	58.3%	40.3%	1.4%
FARMINGTON	206	92	104	10	Gore	44.7%	50.5%	4.9%
FREEPORT	549	315	220	14	Bradley	57.4%	40.1%	2.6%
GARDINER	353	129	209	15	Gore	36.5%	59.2%	4.2%
GORHAM	533	256	246	31	Bradley	48.0%	46.2%	5.8%
GRAY	294	163	130	1	Bradley	55.4%	44.2%	0.3%
HAMPDEN	239	102	127	10	Gore	42.7%	53.1%	4.2%
HARPSWELL	318	177	138	3	Bradley	55.7%	43.4%	0.9%
HOULTON	339	109	196	34	Gore	32.2%	57.8%	10.0%
JAY	189	41	142	6	Gore	21.7%	75.1%	3.2%
KENNEBUNK	680	308	352	20	Gore	45.3%	51.8%	2.9%
KITTERY	631	267	342	22	Gore	42.3%	54.2%	3.5%
LEWISTON	2,301	719	1,486	96	Gore	31.2%	64.6%	4.2%
LIMESTONE	55	16	39	0	Gore	29.1%	70.9%	0.0%
LINCOLN TOWN	166	56	93	17	Gore	33.7%	56.0%	10.2%
LISBON	421	135	251	35	Gore	32.1%	59.6%	8.3%
MILLINOCKET	188	54	123	11	Gore	28.7%	65.4%	5.9%
OAKLAND	204	62	124	18	Gore	30.4%	60.8%	8.8%
OLD ORCHARD BEACH	435	181	236	18	Gore	41.6%	54.3%	4.1%
OLD TOWN	330	114	203	13	Gore	34.5%	61.5%	3.9%
ORONO	396	192	191	13	Bradley	48.5%	48.2%	3.3%
PORTLAND	5,514	2,772	2,635	107	Bradley	50.3%	47.8%	1.9%
PRESQUE ISLE	500	135	313	52	Gore	27.0%	62.6%	10.4%
ROCKLAND	287	119	161	7	Gore	41.5%	56.1%	2.4%
RUMFORD	442	143	271	28	Gore	32.4%	61.3%	6.3%
SACO	878	330	523	25	Gore	37.6%	59.6%	2.8%
SANFORD	1,101	325	703	73	Gore	29.5%	63.9%	6.6%
SCARBOROUGH	822	405	391	26	Bradley	49.3%	47.6%	3.2%

MAINE DEMOCRATIC PRIMARY

2000

City/Town	Total Vote	Bradley	Gore	Other	Winner	Percentage of Total Vote		
						Bradley	Gore	Other
SKOWHEGAN	340	97	224	19	Gore	28.5%	65.9%	5.6%
SOUTH BERWICK	272	155	111	6	Bradley	57.0%	40.8%	2.2%
SOUTH PORTLAND	1,623	692	875	56	Gore	42.6%	53.9%	3.5%
STANDISH	314	133	168	13	Gore	42.4%	53.5%	4.1%
TOPSHAM	414	178	223	13	Gore	43.0%	53.9%	3.1%
WATERVILLE	797	285	488	24	Gore	35.8%	61.2%	3.0%
WELLS	386	163	205	18	Gore	42.2%	53.1%	4.7%
WESTBROOK	876	347	492	37	Gore	39.6%	56.2%	4.2%
WINDHAM	557	261	273	23	Gore	46.9%	49.0%	4.1%
WINSLOW	325	88	221	16	Gore	27.1%	68.0%	4.9%
WINTHROP	478	182	264	32	Gore	38.1%	55.2%	6.7%
YARMOUTH	907	488	378	41	Bradley	53.8%	41.7%	4.5%
YORK TOWN	743	336	380	27	Gore	45.2%	51.1%	3.6%

Note: The cities and towns included are basically those with a population of at least 5,000 in the 2000 Census plus a few other selected communities.

MAINE REPUBLICAN PRIMARY

2000

County	Total Vote	G.W. Bush	McCain	Other	Winner	Percentage of Total Vote		
						G.W. Bush	McCain	Other
ANDROSCOGGIN	5,214	2,828	2,065	321	G.W. Bush	54.2%	39.6%	6.2%
AROOSTOOK	4,999	2,770	1,928	301	G.W. Bush	55.4%	38.6%	6.0%
CUMBERLAND	22,388	11,478	10,059	851	G.W. Bush	51.3%	44.9%	3.8%
FRANKLIN	2,037	897	1,033	107	McCain	44.0%	50.7%	5.3%
HANCOCK	4,727	2,265	2,253	209	G.W. Bush	47.9%	47.7%	4.4%
KENNEBEC	7,363	3,653	3,264	446	G.W. Bush	49.6%	44.3%	6.1%
KNOX	4,098	1,811	2,036	251	McCain	44.2%	49.7%	6.1%
LINCOLN	4,113	1,923	2,017	173	McCain	46.8%	49.0%	4.2%
OXFORD	3,803	1,883	1,758	162	G.W. Bush	49.5%	46.2%	4.3%
PENOBSCOT	9,081	5,284	3,316	481	G.W. Bush	58.2%	36.5%	5.3%
PISCATAQUIS	1,531	847	571	113	G.W. Bush	55.3%	37.3%	7.4%
SAGADAHOC	2,888	1,325	1,411	152	McCain	45.9%	48.9%	5.3%
SOMERSET	3,090	1,607	1,314	169	G.W. Bush	52.0%	42.5%	5.5%
WALDO	3,310	1,662	1,498	150	G.W. Bush	50.2%	45.3%	4.5%
WASHINGTON	2,483	1,320	1,014	149	G.W. Bush	53.2%	40.8%	6.0%
YORK	15,499	7,755	6,973	771	G.W. Bush	50.0%	45.0%	5.0%
TOTAL	96,624	49,308	42,510	4,806	G.W. Bush	51.0%	44.0%	5.0%

Note: Other vote was 2,989 Alan Keyes; 1,038 Uncommitted; 455 Steve Forbes; 324 Gary Bauer.

MAINE REPUBLICAN PRIMARY

2000

City/Town	Total Vote	G.W. Bush	McCain	Other	Winner	Percentage of Total Vote		
						G.W. Bush	McCain	Other
AUBURN	1,405	741	600	64	G.W. Bush	52.7%	42.7%	4.6%
AUGUSTA	1,012	482	488	42	McCain	47.6%	48.2%	4.2%
BANGOR	1,831	1,004	736	91	G.W. Bush	54.8%	40.2%	5.0%
BATH	707	292	380	35	McCain	41.3%	53.7%	5.0%
BELFAST	644	312	308	24	G.W. Bush	48.4%	47.8%	3.7%
BERWICK	477	189	237	51	McCain	39.6%	49.7%	10.7%
BIDDEFORD	472	275	179	18	G.W. Bush	58.3%	37.9%	3.8%
BREWER	753	462	267	24	G.W. Bush	61.4%	35.5%	3.2%
BRUNSWICK	1,576	708	804	64	McCain	44.9%	51.0%	4.1%
BUXTON	669	381	254	34	G.W. Bush	57.0%	38.0%	5.1%
CAMDEN	767	321	412	34	McCain	41.9%	53.7%	4.4%
CAPE ELIZABETH	1,320	624	657	39	McCain	47.3%	49.8%	3.0%
CARIBOU	506	259	211	36	G.W. Bush	51.2%	41.7%	7.1%
CUMBERLAND TOWN	1,083	566	491	26	G.W. Bush	52.3%	45.3%	2.4%
ELIOT	825	320	452	53	McCain	38.8%	54.8%	6.4%
ELLSWORTH	606	326	252	28	G.W. Bush	53.8%	41.6%	4.6%
FAIRFIELD	229	121	101	7	G.W. Bush	52.8%	44.1%	3.1%
FALMOUTH	1,369	701	633	35	G.W. Bush	51.2%	46.2%	2.6%
FARMINGTON	431	174	230	27	McCain	40.4%	53.4%	6.3%
FREEPORT	715	375	307	33	G.W. Bush	52.4%	42.9%	4.6%
GARDINER	392	199	164	29	G.W. Bush	50.8%	41.8%	7.4%
GORHAM	1,087	594	451	42	G.W. Bush	54.6%	41.5%	3.9%
GRAY	628	348	244	36	G.W. Bush	55.4%	38.9%	5.7%
HAMPDEN	602	366	215	21	G.W. Bush	60.8%	35.7%	3.5%
HARPSWELL	565	230	313	22	McCain	40.7%	55.4%	3.9%
HOULTON	676	378	247	51	G.W. Bush	55.9%	36.5%	7.5%
JAY	158	94	54	10	G.W. Bush	59.5%	34.2%	6.3%
KENNEBUNK	1,592	879	662	51	G.W. Bush	55.2%	41.6%	3.2%
KITTERY	891	340	514	37	McCain	38.2%	57.7%	4.2%
LEWISTON	1,156	616	465	75	G.W. Bush	53.3%	40.2%	6.5%
LIMESTONE	121	57	60	4	McCain	47.1%	49.6%	3.3%
LINCOLN TOWN	280	180	86	14	G.W. Bush	64.3%	30.7%	5.0%
LISBON	533	318	184	31	G.W. Bush	59.7%	34.5%	5.8%
MILLINOCKET	249	145	74	30	G.W. Bush	58.2%	29.7%	12.0%
OAKLAND	302	149	132	21	G.W. Bush	49.3%	43.7%	7.0%
OLD ORCHARD BEACH	449	216	208	25	G.W. Bush	48.1%	46.3%	5.6%
OLD TOWN	379	202	147	30	G.W. Bush	53.3%	38.8%	7.9%
ORONO	459	202	238	19	McCain	44.0%	51.9%	4.1%
PORTLAND	3,525	1,727	1,658	140	G.W. Bush	49.0%	47.0%	4.0%
PRESQUE ISLE	906	510	351	45	G.W. Bush	56.3%	38.7%	5.0%
ROCKLAND	596	282	276	38	G.W. Bush	47.3%	46.3%	6.4%
RUMFORD	236	113	114	9	McCain	47.9%	48.3%	3.8%
SACO	891	513	356	22	G.W. Bush	57.6%	40.0%	2.5%
SANFORD	1,183	649	463	71	G.W. Bush	54.9%	39.1%	6.0%
SCARBOROUGH	1,797	997	734	66	G.W. Bush	55.5%	40.8%	3.7%

MAINE REPUBLICAN PRIMARY

2000

City/Town	Total Vote	G.W. Bush	McCain	Other	Winner	Percentage of Total Vote		
						G.W. Bush	McCain	Other
SKOWHEGAN	451	205	218	28	McCain	45.5%	48.3%	6.2%
SOUTH BERWICK	726	270	393	63	McCain	37.2%	54.1%	8.7%
SOUTH PORTLAND	1,691	902	736	53	G.W. Bush	53.3%	43.5%	3.1%
STANDISH	668	362	267	39	G.W. Bush	54.2%	40.0%	5.8%
TOPSHAM	715	345	325	45	G.W. Bush	48.3%	45.5%	6.3%
WATERVILLE	633	303	290	40	G.W. Bush	47.9%	45.8%	6.3%
WELLS	931	459	432	40	G.W. Bush	49.3%	46.4%	4.3%
WESTBROOK	986	543	395	48	G.W. Bush	55.1%	40.1%	4.9%
WINDHAM	1,056	623	395	38	G.W. Bush	59.0%	37.4%	3.6%
WINSLOW	374	200	149	25	G.W. Bush	53.5%	39.8%	6.7%
WINTHROP	701	349	307	45	G.W. Bush	49.8%	43.8%	6.4%
YARMOUTH	1,510	674	779	57	McCain	44.6%	51.6%	3.8%
YORK TOWN	1,620	623	927	70	McCain	38.5%	57.2%	4.3%

Note: The cities and towns included are basically those with a population of at least 5,000 in the 2000 Census plus a few other selected communities.

MARYLAND

When H. L. Mencken was penning his bitingly incisive political essays early in the twentieth century, his hometown of Baltimore dominated the state. But that is no longer the case. Fast-growing suburbs have grown to define Maryland politically.

Yet while large tracts of suburbia give Republicans a strong base in many states, that has not been the case in Maryland, where a large complement of federal workers and minority voters, and a heritage closely linked to the South, has long given Democrats the upper hand and meant the Democratic primary is often where the action takes place.

A generation or so ago, the vote in the Democratic presidential primary reflected the Southern character of this border state. In 1964, George Wallace collected a surprising 43 percent of the vote against the state's favorite-son candidate, Sen. Daniel Brewster. Embarrassed by that outcome, state officials

Recent Maryland Primary Results

Maryland held its first presidential primary in 1912.

Year	DEMOCRATS			REPUBLICANS		
	Turnout	Candidates	%	Turnout	Candidates	%
2004 (March 2)	481,476	JOHN KERRY	60	151,943	GEORGE W. BUSH*	100
		John Edwards	26			
2000 (March 7)	507,462	AL GORE	67	376,034	GEORGE W. BUSH	56
		Bill Bradley	28		John McCain	36
					Alan Keyes	7
1996 (March 5)	293,829	BILL CLINTON*	84	254,246	BOB DOLE	53
		Uncommitted	11		Pat Buchanan	21
					Steve Forbes	13
					Lamar Alexander	6
					Alan Keyes	5
1992 (March 3)	567,243	PAUL TSONGAS	41	240,021	GEORGE BUSH*	70
		Bill Clinton	33		Pat Buchanan	30
		Jerry Brown	8			
		Uncommitted	6			
		Tom Harkin	6			
1988 (March 8)	531,335	MICHAEL DUKAKIS	46	200,754	GEORGE BUSH	53
		Jesse Jackson	29		Bob Dole	32
		Al Gore	9		Pat Robertson	6
		Richard Gephardt	8		Jack Kemp	6
1984 (May 8)	506,886	WALTER MONDALE	42	73,663	RONALD REAGAN*	100
		Jesse Jackson	26			
		Gary Hart	24			
1980 (May 13)	477,090	JIMMY CARTER*	47	167,303	RONALD REAGAN	48
		Edward Kennedy	38		George Bush	41
		Uncommitted	10		John Anderson	10
1976 (May 18)	591,746	JERRY BROWN	48	165,971	GERALD FORD*	58
		Jimmy Carter	37		Ronald Reagan	42
		Morris Udall	6			
1972 (May 16)	568,131	GEORGE WALLACE	39	115,249	RICHARD NIXON*	86
		Hubert Humphrey	27		Paul McCloskey	8
		George McGovern	22		John Ashbrook	6
1968	—	No Primary		—	No Primary	

Note: All candidates are listed who drew at least 5 percent of their party's primary vote. The names of winning candidates are capitalized. An asterisk (*) indicates an incumbent president.

scrubbed the primary in 1968. But when it was reinstituted in 1972, Wallace was back to win it easily, one day after an assassination attempt in Laurel left him paralyzed from the waist down.

Wallace swept not only the conservative counties of Maryland's Eastern Shore, which have a cultural affinity to Dixie, but most of the suburban counties as well. Among the venues he carried that year was Prince George's County outside Washington, then a predominantly white, blue-collar constituency that has since become primarily black.

Yet with the exception of Jimmy Carter's victory in 1980 over Edward Kennedy, the result of late in the Democratic primary has tended to accent the state's ties to the northern side of the Mason-Dixon line. Al Gore drew only 9 percent of the vote in Maryland during his 1988 presidential run (although he did win the primary easily in 2000 after two terms as vice president gave him a more national persona). In 1992, Bill Clinton lost the Maryland primary to Paul Tsongas (who scored his lone primary victory outside his native New England).

Tsongas built up his margin of victory among "Volvo Democrats" in the suburban corridor from Baltimore to Washington, swamping Clinton in Montgomery and Howard counties by margins of more than 2 to 1. Clinton won rural Maryland—the mountainous western panhandle that is part of Appalachia, as well as southern Maryland and the Eastern Shore. And Clinton won the city of Baltimore and Prince George's County, both with black majorities, which had

boosted Jesse Jackson to second-place primary finishes in both 1984 and 1988.

None of the Democratic primary winners from 1972 through 1992 was able to attract a majority of the Maryland vote. Winners on the Republican side, though, have often won by lopsided margins, and moderates have often fared well. President Gerald Ford easily won Maryland's GOP primary in 1976 by beating Ronald Reagan in Baltimore and all the major suburban counties. Reagan triumphed in May 1980 at a time his campaign was moving into overdrive. Yet George Bush still carried Baltimore and much of the suburban corridor, and might have beaten Reagan if John Anderson had not drained away 10 percent of the primary vote.

Bush dominated the Maryland primary in 1988 and 1992, carrying every county each time. Pat Robertson's 6 percent showing in Maryland in 1988 was his weakest in any state south of the Mason-Dixon line. Four years later, Bush defeated Pat Buchanan, a native of nearby Washington, D.C., who lived for a time in the Maryland suburb of Chevy Chase.

In 1996, Buchanan was joined on the ballot by another conservative Marylander, Alan Keyes. But Buchanan (21 percent) and Keyes (5 percent) combined to draw only half the vote of the victorious Bob Dole. Dole won every county, piling up his highest vote share (61 percent) in affluent Montgomery, the prime source of both Republican and Democratic primary votes since 1992.

In 2000, Maryland Republicans opened their presidential primary to independent voters. It helped produce a record GOP turnout of more than 375,000 voters. But it did not appreciably boost John McCain, whose success in many other states had been dependent on votes from non-Republicans. George W. Bush defeated him in every county in the state, winning all but Montgomery and the city of Baltimore with a majority of the vote.

Four years later, John Kerry's victory on the Democratic side in Maryland was even more one-sided. Although the presidential primary was held on the first Tuesday in March for the fourth straight election, Kerry was already on the verge of wrapping up the nomination by the time Maryland voted—so much so that turnout for the Democratic primary fell below 500,000 for only the second time in two decades.

MARYLAND DEMOCRATIC PRIMARY

2000

County	Total Vote	Bradley	Gore	Other	Winner	Percentage of Total Vote		
						Bradley	Gore	Other
ALLEGANY	6,494	1,952	4,234	308	Gore	30.1%	65.2%	4.7%
ANNE ARUNDEL	44,268	14,123	27,225	2,920	Gore	31.9%	61.5%	6.6%
BALTIMORE CITY	68,662	13,814	53,468	1,380	Gore	20.1%	77.9%	2.0%
BALTIMORE COUNTY	75,842	24,698	47,500	3,644	Gore	32.6%	62.6%	4.8%
CALVERT	5,172	1,612	3,254	306	Gore	31.2%	62.9%	5.9%
CAROLINE	1,395	498	784	113	Gore	35.7%	56.2%	8.1%
CARROLL	10,209	3,813	5,659	737	Gore	37.3%	55.4%	7.2%
CECIL	5,189	1,702	3,009	478	Gore	32.8%	58.0%	9.2%
CHARLES	7,122	2,032	4,643	447	Gore	28.5%	65.2%	6.3%
DORCHESTER	2,703	913	1,584	206	Gore	33.8%	58.6%	7.6%
FREDERICK	13,238	4,731	7,733	774	Gore	35.7%	58.4%	5.8%
GARRETT	1,372	426	801	145	Gore	31.0%	58.4%	10.6%
HARFORD	17,134	6,124	9,673	1,337	Gore	35.7%	56.5%	7.8%
HOWARD	25,654	8,800	16,223	631	Gore	34.3%	63.2%	2.5%
KENT	1,851	717	1,024	110	Gore	38.7%	55.3%	5.9%
MONTGOMERY	104,056	34,083	66,765	3,208	Gore	32.8%	64.2%	3.1%
PRINCE GEORGE'S	85,901	13,703	69,470	2,728	Gore	16.0%	80.9%	3.2%
QUEEN ANNE'S	2,936	1,105	1,606	225	Gore	37.6%	54.7%	7.7%
ST. MARY'S	5,702	1,792	3,503	407	Gore	31.4%	61.4%	7.1%
SOMERSET	1,424	506	816	102	Gore	35.5%	57.3%	7.2%
TALBOT	2,381	972	1,283	126	Gore	40.8%	53.9%	5.3%
WASHINGTON	8,765	2,916	5,309	540	Gore	33.3%	60.6%	6.2%
WICOMICO	6,108	1,939	3,812	357	Gore	31.7%	62.4%	5.8%
WORCESTER	3,884	1,416	2,252	216	Gore	36.5%	58.0%	5.6%
TOTAL	507,462	144,387	341,630	21,445	Gore	28.5%	67.3%	4.2%

Note: Other vote was 16,935 Uncommitted; 4,510 Lyndon H. LaRouche Jr.

MARYLAND REPUBLICAN PRIMARY

2000

Country	Total Vote	G.W. Bush	Keyes	McCain	Other	Winner	Percentage of Total Vote			
							G.W. Bush	Keyes	McCain	Other
ALLEGANY	8,504	5,438	443	2,485	138	G.W. Bush	63.9%	5.2%	29.2%	1.6%
ANNE ARUNDEL	51,592	27,845	3,432	19,927	388	G.W. Bush	54.0%	6.7%	38.6%	0.8%
BALTIMORE CITY	8,835	4,206	953	3,484	192	G.W. Bush	47.6%	10.8%	39.4%	2.2%
BALTIMORE COUNTY	45,008	27,009	3,142	14,518	339	G.W. Bush	60.0%	7.0%	32.3%	0.8%
CALVERT	6,758	3,898	496	2,320	44	G.W. Bush	57.7%	7.3%	34.3%	0.7%
CAROLINE	1,806	1,126	165	499	16	G.W. Bush	62.3%	9.1%	27.6%	0.9%
CARROLL	18,366	11,717	1,337	5,191	121	G.W. Bush	63.8%	7.3%	28.3%	0.7%
CECIL	5,536	3,297	373	1,811	55	G.W. Bush	59.6%	6.7%	32.7%	1.0%
CHARLES	8,843	5,263	668	2,857	55	G.W. Bush	59.5%	7.6%	32.3%	0.6%
DORCHESTER	2,216	1,318	149	690	59	G.W. Bush	59.5%	6.7%	31.1%	2.7%
FREDERICK	22,054	13,452	1,352	7,086	164	G.W. Bush	61.0%	6.1%	32.1%	0.7%
GARRETT	3,959	2,663	286	976	34	G.W. Bush	67.3%	7.2%	24.7%	0.9%
HARFORD	19,604	12,244	1,397	5,814	149	G.W. Bush	62.5%	7.1%	29.7%	0.8%
HOWARD	26,359	13,910	1,707	10,580	162	G.W. Bush	52.8%	6.5%	40.1%	0.6%
KENT	1,818	1,068	86	650	14	G.W. Bush	58.7%	4.7%	35.8%	0.8%
MONTGOMERY	79,359	39,373	4,472	34,787	727	G.W. Bush	49.6%	5.6%	43.8%	0.9%
PRINCE GEORGE'S	26,273	14,178	2,181	9,281	633	G.W. Bush	54.0%	8.3%	35.3%	2.4%
QUEEN ANNE'S	3,946	2,379	226	1,320	21	G.W. Bush	60.3%	5.7%	33.5%	0.5%
ST. MARY'S	6,321	3,458	534	2,293	36	G.W. Bush	54.7%	8.4%	36.3%	0.6%
SOMERSET	1,343	923	73	336	11	G.W. Bush	68.7%	5.4%	25.0%	0.8%
TALBOT	4,100	2,398	172	1,509	21	G.W. Bush	58.5%	4.2%	36.8%	0.5%
WASHINGTON	12,560	7,762	779	3,934	85	G.W. Bush	61.8%	6.2%	31.3%	0.7%
WICOMICO	6,832	4,194	403	2,140	95	G.W. Bush	61.4%	5.9%	31.3%	1.4%
WORCESTER	4,042	2,320	194	1,493	35	G.W. Bush	57.4%	4.8%	36.9%	0.9%
TOTAL	376,034	211,439	25,020	135,981	3,594	G.W. Bush	56.2%	6.7%	36.2%	1.0%

Note: Other vote was 1,678 Steve Forbes; 1,328 Gary Bauer; 588 Orrin G. Hatch.

MARYLAND DEMOCRATIC PRIMARY

2004

County	Total Vote	Edwards	Kerry	Other	Winner	Percentage of Total Vote		
						Edwards	Kerry	Other
ALLEGANY	5,769	1,805	3,112	852	Kerry	31.3%	53.9%	14.8%
ANNE ARUNDEL	40,644	12,401	22,395	5,848	Kerry	30.5%	55.1%	14.4%
BALTIMORE CITY	54,987	9,575	34,198	11,214	Kerry	17.4%	62.2%	20.4%
BALTIMORE COUNTY	78,706	20,859	45,017	12,830	Kerry	26.5%	57.2%	16.3%
CALVERT	4,716	1,434	2,686	596	Kerry	30.4%	57.0%	12.6%
CAROLINE	1,815	649	882	284	Kerry	35.8%	48.6%	15.6%
CARROLL	9,270	3,379	4,595	1,296	Kerry	36.5%	49.6%	14.0%
CECIL	5,299	1,799	2,684	816	Kerry	33.9%	50.7%	15.4%
CHARLES	8,584	2,352	5,038	1,194	Kerry	27.4%	58.7%	13.9%
DORCHESTER	2,057	745	994	318	Kerry	36.2%	48.3%	15.5%
FREDERICK	15,037	4,615	8,468	1,954	Kerry	30.7%	56.3%	13.0%
GARRETT	1,372	436	746	190	Kerry	31.8%	54.4%	13.8%
HARFORD	15,423	5,253	7,978	2,192	Kerry	34.1%	51.7%	14.2%
HOWARD	27,191	7,224	16,459	3,508	Kerry	26.6%	60.5%	12.9%
KENT	2,023	653	1,115	255	Kerry	32.3%	55.1%	12.6%
MONTGOMERY	102,187	23,534	67,715	10,938	Kerry	23.0%	66.3%	10.7%
PRINCE GEORGE'S	72,048	14,944	44,641	12,463	Kerry	20.7%	62.0%	17.3%
QUEEN ANNE'S	3,154	1,161	1,602	391	Kerry	36.8%	50.8%	12.4%
ST. MARY'S	7,812	2,360	4,203	1,249	Kerry	30.2%	53.8%	16.0%
SOMERSET	1,572	542	773	257	Kerry	34.5%	49.2%	16.3%
TALBOT	2,954	1,030	1,537	387	Kerry	34.9%	52.0%	13.1%
WASHINGTON	8,457	2,791	4,592	1,074	Kerry	33.0%	54.3%	12.7%
WICOMICO	5,879	1,978	3,102	799	Kerry	33.6%	52.8%	13.6%
WORCESTER	4,520	1,487	2,423	610	Kerry	32.9%	53.6%	13.5%
TOTAL	481,476	123,006	286,955	71,515	Kerry	25.5%	59.6%	14.9%

Note: Other vote was 21,810 Al Sharpton; 12,461 Howard Dean; 8,693 Dennis J. Kucinich; 8,527 Uncommitted; 5,245 Joseph I. Lieberman; 4,230 Wesley Clark; 4,039 Mildred Glover; 2,809 Carol Moseley Braun; 2,146 Richard A. Gephardt; 1,555 Lyndon H. LaRouche Jr.

MASSACHUSETTS

Ever since George McGovern went one for 50 in the presidential election of 1972—carrying Massachusetts but no other—the Bay State has been widely regarded as the premier bastion of Democratic liberalism in the United States. That perception may not be untrue, but it is not as simple as that either. Massachusetts has several faces.

There is Yankee Massachusetts that gave President William Howard Taft his only victory over insurgent Teddy Roosevelt in the 1912 Republican primaries.

There is blue-collar Massachusetts, which gave Henry Jackson his biggest win of the 1976 Democratic primaries.

Recent Massachusetts Primary Results

Massachusetts held its first presidential primary in 1912.

Year	DEMOCRATS			REPUBLICANS		
	Turnout	Candidates	%	Turnout	Candidates	%
2004 (March 2)	615,188	JOHN KERRY	72	70,649	GEORGE W. BUSH*	89
		John Edwards	18		No Preference	9
2000 (March 7)	571,527	AL GORE	60	502,932	JOHN McCAIN	65
		Bill Bradley	37		George W. Bush	32
1996 (March 5)	155,470	BILL CLINTON*	87	284,833	BOB DOLE	48
		No Preference	8		Pat Buchanan	25
					Steve Forbes	14
					Lamar Alexander	8
1992 (March 10)	792,885	PAUL TSONGAS	66	269,701	GEORGE BUSH*	66
		Jerry Brown	15		Pat Buchanan	28
		Bill Clinton	11			
1988 (March 8)	713,447	MICHAEL DUKAKIS	59	241,181	GEORGE BUSH	59
		Jesse Jackson	19		Bob Dole	26
		Richard Gephardt	10		Jack Kemp	7
1984 (March 13)	630,962	GARY HART	39	65,937	RONALD REAGAN*	89
		Walter Mondale	25		No Preference	8
		George McGovern	21			
		John Glenn	7			
		Jesse Jackson	5			
1980 (March 4)	907,323	EDWARD KENNEDY	65	400,826	GEORGE BUSH	31
		Jimmy Carter*	29		John Anderson	31
					Ronald Reagan	29
1976 (March 2)	735,821	HENRY JACKSON	22	188,449	GERALD FORD*	61
		Morris Udall	18		Ronald Reagan	34
		George Wallace	17			
		Jimmy Carter	14			
		Fred Harris	8			
		Sargent Shriver	7			
1972 (April 25)	618,516	GEORGE McGOVERN	53	122,139	RICHARD NIXON*	81
		Edmund Muskie	21		Paul McCloskey	13
		Hubert Humphrey	8			
		George Wallace	7			
1968 (April 30)	248,903	EUGENE McCARTHY	49	106,521	NELSON ROCKEFELLER#	30
		Robert Kennedy#	28		John Volpe	30
		Hubert Humphrey#	18		Richard Nixon#	26
					Eugene McCarthy (D)#	9

Note: All candidates are listed that drew at least 5 percent of their party's primary vote. The names of winning candidates are capitalized. An asterisk (*) indicates an incumbent president. A pound sign (#) indicates a write-in candidate.

And there is the liberal Massachusetts of suburbia and academe, which has given long-shot challengers such as George McGovern and John Anderson a base to build from in the state's presidential primary, as well as helping to provide John McCain with his highest share of the vote in the 2000 Republican primary season.

Much of the Democratic electorate lives within 25 miles of Boston; roughly 10 percent lives within the city itself. Boston contains two key elements of the Democratic Party statewide—ethnic neighborhoods and academic institutions—but it adds a third element not found in large numbers elsewhere in Massachusetts—minorities.

The combustible mixture can produce unexpected results. When the Democratic primary occurred during the height of a school busing crisis in 1976, George Wallace carried the city.

The Democrats used to be the party of the cities, but as Massachusetts has made the transformation from a declining manufacturing-based economy to the bustling world of high technology, the party has taken root in the growing suburbs.

That has not left much room for the Republicans. The dominant party in Massachusetts for nearly a century after the Civil War, the GOP was the choice of less than one of every seven registered voters in Massachusetts by the summer of 2006.

Yet while the Republican Party is small, it is not static. For years, the Massachusetts GOP was dominated by moderate Yankees. President Gerald Ford easily won the Republican

primary over Ronald Reagan in 1976; George Bush was a narrow winner four years later.

Bush, who was born in Milton and educated at the Phillips Academy in Andover, ran well in old-line Yankee Republican communities, barely offsetting Anderson's appeal in liberal suburbs and academic centers. Reagan finished a close third by carrying many of the working-class mill towns.

Bush won the Republican primaries again in 1988 and 1992, but his victories were not nail-biters like 1980. He swept virtually every community in Massachusetts each time.

But there is a conservative element within the state GOP, often of the ethnic, lunch-bucket variety, which Pat Buchanan was able to tap in the 1990s with his message of economic protest. Buchanan made his most conspicuous inroads in the 1996 primary by carrying old industrial cities such as Lawrence, Lowell, and Lynn. Bob Dole, though, still easily won the statewide GOP vote.

A big variable in the Republican equation is turnout, which can vary widely from one primary to another. Unenrolled voters (the Massachusetts parlance for independents) account for nearly half the electorate and have been allowed to vote in either party's primary. They often get swallowed up in large-turnout Democratic contests but can shape the outcome in lower-turnout Republican affairs.

That was the case in 2000, when the appeal of McCain helped bring a flood of independents into the Republican primary.

George W. Bush drew nearly 20,000 more votes than his father did in 1988, but the turnout grew by 260,000 from then—making the younger Bush a big loser in Massachusetts. The only city of size that he managed to carry in the 2000 primary was Springfield, which he won over McCain by a margin of just eight votes.

Meanwhile, Massachusetts Democrats have had their largest turnouts when one of their own has been on the presidential primary ballot. There have been four home-state entries in recent years—Sen. Edward Kennedy in 1980, Gov. Michael S. Dukakis in 1988, former senator Paul Tsongas in 1992, and Sen. John Kerry in 2004. All were easy winners, with Kerry's 72 percent share the highest of the group. His prime challenger at the time of the early March vote, John Edwards, reached 25 percent of the vote in only a handful of Massachusetts' larger towns and cities. Dennis Kucinich did better than that in Northampton, the home of Smith College, where his anti-Iraq war candidacy took 30 percent.

MASSACHUSETTS DEMOCRATIC PRIMARY

2000

City/Town	Total Vote	Bradley	Gore	Other	Winner	Percentage of Total Vote		
						Bradley	Gore	Other
ACTON	2,413	1,204	1,171	38	Bradley	49.9%	48.5%	1.6%
AGAWAM	1,719	515	1,135	69	Gore	30.0%	66.0%	4.0%
AMHERST	2,948	1,440	1,483	25	Gore	48.8%	50.3%	0.8%
ANDOVER	2,892	1,488	1,352	52	Bradley	51.5%	46.7%	1.8%
ARLINGTON	8,625	3,804	4,560	261	Gore	44.1%	52.9%	3.0%
ATTLEBORO	2,029	707	1,267	55	Gore	34.8%	62.4%	2.7%
BARNSTABLE	3,997	1,796	2,127	74	Gore	44.9%	53.2%	1.9%
BELMONT	3,804	1,746	1,993	65	Gore	45.9%	52.4%	1.7%
BEVERLY	3,339	1,368	1,880	91	Gore	41.0%	56.3%	2.7%
BILLERICA	3,305	1,233	1,923	149	Gore	37.3%	58.2%	4.5%
BOSTON	54,160	18,081	34,505	1,574	Gore	33.4%	63.7%	2.9%
BRAINTREE	4,447	1,606	2,608	233	Gore	36.1%	58.6%	5.2%
BROCKTON	3,530	1,256	2,130	144	Gore	35.6%	60.3%	4.1%
BROOKLINE	7,691	3,493	4,147	51	Gore	45.4%	53.9%	0.7%
BURLINGTON	2,124	736	1,325	63	Gore	34.7%	62.4%	3.0%
CAMBRIDGE	13,349	6,340	6,742	267	Gore	47.5%	50.5%	2.0%
CANTON	2,288	879	1,357	52	Gore	38.4%	59.3%	2.3%
CHELMSFORD	3,140	1,346	1,713	81	Gore	42.9%	54.6%	2.6%
CHICOPEE	4,727	1,221	3,297	209	Gore	25.8%	69.7%	4.4%
CONCORD	3,479	1,704	1,717	58	Gore	49.0%	49.4%	1.7%
DANVERS	2,194	785	1,339	70	Gore	35.8%	61.0%	3.2%
DARTMOUTH	2,615	761	1,789	65	Gore	29.1%	68.4%	2.5%
DEDHAM	3,014	1,135	1,746	133	Gore	37.7%	57.9%	4.4%
DRACUT	2,762	997	1,626	139	Gore	36.1%	58.9%	5.0%
EASTON	776	346	403	27	Gore	44.6%	51.9%	3.5%
EVERETT	3,515	972	2,422	121	Gore	27.7%	68.9%	3.4%
FALL RIVER	8,442	1,720	6,413	309	Gore	20.4%	76.0%	3.7%
FALMOUTH	3,399	1,426	1,901	72	Gore	42.0%	55.9%	2.1%
FITCHBURG	2,500	697	1,716	87	Gore	27.9%	68.6%	3.5%
FRAMINGHAM	6,113	2,264	3,670	179	Gore	37.0%	60.0%	2.9%
FRANKLIN	2,063	757	1,272	34	Gore	36.7%	61.7%	1.6%
GLOUCESTER	2,440	900	1,485	55	Gore	36.9%	60.9%	2.3%
HAVERHILL	4,603	1,502	2,940	161	Gore	32.6%	63.9%	3.5%
HINGHAM	2,055	1,041	987	27	Bradley	50.7%	48.0%	1.3%
HOLYOKE	2,749	832	1,802	115	Gore	30.3%	65.6%	4.2%
LAWRENCE	3,906	1,094	2,772	40	Gore	28.0%	71.0%	1.0%
LEOMINSTER	2,368	698	1,609	61	Gore	29.5%	67.9%	2.6%
LEXINGTON	5,204	2,445	2,707	52	Gore	47.0%	52.0%	1.0%
LOWELL	6,777	2,342	4,181	254	Gore	34.6%	61.7%	3.7%
LYNN	7,086	2,191	4,500	395	Gore	30.9%	63.5%	5.6%
MALDEN	5,090	1,532	3,365	193	Gore	30.1%	66.1%	3.8%
MARBLEHEAD	2,337	1,048	1,241	48	Gore	44.8%	53.1%	2.1%
MARLBOROUGH	2,670	923	1,635	112	Gore	34.6%	61.2%	4.2%
MARSHFIELD	2,038	901	1,077	60	Gore	44.2%	52.8%	2.9%
MEDFORD	7,032	2,311	4,470	251	Gore	32.9%	63.6%	3.6%

MASSACHUSETTS DEMOCRATIC PRIMARY

2000

City/Town	Total Vote	Bradley	Gore	Other	Winner	Percentage of Total Vote		
						Bradley	Gore	Other
MELROSE	3,271	1,359	1,828	84	Gore	41.5%	55.9%	2.6%
METHUEN	4,660	1,624	2,750	286	Gore	34.8%	59.0%	6.1%
MILFORD	1,840	510	1,295	35	Gore	27.7%	70.4%	1.9%
MILTON	4,792	2,131	2,468	193	Gore	44.5%	51.5%	4.0%
NATICK	3,880	1,655	2,150	75	Gore	42.7%	55.4%	1.9%
NEEDHAM	3,907	1,833	2,015	59	Gore	46.9%	51.6%	1.5%
NEW BEDFORD	8,350	1,651	6,396	303	Gore	19.8%	76.6%	3.6%
NEWTON	12,394	5,691	6,605	98	Gore	45.9%	53.3%	0.8%
NORTH ANDOVER	2,432	1,065	1,306	61	Gore	43.8%	53.7%	2.5%
NORTH ATTLEBOROUGH	1,464	552	864	48	Gore	37.7%	59.0%	3.3%
NORTHAMPTON	3,498	1,602	1,820	76	Gore	45.8%	52.0%	2.2%
NORWOOD	3,489	1,242	2,097	150	Gore	35.6%	60.1%	4.3%
PEABODY	5,070	1,549	3,331	190	Gore	30.6%	65.7%	3.7%
PITTSFIELD	4,202	1,264	2,759	179	Gore	30.1%	65.7%	4.3%
PLYMOUTH	3,280	1,203	1,976	101	Gore	36.7%	60.2%	3.1%
PROVINCETOWN	696	243	445	8	Gore	34.9%	63.9%	1.1%
QUINCY	10,178	3,518	5,925	735	Gore	34.6%	58.2%	7.2%
RANDOLPH	3,395	965	2,332	98	Gore	28.4%	68.7%	2.9%
READING	3,938	1,610	2,194	134	Gore	40.9%	55.7%	3.4%
REVERE	5,106	1,275	3,592	239	Gore	25.0%	70.3%	4.7%
SALEM	3,969	1,434	2,419	116	Gore	36.1%	60.9%	2.9%
SAUGUS	2,550	766	1,684	100	Gore	30.0%	66.0%	3.9%
SCITUATE	1,967	977	934	56	Bradley	49.7%	47.5%	2.8%
SHREWSBURY	2,463	928	1,465	70	Gore	37.7%	59.5%	2.8%
SOMERVILLE	9,660	3,981	5,382	297	Gore	41.2%	55.7%	3.1%
SPRINGFIELD	9,234	2,595	6,337	302	Gore	28.1%	68.6%	3.3%
STONEHAM	2,467	887	1,505	75	Gore	36.0%	61.0%	3.0%
STOUGHTON	2,653	869	1,730	54	Gore	32.8%	65.2%	2.0%
TAUNTON	3,176	861	2,196	119	Gore	27.1%	69.1%	3.7%
TEWKSBURY	3,108	1,095	1,857	156	Gore	35.2%	59.7%	5.0%
WAKEFIELD	2,859	1,084	1,674	101	Gore	37.9%	58.6%	3.5%
WALPOLE	2,139	923	1,134	82	Gore	43.2%	53.0%	3.8%
WALTHAM	4,645	1,790	2,831	24	Gore	38.5%	60.9%	0.5%
WATERTOWN	4,556	1,884	2,545	127	Gore	41.4%	55.9%	2.8%
WELLESLEY	3,041	1,529	1,462	50	Bradley	50.3%	48.1%	1.6%
WEST SPRINGFIELD	1,729	573	1,098	58	Gore	33.1%	63.5%	3.4%
WESTFIELD	2,095	705	1,298	92	Gore	33.7%	62.0%	4.4%
WESTON	1,061	540	508	13	Bradley	50.9%	47.9%	1.2%
WEYMOUTH	6,107	2,136	3,747	224	Gore	35.0%	61.4%	3.7%
WILLIAMSTOWN	928	412	505	11	Gore	44.4%	54.4%	1.2%
WINCHESTER	2,830	1,337	1,427	66	Gore	47.2%	50.4%	2.3%
WOBURN	4,156	1,542	2,454	160	Gore	37.1%	59.0%	3.8%
WORCESTER	11,049	3,381	7,223	445	Gore	30.6%	65.4%	4.0%
YARMOUTH	2,117	863	1,210	44	Gore	40.8%	57.2%	2.1%
STATE TOTAL	571,527	212,452	341,586	17,489	Gore	37.2%	59.8%	3.1%

Note: Other vote was 11,281 No Preference; 2,135 Lyndon H. LaRouche Jr.; 4,073 write-in. The 2000 Democratic and Republican presidential primary results were not tabulated on a county basis. The cities and towns included are basically those with a population of at least 20,000 in the 2000 Census plus a few other selected communities. The 2000 Democratic and Republican presidential primary results are as published in *Public Document No. 43: Massachusetts Elections Statistics 2000*. The state total is the aggregate vote from all communities in Massachusetts.

MASSACHUSETTS REPUBLICAN PRIMARY

2000

City/Town	Total Vote	G.W. Bush	McCain	Other	Winner	Percentage of Total Vote		
						G.W. Bush	McCain	Other
ACTON	2,787	733	1,988	66	McCain	26.3%	71.3%	2.4%
AGAWAM	1,953	903	975	75	McCain	46.2%	49.9%	3.8%
AMHERST	965	271	653	41	McCain	28.1%	67.7%	4.2%
ANDOVER	4,206	1,452	2,620	134	McCain	34.5%	62.3%	3.2%
ARLINGTON	4,269	1,336	2,788	145	McCain	31.3%	65.3%	3.4%
ATTLEBORO	2,755	920	1,720	115	McCain	33.4%	62.4%	4.2%
BARNSTABLE	6,847	2,383	4,264	200	McCain	34.8%	62.3%	2.9%
BELMONT	3,227	1,134	2,003	90	McCain	35.1%	62.1%	2.8%
BEVERLY	4,271	1,265	2,869	137	McCain	29.6%	67.2%	3.2%
BILLERICA	3,416	1,047	2,245	124	McCain	30.6%	65.7%	3.6%
BOSTON	18,047	5,101	12,138	808	McCain	28.3%	67.3%	4.5%
BRAINTREE	3,762	1,180	2,443	139	McCain	31.4%	64.9%	3.7%
BROCKTON	3,834	1,385	2,274	175	McCain	36.1%	59.3%	4.6%
BROOKLINE	3,189	785	2,325	79	McCain	24.6%	72.9%	2.5%
BURLINGTON	2,429	824	1,531	74	McCain	33.9%	63.0%	3.0%
CAMBRIDGE	3,208	749	2,334	125	McCain	23.3%	72.8%	3.9%
CANTON	2,318	636	1,617	65	McCain	27.4%	69.8%	2.8%
CHELMSFORD	4,525	1,276	3,109	140	McCain	28.2%	68.7%	3.1%
CHICOPEE	1,554	683	797	74	McCain	44.0%	51.3%	4.8%
CONCORD	3,361	1,045	2,236	80	McCain	31.1%	66.5%	2.4%
DANVERS	3,356	983	2,279	94	McCain	29.3%	67.9%	2.8%
DARTMOUTH	2,102	641	1,396	65	McCain	30.5%	66.4%	3.1%
DEDHAM	2,668	797	1,776	95	McCain	29.9%	66.6%	3.6%
DRACUT	2,493	776	1,588	129	McCain	31.1%	63.7%	5.2%
EASTON	1,034	357	646	31	McCain	34.5%	62.5%	3.0%
EVERETT	1,510	491	944	75	McCain	32.5%	62.5%	5.0%
FALL RIVER	1,998	671	1,224	103	McCain	33.6%	61.3%	5.2%
FALMOUTH	4,465	1,323	3,032	110	McCain	29.6%	67.9%	2.5%
FITCHBURG	2,137	684	1,362	91	McCain	32.0%	63.7%	4.3%
FRAMINGHAM	5,190	1,371	3,684	135	McCain	26.4%	71.0%	2.6%
FRANKLIN	3,031	840	2,131	60	McCain	27.7%	70.3%	2.0%
GLOUCESTER	2,774	785	1,903	86	McCain	28.3%	68.6%	3.1%
HAVERHILL	4,429	1,485	2,758	186	McCain	33.5%	62.3%	4.2%
HINGHAM	3,253	1,051	2,106	96	McCain	32.3%	64.7%	3.0%
HOLYOKE	1,416	612	741	63	McCain	43.2%	52.3%	4.4%
LAWRENCE	1,590	635	882	73	McCain	39.9%	55.5%	4.6%
LEOMINSTER	2,904	919	1,860	125	McCain	31.6%	64.0%	4.3%
LEXINGTON	3,420	1,137	2,181	102	McCain	33.2%	63.8%	3.0%
LOWELL	3,809	1,286	2,360	163	McCain	33.8%	62.0%	4.3%
LYNN	3,561	1,103	2,327	131	McCain	31.0%	65.3%	3.7%
MALDEN	2,644	787	1,760	97	McCain	29.8%	66.6%	3.7%
MARBLEHEAD	3,415	996	2,356	63	McCain	29.2%	69.0%	1.8%
MARLBOROUGH	2,837	829	1,914	94	McCain	29.2%	67.5%	3.3%
MARSHFIELD	2,729	724	1,932	73	McCain	26.5%	70.8%	2.7%
MEDFORD	3,889	1,137	2,631	121	McCain	29.2%	67.7%	3.1%

MASSACHUSETTS REPUBLICAN PRIMARY

2000

City/Town	Total Vote	G.W. Bush	McCain	Other	Winner	Percentage of Total Vote		
						G.W. Bush	McCain	Other
MELROSE	3,345	979	2,268	98	McCain	29.3%	67.8%	2.9%
METHUEN	3,131	1,176	1,817	138	McCain	37.6%	58.0%	4.4%
MILFORD	1,652	451	1,144	57	McCain	27.3%	69.2%	3.5%
MILTON	2,958	910	1,965	83	McCain	30.8%	66.4%	2.8%
NATICK	3,597	1,051	2,446	100	McCain	29.2%	68.0%	2.8%
NEEDHAM	3,941	1,227	2,606	108	McCain	31.1%	66.1%	2.7%
NEW BEDFORD	2,786	738	1,686	362	McCain	26.5%	60.5%	13.0%
NEWTON	5,642	1,483	3,997	162	McCain	26.3%	70.8%	2.9%
NORTH ANDOVER	3,322	1,146	2,066	110	McCain	34.5%	62.2%	3.3%
NORTH ATTLEBOROUGH	2,829	927	1,804	98	McCain	32.8%	63.8%	3.5%
NORTHAMPTON	1,452	434	965	53	McCain	29.9%	66.5%	3.7%
NORWOOD	3,013	919	2,009	85	McCain	30.5%	66.7%	2.8%
PEABODY	4,098	1,157	2,818	123	McCain	28.2%	68.8%	3.0%
PITTSFIELD	2,000	712	1,194	94	McCain	35.6%	59.7%	4.7%
PLYMOUTH	5,119	1,575	3,369	175	McCain	30.8%	65.8%	3.4%
PROVINCETOWN	195	39	150	6	McCain	20.0%	76.9%	3.1%
QUINCY	5,881	1,756	3,870	255	McCain	29.9%	65.8%	4.3%
RANDOLPH	1,882	472	1,138	272	McCain	25.1%	60.5%	14.5%
READING	4,364	1,391	2,821	152	McCain	31.9%	64.6%	3.5%
REVERE	2,090	741	1,256	93	McCain	35.5%	60.1%	4.4%
SALEM	2,773	770	1,938	65	McCain	27.8%	69.9%	2.3%
SAUGUS	2,347	748	1,525	74	McCain	31.9%	65.0%	3.2%
SCITUATE	2,953	807	2,065	81	McCain	27.3%	69.9%	2.7%
SHREWSBURY	3,330	1,150	2,086	94	McCain	34.5%	62.6%	2.8%
SOMERVILLE	2,440	660	1,685	95	McCain	27.0%	69.1%	3.9%
SPRINGFIELD	3,440	1,630	1,622	188	G.W. Bush	47.4%	47.2%	5.5%
STONEHAM	2,269	691	1,498	80	McCain	30.5%	66.0%	3.5%
STOUGHTON	2,303	640	1,599	64	McCain	27.8%	69.4%	2.8%
TAUNTON	2,843	835	1,938	70	McCain	29.4%	68.2%	2.5%
TEWKSBURY	3,015	955	1,946	114	McCain	31.7%	64.5%	3.8%
WAKEFIELD	2,983	866	2,017	100	McCain	29.0%	67.6%	3.4%
WALPOLE	2,929	836	2,024	69	McCain	28.5%	69.1%	2.4%
WALTHAM	3,784	1,142	2,518	124	McCain	30.2%	66.5%	3.3%
WATERTOWN	2,286	713	1,506	67	McCain	31.2%	65.9%	2.9%
WELLESLEY	3,847	1,348	2,411	88	McCain	35.0%	62.7%	2.3%
WEST SPRINGFIELD	1,822	824	924	74	McCain	45.2%	50.7%	4.1%
WESTFIELD	2,621	1,159	1,374	88	McCain	44.2%	52.4%	3.4%
WESTON	1,708	556	1,110	42	McCain	32.6%	65.0%	2.5%
WEYMOUTH	5,808	1,719	3,923	166	McCain	29.6%	67.5%	2.9%
WILLIAMSTOWN	622	177	426	19	McCain	28.5%	68.5%	3.1%
WINCHESTER	3,179	1,083	2,008	88	McCain	34.1%	63.2%	2.8%
WOBURN	2,893	967	1,812	114	McCain	33.4%	62.6%	3.9%
WORCESTER	6,588	2,361	3,931	296	McCain	35.8%	59.7%	4.5%
YARMOUTH	3,919	1,457	2,360	102	McCain	37.2%	60.2%	2.6%
STATE TOTAL	502,932	159,826	325,297	17,809	McCain	31.8%	64.7%	3.5%

Note: Other vote was 12,656 Alan Keyes; 1,745 Gary Bauer; 1,411 Steve Forbes; 1,295 No Preference; 262 Orrin G. Hatch; 440 write-in. The cities and towns included are basically those with a population of at least 20,000 in the 2000 Census plus a few other selected communities.

MASSACHUSETTS DEMOCRATIC PRIMARY

2004

City/Town	Total Vote	Edwards	Kerry	Other	Winner	Percentage of Total Vote		
						Edwards	Kerry	Other
ACTON	2,730	501	1,891	338	Kerry	18.4%	69.3%	12.4%
AGAWAM	1,598	252	1,246	100	Kerry	15.8%	78.0%	6.3%
AMHERST	3,703	402	1,993	1,308	Kerry	10.9%	53.8%	35.3%
ANDOVER	3,048	677	2,050	321	Kerry	22.2%	67.3%	10.5%
ARLINGTON	8,528	1,556	5,810	1,162	Kerry	18.2%	68.1%	13.6%
ATTLEBORO	2,768	530	2,005	233	Kerry	19.1%	72.4%	8.4%
BARNSTABLE	4,088	829	2,894	365	Kerry	20.3%	70.8%	8.9%
BELMONT	3,972	786	2,667	519	Kerry	19.8%	67.1%	13.1%
BEVERLY	3,808	702	2,768	338	Kerry	18.4%	72.7%	8.9%
BILLERICA	3,852	957	2,560	335	Kerry	24.8%	66.5%	8.7%
BOSTON	56,964	8,934	40,498	7,532	Kerry	15.7%	71.1%	13.2%
BRAINTREE	4,583	1,020	3,246	317	Kerry	22.3%	70.8%	6.9%
BROCKTON	6,022	1,035	4,553	434	Kerry	17.2%	75.6%	7.2%
BROOKLINE	7,996	1,268	5,467	1,261	Kerry	15.9%	68.4%	15.8%
BURLINGTON	2,317	476	1,673	168	Kerry	20.5%	72.2%	7.3%
CAMBRIDGE	13,532	2,096	8,170	3,266	Kerry	15.5%	60.4%	24.1%
CANTON	2,636	566	1,869	201	Kerry	21.5%	70.9%	7.6%
CHELMSFORD	3,641	969	2,346	326	Kerry	26.6%	64.4%	9.0%
CHICOPEE	4,468	546	3,604	318	Kerry	12.2%	80.7%	7.1%
CONCORD	4,182	764	2,881	537	Kerry	18.3%	68.9%	12.8%
DANVERS	2,488	569	1,757	162	Kerry	22.9%	70.6%	6.5%
DARTMOUTH	2,680	401	2,147	132	Kerry	15.0%	80.1%	4.9%
DEDHAM	3,826	874	2,611	341	Kerry	22.8%	68.2%	8.9%
DRACUT	2,797	722	1,607	468	Kerry	25.8%	57.5%	16.7%
EASTON	1,701	361	1,233	107	Kerry	21.2%	72.5%	6.3%
EVERETT	3,039	504	2,333	202	Kerry	16.6%	76.8%	6.6%
FALL RIVER	7,696	640	6,758	298	Kerry	8.3%	87.8%	3.9%
FALMOUTH	4,555	809	3,274	472	Kerry	17.8%	71.9%	10.4%
FITCHBURG	2,422	375	1,872	175	Kerry	15.5%	77.3%	7.2%
FRAMINGHAM	5,880	1,005	4,400	475	Kerry	17.1%	74.8%	8.1%
FRANKLIN	2,878	571	2,091	216	Kerry	19.8%	72.7%	7.5%
GLOUCESTER	2,895	417	2,111	367	Kerry	14.4%	72.9%	12.7%
HAVERHILL	4,666	989	3,321	356	Kerry	21.2%	71.2%	7.6%
HINGHAM	2,080	439	1,449	192	Kerry	21.1%	69.7%	9.2%
HOLYOKE	2,514	291	1,927	296	Kerry	11.6%	76.7%	11.8%
LAWRENCE	3,638	523	2,883	232	Kerry	14.4%	79.2%	6.4%
LEOMINSTER	2,547	421	1,963	163	Kerry	16.5%	77.1%	6.4%
LEXINGTON	7,993	1,372	5,660	961	Kerry	17.2%	70.8%	12.0%
LOWELL	6,420	1,375	4,561	484	Kerry	21.4%	71.0%	7.5%
LYNN	6,013	880	4,729	404	Kerry	14.6%	78.6%	6.7%
MALDEN	4,667	716	3,503	448	Kerry	15.3%	75.1%	9.6%
MARBLEHEAD	2,768	530	1,946	292	Kerry	19.1%	70.3%	10.5%
MARLBOROUGH	2,619	514	1,910	195	Kerry	19.6%	72.9%	7.4%
MARSHFIELD	2,051	423	1,483	145	Kerry	20.6%	72.3%	7.1%
MEDFORD	7,169	1,148	4,811	1,210	Kerry	16.0%	67.1%	16.9%

MASSACHUSETTS DEMOCRATIC PRIMARY

2004

City/Town	Total Vote	Edwards	Kerry	Other	Winner	Percentage of Total Vote		
						Edwards	Kerry	Other
MELROSE	3,679	741	2,599	339	Kerry	20.1%	70.6%	9.2%
METHUEN	3,445	767	2,456	222	Kerry	22.3%	71.3%	6.4%
MILFORD	2,360	379	1,802	179	Kerry	16.1%	76.4%	7.6%
MILTON	5,200	1,150	3,495	555	Kerry	22.1%	67.2%	10.7%
NATICK	5,135	980	3,686	469	Kerry	19.1%	71.8%	9.1%
NEEDHAM	6,513	1,281	4,636	596	Kerry	19.7%	71.2%	9.2%
NEW BEDFORD	8,042	681	6,870	491	Kerry	8.5%	85.4%	6.1%
NEWTON	13,028	1,876	9,575	1,577	Kerry	14.4%	73.5%	12.1%
NORTH ANDOVER	2,434	588	1,618	228	Kerry	24.2%	66.5%	9.4%
NORTH ATTLEBOROUGH	2,594	549	1,850	195	Kerry	21.2%	71.3%	7.5%
NORTHAMPTON	5,135	529	2,684	1,922	Kerry	10.3%	52.3%	37.4%
NORWOOD	3,553	827	2,416	310	Kerry	23.3%	68.0%	8.7%
PEABODY	5,520	984	4,216	320	Kerry	17.8%	76.4%	5.8%
PITTSFIELD	4,555	571	3,654	330	Kerry	12.5%	80.2%	7.2%
PLYMOUTH	3,699	715	2,748	236	Kerry	19.3%	74.3%	6.4%
PROVINCETOWN	814	121	536	157	Kerry	14.9%	65.8%	19.3%
QUINCY	9,486	1,928	6,666	892	Kerry	20.3%	70.3%	9.4%
RANDOLPH	3,218	518	2,504	196	Kerry	16.1%	77.8%	6.1%
READING	4,001	828	2,827	346	Kerry	20.7%	70.7%	8.6%
REVERE	4,237	642	3,324	271	Kerry	15.2%	78.5%	6.4%
SALEM	4,175	728	3,038	409	Kerry	17.4%	72.8%	9.8%
SAUGUS	2,566	484	1,934	148	Kerry	18.9%	75.4%	5.8%
SCITUATE	1,993	404	1,416	173	Kerry	20.3%	71.0%	8.7%
SHREWSBURY	2,615	447	1,992	176	Kerry	17.1%	76.2%	6.7%
SOMERVILLE	9,529	1,677	5,967	1,885	Kerry	17.6%	62.6%	19.8%
SPRINGFIELD	7,917	812	6,446	659	Kerry	10.3%	81.4%	8.3%
STONEHAM	2,315	445	1,683	187	Kerry	19.2%	72.7%	8.1%
STOUGHTON	3,026	590	2,222	214	Kerry	19.5%	73.4%	7.1%
TAUNTON	3,531	550	2,773	208	Kerry	15.6%	78.5%	5.9%
TEWKSBURY	2,959	759	1,966	234	Kerry	25.7%	66.4%	7.9%
WAKEFIELD	3,027	587	2,200	240	Kerry	19.4%	72.7%	7.9%
WALPOLE	2,369	591	1,588	190	Kerry	24.9%	67.0%	8.0%
WALTHAM	4,454	902	3,085	467	Kerry	20.3%	69.3%	10.5%
WATERTOWN	4,456	827	3,021	608	Kerry	18.6%	67.8%	13.6%
WELLESLEY	3,791	728	2,713	350	Kerry	19.2%	71.6%	9.2%
WEST SPRINGFIELD	1,578	184	1,270	124	Kerry	11.7%	80.5%	7.9%
WESTFIELD	1,962	321	1,440	201	Kerry	16.4%	73.4%	10.2%
WESTON	1,167	209	802	156	Kerry	17.9%	68.7%	13.4%
WEYMOUTH	5,709	1,202	4,155	352	Kerry	21.1%	72.8%	6.2%
WILLIAMSTOWN	1,195	178	807	210	Kerry	14.9%	67.5%	17.6%
WINCHESTER	3,175	667	2,195	313	Kerry	21.0%	69.1%	9.9%
WOBURN	3,813	747	2,810	256	Kerry	19.6%	73.7%	6.7%
WORCESTER	10,952	1,497	8,349	1,106	Kerry	13.7%	76.2%	10.1%
YARMOUTH	2,563	502	1,905	156	Kerry	19.6%	74.3%	6.1%
STATE TOTAL	615,188	108,051	440,964	66,173	Kerry	17.6%	71.7%	10.8%

Note: Other vote was 25,198 Dennis J. Kucinich; 17,076 Howard Dean; 6,123 Al Sharpton; 5,432 Joseph I. Lieberman; 4,451 No Preference; 3,109 Wesley Clark; 1,455 Richard A. Gephardt; 1,019 Carol Moseley Braun; 970 Lyndon H. LaRouche Jr.; 1,340 write-in. The 2004 Democratic and Republican presidential primary results were not tabulated on a county basis. The cities and towns included are basically those with a population of at least 20,000 in the 2000 Census plus a few other selected communities. The 2004 Democratic and Republican presidential primary results are as published in *Public Document No. 43: Massachusetts Elections Statistics 2004*. The state total is the aggregate vote from all communities in Massachusetts.

MASSACHUSETTS REPUBLICAN PRIMARY

2004

City/Town	Total Vote	G.W. Bush	No Preference	Other	Winner	Percentage of Total Vote		
						G.W. Bush	No Preference	Other
ACTON	314	272	31	11	G.W. Bush	86.6%	9.9%	3.5%
AGAWAM	110	93	15	2	G.W. Bush	84.5%	13.6%	1.8%
AMHERST	67	55	9	3	G.W. Bush	82.1%	13.4%	4.5%
ANDOVER	376	346	21	9	G.W. Bush	92.0%	5.6%	2.4%
ARLINGTON	480	438	41	1	G.W. Bush	91.3%	8.5%	0.2%
ATTLEBORO	893	804	72	17	G.W. Bush	90.0%	8.1%	1.9%
BARNSTABLE	495	453	34	8	G.W. Bush	91.5%	6.9%	1.6%
BELMONT	490	446	33	11	G.W. Bush	91.0%	6.7%	2.2%
BEVERLY	515	452	50	13	G.W. Bush	87.8%	9.7%	2.5%
BILLERICA	515	466	41	8	G.W. Bush	90.5%	8.0%	1.6%
BOSTON	2,188	1,856	264	68	G.W. Bush	84.8%	12.1%	3.1%
BRAINTREE	557	518	27	12	G.W. Bush	93.0%	4.8%	2.2%
BROCKTON	564	490	62	12	G.W. Bush	86.9%	11.0%	2.1%
BROOKLINE	261	212	31	18	G.W. Bush	81.2%	11.9%	6.9%
BURLINGTON	241	213	24	4	G.W. Bush	88.4%	10.0%	1.7%
CAMBRIDGE	373	275	60	38	G.W. Bush	73.7%	16.1%	10.2%
CANTON	297	263	28	6	G.W. Bush	88.6%	9.4%	2.0%
CHELMSFORD	506	453	42	11	G.W. Bush	89.5%	8.3%	2.2%
CHICOPEE	273	239	26	8	G.W. Bush	87.5%	9.5%	2.9%
CONCORD	868	751	105	12	G.W. Bush	86.5%	12.1%	1.4%
DANVERS	418	389	21	8	G.W. Bush	93.1%	5.0%	1.9%
DARTMOUTH	212	183	24	5	G.W. Bush	86.3%	11.3%	2.4%
DEDHAM	381	359	22	0	G.W. Bush	94.2%	5.8%	0.0%
DRACUT	345	304	36	5	G.W. Bush	88.1%	10.4%	1.4%
EASTON	246	230	10	6	G.W. Bush	93.5%	4.1%	2.4%
EVERETT	312	285	24	3	G.W. Bush	91.3%	7.7%	1.0%
FALL RIVER	264	227	26	11	G.W. Bush	86.0%	9.8%	4.2%
FALMOUTH	504	438	52	14	G.W. Bush	86.9%	10.3%	2.8%
FITCHBURG	176	163	10	3	G.W. Bush	92.6%	5.7%	1.7%
FRAMINGHAM	452	395	39	18	G.W. Bush	87.4%	8.6%	4.0%
FRANKLIN	789	727	53	9	G.W. Bush	92.1%	6.7%	1.1%
GLOUCESTER	442	405	26	11	G.W. Bush	91.6%	5.9%	2.5%
HAVERHILL	539	483	45	11	G.W. Bush	89.6%	8.3%	2.0%
HINGHAM	689	624	49	16	G.W. Bush	90.6%	7.1%	2.3%
HOLYOKE	206	184	18	4	G.W. Bush	89.3%	8.7%	1.9%
LAWRENCE	317	281	36	0	G.W. Bush	88.6%	11.4%	0.0%
LEOMINSTER	238	222	16	0	G.W. Bush	93.3%	6.7%	0.0%
LEXINGTON	1,202	1,030	146	26	G.W. Bush	85.7%	12.1%	2.2%
LOWELL	660	594	58	8	G.W. Bush	90.0%	8.8%	1.2%
LYNN	318	282	27	9	G.W. Bush	88.7%	8.5%	2.8%
MALDEN	263	241	20	2	G.W. Bush	91.6%	7.6%	0.8%
MARBLEHEAD	369	333	29	7	G.W. Bush	90.2%	7.9%	1.9%
MARLBOROUGH	342	305	31	6	G.W. Bush	89.2%	9.1%	1.8%
MARSHFIELD	378	358	0	20	G.W. Bush	94.7%	0.0%	5.3%
MEDFORD	443	399	33	11	G.W. Bush	90.1%	7.4%	2.5%

MASSACHUSETTS REPUBLICAN PRIMARY

2004

City/Town	Total Vote	G.W. Bush	No Preference	Other	Winner	Percentage of Total Vote		
						G.W. Bush	No Preference	Other
MELROSE	394	332	46	16	G.W. Bush	84.3%	11.7%	4.1%
METHUEN	402	366	35	1	G.W. Bush	91.0%	8.7%	0.2%
MILFORD	209	192	15	2	G.W. Bush	91.9%	7.2%	1.0%
MILTON	521	474	47	0	G.W. Bush	91.0%	9.0%	0.0%
NATICK	1,048	926	103	19	G.W. Bush	88.4%	9.8%	1.8%
NEEDHAM	1,846	1,677	148	21	G.W. Bush	90.8%	8.0%	1.1%
NEW BEDFORD	403	333	9	61	G.W. Bush	82.6%	2.2%	15.1%
NEWTON	499	420	54	25	G.W. Bush	84.2%	10.8%	5.0%
NORTH ANDOVER	474	440	27	7	G.W. Bush	92.8%	5.7%	1.5%
NORTH ATTLEBOROUGH	1,613	1,462	135	16	G.W. Bush	90.6%	8.4%	1.0%
NORTHAMPTON	156	128	24	4	G.W. Bush	82.1%	15.4%	2.6%
NORWOOD	367	341	20	6	G.W. Bush	92.9%	5.4%	1.6%
PEABODY	379	346	30	3	G.W. Bush	91.3%	7.9%	0.8%
PITTSFIELD	199	155	36	8	G.W. Bush	77.9%	18.1%	4.0%
PLYMOUTH	542	486	51	5	G.W. Bush	89.7%	9.4%	0.9%
PROVINCETOWN	16	15	0	1	G.W. Bush	93.8%	0.0%	6.3%
QUINCY	972	811	99	62	G.W. Bush	83.4%	10.2%	6.4%
RANDOLPH	190	173	11	6	G.W. Bush	91.1%	5.8%	3.2%
READING	1,066	953	108	5	G.W. Bush	89.4%	10.1%	0.5%
REVERE	398	350	38	10	G.W. Bush	87.9%	9.5%	2.5%
SALEM	290	257	20	13	G.W. Bush	88.6%	6.9%	4.5%
SAUGUS	280	256	22	2	G.W. Bush	91.4%	7.9%	0.7%
SCITUATE	615	567	42	6	G.W. Bush	92.2%	6.8%	1.0%
SHREWSBURY	341	297	40	4	G.W. Bush	87.1%	11.7%	1.2%
SOMERVILLE	284	252	22	10	G.W. Bush	88.7%	7.7%	3.5%
SPRINGFIELD	322	265	57	0	G.W. Bush	82.3%	17.7%	0.0%
STONEHAM	235	213	12	10	G.W. Bush	90.6%	5.1%	4.3%
STOUGHTON	339	301	32	6	G.W. Bush	88.8%	9.4%	1.8%
TAUNTON	238	213	20	5	G.W. Bush	89.5%	8.4%	2.1%
TEWKSBURY	334	293	30	11	G.W. Bush	87.7%	9.0%	3.3%
WAKEFIELD	412	376	32	4	G.W. Bush	91.3%	7.8%	1.0%
WALPOLE	540	492	40	8	G.W. Bush	91.1%	7.4%	1.5%
WALTHAM	286	257	29	0	G.W. Bush	89.9%	10.1%	0.0%
WATERTOWN	349	323	22	4	G.W. Bush	92.6%	6.3%	1.1%
WELLESLEY	1,043	926	104	13	G.W. Bush	88.8%	10.0%	1.2%
WEST SPRINGFIELD	146	123	17	6	G.W. Bush	84.2%	11.6%	4.1%
WESTFIELD	286	249	28	9	G.W. Bush	87.1%	9.8%	3.1%
WESTON	148	117	16	15	G.W. Bush	79.1%	10.8%	10.1%
WEYMOUTH	1,194	1,110	84	0	G.W. Bush	93.0%	7.0%	0.0%
WILLIAMSTOWN	53	39	10	4	G.W. Bush	73.6%	18.9%	7.5%
WINCHESTER	528	479	41	8	G.W. Bush	90.7%	7.8%	1.5%
WOBURN	283	245	30	8	G.W. Bush	86.6%	10.6%	2.8%
WORCESTER	683	566	89	28	G.W. Bush	82.9%	13.0%	4.1%
YARMOUTH	429	372	49	8	G.W. Bush	86.7%	11.4%	1.9%
STATE TOTAL	70,649	62,773	6,050	1,826	G.W. Bush	88.9%	8.6%	2.6%

Note: Other vote was 1,826 write-in. The Federal Election Commission (FEC) reports 1,831 write-in votes and a Total Vote of 70,654. The FEC vote is used elsewhere in this volume in tallying the aggregate Republican primary vote for 2004. The cities and towns included in this table are basically those with a population of at least 20,000 in the 2000 Census plus a few other selected communities.

MICHIGAN

Leaders of both the Democratic and Republican parties in Michigan have never fully embraced the state's presidential primary, in large part because its open nature has produced an unpredictable environment and unwelcome results—at least for them.

In 1972, a flood of independents and Republicans entered the Democratic primary to vote for then Alabama governor George Wallace, who won easily despite the opposition of Democratic leaders.

In 2000, a flood of independents and Democrats entered the Republican primary to vote for John McCain, who won easily in spite of GOP governor John Engler's enthusiastic support for George W. Bush.

For McCain, victory in Michigan was the last big hurrah of his upstart 2000 presidential campaign. He swept 70 of Michigan's 83 counties, including Wayne (Detroit) and the major suburban counties of Macomb and Oakland. Bush was basically left with only the state's Republican strongholds, such

as Ottawa (Holland) and Kent (Grand Rapids) counties, the latter the longtime congressional base of Gerald Ford.

Voter turnout for the Republican contest in 2000 exceeded one and one-quarter million, a record for a GOP presidential primary in Michigan. The only higher primary turnout for president came on the Democratic side in 1972, when nearly 1.6 million voters took part.

But often, party officials in Michigan have opted to do without the presidential primary, choosing to have tighter control over the process at the expense of lighter turnouts and occasional controversy.

Michigan Democrats have often opted for "firehouse primaries," a party-run affair that in delegate-selection parlance is often termed a caucus. In 2004, the Democratic event attracted more than 160,000 voters, with voters having three ways to cast their ballot—in person, by mail, or over the Internet (an experimental feature that proved popular). More than half the ballots were cast at 590 caucus sites that the state party set up across

Recent Michigan Primary Results

Michigan held its first presidential primary in 1916, although no primary was held between 1928 and 1972.

Year	DEMOCRATS			REPUBLICANS		
	Turnout	Candidates	%	Turnout	Candidates	%
2004	—	No Primary		—	No Primary	
2000 (Feb. 22)	44,850	UNCOMMITTED	71	1,276,770	JOHN McCAIN	51
		Lyndon LaRouche	29		George W. Bush	43
1996 (March 19)	142,750	UNCOMMITTED	87	524,161	BOB DOLE	51
					Pat Buchanan	34
					Steve Forbes	5
1992 (March 17)	585,972	BILL CLINTON	51	449,133	GEORGE BUSH*	67
		Jerry Brown	26		Pat Buchanan	25
		Paul Tsongas	17		Uncommitted	5
1988	—	No Primary		—	No Primary	
1984	—	No Primary		—	No Primary	
1980 (May 20)	78,424	UNCOMMITTED	46	595,176	GEORGE BUSH	57
		Jerry Brown	29		Ronald Reagan	32
		Lyndon LaRouche	11		John Anderson	8
1976 (May 18)	708,666	JIMMY CARTER	43	1,062,814	GERALD FORD*	65
		Morris Udall	43		Ronald Reagan	34
		George Wallace	7			
1972 (May 16)	1,588,073	GEORGE WALLACE	51	336,743	RICHARD NIXON*	96
		George McGovern	27			
		Hubert Humphrey	16			

Note: All candidates are listed that drew at least 5 percent of their party's primary vote. The names of winning candidates are capitalized. An asterisk (*) indicates an incumbent president.

the state, while more than a quarter of the vote was submitted on the Internet. The rest of the ballots were cast by mail.

John Kerry won the bulk of the vote cast by each method, enroute to a statewide victory over runner-up Howard Dean by a ratio of more than 3 to 1. In the process, Kerry swept all 15 of Michigan's congressional districts, with the closest votes coming in the two majority-black Detroit-area districts, where Al Sharpton captured roughly one-third of the ballots.

The turnout in 2004 was a sharp contrast to a similar event in 1980, when the Democratic statewide caucuses attracted only 16,000 voters. Strict rules on caucus participation that reduced turnout in 1980 were relaxed in 1984 so voters did not have to go through a pre-enrollment process. Still, the Democratic turnout barely reached 130,000.

Labor support for Walter Mondale provided him with a big win in the 1984 caucuses. But critics complained that the administration of the event was stacked in Mondale's favor. It was estimated that roughly 10 percent of the voting places were union halls. And separate ballot boxes were set up for each of the candidates, publicly discouraging any union member from casting their vote for anyone but Mondale.

In 1988, it was the Republicans who were the center of controversy. In a bid to be first on the calendar, the GOP held caucuses that were called the "Beirut of American politics."

The caucuses revealed the organizational muscle of George Bush's campaign and the potency of Pat Robertson's "invisible army." But the convoluted and often rancorous nature of the process led many party leaders to favor the primary format in 1992, a move that Democratic leaders were ready to join.

Pat Buchanan targeted Michigan and its large blue-collar constituency in both 1992 and 1996. His first time out Buchanan was thrown on the defensive, as the Bush campaign pounded away at the nationalistic-sounding Buchanan for driving a Mercedes-Benz and for referring to two Cadillacs he had bought as "lemons." It helped Bush win the Michigan primary for the second time. He had won the previous Republican primary in 1980 over Ronald Reagan, and beat Buchanan even more convincingly in 1992.

Jerry Brown made his own effort on the Democratic side to harness the economic discontent of the working class. He regaled union members in his white turtleneck and a blue UAW (United Auto Workers) windbreaker. He managed to win the support of several union locals, and he even drew kind words from filmmaker Michael Moore, who chronicled the decline of Flint in the documentary *Roger and Me*.

But Brown was more successful attracting publicity than votes in the 1992 primary. Going from union hall to union hall, he stirred the passions of the assembled members, but he failed to expand his base beyond them. Clinton beat Brown by a margin of nearly 2 to 1.

Brown was gone by 1996, but Buchanan was back on the GOP side and ran better in Michigan than he had the first time. He carried seven counties and came within 5 percentage points of winning Macomb County, the quintessential suburban blue-collar constituency. Dole easily won the primary vote statewide, but Buchanan's 34 percent vote share was the highest he would receive in the 1996 primaries.

MICHIGAN REPUBLICAN PRIMARY

2000

County	Total Vote	G.W. Bush	McCain	Other	Winner	Percentage of Total Vote		
						G.W. Bush	McCain	Other
ALCONA	1,767	747	962	58	McCain	42.3%	54.4%	3.3%
ALGER	1,188	437	715	36	McCain	36.8%	60.2%	3.0%
ALLEGAN	17,965	8,495	8,065	1,405	G.W. Bush	47.3%	44.9%	7.8%
ALPENA	3,940	1,677	2,114	149	McCain	42.6%	53.7%	3.8%
ANTRIM	4,184	1,807	2,194	183	McCain	43.2%	52.4%	4.4%
ARENAC	1,969	799	1,099	71	McCain	40.6%	55.8%	3.6%
BARAGA	886	371	446	69	McCain	41.9%	50.3%	7.8%
BARRY	9,132	3,916	4,512	704	McCain	42.9%	49.4%	7.7%
BAY	17,059	6,935	9,304	820	McCain	40.7%	54.5%	4.8%
BENZIE	2,922	1,111	1,720	91	McCain	38.0%	58.9%	3.1%
BERRIEN	20,861	10,442	9,512	907	G.W. Bush	50.1%	45.6%	4.3%
BRANCH	5,036	2,269	2,556	211	McCain	45.1%	50.8%	4.2%
CALHOUN	15,940	6,559	8,375	1,006	McCain	41.1%	52.5%	6.3%
CASS	5,354	2,462	2,675	217	McCain	46.0%	50.0%	4.1%
CHARLEVOIX	3,909	1,579	2,194	136	McCain	40.4%	56.1%	3.5%
CHEBOYGAN	3,906	1,525	2,257	124	McCain	39.0%	57.8%	3.2%
CHIPPEWA	4,746	1,792	2,781	173	McCain	37.8%	58.6%	3.6%
CLARE	3,770	1,426	2,220	124	McCain	37.8%	58.9%	3.3%
CLINTON	11,219	5,205	5,537	477	McCain	46.4%	49.4%	4.3%
CRAWFORD	2,062	711	1,276	75	McCain	34.5%	61.9%	3.6%
DELTA	3,593	1,594	1,795	204	McCain	44.4%	50.0%	5.7%
DICKINSON	2,834	1,229	1,479	126	McCain	43.4%	52.2%	4.4%
EATON	17,280	7,430	8,977	873	McCain	43.0%	52.0%	5.1%
EMMET	4,504	1,954	2,375	175	McCain	43.4%	52.7%	3.9%
GENESEE	41,614	16,384	22,800	2,430	McCain	39.4%	54.8%	5.8%
GLADWIN	3,202	1,288	1,767	147	McCain	40.2%	55.2%	4.6%
GOGEBIC	1,742	645	1,020	77	McCain	37.0%	58.6%	4.4%
GRAND TRAVERSE	15,950	7,017	8,148	785	McCain	44.0%	51.1%	4.9%
GRATIOT	4,986	2,268	2,566	152	McCain	45.5%	51.5%	3.0%
HILLSDALE	5,515	2,729	2,486	300	G.W. Bush	49.5%	45.1%	5.4%
HOUGHTON	3,787	1,733	1,794	260	McCain	45.8%	47.4%	6.9%
HURON	5,226	2,281	2,699	246	McCain	43.6%	51.6%	4.7%
INGHAM	37,461	14,492	21,245	1,724	McCain	38.7%	56.7%	4.6%
IONIA	8,005	3,379	4,016	610	McCain	42.2%	50.2%	7.6%
IOSCO	3,895	1,438	2,276	181	McCain	36.9%	58.4%	4.6%
IRON	1,559	552	927	80	McCain	35.4%	59.5%	5.1%
ISABELLA	6,520	2,416	3,777	327	McCain	37.1%	57.9%	5.0%
JACKSON	17,344	8,860	7,676	808	G.W. Bush	51.1%	44.3%	4.7%
KALAMAZOO	34,019	13,799	18,283	1,937	McCain	40.6%	53.7%	5.7%
KALKASKA	2,317	945	1,271	101	McCain	40.8%	54.9%	4.4%
KENT	101,771	46,428	45,269	10,074	G.W. Bush	45.6%	44.5%	9.9%
KEWEENAW	437	172	225	40	McCain	39.4%	51.5%	9.2%
LAKE	1,303	423	817	63	McCain	32.5%	62.7%	4.8%
LAPEER	10,336	4,820	4,784	732	G.W. Bush	46.6%	46.3%	7.1%
LEELANAU	5,164	2,157	2,833	174	McCain	41.8%	54.9%	3.4%

MICHIGAN REPUBLICAN PRIMARY

2000

County	Total Vote	G.W. Bush	McCain	Other	Winner	Percentage of Total Vote		
						G.W. Bush	McCain	Other
LENAWEE	10,889	5,249	5,046	594	G.W. Bush	48.2%	46.3%	5.5%
LIVINGSTON	22,233	10,724	10,192	1,317	G.W. Bush	48.2%	45.8%	5.9%
LUCE	922	334	553	35	McCain	36.2%	60.0%	3.8%
MACKINAC	2,557	953	1,478	126	McCain	37.3%	57.8%	4.9%
MACOMB	100,514	45,317	49,964	5,233	McCain	45.1%	49.7%	5.2%
MANISTEE	3,645	1,255	2,282	108	McCain	34.4%	62.6%	3.0%
MARQUETTE	6,293	2,443	3,552	298	McCain	38.8%	56.4%	4.7%
MASON	5,017	2,117	2,695	205	McCain	42.2%	53.7%	4.1%
MECOSTA	4,928	1,981	2,745	202	McCain	40.2%	55.7%	4.1%
MENOMINEE	2,126	973	1,058	95	McCain	45.8%	49.8%	4.5%
MIDLAND	15,148	6,782	7,613	753	McCain	44.8%	50.3%	5.0%
MISSAUKEE	2,429	1,258	1,065	106	G.W. Bush	51.8%	43.8%	4.4%
MONROE	15,119	7,141	7,064	914	G.W. Bush	47.2%	46.7%	6.0%
MONTCALM	7,784	3,174	4,117	493	McCain	40.8%	52.9%	6.3%
MONTMORENCY	1,897	726	1,079	92	McCain	38.3%	56.9%	4.8%
MUSKEGON	19,624	8,414	10,146	1,064	McCain	42.9%	51.7%	5.4%
NEWAYGO	7,078	3,335	3,301	442	G.W. Bush	47.1%	46.6%	6.2%
OAKLAND	184,689	83,071	91,434	10,184	McCain	45.0%	49.5%	5.5%
OCEANA	3,852	1,595	2,074	183	McCain	41.4%	53.8%	4.8%
OGEMAW	2,689	978	1,599	112	McCain	36.4%	59.5%	4.2%
ONTONAGON	1,265	479	725	61	McCain	37.9%	57.3%	4.8%
OSCEOLA	3,311	1,442	1,767	102	McCain	43.6%	53.4%	3.1%
OSCODA	1,358	507	794	57	McCain	37.3%	58.5%	4.2%
OTSEGO	3,272	1,376	1,792	104	McCain	42.1%	54.8%	3.2%
OTTAWA	47,583	25,957	17,428	4,198	G.W. Bush	54.6%	36.6%	8.8%
PRESQUE ISLE	2,234	864	1,281	89	McCain	38.7%	57.3%	4.0%
ROSCOMMON	4,006	1,406	2,501	99	McCain	35.1%	62.4%	2.5%
SAGINAW	25,658	11,901	12,709	1,048	McCain	46.4%	49.5%	4.1%
ST. CLAIR	19,542	8,489	10,018	1,035	McCain	43.4%	51.3%	5.3%
ST. JOSEPH	6,573	2,986	3,263	324	McCain	45.4%	49.6%	4.9%
SANILAC	6,022	3,108	2,618	296	G.W. Bush	51.6%	43.5%	4.9%
SCHOOLCRAFT	1,248	434	760	54	McCain	34.8%	60.9%	4.3%
SHIAWASSEE	9,717	4,267	4,981	469	McCain	43.9%	51.3%	4.8%
TUSCOLA	7,718	3,476	3,844	398	McCain	45.0%	49.8%	5.2%
VAN BUREN	9,693	3,748	5,382	563	McCain	38.7%	55.5%	5.8%
WASHTENAW	39,533	13,865	23,681	1,987	McCain	35.1%	59.9%	5.0%
WAYNE	186,071	69,099	103,937	13,035	McCain	37.1%	55.9%	7.0%
WEXFORD	4,354	1,743	2,448	163	McCain	40.0%	56.2%	3.7%
TOTAL	1,276,770	549,665	650,805	76,300	McCain	43.1%	51.0%	6.0%

Note: Other vote was 59,032 Alan Keyes; 8,714 Uncommitted; 4,894 Steve Forbes; 2,733 Gary Bauer; 905 Orrin G. Hatch; 22 Joe Schriner (write-in).

MINNESOTA

Every generation or so, a presidential primary appears in Minnesota like Brigadoon. There was one in 1916, a pair in the 1950s, and another in 1992. The rest of the time the residents of Minnesota have been content to elect their delegates through caucuses.

The state's presidential primary, though occasional, has often been memorable. In 1952, Dwight D. Eisenhower showed his vote-getting appeal by generating over 100,000 write-in votes in the Republican primary.

In 1956, Sen. Estes Kefauver of Tennessee upset Adlai Stevenson in the state's Democratic balloting. Stevenson had won the Democratic presidential nomination in 1952 and was to win it again in 1956.

And Bill Clinton's narrow victory over Jerry Brown in the 1992 Democratic primary was the closest of any presidential primary that year.

Yet the caucus system reigns supreme in Minnesota, in part because it heightens the role of activists in both parties. In the Republican camp, many of those activists are evangelical Christians energized by social issues such as abortion.

The Democrats, too, have an ardent anti-abortion element that sent more than a dozen delegates to the 1984 Democratic convention. On the whole, however, the state party that nursed the presidential aspirations of Hubert Humphrey and Walter Mondale remains one of the most liberal in the country.

That was evident in 2004. Even as John Kerry was driving his last major challenger from the field, 17 percent of the more than 50,000 participants in the early March caucuses voted for the anti-Iraq war candidacy of Dennis Kucinich. Support for the Ohio congressman was particularly strong in the Minneapolis-based 5th District, where he drew one-quarter of the vote.

As they had throughout much of the 2004 primary season, Kerry and John Edwards finished one-two in the Minnesota caucuses, with 51 percent and 27 percent of the vote, respectively. Edwards had picked Minnesota as one of a handful of states to make a last stand in the cross-country Super Tuesday balloting. And he received a late boost from Minnesota leaders of the Howard Dean campaign, who threw Edwards their support after their candidate quit the race. But even that influx of grass-roots support was not enough to offset the wave of momentum that Kerry had generated with victories in Iowa, New Hampshire, and virtually all the February primaries that followed. Kerry swept all eight Minnesota congressional districts, with Edwards reaching 30 percent of the vote only in the 2nd District, just south of the Twin Cities (Minneapolis and St. Paul).

The strong liberal pull within the Minnesota Democratic-Farmer-Labor Party (as it is officially known) was also evident during the party's last presidential primary, a nonbinding event held in April 1992. Although Clinton's campaign was rolling into high gear nationally, he prevailed over Brown in Minnesota by a margin of barely 1,000 votes out of more than 200,000 cast. Clinton offset Brown's edge in the Twin Cities area with a stronger showing in rural parts of the state.

On the Republican side, George Bush was a big winner. He swept every county and nearly two-thirds of the 130,000 ballots

Recent Minnesota Primary Results

Minnesota held its first presidential primary in 1916, but it has taken place only three times since then—1952, 1956 and 1992.

	DEMOCRATS				REPUBLICANS		
Year	Turnout	Candidates	%	Turnout	Candidates	%
2004	—	No Primary		—	No Primary	
2000	—	No Primary		—	No Primary	
1996	—	No Primary		—	No Primary	
1992 (April 7)	204,170	BILL CLINTON	31	132,756	GEORGE BUSH*	64
		Jerry Brown	31		Pat Buchanan	24
		Paul Tsongas	21			
		Uncommitted	6			

Note: All candidates are listed that drew at least 5 percent of their party's primary vote. The names of winning candidates are capitalized. An asterisk (*) indicates an incumbent president.

208

cast. Former Minnesota governor Harold Stassen, who had beaten back Eisenhower's write-in campaign to win the state's Republican presidential primary in 1952, drew only 3 percent of the primary vote in 1992 but qualified for a delegate. Stassen wanted to cast his one vote for himself at the national convention, but the state convention refused to elect him as a delegate.

Sandwiched around Bush's primary victory in 1992 were two caucus triumphs by Bob Dole. His successful effort in 1988 capitalized on his farm-state ties and the momentum from his win in Iowa barely two weeks earlier. In 1996, Dole had the backing of Minnesota's moderate Republican governor, Arne Carlson.

But with the strong conservative presence among GOP activists, neither of Dole's caucus victories was a landslide. In 1988, he defeated Pat Robertson, 43 to 28 percent, with Robertson running best in the Twin Cities' suburbs and the hardscrabble Iron Range, a Democratic stronghold in northeast Minnesota.

In 1996, Dole defeated Pat Buchanan, 41 to 33 percent—about a 10 percentage point improvement for Buchanan over his primary showing in 1992.

MISSISSIPPI

Mississippi's presidential primary has been distinguished more by who has not done well in it than who has.

Mississippi is in the midst of the Bible Belt and would seem to have been favorable terrain for religious broadcaster Pat Robertson. But Robertson drew only 13 percent of the vote in the 1988 Republican primary.

Mississippi has a reputation for rock-ribbed conservatism. Yet Pat Buchanan never reached 30 percent of the vote there in two tries for the Republican presidential nomination.

And Mississippi has a larger proportion of African Americans (36 percent, according to the 2000 Census) than any other state in the country. Yet recent black presidential candidates, Republican Alan Keyes in 1996 and 2000 and Democrat Al Sharpton in 2004, each had trouble reaching 5 percent of the vote in the Mississippi primary.

Voters in the Magnolia State's primary have seemed comfortable casting a pragmatic vote for the presidential front-runner, especially in Republican balloting.

In 1988, Mississippi provided George Bush with his highest percentage of the vote in any Southern primary—66 percent, with Robertson and Bob Dole dividing most of the other ballots.

Bush won an even larger share in the 1992 primary, even though Buchanan bought TV ads and paid a well-publicized visit to a Confederate cemetery. Buchanan netted only 17 percent of the vote and had to share the anti-Bush element of the primary electorate with David Duke, who reached his only double-digit percentage of the primary season in Mississippi.

The state's only close presidential primary was on the Democratic side four years earlier, when Jesse Jackson defeated Al Gore, 45 to 33 percent. Unlike Keyes and Sharpton, Jackson was able to find considerable support among Mississippi's large black population, the source of nearly half the Democratic ballots in 1988 according to exit polls. By all indications, they voted almost unanimously for Jackson. And he won in most parts of the state, including virtually all the major population centers.

Recent Mississippi Primary Results

Mississippi Republicans held a presidential primary to select delegates in 1980. Both parties held their first primary with a direct vote for candidates in 1988.

Year	DEMOCRATS			REPUBLICANS		
	Turnout	Candidates	%	Turnout	Candidates	%
2004 (March 9)	76,298	JOHN KERRY	78	—	No Primary	
		John Edwards	7			
		Al Sharpton	5			
2000 (March 14)	88,602	AL GORE	90	114,979	GEORGE W. BUSH	88
		Bill Bradley	9		Alan Keyes	6
					John McCain	5
1996 (March 12)	93,788	BILL CLINTON*	92	151,925	BOB DOLE	60
		Lyndon LaRouche	8		Pat Buchanan	26
					Steve Forbes	8
1992 (March 10)	191,357	BILL CLINTON	73	154,708	GEORGE BUSH*	72
		Jerry Brown	10		Pat Buchanan	17
		Paul Tsongas	8		David Duke	11
		Uncommitted	6			
1988 (March 8)	359,417	JESSE JACKSON	45	158,526	GEORGE BUSH	66
		Al Gore	33		Bob Dole	17
		Michael Dukakis	8		Pat Robertson	13
		Richard Gephardt	5			
1984	—	No Primary		—	No Primary	
1980 (June 3)	—	No Primary		25,751	RONALD REAGAN	89
					George Bush	8

Note: All candidates are listed that drew at least 5 percent of their party's primary vote. The names of winning candidates are capitalized. An asterisk (*) indicates an incumbent president. There was no direct vote for candidates in the 1980 Republican primary; results that year are based on the vote for delegates.

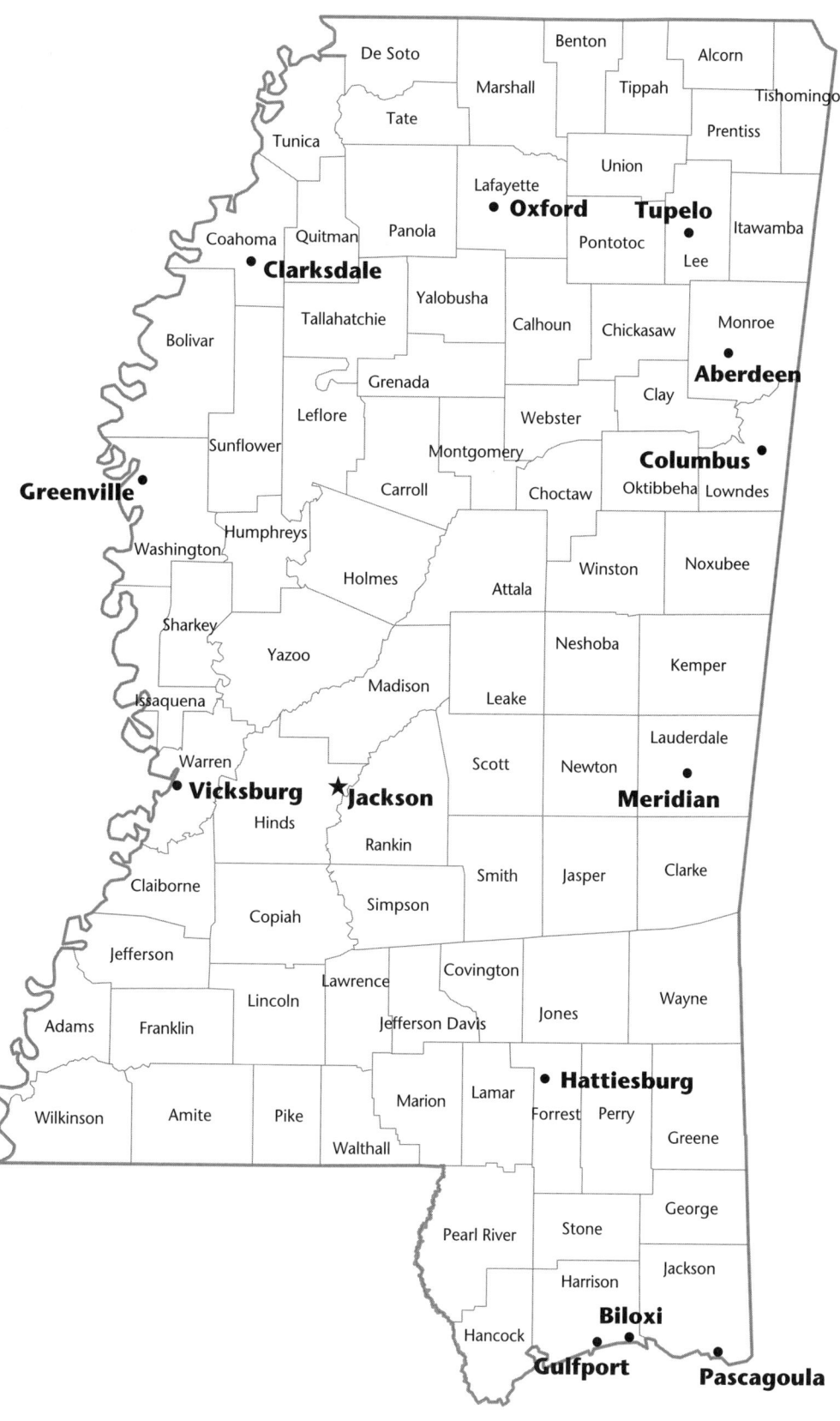

Gore swept most of the predominantly white Hill Country of northeast Mississippi (which borders Gore's home state of Tennessee), the high-growth suburbs of Jackson and Memphis, Tenn., and a scattering of majority-white counties in other parts of the state.

Several of those counties that Gore carried were long-time symbols of the white South. Lafayette County (Oxford) includes "Ole Miss," the University of Mississippi, as well as the home of novelist William Faulkner. Lee County (Tupelo) was the birthplace of Elvis Presley. And Neshoba County has been best known for its annual county fair that draws politicians from across the state, although Neshoba acquired a more infamous reputation in 1964 when three civil rights workers were slain near the county seat of Philadelphia.

In those days, the state Democratic Party was bitterly divided. The conservative "regular" faction held control of the party machinery at the state and local level, while a "loyalist" faction of blacks and liberal whites controlled the presidential delegate-selection process.

The two factions merged before the 1976 election. And since then, the state party has been in the mainstream of Southern Democratic politics. That biracial spirit was evident in the party's presidential primary in 1992, when Bill Clinton swept all parts of Mississippi and nearly three-fourths of the vote.

Yet like other states voting in March or later, Mississippi has seen voter interest in its presidential primary decline sharply over the years as the party nominations have been settled earlier and earlier. In 1988, when the South voted as a virtual bloc on the second Tuesday in March, the combined Democratic and Republican primary turnout in Mississippi topped a half million. By 1996, the combined figure was less than a quarter million. And in 2004 barely 75,000 voters participated in Mississippi's Democratic primary. Mississippi Republicans did not even bother to hold a presidential primary in 2004, as President George W. Bush drew no serious opposition for renomination.

MISSISSIPPI DEMOCRATIC PRIMARY

2000

County	Total Vote	Bradley	Gore	LaRouche	Winner	Percentage of Total Vote		
						Bradley	Gore	LaRouche
ADAMS	1,765	84	1,668	13	Gore	4.8%	94.5%	0.7%
ALCORN	594	66	519	9	Gore	11.1%	87.4%	1.5%
AMITE	905	91	791	23	Gore	10.1%	87.4%	2.5%
ATTALA	729	63	656	10	Gore	8.6%	90.0%	1.4%
BENTON	493	35	455	3	Gore	7.1%	92.3%	0.6%
BOLIVAR	1,510	85	1,390	35	Gore	5.6%	92.1%	2.3%
CALHOUN	565	36	521	8	Gore	6.4%	92.2%	1.4%
CARROLL	388	39	346	3	Gore	10.1%	89.2%	0.8%
CHICKASAW	655	48	595	12	Gore	7.3%	90.8%	1.8%
CHOCTAW	384	54	320	10	Gore	14.1%	83.3%	2.6%
CLAIBORNE	896	70	820	6	Gore	7.8%	91.5%	0.7%
CLARKE	803	82	713	8	Gore	10.2%	88.8%	1.0%
CLAY	654	58	584	12	Gore	8.9%	89.3%	1.8%
COAHOMA	2,090	288	1,736	66	Gore	13.8%	83.1%	3.2%
COPIAH	1,346	103	1,229	14	Gore	7.7%	91.3%	1.0%
COVINGTON	581	66	493	22	Gore	11.4%	84.9%	3.8%
DE SOTO	791	39	745	7	Gore	4.9%	94.2%	0.9%
FORREST	1,737	151	1,566	20	Gore	8.7%	90.2%	1.2%
FRANKLIN	567	76	474	17	Gore	13.4%	83.6%	3.0%
GEORGE	586	80	481	25	Gore	13.7%	82.1%	4.3%
GREENE	317	26	287	4	Gore	8.2%	90.5%	1.3%
GRENADA	473	41	422	10	Gore	8.7%	89.2%	2.1%
HANCOCK	931	128	776	27	Gore	13.7%	83.4%	2.9%
HARRISON	2,955	258	2,672	25	Gore	8.7%	90.4%	0.8%
HINDS	12,074	558	11,408	108	Gore	4.6%	94.5%	0.9%
HOLMES	1,676	143	1,502	31	Gore	8.5%	89.6%	1.8%
HUMPHREYS	1,200	246	911	43	Gore	20.5%	75.9%	3.6%
ISSAQUENA	147	15	129	3	Gore	10.2%	87.8%	2.0%
ITAWAMBA	668	55	604	9	Gore	8.2%	90.4%	1.3%
JACKSON	2,387	191	2,154	42	Gore	8.0%	90.2%	1.8%
JASPER	741	67	652	22	Gore	9.0%	88.0%	3.0%
JEFFERSON	860	66	774	20	Gore	7.7%	90.0%	2.3%
JEFFERSON DAVIS	1,077	98	959	20	Gore	9.1%	89.0%	1.9%
JONES	2,247	251	1,940	56	Gore	11.2%	86.3%	2.5%
KEMPER	575	60	511	4	Gore	10.4%	88.9%	0.7%
LAFAYETTE	671	60	606	5	Gore	8.9%	90.3%	0.7%
LAMAR	613	62	539	12	Gore	10.1%	87.9%	2.0%
LAUDERDALE	1,300	71	1,193	36	Gore	5.5%	91.8%	2.8%
LAWRENCE	786	79	687	20	Gore	10.1%	87.4%	2.5%
LEAKE	794	53	726	15	Gore	6.7%	91.4%	1.9%
LEE	1,568	132	1,405	31	Gore	8.4%	89.6%	2.0%
LEFLORE	814	48	713	53	Gore	5.9%	87.6%	6.5%
LINCOLN	1,104	101	982	21	Gore	9.1%	88.9%	1.9%
LOWNDES	762	59	692	11	Gore	7.7%	90.8%	1.4%
MADISON	1,753	103	1,634	16	Gore	5.9%	93.2%	0.9%

MISSISSIPPI DEMOCRATIC PRIMARY

2000

County	Total Vote	Bradley	Gore	LaRouche	Winner	Percentage of Total Vote		
						Bradley	Gore	LaRouche
MARION	1,175	102	1,044	29	Gore	8.7%	88.9%	2.5%
MARSHALL	1,166	82	1,064	20	Gore	7.0%	91.3%	1.7%
MONROE	1,239	126	1,097	16	Gore	10.2%	88.5%	1.3%
MONTGOMERY	537	41	492	4	Gore	7.6%	91.6%	0.7%
NESHOBA	665	70	586	9	Gore	10.5%	88.1%	1.4%
NEWTON	496	50	426	20	Gore	10.1%	85.9%	4.0%
NOXUBEE	565	45	509	11	Gore	8.0%	90.1%	1.9%
OKTIBBEHA	992	127	852	13	Gore	12.8%	85.9%	1.3%
PANOLA	1,330	84	1,233	13	Gore	6.3%	92.7%	1.0%
PEARL RIVER	1,152	190	930	32	Gore	16.5%	80.7%	2.8%
PERRY	325	48	272	5	Gore	14.8%	83.7%	1.5%
PIKE	1,619	111	1,490	18	Gore	6.9%	92.0%	1.1%
PONTOTOC	666	69	588	9	Gore	10.4%	88.3%	1.4%
PRENTISS	501	40	456	5	Gore	8.0%	91.0%	1.0%
QUITMAN	439	39	390	10	Gore	8.9%	88.8%	2.3%
RANKIN	1,703	79	1,606	18	Gore	4.6%	94.3%	1.1%
SCOTT	1,006	99	890	17	Gore	9.8%	88.5%	1.7%
SHARKEY	286	23	262	1	Gore	8.0%	91.6%	0.3%
SIMPSON	966	80	879	7	Gore	8.3%	91.0%	0.7%
SMITH	578	56	510	12	Gore	9.7%	88.2%	2.1%
STONE	487	70	409	8	Gore	14.4%	84.0%	1.6%
SUNFLOWER	1,034	73	953	8	Gore	7.1%	92.2%	0.8%
TALLAHATCHIE	951	101	837	13	Gore	10.6%	88.0%	1.4%
TATE	722	53	665	4	Gore	7.3%	92.1%	0.6%
TIPPAH	481	49	424	8	Gore	10.2%	88.1%	1.7%
TISHOMINGO	618	50	557	11	Gore	8.1%	90.1%	1.8%
TUNICA	213	19	190	4	Gore	8.9%	89.2%	1.9%
UNION	794	70	711	13	Gore	8.8%	89.5%	1.6%
WALTHALL	732	91	619	22	Gore	12.4%	84.6%	3.0%
WARREN	1,313	89	1,214	10	Gore	6.8%	92.5%	0.8%
WASHINGTON	1,748	115	1,610	23	Gore	6.6%	92.1%	1.3%
WAYNE	687	86	591	10	Gore	12.5%	86.0%	1.5%
WEBSTER	379	42	331	6	Gore	11.1%	87.3%	1.6%
WILKINSON	835	48	776	11	Gore	5.7%	92.9%	1.3%
WINSTON	846	66	766	14	Gore	7.8%	90.5%	1.7%
YALOBUSHA	638	35	589	14	Gore	5.5%	92.3%	2.2%
YAZOO	2,186	418	1,610	158	Gore	19.1%	73.7%	7.2%
TOTAL	88,602	7,621	79,408	1,573	Gore	8.6%	89.6%	1.8%

MISSISSIPPI REPUBLICAN PRIMARY

2000

County	Total Vote	G.W. Bush	Keyes	McCain	Other	Winner	Percentage of Total Vote			
							G.W. Bush	Keyes	McCain	Other
ADAMS	1,025	917	40	59	9	G.W. Bush	89.5%	3.9%	5.8%	0.9%
ALCORN	500	428	42	29	1	G.W. Bush	85.6%	8.4%	5.8%	0.2%
AMITE	812	739	32	27	14	G.W. Bush	91.0%	3.9%	3.3%	1.7%
ATTALA	902	800	64	28	10	G.W. Bush	88.7%	7.1%	3.1%	1.1%
BENTON	182	158	2	20	2	G.W. Bush	86.8%	1.1%	11.0%	1.1%
BOLIVAR	849	757	31	48	13	G.W. Bush	89.2%	3.7%	5.7%	1.5%
CALHOUN	608	550	32	23	3	G.W. Bush	90.5%	5.3%	3.8%	0.5%
CARROLL	529	443	31	53	2	G.W. Bush	83.7%	5.9%	10.0%	0.4%
CHICKASAW	491	439	26	23	3	G.W. Bush	89.4%	5.3%	4.7%	0.6%
CHOCTAW	575	474	27	34	40	G.W. Bush	82.4%	4.7%	5.9%	7.0%
CLAIBORNE	179	166	5	7	1	G.W. Bush	92.7%	2.8%	3.9%	0.6%
CLARKE	1,178	1,087	48	35	8	G.W. Bush	92.3%	4.1%	3.0%	0.7%
CLAY	354	306	20	0	28	G.W. Bush	86.4%	5.6%	0.0%	7.9%
COAHOMA	227	201	7	18	1	G.W. Bush	88.5%	3.1%	7.9%	0.4%
COPIAH	1,628	1,461	69	84	14	G.W. Bush	89.7%	4.2%	5.2%	0.9%
COVINGTON	778	706	29	33	10	G.W. Bush	90.7%	3.7%	4.2%	1.3%
DE SOTO	2,978	2,541	208	197	32	G.W. Bush	85.3%	7.0%	6.6%	1.1%
FORREST	2,927	2,603	154	146	24	G.W. Bush	88.9%	5.3%	5.0%	0.8%
FRANKLIN	722	579	21	0	122	G.W. Bush	80.2%	2.9%	0.0%	16.9%
GEORGE	853	779	34	22	18	G.W. Bush	91.3%	4.0%	2.6%	2.1%
GREENE	471	435	14	13	9	G.W. Bush	92.4%	3.0%	2.8%	1.9%
GRENADA	767	674	53	35	5	G.W. Bush	87.9%	6.9%	4.6%	0.7%
HANCOCK	1,569	1,261	116	170	22	G.W. Bush	80.4%	7.4%	10.8%	1.4%
HARRISON	6,617	5,464	393	691	69	G.W. Bush	82.6%	5.9%	10.4%	1.0%
HINDS	12,688	11,030	864	696	98	G.W. Bush	86.9%	6.8%	5.5%	0.8%
HOLMES	377	340	23	9	5	G.W. Bush	90.2%	6.1%	2.4%	1.3%
HUMPHREYS	156	148	3	4	1	G.W. Bush	94.9%	1.9%	2.6%	0.6%
ISSAQUENA	83	74	6	3	0	G.W. Bush	89.2%	7.2%	3.6%	0.0%
ITAWAMBA	710	643	31	34	2	G.W. Bush	90.6%	4.4%	4.8%	0.3%
JACKSON	6,328	5,544	313	411	60	G.W. Bush	87.6%	4.9%	6.5%	0.9%
JASPER	544	500	23	18	3	G.W. Bush	91.9%	4.2%	3.3%	0.6%
JEFFERSON	125	119	3	3	0	G.W. Bush	95.2%	2.4%	2.4%	0.0%
JEFFERSON DAVIS	516	474	26	12	4	G.W. Bush	91.9%	5.0%	2.3%	0.8%
JONES	3,092	2,782	180	105	25	G.W. Bush	90.0%	5.8%	3.4%	0.8%
KEMPER	585	531	25	27	2	G.W. Bush	90.8%	4.3%	4.6%	0.3%
LAFAYETTE	872	698	67	100	7	G.W. Bush	80.0%	7.7%	11.5%	0.8%
LAMAR	2,216	1,989	99	113	15	G.W. Bush	89.8%	4.5%	5.1%	0.7%
LAUDERDALE	4,166	3,715	225	200	26	G.W. Bush	89.2%	5.4%	4.8%	0.6%
LAWRENCE	716	643	29	31	13	G.W. Bush	89.8%	4.1%	4.3%	1.8%
LEAKE	984	903	49	26	6	G.W. Bush	91.8%	5.0%	2.6%	0.6%
LEE	2,393	2,004	192	173	24	G.W. Bush	83.7%	8.0%	7.2%	1.0%
LEFLORE	810	698	36	62	14	G.W. Bush	86.2%	4.4%	7.7%	1.7%
LINCOLN	2,134	1,933	92	90	19	G.W. Bush	90.6%	4.3%	4.2%	0.9%
LOWNDES	1,855	1,568	121	138	28	G.W. Bush	84.5%	6.5%	7.4%	1.5%
MADISON	4,692	4,055	366	242	29	G.W. Bush	86.4%	7.8%	5.2%	0.6%

MISSISSIPPI REPUBLICAN PRIMARY

2000

County	Total Vote	G.W. Bush	Keyes	McCain	Other	Winner	Percentage of Total Vote			
							G.W. Bush	Keyes	McCain	Other
MARION	1,056	964	55	33	4	G.W. Bush	91.3%	5.2%	3.1%	0.4%
MARSHALL	668	594	43	27	4	G.W. Bush	88.9%	6.4%	4.0%	0.6%
MONROE	1,008	878	55	59	16	G.W. Bush	87.1%	5.5%	5.9%	1.6%
MONTGOMERY	484	431	29	20	4	G.W. Bush	89.0%	6.0%	4.1%	0.8%
NESHOBA	1,429	1,298	77	52	2	G.W. Bush	90.8%	5.4%	3.6%	0.1%
NEWTON	1,287	1,187	57	28	15	G.W. Bush	92.2%	4.4%	2.2%	1.2%
NOXUBEE	363	319	27	16	1	G.W. Bush	87.9%	7.4%	4.4%	0.3%
OKTIBBEHA	1,441	1,197	124	106	14	G.W. Bush	83.1%	8.6%	7.4%	1.0%
PANOLA	889	788	49	49	3	G.W. Bush	88.6%	5.5%	5.5%	0.3%
PEARL RIVER	2,136	1,833	149	127	27	G.W. Bush	85.8%	7.0%	5.9%	1.3%
PERRY	436	408	11	15	2	G.W. Bush	93.6%	2.5%	3.4%	0.5%
PIKE	2,467	2,186	97	162	22	G.W. Bush	88.6%	3.9%	6.6%	0.9%
PONTOTOC	1,154	994	101	44	15	G.W. Bush	86.1%	8.8%	3.8%	1.3%
PRENTISS	517	465	30	16	6	G.W. Bush	89.9%	5.8%	3.1%	1.2%
QUITMAN	181	167	8	5	1	G.W. Bush	92.3%	4.4%	2.8%	0.6%
RANKIN	8,400	7,467	523	374	36	G.W. Bush	88.9%	6.2%	4.5%	0.4%
SCOTT	1,300	1,214	42	44	0	G.W. Bush	93.4%	3.2%	3.4%	0.0%
SHARKEY	203	179	6	16	2	G.W. Bush	88.2%	3.0%	7.9%	1.0%
SIMPSON	1,500	1,327	71	65	37	G.W. Bush	88.5%	4.7%	4.3%	2.5%
SMITH	953	896	31	13	13	G.W. Bush	94.0%	3.3%	1.4%	1.4%
STONE	820	696	51	59	14	G.W. Bush	84.9%	6.2%	7.2%	1.7%
SUNFLOWER	734	662	26	40	6	G.W. Bush	90.2%	3.5%	5.4%	0.8%
TALLAHATCHIE	470	442	4	18	6	G.W. Bush	94.0%	0.9%	3.8%	1.3%
TATE	758	677	40	39	2	G.W. Bush	89.3%	5.3%	5.1%	0.3%
TIPPAH	553	498	28	21	6	G.W. Bush	90.1%	5.1%	3.8%	1.1%
TISHOMINGO	507	439	34	28	6	G.W. Bush	86.6%	6.7%	5.5%	1.2%
TUNICA	36	29	2	4	1	G.W. Bush	80.6%	5.6%	11.1%	2.8%
UNION	1,039	924	53	54	8	G.W. Bush	88.9%	5.1%	5.2%	0.8%
WALTHALL	802	716	38	38	10	G.W. Bush	89.3%	4.7%	4.7%	1.2%
WARREN	2,345	2,025	123	154	43	G.W. Bush	86.4%	5.2%	6.6%	1.8%
WASHINGTON	1,504	1,382	57	59	6	G.W. Bush	91.9%	3.8%	3.9%	0.4%
WAYNE	880	821	15	39	5	G.W. Bush	93.3%	1.7%	4.4%	0.6%
WEBSTER	712	638	31	41	2	G.W. Bush	89.6%	4.4%	5.8%	0.3%
WILKINSON	222	207	5	9	1	G.W. Bush	93.2%	2.3%	4.1%	0.5%
WINSTON	884	777	61	41	5	G.W. Bush	87.9%	6.9%	4.6%	0.6%
YALOBUSHA	378	321	30	23	4	G.W. Bush	84.9%	7.9%	6.1%	1.1%
YAZOO	700	637	24	33	6	G.W. Bush	91.0%	3.4%	4.7%	0.9%
TOTAL	114,979	101,042	6,478	6,263	1,196	G.W. Bush	87.9%	5.6%	5.4%	1.0%

Note: Other vote was 588 Steve Forbes; 475 Gary Bauer; 133 Orrin Hatch.

MISSISSIPPI DEMOCRATIC PRIMARY

2004

County	Total Vote	Edwards	Kerry	Sharpton	Other	Winner	Edwards	Kerry	Sharpton	Other
							Percentage of Total Vote			
ADAMS	1,367	59	1,187	57	64	Kerry	4.3%	86.8%	4.2%	4.7%
ALCORN	472	54	350	11	57	Kerry	11.4%	74.2%	2.3%	12.1%
AMITE	640	42	494	40	64	Kerry	6.6%	77.2%	6.3%	10.0%
ATTALA	767	59	599	30	79	Kerry	7.7%	78.1%	3.9%	10.3%
BENTON	410	42	302	15	51	Kerry	10.2%	73.7%	3.7%	12.4%
BOLIVAR	1,322	51	999	168	104	Kerry	3.9%	75.6%	12.7%	7.9%
CALHOUN	442	62	296	22	62	Kerry	14.0%	67.0%	5.0%	14.0%
CARROLL	473	38	385	18	32	Kerry	8.0%	81.4%	3.8%	6.8%
CHICKASAW	435	40	329	20	46	Kerry	9.2%	75.6%	4.6%	10.6%
CHOCTAW	431	46	259	50	76	Kerry	10.7%	60.1%	11.6%	17.6%
CLAIBORNE	1,139	58	910	52	119	Kerry	5.1%	79.9%	4.6%	10.4%
CLARKE	803	67	594	83	59	Kerry	8.3%	74.0%	10.3%	7.3%
CLAY	900	75	718	50	57	Kerry	8.3%	79.8%	5.6%	6.3%
COAHOMA	1,630	190	1,056	134	250	Kerry	11.7%	64.8%	8.2%	15.3%
COPIAH	1,420	76	1,201	56	87	Kerry	5.4%	84.6%	3.9%	6.1%
COVINGTON	457	47	352	26	32	Kerry	10.3%	77.0%	5.7%	7.0%
DE SOTO	964	82	770	24	88	Kerry	8.5%	79.9%	2.5%	9.1%
FORREST	1,106	67	884	67	88	Kerry	6.1%	79.9%	6.1%	8.0%
FRANKLIN	436	43	318	26	49	Kerry	9.9%	72.9%	6.0%	11.2%
GEORGE	532	70	356	17	89	Kerry	13.2%	66.9%	3.2%	16.7%
GREENE	355	40	251	14	50	Kerry	11.3%	70.7%	3.9%	14.1%
GRENADA	385	43	259	22	61	Kerry	11.2%	67.3%	5.7%	15.8%
HANCOCK	722	91	512	28	91	Kerry	12.6%	70.9%	3.9%	12.6%
HARRISON	3,289	274	2,560	212	243	Kerry	8.3%	77.8%	6.4%	7.4%
HINDS	10,494	388	8,919	539	648	Kerry	3.7%	85.0%	5.1%	6.2%
HOLMES	1,463	25	1,257	92	89	Kerry	1.7%	85.9%	6.3%	6.1%
HUMPHREYS	689	32	533	43	81	Kerry	4.6%	77.4%	6.2%	11.8%
ISSAQUENA	162	9	112	7	34	Kerry	5.6%	69.1%	4.3%	21.0%
ITAWAMBA	603	79	440	15	69	Kerry	13.1%	73.0%	2.5%	11.4%
JACKSON	2,127	175	1,692	110	150	Kerry	8.2%	79.5%	5.2%	7.1%
JASPER	882	59	691	44	88	Kerry	6.7%	78.3%	5.0%	10.0%
JEFFERSON	1,011	20	902	31	58	Kerry	2.0%	89.2%	3.1%	5.7%
JEFFERSON DAVIS	749	46	573	55	75	Kerry	6.1%	76.5%	7.3%	10.0%
JONES	1,179	82	924	55	118	Kerry	7.0%	78.4%	4.7%	10.0%
KEMPER	576	45	439	33	59	Kerry	7.8%	76.2%	5.7%	10.2%
LAFAYETTE	693	57	552	12	72	Kerry	8.2%	79.7%	1.7%	10.4%
LAMAR	421	41	328	21	31	Kerry	9.7%	77.9%	5.0%	7.4%
LAUDERDALE	1,114	51	958	56	49	Kerry	4.6%	86.0%	5.0%	4.4%
LAWRENCE	682	58	489	41	94	Kerry	8.5%	71.7%	6.0%	13.8%
LEAKE	751	59	587	32	73	Kerry	7.9%	78.2%	4.3%	9.7%
LEE	1,205	134	904	61	106	Kerry	11.1%	75.0%	5.1%	8.8%
LEFLORE	929	36	785	45	63	Kerry	3.9%	84.5%	4.8%	6.8%
LINCOLN	844	77	630	41	96	Kerry	9.1%	74.6%	4.9%	11.4%
LOWNDES	687	49	572	25	41	Kerry	7.1%	83.3%	3.6%	6.0%
MADISON	2,201	114	1,794	103	190	Kerry	5.2%	81.5%	4.7%	8.6%

MISSISSIPPI DEMOCRATIC PRIMARY

2004

County	Total Vote	Edwards	Kerry	Sharpton	Other	Winner	Percentage of Total Vote			
							Edwards	Kerry	Sharpton	Other
MARION	778	68	604	31	75	Kerry	8.7%	77.6%	4.0%	9.6%
MARSHALL	1,098	61	911	38	88	Kerry	5.6%	83.0%	3.5%	8.0%
MONROE	992	113	748	56	75	Kerry	11.4%	75.4%	5.6%	7.6%
MONTGOMERY	516	39	366	40	71	Kerry	7.6%	70.9%	7.8%	13.8%
NESHOBA	592	77	391	28	96	Kerry	13.0%	66.0%	4.7%	16.2%
NEWTON	417	33	285	51	48	Kerry	7.9%	68.3%	12.2%	11.5%
NOXUBEE	348	6	295	23	24	Kerry	1.7%	84.8%	6.6%	6.9%
OKTIBBEHA	880	63	703	49	65	Kerry	7.2%	79.9%	5.6%	7.4%
PANOLA	1,060	80	852	34	94	Kerry	7.5%	80.4%	3.2%	8.9%
PEARL RIVER	821	100	604	33	84	Kerry	12.2%	73.6%	4.0%	10.2%
PERRY	242	21	182	15	24	Kerry	8.7%	75.2%	6.2%	9.9%
PIKE	1,112	78	918	37	79	Kerry	7.0%	82.6%	3.3%	7.1%
PONTOTOC	508	71	332	16	89	Kerry	14.0%	65.4%	3.1%	17.5%
PRENTISS	403	59	303	5	36	Kerry	14.6%	75.2%	1.2%	8.9%
QUITMAN	488	26	379	22	61	Kerry	5.3%	77.7%	4.5%	12.5%
RANKIN	1,613	115	1,340	56	102	Kerry	7.1%	83.1%	3.5%	6.3%
SCOTT	916	73	710	25	108	Kerry	8.0%	77.5%	2.7%	11.8%
SHARKEY	288	18	223	15	32	Kerry	6.3%	77.4%	5.2%	11.1%
SIMPSON	737	59	571	24	83	Kerry	8.0%	77.5%	3.3%	11.3%
SMITH	505	65	334	21	85	Kerry	12.9%	66.1%	4.2%	16.8%
STONE	362	37	256	14	55	Kerry	10.2%	70.7%	3.9%	15.2%
SUNFLOWER	878	54	667	58	99	Kerry	6.2%	76.0%	6.6%	11.3%
TALLAHATCHIE	789	61	536	95	97	Kerry	7.7%	67.9%	12.0%	12.3%
TATE	610	64	448	23	75	Kerry	10.5%	73.4%	3.8%	12.3%
TIPPAH	402	55	284	9	54	Kerry	13.7%	70.6%	2.2%	13.4%
TISHOMINGO	633	77	499	6	51	Kerry	12.2%	78.8%	0.9%	8.1%
TUNICA	244	16	174	17	37	Kerry	6.6%	71.3%	7.0%	15.2%
UNION	649	100	436	22	91	Kerry	15.4%	67.2%	3.4%	14.0%
WALTHALL	635	65	483	25	62	Kerry	10.2%	76.1%	3.9%	9.8%
WARREN	1,456	57	1,227	82	90	Kerry	3.9%	84.3%	5.6%	6.2%
WASHINGTON	1,303	134	927	101	141	Kerry	10.3%	71.1%	7.8%	10.8%
WAYNE	724	56	494	52	122	Kerry	7.7%	68.2%	7.2%	16.9%
WEBSTER	325	55	216	7	47	Kerry	16.9%	66.5%	2.2%	14.5%
WILKINSON	530	38	424	29	39	Kerry	7.2%	80.0%	5.5%	7.4%
WINSTON	737	56	607	24	50	Kerry	7.6%	82.4%	3.3%	6.8%
YALOBUSHA	376	34	297	14	31	Kerry	9.0%	79.0%	3.7%	8.2%
YAZOO	972	46	767	33	126	Kerry	4.7%	78.9%	3.4%	13.0%
TOTAL	76,298	5,582	59,815	3,933	6,968	Kerry	7.3%	78.4%	5.2%	9.1%

Note: Other vote was 1,997 Howard Dean; 1,878 Wesley Clark; 1,370 Uncommitted; 768 Dennis J. Kucinich; 716 Joseph I. Lieberman; 239 Lyndon H. LaRouche Jr.

MISSOURI

Situated at the juncture of the industrial Frost Belt, the agrarian Midwest and the rural South, Missouri likes to present itself as one of the nation's foremost political bellwethers. In all but two presidential elections since 1900, it has voted for the winning candidate.

But Missouri has not had much chance to prove its perspicacity in presidential primaries. The first–in 1988–was skewed toward the home-state candidacy of Rep. Richard Gephardt.

The primary itself had been created largely to aid Gephardt, as state party officials thought such an event would do their native son more good than the traditional caucuses the state had held previously.

None of the other Democratic presidential hopefuls seriously challenged Gephardt in Missouri. He rolled up nearly 60 percent of the vote, easily his best showing of the primary season.

There was some embarrassment for Gephardt, though, in the returns. He narrowly lost his home base, the city of St. Louis, to Jesse Jackson, who won handily in the heavily black precincts in the northern part of the city. Gephardt, though, did swamp Jackson in that southern portion of St. Louis that was part of his congressional district. Meanwhile, Al Gore had trouble finding a toehold anywhere in Missouri and drew only 3 percent of the vote statewide.

The tables were turned, though, in 2000, as Gore handily defeated Missouri native Bill Bradley in the state's second Democratic presidential primary. Bradley carried only two counties, one of which—Jefferson—included his birthplace of Crystal City.

The Missouri Democratic primary in 2004 again featured Gephardt's name on the ballot. But even with the early February date, a month earlier than in 2000, Gephardt had already retreated to the sidelines. A victim of a distant fourth-place finish in the Iowa caucuses, Gephardt threw his support to John Kerry after the Missouri vote. Nonetheless, Kerry was riding a wave of momentum following his opening victories in Iowa and New Hampshire. And with other candidates making a minimal effort in Missouri, Kerry swept all but two rural counties, which went to runner-up John Edwards.

Thus far, the only competitive primary for president was on the Republican side in 1988. Bob Dole, who did not win any Super Tuesday primary that year, came closest in Missouri. For much of the night it appeared that he might defeat George Bush in the Show Me State, and in the end he lost by less than 5,000 votes out of 400,000 cast.

Dole's basic asset was the proximity of western Missouri to his home state of Kansas. Dole swept most of western Missouri, including the Kansas City area. Bush won most of the eastern half, including St. Louis and its suburbs.

In its caucus days, Democrats in Harry Truman's home state showed a clear preference for traditional "New Deal" Democrats, such as Hubert Humphrey, Henry Jackson, and Walter Mondale. Bill Clinton won Missouri's first-round caucuses in 1992, although the turnout of about 25,000 was less

Recent Missouri Primary Results

Missouri held its first presidential primary in 1988.

| Year | DEMOCRATS | | | REPUBLICANS | | |
	Turnout	Candidates	%	Turnout	Candidates	%
2004 (Feb. 3)	418,339	JOHN KERRY	51	123,086	GEORGE W. BUSH*	95
		John Edwards	25			
		Howard Dean	9			
2000 (March 7)	265,489	AL GORE	65	475,363	GEORGE W. BUSH	58
		Bill Bradley	34		John McCain	35
					Alan Keyes	6
1996	—	No Primary		—	No Primary	
1992	—	No Primary		—	No Primary	
1988 (March 8)	527,805	RICHARD GEPHARDT	58	400,300	GEORGE BUSH	42
		Jesse Jackson	20		Bob Dole	41
		Michael Dukakis	12		Pat Robertson	11

Note: All candidates are listed that drew at least 5 percent of their party's primary vote. The names of winning candidates are capitalized. An asterisk (*) indicates an incumbent president.

than 5 percent of the number that participated in the Democratic primary four years earlier.

Meanwhile, if Missouri Republicans needed an excuse to reinstitute the presidential primary, their 1996 caucus process gave them one. Tapping into strong anti-abortion sentiment in suburban St. Louis County, Pat Buchanan won the first-round caucuses over Dole by 8 percentage points, with 9 percent going to Alan Keyes. But to the chagrin of the Buchanan legions, Keyes's supporters aligned with the Dole forces at the state convention to give Dole a majority of the Missouri delegates.

With the presidential primary back in business in 2000, George W. Bush was able to fashion a much more comfortable victory among Missouri Republicans than his father had in 1988. John McCain triumphed in the state's two largest cities, St. Louis and Kansas City, but lost virtually everywhere else to Bush. In 2004, President Bush's support in Missouri's Republican primary was close to unanimous, as he fell below 90 percent in only one county, Grundy, in the rural north-central part of the state.

MISSOURI DEMOCRATIC PRIMARY

2000

County	Total Vote	Bradley	Gore	Other	Winner	Percentage of Total Vote		
						Bradley	Gore	Other
ADAIR	876	316	541	19	Gore	36.1%	61.8%	2.2%
ANDREW	522	158	352	12	Gore	30.3%	67.4%	2.3%
ATCHISON	225	79	142	4	Gore	35.1%	63.1%	1.8%
AUDRAIN	1,124	418	687	19	Gore	37.2%	61.1%	1.7%
BARRY	779	179	572	28	Gore	23.0%	73.4%	3.6%
BARTON	284	84	191	9	Gore	29.6%	67.3%	3.2%
BATES	675	184	472	19	Gore	27.3%	69.9%	2.8%
BENTON	642	106	523	13	Gore	16.5%	81.5%	2.0%
BOLLINGER	340	117	211	12	Gore	34.4%	62.1%	3.5%
BOONE	6,249	2,760	3,402	87	Gore	44.2%	54.4%	1.4%
BUCHANAN	3,700	1,104	2,488	108	Gore	29.8%	67.2%	2.9%
BUTLER	960	299	638	23	Gore	31.1%	66.5%	2.4%
CALDWELL	237	75	156	6	Gore	31.6%	65.8%	2.5%
CALLAWAY	1,477	557	873	47	Gore	37.7%	59.1%	3.2%
CAMDEN	1,031	267	755	9	Gore	25.9%	73.2%	0.9%
CAPE GIRARDEAU	2,045	798	1,206	41	Gore	39.0%	59.0%	2.0%
CARROLL	353	101	233	19	Gore	28.6%	66.0%	5.4%
CARTER	263	96	159	8	Gore	36.5%	60.5%	3.0%
CASS	2,560	666	1,821	73	Gore	26.0%	71.1%	2.9%
CEDAR	417	97	313	7	Gore	23.3%	75.1%	1.7%
CHARITON	461	167	279	15	Gore	36.2%	60.5%	3.3%
CHRISTIAN	1,184	299	870	15	Gore	25.3%	73.5%	1.3%
CLARK	405	109	285	11	Gore	26.9%	70.4%	2.7%
CLAY	5,988	1,639	4,244	105	Gore	27.4%	70.9%	1.8%
CLINTON	727	234	468	25	Gore	32.2%	64.4%	3.4%
COLE	2,773	1,251	1,481	41	Gore	45.1%	53.4%	1.5%
COOPER	546	186	353	7	Gore	34.1%	64.7%	1.3%
CRAWFORD	686	273	396	17	Gore	39.8%	57.7%	2.5%
DADE	227	66	159	2	Gore	29.1%	70.0%	0.9%
DALLAS	463	121	332	10	Gore	26.1%	71.7%	2.2%
DAVIESS	301	76	216	9	Gore	25.2%	71.8%	3.0%
DE KALB	349	135	202	12	Gore	38.7%	57.9%	3.4%
DENT	569	234	318	17	Gore	41.1%	55.9%	3.0%
DOUGLAS	267	84	177	6	Gore	31.5%	66.3%	2.2%
DUNKLIN	925	203	693	29	Gore	21.9%	74.9%	3.1%
FRANKLIN	4,134	1,647	2,414	73	Gore	39.8%	58.4%	1.8%
GASCONADE	435	165	259	11	Gore	37.9%	59.5%	2.5%
GENTRY	309	127	178	4	Gore	41.1%	57.6%	1.3%
GREENE	8,337	1,892	6,287	158	Gore	22.7%	75.4%	1.9%
GRUNDY	322	90	226	6	Gore	28.0%	70.2%	1.9%
HARRISON	253	80	167	6	Gore	31.6%	66.0%	2.4%
HENRY	1,117	349	737	31	Gore	31.2%	66.0%	2.8%
HICKORY	500	80	410	10	Gore	16.0%	82.0%	2.0%
HOLT	163	45	116	2	Gore	27.6%	71.2%	1.2%
HOWARD	502	197	295	10	Gore	39.2%	58.8%	2.0%

MISSOURI DEMOCRATIC PRIMARY

2000

County	Total Vote	Bradley	Gore	Other	Winner	Percentage of Total Vote		
						Bradley	Gore	Other
HOWELL	826	188	625	13	Gore	22.8%	75.7%	1.6%
IRON	582	237	336	9	Gore	40.7%	57.7%	1.5%
JACKSON	15,607	4,039	11,177	391	Gore	25.9%	71.6%	2.5%
JASPER	1,866	476	1,342	48	Gore	25.5%	71.9%	2.6%
JEFFERSON	12,458	7,361	4,969	128	Bradley	59.1%	39.9%	1.0%
JOHNSON	1,287	403	853	31	Gore	31.3%	66.3%	2.4%
KANSAS CITY	18,744	4,397	14,055	292	Gore	23.5%	75.0%	1.6%
KNOX	229	69	154	6	Gore	30.1%	67.2%	2.6%
LACLEDE	828	198	602	28	Gore	23.9%	72.7%	3.4%
LAFAYETTE	1,129	275	825	29	Gore	24.4%	73.1%	2.6%
LAWRENCE	804	217	568	19	Gore	27.0%	70.6%	2.4%
LEWIS	601	195	395	11	Gore	32.4%	65.7%	1.8%
LINCOLN	1,636	579	1,015	42	Gore	35.4%	62.0%	2.6%
LINN	708	219	470	19	Gore	30.9%	66.4%	2.7%
LIVINGSTON	428	132	279	17	Gore	30.8%	65.2%	4.0%
MCDONALD	426	109	300	17	Gore	25.6%	70.4%	4.0%
MACON	620	189	420	11	Gore	30.5%	67.7%	1.8%
MADISON	539	211	313	15	Gore	39.1%	58.1%	2.8%
MARIES	410	124	270	16	Gore	30.2%	65.9%	3.9%
MARION	1,607	631	938	38	Gore	39.3%	58.4%	2.4%
MERCER	90	28	59	3	Gore	31.1%	65.6%	3.3%
MILLER	530	163	358	9	Gore	30.8%	67.5%	1.7%
MISSISSIPPI	572	121	432	19	Gore	21.2%	75.5%	3.3%
MONITEAU	435	130	298	7	Gore	29.9%	68.5%	1.6%
MONROE	541	185	342	14	Gore	34.2%	63.2%	2.6%
MONTGOMERY	425	140	275	10	Gore	32.9%	64.7%	2.4%
MORGAN	678	153	510	15	Gore	22.6%	75.2%	2.2%
NEW MADRID	790	201	566	23	Gore	25.4%	71.6%	2.9%
NEWTON	1,036	259	752	25	Gore	25.0%	72.6%	2.4%
NODAWAY	580	214	354	12	Gore	36.9%	61.0%	2.1%
OREGON	484	135	325	24	Gore	27.9%	67.1%	5.0%
OSAGE	503	194	300	9	Gore	38.6%	59.6%	1.8%
OZARK	280	43	233	4	Gore	15.4%	83.2%	1.4%
PEMISCOT	518	121	382	15	Gore	23.4%	73.7%	2.9%
PERRY	455	151	294	10	Gore	33.2%	64.6%	2.2%
PETTIS	1,244	381	832	31	Gore	30.6%	66.9%	2.5%
PHELPS	1,679	693	943	43	Gore	41.3%	56.2%	2.6%
PIKE	940	334	584	22	Gore	35.5%	62.1%	2.3%
PLATTE	2,334	675	1,624	35	Gore	28.9%	69.6%	1.5%
POLK	622	134	480	8	Gore	21.5%	77.2%	1.3%
PULASKI	1,034	309	686	39	Gore	29.9%	66.3%	3.8%
PUTNAM	150	52	97	1	Gore	34.7%	64.7%	0.7%
RALLS	576	228	339	9	Gore	39.6%	58.9%	1.6%
RANDOLPH	1,036	412	593	31	Gore	39.8%	57.2%	3.0%
RAY	843	233	581	29	Gore	27.6%	68.9%	3.4%

MISSOURI DEMOCRATIC PRIMARY

2000

County	Total Vote	Bradley	Gore	Other	Winner	Percentage of Total Vote		
						Bradley	Gore	Other
REYNOLDS	473	195	258	20	Gore	41.2%	54.5%	4.2%
RIPLEY	397	112	277	8	Gore	28.2%	69.8%	2.0%
ST. CHARLES	12,350	4,403	7,706	241	Gore	35.7%	62.4%	2.0%
ST. CLAIR	572	127	423	22	Gore	22.2%	74.0%	3.8%
ST. FRANCOIS	2,507	1,147	1,316	44	Gore	45.8%	52.5%	1.8%
ST. LOUIS COUNTY	66,907	26,116	39,951	840	Gore	39.0%	59.7%	1.3%
ST. LOUIS CITY	32,124	8,525	23,136	463	Gore	26.5%	72.0%	1.4%
STE. GENEVIEVE	1,085	563	496	26	Bradley	51.9%	45.7%	2.4%
SALINE	1,082	336	726	20	Gore	31.1%	67.1%	1.8%
SCHUYLER	259	74	175	10	Gore	28.6%	67.6%	3.9%
SCOTLAND	302	122	174	6	Gore	40.4%	57.6%	2.0%
SCOTT	1,547	452	1,046	49	Gore	29.2%	67.6%	3.2%
SHANNON	398	109	276	13	Gore	27.4%	69.3%	3.3%
SHELBY	510	211	290	9	Gore	41.4%	56.9%	1.8%
STODDARD	989	298	675	16	Gore	30.1%	68.3%	1.6%
STONE	687	160	512	15	Gore	23.3%	74.5%	2.2%
SULLIVAN	316	81	225	10	Gore	25.6%	71.2%	3.2%
TANEY	857	205	631	21	Gore	23.9%	73.6%	2.5%
TEXAS	1,027	317	675	35	Gore	30.9%	65.7%	3.4%
VERNON	970	250	676	44	Gore	25.8%	69.7%	4.5%
WARREN	785	308	466	11	Gore	39.2%	59.4%	1.4%
WASHINGTON	1,007	373	612	22	Gore	37.0%	60.8%	2.2%
WAYNE	678	204	453	21	Gore	30.1%	66.8%	3.1%
WEBSTER	760	144	589	27	Gore	18.9%	77.5%	3.6%
WORTH	147	38	101	8	Gore	25.9%	68.7%	5.4%
WRIGHT	341	74	255	12	Gore	21.7%	74.8%	3.5%
TOTAL	265,489	89,092	171,562	4,835	Gore	33.6%	64.6%	1.8%

Note: Other vote was 3,364 Uncommitted; 906 Lyndon H. LaRouche Jr.; 565 Pat Price.

MISSOURI REPUBLICAN PRIMARY

2000

County	Total Vote	G.W. Bush	Keyes	McCain	Other	Winner	Percentage of Total Vote			
							G.W. Bush	Keyes	McCain	Other
ADAIR	1,909	1,191	88	591	39	G.W. Bush	62.4%	4.6%	31.0%	2.0%
ANDREW	1,431	897	58	454	22	G.W. Bush	62.7%	4.1%	31.7%	1.5%
ATCHISON	568	373	25	161	9	G.W. Bush	65.7%	4.4%	28.3%	1.6%
AUDRAIN	2,061	1,184	95	762	20	G.W. Bush	57.4%	4.6%	37.0%	1.0%
BARRY	3,296	2,060	186	1,018	32	G.W. Bush	62.5%	5.6%	30.9%	1.0%
BARTON	1,532	1,036	79	402	15	G.W. Bush	67.6%	5.2%	26.2%	1.0%
BATES	1,241	723	61	428	29	G.W. Bush	58.3%	4.9%	34.5%	2.3%
BENTON	1,549	890	48	597	14	G.W. Bush	57.5%	3.1%	38.5%	0.9%
BOLLINGER	1,153	824	42	278	9	G.W. Bush	71.5%	3.6%	24.1%	0.8%
BOONE	12,695	6,988	550	5,074	83	G.W. Bush	55.0%	4.3%	40.0%	0.7%
BUCHANAN	5,943	3,203	350	2,307	83	G.W. Bush	53.9%	5.9%	38.8%	1.4%
BUTLER	2,834	2,059	59	699	17	G.W. Bush	72.7%	2.1%	24.7%	0.6%
CALDWELL	693	415	35	233	10	G.W. Bush	59.9%	5.1%	33.6%	1.4%
CALLAWAY	3,001	1,768	133	1,062	38	G.W. Bush	58.9%	4.4%	35.4%	1.3%
CAMDEN	4,425	2,495	179	1,709	42	G.W. Bush	56.4%	4.0%	38.6%	0.9%
CAPE GIRARDEAU	7,469	5,458	242	1,708	61	G.W. Bush	73.1%	3.2%	22.9%	0.8%
CARROLL	942	601	25	295	21	G.W. Bush	63.8%	2.7%	31.3%	2.2%
CARTER	503	333	23	145	2	G.W. Bush	66.2%	4.6%	28.8%	0.4%
CASS	6,052	3,523	414	2,045	70	G.W. Bush	58.2%	6.8%	33.8%	1.2%
CEDAR	1,638	928	100	598	12	G.W. Bush	56.7%	6.1%	36.5%	0.7%
CHARITON	721	446	27	238	10	G.W. Bush	61.9%	3.7%	33.0%	1.4%
CHRISTIAN	6,098	3,493	566	1,986	53	G.W. Bush	57.3%	9.3%	32.6%	0.9%
CLARK	592	344	32	207	9	G.W. Bush	58.1%	5.4%	35.0%	1.5%
CLAY	12,789	6,854	817	4,990	128	G.W. Bush	53.6%	6.4%	39.0%	1.0%
CLINTON	1,216	638	75	493	10	G.W. Bush	52.5%	6.2%	40.5%	0.8%
COLE	7,998	5,263	274	2,408	53	G.W. Bush	65.8%	3.4%	30.1%	0.7%
COOPER	1,704	986	61	638	19	G.W. Bush	57.9%	3.6%	37.4%	1.1%
CRAWFORD	1,571	962	67	529	13	G.W. Bush	61.2%	4.3%	33.7%	0.8%
DADE	1,262	731	79	438	14	G.W. Bush	57.9%	6.3%	34.7%	1.1%
DALLAS	1,809	1,004	122	673	10	G.W. Bush	55.5%	6.7%	37.2%	0.6%
DAVIESS	630	368	25	232	5	G.W. Bush	58.4%	4.0%	36.8%	0.8%
DE KALB	721	450	36	222	13	G.W. Bush	62.4%	5.0%	30.8%	1.8%
DENT	1,309	888	65	337	19	G.W. Bush	67.8%	5.0%	25.7%	1.5%
DOUGLAS	1,577	958	82	519	18	G.W. Bush	60.7%	5.2%	32.9%	1.1%
DUNKLIN	1,411	999	53	315	44	G.W. Bush	70.8%	3.8%	22.3%	3.1%
FRANKLIN	8,893	5,014	503	3,305	71	G.W. Bush	56.4%	5.7%	37.2%	0.8%
GASCONADE	1,685	1,033	58	571	23	G.W. Bush	61.3%	3.4%	33.9%	1.4%
GENTRY	562	347	11	180	24	G.W. Bush	61.7%	2.0%	32.0%	4.3%
GREENE	29,939	17,617	2,641	9,486	195	G.W. Bush	58.8%	8.8%	31.7%	0.7%
GRUNDY	908	514	58	324	12	G.W. Bush	56.6%	6.4%	35.7%	1.3%
HARRISON	888	547	38	292	11	G.W. Bush	61.6%	4.3%	32.9%	1.2%
HENRY	1,570	886	61	598	25	G.W. Bush	56.4%	3.9%	38.1%	1.6%
HICKORY	1,283	602	65	606	10	McCain	46.9%	5.1%	47.2%	0.8%
HOLT	586	403	18	156	9	G.W. Bush	68.8%	3.1%	26.6%	1.5%
HOWARD	875	488	46	336	5	G.W. Bush	55.8%	5.3%	38.4%	0.6%

MISSOURI REPUBLICAN PRIMARY

2000

County	Total Vote	G.W. Bush	Keyes	McCain	Other	Winner	Percentage of Total Vote			
							G.W. Bush	Keyes	McCain	Other
HOWELL	3,634	2,178	237	1,192	27	G.W. Bush	59.9%	6.5%	32.8%	0.7%
IRON	686	405	43	232	6	G.W. Bush	59.0%	6.3%	33.8%	0.9%
JACKSON	29,614	16,961	1,746	10,471	436	G.W. Bush	57.3%	5.9%	35.4%	1.5%
JASPER	9,577	6,143	512	2,830	92	G.W. Bush	64.1%	5.3%	29.5%	1.0%
JEFFERSON	12,924	7,466	870	4,443	145	G.W. Bush	57.8%	6.7%	34.4%	1.1%
JOHNSON	2,797	1,519	128	1,113	37	G.W. Bush	54.3%	4.6%	39.8%	1.3%
KANSAS CITY	15,092	6,949	914	7,085	144	McCain	46.0%	6.1%	46.9%	1.0%
KNOX	409	286	18	96	9	G.W. Bush	69.9%	4.4%	23.5%	2.2%
LACLEDE	3,557	2,213	207	1,103	34	G.W. Bush	62.2%	5.8%	31.0%	1.0%
LAFAYETTE	2,573	1,546	137	851	39	G.W. Bush	60.1%	5.3%	33.1%	1.5%
LAWRENCE	3,761	2,121	324	1,280	36	G.W. Bush	56.4%	8.6%	34.0%	1.0%
LEWIS	667	439	23	194	11	G.W. Bush	65.8%	3.4%	29.1%	1.6%
LINCOLN	2,642	1,579	188	853	22	G.W. Bush	59.8%	7.1%	32.3%	0.8%
LINN	978	631	44	285	18	G.W. Bush	64.5%	4.5%	29.1%	1.8%
LIVINGSTON	944	571	43	319	11	G.W. Bush	60.5%	4.6%	33.8%	1.2%
MCDONALD	1,556	1,012	63	457	24	G.W. Bush	65.0%	4.0%	29.4%	1.5%
MACON	1,161	741	57	344	19	G.W. Bush	63.8%	4.9%	29.6%	1.6%
MADISON	777	488	20	262	7	G.W. Bush	62.8%	2.6%	33.7%	0.9%
MARIES	860	519	39	298	4	G.W. Bush	60.3%	4.5%	34.7%	0.5%
MARION	2,226	1,603	127	481	15	G.W. Bush	72.0%	5.7%	21.6%	0.7%
MERCER	395	240	14	128	13	G.W. Bush	60.8%	3.5%	32.4%	3.3%
MILLER	2,441	1,564	67	790	20	G.W. Bush	64.1%	2.7%	32.4%	0.8%
MISSISSIPPI	772	542	22	203	5	G.W. Bush	70.2%	2.8%	26.3%	0.6%
MONITEAU	1,520	989	33	481	17	G.W. Bush	65.1%	2.2%	31.6%	1.1%
MONROE	598	360	22	211	5	G.W. Bush	60.2%	3.7%	35.3%	0.8%
MONTGOMERY	1,384	694	56	622	12	G.W. Bush	50.1%	4.0%	44.9%	0.9%
MORGAN	1,899	1,151	63	658	27	G.W. Bush	60.6%	3.3%	34.6%	1.4%
NEW MADRID	911	608	37	256	10	G.W. Bush	66.7%	4.1%	28.1%	1.1%
NEWTON	5,428	3,489	245	1,654	40	G.W. Bush	64.3%	4.5%	30.5%	0.7%
NODAWAY	1,227	734	48	427	18	G.W. Bush	59.8%	3.9%	34.8%	1.5%
OREGON	809	460	57	281	11	G.W. Bush	56.9%	7.0%	34.7%	1.4%
OSAGE	1,470	900	44	517	9	G.W. Bush	61.2%	3.0%	35.2%	0.6%
OZARK	1,230	669	54	495	12	G.W. Bush	54.4%	4.4%	40.2%	1.0%
PEMISCOT	595	413	14	163	5	G.W. Bush	69.4%	2.4%	27.4%	0.8%
PERRY	1,780	1,141	54	566	19	G.W. Bush	64.1%	3.0%	31.8%	1.1%
PETTIS	3,210	2,089	81	1,008	32	G.W. Bush	65.1%	2.5%	31.4%	1.0%
PHELPS	3,807	2,287	210	1,281	29	G.W. Bush	60.1%	5.5%	33.6%	0.8%
PIKE	1,225	662	96	462	5	G.W. Bush	54.0%	7.8%	37.7%	0.4%
PLATTE	5,833	3,030	362	2,377	64	G.W. Bush	51.9%	6.2%	40.8%	1.1%
POLK	2,923	1,727	215	939	42	G.W. Bush	59.1%	7.4%	32.1%	1.4%
PULASKI	2,380	1,433	115	813	19	G.W. Bush	60.2%	4.8%	34.2%	0.8%
PUTNAM	600	433	22	122	23	G.W. Bush	72.2%	3.7%	20.3%	3.8%
RALLS	646	422	34	185	5	G.W. Bush	65.3%	5.3%	28.6%	0.8%
RANDOLPH	1,557	983	65	493	16	G.W. Bush	63.1%	4.2%	31.7%	1.0%
RAY	1,083	614	80	373	16	G.W. Bush	56.7%	7.4%	34.4%	1.5%

MISSOURI REPUBLICAN PRIMARY

2000

County	Total Vote	G.W. Bush	Keyes	McCain	Other	Winner	Percentage of Total Vote			
							G.W. Bush	Keyes	McCain	Other
REYNOLDS	472	276	27	163	6	G.W. Bush	58.5%	5.7%	34.5%	1.3%
RIPLEY	793	536	38	214	5	G.W. Bush	67.6%	4.8%	27.0%	0.6%
ST. CHARLES	29,249	16,881	1,709	10,269	390	G.W. Bush	57.7%	5.8%	35.1%	1.3%
ST. CLAIR	1,245	764	45	418	18	G.W. Bush	61.4%	3.6%	33.6%	1.4%
ST. FRANCOIS	3,163	1,923	152	1,061	27	G.W. Bush	60.8%	4.8%	33.5%	0.9%
ST. LOUIS COUNTY	102,794	56,978	6,059	38,832	925	G.W. Bush	55.4%	5.9%	37.8%	0.9%
ST. LOUIS CITY	13,495	6,109	1,004	6,244	138	McCain	45.3%	7.4%	46.3%	1.0%
STE. GENEVIEVE	928	525	50	329	24	G.W. Bush	56.6%	5.4%	35.5%	2.6%
SALINE	1,487	848	49	579	11	G.W. Bush	57.0%	3.3%	38.9%	0.7%
SCHUYLER	351	238	8	91	14	G.W. Bush	67.8%	2.3%	25.9%	4.0%
SCOTLAND	439	291	26	108	14	G.W. Bush	66.3%	5.9%	24.6%	3.2%
SCOTT	2,918	2,106	66	735	11	G.W. Bush	72.2%	2.3%	25.2%	0.4%
SHANNON	652	335	53	255	9	G.W. Bush	51.4%	8.1%	39.1%	1.4%
SHELBY	551	360	26	155	10	G.W. Bush	65.3%	4.7%	28.1%	1.8%
STODDARD	2,047	1,495	50	492	10	G.W. Bush	73.0%	2.4%	24.0%	0.5%
STONE	3,588	2,118	198	1,248	24	G.W. Bush	59.0%	5.5%	34.8%	0.7%
SULLIVAN	581	401	25	142	13	G.W. Bush	69.0%	4.3%	24.4%	2.2%
TANEY	4,163	2,458	320	1,340	45	G.W. Bush	59.0%	7.7%	32.2%	1.1%
TEXAS	2,427	1,375	151	874	27	G.W. Bush	56.7%	6.2%	36.0%	1.1%
VERNON	1,807	1,078	81	629	19	G.W. Bush	59.7%	4.5%	34.8%	1.1%
WARREN	2,254	1,239	143	850	22	G.W. Bush	55.0%	6.3%	37.7%	1.0%
WASHINGTON	1,214	726	56	420	12	G.W. Bush	59.8%	4.6%	34.6%	1.0%
WAYNE	1,129	778	35	304	12	G.W. Bush	68.9%	3.1%	26.9%	1.1%
WEBSTER	3,208	1,994	213	973	28	G.W. Bush	62.2%	6.6%	30.3%	0.9%
WORTH	264	168	4	89	3	G.W. Bush	63.6%	1.5%	33.7%	1.1%
WRIGHT	2,454	1,578	172	678	26	G.W. Bush	64.3%	7.0%	27.6%	1.1%
TOTAL	475,363	275,366	27,282	167,831	4,884	G.W. Bush	57.9%	5.7%	35.3%	1.0%

Note: Other vote was 2,044 Steve Forbes; 1,345 Uncommitted; 1,038 Gary Bauer; 363 Orrin G. Hatch; 94 Lawrence Hornung.

MISSOURI DEMOCRATIC PRIMARY

2004

County	Total Vote	Dean	Edwards	Kerry	Other	Winner	Percentage of Total Vote			
							Dean	Edwards	Kerry	Other
ADAIR	1,716	218	567	721	210	Kerry	12.7%	33.0%	42.0%	12.2%
ANDREW	738	62	197	406	73	Kerry	8.4%	26.7%	55.0%	9.9%
ATCHISON	311	16	77	177	41	Kerry	5.1%	24.8%	56.9%	13.2%
AUDRAIN	1,405	104	452	700	149	Kerry	7.4%	32.2%	49.8%	10.6%
BARRY	1,777	90	697	762	228	Kerry	5.1%	39.2%	42.9%	12.8%
BARTON	1,250	80	291	579	300	Kerry	6.4%	23.3%	46.3%	24.0%
BATES	1,217	98	352	615	152	Kerry	8.1%	28.9%	50.5%	12.5%
BENTON	1,237	73	438	634	92	Kerry	5.9%	35.4%	51.3%	7.4%
BOLLINGER	510	35	175	249	51	Kerry	6.9%	34.3%	48.8%	10.0%
BOONE	12,974	1,883	3,049	5,756	2,286	Kerry	14.5%	23.5%	44.4%	17.6%
BUCHANAN	11,749	1,119	2,271	5,643	2,716	Kerry	9.5%	19.3%	48.0%	23.1%
BUTLER	1,330	93	418	664	155	Kerry	7.0%	31.4%	49.9%	11.7%
CALDWELL	406	21	137	212	36	Kerry	5.2%	33.7%	52.2%	8.9%
CALLAWAY	2,088	185	728	928	247	Kerry	8.9%	34.9%	44.4%	11.8%
CAMDEN	1,984	169	670	922	223	Kerry	8.5%	33.8%	46.5%	11.2%
CAPE GIRARDEAU	2,820	253	760	1,436	371	Kerry	9.0%	27.0%	50.9%	13.2%
CARROLL	533	41	130	287	75	Kerry	7.7%	24.4%	53.8%	14.1%
CARTER	364	15	99	184	66	Kerry	4.1%	27.2%	50.5%	18.1%
CASS	5,178	428	1,554	2,586	610	Kerry	8.3%	30.0%	49.9%	11.8%
CEDAR	951	65	338	442	106	Kerry	6.8%	35.5%	46.5%	11.1%
CHARITON	715	47	214	360	94	Kerry	6.6%	29.9%	50.3%	13.1%
CHRISTIAN	4,328	271	1,689	1,734	634	Kerry	6.3%	39.0%	40.1%	14.6%
CLARK	494	63	134	258	39	Kerry	12.8%	27.1%	52.2%	7.9%
CLAY	11,141	966	3,040	5,741	1,394	Kerry	8.7%	27.3%	51.5%	12.5%
CLINTON	1,691	119	458	830	284	Kerry	7.0%	27.1%	49.1%	16.8%
COLE	3,921	402	1,304	1,560	655	Kerry	10.3%	33.3%	39.8%	16.7%
COOPER	759	72	203	365	119	Kerry	9.5%	26.7%	48.1%	15.7%
CRAWFORD	887	62	249	495	81	Kerry	7.0%	28.1%	55.8%	9.1%
DADE	481	19	202	213	47	Kerry	4.0%	42.0%	44.3%	9.8%
DALLAS	975	63	405	419	88	Kerry	6.5%	41.5%	43.0%	9.0%
DAVIESS	430	29	128	232	41	Kerry	6.7%	29.8%	54.0%	9.5%
DE KALB	538	42	159	256	81	Kerry	7.8%	29.6%	47.6%	15.1%
DENT	867	45	343	392	87	Kerry	5.2%	39.6%	45.2%	10.0%
DOUGLAS	677	62	252	269	94	Kerry	9.2%	37.2%	39.7%	13.9%
DUNKLIN	1,185	76	288	610	211	Kerry	6.4%	24.3%	51.5%	17.8%
FRANKLIN	6,168	507	1,495	3,533	633	Kerry	8.2%	24.2%	57.3%	10.3%
GASCONADE	664	49	157	368	90	Kerry	7.4%	23.6%	55.4%	13.6%
GENTRY	430	32	128	220	50	Kerry	7.4%	29.8%	51.2%	11.6%
GREENE	21,656	1,594	8,066	9,058	2,938	Kerry	7.4%	37.2%	41.8%	13.6%
GRUNDY	1,278	103	330	591	254	Kerry	8.1%	25.8%	46.2%	19.9%
HARRISON	497	34	135	263	65	Kerry	6.8%	27.2%	52.9%	13.1%
HENRY	1,663	91	497	897	178	Kerry	5.5%	29.9%	53.9%	10.7%
HICKORY	973	47	387	469	70	Kerry	4.8%	39.8%	48.2%	7.2%
HOLT	241	15	69	119	38	Kerry	6.2%	28.6%	49.4%	15.8%
HOWARD	692	70	209	323	90	Kerry	10.1%	30.2%	46.7%	13.0%

MISSOURI DEMOCRATIC PRIMARY

2004

County	Total Vote	Dean	Edwards	Kerry	Other	Winner	Percentage of Total Vote			
							Dean	Edwards	Kerry	Other
HOWELL	1,938	125	642	932	239	Kerry	6.4%	33.1%	48.1%	12.3%
IRON	756	43	215	418	80	Kerry	5.7%	28.4%	55.3%	10.6%
JACKSON	25,840	2,136	6,949	13,225	3,530	Kerry	8.3%	26.9%	51.2%	13.7%
JASPER	3,591	296	949	1,851	495	Kerry	8.2%	26.4%	51.5%	13.8%
JEFFERSON	22,301	1,693	4,787	12,362	3,459	Kerry	7.6%	21.5%	55.4%	15.5%
JOHNSON	2,535	232	739	1,227	337	Kerry	9.2%	29.2%	48.4%	13.3%
KANSAS CITY	26,999	3,043	5,194	14,176	4,586	Kerry	11.3%	19.2%	52.5%	17.0%
KNOX	320	15	144	131	30	Edwards	4.7%	45.0%	40.9%	9.4%
LACLEDE	2,374	129	947	1,030	268	Kerry	5.4%	39.9%	43.4%	11.3%
LAFAYETTE	1,968	158	626	963	221	Kerry	8.0%	31.8%	48.9%	11.2%
LAWRENCE	1,713	112	713	707	181	Edwards	6.5%	41.6%	41.3%	10.6%
LEWIS	689	78	178	344	89	Kerry	11.3%	25.8%	49.9%	12.9%
LINCOLN	2,127	145	523	1,217	242	Kerry	6.8%	24.6%	57.2%	11.4%
LINN	866	78	251	439	98	Kerry	9.0%	29.0%	50.7%	11.3%
LIVINGSTON	753	56	195	406	96	Kerry	7.4%	25.9%	53.9%	12.7%
MCDONALD	996	56	250	483	207	Kerry	5.6%	25.1%	48.5%	20.8%
MACON	990	76	311	483	120	Kerry	7.7%	31.4%	48.8%	12.1%
MADISON	636	39	163	366	68	Kerry	6.1%	25.6%	57.5%	10.7%
MARIES	611	31	213	302	65	Kerry	5.1%	34.9%	49.4%	10.6%
MARION	1,435	103	418	705	209	Kerry	7.2%	29.1%	49.1%	14.6%
MERCER	391	27	128	195	41	Kerry	6.9%	32.7%	49.9%	10.5%
MILLER	1,061	58	381	477	145	Kerry	5.5%	35.9%	45.0%	13.7%
MISSISSIPPI	646	24	176	343	103	Kerry	3.7%	27.2%	53.1%	15.9%
MONITEAU	638	41	235	290	72	Kerry	6.4%	36.8%	45.5%	11.3%
MONROE	518	26	166	253	73	Kerry	5.0%	32.0%	48.8%	14.1%
MONTGOMERY	676	52	230	326	68	Kerry	7.7%	34.0%	48.2%	10.1%
MORGAN	1,010	65	316	512	117	Kerry	6.4%	31.3%	50.7%	11.6%
NEW MADRID	1,052	53	318	518	163	Kerry	5.0%	30.2%	49.2%	15.5%
NEWTON	2,043	173	539	1,028	303	Kerry	8.5%	26.4%	50.3%	14.8%
NODAWAY	864	74	219	452	119	Kerry	8.6%	25.3%	52.3%	13.8%
OREGON	834	55	278	353	148	Kerry	6.6%	33.3%	42.3%	17.7%
OSAGE	609	37	223	286	63	Kerry	6.1%	36.6%	47.0%	10.3%
OZARK	672	42	239	313	78	Kerry	6.3%	35.6%	46.6%	11.6%
PEMISCOT	607	29	152	264	162	Kerry	4.8%	25.0%	43.5%	26.7%
PERRY	700	40	201	378	81	Kerry	5.7%	28.7%	54.0%	11.6%
PETTIS	1,710	122	497	890	201	Kerry	7.1%	29.1%	52.0%	11.8%
PHELPS	2,255	210	644	1,079	322	Kerry	9.3%	28.6%	47.8%	14.3%
PIKE	1,082	79	284	585	134	Kerry	7.3%	26.2%	54.1%	12.4%
PLATTE	4,541	435	1,275	2,278	553	Kerry	9.6%	28.1%	50.2%	12.2%
POLK	1,627	96	596	762	173	Kerry	5.9%	36.6%	46.8%	10.6%
PULASKI	1,378	75	511	577	215	Kerry	5.4%	37.1%	41.9%	15.6%
PUTNAM	263	11	102	122	28	Kerry	4.2%	38.8%	46.4%	10.6%
RALLS	714	63	257	314	80	Kerry	8.8%	36.0%	44.0%	11.2%
RANDOLPH	1,012	61	305	489	157	Kerry	6.0%	30.1%	48.3%	15.5%
RAY	1,503	114	468	771	150	Kerry	7.6%	31.1%	51.3%	10.0%

MISSOURI DEMOCRATIC PRIMARY

2004

County	Total Vote	Dean	Edwards	Kerry	Other	Winner	Percentage of Total Vote			
							Dean	Edwards	Kerry	Other
REYNOLDS	663	34	208	361	60	Kerry	5.1%	31.4%	54.4%	9.0%
RIPLEY	1,359	108	296	645	310	Kerry	7.9%	21.8%	47.5%	22.8%
ST. CHARLES	20,596	1,597	4,748	11,753	2,498	Kerry	7.8%	23.1%	57.1%	12.1%
ST. CLAIR	850	51	339	366	94	Kerry	6.0%	39.9%	43.1%	11.1%
ST. FRANCOIS	2,906	187	709	1,715	295	Kerry	6.4%	24.4%	59.0%	10.2%
ST. LOUIS COUNTY	94,097	9,017	17,587	50,433	17,060	Kerry	9.6%	18.7%	53.6%	18.1%
ST. LOUIS CITY	32,117	3,035	4,274	15,929	8,879	Kerry	9.4%	13.3%	49.6%	27.6%
STE. GENEVIEVE	1,059	48	228	668	115	Kerry	4.5%	21.5%	63.1%	10.9%
SALINE	1,613	177	508	734	194	Kerry	11.0%	31.5%	45.5%	12.0%
SCHUYLER	359	31	136	172	20	Kerry	8.6%	37.9%	47.9%	5.6%
SCOTLAND	347	39	114	152	42	Kerry	11.2%	32.9%	43.8%	12.1%
SCOTT	2,623	205	697	1,177	544	Kerry	7.8%	26.6%	44.9%	20.7%
SHANNON	740	30	287	327	96	Kerry	4.1%	38.8%	44.2%	13.0%
SHELBY	540	31	169	259	81	Kerry	5.7%	31.3%	48.0%	15.0%
STODDARD	1,382	92	434	665	191	Kerry	6.7%	31.4%	48.1%	13.8%
STONE	1,790	105	706	809	170	Kerry	5.9%	39.4%	45.2%	9.5%
SULLIVAN	404	33	114	212	45	Kerry	8.2%	28.2%	52.5%	11.1%
TANEY	2,169	132	754	1,016	267	Kerry	6.1%	34.8%	46.8%	12.3%
TEXAS	1,986	115	763	853	255	Kerry	5.8%	38.4%	43.0%	12.8%
VERNON	1,452	150	389	687	226	Kerry	10.3%	26.8%	47.3%	15.6%
WARREN	1,383	89	361	797	136	Kerry	6.4%	26.1%	57.6%	9.8%
WASHINGTON	1,164	62	291	699	112	Kerry	5.3%	25.0%	60.1%	9.6%
WAYNE	976	47	320	480	129	Kerry	4.8%	32.8%	49.2%	13.2%
WEBSTER	2,202	121	897	950	234	Kerry	5.5%	40.7%	43.1%	10.6%
WORTH	199	17	41	99	42	Kerry	8.5%	20.6%	49.7%	21.1%
WRIGHT	1,630	101	630	687	212	Kerry	6.2%	38.7%	42.1%	13.0%
TOTAL	418,339	36,288	103,088	211,745	67,218	Kerry	8.7%	24.6%	50.6%	16.1%

Note: Other vote was 18,340 Wesley Clark; 14,727 Joseph I. Lieberman; 14,308 Al Sharpton; 8,281 Richard A. Gephardt; 4,875 Dennis J. Kucinich; 4,311 Uncommitted; 1,088 Carol Moseley Braun; 953 Lyndon H. LaRouche Jr.; 335 Fern Penna.

MISSOURI REPUBLICAN PRIMARY

2004

| County | Total Vote | G.W. Bush | Other | Winner | Percentage of Total Vote | |
					G.W. Bush	Other
ADAIR	504	478	26	G.W. Bush	94.8%	5.2%
ANDREW	343	328	15	G.W. Bush	95.6%	4.4%
ATCHISON	143	139	4	G.W. Bush	97.2%	2.8%
AUDRAIN	241	234	7	G.W. Bush	97.1%	2.9%
BARRY	962	928	34	G.W. Bush	96.5%	3.5%
BARTON	1,565	1,487	78	G.W. Bush	95.0%	5.0%
BATES	341	329	12	G.W. Bush	96.5%	3.5%
BENTON	451	436	15	G.W. Bush	96.7%	3.3%
BOLLINGER	244	235	9	G.W. Bush	96.3%	3.7%
BOONE	2,596	2,491	105	G.W. Bush	96.0%	4.0%
BUCHANAN	4,219	3,886	333	G.W. Bush	92.1%	7.9%
BUTLER	370	361	9	G.W. Bush	97.6%	2.4%
CALDWELL	120	117	3	G.W. Bush	97.5%	2.5%
CALLAWAY	374	362	12	G.W. Bush	96.8%	3.2%
CAMDEN	752	707	45	G.W. Bush	94.0%	6.0%
CAPE GIRARDEAU	863	824	39	G.W. Bush	95.5%	4.5%
CARROLL	255	242	13	G.W. Bush	94.9%	5.1%
CARTER	77	74	3	G.W. Bush	96.1%	3.9%
CASS	967	924	43	G.W. Bush	95.6%	4.4%
CEDAR	445	418	27	G.W. Bush	93.9%	6.1%
CHARITON	153	149	4	G.W. Bush	97.4%	2.6%
CHRISTIAN	3,411	3,234	177	G.W. Bush	94.8%	5.2%
CLARK	86	79	7	G.W. Bush	91.9%	8.1%
CLAY	1,593	1,487	106	G.W. Bush	93.3%	6.7%
CLINTON	438	409	29	G.W. Bush	93.4%	6.6%
COLE	884	858	26	G.W. Bush	97.1%	2.9%
COOPER	230	218	12	G.W. Bush	94.8%	5.2%
CRAWFORD	300	279	21	G.W. Bush	93.0%	7.0%
DADE	415	400	15	G.W. Bush	96.4%	3.6%
DALLAS	468	447	21	G.W. Bush	95.5%	4.5%
DAVIESS	156	145	11	G.W. Bush	92.9%	7.1%
DE KALB	182	174	8	G.W. Bush	95.6%	4.4%
DENT	223	219	4	G.W. Bush	98.2%	1.8%
DOUGLAS	466	445	21	G.W. Bush	95.5%	4.5%
DUNKLIN	197	189	8	G.W. Bush	95.9%	4.1%
FRANKLIN	2,099	1,998	101	G.W. Bush	95.2%	4.8%
GASCONADE	324	302	22	G.W. Bush	93.2%	6.8%
GENTRY	143	136	7	G.W. Bush	95.1%	4.9%
GREENE	12,207	11,768	439	G.W. Bush	96.4%	3.6%
GRUNDY	1,120	998	122	G.W. Bush	89.1%	10.9%
HARRISON	242	219	23	G.W. Bush	90.5%	9.5%
HENRY	344	328	16	G.W. Bush	95.3%	4.7%
HICKORY	355	342	13	G.W. Bush	96.3%	3.7%
HOLT	163	152	11	G.W. Bush	93.3%	6.7%
HOWARD	106	106	0	G.W. Bush	100.0%	0.0%

MISSOURI REPUBLICAN PRIMARY

2004

County	Total Vote	G.W. Bush	Other	Winner	Percentage of Total Vote	
					G.W. Bush	Other
HOWELL	780	751	29	G.W. Bush	96.3%	3.7%
IRON	116	111	5	G.W. Bush	95.7%	4.3%
JACKSON	6,522	6,170	352	G.W. Bush	94.6%	5.4%
JASPER	1,734	1,665	69	G.W. Bush	96.0%	4.0%
JEFFERSON	7,647	7,177	470	G.W. Bush	93.9%	6.1%
JOHNSON	937	893	44	G.W. Bush	95.3%	4.7%
KANSAS CITY	2,058	1,915	143	G.W. Bush	93.1%	6.9%
KNOX	57	56	1	G.W. Bush	98.2%	1.8%
LACLEDE	2,060	1,963	97	G.W. Bush	95.3%	4.7%
LAFAYETTE	509	494	15	G.W. Bush	97.1%	2.9%
LAWRENCE	933	887	46	G.W. Bush	95.1%	4.9%
LEWIS	136	132	4	G.W. Bush	97.1%	2.9%
LINCOLN	366	357	9	G.W. Bush	97.5%	2.5%
LINN	183	176	7	G.W. Bush	96.2%	3.8%
LIVINGSTON	168	164	4	G.W. Bush	97.6%	2.4%
MCDONALD	743	693	50	G.W. Bush	93.3%	6.7%
MACON	208	200	8	G.W. Bush	96.2%	3.8%
MADISON	158	150	8	G.W. Bush	94.9%	5.1%
MARIES	158	153	5	G.W. Bush	96.8%	3.2%
MARION	270	261	9	G.W. Bush	96.7%	3.3%
MERCER	292	273	19	G.W. Bush	93.5%	6.5%
MILLER	1,134	1,077	57	G.W. Bush	95.0%	5.0%
MISSISSIPPI	118	113	5	G.W. Bush	95.8%	4.2%
MONITEAU	257	247	10	G.W. Bush	96.1%	3.9%
MONROE	81	79	2	G.W. Bush	97.5%	2.5%
MONTGOMERY	219	208	11	G.W. Bush	95.0%	5.0%
MORGAN	380	365	15	G.W. Bush	96.1%	3.9%
NEW MADRID	175	170	5	G.W. Bush	97.1%	2.9%
NEWTON	958	924	34	G.W. Bush	96.5%	3.5%
NODAWAY	222	205	17	G.W. Bush	92.3%	7.7%
OREGON	174	169	5	G.W. Bush	97.1%	2.9%
OSAGE	291	284	7	G.W. Bush	97.6%	2.4%
OZARK	334	311	23	G.W. Bush	93.1%	6.9%
PEMISCOT	75	74	1	G.W. Bush	98.7%	1.3%
PERRY	320	307	13	G.W. Bush	95.9%	4.1%
PETTIS	591	563	28	G.W. Bush	95.3%	4.7%
PHELPS	644	620	24	G.W. Bush	96.3%	3.7%
PIKE	162	149	13	G.W. Bush	92.0%	8.0%
PLATTE	608	570	38	G.W. Bush	93.8%	6.3%
POLK	753	722	31	G.W. Bush	95.9%	4.1%
PULASKI	539	517	22	G.W. Bush	95.9%	4.1%
PUTNAM	149	140	9	G.W. Bush	94.0%	6.0%
RALLS	76	74	2	G.W. Bush	97.4%	2.6%
RANDOLPH	182	178	4	G.W. Bush	97.8%	2.2%
RAY	135	127	8	G.W. Bush	94.1%	5.9%

MISSOURI REPUBLICAN PRIMARY

2004

County	Total Vote	G.W. Bush	Other	Winner	Percentage of Total Vote	
					G.W. Bush	Other
REYNOLDS	84	84	0	G.W. Bush	100.0%	0.0%
RIPLEY	804	775	29	G.W. Bush	96.4%	3.6%
ST. CHARLES	6,879	6,612	267	G.W. Bush	96.1%	3.9%
ST. CLAIR	361	351	10	G.W. Bush	97.2%	2.8%
ST. FRANCOIS	533	494	39	G.W. Bush	92.7%	7.3%
ST. LOUIS COUNTY	25,750	24,415	1,335	G.W. Bush	94.8%	5.2%
ST. LOUIS CITY	2,065	1,902	163	G.W. Bush	92.1%	7.9%
STE. GENEVIEVE	139	127	12	G.W. Bush	91.4%	8.6%
SALINE	231	218	13	G.W. Bush	94.4%	5.6%
SCHUYLER	80	73	7	G.W. Bush	91.3%	8.8%
SCOTLAND	75	70	5	G.W. Bush	93.3%	6.7%
SCOTT	1,097	1,066	31	G.W. Bush	97.2%	2.8%
SHANNON	154	144	10	G.W. Bush	93.5%	6.5%
SHELBY	149	148	1	G.W. Bush	99.3%	0.7%
STODDARD	285	282	3	G.W. Bush	98.9%	1.1%
STONE	965	926	39	G.W. Bush	96.0%	4.0%
SULLIVAN	158	146	12	G.W. Bush	92.4%	7.6%
TANEY	1,294	1,241	53	G.W. Bush	95.9%	4.1%
TEXAS	741	701	40	G.W. Bush	94.6%	5.4%
VERNON	416	404	12	G.W. Bush	97.1%	2.9%
WARREN	384	369	15	G.W. Bush	96.1%	3.9%
WASHINGTON	230	220	10	G.W. Bush	95.7%	4.3%
WAYNE	319	314	5	G.W. Bush	98.4%	1.6%
WEBSTER	1,117	1,080	37	G.W. Bush	96.7%	3.3%
WORTH	68	64	4	G.W. Bush	94.1%	5.9%
WRIGHT	1,959	1,866	93	G.W. Bush	95.3%	4.7%
TOTAL	123,086	117,007	6,079	G.W. Bush	95.1%	4.9%

Note: Other vote was 3,830 Uncommitted; 1,268 Bill Wyatt; 981 Blake Ashby.

MONTANA

Since its inception, Montana's presidential primary has been an afterthought to an afterthought. It has often been the least populous state to vote on the last big day of the primary season.

The only presidential candidate in recent times to make a significant effort in Montana was Frank Church of neighboring Idaho. His 10 visits in 1976 earned him nearly 60 percent of the Democratic primary vote and victory over Jimmy Carter. Carter followed the norm of most candidates: he did not visit the state at all.

The last time a Republican presidential contest seriously involved Montana was that same year, when Ronald Reagan and President Gerald Ford were nearing the end of their long-running battle for the nomination. Reagan won the Montana primary with 63 percent of the vote, then swept all the delegates (traditionally chosen separately at the GOP state convention).

Generally, a libertarian rather than moralistic strain of Republicanism is dominant in Montana. President George Bush won the primary easily in 1992, with Pat Buchanan running a distant third behind the "no preference" line. Buchanan managed to beat the "no preference" line in 1996, but still trailed Bob Dole by a wide margin.

The last Democratic presidential primary in Montana with much significance came in 1980, when President Carter defeated Edward Kennedy, 51 to 37 percent. While Carter carried most of the state, including its leading population centers, Kennedy took the Native American counties of Big Horn

Recent Montana Primary Results

Montana held its first presidential primary in 1916, but only one between 1924 and 1976, that in 1956.

	DEMOCRATS				REPUBLICANS		
Year	Turnout	Candidates	%	Turnout	Candidates	%
2004 (June 8)	93,543	JOHN KERRY	68	112,748	GEORGE W. BUSH*	94
		Dennis Kucinich	10		No Preference	6
		John Edwards	9			
		No Preference	7			
2000 (June 6)	87,867	AL GORE	78	113,671	GEORGE W. BUSH	78
		No Preference	22		Alan Keyes	18
1996 (June 4)	91,725	BILL CLINTON*	90	117,746	BOB DOLE	61
		No Preference	10		Pat Buchanan	24
					No Preference	7
					Steve Forbes	7
1992 (June 2)	117,471	BILL CLINTON	47	90,975	GEORGE BUSH*	72
		No Preference	24		No Preference	17
		Jerry Brown	18		Pat Buchanan	12
		Paul Tsongas	11			
1988 (June 7)	121,871	MICHAEL DUKAKIS	69	86,380	GEORGE BUSH	73
		Jesse Jackson	22		Bob Dole	19
					No Preference	8
1984 (June 5)	34,214	NO PREFERENCE	83	71,887	RONALD REAGAN*	92
		Gary Hart#	9		No Preference	7
		Walter Mondale#	6			
1980 (June 3)	130,059	JIMMY CARTER*	51	79,423	RONALD REAGAN	87
		Edward Kennedy	37		George Bush	10
		No Preference	12			
1976 (June 1)	106,841	FRANK CHURCH	59	89,779	RONALD REAGAN	63
		Jimmy Carter	25		Gerald Ford*	35
		Morris Udall	6			

Note: All candidates are listed that drew at least 5 percent of their party's primary vote. The names of winning candidates are capitalized. An asterisk (*) indicates an incumbent president. A pound sign (#) indicates a write-in candidate.

and Glacier and a number of politically volatile wheat-growing counties in northeast Montana, where farmers were unhappy with the Carter administration's grain embargo.

Conspicuously, though, Kennedy failed to win in the Democratic counties of western Montana, such as Deer Lodge (Anaconda) and Silver Bow (Butte), where there is a large ethnic population and a strong union tradition built around the copper mines. Silver Bow is among the largest source of votes in a Democratic primary, even though it is not one of Montana's more populous counties.

Bill Clinton scored a lackluster win in Democratic voting in 1992, the party's last presidential primary that was even vaguely competitive. Even though Clinton was already the apparent

nominee, he drew less than a majority of the primary vote. He was ambushed by the "no preference" forces in rural Treasure County, which is in the vicinity of the Little Bighorn battlefield.

While Montana's late primary makes little difference in the nominating race, it does allow indefatigable dark horse candidates a chance to make one last bid for attention. In 2000, Alan Keyes drew 18 percent of the Republican primary vote in Montana, approaching one-quarter of the vote in the counties that include the college towns of Bozeman and Missoula as well as the state capital of Helena. In 2004, Dennis Kucinich polled 10 percent of the Democratic primary vote, taking nearly 25 percent in Missoula County (the home of the University of Montana).

MONTANA DEMOCRATIC PRIMARY

2000

County	Total Vote	Gore	No Preference	Winner	Percentage of Total Vote Gore	No Preference
BEAVERHEAD	390	329	61	Gore	84.4%	15.6%
BIG HORN	912	753	159	Gore	82.6%	17.4%
BLAINE	605	476	129	Gore	78.7%	21.3%
BROADWATER	398	262	136	Gore	65.8%	34.2%
CARBON	873	685	188	Gore	78.5%	21.5%
CARTER	51	37	14	Gore	72.5%	27.5%
CASCADE	8,756	6,770	1,986	Gore	77.3%	22.7%
CHOUTEAU	434	327	107	Gore	75.3%	24.7%
CUSTER	1,046	824	222	Gore	78.8%	21.2%
DANIELS	133	120	13	Gore	90.2%	9.8%
DAWSON	762	627	135	Gore	82.3%	17.7%
DEER LODGE	2,666	2,160	506	Gore	81.0%	19.0%
FALLON	207	139	68	Gore	67.1%	32.9%
FERGUS	1,052	784	268	Gore	74.5%	25.5%
FLATHEAD	4,745	3,507	1,238	Gore	73.9%	26.1%
GALLATIN	3,607	2,984	623	Gore	82.7%	17.3%
GARFIELD	51	26	25	Gore	51.0%	49.0%
GLACIER	1,598	1,153	445	Gore	72.2%	27.8%
GOLDEN VALLEY	66	46	20	Gore	69.7%	30.3%
GRANITE	201	133	68	Gore	66.2%	33.8%
HILL	2,122	1,646	476	Gore	77.6%	22.4%
JEFFERSON	1,334	905	429	Gore	67.8%	32.2%
JUDITH BASIN	237	173	64	Gore	73.0%	27.0%
LAKE	1,788	1,456	332	Gore	81.4%	18.6%
LEWIS AND CLARK	9,677	7,082	2,595	Gore	73.2%	26.8%
LIBERTY	197	133	64	Gore	67.5%	32.5%
LINCOLN	1,145	752	393	Gore	65.7%	34.3%
MCCONE	194	153	41	Gore	78.9%	21.1%
MADISON	471	361	110	Gore	76.6%	23.4%
MEAGHER	117	85	32	Gore	72.6%	27.4%
MINERAL	434	234	200	Gore	53.9%	46.1%
MISSOULA	11,115	8,750	2,365	Gore	78.7%	21.3%
MUSSELSHELL	336	276	60	Gore	82.1%	17.9%
PARK	1,114	889	225	Gore	79.8%	20.2%
PETROLEUM	28	23	5	Gore	82.1%	17.9%
PHILLIPS	202	158	44	Gore	78.2%	21.8%
PONDERA	757	544	213	Gore	71.9%	28.1%
POWDER RIVER	46	42	4	Gore	91.3%	8.7%
POWELL	516	367	149	Gore	71.1%	28.9%
PRAIRIE	108	95	13	Gore	88.0%	12.0%
RAVALLI	2,416	1,971	445	Gore	81.6%	18.4%
RICHLAND	690	501	189	Gore	72.6%	27.4%
ROOSEVELT	901	667	234	Gore	74.0%	26.0%
ROSEBUD	680	532	148	Gore	78.2%	21.8%
SANDERS	880	632	248	Gore	71.8%	28.2%

MONTANA DEMOCRATIC PRIMARY

2000

County	Total Vote	Gore	No Preference	Winner	Percentage of Total Vote	
					Gore	No Preference
SHERIDAN	445	348	97	Gore	78.2%	21.8%
SILVER BOW	8,591	7,037	1,554	Gore	81.9%	18.1%
STILLWATER	614	498	116	Gore	81.1%	18.9%
SWEET GRASS	154	117	37	Gore	76.0%	24.0%
TETON	560	473	87	Gore	84.5%	15.5%
TOOLE	480	370	110	Gore	77.1%	22.9%
TREASURE	88	59	29	Gore	67.0%	33.0%
VALLEY	863	648	215	Gore	75.1%	24.9%
WHEATLAND	132	126	6	Gore	95.5%	4.5%
WIBAUX	121	73	48	Gore	60.3%	39.7%
YELLOWSTONE	9,761	8,102	1,659	Gore	83.0%	17.0%
TOTAL	87,867	68,420	19,447	Gore	77.9%	22.1%

MONTANA REPUBLICAN PRIMARY

2000

County	Total Vote	G.W. Bush	Keyes	Other	Winner	Percentage of Total Vote		
						G.W. Bush	Keyes	Other
BEAVERHEAD	2,041	1,757	192	92	G.W. Bush	86.1%	9.4%	4.5%
BIG HORN	825	685	105	35	G.W. Bush	83.0%	12.7%	4.2%
BLAINE	649	553	80	16	G.W. Bush	85.2%	12.3%	2.5%
BROADWATER	775	588	155	32	G.W. Bush	75.9%	20.0%	4.1%
CARBON	1,450	1,182	212	56	G.W. Bush	81.5%	14.6%	3.9%
CARTER	457	380	61	16	G.W. Bush	83.2%	13.3%	3.5%
CASCADE	7,703	6,209	1,180	314	G.W. Bush	80.6%	15.3%	4.1%
CHOUTEAU	1,436	1,153	190	93	G.W. Bush	80.3%	13.2%	6.5%
CUSTER	1,508	1,299	153	56	G.W. Bush	86.1%	10.1%	3.7%
DANIELS	509	411	84	14	G.W. Bush	80.7%	16.5%	2.8%
DAWSON	1,516	1,157	272	87	G.W. Bush	76.3%	17.9%	5.7%
DEER LODGE	665	520	89	56	G.W. Bush	78.2%	13.4%	8.4%
FALLON	641	531	84	26	G.W. Bush	82.8%	13.1%	4.1%
FERGUS	2,750	2,238	409	103	G.W. Bush	81.4%	14.9%	3.7%
FLATHEAD	10,642	7,760	2,393	489	G.W. Bush	72.9%	22.5%	4.6%
GALLATIN	7,313	5,262	1,793	258	G.W. Bush	72.0%	24.5%	3.5%
GARFIELD	409	373	31	5	G.W. Bush	91.2%	7.6%	1.2%
GLACIER	618	511	77	30	G.W. Bush	82.7%	12.5%	4.9%
GOLDEN VALLEY	244	207	34	3	G.W. Bush	84.8%	13.9%	1.2%
GRANITE	711	528	128	55	G.W. Bush	74.3%	18.0%	7.7%
HILL	1,355	1,119	174	62	G.W. Bush	82.6%	12.8%	4.6%
JEFFERSON	1,656	1,183	416	57	G.W. Bush	71.4%	25.1%	3.4%
JUDITH BASIN	604	512	66	26	G.W. Bush	84.8%	10.9%	4.3%
LAKE	3,860	2,586	1,069	205	G.W. Bush	67.0%	27.7%	5.3%
LEWIS AND CLARK	5,966	4,369	1,486	111	G.W. Bush	73.2%	24.9%	1.9%

MONTANA REPUBLICAN PRIMARY

2000

County	Total Vote	G.W. Bush	Keyes	Other	Winner	Percentage of Total Vote		
						G.W. Bush	Keyes	Other
LIBERTY	515	427	68	20	G.W. Bush	82.9%	13.2%	3.9%
LINCOLN	2,461	1,992	394	75	G.W. Bush	80.9%	16.0%	3.0%
MCCONE	437	368	59	10	G.W. Bush	84.2%	13.5%	2.3%
MADISON	1,517	1,240	204	73	G.W. Bush	81.7%	13.4%	4.8%
MEAGHER	386	323	47	16	G.W. Bush	83.7%	12.2%	4.1%
MINERAL	397	295	83	19	G.W. Bush	74.3%	20.9%	4.8%
MISSOULA	8,557	6,166	2,106	285	G.W. Bush	72.1%	24.6%	3.3%
MUSSELSHELL	1,099	927	130	42	G.W. Bush	84.3%	11.8%	3.8%
PARK	2,198	1,705	417	76	G.W. Bush	77.6%	19.0%	3.5%
PETROLEUM	134	111	22	1	G.W. Bush	82.8%	16.4%	0.7%
PHILLIPS	1,209	1,011	135	63	G.W. Bush	83.6%	11.2%	5.2%
PONDERA	1,067	887	142	38	G.W. Bush	83.1%	13.3%	3.6%
POWDER RIVER	573	480	67	26	G.W. Bush	83.8%	11.7%	4.5%
POWELL	1,037	807	179	51	G.W. Bush	77.8%	17.3%	4.9%
PRAIRIE	427	356	57	14	G.W. Bush	83.4%	13.3%	3.3%
RAVALLI	7,054	5,044	1,570	440	G.W. Bush	71.5%	22.3%	6.2%
RICHLAND	1,217	989	163	65	G.W. Bush	81.3%	13.4%	5.3%
ROOSEVELT	610	489	98	23	G.W. Bush	80.2%	16.1%	3.8%
ROSEBUD	734	617	88	29	G.W. Bush	84.1%	12.0%	4.0%
SANDERS	1,450	1,134	267	49	G.W. Bush	78.2%	18.4%	3.4%
SHERIDAN	523	462	43	18	G.W. Bush	88.3%	8.2%	3.4%
SILVER BOW	3,027	2,344	487	196	G.W. Bush	77.4%	16.1%	6.5%
STILLWATER	1,370	1,137	185	48	G.W. Bush	83.0%	13.5%	3.5%
SWEET GRASS	915	780	94	41	G.W. Bush	85.2%	10.3%	4.5%
TETON	1,475	1,195	230	50	G.W. Bush	81.0%	15.6%	3.4%
TOOLE	1,010	811	138	61	G.W. Bush	80.3%	13.7%	6.0%
TREASURE	180	154	22	4	G.W. Bush	85.6%	12.2%	2.2%
VALLEY	1,490	1,193	217	80	G.W. Bush	80.1%	14.6%	5.4%
WHEATLAND	398	345	51	2	G.W. Bush	86.7%	12.8%	0.5%
WIBAUX	169	134	22	13	G.W. Bush	79.3%	13.0%	7.7%
YELLOWSTONE	13,734	11,198	2,104	432	G.W. Bush	81.5%	15.3%	3.1%
TOTAL	113,673	88,194	20,822	4,657	G.W. Bush	77.6%	18.3%	4.1%

Note: Other vote was 4,655 No Preference; 2 John McCain (write-in).

MONTANA DEMOCRATIC PRIMARY

2004

County	Total Vote	Edwards	Kerry	Kucinich	No Preference	Other	Winner	Percentage of Total Vote				
								Edwards	Kerry	Kucinich	No Preference	Other
BEAVERHEAD	494	35	348	66	16	29	Kerry	7.1%	70.4%	13.4%	3.2%	5.9%
BIG HORN	643	66	464	31	35	47	Kerry	10.3%	72.2%	4.8%	5.4%	7.3%
BLAINE	815	82	502	69	106	56	Kerry	10.1%	61.6%	8.5%	13.0%	6.9%
BROADWATER	324	34	217	20	29	24	Kerry	10.5%	67.0%	6.2%	9.0%	7.4%
CARBON	931	87	705	50	50	39	Kerry	9.3%	75.7%	5.4%	5.4%	4.2%
CARTER	54	3	44	4	2	1	Kerry	5.6%	81.5%	7.4%	3.7%	1.9%
CASCADE	12,458	1,407	7,568	801	1,812	870	Kerry	11.3%	60.7%	6.4%	14.5%	7.0%
CHOUTEAU	398	37	308	25	0	28	Kerry	9.3%	77.4%	6.3%	0.0%	7.0%
CUSTER	1,080	111	835	33	62	39	Kerry	10.3%	77.3%	3.1%	5.7%	3.6%
DANIELS	131	10	107	1	4	9	Kerry	7.6%	81.7%	0.8%	3.1%	6.9%
DAWSON	703	53	563	14	52	21	Kerry	7.5%	80.1%	2.0%	7.4%	3.0%
DEER LODGE	2,595	175	1,856	205	239	120	Kerry	6.7%	71.5%	7.9%	9.2%	4.6%
FALLON	186	20	133	1	18	14	Kerry	10.8%	71.5%	0.5%	9.7%	7.5%
FERGUS	1,093	110	764	56	120	43	Kerry	10.1%	69.9%	5.1%	11.0%	3.9%
FLATHEAD	3,863	322	2,632	478	264	167	Kerry	8.3%	68.1%	12.4%	6.8%	4.3%
GALLATIN	5,479	476	3,454	1,082	261	206	Kerry	8.7%	63.0%	19.7%	4.8%	3.8%
GARFIELD	24	5	15	0	1	3	Kerry	20.8%	62.5%	0.0%	4.2%	12.5%
GLACIER	1,640	168	1,099	127	143	103	Kerry	10.2%	67.0%	7.7%	8.7%	6.3%
GOLDEN VALLEY	82	9	60	4	0	9	Kerry	11.0%	73.2%	4.9%	0.0%	11.0%
GRANITE	172	16	104	29	13	10	Kerry	9.3%	60.5%	16.9%	7.6%	5.8%
HILL	2,231	279	1,377	134	326	115	Kerry	12.5%	61.7%	6.0%	14.6%	5.2%
JEFFERSON	1,289	106	850	157	96	80	Kerry	8.2%	65.9%	12.2%	7.4%	6.2%
JUDITH BASIN	250	41	175	16	0	18	Kerry	16.4%	70.0%	6.4%	0.0%	7.2%
LAKE	1,986	140	1,284	391	86	85	Kerry	7.0%	64.7%	19.7%	4.3%	4.3%
LEWIS AND CLARK	7,965	722	5,376	811	495	561	Kerry	9.1%	67.5%	10.2%	6.2%	7.0%
LIBERTY	219	26	129	15	21	28	Kerry	11.9%	58.9%	6.8%	9.6%	12.8%
LINCOLN	1,161	120	774	78	108	81	Kerry	10.3%	66.7%	6.7%	9.3%	7.0%
MCCONE	201	18	150	5	10	18	Kerry	9.0%	74.6%	2.5%	5.0%	9.0%
MADISON	496	48	340	54	30	24	Kerry	9.7%	68.5%	10.9%	6.0%	4.8%
MEAGHER	139	16	101	5	9	8	Kerry	11.5%	72.7%	3.6%	6.5%	5.8%
MINERAL	330	30	209	42	32	17	Kerry	9.1%	63.3%	12.7%	9.7%	5.2%
MISSOULA	10,241	808	6,622	2,393	0	418	Kerry	7.9%	64.7%	23.4%	0.0%	4.1%
MUSSELSHELL	291	33	209	10	21	18	Kerry	11.3%	71.8%	3.4%	7.2%	6.2%
PARK	1,583	130	1,160	118	98	77	Kerry	8.2%	73.3%	7.5%	6.2%	4.9%
PETROLEUM	34	8	23	0	0	3	Kerry	23.5%	67.6%	0.0%	0.0%	8.8%
PHILLIPS	197	15	144	9	16	13	Kerry	7.6%	73.1%	4.6%	8.1%	6.6%
PONDERA	525	46	369	34	44	32	Kerry	8.8%	70.3%	6.5%	8.4%	6.1%
POWDER RIVER	46	7	30	2	4	3	Kerry	15.2%	65.2%	4.3%	8.7%	6.5%
POWELL	473	44	310	42	43	34	Kerry	9.3%	65.5%	8.9%	9.1%	7.2%
PRAIRIE	106	16	84	2	0	4	Kerry	15.1%	79.2%	1.9%	0.0%	3.8%
RAVALLI	2,698	230	1,757	454	141	116	Kerry	8.5%	65.1%	16.8%	5.2%	4.3%
RICHLAND	807	93	546	13	94	61	Kerry	11.5%	67.7%	1.6%	11.6%	7.6%
ROOSEVELT	1,014	92	687	45	119	71	Kerry	9.1%	67.8%	4.4%	11.7%	7.0%
ROSEBUD	849	68	620	52	60	49	Kerry	8.0%	73.0%	6.1%	7.1%	5.8%
SANDERS	1,088	99	624	123	148	94	Kerry	9.1%	57.4%	11.3%	13.6%	8.6%

MONTANA DEMOCRATIC PRIMARY

2004

| County | Total Vote | Edwards | Kerry | Kucinich | No Preference | Other | Winner | Percentage of Total Vote | | | | |
								Edwards	Kerry	Kucinich	No Preference	Other
SHERIDAN	380	27	307	8	20	18	Kerry	7.1%	80.8%	2.1%	5.3%	4.7%
SILVER BOW	8,652	620	5,978	946	742	366	Kerry	7.2%	69.1%	10.9%	8.6%	4.2%
STILLWATER	525	67	379	19	43	17	Kerry	12.8%	72.2%	3.6%	8.2%	3.2%
SWEET GRASS	235	45	159	14	10	7	Kerry	19.1%	67.7%	6.0%	4.3%	3.0%
TETON	722	98	516	44	5	59	Kerry	13.6%	71.5%	6.1%	0.7%	8.2%
TOOLE	425	37	315	14	36	23	Kerry	8.7%	74.1%	3.3%	8.5%	5.4%
TREASURE	50	5	37	2	0	6	Kerry	10.0%	74.0%	4.0%	0.0%	12.0%
VALLEY	676	47	528	15	54	32	Kerry	7.0%	78.1%	2.2%	8.0%	4.7%
WHEATLAND	121	13	93	5	2	8	Kerry	10.7%	76.9%	4.1%	1.7%	6.6%
WIBAUX	68	8	47	1	9	3	Kerry	11.8%	69.1%	1.5%	13.2%	4.4%
YELLOWSTONE	12,305	1,088	9,524	517	750	426	Kerry	8.8%	77.4%	4.2%	6.1%	3.5%
TOTAL	93,543	8,516	63,611	9,686	6,899	4,831	Kerry	9.1%	68.0%	10.4%	7.4%	5.2%

Note: Other vote was 4,081 Wesley Clark; 750 Lyndon H. LaRouche Jr.

MONTANA REPUBLICAN PRIMARY

2004

| County | Total Vote | G.W. Bush | No Preference | Other | Winner | Percentage of Total Vote | | |
						G.W. Bush	No Preference	Other
BEAVERHEAD	1,355	1,304	51	0	G.W. Bush	96.2%	3.8%	0.0%
BIG HORN	663	630	33	0	G.W. Bush	95.0%	5.0%	0.0%
BLAINE	488	475	13	0	G.W. Bush	97.3%	2.7%	0.0%
BROADWATER	826	798	28	0	G.W. Bush	96.6%	3.4%	0.0%
CARBON	1,381	1,299	82	0	G.W. Bush	94.1%	5.9%	0.0%
CARTER	379	374	5	0	G.W. Bush	98.7%	1.3%	0.0%
CASCADE	5,464	5,232	232	0	G.W. Bush	95.8%	4.2%	0.0%
CHOUTEAU	1,250	1,250	0	0	G.W. Bush	100.0%	0.0%	0.0%
CUSTER	1,755	1,641	114	0	G.W. Bush	93.5%	6.5%	0.0%
DANIELS	336	330	6	0	G.W. Bush	98.2%	1.8%	0.0%
DAWSON	1,925	1,693	232	0	G.W. Bush	87.9%	12.1%	0.0%
DEER LODGE	752	698	54	0	G.W. Bush	92.8%	7.2%	0.0%
FALLON	586	554	32	0	G.W. Bush	94.5%	5.5%	0.0%
FERGUS	2,968	2,769	199	0	G.W. Bush	93.3%	6.7%	0.0%
FLATHEAD	11,775	10,723	1,051	1	G.W. Bush	91.1%	8.9%	0.0%
GALLATIN	7,424	7,034	390	0	G.W. Bush	94.7%	5.3%	0.0%
GARFIELD	446	417	29	0	G.W. Bush	93.5%	6.5%	0.0%
GLACIER	905	865	40	0	G.W. Bush	95.6%	4.4%	0.0%
GOLDEN VALLEY	202	198	4	0	G.W. Bush	98.0%	2.0%	0.0%
GRANITE	756	678	78	0	G.W. Bush	89.7%	10.3%	0.0%
HILL	1,018	978	40	0	G.W. Bush	96.1%	3.9%	0.0%
JEFFERSON	2,024	1,931	93	0	G.W. Bush	95.4%	4.6%	0.0%
JUDITH BASIN	478	478	0	0	G.W. Bush	100.0%	0.0%	0.0%
LAKE	3,306	3,092	214	0	G.W. Bush	93.5%	6.5%	0.0%
LEWIS AND CLARK	7,004	6,639	365	0	G.W. Bush	94.8%	5.2%	0.0%

MONTANA REPUBLICAN PRIMARY

2004

County	Total Vote	G.W. Bush	No Preference	Other	Winner	Percentage of Total Vote		
						G.W. Bush	No Preference	Other
LIBERTY	404	386	18	0	G.W. Bush	95.5%	4.5%	0.0%
LINCOLN	1,836	1,779	57	0	G.W. Bush	96.9%	3.1%	0.0%
MCCONE	455	427	28	0	G.W. Bush	93.8%	6.2%	0.0%
MADISON	1,464	1,372	92	0	G.W. Bush	93.7%	6.3%	0.0%
MEAGHER	458	428	30	0	G.W. Bush	93.4%	6.6%	0.0%
MINERAL	519	486	33	0	G.W. Bush	93.6%	6.4%	0.0%
MISSOULA	7,218	7,218	0	0	G.W. Bush	100.0%	0.0%	0.0%
MUSSELSHELL	877	833	44	0	G.W. Bush	95.0%	5.0%	0.0%
PARK	2,258	2,130	128	0	G.W. Bush	94.3%	5.7%	0.0%
PETROLEUM	128	128	0	0	G.W. Bush	100.0%	0.0%	0.0%
PHILLIPS	1,213	1,125	88	0	G.W. Bush	92.7%	7.3%	0.0%
PONDERA	1,342	1,209	133	0	G.W. Bush	90.1%	9.9%	0.0%
POWDER RIVER	583	536	47	0	G.W. Bush	91.9%	8.1%	0.0%
POWELL	1,062	996	66	0	G.W. Bush	93.8%	6.2%	0.0%
PRAIRIE	335	335	0	0	G.W. Bush	100.0%	0.0%	0.0%
RAVALLI	4,947	4,719	228	0	G.W. Bush	95.4%	4.6%	0.0%
RICHLAND	1,043	997	46	0	G.W. Bush	95.6%	4.4%	0.0%
ROOSEVELT	650	626	24	0	G.W. Bush	96.3%	3.7%	0.0%
ROSEBUD	766	732	34	0	G.W. Bush	95.6%	4.4%	0.0%
SANDERS	1,213	1,162	51	0	G.W. Bush	95.8%	4.2%	0.0%
SHERIDAN	520	481	39	0	G.W. Bush	92.5%	7.5%	0.0%
SILVER BOW	3,017	2,818	199	0	G.W. Bush	93.4%	6.6%	0.0%
STILLWATER	1,505	1,403	102	0	G.W. Bush	93.2%	6.8%	0.0%
SWEET GRASS	742	717	25	0	G.W. Bush	96.6%	3.4%	0.0%
TETON	951	947	4	0	G.W. Bush	99.6%	0.4%	0.0%
TOOLE	1,133	1,040	93	0	G.W. Bush	91.8%	8.2%	0.0%
TREASURE	281	251	30	0	G.W. Bush	89.3%	10.7%	0.0%
VALLEY	1,610	1,415	195	0	G.W. Bush	87.9%	12.1%	0.0%
WHEATLAND	419	412	7	0	G.W. Bush	98.3%	1.7%	0.0%
WIBAUX	271	234	37	0	G.W. Bush	86.3%	13.7%	0.0%
YELLOWSTONE	18,062	16,985	1,077	0	G.W. Bush	94.0%	6.0%	0.0%
TOTAL	112,748	106,407	6,340	1	G.W. Bush	94.4%	5.6%	0.0%

Note: Other vote was 1 Nancy Warrick (write-in).

NEBRASKA

Nebraska's presidential primary is not nearly as important as it once was. A generation ago, when there were only a handful of primaries, Nebraska served as a connecting rod between the opening round of contests in states such as New Hampshire and Wisconsin and the climactic round of voting in Oregon and California.

That was true as late as 1968, when Robert Kennedy scored a notable victory over Eugene McCarthy in Nebraska. But as primaries have become more important since then, Nebraska's became less so. The proliferation of such events, coupled with Nebraska's late date and small delegate yield, robbed the event of much of its significance.

From time to time, though, Nebraska voters still use their primary to send a message. Disenchanted with President Jimmy Carter in 1980 for imposing a grain embargo on the Soviet Union (and canceling the state's grain sales), farmers in many

Recent Nebraska Primary Results

Nebraska held its first presidential primary in 1912.

	DEMOCRATS				REPUBLICANS		
Year	Turnout	Candidates	%	Turnout	Candidates	%
2004 (May 11)	71,572	JOHN KERRY	73	121,355	GEORGE W. BUSH*	100
		John Edwards	14			
		Howard Dean	8			
2000 (May 9)	105,271	AL GORE	70	185,758	GEORGE W. BUSH	78
		Bill Bradley	26		John McCain	15
					Alan Keyes	6
1996 (May 14)	94,176	BILL CLINTON*	87	170,591	BOB DOLE	76
		Lyndon LaRouche	11		Pat Buchanan	10
					Steve Forbes	6
1992 (May 12)	150,587	BILL CLINTON	46	192,098	GEORGE BUSH*	81
		Jerry Brown	21		Pat Buchanan	13
		Uncommitted	16			
		Paul Tsongas	7			
1988 (May 10)	169,008	MICHAEL DUKAKIS	63	204,049	GEORGE BUSH	68
		Jesse Jackson	26		Bob Dole	22
					Pat Robertson	5
1984 (May 15)	148,855	GARY HART	58	146,648	RONALD REAGAN*	99
		Walter Mondale	27			
		Jesse Jackson	9			
1980 (May 13)	153,881	JIMMY CARTER*	47	205,203	RONALD REAGAN	76
		Edward Kennedy	38		George Bush	15
		Uncommitted	10		John Anderson	6
1976 (May 11)	175,013	FRANK CHURCH	38	208,414	RONALD REAGAN	54
		Jimmy Carter	38		Gerald Ford*	45
		Hubert Humphrey	7			
1972 (May 9)	192,137	GEORGE McGOVERN	41	194,272	RICHARD NIXON*	92
		Hubert Humphrey	34			
		George Wallace	12			
1968 (May 14)	162,611	ROBERT KENNEDY	52	200,476	RICHARD NIXON	70
		Eugene McCarthy	31		Ronald Reagan	21
		Hubert Humphrey#	7		Nelson Rockefeller#	5
		Lyndon Johnson*	6			

Note: All candidates are listed that drew at least 5 percent of their party's primary vote. The names of winning candidates are capitalized. An asterisk (*) indicates an incumbent president. A pound sign (#) indicates a write-in candidate.

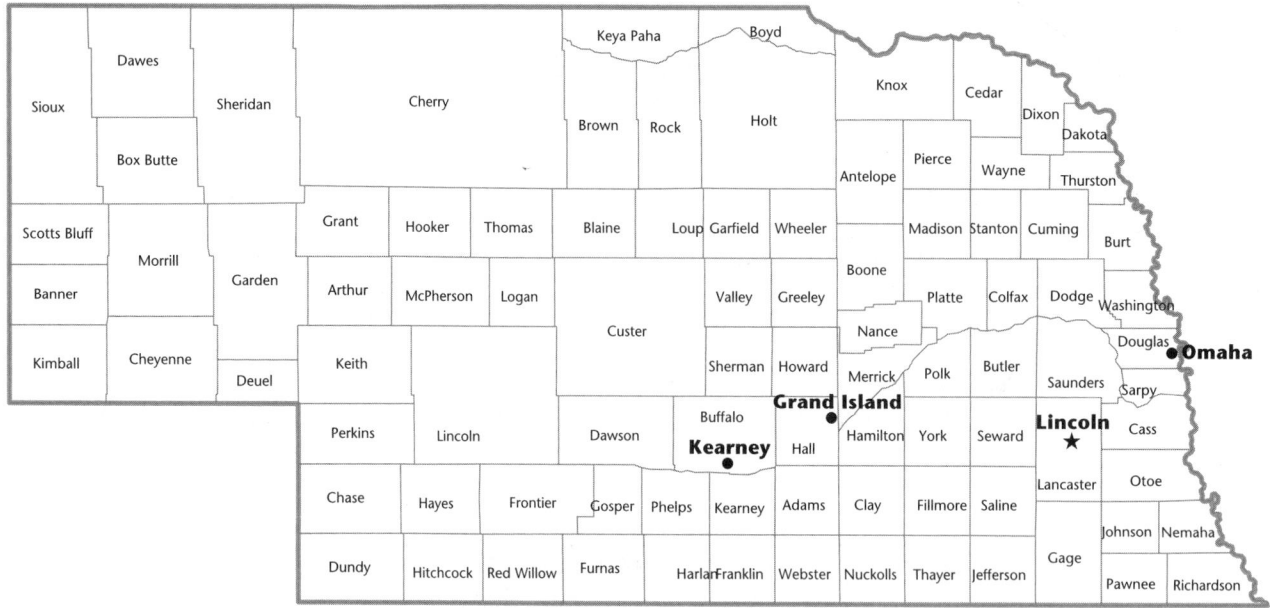

of the crop-growing counties in eastern Nebraska cast their primary ballots for Edward Kennedy.

In 1976, Republican primary voters turned their back on President Gerald Ford, who was born in Omaha under the name Leslie King Jr. Ford carried Douglas (Omaha) and Lancaster (Lincoln) counties, but was crushed by Ronald Reagan in the state's vast rural sector.

Reagan's victory was in line with the previous voting behavior of Nebraska Republicans, who had tended to prefer the most doctrinaire conservative in the primary field. They chose Robert A. Taft over Dwight Eisenhower in 1952, and Barry Goldwater over several more moderate alternatives in 1964.

Nebraska Democrats have a quite different tradition that goes back to the prairie populism of the state's most famous Democrat, William Jennings Bryan. Given a choice, Democratic voters have preferred "new ideas" Democrats over more traditional "New Dealers." In 1972, George McGovern defeated Hubert Humphrey. Twelve years later, McGovern's former campaign manager, Gary Hart, beat Humphrey's protégé, Walter Mondale.

The McGovern-Humphrey race was fairly close; the Hart-Mondale race was not. While Humphrey carried the Omaha area and a sprinkling of counties elsewhere, Mondale lost all 93 counties. Hart ran particularly well in the western part of the state, where the Corn Belt gives way to wheat growing and ranching.

Democratic candidates from the South, even those with campaigns that arrived in Nebraska in overdrive, have had only mixed success in the state's primary. In 1976, peanut farmer Carter lost narrowly to Frank Church. In 1980, Carter won the Nebraska primary but with less than a majority of the vote. In 1992, Bill Clinton also won the Democratic primary with less than 50 percent. Part of the antipathy to Clinton, no doubt was due to his rivalry with the state's popular senator, Bob Kerrey, who had been forced from the Democratic presidential race long before his home state voted. And in 2000, Al Gore's erstwhile opponent, Bill Bradley, drew more than 25 percent of the vote in Nebraska, his best showing in any primary state after he quit the Democratic race in early March. The former professional basketball star even outpolled Gore in two small counties in western Nebraska.

The presidential contest is traditionally just one race on the Nebraska primary ballot. But the variety of action has not kept the primary turnout from falling sharply in recent years. Fewer ballots were cast in the Democratic presidential primary in 2004 than any since 1964, while the Republican primary turnout was the lowest since 1960.

NEBRASKA DEMOCRATIC PRIMARY

2000

County	Total Vote	Bradley	Gore	Other	Winner	Percentage of Total Vote		
						Bradley	Gore	Other
ADAMS	1,984	593	1,310	81	Gore	29.9%	66.0%	4.1%
ANTELOPE	543	192	326	25	Gore	35.4%	60.0%	4.6%
ARTHUR	35	18	13	4	Bradley	51.4%	37.1%	11.4%
BANNER	41	10	30	1	Gore	24.4%	73.2%	2.4%
BLAINE	31	10	21	0	Gore	32.3%	67.7%	0.0%
BOONE	382	142	211	29	Gore	37.2%	55.2%	7.6%
BOX BUTTE	610	174	412	24	Gore	28.5%	67.5%	3.9%
BOYD	164	63	91	10	Gore	38.4%	55.5%	6.1%
BROWN	133	39	83	11	Gore	29.3%	62.4%	8.3%
BUFFALO	1,437	480	894	63	Gore	33.4%	62.2%	4.4%
BURT	452	97	344	11	Gore	21.5%	76.1%	2.4%
BUTLER	853	280	534	39	Gore	32.8%	62.6%	4.6%
CASS	1,164	279	824	61	Gore	24.0%	70.8%	5.2%
CEDAR	636	205	396	35	Gore	32.2%	62.3%	5.5%
CHASE	245	110	122	13	Gore	44.9%	49.8%	5.3%
CHERRY	334	137	184	13	Gore	41.0%	55.1%	3.9%
CHEYENNE	487	155	311	21	Gore	31.8%	63.9%	4.3%
CLAY	429	144	265	20	Gore	33.6%	61.8%	4.7%
COLFAX	587	178	368	41	Gore	30.3%	62.7%	7.0%
CUMING	368	126	222	20	Gore	34.2%	60.3%	5.4%
CUSTER	577	188	373	16	Gore	32.6%	64.6%	2.8%
DAKOTA	651	153	475	23	Gore	23.5%	73.0%	3.5%
DAWES	260	83	159	18	Gore	31.9%	61.2%	6.9%
DAWSON	758	245	482	31	Gore	32.3%	63.6%	4.1%
DEUEL	88	24	62	2	Gore	27.3%	70.5%	2.3%
DIXON	968	260	660	48	Gore	26.9%	68.2%	5.0%
DODGE	1,566	399	1,096	71	Gore	25.5%	70.0%	4.5%
DOUGLAS	39,776	9,507	28,621	1,648	Gore	23.9%	72.0%	4.1%
DUNDY	89	37	45	7	Gore	41.6%	50.6%	7.9%
FILLMORE	464	110	336	18	Gore	23.7%	72.4%	3.9%
FRANKLIN	226	83	138	5	Gore	36.7%	61.1%	2.2%
FRONTIER	165	54	104	7	Gore	32.7%	63.0%	4.2%
FURNAS	331	107	217	7	Gore	32.3%	65.6%	2.1%
GAGE	1,092	259	787	46	Gore	23.7%	72.1%	4.2%
GARDEN	108	39	61	8	Gore	36.1%	56.5%	7.4%
GARFIELD	98	28	68	2	Gore	28.6%	69.4%	2.0%
GOSPER	101	34	63	4	Gore	33.7%	62.4%	4.0%
GRANT	52	17	28	7	Gore	32.7%	53.8%	13.5%
GREELEY	382	105	254	23	Gore	27.5%	66.5%	6.0%
HALL	3,225	782	2,305	138	Gore	24.2%	71.5%	4.3%
HAMILTON	361	119	226	16	Gore	33.0%	62.6%	4.4%
HARLAN	312	101	200	11	Gore	32.4%	64.1%	3.5%
HAYES	38	20	15	3	Bradley	52.6%	39.5%	7.9%
HITCHCOCK	179	64	106	9	Gore	35.8%	59.2%	5.0%
HOLT	517	188	299	30	Gore	36.4%	57.8%	5.8%
HOOKER	33	7	23	3	Gore	21.2%	69.7%	9.1%
HOWARD	688	217	441	30	Gore	31.5%	64.1%	4.4%
JEFFERSON	446	94	344	8	Gore	21.1%	77.1%	1.8%
JOHNSON	332	100	222	10	Gore	30.1%	66.9%	3.0%
KEARNEY	412	150	245	17	Gore	36.4%	59.5%	4.1%

NEBRASKA DEMOCRATIC PRIMARY

2000

County	Total Vote	Bradley	Gore	Other	Winner	Percentage of Total Vote		
						Bradley	Gore	Other
KEITH	485	161	307	17	Gore	33.2%	63.3%	3.5%
KEYA PAHA	73	32	38	3	Gore	43.8%	52.1%	4.1%
KIMBALL	162	46	100	16	Gore	28.4%	61.7%	9.9%
KNOX	546	143	368	35	Gore	26.2%	67.4%	6.4%
LANCASTER	13,722	3,330	9,889	503	Gore	24.3%	72.1%	3.7%
LINCOLN	2,651	667	1,852	132	Gore	25.2%	69.9%	5.0%
LOGAN	30	13	15	2	Gore	43.3%	50.0%	6.7%
LOUP	23	3	20	0	Gore	13.0%	87.0%	0.0%
MCPHERSON	48	19	27	2	Gore	39.6%	56.3%	4.2%
MADISON	1,378	429	889	60	Gore	31.1%	64.5%	4.4%
MERRICK	354	103	240	11	Gore	29.1%	67.8%	3.1%
MORRILL	166	49	109	8	Gore	29.5%	65.7%	4.8%
NANCE	265	84	167	14	Gore	31.7%	63.0%	5.3%
NEMAHA	392	103	280	9	Gore	26.3%	71.4%	2.3%
NUCKOLLS	405	136	246	23	Gore	33.6%	60.7%	5.7%
OTOE	818	224	555	39	Gore	27.4%	67.8%	4.8%
PAWNEE	243	69	167	7	Gore	28.4%	68.7%	2.9%
PERKINS	209	88	107	14	Gore	42.1%	51.2%	6.7%
PHELPS	448	163	258	27	Gore	36.4%	57.6%	6.0%
PIERCE	315	103	200	12	Gore	32.7%	63.5%	3.8%
PLATTE	1,626	539	955	132	Gore	33.1%	58.7%	8.1%
POLK	290	86	196	8	Gore	29.7%	67.6%	2.8%
RED WILLOW	762	232	493	37	Gore	30.4%	64.7%	4.9%
RICHARDSON	553	132	394	27	Gore	23.9%	71.2%	4.9%
ROCK	106	42	55	9	Gore	39.6%	51.9%	8.5%
SALINE	1,374	305	980	89	Gore	22.2%	71.3%	6.5%
SARPY	5,620	1,392	3,949	279	Gore	24.8%	70.3%	5.0%
SAUNDERS	1,239	382	785	72	Gore	30.8%	63.4%	5.8%
SCOTTS BLUFF	1,391	335	996	60	Gore	24.1%	71.6%	4.3%
SEWARD	944	246	666	32	Gore	26.1%	70.6%	3.4%
SHERIDAN	205	70	127	8	Gore	34.1%	62.0%	3.9%
SHERMAN	518	146	350	22	Gore	28.2%	67.6%	4.2%
SIOUX	62	20	41	1	Gore	32.3%	66.1%	1.6%
STANTON	216	64	143	9	Gore	29.6%	66.2%	4.2%
THAYER	484	136	334	14	Gore	28.1%	69.0%	2.9%
THOMAS	22	10	11	1	Gore	45.5%	50.0%	4.5%
THURSTON	345	98	236	11	Gore	28.4%	68.4%	3.2%
VALLEY	314	80	219	15	Gore	25.5%	69.7%	4.8%
WASHINGTON	655	184	455	16	Gore	28.1%	69.5%	2.4%
WAYNE	541	148	379	14	Gore	27.4%	70.1%	2.6%
WEBSTER	374	117	243	14	Gore	31.3%	65.0%	3.7%
WHEELER	59	20	34	5	Gore	33.9%	57.6%	8.5%
YORK	502	129	348	25	Gore	25.7%	69.3%	5.0%
TOTAL	106,145	27,884	73,639	4,622	Gore	26.3%	69.4%	4.4%
Certified Totals	105,271	27,884	73,639	3,748	Gore	26.5%	70.0%	3.6%

Note: Other vote was 3,191 Lyndon H. LaRouche Jr.; 1,431 write-in. The certified statewide total for write-in votes was 557, although on a county-by-county basis they added to 1,431. The certified vote is used elsewhere in this volume.

NEBRASKA REPUBLICAN PRIMARY

2000

County	Total Vote	G.W. Bush	Keyes	McCain	Other	Winner	Percentage of Total Vote			
							G.W. Bush	Keyes	McCain	Other
ADAMS	4,007	3,119	256	629	3	G.W. Bush	77.8%	6.4%	15.7%	0.1%
ANTELOPE	1,295	1,049	59	187	0	G.W. Bush	81.0%	4.6%	14.4%	0.0%
ARTHUR	175	147	12	16	0	G.W. Bush	84.0%	6.9%	9.1%	0.0%
BANNER	285	216	26	43	0	G.W. Bush	75.8%	9.1%	15.1%	0.0%
BLAINE	151	129	3	19	0	G.W. Bush	85.4%	2.0%	12.6%	0.0%
BOONE	886	710	39	137	0	G.W. Bush	80.1%	4.4%	15.5%	0.0%
BOX BUTTE	1,367	1,064	67	236	0	G.W. Bush	77.8%	4.9%	17.3%	0.0%
BOYD	438	308	32	98	0	G.W. Bush	70.3%	7.3%	22.4%	0.0%
BROWN	915	702	51	162	0	G.W. Bush	76.7%	5.6%	17.7%	0.0%
BUFFALO	4,193	3,412	228	537	16	G.W. Bush	81.4%	5.4%	12.8%	0.4%
BURT	826	646	42	136	2	G.W. Bush	78.2%	5.1%	16.5%	0.2%
BUTLER	810	648	46	116	0	G.W. Bush	80.0%	5.7%	14.3%	0.0%
CASS	1,880	1,463	129	285	3	G.W. Bush	77.8%	6.9%	15.2%	0.2%
CEDAR	931	736	65	130	0	G.W. Bush	79.1%	7.0%	14.0%	0.0%
CHASE	718	579	29	110	0	G.W. Bush	80.6%	4.0%	15.3%	0.0%
CHERRY	1,427	1,156	65	205	1	G.W. Bush	81.0%	4.6%	14.4%	0.1%
CHEYENNE	1,674	1,327	109	238	0	G.W. Bush	79.3%	6.5%	14.2%	0.0%
CLAY	1,078	845	65	68	0	G.W. Bush	78.4%	6.0%	15.6%	0.0%
COLFAX	761	617	42	100	2	G.W. Bush	81.1%	5.5%	13.1%	0.3%
CUMING	1,014	826	60	126	2	G.W. Bush	81.5%	5.9%	12.4%	0.2%
CUSTER	2,011	1,591	162	258	0	G.W. Bush	79.1%	8.1%	12.8%	0.0%
DAKOTA	927	720	78	127	2	G.W. Bush	77.7%	8.4%	13.7%	0.2%
DAWES	1,020	764	76	180	0	G.W. Bush	74.9%	7.5%	17.6%	0.0%
DAWSON	2,377	1,941	113	323	0	G.W. Bush	81.7%	4.8%	13.6%	0.0%
DEUEL	448	356	13	79	0	G.W. Bush	79.5%	2.9%	17.6%	0.0%
DIXON	1,746	1,418	128	196	4	G.W. Bush	81.2%	7.3%	11.2%	0.2%
DODGE	3,056	2,429	138	479	10	G.W. Bush	79.5%	4.5%	15.7%	0.3%
DOUGLAS	47,777	37,082	3,521	6,989	185	G.W. Bush	77.6%	7.4%	14.6%	0.4%
DUNDY	396	316	22	58	0	G.W. Bush	79.8%	5.6%	14.6%	0.0%
FILLMORE	863	681	42	140	0	G.W. Bush	78.9%	4.9%	16.2%	0.0%
FRANKLIN	544	444	19	81	0	G.W. Bush	81.6%	3.5%	14.9%	0.0%
FRONTIER	590	476	36	78	0	G.W. Bush	80.7%	6.1%	13.2%	0.0%
FURNAS	925	745	43	137	0	G.W. Bush	80.5%	4.6%	14.8%	0.0%
GAGE	1,891	1,392	111	379	9	G.W. Bush	73.6%	5.9%	20.0%	0.5%
GARDEN	581	463	18	100	0	G.W. Bush	79.7%	3.1%	17.2%	0.0%
GARFIELD	439	328	43	68		G.W. Bush	74.7%	9.8%	15.5%	0.0%
GOSPER	318	255	19	44	0	G.W. Bush	80.2%	6.0%	13.8%	0.0%
GRANT	252	197	11	44	0	G.W. Bush	78.2%	4.4%	17.5%	0.0%
GREELEY	261	210	15	36	0	G.W. Bush	80.5%	5.7%	13.8%	0.0%
HALL	5,904	4,644	301	942	17	G.W. Bush	78.7%	5.1%	16.0%	0.3%
HAMILTON	1,299	1,035	104	160	0	G.W. Bush	79.7%	8.0%	12.3%	0.0%
HARLAN	678	567	35	76	0	G.W. Bush	83.6%	5.2%	11.2%	0.0%
HAYES	302	258	24	20	0	G.W. Bush	85.4%	7.9%	6.6%	0.0%
HITCHCOCK	513	417	20	76	0	G.W. Bush	81.3%	3.9%	14.8%	0.0%
HOLT	1,664	1,332	115	214	3	G.W. Bush	80.0%	6.9%	12.9%	0.2%
HOOKER	156	118	5	33	0	G.W. Bush	75.6%	3.2%	21.2%	0.0%
HOWARD	858	651	42	165	0	G.W. Bush	75.9%	4.9%	19.2%	0.0%
JEFFERSON	925	723	48	152	2	G.W. Bush	78.2%	5.2%	16.4%	0.2%
JOHNSON	560	410	38	111	1	G.W. Bush	73.2%	6.8%	19.8%	0.2%
KEARNEY	978	811	46	121	0	G.W. Bush	82.9%	4.7%	12.4%	0.0%

NEBRASKA REPUBLICAN PRIMARY

2000

| County | Total Vote | G.W. Bush | Keyes | McCain | Other | Winner | Percentage of Total Vote | | | |
							G.W. Bush	Keyes	McCain	Other
KEITH	1,769	1,435	71	263	0	G.W. Bush	81.1%	4.0%	14.9%	0.0%
KEYA PAHA	299	234	19	44	2	G.W. Bush	78.3%	6.4%	14.7%	0.7%
KIMBALL	746	589	24	132	1	G.W. Bush	79.0%	3.2%	17.7%	0.1%
KNOX	1,084	900	46	136	2	G.W. Bush	83.0%	4.2%	12.5%	0.2%
LANCASTER	20,367	14,971	1,558	3,765	73	G.W. Bush	73.5%	7.6%	18.5%	0.4%
LINCOLN	4,771	3,720	250	787	14	G.W. Bush	78.0%	5.2%	16.5%	0.3%
LOGAN	196	151	20	25	0	G.W. Bush	77.0%	10.2%	12.8%	0.0%
LOUP	122	103	7	12	0	G.W. Bush	84.4%	5.7%	9.8%	0.0%
MCPHERSON	176	140	16	20	0	G.W. Bush	79.5%	9.1%	1.4%	0.0%
MADISON	4,270	3,435	239	587	9	G.W. Bush	80.4%	5.6%	13.7%	0.2%
MERRICK	1,130	886	74	169	1	G.W. Bush	78.4%	6.5%	15.0%	0.1%
MORRILL	760	74	79	106	1	G.W. Bush	75.5%	10.4%	13.9%	0.1%
NANCE	370	300	21	49	0	G.W. Bush	81.1%	5.7%	13.2%	0.0%
NEMAHA	809	621	50	138	0	G.W. Bush	76.8%	6.2%	17.1%	0.0%
NUCKOLLS	630	526	28	74	2	G.W. Bush	83.5%	4.4%	11.7%	0.3%
OTOE	1,647	1,298	85	263	1	G.W. Bush	78.8%	5.2%	16.0%	0.1%
PAWNEE	408	311	24	73	0	G.W. Bush	76.2%	5.9%	17.9%	0.0%
PERKINS	526	447	34	45	0	G.W. Bush	85.0%	6.5%	8.6%	0.0%
PHELPS	1,554	1,316	77	161	0	G.W. Bush	84.7%	5.0%	10.4%	0.0%
PIERCE	1,013	831	59	123	0	G.W. Bush	82.0%	5.8%	12.1%	0.0%
PLATTE	3,372	2,745	157	464	6	G.W. Bush	81.4%	4.7%	13.8%	0.2%
POLK	884	690	56	138	0	G.W. Bush	78.1%	6.3%	15.6%	0.0%
RED WILLOW	1,976	1,594	117	265	0	G.W. Bush	80.7%	5.9%	13.4%	0.0%
RICHARDSON	1,027	812	62	153	0	G.W. Bush	79.1%	6.0%	14.9%	0.0%
ROCK	499	424	18	57	0	G.W. Bush	85.0%	3.6%	11.4%	0.0%
SALINE	948	685	62	199	2	G.W. Bush	72.3%	6.5%	21.0%	0.2%
SARPY	9,752	7,587	796	1,326	43	G.W. Bush	77.8%	8.2%	13.6%	0.4%
SAUNDERS	1,838	1,421	112	305	0	G.W. Bush	77.3%	6.1%	16.6%	0.0%
SCOTTS BLUFF	4,251	3,366	274	602	9	G.W. Bush	79.2%	6.4%	14.2%	0.2%
SEWARD	1,813	1,378	133	297	5	G.W. Bush	76.0%	7.3%	16.4%	0.3%
SHERIDAN	901	742	36	123	0	G.W. Bush	82.4%	4.0%	13.7%	0.0%
SHERMAN	397	309	14	74	0	G.W. Bush	77.8%	3.5%	18.6%	0.0%
SIOUX	399	321	17	61	0	G.W. Bush	80.5%	4.3%	15.3%	0.0%
STANTON	876	691	42	140	3	G.W. Bush	78.9%	4.8%	16.0%	0.3%
THAYER	1,006	772	46	188	0	G.W. Bush	76.7%	4.6%	18.7%	0.0%
THOMAS	191	155	10	26	0	G.W. Bush	81.2%	5.2%	13.6%	0.0%
THURSTON	306	243	14	49	0	G.W. Bush	79.4%	4.6%	16.0%	0.0%
VALLEY	721	555	69	95	2	G.W. Bush	77.0%	9.6%	13.2%	0.3%
WASHINGTON	2,111	1,643	144	324	0	G.W. Bush	77.8%	6.8%	15.3%	0.0%
WAYNE	1,459	1,132	115	212	0	G.W. Bush	77.6%	7.9%	14.5%	0.0%
WEBSTER	688	579	28	81	0	G.W. Bush	84.2%	4.1%	11.8%	0.0%
WHEELER	182	148	11	23	0	G.W. Bush	81.3%	6.0%	12.6%	0.0%
YORK	2,424	1,923	148	347	6	G.W. Bush	79.3%	6.1%	14.3%	0.2%
TOTAL	185,758	145,176	12,073	28,065	444	G.W. Bush	78.2%	6.5%	15.1%	0.2%

Note: Other vote was 444 write-in.

NEBRASKA DEMOCRATIC PRIMARY

2004

County	Total Vote	Dean	Edwards	Kerry	Other	Winner	Percentage of Total Vote			
							Dean	Edwards	Kerry	Other
ADAMS	1,339	122	204	954	59	Kerry	9.1%	15.2%	71.2%	4.4%
ANTELOPE	312	26	63	205	18	Kerry	8.3%	20.2%	65.7%	5.8%
ARTHUR	22	1	1	18	2	Kerry	4.5%	4.5%	81.8%	9.1%
BANNER	12	0	2	10	0	Kerry	0.0%	16.7%	83.3%	0.0%
BLAINE	33	1	6	23	3	Kerry	3.0%	18.2%	69.7%	9.1%
BOONE	234	31	42	147	14	Kerry	13.2%	17.9%	62.8%	6.0%
BOX BUTTE	477	27	56	374	20	Kerry	5.7%	11.7%	78.4%	4.2%
BOYD	105	14	20	67	4	Kerry	13.3%	19.0%	63.8%	3.8%
BROWN	126	18	14	85	9	Kerry	14.3%	11.1%	67.5%	7.1%
BUFFALO	868	83	151	601	33	Kerry	9.6%	17.4%	69.2%	3.8%
BURT	480	25	56	383	16	Kerry	5.2%	11.7%	79.8%	3.3%
BUTLER	594	64	83	410	37	Kerry	10.8%	14.0%	69.0%	6.2%
CASS	815	57	116	605	37	Kerry	7.0%	14.2%	74.2%	4.5%
CEDAR	336	35	60	230	1	Kerry	10.4%	17.9%	68.5%	3.3%
CHASE	158	27	10	114	7	Kerry	17.1%	6.3%	72.2%	4.4%
CHERRY	255	25	33	181	16	Kerry	9.8%	12.9%	71.0%	6.3%
CHEYENNE	259	36	39	175	9	Kerry	13.9%	15.1%	67.6%	3.5%
CLAY	295	39	48	193	15	Kerry	13.2%	16.3%	65.4%	5.1%
COLFAX	576	66	73	399	38	Kerry	11.5%	12.7%	69.3%	6.6%
CUMING	284	30	43	188	23	Kerry	10.6%	15.1%	66.2%	8.1%
CUSTER	563	65	78	394	26	Kerry	11.5%	13.9%	70.0%	4.6%
DAKOTA	723	37	87	585	14	Kerry	5.1%	12.0%	80.9%	1.9%
DAWES	182	1	34	137	10	Kerry	0.5%	18.7%	75.3%	5.5%
DAWSON	723	66	103	527	27	Kerry	9.1%	14.2%	72.9%	3.7%
DEUEL	62	3	10	48	1	Kerry	4.8%	16.1%	77.4%	1.6%
DIXON	284	24	46	206	8	Kerry	8.5%	16.2%	72.5%	2.8%
DODGE	1,597	113	213	1,201	70	Kerry	7.1%	13.3%	75.2%	4.4%
DOUGLAS	16,785	981	2,070	12,630	1,104	Kerry	5.8%	12.3%	75.2%	6.6%
DUNDY	105	11	14	74	6	Kerry	10.5%	13.3%	70.5%	5.7%
FILLMORE	298	28	52	206	12	Kerry	9.4%	17.4%	69.1%	4.0%
FRANKLIN	204	23	34	141	6	Kerry	11.3%	16.7%	69.1%	2.9%
FRONTIER	128	11	23	89	5	Kerry	8.6%	18.0%	69.5%	3.9%
FURNAS	226	26	38	155	7	Kerry	11.5%	16.8%	68.6%	3.1%
GAGE	1,129	79	167	836	47	Kerry	7.0%	14.8%	74.0%	4.2%
GARDEN	85	12	15	56	2	Kerry	14.1%	17.6%	65.9%	2.4%
GARFIELD	82	10	7	62	3	Kerry	12.2%	8.5%	75.6%	3.7%
GOSPER	81	8	12	58	3	Kerry	9.9%	14.8%	71.6%	3.7%
GRANT	38	6	3	27	2	Kerry	15.8%	7.9%	71.1%	5.3%
GREELEY	217	25	49	135	8	Kerry	11.5%	22.6%	62.2%	3.7%
HALL	2,383	204	355	1,743	81	Kerry	8.6%	14.9%	73.1%	3.4%
HAMILTON	213	13	29	161	10	Kerry	6.1%	13.6%	75.6%	4.7%
HARLAN	217	19	34	149	15	Kerry	8.8%	15.7%	68.7%	6.9%
HAYES	37	8	8	19	2	Kerry	21.6%	21.6%	51.4%	5.4%
HITCHCOCK	132	9	17	100	6	Kerry	6.8%	12.9%	75.8%	4.5%
HOLT	455	43	85	287	0	Kerry	9.5%	18.7%	63.1%	8.8%
HOOKER	32	5	3	23	1	Kerry	15.6%	9.4%	71.9%	3.1%
HOWARD	396	45	53	279	19	Kerry	11.4%	13.4%	70.5%	4.8%
JEFFERSON	357	22	46	281	8	Kerry	6.2%	12.9%	78.7%	2.2%
JOHNSON	417	39	66	300	12	Kerry	9.4%	15.8%	71.9%	2.9%
KEARNEY	308	31	52	208	17	Kerry	10.1%	16.9%	67.5%	5.5%

NEBRASKA DEMOCRATIC PRIMARY

2004

County	Total Vote	Dean	Edwards	Kerry	Other	Winner	Percentage of Total Vote			
							Dean	Edwards	Kerry	Other
KEITH	282	24	44	204	10	Kerry	8.5%	15.6%	72.3%	3.5%
KEYA PAHA	47	5	6	32	4	Kerry	10.6%	12.8%	68.1%	8.5%
KIMBALL	128	11	10	103	4	Kerry	8.6%	7.8%	80.5%	3.1%
KNOX	398	45	66	271	16	Kerry	11.3%	16.6%	68.1%	4.0%
LANCASTER	14,312	923	1,843	10,805	741	Kerry	6.4%	12.9%	75.5%	5.2%
LINCOLN	2,294	166	303	1,722	103	Kerry	7.2%	13.2%	75.1%	4.5%
LOGAN	16	3	4	9	0	Kerry	18.8%	25.0%	56.3%	0.0%
LOUP	24	2	4	17	1	Kerry	8.3%	16.7%	70.8%	4.2%
MCPHERSON	39	2	5	32	0	Kerry	5.1%	12.8%	82.1%	0.0%
MADISON	968	91	149	671	57	Kerry	9.4%	15.4%	69.3%	5.9%
MERRICK	273	20	41	196	16	Kerry	7.3%	15.0%	71.8%	5.9%
MORRILL	164	15	27	116	6	Kerry	9.1%	16.5%	70.7%	3.7%
NANCE	290	23	55	196	16	Kerry	7.9%	19.0%	67.6%	5.5%
NEMAHA	498	37	68	370	23	Kerry	7.4%	13.7%	74.3%	4.6%
NUCKOLLS	269	31	49	181	8	Kerry	11.5%	18.2%	67.3%	3.0%
OTOE	802	63	114	580	45	Kerry	7.9%	14.2%	72.3%	5.6%
PAWNEE	238	19	50	161	8	Kerry	8.0%	21.0%	67.6%	3.4%
PERKINS	132	23	17	88	4	Kerry	17.4%	12.9%	66.7%	3.0%
PHELPS	250	26	42	163	19	Kerry	10.4%	16.8%	65.2%	7.6%
PIERCE	216	28	38	133	17	Kerry	13.0%	17.6%	61.6%	7.9%
PLATTE	1,444	161	345	848	90	Kerry	11.1%	23.9%	58.7%	6.2%
POLK	197	26	41	122	8	Kerry	13.2%	20.8%	61.9%	4.1%
RED WILLOW	747	67	107	542	31	Kerry	9.0%	14.3%	72.6%	4.1%
RICHARDSON	790	52	109	607	22	Kerry	6.6%	13.8%	76.8%	2.8%
ROCK	65	12	15	33	5	Kerry	18.5%	23.1%	50.8%	7.7%
SALINE	1,152	108	179	811	54	Kerry	9.4%	15.5%	70.4%	4.7%
SARPY	3,325	213	517	2,440	155	Kerry	6.4%	15.5%	73.4%	4.7%
SAUNDERS	1,146	113	175	791	7	Kerry	9.9%	15.3%	69.0%	5.8%
SCOTTS BLUFF	854	60	101	675	18	Kerry	7.0%	11.8%	79.0%	2.1%
SEWARD	628	58	96	455	19	Kerry	9.2%	15.3%	72.5%	3.0%
SHERIDAN	128	11	26	84	7	Kerry	8.6%	20.3%	65.6%	5.5%
SHERMAN	245	22	32	179	12	Kerry	9.0%	13.1%	73.1%	4.9%
SIOUX	35	2	4	28	1	Kerry	5.7%	11.4%	80.0%	2.9%
STANTON	173	12	27	132	2	Kerry	6.9%	15.6%	76.3%	1.2%
THAYER	250	14	39	187	10	Kerry	5.6%	15.6%	74.8%	4.0%
THOMAS	39	3	7	25	4	Kerry	7.7%	17.9%	64.1%	10.3%
THURSTON	671	53	65	516	37	Kerry	7.9%	9.7%	76.9%	5.5%
VALLEY	432	35	55	328	14	Kerry	8.1%	12.7%	75.9%	3.2%
WASHINGTON	524	32	52	415	25	Kerry	6.1%	9.9%	79.2%	4.8%
WAYNE	363	27	63	256	17	Kerry	7.4%	17.4%	70.5%	4.7%
WEBSTER	228	20	41	158	9	Kerry	8.8%	18.0%	69.3%	3.9%
WHEELER	38	5	3	29	1	Kerry	13.2%	7.9%	76.3%	2.6%
YORK	419	43	74	289	13	Kerry	10.3%	17.7%	69.0%	3.1%
TOTAL	71,572	5,400	10,031	52,479	3,662	Kerry	7.5%	14.0%	73.3%	5.1%

Note: Other vote was 1,490 Dennis J. Kucinich; 1,367 Al Sharpton; 805 Lyndon H. LaRouche Jr.

NEVADA

The mention of Nevada often conjures up images of garish gambling palaces, quickie marriages, and speedy divorces. And when it comes to presidential nominating politics, there is an open climate as well.

Nevada has been willing to bet its chips on candidates that face long odds at the national level, or to vote "no" on all the candidates when dissatisfied with the choices. It has even turned thumbs down on its presidential primary, holding ones in 1976 and 1980, then taking an hiatus until 1996, before abandoning the primary again in 2000 and 2004.

Nevada's free-wheeling behavior was evident from the start. In 1976, its primary voters opted for two Californians, Jerry Brown and Ronald Reagan, neither of whom was to win his party's nomination that year. Faced with a choice in 1980 between Jimmy Carter and Edward Kennedy, one-third of Nevada primary voters cast ballots for the line labeled "None of These Candidates."

In 1988, Nevada Democrats gave a first-round caucus victory to Al Gore, one of only two caucus states that Gore was to win on his first try for the White House. (Wyoming was the other.) Gore had help from his Senate colleague, Harry Reid, and won the state by combining support in Reid's home base of Clark County (Las Vegas) with a strong showing in many of the more conservative, lightly populated "Cow Counties" to the north.

But the real action that year was on the Republican side, where well-organized and procedure-savvy supporters of Pat Robertson not only took over the caucus process but stayed to contend for control of the state GOP apparatus. In the end, Robertson's followers won a majority of the Nevada delegation.

In 1992, Nevada Democrats were back in Brown's corner, giving him a first-round caucus victory over Bill Clinton. While campaigning in Nevada, Brown took an unusual step to cultivate labor support, grabbing a picket sign and joining striking culinary workers outside a Las Vegas hotel. The Culinary Union, a major factor in a state dependent on the tourist industry, returned the favor with a caucus-eve endorsement of Brown.

In 1996, the presidential primary was back, but only for the Republicans, and only with balloting by mail. Bob Dole won the late March event easily, a vote that also served to underscore the booming population growth of the state in general and the Republican Party in particular. Roughly 140,000 GOP primary ballots were cast, nearly double the number in any previous

Recent Nevada Primary Results

Nevada held its first presidential primary in 1976.

| Year | DEMOCRATS | | | REPUBLICANS | | |
	Turnout	Candidates	%	Turnout	Candidates	%
2004	—	No Primary		—	No Primary	
2000	—	No Primary		—	No Primary	
1996 (March 26)	—	No Primary		140,637	BOB DOLE	52
					Steve Forbes	19
					Pat Buchanan	15
					"None"	9
1992	—	No Primary		—	No Primary	
1988	—	No Primary		—	No Primary	
1984	—	No Primary		—	No Primary	
1980 (May 27)	66,948	JIMMY CARTER*	38	47,395	RONALD REAGAN	83
		"None"	34		"None"	10
		Edward Kennedy	29		George Bush	6
1976 (May 25)	75,242	JERRY BROWN	53	47,749	RONALD REAGAN	66
		Jimmy Carter	23		Gerald Ford*	29
		Frank Church	9		"None"	5
		"None"	6			

Note: All candidates are listed that drew at least 5 percent of their party's primary vote. The names of winning candidates are capitalized. An asterisk (*) indicates an incumbent president.

presidential primary in Nevada, Democratic or Republican. Slightly more than half the ballots were cast in Clark County and one-quarter in Washoe County (Reno).

Returning to the caucus system in 2000 and 2004, Nevada once again retreated to the shadows of the presidential nominating process. The state's closest brush with relevance came in 2004 when an estimated 9,000 Nevada Democrats turned out on Valentine's Day to give John Kerry 63 percent of the caucus vote, his highest share in any Democratic primary or caucus held through February. Kerry campaigned personally in Las Vegas as the caucuses convened. Yet much of the Democratic enthusiasm was more generic, as many caucus attendees wore shirts and bore signs that read "A.B.B" (for "Anybody But Bush").

NEW HAMPSHIRE

Like the New York Yankees, the New Hampshire presidential primary has never been willing to settle for anything less than first.

A state, of course, has means beyond a baseball team: New Hampshire has decreed that its primary be held before that of any other state as a matter of law. Despite all the frowning and frustration in other states, New Hampshire has attracted candidates to its first-in-the-nation presidential primary since it became a major part of the political landscape in 1952.

The primary lost a bit of its luster in the 1990s. In 1992 Bill Clinton became the first candidate since 1952 to be elected president without first winning the New Hampshire primary; he was second in the state's Democratic voting. In 1996 Pat Buchanan won the Republican balloting in New Hampshire but no other primary that followed, throwing into question the whole idea that momentum accrues to a Granite State winner.

But in the new millennium, New Hampshire has been back in its glory. Republican John McCain vaulted onto the national stage in 2000 with a lopsided victory in New Hampshire over the early GOP front-runner and eventual nominee, George W. Bush. Four years later, Democrat John Kerry amplified the momentum from his victory in the Iowa caucuses with a clear-cut victory in New Hampshire. In retrospect, it was a knockout punch for the Massachusetts senator, as none of his rivals could draw close to him in the plethora of primaries that voted afterwards.

In short, New Hampshire has remained a rite of passage for anyone who seriously covets the White House, and for long shots it is a place where hope springs eternal. In a state whose motto is "Live Free or Die," voters have never been reluctant to deliver a blow against the politically high and mighty.

Two presidents—Harry Truman and Lyndon Johnson—decided not to seek reelection after poor showings in New Hampshire. Truman was upset in the 1952 Democratic primary by Sen. Estes Kefauver of Tennessee. A write-in campaign for Johnson in the 1968 Democratic balloting could muster only 49.6 percent of the vote against the lightly regarded anti–Vietnam War candidacy of Eugene McCarthy.

Since then, Presidents Gerald Ford (in 1976), Jimmy Carter (in 1980), and George Bush (in 1992) have also been chastened by New Hampshire primary voters. They won, but with less than 55 percent of the vote, and all three lost the general election that followed.

New Hampshire is a great leveler. It is small enough that any candidate with time, energy, and a knack for grass-roots organization has a good chance of winning. As Kefauver and McCarthy came to national prominence in New Hampshire, so did George McGovern in 1972, Gary Hart in 1984, and McCain in 2000.

McGovern did not beat the Democratic front-runner, Sen. Edmund Muskie of Maine, but he ran so far above expectations that Muskie's campaign lost respect and soon slid into political oblivion. Hart defeated Walter Mondale in the 1984 Democratic contest, sending the erstwhile front-runner into a tailspin from which he barely recovered.

McCain's upset of Bush in 2000 enabled the Arizona senator to battle the well-funded Texas governor on even terms throughout the first month of primaries—a window of opportunity that closed, though, with the nationwide array of contests in early March that Bush was better prepared to contest.

For all its traditionalism, New Hampshire lacks strong party structures and the politically potent interest groups that all but rule in other states. But for all the opportunity the state provides, its primary places great pressure on dark-horse hopefuls. For those who do not make a breakthrough in Iowa, a caucus state, New Hampshire can be their last chance.

McCain in 2000 was one of the few candidates to skip Iowa and successfully jump-start their campaign in New Hampshire. Democrats Wesley Clark and Joe Lieberman tried the same tactic in 2004 but were less fortunate. They were no shows in Iowa and finished well back in the pack in New Hampshire.

Yet one fact is certain. Over the years New Hampshire has been the final opportunity for candidates to extensively woo voters personally before the whirl of subsequent primaries forces surviving candidates to focus on media advertising campaigns. And that role of "focus group for the nation" is one that the Granite State takes very seriously.

New Hampshire's Republican electorate has a conservative hue, but in presidential primaries it has not always supported the champion of the GOP right. Robert Taft lost to Dwight Eisenhower in 1952; Barry Goldwater ran far behind the 1964 write-in winner, Henry Cabot Lodge; and in 1976, Ronald Reagan lost narrowly to President Ford.

Voices on the right are amplified by the unabashedly conservative Manchester *Union Leader,* which plays a role in shaping political debate within the state. In 1992 and 1996, the *Union Leader* backed the insurgent candidacy of Pat Buchanan, who staggered President Bush by taking 37 percent of the vote in the 1992 GOP primary and won the event over a crowded Republican field four years later.

For conservative candidates from Taft to Buchanan, the city of Manchester has been a most reliable source of votes. The

Recent New Hampshire Primary Results

New Hampshire held its first presidential primary in 1916.

Year	Turnout	DEMOCRATS Candidates	%	Turnout	REPUBLICANS Candidates	%
2004 (Jan. 27)	219,787	JOHN KERRY	38	67,624	GEORGE W. BUSH*	80
		Howard Dean	26			
		Wesley Clark	12			
		John Edwards	12			
		Joe Lieberman	9			
2000 (Feb. 1)	154,639	AL GORE	50	238,206	JOHN McCAIN	49
		Bill Bradley	46		George W. Bush	30
					Steve Forbes	13
					Alan Keyes	6
1996 (Feb. 20)	91,562	BILL CLINTON*	84	208,938	PAT BUCHANAN	27
					Bob Dole	26
					Lamar Alexander	23
					Steve Forbes	12
					Richard Lugar	5
1992 (Feb. 18)	167,819	PAUL TSONGAS	33	174,165	GEORGE BUSH*	53
		Bill Clinton	25		Pat Buchanan	37
		Bob Kerrey	11			
		Tom Harkin	10			
		Jerry Brown	8			
1988 (Feb. 16)	123,512	MICHAEL DUKAKIS	36	157,644	GEORGE BUSH	38
		Richard Gephardt	20		Bob Dole	28
		Paul Simon	17		Jack Kemp	13
		Jesse Jackson	8		Pierre du Pont	10
		Al Gore	7		Pat Robertson	9
1984 (Feb. 28)	101,131	GARY HART	37	75,570	RONALD REAGAN*	86
		Walter Mondale	28			
		John Glenn	12			
		Jesse Jackson	5			
		George McGovern	5			
1980 (Feb. 26)	111,930	JIMMY CARTER*	47	147,157	RONALD REAGAN	50
		Edward Kennedy	37		George Bush	23
		Jerry Brown	10		Howard Baker	13
					John Anderson	10
1976 (Feb. 24)	82,381	JIMMY CARTER	28	111,674	GERALD FORD*	49
		Morris Udall	23		Ronald Reagan	48
		Birch Bayh	15			
		Fred Harris	11			
		Sargent Shriver	8			
		Hubert Humphrey#	6			
1972 (March 7)	88,854	EDMUND MUSKIE	46	117,208	RICHARD NIXON*	68
		George McGovern	37		Paul McCloskey	20
		Sam Yorty	6		John Ashbrook	10
1968 (March 12)	55,464	LYNDON JOHNSON*#	50	103,938	RICHARD NIXON	78
		Eugene McCarthy	42		Nelson Rockefeller#	11
					Eugene McCarthy (D)#	5

Note: All candidates are listed that drew at least 5 percent of their party's primary vote. The names of winning candidates are capitalized. An asterisk (*) indicates an incumbent president. A pound sign (#) indicates a write-in candidate.

New Hampshire), and the state capital of Concord and its environs. McCain ran particularly well in these areas in 2000, in posting a victory that was stunning for its completeness.

Traversing the state in his campaign bus, the "Straight Talk Express," and holding scores of town meetings along the way, McCain masterfully tapped into the grass-roots nature of New Hampshire politics. On primary day, he swamped Bush in all 10 counties and won communities of all stripes. McCain's statewide margin of victory over Bush was nearly 20 percentage points.

On the Democratic side that year, Al Gore's 4-point victory over Bill Bradley was about as decisive as a close victory could be and essentially extinguished the former New Jersey senator's chances for the party's nomination in 2000. Gore easily won New Hampshire's two largest cities, Manchester and Nashua, swept most of the old mill towns, and carried many of the smaller cities across the state. Bradley found a toehold in upscale suburbs and academic communities. But any prospect of an upset victory by Bradley was blunted by McCain's greater success at winning independent voters, which in New Hampshire can participate in either party's primary.

Kerry's victory over a crowded field in 2004 was one of the most one-sided in a contested Democratic primary in New Hampshire in the last half century. Since 1952, only Michael Dukakis' 16-point triumph in 1988 was larger than Kerry's 12-point margin in a competitive contest.

Kerry ran particularly well in the populous southeastern corner of the state, not far from his home base of Massachusetts. Half the Democratic primary vote was cast in Hillsborough and Rockingham counties, and Kerry swept each by margins approaching 20 percentage points. Meanwhile, the only three counties carried by runner-up Howard Dean were along New Hampshire's sparsely populated western border with Dean's home state of Vermont.

But possibly the most critical showing by any Democratic candidate in New Hampshire came 12 years earlier and did not result in a victory. A month or so before the 1992 New Hampshire primary, it looked like Clinton was well positioned to win. But in short order, he suffered two big blows: a tabloid tale of womanizing and hints of draft evasion during the Vietnam War. Yet by finishing a clear second in New Hampshire behind former Massachusetts senator Paul Tsongas, Clinton survived, and he could leave New Hampshire boasting that he was the "Comeback Kid."

state's largest urban center, it was the only New Hampshire city to back Taft in 1952 and Goldwater in the 1964 GOP contest. It also went overwhelmingly for Reagan in both 1976 and 1980, as well as Buchanan in 1996.

That year, Buchanan also won old mill towns around the state, much of the conservative mountainous North Country, communities near Manchester that were loyal readers of the *Union Leader,* and communities where Ross Perot ran particularly well as an independent presidential candidate in 1992.

Generally, the strongholds of moderate Republicanism mirror the hotbeds of liberal Democrats—the seacoast area of southeast New Hampshire, the major academic communities of Hanover (Dartmouth College) and Durham (University of

NEW HAMPSHIRE DEMOCRATIC PRIMARY

2000

County	Total Vote	Bradley	Gore	Other	Winner	Percentage of Total Vote Bradley	Gore	Other
BELKNAP	5,972	2,711	2,837	424	Gore	45.4%	47.5%	7.1%
CARROLL	4,311	2,139	1,968	204	Bradley	49.6%	45.7%	4.7%
CHESHIRE	9,836	4,567	4,766	503	Gore	46.4%	48.5%	5.1%
COOS	4,192	1,478	2,394	320	Gore	35.3%	57.1%	7.6%
GRAFTON	9,612	5,321	3,824	467	Bradley	55.4%	39.8%	4.9%
HILLSBOROUGH	48,219	21,276	24,919	2,024	Gore	44.1%	51.7%	4.2%
MERRIMACK	18,122	8,145	9,156	821	Gore	44.9%	50.5%	4.5%
ROCKINGHAM	33,963	16,054	16,572	1,337	Gore	47.3%	48.8%	3.9%
STRAFFORD	15,553	6,659	8,112	782	Gore	42.8%	52.2%	5.0%
SULLIVAN	4,859	2,152	2,349	358	Gore	44.3%	48.3%	7.4%
TOTAL	154,639	70,502	76,897	7,240	Gore	45.6%	49.7%	4.7%

Note: Other vote was 3,320 John McCain (R write-in); 998 Steve Forbes (R write-in); 827 George W. Bush (R write-in); 424 Alan Keyes (R write-in); 322 Charles Buckley; 192 Heather Harder; 156 Jeffrey Peters; 134 John Eaton; 124 Lyndon H. LaRouche Jr.; 87 Jim Taylor; 75 Mark Greenstein; 44 Gary Bauer (R write-in); 35 Nathaniel Mullins; 35 Edward O'Donnell; 30 Willie Carter; 29 Randolph Crow; 22 Vincent Hamm; 19 Thomas Koos; 18 Michael Skok; 7 Mark Harnes (R write-in); 2 Andy Martin (R write-in); 340 scattered write-in.

City/Town								
AMHERST	1,518	920	559	39	Bradley	60.6%	36.8%	2.6%
ATKINSON	754	388	354	12	Bradley	51.5%	46.9%	1.6%
BARRINGTON	920	420	444	56	Gore	45.7%	48.3%	6.1%
BEDFORD	2,179	1,073	1,029	77	Bradley	49.2%	47.2%	3.5%
BELMONT	553	186	294	73	Gore	33.6%	53.2%	13.2%
BERLIN	2,012	636	1,215	161	Gore	31.6%	60.4%	8.0%
BOW	971	461	489	21	Gore	47.5%	50.4%	2.2%
CLAREMONT	1,596	510	930	156	Gore	32.0%	58.3%	9.8%
CONCORD	6,211	2,787	3,204	220	Gore	44.9%	51.6%	3.5%
CONWAY	826	401	379	46	Bradley	48.5%	45.9%	5.6%
DERRY	2,902	1,234	1,565	103	Gore	42.5%	53.9%	3.5%
DOVER	4,317	1,880	2,226	211	Gore	43.5%	51.6%	4.9%
DURHAM	2,156	1,333	802	21	Bradley	61.8%	37.2%	1.0%
EPPING	561	200	344	17	Gore	35.7%	61.3%	3.0%
EXETER	2,132	1,211	840	81	Bradley	56.8%	39.4%	3.8%
FARMINGTON	503	183	293	27	Gore	36.4%	58.3%	5.4%
FRANKLIN	795	299	430	66	Gore	37.6%	54.1%	8.3%
GILFORD	793	394	345	54	Bradley	49.7%	43.5%	6.8%
GOFFSTOWN	2,013	832	1,106	75	Gore	41.3%	54.9%	3.7%
HAMPSTEAD	875	426	414	35	Bradley	48.7%	47.3%	4.0%
HAMPTON	2,406	1,195	1,157	54	Bradley	49.7%	48.1%	2.2%
HANOVER	2,074	1,380	667	27	Bradley	66.5%	32.2%	1.3%
HOLLIS	976	577	375	24	Bradley	59.1%	38.4%	2.5%
HOOKSETT	1,211	467	671	73	Gore	38.6%	55.4%	6.0%
HUDSON	2,482	1,135	1,317	30	Gore	45.7%	53.1%	1.2%
JAFFREY	648	285	329	34	Gore	44.0%	50.8%	5.2%
KEENE	3,594	1,657	1,803	134	Gore	46.1%	50.2%	3.7%
KINGSTON	628	291	299	38	Gore	46.3%	47.6%	6.1%
LACONIA	1,751	767	884	100	Gore	43.8%	50.5%	5.7%
LEBANON	1,638	853	734	51	Bradley	52.1%	44.8%	3.1%

NEW HAMPSHIRE DEMOCRATIC PRIMARY

2000

| County | Total Vote | Bradley | Gore | Other | Winner | Percentage of Total Vote | | |
						Bradley	Gore	Other
LITCHFIELD	761	324	408	29	Gore	42.6%	53.6%	3.8%
LITTLETON	467	206	240	21	Gore	44.1%	51.4%	4.5%
LONDONDERRY	2,404	1,241	1,059	104	Bradley	51.6%	44.1%	4.3%
MANCHESTER	14,960	5,477	8,618	865	Gore	36.6%	57.6%	5.8%
MERRIMACK TOWN	3,005	1,326	1,546	133	Gore	44.1%	51.4%	4.4%
MILFORD	1,439	687	693	59	Gore	47.7%	48.2%	4.1%
NASHUA	10,938	4,781	5,828	329	Gore	43.7%	53.3%	3.0%
NEWMARKET	1,408	708	661	39	Bradley	50.3%	46.9%	2.8%
NEWPORT	616	240	328	48	Gore	39.0%	53.2%	7.8%
PELHAM	1,317	619	605	93	Bradley	47.0%	45.9%	7.1%
PEMBROKE	836	301	494	41	Gore	36.0%	59.1%	4.9%
PETERBOROUGH	987	596	369	22	Bradley	60.4%	37.4%	2.2%
PLAISTOW	717	282	387	48	Gore	39.3%	54.0%	6.7%
PLYMOUTH	648	404	233	11	Bradley	62.3%	36.0%	1.7%
PORTSMOUTH	4,234	1,999	2,155	80	Gore	47.2%	50.9%	1.9%
RAYMOND	818	299	476	43	Gore	36.6%	58.2%	5.3%
ROCHESTER	3,247	1,097	1,899	251	Gore	33.8%	58.5%	7.7%
SALEM	3,385	1,467	1,785	133	Gore	43.3%	52.7%	3.9%
SEABROOK	810	292	480	38	Gore	36.0%	59.3%	4.7%
SOMERSWORTH	1,665	555	1,050	60	Gore	33.3%	63.1%	3.6%
SWANZEY	756	326	367	63	Gore	43.1%	48.5%	8.3%
WEARE	710	330	340	40	Gore	46.5%	47.9%	5.6%
WINDHAM	1,130	577	480	73	Bradley	51.1%	42.5%	6.5%

Note: The 2000 Democratic county table includes scattered write-in votes that were not included in the New Hampshire Manual for the General Court 2001, where the official returns were published. But they were tallied and distributed by state election officials immediately after the primary. City and town results are as they appeared in the Manual, without scattered write-in votes. Basically, communities are included with a population of at least 5,000 in the 2000 Census.

NEW HAMPSHIRE REPUBLICAN PRIMARY

2000

County	Total Vote	G.W. Bush	Forbes	Keyes	McCain	Other	Winner	Percentage of Total Vote				
								G.W. Bush	Forbes	Keyes	McCain	Other
BELKNAP	13,027	4,192	1,696	827	6,009	303	McCain	32.2%	13.0%	6.3%	46.1%	2.3%
CARROLL	11,453	3,565	1,357	509	5,794	228	McCain	31.1%	11.8%	4.4%	50.6%	2.0%
CHESHIRE	12,871	3,666	1,547	776	6,583	299	McCain	28.5%	12.0%	6.0%	51.1%	2.3%
COOS	5,223	1,642	812	315	2,266	188	McCain	31.4%	15.5%	6.0%	43.4%	3.6%
GRAFTON	15,331	4,574	1,837	857	7,750	313	McCain	29.8%	12.0%	5.6%	50.6%	2.0%
HILLSBOROUGH	69,968	21,223	10,365	5,051	31,896	1,433	McCain	30.3%	14.8%	7.2%	45.6%	2.0%
MERRIMACK	29,636	8,263	3,561	1,871	15,302	639	McCain	27.9%	12.0%	6.3%	51.6%	2.2%
ROCKINGHAM	55,807	17,353	6,534	3,160	27,806	954	McCain	31.1%	11.7%	5.7%	49.8%	1.7%
STRAFFORD	17,344	5,581	1,514	1,328	8,479	442	McCain	32.2%	8.7%	7.7%	48.9%	2.5%
SULLIVAN	7,546	2,271	943	485	3,721	126	McCain	30.1%	12.5%	6.4%	49.3%	1.7%
TOTAL	238,206	72,330	30,166	15,179	115,606	4,925	McCain	30.4%	12.7%	6.4%	48.5%	2.1%

Note: Other vote was 1,640 Gary Bauer; 1,155 Al Gore (D write-in); 1,025 Bill Bradley (D write-in); 231 Elizabeth Dole (R write-in); 163 Orrin G. Hatch; 98 Dorian Yeager; 81 Andy Martin; 61 Samuel Berry; 51 Kenneth Capalbo; 41 Timothy Mosby; 34 Mark Harnes; 23 Richard Peet; 14 Tom Oyler; 3 Lyndon H. LaRouche Jr. (D write-in); 3 Jeffrey Peters (D write-in); 2 Charles Buckley (D write-in); 2 Willie Carter (D write-in); 2 Mark Greenstein (D write-in); 1 Vincent Hamm (D write-in); 1 Heather Harder (D write-in); 1 Michael Skok (D write-in); 293 scattered write-in.

City/Town	Total Vote	G.W. Bush	Forbes	Keyes	McCain	Other	Winner	G.W. Bush	Forbes	Keyes	McCain	Other
AMHERST	3,101	1,002	285	146	1,631	37	McCain	32.3%	9.2%	4.7%	52.6%	1.2%
ATKINSON	1,636	572	163	61	818	22	McCain	35.0%	10.0%	3.7%	50.0%	1.3%
BARRINGTON	1,465	421	158	132	726	28	McCain	28.7%	10.8%	9.0%	49.6%	1.9%
BEDFORD	5,379	1,859	881	310	2,265	64	McCain	34.6%	16.4%	5.8%	42.1%	1.2%
BELMONT	1,161	338	143	110	535	35	McCain	29.1%	12.3%	9.5%	46.1%	3.0%
BERLIN	1,162	295	184	80	562	41	McCain	25.4%	15.8%	6.9%	48.4%	3.5%
BOW	2,176	680	222	111	1,140	23	McCain	31.3%	10.2%	5.1%	52.4%	1.1%
CLAREMONT	1,799	534	246	133	831	55	McCain	29.7%	13.7%	7.4%	46.2%	3.1%
CONCORD	7,603	2,139	666	447	4,119	232	McCain	28.1%	8.8%	5.9%	54.2%	3.1%
CONWAY	1,660	460	174	60	920	46	McCain	27.7%	10.5%	3.6%	55.4%	2.8%
DERRY	5,132	1,597	699	371	2,384	81	McCain	31.1%	13.6%	7.2%	46.5%	1.6%
DOVER	4,298	1,403	344	248	2,142	161	McCain	32.6%	8.0%	5.8%	49.8%	3.7%
DURHAM	1,519	440	82	95	882	20	McCain	29.0%	5.4%	6.3%	58.1%	1.3%
EPPING	979	267	151	78	462	21	McCain	27.3%	15.4%	8.0%	47.2%	2.1%
EXETER	3,389	963	311	140	1,673	302	McCain	28.4%	9.2%	4.1%	49.4%	8.9%
FARMINGTON	780	242	76	72	381	9	McCain	31.0%	9.7%	9.2%	48.8%	1.2%
FRANKLIN	1,377	341	182	114	719	21	McCain	24.8%	13.2%	8.3%	52.2%	1.5%
GILFORD	1,940	678	176	63	985	38	McCain	34.9%	9.1%	3.2%	50.8%	2.0%
GOFFSTOWN	3,497	1,049	790	286	1,340	32	McCain	30.0%	22.6%	8.2%	38.3%	0.9%
HAMPSTEAD	1,904	563	233	106	975	27	McCain	29.6%	12.2%	5.6%	51.2%	1.4%
HAMPTON	3,326	1,118	309	112	1,754	33	McCain	33.6%	9.3%	3.4%	52.7%	1.0%
HANOVER	1,429	376	61	42	939	11	McCain	26.3%	4.3%	2.9%	65.7%	0.8%
HOLLIS	1,971	617	149	79	1,105	21	McCain	31.3%	7.6%	4.0%	56.1%	1.1%
HOOKSETT	2,406	736	495	168	966	41	McCain	30.6%	20.6%	7.0%	40.1%	1.7%
HUDSON	3,997	1,222	394	317	1,945	119	McCain	30.6%	9.9%	7.9%	48.7%	3.0%
JAFFREY	1,036	311	119	55	543	8	McCain	30.0%	11.5%	5.3%	52.4%	0.8%
KEENE	3,654	983	388	193	2,002	88	McCain	26.9%	10.6%	5.3%	54.8%	2.4%
KINGSTON	1,289	396	159	58	648	28	McCain	30.7%	12.3%	4.5%	50.3%	2.2%
LACONIA	3,326	1,150	470	177	1,447	82	McCain	34.6%	14.1%	5.3%	43.5%	2.5%
LEBANON	1,979	507	112	108	1,208	44	McCain	25.6%	5.7%	5.5%	61.0%	2.2%

NEW HAMPSHIRE REPUBLICAN PRIMARY

2000

County	Total Vote	G.W. Bush	Forbes	Keyes	McCain	Other	Winner	Percentage of Total Vote				
								G.W. Bush	Forbes	Keyes	McCain	Other
LITCHFIELD	1,466	428	183	108	722	25	McCain	29.2%	12.5%	7.4%	49.2%	1.7%
LITTLETON	1,145	384	202	47	499	13	McCain	33.5%	17.6%	4.1%	43.6%	1.1%
LONDONDERRY	4,727	1,465	613	358	2,215	76	McCain	31.0%	13.0%	7.6%	46.9%	1.6%
MANCHESTER	15,648	4,721	3,421	1,304	5,832	370	McCain	30.2%	21.9%	8.3%	37.3%	2.4%
MERRIMACK TOWN	5,421	1,707	652	424	2,531	107	McCain	31.5%	12.0%	7.8%	46.7%	2.0%
MILFORD	2,767	839	332	215	1,314	67	McCain	30.3%	12.0%	7.8%	47.5%	2.4%
NASHUA	12,587	3,713	1,296	863	6,472	243	McCain	29.5%	10.3%	6.9%	51.4%	1.9%
NEWMARKET	1,297	312	107	86	771	21	McCain	24.1%	8.2%	6.6%	59.4%	1.6%
NEWPORT	1,026	381	145	63	429	8	McCain	37.1%	14.1%	6.1%	41.8%	0.8%
PELHAM	1,826	602	192	119	870	43	McCain	33.0%	10.5%	6.5%	47.6%	2.4%
PEMBROKE	1,406	378	196	113	691	28	McCain	26.9%	13.9%	8.0%	49.1%	2.0%
PETERBOROUGH	1,418	429	110	47	810	22	McCain	30.3%	7.8%	3.3%	57.1%	1.6%
PLAISTOW	1,325	452	130	61	654	28	McCain	34.1%	9.8%	4.6%	49.4%	2.1%
PLYMOUTH	856	219	132	65	416	24	McCain	25.6%	15.4%	7.6%	48.6%	2.8%
PORTSMOUTH	3,349	1,005	238	121	1,933	52	McCain	30.0%	7.1%	3.6%	57.7%	1.6%
RAYMOND	1,719	467	273	136	822	21	McCain	27.2%	15.9%	7.9%	47.8%	1.2%
ROCHESTER	4,153	1,442	376	375	1,843	117	McCain	34.7%	9.1%	9.0%	44.4%	2.8%
SALEM	4,364	1,513	594	198	1,989	70	McCain	34.7%	13.6%	4.5%	45.6%	1.6%
SEABROOK	1,184	449	154	53	512	16	McCain	37.9%	13.0%	4.5%	43.2%	1.4%
SOMERSWORTH	1,380	475	113	134	631	27	McCain	34.4%	8.2%	9.7%	45.7%	2.0%
SWANZEY	1,148	350	146	66	559	27	McCain	30.5%	12.7%	5.7%	48.7%	2.4%
WEARE	1,675	430	254	182	771	38	McCain	25.7%	15.2%	10.9%	46.0%	2.3%
WINDHAM	2,586	831	235	125	1,339	56	McCain	32.1%	9.1%	4.8%	51.8%	2.2%

Note: The 2000 Republican county table includes scattered write-in votes that were not included in the New Hampshire Manual for the General Court 2001, where the official returns were published. But they were tallied and distributed by state election officials immediately after the primary. City and town results are as they appeared in the Manual, without scattered write-in votes. Basically, communities are included with a population of at least 5,000 in the 2000 Census.

NEW HAMPSHIRE DEMOCRATIC PRIMARY

2004

County	Total Vote	Clark	Dean	Edwards	Kerry	Lieberman	Other	Winner	Percentage of Total Vote					
									Clark	Dean	Edwards	Kerry	Lieberman	Other
BELKNAP	9,099	1,176	2,238	1,189	3,462	846	188	Kerry	12.9%	24.6%	13.1%	38.0%	9.3%	2.1%
CARROLL	7,930	1,098	2,391	817	2,934	486	204	Kerry	13.8%	30.2%	10.3%	37.0%	6.1%	2.6%
CHESHIRE	15,047	2,184	5,042	1,742	4,706	766	607	Dean	14.5%	33.5%	11.6%	31.3%	5.1%	4.0%
COOS	5,641	832	1,273	656	2,469	301	110	Kerry	14.7%	22.6%	11.6%	43.8%	5.3%	2.0%
GRAFTON	15,984	1,853	6,486	1,534	5,004	778	329	Dean	11.6%	40.6%	9.6%	31.3%	4.9%	2.1%
HILLSBOROUGH	62,424	7,684	13,665	7,817	24,973	6,949	1,336	Kerry	12.3%	21.9%	12.5%	40.0%	11.1%	2.1%
MERRIMACK	27,606	3,408	7,570	3,499	10,383	2,179	567	Kerry	12.3%	27.4%	12.7%	37.6%	7.9%	2.1%
ROCKINGHAM	48,163	5,808	11,243	5,684	19,893	4,679	856	Kerry	12.1%	23.3%	11.8%	41.3%	9.7%	1.8%
STRAFFORD	20,321	2,639	4,843	2,641	8,093	1,561	544	Kerry	13.0%	23.8%	13.0%	39.8%	7.7%	2.7%
SULLIVAN	7,572	632	3,010	908	2,460	366	196	Dean	8.3%	39.8%	12.0%	32.5%	4.8%	2.6%
TOTAL	219,787	27,314	57,761	26,487	84,377	18,911	4,937	Kerry	12.4%	26.3%	12.1%	38.4%	8.6%	2.2%

Note: Other vote was 3,114 Dennis J. Kucinich; 419 Richard A. Gephardt; 347 Al Sharpton; 257 George W. Bush (R write-in); 90 Lyndon H. LaRouche Jr.; 86 Willie Carter; 81 Carol Moseley Braun; 79 Edward O'Donnell; 68 Katherine Bateman; 60 Randy Crow; 58 Vincent Hamm; 49 Robert Linnell; 42 Gerry Dokka; 31 Caroline Killeen; 15 Randy Lee; 13 Harry Braun; 11 Mildred Glover; 8 Fern Penna; 8 Leonard Talbow; 5 John Rigazio (R write-in); 2 Blake Ashby (R write-in); 2 John Buchanan (R write-in); 92 scattered write-in.

City/Town	Total Vote	Clark	Dean	Edwards	Kerry	Lieberman	Other	Winner	Clark	Dean	Edwards	Kerry	Lieberman	Other
AMHERST	2,172	283	611	258	802	191	27	Kerry	13.0%	28.1%	11.9%	36.9%	8.8%	1.2%
ATKINSON	1,205	112	233	125	573	153	9	Kerry	9.3%	19.3%	10.4%	47.6%	12.7%	0.7%
BARRINGTON	1,385	208	356	174	500	108	39	Kerry	15.0%	25.7%	12.6%	36.1%	7.8%	2.8%
BEDFORD	2,964	355	638	344	1,113	478	36	Kerry	12.0%	21.5%	11.6%	37.6%	16.1%	1.2%
BELMONT	836	106	168	119	348	79	16	Kerry	12.7%	20.1%	14.2%	41.6%	9.4%	1.9%
BERLIN	2,316	343	394	245	1,149	143	42	Kerry	14.8%	17.0%	10.6%	49.6%	6.2%	1.8%
BOW	1,577	173	382	234	606	158	24	Kerry	11.0%	24.2%	14.8%	38.4%	10.0%	1.5%
CLAREMONT	2,159	161	740	296	813	95	54	Kerry	7.5%	34.3%	13.7%	37.7%	4.4%	2.5%
CONCORD	8,812	1,005	2,445	1,142	3,439	604	177	Kerry	11.4%	27.7%	13.0%	39.0%	6.9%	2.0%
CONWAY	1,481	250	445	132	558	59	37	Kerry	16.9%	30.0%	8.9%	37.7%	4.0%	2.5%
DERRY	3,899	442	757	534	1,702	413	51	Kerry	11.3%	19.4%	13.7%	43.7%	10.6%	1.3%
DOVER	5,676	690	1,350	679	2,393	409	155	Kerry	12.2%	23.8%	12.0%	42.2%	7.2%	2.7%
DURHAM	2,439	362	837	240	757	134	109	Dean	14.8%	34.3%	9.8%	31.0%	5.5%	4.5%
EPPING	952	198	217	107	336	81	13	Kerry	20.8%	22.8%	11.2%	35.3%	8.5%	1.4%
EXETER	2,929	364	843	322	1,153	210	37	Kerry	12.4%	28.8%	11.0%	39.4%	7.2%	1.3%
FARMINGTON	763	135	159	107	288	58	16	Kerry	17.7%	20.8%	14.0%	37.7%	7.6%	2.1%
FRANKLIN	1,288	172	280	180	527	105	24	Kerry	13.4%	21.7%	14.0%	40.9%	8.2%	1.9%
GILFORD	1,198	170	299	137	453	115	24	Kerry	14.2%	25.0%	11.4%	37.8%	9.6%	2.0%
GOFFSTOWN	2,564	332	478	335	1,018	343	58	Kerry	12.9%	18.6%	13.1%	39.7%	13.4%	2.3%
HAMPSTEAD	1,345	150	287	158	575	156	19	Kerry	11.2%	21.3%	11.7%	42.8%	11.6%	1.4%
HAMPTON	3,235	299	646	397	1,554	297	42	Kerry	9.2%	20.0%	12.3%	48.0%	9.2%	1.3%
HANOVER	3,436	453	1,499	302	1,010	116	56	Dean	13.2%	43.6%	8.8%	29.4%	3.4%	1.6%
HOLLIS	1,583	200	449	178	556	158	42	Kerry	12.6%	28.4%	11.2%	35.1%	10.0%	2.7%
HOOKSETT	1,704	224	332	222	685	219	22	Kerry	13.1%	19.5%	13.0%	40.2%	12.9%	1.3%
HUDSON	3,342	447	674	400	1,449	330	42	Kerry	13.4%	20.2%	12.0%	43.4%	9.9%	1.3%
JAFFREY	1,013	144	253	107	415	65	29	Kerry	14.2%	25.0%	10.6%	41.0%	6.4%	2.9%
KEENE	4,972	739	1,719	575	1,485	214	240	Dean	14.9%	34.6%	11.6%	29.9%	4.3%	4.8%
KINGSTON	798	91	156	96	364	71	20	Kerry	11.4%	19.5%	12.0%	45.6%	8.9%	2.5%
LACONIA	2,334	289	520	298	916	265	46	Kerry	12.4%	22.3%	12.8%	39.2%	11.4%	2.0%
LEBANON	2,627	233	1,192	232	810	103	57	Dean	8.9%	45.4%	8.8%	30.8%	3.9%	2.2%

NEW HAMPSHIRE DEMOCRATIC PRIMARY

2004

County	Total Vote	Clark	Dean	Edwards	Kerry	Lieberman	Other	Winner	Percentage of Total Vote					
									Clark	Dean	Edwards	Kerry	Lieberman	Other
LITCHFIELD	1,074	140	215	129	458	123	9	Kerry	13.0%	20.0%	12.0%	42.6%	11.5%	0.8%
LITTLETON	736	83	239	89	272	42	11	Kerry	11.3%	32.5%	12.1%	37.0%	5.7%	1.5%
LONDONDERRY	3,454	382	763	402	1,477	399	31	Kerry	11.1%	22.1%	11.6%	42.8%	11.6%	0.9%
MANCHESTER	16,381	1,982	3,092	2,167	6,375	2,318	447	Kerry	12.1%	18.9%	13.2%	38.9%	14.2%	2.7%
MERRIMACK TOWN	4,216	594	797	560	1,774	445	46	Kerry	14.1%	18.9%	13.3%	42.1%	10.6%	1.1%
MILFORD	2,132	270	497	260	894	174	37	Kerry	12.7%	23.3%	12.2%	41.9%	8.2%	1.7%
NASHUA	13,561	1,500	2,596	1,742	6,179	1,338	206	Kerry	11.1%	19.1%	12.8%	45.6%	9.9%	1.5%
NEWMARKET	2,018	247	585	297	696	142	51	Kerry	12.2%	29.0%	14.7%	34.5%	7.0%	2.5%
NEWPORT	853	100	293	115	288	44	13	Dean	11.7%	34.3%	13.5%	33.8%	5.2%	1.5%
PELHAM	1,696	187	317	176	816	175	25	Kerry	11.0%	18.7%	10.4%	48.1%	10.3%	1.5%
PEMBROKE	1,176	155	264	170	482	90	15	Kerry	13.2%	22.4%	14.5%	41.0%	7.7%	1.3%
PETERBOROUGH	1,612	229	580	141	509	91	62	Dean	14.2%	36.0%	8.7%	31.6%	5.6%	3.8%
PLAISTOW	1,104	106	248	123	472	139	16	Kerry	9.6%	22.5%	11.1%	42.8%	12.6%	1.4%
PLYMOUTH	929	87	383	100	274	56	29	Dean	9.4%	41.2%	10.8%	29.5%	6.0%	3.1%
PORTSMOUTH	5,449	717	1,604	650	2,007	314	157	Kerry	13.2%	29.4%	11.9%	36.8%	5.8%	2.9%
RAYMOND	1,253	206	270	158	473	127	19	Kerry	16.4%	21.5%	12.6%	37.7%	10.1%	1.5%
ROCHESTER	4,058	564	734	613	1,680	399	68	Kerry	13.9%	18.1%	15.1%	41.4%	9.8%	1.7%
SALEM	4,205	435	798	416	2,009	498	49	Kerry	10.3%	19.0%	9.9%	47.8%	11.8%	1.2%
SEABROOK	1,043	98	184	122	549	68	22	Kerry	9.4%	17.6%	11.7%	52.6%	6.5%	2.1%
SOMERSWORTH	2,030	188	359	291	1,007	152	33	Kerry	9.3%	17.7%	14.3%	49.6%	7.5%	1.6%
SWANZEY	1,097	199	336	123	364	52	23	Kerry	18.1%	30.6%	11.2%	33.2%	4.7%	2.1%
WEARE	1,157	165	316	132	416	107	21	Kerry	14.3%	27.3%	11.4%	36.0%	9.2%	1.8%
WINDHAM	1,851	215	437	174	781	229	15	Kerry	11.6%	23.6%	9.4%	42.2%	12.4%	0.8%

Note: The 2004 Democratic county table includes scattered write-in votes that were not included in the New Hampshire Manual for the General Court 2005, where the official returns were published. But they were tallied and distributed by state election officials immediately after the primary. City and town results are as they appeared in the Manual, without scattered write-in votes. Basically, communities are included with a population of at least 5,000 in the 2000 Census.

NEW HAMPSHIRE REPUBLICAN PRIMARY

2004

| County | Total Vote | G.W. Bush | Other | Winner | Percentage of Total Vote | |
					Clinton	Other
BELKNAP	3,877	3,027	850	G.W. Bush	78.1%	21.9%
CARROLL	3,119	2,468	651	G.W. Bush	79.1%	20.9%
CHESHIRE	3,713	2,719	994	G.W. Bush	73.2%	26.8%
COOS	1,781	1,350	431	G.W. Bush	75.8%	24.2%
GRAFTON	4,523	3,571	952	G.W. Bush	79.0%	21.0%
HILLSBOROUGH	19,669	15,970	3,699	G.W. Bush	81.2%	18.8%
MERRIMACK	9,234	7,450	1,784	G.W. Bush	80.7%	19.3%
ROCKINGHAM	14,814	12,199	2,615	G.W. Bush	82.3%	17.7%
STRAFFORD	4,651	3,422	1,229	G.W. Bush	73.6%	26.4%
SULLIVAN	2,243	1,786	457	G.W. Bush	79.6%	20.4%
TOTAL	67,624	53,962	13,662	G.W. Bush	79.8%	20.2%

Note: Other vote was 2,819 John Kerry (D write-in); 1,789 Howard Dean (D write-in); 1,407 Wesley Clark (D write-in); 1,088 John Edwards (D write-in); 914 Joseph I. Lieberman (D write-in); 841 Richard Bosa; 836 John Buchanan; 803 John Rigazio; 579 Robert Haines; 388 Michael Callis; 264 Blake Ashby; 239 Millie Howard; 154 Tom Laughlin; 153 Bill Wyatt; 124 Jim Taylor; 87 Mark Harnes; 77 Cornelius O'Connor; 52 George Gostigian; 38 Dennis J. Kucinich (D write-in); 15 Al Sharpton (D write-in); 6 Carol Moseley Braun (D write-in); 5 Lyndon H. LaRouche Jr. (D write-in); 4 Richard A. Gephardt (D write-in); 3 Katherine Bateman (D write-in); 1 Willie Carter (D write-in); 1 Robert Linnell (D write-in); 1 Edward O'Donnell (D write-in); 1 Fern Penna (D write-in); 973 scattered write-in.

City/Town	Total Vote	G.W. Bush	Other	Winner	Clinton	Other
AMHERST	775	623	152	G.W. Bush	80.4%	19.6%
ATKINSON	354	307	47	G.W. Bush	86.7%	13.3%
BARRINGTON	421	288	133	G.W. Bush	68.4%	31.6%
BEDFORD	1,551	1,358	193	G.W. Bush	87.6%	12.4%
BELMONT	386	275	111	G.W. Bush	71.2%	28.8%
BERLIN	362	246	116	G.W. Bush	68.0%	32.0%
BOW	685	562	123	G.W. Bush	82.0%	18.0%
CLAREMONT	553	440	113	G.W. Bush	79.6%	20.4%
CONCORD	2,265	1,743	522	G.W. Bush	77.0%	23.0%
CONWAY	390	270	120	G.W. Bush	69.2%	30.8%
DERRY	1,376	1,181	195	G.W. Bush	85.8%	14.2%
DOVER	1,037	785	252	G.W. Bush	75.7%	24.3%
DURHAM	300	226	74	G.W. Bush	75.3%	24.7%
EPPING	211	177	34	G.W. Bush	83.9%	16.1%
EXETER	809	585	224	G.W. Bush	72.3%	27.7%
FARMINGTON	237	180	57	G.W. Bush	75.9%	24.1%
FRANKLIN	434	348	86	G.W. Bush	80.2%	19.8%
GILFORD	495	387	108	G.W. Bush	78.2%	21.8%
GOFFSTOWN	1,057	888	169	G.W. Bush	84.0%	16.0%
HAMPSTEAD	505	431	74	G.W. Bush	85.3%	14.7%
HAMPTON	803	691	112	G.W. Bush	86.1%	13.9%
HANOVER	285	227	58	G.W. Bush	79.6%	20.4%
HOLLIS	476	403	73	G.W. Bush	84.7%	15.3%
HOOKSETT	786	636	150	G.W. Bush	80.9%	19.1%
HUDSON	912	675	237	G.W. Bush	74.0%	26.0%
JAFFREY	344	282	62	G.W. Bush	82.0%	18.0%
KEENE	1,028	709	319	G.W. Bush	69.0%	31.0%
KINGSTON	344	268	76	G.W. Bush	77.9%	22.1%
LACONIA	970	763	207	G.W. Bush	78.7%	21.3%
LEBANON	534	433	101	G.W. Bush	81.1%	18.9%

NEW HAMPSHIRE REPUBLICAN PRIMARY

2004

| County | Total Vote | G.W. Bush | Other | Winner | Percentage of Total Vote | |
					Clinton	Other
LITCHFIELD	398	332	66	G.W. Bush	83.4%	16.6%
LITTLETON	422	340	82	G.W. Bush	80.6%	19.4%
LONDONDERRY	1,082	918	164	G.W. Bush	84.8%	15.2%
MANCHESTER	5,003	4,148	855	G.W. Bush	82.9%	17.1%
MERRIMACK TOWN	1,353	1,098	255	G.W. Bush	81.2%	18.8%
MILFORD	779	637	142	G.W. Bush	81.8%	18.2%
NASHUA	2,960	2,415	545	G.W. Bush	81.6%	18.4%
NEWMARKET	317	220	97	G.W. Bush	69.4%	30.6%
NEWPORT	245	206	39	G.W. Bush	84.1%	15.9%
PELHAM	483	429	54	G.W. Bush	88.8%	11.2%
PEMBROKE	381	329	52	G.W. Bush	86.4%	13.6%
PETERBOROUGH	356	294	62	G.W. Bush	82.6%	17.4%
PLAISTOW	292	237	55	G.W. Bush	81.2%	18.8%
PLYMOUTH	219	155	64	G.W. Bush	70.8%	29.2%
PORTSMOUTH	742	612	130	G.W. Bush	82.5%	17.5%
RAYMOND	430	349	81	G.W. Bush	81.2%	18.8%
ROCHESTER	1,259	898	361	G.W. Bush	71.3%	28.7%
SALEM	1,271	1,085	186	G.W. Bush	85.4%	14.6%
SEABROOK	342	289	53	G.W. Bush	84.5%	15.5%
SOMERSWORTH	313	261	52	G.W. Bush	83.4%	16.6%
SWANZEY	364	232	132	G.W. Bush	63.7%	36.3%
WEARE	360	298	62	G.W. Bush	82.8%	17.2%
WINDHAM	767	616	151	G.W. Bush	80.3%	19.7%

Note: The 2004 Republican county table includes scattered write-in votes that were not included in the New Hampshire Manual for the General Court 2005, where the official returns were published. But they were tallied and distributed by state election officials immediately after the primary. City and town results are as they appeared in the Manual, without scattered write-in votes. Basically, communities are included with a population of at least 5,000 in the 2000 Census.

NEW JERSEY

New Jersey once joined with California to provide bicoastal bookends for the final big day of the primary season. But since 1996, the two have held separate spots on the calendar, as California moved its primary forward to March in a bid to regain its status as a major player in the nominating process.

Occasionally, New Jersey's role has been noteworthy even on its June date. In 1984, Walter Mondale essentially nailed down the Democratic nomination with a victory in the Garden State over Gary Hart. And in 1980, Edward Kennedy scored a last hurrah of sorts with Democratic primary wins over the front-running Jimmy Carter in both New Jersey and California.

More typically, the exercise has been a yawn, as primary voters often were asked merely to ratify delegate slates put together by their parties' leadership. New Jersey Republicans have not had a competitive primary since 1952, when Dwight Eisenhower swamped Robert Taft by a margin of nearly 2 to 1. And the moderate tone of the state GOP has not seemed to change a lot since then.

Recent New Jersey Primary Results

New Jersey held its first presidential primary in 1912.

Year	DEMOCRATS			REPUBLICANS		
	Turnout	Candidates	%	Turnout	Candidates	%
2004 (June 8)	214,804	JOHN KERRY	92	141,752	GEORGE W. BUSH*	100
2000 (June 6)	378,272	AL GORE	95	240,810	GEORGE W. BUSH	84
		Lyndon LaRouche	5		Alan Keyes	16
1996 (June 4)	266,740	BILL CLINTON*	95	218,812	BOB DOLE	82
					Pat Buchanan	11
					Alan Keyes	7
1992 (June 2)	392,626	BILL CLINTON	62	310,270	GEORGE BUSH*	78
		Jerry Brown	20		Pat Buchanan	15
		Paul Tsongas	12		Ross Perot#	8
1988 (June 7)	654,302	MICHAEL DUKAKIS	63	241,033	GEORGE BUSH	100
		Jesse Jackson	33			
1984 (June 5)	676,561	WALTER MONDALE	45	240,054	RONALD REAGAN*	100
		Gary Hart	30			
		Jesse Jackson	24			
1980 (June 3)	560,908	EDWARD KENNEDY	56	277,977	RONALD REAGAN	81
		Jimmy Carter*	38		George Bush	17
1976 (June 8)	360,839	JIMMY CARTER	58	242,122	GERALD FORD*	100
		Frank Church	14			
		Henry Jackson	9			
		George Wallace	9			
		Ellen McCormack	6			
1972 (June 6)	76,834	SHIRLEY CHISHOLM	67	—	No candidates entered	
		Terry Sanford	33			
1968 (June 4)	27,446	EUGENE McCARTHY#	36	88,592	RICHARD NIXON#	81
		Robert Kennedy#	31		Nelson Rockefeller#	13
		Hubert Humphrey#	20			
		George Wallace#	5			
		Richard Nixon (R)#	5			

Note: All candidates are listed that drew at least 5 percent of their party's primary vote. The names of winning candidates are capitalized. An asterisk (*) indicates an incumbent president. A pound sign (#) indicates a write-in candidate.

Ronald Reagan did not even enter the 1976 preference primary, and President Gerald Ford took all but four of the state's delegates. In 1980, Reagan entered the primary, but his competition evaporated before the June vote. It has been a similar story since then; the eventual nominees have been acceptable to the state party establishment and have won the New Jersey primary with little or no opposition.

For many years, New Jersey held a nonbinding presidential preference vote with delegates elected elsewhere on the ballot. The multiple votes at times produced some widely varying expressions of voter sentiment. In 1972, for instance, New York City congresswoman Shirley Chisholm defeated former North Carolina governor Terry Sanford in the Democratic "beauty contest" that attracted barely 75,000 voters, while

George McGovern outpolled Hubert Humphrey in the separate, more meaningful contest for at-large delegates that drew more than 400,000 voters.

New Jersey Democrats have since moved to a binding presidential preference vote, something the Republicans have been slower to do. And what consequential primaries there have been of late have been on the Democratic side.

In 1980, Kennedy swept New Jersey by a margin of 3 to 2, helping keep alive his challenge for the Democratic nomination—at least in spirit.

In 1984, New Jersey gave Mondale a desperately needed win that offset a loss the same day to Gary Hart in California. Mondale beat Hart by a decisive 15 percentage points in New Jersey, winning virtually all the major suburban counties of northern New Jersey, as well as Camden and Mercer (Trenton) to the south. Mondale's New Jersey win ensured that he would have enough delegates at the convention to secure a first-ballot nomination.

Winning margins in the Democratic primary have grown wider since then, with New Jersey giving Bill Clinton one of his more convincing primary victories in 1992 outside the South. Clinton won more than 60 percent of the vote, running best in Essex County (Newark) with its large minority population; Jesse Jackson had carried the county in Democratic primary voting in 1984 and 1988.

Since 1996, New Jersey has been the last major stop on the campaign trail and has found it hard to match the glitz and glitter that California routinely offers. But at least New Jersey has been spared the comparisons between the two. (Hart got himself in trouble in 1984 with a joke about the state's reputation for toxic-waste dumps.)

And occasionally, New Jersey has been able to offer some glamour of its own. Among its Democratic delegates in 1988 was Academy Award-winning actress Olympia Dukakis, a cousin of the New Jersey primary winner that year and the party's eventual nominee, Michael Dukakis.

NEW JERSEY DEMOCRATIC PRIMARY

2000

| County | Total Vote | Gore | LaRouche | Winner | Percentage of Total Vote | |
					Gore	LaRouche
ATLANTIC	8,739	8,156	583	Gore	93.3%	6.7%
BERGEN	33,068	31,696	1,372	Gore	95.9%	4.1%
BURLINGTON	19,889	18,753	1,136	Gore	94.3%	5.7%
CAMDEN	31,247	29,728	1,519	Gore	95.1%	4.9%
CAPE MAY	2,819	2,600	219	Gore	92.2%	7.8%
CUMBERLAND	4,489	4,264	225	Gore	95.0%	5.0%
ESSEX	54,196	51,803	2,393	Gore	95.6%	4.4%
GLOUCESTER	16,620	15,731	889	Gore	94.7%	5.3%
HUDSON	37,964	36,055	1,909	Gore	95.0%	5.0%
HUNTERDON	3,316	3,089	227	Gore	93.2%	6.8%
MERCER	16,993	16,093	900	Gore	94.7%	5.3%
MIDDLESEX	33,524	31,820	1,704	Gore	94.9%	5.1%
MONMOUTH	22,010	20,677	1,333	Gore	93.9%	6.1%
MORRIS	13,029	12,351	678	Gore	94.8%	5.2%
OCEAN	14,336	13,497	839	Gore	94.1%	5.9%
PASSAIC	15,041	14,233	808	Gore	94.6%	5.4%
SALEM	2,548	2,255	293	Gore	88.5%	11.5%
SOMERSET	9,690	9,335	355	Gore	96.3%	3.7%
SUSSEX	3,146	2,784	362	Gore	88.5%	11.5%
UNION	32,386	31,170	1,216	Gore	96.2%	3.8%
WARREN	3,222	2,861	361	Gore	88.8%	11.2%
TOTAL	378,272	358,951	19,321	Gore	94.9%	5.1%

NEW JERSEY REPUBLICAN PRIMARY

2000

County	Total Vote	G.W. Bush	Keyes	Winner	Percentage of Total Vote	
					G.W. Bush	Keyes
ATLANTIC	8,855	7,435	1,420	G.W. Bush	84.0%	16.0%
BERGEN	23,019	19,513	3,506	G.W. Bush	84.8%	15.2%
BURLINGTON	15,338	12,660	2,678	G.W. Bush	82.5%	17.5%
CAMDEN	8,115	6,416	1,699	G.W. Bush	79.1%	20.9%
CAPE MAY	8,947	7,761	1,186	G.W. Bush	86.7%	13.3%
CUMBERLAND	3,462	3,045	417	G.W. Bush	88.0%	12.0%
ESSEX	11,870	10,115	1,755	G.W. Bush	85.2%	14.8%
GLOUCESTER	6,877	5,650	1,227	G.W. Bush	82.2%	17.8%
HUDSON	5,473	4,649	824	G.W. Bush	84.9%	15.1%
HUNTERDON	9,098	7,449	1,649	G.W. Bush	81.9%	18.1%
MERCER	7,442	5,488	1,954	G.W. Bush	73.7%	26.3%
MIDDLESEX	10,771	8,669	2,102	G.W. Bush	80.5%	19.5%
MONMOUTH	19,495	16,340	3,155	G.W. Bush	83.8%	16.2%
MORRIS	27,523	24,067	3,456	G.W. Bush	87.4%	12.6%
OCEAN	14,255	11,704	2,551	G.W. Bush	82.1%	17.9%
PASSAIC	11,468	9,742	1,726	G.W. Bush	84.9%	15.1%
SALEM	2,369	1,977	392	G.W. Bush	83.5%	16.5%
SOMERSET	14,034	12,098	1,936	G.W. Bush	86.2%	13.8%
SUSSEX	12,658	9,789	2,869	G.W. Bush	77.3%	22.7%
UNION	12,796	11,056	1,740	G.W. Bush	86.4%	13.6%
WARREN	6,945	5,586	1,359	G.W. Bush	80.4%	19.6%
TOTAL	240,810	201,209	39,601	G.W. Bush	83.6%	16.4%

NEW JERSEY DEMOCRATIC PRIMARY

2004

| County | Total Vote | Kerry | Other | Winner | Percentage of Total Vote | |
					Kerry	Other
ATLANTIC	6,142	5,659	483	Kerry	92.1%	7.9%
BERGEN	19,086	17,655	1,431	Kerry	92.5%	7.5%
BURLINGTON	10,090	9,212	878	Kerry	91.3%	8.7%
CAMDEN	12,727	11,583	1,144	Kerry	91.0%	9.0%
CAPE MAY	1,672	1,520	152	Kerry	90.9%	9.1%
CUMBERLAND	2,374	2,145	229	Kerry	90.4%	9.6%
ESSEX	26,118	23,689	2,429	Kerry	90.7%	9.3%
GLOUCESTER	10,797	9,814	983	Kerry	90.9%	9.1%
HUDSON	37,613	36,054	1,559	Kerry	95.9%	4.1%
HUNTERDON	1,942	1,736	206	Kerry	89.4%	10.6%
MERCER	8,763	8,089	674	Kerry	92.3%	7.7%
MIDDLESEX	15,758	14,470	1,288	Kerry	91.8%	8.2%
MONMOUTH	9,232	8,424	808	Kerry	91.2%	8.8%
MORRIS	6,914	6,291	623	Kerry	91.0%	9.0%
OCEAN	8,500	8,010	490	Kerry	94.2%	5.8%
PASSAIC	8,167	7,696	471	Kerry	94.2%	5.8%
SALEM	2,087	1,783	304	Kerry	85.4%	14.6%
SOMERSET	4,620	4,238	382	Kerry	91.7%	8.3%
SUSSEX	1,870	1,576	294	Kerry	84.3%	15.7%
UNION	18,531	16,967	1,564	Kerry	91.6%	8.4%
WARREN	1,801	1,602	199	Kerry	89.0%	11.0%
TOTAL	214,804	198,213	16,591	Kerry	92.3%	7.7%

Note: Other vote was 9,251 Dennis J. Kucinich; 4,514 Lyndon H. LaRouche Jr.; 2,826 George H. Ballard III.

NEW MEXICO

New Mexico is different than other states in the Mountain West in the degree to which minorities affect its demographics. The state is more than 40 percent Hispanic and almost 10 percent Native American, so that anyone who wants to win comfortably, especially in the Democratic primary, must be able to bridge the gap between non-Hispanic whites and minorities.

John Kerry was able to do so in 2004, easily sweeping all three of New Mexico's congressional districts en route to a 2-to-1 statewide victory over runner-up Wesley Clark.

Clinton was able to do so in 1992, carrying every county, from those of Hispanic northern New Mexico to conservative, overwhelmingly non-Hispanic "Little Texas" in the southeast part of the state. New Mexico was the only Western state where Clinton captured a majority of the primary vote.

Michael Dukakis also ran well in both parts of New Mexico in the 1988 Democratic primary. Jesse Jackson carried McKinley County (Gallup), the lone Native American-majority county in New Mexico, but Jackson's limited appeal to the Hispanic vote was apparent in his failure to win any of the Hispanic-majority counties. Jackson came fairly close in a few, such as Taos County, which has a large artists' colony and a more liberal bent. In others, he was beaten soundly by Dukakis, whose ability to speak fluent Spanish was widely publicized.

But in some of the earlier Democratic primaries, there were racial fault lines. In the state's first presidential primary in 1972, "Little Texas" went for George Wallace, enabling him to finish within 5 percentage points of statewide winner George McGovern. In 1980, the region voted virtually en masse for

Recent New Mexico Primary Results

New Mexico held its first presidential primary in 1972.

	DEMOCRATS			REPUBLICANS		
Year	Turnout	Candidates	%	Turnout	Candidates	%
2004 (June 1)	—	No Primary		49,165	GEORGE W. BUSH*	100
2000 (June 6)	132,280	AL GORE	75	75,230	GEORGE W. BUSH	83
		Bill Bradley	21		John McCain	10
					Alan Keyes	6
1996 (June 4)	121,362	BILL CLINTON*	90	70,464	BOB DOLE	76
		Uncommitted	10		Pat Buchanan	8
					Steve Forbes	6
1992 (June 2)	181,443	BILL CLINTON	53	86,967	GEORGE BUSH*	64
		Uncommitted	19		Uncommitted	27
		Jerry Brown	17		Pat Buchanan	9
		Paul Tsongas	6			
1988 (June 7)	188,610	MICHAEL DUKAKIS	61	88,744	GEORGE BUSH	78
		Jesse Jackson	28		Bob Dole	10
					Pat Robertson	6
1984 (June 5)	187,403	GARY HART	47	42,994	RONALD REAGAN*	95
		Walter Mondale	36		Uncommitted	5
		Jesse Jackson	12			
1980 (June 3)	159,364	EDWARD KENNEDY	46	59,546	RONALD REAGAN	64
		Jimmy Carter*	42		John Anderson	12
		Uncommitted	6		George Bush	10
					Phil Crane	7
1976	—	No Primary		—	No Primary	
1972 (June 6)	153,293	GEORGE McGOVERN	33	55,469	RICHARD NIXON*	88
		George Wallace	29		Paul McCloskey	6
		Hubert Humphrey	26		"None"	5

Note: All candidates are listed that drew at least 5 percent of their party's primary vote. The names of winning candidates are capitalized. An asterisk (*) indicates an incumbent president.

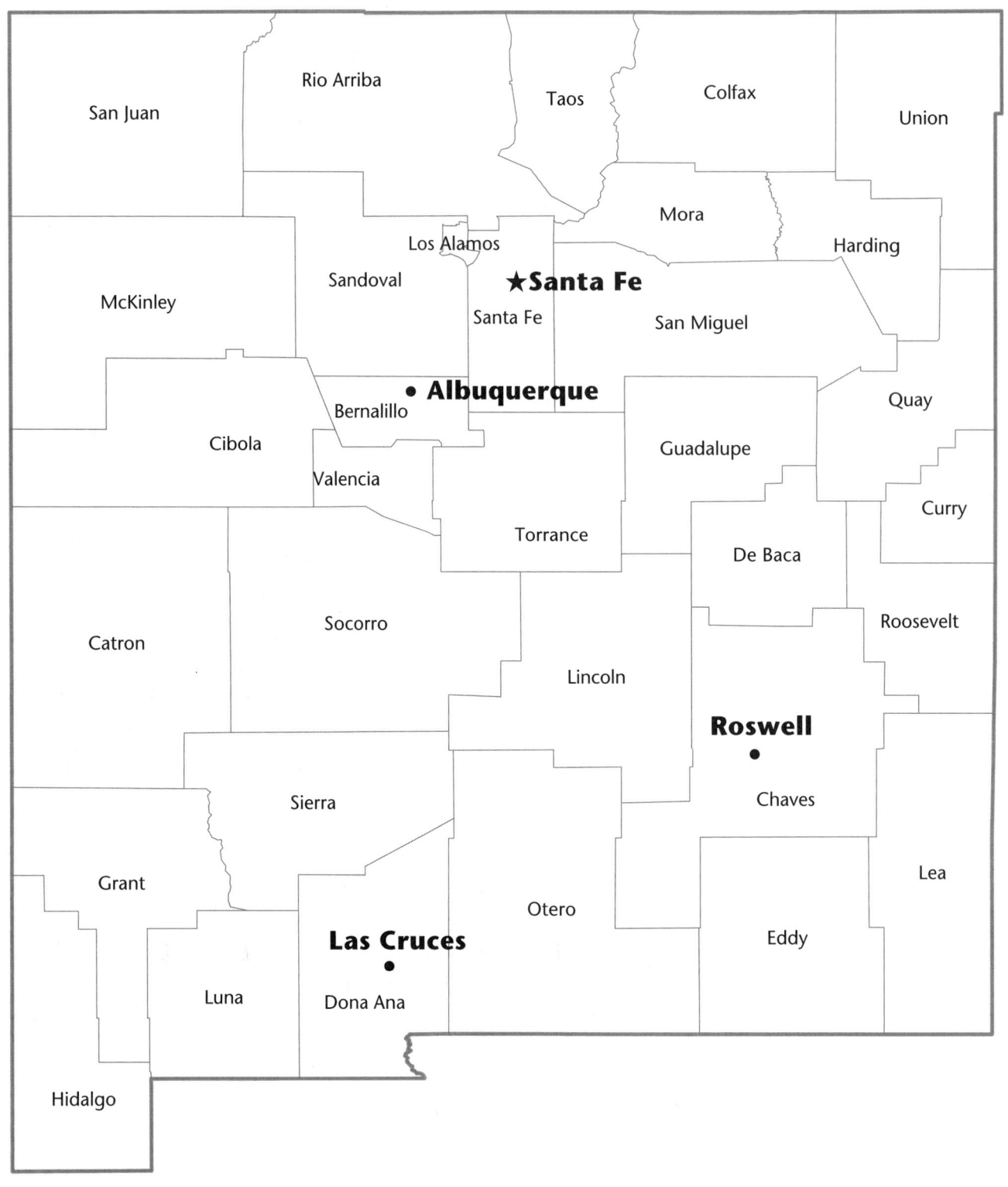

President Jimmy Carter, as he nearly offset the large lead that Edward Kennedy built up in populous Bernalillo County (Albuquerque), Santa Fe, and heavily Catholic Hispanic counties to the north.

New Mexico has traditionally held its presidential primary in June. But in 2004, Democrats in the Land of Enchantment opted for an early February party-run "firehouse" primary (which they formally termed a caucus) in a bid for a more consequential role in the party's presidential nominating process. The move paid off, as many of the Democratic candidates campaigned in New Mexico and roughly 100,000 voters participated in the caucus vote. Nearly one-quarter of the ballots were cast absentee before the end of January and broke almost evenly between Kerry, Clark, and Howard Dean—all viable alternatives at the time. But of the voters who cast ballots on February 3 at the 166 voting sites set up around the state, Kerry—by then the clear front-runner—had the edge.

New Mexico Republicans have not had much luck with their presidential primary. It was created just in time to elect the only delegate to vote against the renomination of President Richard Nixon. (The delegate went to GOP representative Paul McCloskey of California, who mounted a quixotic antiwar challenge to Nixon in the 1972 primaries.)

The primary was abandoned in 1976, just in time to miss the party's hottest nominating battle of the last half century. Since the primary's revival in 1980, the state has seen a succession of GOP contests that were decided long before New Mexico voted in June.

When New Mexico Republicans have put together their delegation through the caucus process, it has tended to mirror the conservatism of their GOP counterparts in other Rocky Mountain states. The delegation voted as a bloc for Barry Goldwater in 1964 and Ronald Reagan in 1976.

NEW MEXICO DEMOCRATIC PRIMARY

2000

County	Total Vote	Bradley	Gore	Other	Winner	Percentage of Total Vote		
						Bradley	Gore	Other
BERNALILLO	34,618	5,943	27,030	1,645	Gore	17.2%	78.1%	4.8%
CATRON	194	101	74	19	Bradley	52.1%	38.1%	9.8%
CHAVES	1,969	495	1,373	101	Gore	25.1%	69.7%	5.1%
CIBOLA	3,211	690	2,344	177	Gore	21.5%	73.0%	5.5%
COLFAX	1,567	355	1,125	87	Gore	22.7%	71.8%	5.6%
CURRY	1,941	744	1,044	153	Gore	38.3%	53.8%	7.9%
DE BACA	364	121	220	23	Gore	33.2%	60.4%	6.3%
DONA ANA	8,013	1,526	6,141	346	Gore	19.0%	76.6%	4.3%
EDDY	5,358	1,477	3,491	390	Gore	27.6%	65.2%	7.3%
GRANT	4,326	990	3,067	269	Gore	22.9%	70.9%	6.2%
GUADALUPE	1,128	182	913	33	Gore	16.1%	80.9%	2.9%
HARDING	204	49	145	10	Gore	24.0%	71.1%	4.9%
HIDALGO	669	211	413	45	Gore	31.5%	61.7%	6.7%
LEA	1,447	429	943	75	Gore	29.6%	65.2%	5.2%
LINCOLN	786	219	531	36	Gore	27.9%	67.6%	4.6%
LOS ALAMOS	1,541	433	1,016	92	Gore	28.1%	65.9%	6.0%
LUNA	728	151	528	49	Gore	20.7%	72.5%	6.7%
MCKINLEY	7,092	1,711	4,966	415	Gore	24.1%	70.0%	5.9%
MORA	1,472	243	1,163	66	Gore	16.5%	79.0%	4.5%
OTERO	2,003	574	1,315	114	Gore	28.7%	65.7%	5.7%
QUAY	1,524	465	935	124	Gore	30.5%	61.4%	8.1%
RIO ARRIBA	7,048	998	5,842	208	Gore	14.2%	82.9%	3.0%
ROOSEVELT	1,388	481	822	85	Gore	34.7%	59.2%	6.1%
SANDOVAL	5,050	1,183	3,618	249	Gore	23.4%	71.6%	4.9%
SAN JUAN	4,668	1,424	2,975	269	Gore	30.5%	63.7%	5.8%
SAN MIGUEL	5,121	716	4,235	170	Gore	14.0%	82.7%	3.3%
SANTA FE	15,325	2,466	12,396	463	Gore	16.1%	80.9%	3.0%
SIERRA	737	195	495	47	Gore	26.5%	67.2%	6.4%
SOCORRO	2,123	491	1,526	106	Gore	23.1%	71.9%	5.0%
TAOS	4,349	770	3,418	161	Gore	17.7%	78.6%	3.7%
TORRANCE	1,041	248	742	51	Gore	23.8%	71.3%	4.9%
UNION	513	169	292	52	Gore	32.9%	56.9%	10.1%
VALENCIA	4,762	954	3,577	231	Gore	20.0%	75.1%	4.9%
TOTAL	132,280	27,204	98,715	6,361	Gore	20.6%	74.6%	4.8%

Note: Other vote was 3,298 Uncommitted; 3,063 Lyndon H. LaRouche Jr.

NEW MEXICO REPUBLICAN PRIMARY

2000

County	Total Vote	G.W. Bush	Keyes	McCain	Uncommitted	Winner	Percentage of Total Vote			
							G.W. Bush	Keyes	McCain	Uncommitted
BERNALILLO	25,941	21,314	1,570	2,760	297	G.W. Bush	82.2%	6.1%	10.6%	1.1%
CATRON	401	311	43	46	1	G.W. Bush	77.6%	10.7%	11.5%	0.2%
CHAVES	3,658	3,148	187	309	14	G.W. Bush	86.1%	5.1%	8.4%	0.4%
CIBOLA	848	707	42	86	13	G.W. Bush	83.4%	5.0%	10.1%	1.5%
COLFAX	493	410	29	49	5	G.W. Bush	83.2%	5.9%	9.9%	1.0%
CURRY	1,920	1,713	111	85	11	G.W. Bush	89.2%	5.8%	4.4%	0.6%
DE BACA	109	94	6	9	0	G.W. Bush	86.2%	5.5%	8.3%	0.0%
DONA ANA	4,641	3,725	375	520	21	G.W. Bush	80.3%	8.1%	11.2%	0.5%
EDDY	1,692	1,419	80	176	17	G.W. Bush	83.9%	4.7%	10.4%	1.0%
GRANT	1,070	827	101	136	6	G.W. Bush	77.3%	9.4%	12.7%	0.6%
GUADALUPE	118	95	7	14	2	G.W. Bush	80.5%	5.9%	11.9%	1.7%
HARDING	143	123	6	13	1	G.W. Bush	86.0%	4.2%	9.1%	0.7%
HIDALGO	134	104	12	18	0	G.W. Bush	77.6%	9.0%	13.4%	0.0%
LEA	2,200	1,973	139	81	7	G.W. Bush	89.7%	6.3%	3.7%	0.3%
LINCOLN	2,043	1,721	117	195	10	G.W. Bush	84.2%	5.7%	9.5%	0.5%
LOS ALAMOS	1,678	1,200	170	296	12	G.W. Bush	71.5%	10.1%	17.6%	0.7%
LUNA	554	420	61	67	6	G.W. Bush	75.8%	11.0%	12.1%	1.1%
MCKINLEY	1,453	1,108	101	231	13	G.W. Bush	76.3%	7.0%	15.9%	0.9%
MORA	208	187	7	9	5	G.W. Bush	89.9%	3.4%	4.3%	2.4%
OTERO	3,586	2,939	249	383	15	G.W. Bush	82.0%	6.9%	10.7%	0.4%
QUAY	518	444	28	44	2	G.W. Bush	85.7%	5.4%	8.5%	0.4%
RIO ARRIBA	603	518	33	49	3	G.W. Bush	85.9%	5.5%	8.1%	0.5%
ROOSEVELT	786	693	44	46	3	G.W. Bush	88.2%	5.6%	5.9%	0.4%
SANDOVAL	3,288	2,674	242	348	24	G.W. Bush	81.3%	7.4%	10.6%	0.7%
SAN JUAN	6,751	5,764	449	524	14	G.W. Bush	85.4%	6.7%	7.8%	0.2%
SAN MIGUEL	514	437	29	46	2	G.W. Bush	85.0%	5.6%	8.9%	0.4%
SANTA FE	2,969	2,299	204	432	34	G.W. Bush	77.4%	6.9%	14.6%	1.1%
SIERRA	844	703	38	98	5	G.W. Bush	83.3%	4.5%	11.6%	0.6%
SOCORRO	1,352	1,122	70	141	19	G.W. Bush	83.0%	5.2%	10.4%	1.4%
TAOS	715	594	33	76	12	G.W. Bush	83.1%	4.6%	10.6%	1.7%
TORRANCE	876	729	66	78	3	G.W. Bush	83.2%	7.5%	8.9%	0.3%
UNION	382	341	18	22	1	G.W. Bush	89.3%	4.7%	5.8%	0.3%
VALENCIA	2,742	2,305	183	232	22	G.W. Bush	84.1%	6.7%	8.5%	0.8%
TOTAL	75,230	62,161	4,850	7,619	600	G.W. Bush	82.6%	6.4%	10.1%	0.8%

NEW YORK

For much of the twentieth century, New York's political leaders chose control of their state's nominating process over widespread voter participation. The Empire State held a presidential primary, but it was often a late spring event devoted solely to the election of delegates on a district-by-district basis; it produced a delegation that was readily transferable to the preferred candidate of the party's kingpins. That ballot access was difficult and voter interest often minimal was just fine with party leaders.

It was not until 1980 that New York Democrats held their first presidential primary with voters able to ballot directly for the candidates. But New York GOP leaders have been slow to jettison the old system, and in 2000 lined up early behind George W. Bush.

Roughly 750,000 Republicans participated in the primary—by then in early March. John McCain won delegates in a dozen congressional districts, most of them in New York City and the suburbs of Long Island. But the arcane nature of the system prevented McCain from making deeper inroads in this citadel of moderate Republicanism. GOP governor George Pataki lined up early behind his gubernatorial colleague from Texas, and many of the Bush district delegate slates were anchored by Republican congressmen, from Rick Lazio on Long Island to Jack Quinn in Buffalo.

Bob Dole had used a similar strategy to sweep the New York Republican primary four years earlier. He enlisted members of Congress, state lawmakers, and prominent local party leaders to run as Dole delegates. His main challengers, Steve Forbes

Recent New York Primary Results

New York Democrats instituted a presidential primary with a direct vote for candidates in 1980. Through 2004, New York Republicans cast their primary ballots for delegates without a direct vote for presidential candidates.

Year	DEMOCRATS			REPUBLICANS		
	Turnout	Candidates	%	Turnout	Candidates	%
2004 (March 2)	715,633	JOHN KERRY	61	—	No Primary	
		John Edwards	20			
		Al Sharpton	8			
		Dennis Kucinich	5			
2000 (March 7)	974,463	AL GORE	66	771,882#	GEORGE W. BUSH	50
		Bill Bradley	33		John McCain	43
1996 (March 7)	—	No Primary		360,000#	BOB DOLE	55
					Steve Forbes	30
					Pat Buchanan	15
1992 (April 7)	1,007,726	BILL CLINTON	41	—	No Primary	
		Paul Tsongas	29			
		Jerry Brown	26			
1988 (April 19)	1,575,186	MICHAEL DUKAKIS	51	—	No Primary	
		Jesse Jackson	37			
		Al Gore	10			
1984 (April 3)	1,387,950	WALTER MONDALE	45	—	No Primary	
		Gary Hart	27			
		Jesse Jackson	26			
1980 (March 25)	989,062	EDWARD KENNEDY	59	—	No Primary	
		Jimmy Carter*	41			

Note: All candidates are listed that drew at least 5 percent of their party's primary vote. The names of winning candidates are capitalized. An asterisk (*) indicates an incumbent president. A pound sign (#) denotes that the Republican turnout is based on the vote for delegates. The 1996 turnout was an estimate and the candidate results were based on the combined vote for all the delegates of each candidate. The 2000 GOP turnout and results were based on the aggregate tally of each candidate's highest delegate vote-getter in each congressional district.

and Pat Buchanan, had to go to court just to get their delegates on the primary ballot. And though Forbes mounted a late drive, with a saturation media campaign and a last-minute endorsement from former New York representative Jack Kemp (who Dole would later pick as his vice-presidential running mate), Forbes was unable to stir much voter interest or stem the Dole bandwagon. With turnout an estimated 360,000, or barely 10 percent of the state's registered Republicans, Dole swept all 93 delegates at stake.

Compared with the Republicans, New York's Democratic presidential primary has often been open and showy, and in some years, hotly contested.

Through much of the last quarter of the twentieth century, the state's ethnically variegated Democratic electorate was comfortable with traditional New Deal-style politicians. Henry Jackson won more delegates than anyone else in New York in 1976; Edward Kennedy won easily in 1980, as did Walter Mondale in 1984 and Michael Dukakis in 1988.

Bill Clinton won the primary in 1992 by piecing together a biracial coalition in New York City and holding his own in the rest of the state. But like many of Clinton's other primary triumphs in 1992, his New York victory was not overwhelming. He took barely 40 percent of the vote against Jerry Brown and Paul Tsongas, who had suspended his campaign more than two weeks before the April balloting, but still placed second. Only in one county, the Bronx, did Clinton win a majority of the vote.

Clinton's winning coalition was different than the one Dukakis had fashioned four years earlier. In 1988, Dukakis narrowly lost New York City to Jesse Jackson, but swamped Jackson in the more conservative suburbs and upstate. In contrast, Clinton built up a big lead in New York City but barely beat Tsongas in the suburbs and was caught in a close battle with Brown and Tsongas in the small cities and towns of upstate New York. Clinton was strong in the western end of the state, which faces the Midwest. Tsongas and Brown dominated voting in the Hudson River Valley, which is adjacent to New England.

But the prime battleground was New York City, where roughly half the Democratic primary ballots are cast, and there Clinton readily prevailed with a significant edge among the city's large component of Jewish and black voters. It enabled him to become the first Southern Democrat to win the New York primary.

Jimmy Carter had lost it twice, denouncing the primary in 1976 as boss-dominated. Al Gore finished a weak third in New York in 1988—despite heavy emphasis on the event—and shortly thereafter suspended his campaign. Gore drew less than 10 percent of the primary vote in the city, less than 15 percent in the suburbs, and could crack 20 percent in only two small upstate counties.

Gore enjoyed a reversal of fortune when he ran again in the New York primary in 2000. Then, the sitting vice president and the favorite of the party establishment, he outpolled Bill Bradley in every New York county. Even in New York City, where Bradley was a household name from his days as a professional basketball star with the New York Knicks, Gore won by a margin of better than 2 to 1.

John Kerry scored a similar statewide sweep in the Democratic primary in 2004, as he trounced his last major challenger, John Edwards, by a margin of better than 3-to-1. The lopsided nature of the balloting allowed room for dark horse candidates to find toeholds. Al Sharpton, a native of New York City, took roughly 20 percent of the vote in two Gotham boroughs, Bronx and Brooklyn (Kings County). Meanwhile, Dennis Kucinich topped 15 percent in two counties with a large academic population, Tompkins (Cornell University at Ithaca) and Ulster (SUNY-New Paltz).

Yet as the competitive nature of New York's Democratic presidential primary has declined, so has voter interest. From more than 1.5 million participants in 1988, the turnout declined to slightly more than 1 million in 1992, slightly less than 1 million in 2000, and to barely 700,000 voters in 2004. The latter figure was the lowest for a Democratic primary for president in New York since the direct vote for candidates was initiated nearly a quarter century earlier.

NEW YORK DEMOCRATIC PRIMARY

2000

County	Total Vote	Bradley	Gore	LaRouche	Winner	Percentage of Total Vote		
						Bradley	Gore	LaRouche
ALBANY	22,596	8,563	13,885	148	Gore	37.9%	61.4%	0.7%
ALLEGANY	1,251	489	730	32	Gore	39.1%	58.4%	2.6%
BRONX	84,327	18,688	64,729	910	Gore	22.2%	76.8%	1.1%
BROOME	9,798	4,016	5,686	96	Gore	41.0%	58.0%	1.0%
CATTARAUGUS	2,757	1,003	1,705	49	Gore	36.4%	61.8%	1.8%
CAYUGA	2,534	948	1,556	30	Gore	37.4%	61.4%	1.2%
CHAUTAUQUA	4,247	1,418	2,769	60	Gore	33.4%	65.2%	1.4%
CHEMUNG	3,159	1,011	2,121	27	Gore	32.0%	67.1%	0.9%
CHENANGO	1,396	586	787	23	Gore	42.0%	56.4%	1.6%
CLINTON	2,023	682	1,310	31	Gore	33.7%	64.8%	1.5%
COLUMBIA	2,155	896	1,248	11	Gore	41.6%	57.9%	0.5%
CORTLAND	1,789	687	1,086	16	Gore	38.4%	60.7%	0.9%
DELAWARE	1,669	679	968	22	Gore	40.7%	58.0%	1.3%
DUTCHESS	8,685	3,855	4,743	87	Gore	44.4%	54.6%	1.0%
ERIE	63,857	20,163	42,615	1,079	Gore	31.6%	66.7%	1.7%
ESSEX	1,154	465	673	16	Gore	40.3%	58.3%	1.4%
FRANKLIN	1,371	501	850	20	Gore	36.5%	62.0%	1.5%
FULTON	1,300	418	865	17	Gore	32.2%	66.5%	1.3%
GENESEE	1,429	525	879	25	Gore	36.7%	61.5%	1.7%
GREENE	1,124	457	653	14	Gore	40.7%	58.1%	1.2%
HAMILTON	246	113	127	6	Gore	45.9%	51.6%	2.4%
HERKIMER	2,001	740	1,234	27	Gore	37.0%	61.7%	1.3%
JEFFERSON	2,649	838	1,779	32	Gore	31.6%	67.2%	1.2%
KINGS	145,035	40,210	103,581	1,244	Gore	27.7%	71.4%	0.9%
LEWIS	561	184	365	12	Gore	32.8%	65.1%	2.1%
LIVINGSTON	1,770	686	1,070	14	Gore	38.8%	60.5%	0.8%
MADISON	1,895	776	1,088	31	Gore	40.9%	57.4%	1.6%
MONROE	32,913	11,733	20,914	266	Gore	35.6%	63.5%	0.8%
MONTGOMERY	4,254	1,394	2,820	40	Gore	32.8%	66.3%	0.9%
NASSAU	56,237	20,208	35,338	691	Gore	35.9%	62.8%	1.2%
NEW YORK	157,948	57,653	99,409	886	Gore	36.5%	62.9%	0.6%
NIAGARA	11,287	3,477	7,635	175	Gore	30.8%	67.6%	1.6%
ONEIDA	8,049	2,946	5,010	93	Gore	36.6%	62.2%	1.2%
ONONDAGA	16,848	6,584	10,113	151	Gore	39.1%	60.0%	0.9%
ONTARIO	3,567	1,446	2,090	31	Gore	40.5%	58.6%	0.9%
ORANGE	9,976	4,351	5,530	95	Gore	43.6%	55.4%	1.0%
ORLEANS	913	278	610	25	Gore	30.4%	66.8%	2.7%
OSWEGO	2,627	904	1,680	43	Gore	34.4%	64.0%	1.6%
OTSEGO	2,295	1,006	1,265	24	Gore	43.8%	55.1%	1.0%
PUTNAM	2,860	1,355	1,478	27	Gore	47.4%	51.7%	0.9%
QUEENS	113,737	31,170	81,746	821	Gore	27.4%	71.9%	0.7%
RENSSELAER	4,676	1,899	2,739	38	Gore	40.6%	58.6%	0.8%
RICHMOND	16,662	6,605	9,871	186	Gore	39.6%	59.2%	1.1%
ROCKLAND	18,768	7,286	11,322	160	Gore	38.8%	60.3%	0.9%
ST. LAWRENCE	3,517	1,115	2,361	41	Gore	31.7%	67.1%	1.2%

NEW YORK DEMOCRATIC PRIMARY

2000

County	Total Vote	Bradley	Gore	LaRouche	Winner	Percentage of Total Vote		
						Bradley	Gore	LaRouche
SARATOGA	5,859	2,547	3,252	60	Gore	43.5%	55.5%	1.0%
SCHENECTADY	6,175	2,609	3,505	61	Gore	42.3%	56.8%	1.0%
SCHOHARIE	894	357	532	5	Gore	39.9%	59.5%	0.6%
SCHUYLER	615	237	366	12	Gore	38.5%	59.5%	2.0%
SENECA	1,133	414	705	14	Gore	36.5%	62.2%	1.2%
STEUBEN	2,753	1,096	1,607	50	Gore	39.8%	58.4%	1.8%
SUFFOLK	37,987	14,668	23,025	294	Gore	38.6%	60.6%	0.8%
SULLIVAN	2,550	1,093	1,420	37	Gore	42.9%	55.7%	1.5%
TIOGA	1,938	813	1,104	21	Gore	42.0%	57.0%	1.1%
TOMPKINS	5,740	2,776	2,940	24	Gore	48.4%	51.2%	0.4%
ULSTER	6,522	2,912	3,575	35	Gore	44.6%	54.8%	0.5%
WARREN	1,892	757	1,104	31	Gore	40.0%	58.4%	1.6%
WASHINGTON	1,421	591	808	22	Gore	41.6%	56.9%	1.5%
WAYNE	1,963	767	1,169	27	Gore	39.1%	59.6%	1.4%
WESTCHESTER	55,389	22,737	32,246	406	Gore	41.0%	58.2%	0.7%
WYOMING	945	345	577	23	Gore	36.5%	61.1%	2.4%
YATES	775	312	449	14	Gore	40.3%	57.9%	1.8%
TOTAL	974,463	326,038	639,417	9,008	Gore	33.5%	65.6%	0.9%

Note: The vote in New York City was Gore 359,336 (69.4 percent); Bradley 154,326 (29.8 percent); LaRouche 4,047 (0.8 percent). A total of 517,709 votes were cast, based on an aggregate of the vote from New York City's five boroughs (or counties): Bronx, Kings (Brooklyn), New York (Manhattan), Queens and Richmond (Staten Island).

NEW YORK REPUBLICAN PRIMARY

2000

County	Total Vote	G.W. Bush	McCain	Other	Winner	Percentage of Total Vote		
						G.W. Bush	McCain	Other
ALBANY	13,734	6,159	6,778	797	McCain	44.8%	49.4%	5.8%
ALLEGANY	3,533	2,009	1,293	231	G.W. Bush	56.9%	36.6%	6.5%
BRONX	6,737	3,584	2,739	414	G.W. Bush	53.2%	40.7%	6.1%
BROOME	19,797	10,591	8,039	1,167	G.W. Bush	53.5%	40.6%	5.9%
CATTARAUGUS	5,063	2,799	1,907	357	G.W. Bush	55.3%	37.7%	7.1%
CAYUGA	5,178	2,682	2,144	352	G.W. Bush	51.8%	41.4%	6.8%
CHAUTAUQUA	8,099	4,554	2,920	625	G.W. Bush	56.2%	36.1%	7.7%
CHEMUNG	8,289	4,672	3,132	485	G.W. Bush	56.4%	37.8%	5.9%
CHENANGO	4,831	2,534	2,067	230	G.W. Bush	52.5%	42.8%	4.8%
CLINTON	3,265	1,807	1,285	173	G.W. Bush	55.3%	39.4%	5.3%
COLUMBIA	4,555	2,498	1,834	223	G.W. Bush	54.8%	40.3%	4.9%
CORTLAND	3,870	2,081	1,518	271	G.W. Bush	53.8%	39.2%	7.0%
DELAWARE	5,092	2,764	2,027	301	G.W. Bush	54.3%	39.8%	5.9%
DUTCHESS	15,641	7,780	6,808	1,053	G.W. Bush	49.7%	43.5%	6.7%
ERIE	54,066	27,689	23,066	3,311	G.W. Bush	51.2%	42.7%	6.1%
ESSEX	3,889	2,058	1,565	266	G.W. Bush	52.9%	40.2%	6.8%
FRANKLIN	2,449	1,144	1,124	181	G.W. Bush	46.7%	45.9%	7.4%
FULTON	5,346	2,532	2,506	308	G.W. Bush	47.4%	46.9%	5.8%
GENESEE	4,466	2,659	1,492	315	G.W. Bush	59.5%	33.4%	7.1%
GREENE	3,547	1,958	1,402	187	G.W. Bush	55.2%	39.5%	5.3%

NEW YORK REPUBLICAN PRIMARY

2000

County	Total Vote	G.W. Bush	McCain	Other	Winner	Percentage of Total Vote		
						G.W. Bush	McCain	Other
HAMILTON	1,232	659	509	64	G.W. Bush	53.5%	41.3%	5.2%
HERKIMER	6,773	3,547	2,726	500	G.W. Bush	52.4%	40.2%	7.4%
JEFFERSON	7,921	4,457	3,104	360	G.W. Bush	56.3%	39.2%	4.5%
KINGS	17,470	8,752	7,542	1,176	G.W. Bush	50.1%	43.2%	6.7%
LEWIS	2,601	1,402	1,033	166	G.W. Bush	53.9%	39.7%	6.4%
LIVINGSTON	5,224	2,978	1,833	413	G.W. Bush	57.0%	35.1%	7.9%
MADISON	5,197	2,674	2,130	393	G.W. Bush	51.5%	41.0%	7.6%
MONROE	49,406	27,791	18,298	3,317	G.W. Bush	56.3%	37.0%	6.7%
MONTGOMERY	3,563	2,060	1,258	245	G.W. Bush	57.8%	35.3%	6.9%
NASSAU	80,458	33,858	41,300	5,300	McCain	42.1%	51.3%	6.6%
NEW YORK	24,299	10,566	12,559	1,174	McCain	43.5%	51.7%	4.8%
NIAGARA	14,855	7,795	6,008	1,052	G.W. Bush	52.5%	40.4%	7.1%
ONEIDA	17,618	9,445	6,834	1,339	G.W. Bush	53.6%	38.8%	7.6%
ONONDAGA	29,049	14,704	12,263	2,082	G.W. Bush	50.6%	42.2%	7.2%
ONTARIO	8,286	4,326	3,303	657	G.W. Bush	52.2%	39.9%	7.9%
ORANGE	21,007	10,947	8,683	1,377	G.W. Bush	52.1%	41.3%	6.6%
ORLEANS	3,231	1,894	1,039	298	G.W. Bush	58.6%	32.2%	9.2%
OSWEGO	10,424	5,541	4,208	675	G.W. Bush	53.2%	40.4%	6.5%
OTSEGO	4,753	2,521	1,970	262	G.W. Bush	53.0%	41.4%	5.5%
PUTNAM	5,241	2,667	2,299	275	G.W. Bush	50.9%	43.9%	5.2%
QUEENS	24,636	12,426	10,332	1,878	G.W. Bush	50.4%	41.9%	7.6%
RENSSELAER	7,475	3,808	3,298	369	G.W. Bush	50.9%	44.1%	4.9%
RICHMOND	15,282	7,593	7,038	651	G.W. Bush	49.7%	46.1%	4.3%
ROCKLAND	12,117	6,623	4,737	757	G.W. Bush	54.7%	39.1%	6.2%
ST. LAWRENCE	7,184	3,497	3,291	396	G.W. Bush	48.7%	45.8%	5.5%
SARATOGA	19,706	9,801	8,995	910	G.W. Bush	49.7%	45.6%	4.6%
SCHENECTADY	9,774	5,087	4,143	544	G.W. Bush	52.0%	42.4%	5.6%
SCHOHARIE	2,202	1,233	852	117	G.W. Bush	56.0%	38.7%	5.3%
SCHUYLER	1,655	996	549	110	G.W. Bush	60.2%	33.2%	6.6%
SENECA	2,315	1,265	881	169	G.W. Bush	54.6%	38.1%	7.3%
STEUBEN	11,389	7,003	3,651	735	G.W. Bush	61.5%	32.1%	6.5%
SUFFOLK	66,251	30,684	31,302	4,265	McCain	46.3%	47.2%	6.4%
SULLIVAN	2,990	1,471	1,296	223	G.W. Bush	49.2%	43.3%	7.5%
TIOGA	6,343	3,441	2,481	421	G.W. Bush	54.2%	39.1%	6.6%
TOMPKINS	5,311	2,669	2,270	372	G.W. Bush	50.3%	42.7%	7.0%
ULSTER	8,971	3,955	4,394	622	McCain	44.1%	49.0%	6.9%
WARREN	7,145	3,462	3,361	322	G.W. Bush	48.5%	47.0%	4.5%
WASHINGTON	4,957	2,508	2,201	248	G.W. Bush	50.6%	44.4%	5.0%
WAYNE	6,272	3,476	2,258	538	G.W. Bush	55.4%	36.0%	8.6%
WESTCHESTER	43,720	21,951	19,612	2,157	G.W. Bush	50.2%	44.9%	4.9%
WYOMING	3,120	1,772	1,105	243	G.W. Bush	56.8%	35.4%	7.8%
YATES	3,012	1,570	1,226	216	G.W. Bush	52.1%	40.7%	7.2%
TOTAL	771,882	389,429	333,818	48,635	G.W. Bush	50.5%	43.2%	6.3%

Note: New York Republicans did not hold a presidential preference vote in 2000. Instead the vote was for delegates, with three elected per district. The vote total for each candidate in this table is based on the aggregate county-by-county vote for their highest delegate vote-getter in each of New York's 31 congressional districts. Based on this methodology, the other vote was 27,719 Alan Keyes; 20,916 Steve Forbes. The Republican primary vote in New York City was Bush 42,921 (48.5 percent); McCain 40,210 (45.5 percent); Other 5,293 (6.0 percent). A total of 88,424 votes were cast in the city's five boroughs (or counties).

NEW YORK DEMOCRATIC PRIMARY

2004

County	Total Vote	Edwards	Kerry	Kucinich	Sharpton	Other	Winner	Percentage of Total Vote				
								Edwards	Kerry	Kucinich	Sharpton	Other
ALBANY	22,531	6,300	12,666	1,196	694	1,675	Kerry	28.0%	56.2%	5.3%	3.1%	7.4%
ALLEGANY	975	345	520	40	10	60	Kerry	35.4%	53.3%	4.1%	1.0%	6.2%
BRONX	46,125	5,119	27,338	2,034	9,418	2,216	Kerry	11.1%	59.3%	4.4%	20.4%	4.8%
BROOME	8,534	2,577	4,911	567	69	410	Kerry	30.2%	57.5%	6.6%	0.8%	4.8%
CATTARAUGUS	1,947	712	1,043	69	20	103	Kerry	36.6%	53.6%	3.5%	1.0%	5.3%
CAYUGA	2,529	847	1,441	112	15	114	Kerry	33.5%	57.0%	4.4%	0.6%	4.5%
CHAUTAUQUA	3,700	1,252	2,025	135	38	250	Kerry	33.8%	54.7%	3.6%	1.0%	6.8%
CHEMUNG	2,493	669	1,594	70	32	128	Kerry	26.8%	63.9%	2.8%	1.3%	5.1%
CHENANGO	1,309	403	772	51	12	71	Kerry	30.8%	59.0%	3.9%	0.9%	5.4%
CLINTON	1,878	520	647	63	17	631	Kerry	27.7%	34.5%	3.4%	0.9%	33.6%
COLUMBIA	2,638	626	1,466	232	35	279	Kerry	23.7%	55.6%	8.8%	1.3%	10.6%
CORTLAND	1,663	551	925	57	11	119	Kerry	33.1%	55.6%	3.4%	0.7%	7.2%
DELAWARE	1,363	426	758	68	17	94	Kerry	31.3%	55.6%	5.0%	1.2%	6.9%
DUTCHESS	7,629	1,677	4,589	573	311	479	Kerry	22.0%	60.2%	7.5%	4.1%	6.3%
ERIE	40,892	12,279	23,781	1,331	1,499	2,002	Kerry	30.0%	58.2%	3.3%	3.7%	4.9%
ESSEX	1,162	300	498	53	6	305	Kerry	25.8%	42.9%	4.6%	0.5%	26.2%
FRANKLIN	1,381	397	675	40	6	263	Kerry	28.7%	48.9%	2.9%	0.4%	19.0%
FULTON	1,149	376	647	45	9	72	Kerry	32.7%	56.3%	3.9%	0.8%	6.3%
GENESEE	1,213	400	707	22	17	67	Kerry	33.0%	58.3%	1.8%	1.4%	5.5%
GREENE	1,006	319	539	64	13	71	Kerry	31.7%	53.6%	6.4%	1.3%	7.1%
HAMILTON	263	92	139	10	4	18	Kerry	35.0%	52.9%	3.8%	1.5%	6.8%
HERKIMER	1,719	491	1,061	49	16	102	Kerry	28.6%	61.7%	2.9%	0.9%	5.9%
JEFFERSON	1,988	570	1,239	34	11	134	Kerry	28.7%	62.3%	1.7%	0.6%	6.7%
KINGS	90,732	13,576	50,772	5,180	16,535	4,669	Kerry	15.0%	56.0%	5.7%	18.2%	5.1%
LEWIS	518	142	328	15	0	33	Kerry	27.4%	63.3%	2.9%	0.0%	6.4%
LIVINGSTON	1,568	538	872	43	8	107	Kerry	34.3%	55.6%	2.7%	0.5%	6.8%
MADISON	1,862	563	1,077	54	11	157	Kerry	30.2%	57.8%	2.9%	0.6%	8.4%
MONROE	26,352	8,391	15,006	1,053	406	1,496	Kerry	31.8%	56.9%	4.0%	1.5%	5.7%
MONTGOMERY	1,489	545	788	44	21	91	Kerry	36.6%	52.9%	3.0%	1.4%	6.1%
NASSAU	39,151	6,273	27,102	1,261	2,087	2,428	Kerry	16.0%	69.2%	3.2%	5.3%	6.2%
NEW YORK	133,188	20,707	86,679	9,365	10,215	6,222	Kerry	15.5%	65.1%	7.0%	7.7%	4.7%
NIAGARA	7,403	2,491	4,210	188	177	337	Kerry	33.6%	56.9%	2.5%	2.4%	4.6%
ONEIDA	6,428	1,857	3,860	201	63	447	Kerry	28.9%	60.0%	3.1%	1.0%	7.0%
ONONDAGA	15,884	4,566	9,420	658	283	957	Kerry	28.7%	59.3%	4.1%	1.8%	6.0%
ONTARIO	2,848	899	1,644	108	25	172	Kerry	31.6%	57.7%	3.8%	0.9%	6.0%
ORANGE	7,998	1,726	5,064	408	329	471	Kerry	21.6%	63.3%	5.1%	4.1%	5.9%
ORLEANS	712	274	385	14	4	35	Kerry	38.5%	54.1%	2.0%	0.6%	4.9%
OSWEGO	2,443	874	1,389	56	13	111	Kerry	35.8%	56.9%	2.3%	0.5%	4.5%
OTSEGO	2,166	643	1,216	139	22	146	Kerry	29.7%	56.1%	6.4%	1.0%	6.7%
PUTNAM	2,496	572	1,598	145	44	137	Kerry	22.9%	64.0%	5.8%	1.8%	5.5%
QUEENS	70,779	11,118	44,914	2,384	9,144	3,219	Kerry	15.7%	63.5%	3.4%	12.9%	4.5%
RENSSELAER	4,042	1,203	2,215	233	64	327	Kerry	29.8%	54.8%	5.8%	1.6%	8.1%
RICHMOND	10,034	2,291	6,076	383	778	506	Kerry	22.8%	60.6%	3.8%	7.8%	5.0%
ROCKLAND	13,040	2,892	8,360	543	544	701	Kerry	22.2%	64.1%	4.2%	4.2%	5.4%
ST. LAWRENCE	2,836	752	1,671	111	22	280	Kerry	26.5%	58.9%	3.9%	0.8%	9.9%

NEW YORK DEMOCRATIC PRIMARY

2004

| County | Total Vote | Edwards | Kerry | Kucinich | Sharpton | Other | Winner | Percentage of Total Vote | | | | |
								Edwards	Kerry	Kucinich	Sharpton	Other
SARATOGA	5,433	1,668	2,999	334	31	401	Kerry	30.7%	55.2%	6.1%	0.6%	7.4%
SCHENECTADY	5,391	1,831	2,908	233	100	319	Kerry	34.0%	53.9%	4.3%	1.9%	5.9%
SCHOHARIE	848	297	427	53	7	64	Kerry	35.0%	50.4%	6.3%	0.8%	7.5%
SCHUYLER	543	143	304	51	7	38	Kerry	26.3%	56.0%	9.4%	1.3%	7.0%
SENECA	1,082	321	632	53	8	68	Kerry	29.7%	58.4%	4.9%	0.7%	6.3%
STEUBEN	2,033	652	1,152	71	20	138	Kerry	32.1%	56.7%	3.5%	1.0%	6.8%
SUFFOLK	31,843	5,600	21,863	1,434	1,150	1,796	Kerry	17.6%	68.7%	4.5%	3.6%	5.6%
SULLIVAN	2,111	467	1,274	165	57	148	Kerry	22.1%	60.4%	7.8%	2.7%	7.0%
TIOGA	1,672	552	906	111	5	98	Kerry	33.0%	54.2%	6.6%	0.3%	5.9%
TOMPKINS	7,101	1,711	3,485	1,351	113	441	Kerry	24.1%	49.1%	19.0%	1.6%	6.2%
ULSTER	7,190	1,385	3,897	1,181	177	550	Kerry	19.3%	54.2%	16.4%	2.5%	7.6%
WARREN	1,707	460	974	69	15	189	Kerry	26.9%	57.1%	4.0%	0.9%	11.1%
WASHINGTON	1,461	455	740	113	10	143	Kerry	31.1%	50.7%	7.7%	0.7%	9.8%
WAYNE	1,749	653	934	56	13	93	Kerry	37.3%	53.4%	3.2%	0.7%	5.3%
WESTCHESTER	44,008	7,130	29,859	1,852	2,659	2,508	Kerry	16.2%	67.8%	4.2%	6.0%	5.7%
WYOMING	764	305	384	25	5	45	Kerry	39.9%	50.3%	3.3%	0.7%	5.9%
YATES	641	189	389	27	4	32	Kerry	29.5%	60.7%	4.2%	0.6%	5.0%
TOTAL	715,633	143,960	437,754	36,680	57,456	39,783	Kerry	20.1%	61.2%	5.1%	8.0%	5.6%

Note: Other vote was 20,471 Howard Dean; 9,314 Joseph I. Lieberman; 3,954 Richard A. Gephardt; 3,517 Wesley Clark; 2,527 Lyndon H. LaRouche Jr. The vote in New York City was Kerry 215,779 (61.5 percent); Edwards 52,811 (15.1 percent); Sharpton 46,090 (13.1 percent); Kucinich 19,346 (5.5 percent); Other 16,832 (4.8 percent). A total of 350,858 votes were cast in the city's five boroughs (or counties).

NORTH CAROLINA

The best known of North Carolina's presidential primaries remains the 1976 duel between Ronald Reagan and President Gerald Ford. Had Reagan not won, his political career probably would have ended there.

Reagan had lost the first five primaries of 1976. But with backing from Sen. Jesse Helms and his potent political organization, Reagan edged Ford in the Tarheel State by about 12,500 votes out of nearly 200,000 cast. It proved a pivotal victory for Reagan that revived his 1976 campaign and helped position him to win the nomination and the White House in 1980.

In besting Ford, Reagan ran well in parts of the state where Helms had demonstrated strength—in the blue-collar, textile-producing centers of the Piedmont, in Helms's home base in the Raleigh area, and in tobacco-growing eastern North Carolina. Ford held his own in populous Mecklenburg County (Charlotte) and beat Reagan in the western mountains, the historic cornerstone of the North Carolina GOP since the Civil War.

At the same time that North Carolina Republicans were resurrecting Reagan's presidential ambitions, the state's Democratic voters were sounding the death knell for those of George Wallace. In the 1972 primary, Wallace had swamped the favorite-son candidacy of former North Carolina governor Terry Sanford by putting together much the same coalition on the Democratic side that Reagan did on the Republican.

Recent North Carolina Primary Results

North Carolina held its first presidential primary in 1920, but did not hold another until 1972.

Year	Turnout	Candidates (DEMOCRATS)	%	Turnout	Candidates (REPUBLICANS)	%
2004	—	No Primary		—	No Primary	
2000 (May 2)	544,922	AL GORE	70	322,517	GEORGE W. BUSH	79
		Bill Bradley	18		John McCain	11
		No Preference	9		Alan Keyes	8
1996 (May 7)	572,160	BILL CLINTON*	81	284,212	BOB DOLE	71
		No Preference	12		Pat Buchanan	13
		Lyndon LaRouche	7			
1992 (May 5)	691,875	BILL CLINTON	64	283,571	GEORGE BUSH*	71
		No Preference	15		Pat Buchanan	20
		Jerry Brown	10		No Preference	10
		Paul Tsongas	8			
1988 (March 8)	679,958	AL GORE	35	273,801	GEORGE BUSH	45
		Jesse Jackson	33		Bob Dole	39
		Michael Dukakis	20		Pat Robertson	10
		Richard Gephardt	6			
1984 (May 8)	960,857	WALTER MONDALE	36	—	No Primary	
		Gary Hart	30			
		Jesse Jackson	25			
1980 (May 6)	737,262	JIMMY CARTER*	70	168,391	RONALD REAGAN	68
		Edward Kennedy	18		George Bush	22
		No Preference	9		John Anderson	5
1976 (March 23)	604,832	JIMMY CARTER	54	193,727	RONALD REAGAN	52
		George Wallace	35		Gerald Ford*	46
1972 (May 6)	821,410	GEORGE WALLACE	50	167,899	RICHARD NIXON*	95
		Terry Sanford	37		Paul McCloskey	5
		Shirley Chisholm	8			

Note: All candidates are listed that drew at least 5 percent of their party's primary vote. The names of winning candidates are capitalized. An asterisk (*) indicates an incumbent president.

But when North Carolina voted in 1976, Wallace was a fading force, both nationally and in the South. Jimmy Carter had gone head-to-head with him in Florida in early March and won by 4 percentage points. Two weeks later in North Carolina, Carter's margin expanded to nearly 20 points, and Wallace was done as a serious presidential contender.

The only other time that the North Carolina primary had a make-or-break quality was in 1988, when Bob Dole suffered a critical loss that enabled George Bush to sweep the South and essentially wrap up the Republican nomination in early March. North Carolina was one of Dole's best chances for a Super Tuesday victory that year, due in no small part to his wife, Elizabeth, who was born in the textile-producing town of Salisbury and graduated from Duke University in Durham. Dole carried several urban counties, including Mecklenburg and Wake (Raleigh). But Bush won most of the rest of the state, and prevailed narrowly.

It was a considerably better showing for Bush than his first presidential run against Reagan in 1980. Then, he could carry only the most liberal of North Carolina's 100 counties—Orange, home of the University of North Carolina at Chapel Hill and a cornerstone of the state's Research Triangle.

Pat Buchanan tried to emulate Reagan's success in his 1992 challenge to Bush, highlighting themes tailored to conservative Republicans—from criticism of the Voting Rights Act to putting the Confederate stars and bars on his North Carolina bumper stickers. But Buchanan could not come close to carrying a single county, either in 1992 against Bush or in 1996 against Dole.

The Dole family has actually done quite well in North Carolina since 1988. Besides winning the Republican primary in 1996, Bob Dole carried the state in the fall presidential election against Bill Clinton. And in 2002, Elizabeth Dole was elected to the Senate from her home state.

The Bush family has also continued to do well in North Carolina. George W. Bush handily won the state's GOP primary in the spring of 2000 when his campaign was in the process of running victory laps. And the younger Bush kept North Carolina's electoral votes in the Republican column in both 2000 and 2004.

With its traditional May date, the North Carolina presidential primary has lost much of its competitive edge in recent years. But the comparative Democratic and Republican primary turnout figures hint at the shifting partisan advantage within the state from Democratic to Republican. Although more primary ballots continue to be cast on the Democratic side, the number that participated in the Democratic primary in 2000 was the lowest since 1972, while the Republican turnout in 2000 was the highest.

Over the course of much of the twentieth century, North Carolina was a model for peace and prosperity in the South. And from 1972 through 2004, every Democratic winner except one (Walter Mondale in 1984) was a son of the South. Wallace, Carter (twice), Clinton (twice), Al Gore (twice), and John Edwards all won North Carolina's Democratic voting.

Gore's 2-percentage point victory over Jesse Jackson in 1988 was the closest of the recent Democratic contests. Gore swept most of the western half of the state, which is adjacent to Tennessee; Jackson won most of the eastern half, which includes the state's largest concentration of black voters. The party's eventual nominee, Michael Dukakis, carried Orange County.

North Carolina temporarily shelved its presidential primary in 2004 when a legal challenge to the state legislative map forced a delay in the traditional May primary to a summer date too late to elect national convention delegates. Democrats instituted an April county caucus system that Edwards won with 52 percent of the 17,420 votes cast, followed by John Kerry with 27 percent, and Dennis Kucinich with 12 percent. It was a last tip of the cap to Edwards, then a senator from North Carolina, who had quit the presidential race a month earlier.

Yet there was something for everyone in the Democratic caucus results. Kerry won several scattered counties—from Dare (Manteo) on the Atlantic coast to Durham near the center of the state to Henderson in the western mountains near Asheville. Kucinich carried the county that includes Asheville (Buncombe), as well as academically-oriented Orange and Watauga (Appalachian State University at Boone) counties. Al Sharpton won Granville County outside Durham, which has a population fully one-third black.

NORTH CAROLINA DEMOCRATIC PRIMARY

2000

County	Total Vote	Bradley	Gore	LaRouche	No Preference	Winner	Percentage of Total Vote			
							Bradley	Gore	LaRouche	No Preference
ALAMANCE	7,501	1,558	4,998	237	708	Gore	20.8%	66.6%	3.2%	9.4%
ALEXANDER	1,230	169	963	26	72	Gore	13.7%	78.3%	2.1%	5.9%
ALLEGHANY	1,060	164	771	20	105	Gore	15.5%	72.7%	1.9%	9.9%
ANSON	2,975	374	2,216	65	320	Gore	12.6%	74.5%	2.2%	10.8%
ASHE	1,444	125	1,225	19	75	Gore	8.7%	84.8%	1.3%	5.2%
AVERY	325	34	249	6	36	Gore	10.5%	76.6%	1.8%	11.1%
BEAUFORT	4,985	1,088	3,062	188	647	Gore	21.8%	61.4%	3.8%	13.0%
BERTIE	2,875	453	2,097	66	259	Gore	15.8%	72.9%	2.3%	9.0%
BLADEN	5,536	796	3,899	149	692	Gore	14.4%	70.4%	2.7%	12.5%
BRUNSWICK	5,835	899	4,323	141	472	Gore	15.4%	74.1%	2.4%	8.1%
BUNCOMBE	14,368	2,610	10,166	324	1,268	Gore	18.2%	70.8%	2.3%	8.8%
BURKE	3,988	553	3,107	80	248	Gore	13.9%	77.9%	2.0%	6.2%
CABARRUS	5,261	1,079	3,543	135	504	Gore	20.5%	67.3%	2.6%	9.6%
CALDWELL	2,180	284	1,693	50	153	Gore	13.0%	77.7%	2.3%	7.0%
CAMDEN	1,242	239	708	31	264	Gore	19.2%	57.0%	2.5%	21.3%
CARTERET	4,447	861	3,047	109	430	Gore	19.4%	68.5%	2.5%	9.7%
CASWELL	3,188	628	2,175	82	303	Gore	19.7%	68.2%	2.6%	9.5%
CATAWBA	4,468	729	3,286	95	358	Gore	16.3%	73.5%	2.1%	8.0%
CHATHAM	6,959	1,638	4,557	154	610	Gore	23.5%	65.5%	2.2%	8.8%
CHEROKEE	822	132	643	15	32	Gore	16.1%	78.2%	1.8%	3.9%
CHOWAN	1,078	209	742	18	109	Gore	19.4%	68.8%	1.7%	10.1%
CLAY	269	37	216	0	16	Gore	13.8%	80.3%	0.0%	5.9%
CLEVELAND	8,131	1,474	5,318	192	1,147	Gore	18.1%	65.4%	2.4%	14.1%
COLUMBUS	8,505	1,095	6,311	146	953	Gore	12.9%	74.2%	1.7%	11.2%
CRAVEN	5,810	1,196	3,902	161	551	Gore	20.6%	67.2%	2.8%	9.5%
CUMBERLAND	19,274	2,915	13,976	401	1,982	Gore	15.1%	72.5%	2.1%	10.3%
CURRITUCK	1,558	337	898	55	268	Gore	21.6%	57.6%	3.5%	17.2%
DARE	3,681	850	2,193	64	574	Gore	23.1%	59.6%	1.7%	15.6%
DAVIDSON	4,981	904	3,620	121	336	Gore	18.1%	72.7%	2.4%	6.7%
DAVIE	1,537	297	1,040	51	149	Gore	19.3%	67.7%	3.3%	9.7%
DUPLIN	5,165	937	3,485	164	579	Gore	18.1%	67.5%	3.2%	11.2%
DURHAM	20,770	3,850	15,395	244	1,281	Gore	18.5%	74.1%	1.2%	6.2%
EDGECOMBE	6,552	933	4,971	106	542	Gore	14.2%	75.9%	1.6%	8.3%
FORSYTH	16,515	3,054	12,189	317	955	Gore	18.5%	73.8%	1.9%	5.8%
FRANKLIN	4,463	870	2,978	124	491	Gore	19.5%	66.7%	2.8%	11.0%
GASTON	5,907	1,105	3,980	175	647	Gore	18.7%	67.4%	3.0%	11.0%
GATES	1,102	183	806	6	107	Gore	16.6%	73.1%	0.5%	9.7%
GRAHAM	414	55	309	5	45	Gore	13.3%	74.6%	1.2%	10.9%
GRANVILLE	5,173	940	3,533	120	580	Gore	18.2%	68.3%	2.3%	11.2%
GREENE	2,787	619	1,555	96	517	Gore	22.2%	55.8%	3.4%	18.6%
GUILFORD	33,910	6,551	24,780	562	2,017	Gore	19.3%	73.1%	1.7%	5.9%
HALIFAX	6,060	930	4,404	129	597	Gore	15.3%	72.7%	2.1%	9.9%
HARNETT	6,430	1,277	4,158	190	805	Gore	19.9%	64.7%	3.0%	12.5%
HAYWOOD	5,199	880	3,658	125	536	Gore	16.9%	70.4%	2.4%	10.3%
HENDERSON	2,598	437	1,923	43	195	Gore	16.8%	74.0%	1.7%	7.5%

NORTH CAROLINA DEMOCRATIC PRIMARY

2000

County	Total Vote	Bradley	Gore	LaRouche	No Preference	Winner	Percentage of Total Vote			
							Bradley	Gore	LaRouche	No Preference
HERTFORD	3,178	381	2,552	42	203	Gore	12.0%	80.3%	1.3%	6.4%
HOKE	3,174	434	2,392	71	277	Gore	13.7%	75.4%	2.2%	8.7%
HYDE	1,197	213	707	37	240	Gore	17.8%	59.1%	3.1%	20.1%
IREDELL	5,241	932	3,554	158	597	Gore	17.8%	67.8%	3.0%	11.4%
JACKSON	2,016	283	1,581	35	117	Gore	14.0%	78.4%	1.7%	5.8%
JOHNSTON	7,515	1,712	4,788	216	799	Gore	22.8%	63.7%	2.9%	10.6%
JONES	1,526	280	965	46	235	Gore	18.3%	63.2%	3.0%	15.4%
LEE	6,485	1,358	4,149	180	798	Gore	20.9%	64.0%	2.8%	12.3%
LENOIR	6,500	1,311	4,003	228	958	Gore	20.2%	61.6%	3.5%	14.7%
LINCOLN	4,759	735	3,548	70	406	Gore	15.4%	74.6%	1.5%	8.5%
MCDOWELL	2,226	385	1,556	79	206	Gore	17.3%	69.9%	3.5%	9.3%
MACON	1,544	263	1,121	33	127	Gore	17.0%	72.6%	2.1%	8.2%
MADISON	1,945	271	1,508	32	134	Gore	13.9%	77.5%	1.6%	6.9%
MARTIN	3,492	612	2,339	73	468	Gore	17.5%	67.0%	2.1%	13.4%
MECKLENBURG	23,902	3,919	18,544	351	1,088	Gore	16.4%	77.6%	1.5%	4.6%
MITCHELL	219	22	181	4	12	Gore	10.0%	82.6%	1.8%	5.5%
MONTGOMERY	2,626	450	1,845	59	272	Gore	17.1%	70.3%	2.2%	10.4%
MOORE	3,825	657	2,870	59	239	Gore	17.2%	75.0%	1.5%	6.2%
NASH	6,865	1,412	4,561	167	725	Gore	20.6%	66.4%	2.4%	10.6%
NEW HANOVER	13,629	2,325	9,877	223	1,204	Gore	17.1%	72.5%	1.6%	8.8%
NORTHAMPTON	4,564	634	3,428	59	443	Gore	13.9%	75.1%	1.3%	9.7%
ONSLOW	6,572	1,223	4,139	194	1,016	Gore	18.6%	63.0%	3.0%	15.5%
ORANGE	11,063	3,120	7,125	166	652	Gore	28.2%	64.4%	1.5%	5.9%
PAMLICO	1,518	302	1,026	56	134	Gore	19.9%	67.6%	3.7%	8.8%
PASQUOTANK	2,952	529	2,016	62	345	Gore	17.9%	68.3%	2.1%	11.7%
PENDER	2,944	477	2,218	58	191	Gore	16.2%	75.3%	2.0%	6.5%
PERQUIMANS	1,507	314	929	37	227	Gore	20.8%	61.6%	2.5%	15.1%
PERSON	4,185	864	2,533	105	683	Gore	20.6%	60.5%	2.5%	16.3%
PITT	12,244	2,591	8,160	197	1,296	Gore	21.2%	66.6%	1.6%	10.6%
POLK	1,227	187	921	24	95	Gore	15.2%	75.1%	2.0%	7.7%
RANDOLPH	3,000	516	2,172	63	249	Gore	17.2%	72.4%	2.1%	8.3%
RICHMOND	5,244	767	3,687	136	654	Gore	14.6%	70.3%	2.6%	12.5%
ROBESON	14,498	1,920	10,464	265	1,849	Gore	13.2%	72.2%	1.8%	12.8%
ROCKINGHAM	5,908	1,201	3,867	148	692	Gore	20.3%	65.5%	2.5%	11.7%
ROWAN	4,579	874	3,187	104	414	Gore	19.1%	69.6%	2.3%	9.0%
RUTHERFORD	2,105	386	1,464	51	204	Gore	18.3%	69.5%	2.4%	9.7%
SAMPSON	5,246	727	4,058	77	384	Gore	13.9%	77.4%	1.5%	7.3%
SCOTLAND	3,134	383	2,506	52	193	Gore	12.2%	80.0%	1.7%	6.2%
STANLY	5,264	1,086	3,484	154	540	Gore	20.6%	66.2%	2.9%	10.3%
STOKES	1,827	285	1,303	56	183	Gore	15.6%	71.3%	3.1%	10.0%
SURRY	3,448	571	2,446	72	359	Gore	16.6%	70.9%	2.1%	10.4%
SWAIN	658	105	530	23	0	Gore	16.0%	80.5%	3.5%	0.0%
TRANSYLVANIA	1,799	348	1,287	41	123	Gore	19.3%	71.5%	2.3%	6.8%
TYRRELL	786	115	510	25	136	Gore	14.6%	64.9%	3.2%	17.3%
UNION	4,495	687	3,289	98	421	Gore	15.3%	73.2%	2.2%	9.4%

NORTH CAROLINA DEMOCRATIC PRIMARY

2000

County	Total Vote	Bradley	Gore	LaRouche	No Preference	Winner	Percentage of Total Vote			
							Bradley	Gore	LaRouche	No Preference
VANCE	4,307	927	2,799	94	487	Gore	21.5%	65.0%	2.2%	11.3%
WAKE	42,661	9,704	29,479	756	2,722	Gore	22.7%	69.1%	1.8%	6.4%
WARREN	3,258	558	2,377	72	251	Gore	17.1%	73.0%	2.2%	7.7%
WASHINGTON	1,937	358	1,279	61	239	Gore	18.5%	66.0%	3.1%	12.3%
WATAUGA	2,774	438	2,114	43	179	Gore	15.8%	76.2%	1.6%	6.5%
WAYNE	8,450	1,598	5,614	214	1,024	Gore	18.9%	66.4%	2.5%	12.1%
WILKES	2,958	387	2,310	44	217	Gore	13.1%	78.1%	1.5%	7.3%
WILSON	4,588	909	3,180	90	409	Gore	19.8%	69.3%	2.0%	8.9%
YADKIN	1,173	210	826	28	109	Gore	17.9%	70.4%	2.4%	9.3%
YANCEY	1,627	192	1,260	30	145	Gore	11.8%	77.4%	1.8%	8.9%
TOTAL	544,922	99,796	383,696	11,525	49,905	Gore	18.3%	70.4%	2.1%	9.2%

NORTH CAROLINA REPUBLICAN PRIMARY

2000

County	Total Vote	G.W. Bush	Keyes	McCain	Other	Winner	Percentage of Total Vote			
							G.W. Bush	Keyes	McCain	Other
ALAMANCE	4,665	3,756	402	424	83	G.W. Bush	80.5%	8.6%	9.1%	1.8%
ALEXANDER	1,202	1,023	67	86	26	G.W. Bush	85.1%	5.6%	7.2%	2.2%
ALLEGHANY	433	364	29	33	7	G.W. Bush	84.1%	6.7%	7.6%	1.6%
ANSON	273	215	25	17	16	G.W. Bush	78.8%	9.2%	6.2%	5.9%
ASHE	1,614	1,323	90	158	43	G.W. Bush	82.0%	5.6%	9.8%	2.7%
AVERY	2,889	2,175	184	358	172	G.W. Bush	75.3%	6.4%	12.4%	6.0%
BEAUFORT	2,031	1,649	138	209	35	G.W. Bush	81.2%	6.8%	10.3%	1.7%
BERTIE	142	107	13	12	10	G.W. Bush	75.4%	9.2%	8.5%	7.0%
BLADEN	530	434	34	44	18	G.W. Bush	81.9%	6.4%	8.3%	3.4%
BRUNSWICK	2,845	2,109	155	490	91	G.W. Bush	74.1%	5.4%	17.2%	3.2%
BUNCOMBE	8,455	5,883	1,294	1,049	229	G.W. Bush	69.6%	15.3%	12.4%	2.7%
BURKE	2,969	2,475	175	214	105	G.W. Bush	83.4%	5.9%	7.2%	3.5%
CABARRUS	5,166	4,059	467	493	147	G.W. Bush	78.6%	9.0%	9.5%	2.8%
CALDWELL	2,675	2,167	195	228	85	G.W. Bush	81.0%	7.3%	8.5%	3.2%
CAMDEN	127	94	12	20	1	G.W. Bush	74.0%	9.4%	15.7%	0.8%
CARTERET	3,789	2,961	313	441	74	G.W. Bush	78.1%	8.3%	11.6%	2.0%
CASWELL	852	725	48	59	20	G.W. Bush	85.1%	5.6%	6.9%	2.3%
CATAWBA	8,326	6,722	522	786	296	G.W. Bush	80.7%	6.3%	9.4%	3.6%
CHATHAM	2,376	1,882	128	315	51	G.W. Bush	79.2%	5.4%	13.3%	2.1%
CHEROKEE	816	634	59	95	28	G.W. Bush	77.7%	7.2%	11.6%	3.4%
CHOWAN	303	234	22	37	10	G.W. Bush	77.2%	7.3%	12.2%	3.3%
CLAY	365	312	26	23	4	G.W. Bush	85.5%	7.1%	6.3%	1.1%
CLEVELAND	3,162	2,578	201	254	129	G.W. Bush	81.5%	6.4%	8.0%	4.1%
COLUMBUS	858	706	42	79	31	G.W. Bush	82.3%	4.9%	9.2%	3.6%
CRAVEN	3,067	2,367	237	406	57	G.W. Bush	77.2%	7.7%	13.2%	1.9%

NORTH CAROLINA REPUBLICAN PRIMARY

2000

County	Total Vote	G.W. Bush	Keyes	McCain	Other	Winner	Percentage of Total Vote			
							G.W. Bush	Keyes	McCain	Other
CUMBERLAND	6,547	5,128	620	613	186	G.W. Bush	78.3%	9.5%	9.4%	2.8%
CURRITUCK	330	248	26	50	6	G.W. Bush	75.2%	7.9%	15.2%	1.8%
DARE	1,541	1,101	83	303	54	G.W. Bush	71.4%	5.4%	19.7%	3.5%
DAVIDSON	6,860	5,642	466	602	150	G.W. Bush	82.2%	6.8%	8.8%	2.2%
DAVIE	4,740	3,865	205	497	173	G.W. Bush	81.5%	4.3%	10.5%	3.6%
DUPLIN	1,433	1,236	67	87	43	G.W. Bush	86.3%	4.7%	6.1%	3.0%
DURHAM	5,212	3,814	577	694	127	G.W. Bush	73.2%	11.1%	13.3%	2.4%
EDGECOMBE	582	481	41	45	15	G.W. Bush	82.6%	7.0%	7.7%	2.6%
FORSYTH	13,312	10,518	1,269	1,243	282	G.W. Bush	79.0%	9.5%	9.3%	2.1%
FRANKLIN	1,298	1,058	112	94	34	G.W. Bush	81.5%	8.6%	7.2%	2.6%
GASTON	5,747	4,699	416	480	152	G.W. Bush	81.8%	7.2%	8.4%	2.6%
GATES	75	57	2	16	0	G.W. Bush	76.0%	2.7%	21.3%	0.0%
GRAHAM	504	421	35	43	5	G.W. Bush	83.5%	6.9%	8.5%	1.0%
GRANVILLE	717	579	70	55	13	G.W. Bush	80.8%	9.8%	7.7%	1.8%
GREENE	250	224	8	10	8	G.W. Bush	89.6%	3.2%	4.0%	3.2%
GUILFORD	24,643	19,307	1,868	2,839	629	G.W. Bush	78.3%	7.6%	11.5%	2.6%
HALIFAX	542	440	41	49	12	G.W. Bush	81.2%	7.6%	9.0%	2.2%
HARNETT	2,514	2,075	206	174	59	G.W. Bush	82.5%	8.2%	6.9%	2.3%
HAYWOOD	1,444	1,020	176	212	36	G.W. Bush	70.6%	12.2%	14.7%	2.5%
HENDERSON	7,799	5,507	865	1,162	265	G.W. Bush	70.6%	11.1%	14.9%	3.4%
HERTFORD	233	187	15	20	11	G.W. Bush	80.3%	6.4%	8.6%	4.7%
HOKE	397	325	22	36	14	G.W. Bush	81.9%	5.5%	9.1%	3.5%
HYDE	113	98	5	10	0	G.W. Bush	86.7%	4.4%	8.8%	0.0%
IREDELL	5,694	4,551	441	513	189	G.W. Bush	79.9%	7.7%	9.0%	3.3%
JACKSON	650	484	79	71	16	G.W. Bush	74.5%	12.2%	10.9%	2.5%
JOHNSTON	6,094	5,183	326	462	123	G.W. Bush	85.1%	5.3%	7.6%	2.0%
JONES	163	137	18	6	2	G.W. Bush	84.0%	11.0%	3.7%	1.2%
LEE	2,535	2,045	127	283	80	G.W. Bush	80.7%	5.0%	11.2%	3.2%
LENOIR	1,276	1,109	58	75	34	G.W. Bush	86.9%	4.5%	5.9%	2.7%
LINCOLN	4,176	3,525	227	316	108	G.W. Bush	84.4%	5.4%	7.6%	2.6%
MCDOWELL	1,534	1,180	156	159	39	G.W. Bush	76.9%	10.2%	10.4%	2.5%
MACON	1,088	788	148	130	22	G.W. Bush	72.4%	13.6%	11.9%	2.0%
MADISON	951	771	69	84	27	G.W. Bush	81.1%	7.3%	8.8%	2.8%
MARTIN	399	333	20	36	10	G.W. Bush	83.5%	5.0%	9.0%	2.5%
MECKLENBURG	26,297	19,950	2,249	3,486	612	G.W. Bush	75.9%	8.6%	13.3%	2.3%
MITCHELL	2,484	1,891	158	315	120	G.W. Bush	76.1%	6.4%	12.7%	4.8%
MONTGOMERY	689	607	25	48	9	G.W. Bush	88.1%	3.6%	7.0%	1.3%
MOORE	5,680	4,453	315	802	110	G.W. Bush	78.4%	5.5%	14.1%	1.9%
NASH	2,580	2,108	233	192	47	G.W. Bush	81.7%	9.0%	7.4%	1.8%
NEW HANOVER	10,968	8,109	747	1,751	361	G.W. Bush	73.9%	6.8%	16.0%	3.3%
NORTHAMPTON	139	107	10	16	6	G.W. Bush	77.0%	7.2%	11.5%	4.3%
ONSLOW	3,721	2,780	382	462	97	G.W. Bush	74.7%	10.3%	12.4%	2.6%
ORANGE	2,848	2,004	268	496	80	G.W. Bush	70.4%	9.4%	17.4%	2.8%
PAMLICO	479	368	27	68	16	G.W. Bush	76.8%	5.6%	14.2%	3.3%
PASQUOTANK	520	379	45	74	22	G.W. Bush	72.9%	8.7%	14.2%	4.2%

NORTH CAROLINA REPUBLICAN PRIMARY

2000

County	Total Vote	G.W. Bush	Keyes	McCain	Other	Winner	Percentage of Total Vote			
							G.W. Bush	Keyes	McCain	Other
PENDER	1,251	936	83	197	35	G.W. Bush	74.8%	6.6%	15.7%	2.8%
PERQUIMANS	391	288	34	55	14	G.W. Bush	73.7%	8.7%	14.1%	3.6%
PERSON	1,068	834	62	117	55	G.W. Bush	78.1%	5.8%	11.0%	5.1%
PITT	3,424	2,832	186	341	65	G.W. Bush	82.7%	5.4%	10.0%	1.9%
POLK	1,302	974	99	190	39	G.W. Bush	74.8%	7.6%	14.6%	3.0%
RANDOLPH	5,036	4,151	346	414	125	G.W. Bush	82.4%	6.9%	8.2%	2.5%
RICHMOND	650	516	43	73	18	G.W. Bush	79.4%	6.6%	11.2%	2.8%
ROBESON	843	627	58	86	72	G.W. Bush	74.4%	6.9%	10.2%	8.5%
ROCKINGHAM	2,810	2,248	191	274	97	G.W. Bush	80.0%	6.8%	9.8%	3.5%
ROWAN	6,171	4,865	388	708	210	G.W. Bush	78.8%	6.3%	11.5%	3.4%
RUTHERFORD	1,487	1,192	130	121	44	G.W. Bush	80.2%	8.7%	8.1%	3.0%
SAMPSON	3,853	3,453	90	193	117	G.W. Bush	89.6%	2.3%	5.0%	3.0%
SCOTLAND	440	339	32	55	14	G.W. Bush	77.0%	7.3%	12.5%	3.2%
STANLY	5,128	4,396	231	360	141	G.W. Bush	85.7%	4.5%	7.0%	2.7%
STOKES	2,682	2,306	180	140	56	G.W. Bush	86.0%	6.7%	5.2%	2.1%
SURRY	1,969	1,666	124	130	49	G.W. Bush	84.6%	6.3%	6.6%	2.5%
SWAIN	271	209	31	26	5	G.W. Bush	77.1%	11.4%	9.6%	1.8%
TRANSYLVANIA	2,486	1,694	304	426	62	G.W. Bush	68.1%	12.2%	17.1%	2.5%
TYRRELL	90	74	10	5	1	G.W. Bush	82.2%	11.1%	5.6%	1.1%
UNION	5,031	3,829	668	423	111	G.W. Bush	76.1%	13.3%	8.4%	2.2%
VANCE	352	277	27	37	11	G.W. Bush	78.7%	7.7%	10.5%	3.1%
WAKE	28,342	21,508	2,745	3,501	588	G.W. Bush	75.9%	9.7%	12.4%	2.1%
WARREN	221	154	17	39	11	G.W. Bush	69.7%	7.7%	17.6%	5.0%
WASHINGTON	175	147	14	11	3	G.W. Bush	84.0%	8.0%	6.3%	1.7%
WATAUGA	1,807	1,420	151	188	48	G.W. Bush	78.6%	8.4%	10.4%	2.7%
WAYNE	3,366	2,860	220	220	66	G.W. Bush	85.0%	6.5%	6.5%	2.0%
WILKES	7,073	5,877	304	627	265	G.W. Bush	83.1%	4.3%	8.9%	3.7%
WILSON	1,397	1,186	90	96	25	G.W. Bush	84.9%	6.4%	6.9%	1.8%
YADKIN	4,531	3,871	144	377	139	G.W. Bush	85.4%	3.2%	8.3%	3.1%
YANCEY	1,232	978	124	94	36	G.W. Bush	79.4%	10.1%	7.6%	2.9%
TOTAL	322,607	253,553	25,327	35,033	8,694	G.W. Bush	78.6%	7.9%	10.9%	2.7%
Certified Totals	322,517	253,485	25,320	35,018	8,694	G.W. Bush	78.6%	7.9%	10.9%	2.7%

Note: Other vote was 5,383 No Preference; 3,311 Gary Bauer.

NORTH DAKOTA

North Dakota has a long populist tradition characterized by a suspicion of concentrated business interests—such as railroads, banks, and grain companies. When the new innovation of the presidential primary blossomed across the country in 1912, it was North Dakota that was first in line to vote.

But the idea of a late-winter primary on the frigid upper Plains did not last long, and it was put on ice in the 1930s. The presidential primary was resurrected in the 1980s. But again it failed to take root, as candidates relegated North Dakota to the ranks of states whose scant prize was appraised as less precious than the time needed to win it.

George Bush's lone opponent in the Republican primary in 1988 was Mary Jane Rachner, a retired teacher from Minnesota who sought to buy billboard space to read: "Stamp Out Homosexuality." Bush won with 94 percent of the vote. The primary ballot in 1992 included Lyndon LaRouche and two comedians. Bush won the GOP primary again; Ross Perot won the Democratic primary on write-ins.

From 1984 through 1992, North Dakota held its presidential primary in June after all the other states had balloted. In 1996, it moved to the front end of the calendar, joining South Dakota on a date in late February. Bob Dole carried both Dakotas to win his first primaries of the year. With his farm-state roots, Dole garnered more votes in North Dakota's Republican primary than runner-up Steve Forbes and third-place finisher Pat Buchanan combined.

Buchanan had the benefit of momentum from his victory the previous week in New Hampshire. But he failed to connect in North Dakota. On one hand, he had to deal with the "ghost" of Phil Gramm in bidding for votes on the right side of the Republican spectrum. By the time of the North Dakota primary, Gramm was out of the race. But with North Dakota allowing ballots to be cast by mail beginning in January (when Gramm was still an active candidate), the Texas senator drew nearly 10 percent.

Nor was Buchanan, a native of Washington, D.C., helped by his urban roots. "Buchanan is a city kid," read an editorial in North Dakota's largest newspaper, the *Forum* of Fargo. "If he knows the difference between production agriculture and 'Green Acres,' he's yet to articulate it."

The early primary date in 1996, though, was unable to make the event a rousing hit at the ballot box. Turnout on

Recent North Dakota Primary Results

North Dakota held its first presidential primary in 1912, but none were held between 1932 and 1984.

| Year | DEMOCRATS | | | REPUBLICANS | | |
	Turnout	Candidates	%	Turnout	Candidates	%
2004	—	No Primary		—	No Primary	
2000	—	No Primary		—	No Primary	
1996 (Feb. 27)	1,584	ROLAND RIEMERS	41	63,734	BOB DOLE	42
		Lyndon LaRouche	35		Steve Forbes	20
		Vernon Clemenson	24		Pat Buchanan	18
					Phil Gramm	9
					Lamar Alexander	6
1992 (June 9)	32,786	ROSS PEROT#	29	47,808	GEORGE BUSH*	83
		Lyndon LaRouche	21		Pat Paulsen	9
		Charles Woods	20		Ross Perot#	8
		Tom Shiekman	15			
		Bill Clinton#	15			
1988 (June 14)	3,405	MICHAEL DUKAKIS#	85	39,434	GEORGE BUSH	94
		Jesse Jackson#	15		Mary Jane Rachner	6
1984 (June 12)	33,555	GARY HART	85	44,109	RONALD REAGAN*	100
		Lyndon LaRouche	12			

Note: All candidates are listed that drew at least 5 percent of their party's primary vote. The names of winning candidates are capitalized. An asterisk (*) indicates an incumbent president. A pound sign (#) indicates a write-in candidate.

the Republican side was barely half the number that voted in the GOP primary in 1924, which was won by President Calvin Coolidge. Barely 1,500 North Dakotans voted in the Democratic primary in 1996, which President Bill Clinton skipped. The state's presidential primary was abandoned after that.

But both parties in North Dakota have sought to enhance what influence they have by scheduling their caucuses early in the nominating season. In 2000, Republicans voted in late February, Democrats in early March, with voters in each party giving their party's front-runners, George W. Bush and Al Gore, respectively, landslide victories. In 2004, Democratic caucus-goers voted in early February and gave John Kerry a better than 2-to-1 victory over runner-up Wesley Clark.

Turnout was in the vicinity of 10,000 North Dakotans for the Republican caucuses in 2000 and the Democratic caucuses in 2004. The latter event was conducted at nearly 100 venues across the state, at a variety of sites ranging from the Bismarck Labor Temple to the Good Friends Bar and Grill outside Grand Forks.

OHIO

Ohio likes to portray itself as a bellwether, a microcosm of the national mood. In the 25 presidential elections held in the twentieth century, Ohio voted for the winner 23 times, a success rate exceeded by no other state and matched by just one, Missouri. And like Missouri, it voted for the winner in both 2000 and 2004.

For its part, Ohio's presidential primary has been as much a harbinger as a bellwether, particularly on the Democratic side. Nominees who have struggled in the primary have rarely had much success in winning the pivotal Buckeye State in the general election. Hubert Humphrey edged George McGovern in

the 1972 Democratic primary, giving the party an early warning of McGovern's lackluster appeal among blue-collar Democrats. Jimmy Carter scored a big win in Ohio on the final day of the primary season in 1976, offsetting a loss the same day in California and taking the air out of an incipient stop-Carter movement. Five months later he won the White House.

As president, Carter won the Ohio primary again in 1980. But with much of the state in the economic doldrums, the vote was much closer. Edward Kennedy had strong labor backing and ran tough television ads. ("Carter equals Hoover equals Depression," said one.) Kennedy carried much of the state's

Recent Ohio Primary Results

Ohio held its first presidential primary in 1912.

	DEMOCRATS				REPUBLICANS	
Year	Turnout	Candidates	%	Turnout	Candidates	%
2004 (March 2)	1,221,026	JOHN KERRY	52	793,833	GEORGE W. BUSH*	100
		John Edwards	34			
		Dennis Kucinich	9			
2000 (March 7)	978,512	AL GORE	74	1,397,528	GEORGE W. BUSH	58
		Bill Bradley	25		John McCain	37
1996 (March 19)	776,530	BILL CLINTON*	92	963,422	BOB DOLE	67
		Lyndon LaRouche	8		Pat Buchanan	22
					Steve Forbes	6
1992 (June 2)	1,042,335	BILL CLINTON	61	860,453	GEORGE BUSH*	83
		Jerry Brown	19		Pat Buchanan	17
		Paul Tsongas	11			
1988 (May 3)	1,383,572	MICHAEL DUKAKIS	63	794,904	GEORGE BUSH	81
		Jesse Jackson	27		Bob Dole	12
					Pat Robertson	7
1984 (May 8)	1,447,236	GARY HART	42	658,169	RONALD REAGAN*	100
		Walter Mondale	40			
		Jesse Jackson	16			
1980 (June 3)	1,186,410	JIMMY CARTER*	51	856,773	RONALD REAGAN	81
		Edward Kennedy	44		George Bush	19
1976 (June 8)	1,134,374	JIMMY CARTER	52	935,757	GERALD FORD*	55
		Morris Udall	21		Ronald Reagan	45
		Frank Church	14			
		George Wallace	6			
1972 (May 2)	1,212,330	HUBERT HUMPHREY	41	692,828	RICHARD NIXON*	100
		George McGovern	40			
		Edmund Muskie	9			
		Henry Jackson	8			
1968 (May 7)	549,140	STEPHEN YOUNG	100	614,492	JAMES RHODES	100

Note: All candidates are listed that drew at least 5 percent of their party's primary vote. The names of winning candidates are capitalized. An asterisk (*) indicates an incumbent president.

industrial northern tier from Toledo to Youngstown, traditionally the source of about half the Democratic primary vote. But Kennedy did not have enough strength elsewhere in the state to win the primary.

Four years later, Gary Hart appropriated a similar message, tying Walter Mondale to the Carter administration's economic record. Hart ended up running virtually even with Mondale in northern Ohio's industrial belt. And with his edge in rural Ohio, Hart scored a narrow victory that revitalized his struggling campaign for the final wave of primaries.

The Democratic primaries since then have been more one-sided. Michael Dukakis lost Franklin (Columbus) and Hamilton (Cincinnati) counties to Jesse Jackson in 1988, but still rolled up more than 60 percent of the vote statewide. Bill Clinton also surpassed 60 percent in 1992, with his "weakest" showing in Cuyahoga County (Cleveland), where he was held to 53 percent.

John Kerry won a more modest 52 percent of the vote in the Democratic primary in 2004, but it was still 18 percentage points better than John Edwards, who sought to keep his struggling candidacy alive with a strong Super Tuesday showing in the Buckeye State. Edwards tended to run better in the countryside than the cities of Ohio, but he ended up carrying only one county, Trumbull, located along the Pennsylvania border in the populous northeastern part of the state.

Edwards was crippled in his bid for anti-Kerry votes by the localized appeal of Dennis Kucinich. The Cleveland congressman and former mayor took nearly a quarter of the Democratic primary vote in Cuyahoga County and better than 10 percent in a number of northeast Ohio counties.

The Republican side of the presidential primary ballot in Ohio has not tended to be very competitive. Since Ray Bliss chaired the Ohio GOP in the 1950s and early 1960s, the party has emphasized nuts-and-bolts organization and political pragmatism. It gave President Gerald Ford an early endorsement that discouraged Ronald Reagan from mounting a full-scale effort in Ohio in 1976. Although Ford won the primary with a modest 55 percent of the vote, his tally was remarkably consistent around the state and gave him the delegates he needed to stake his claim to a first-ballot nomination.

For all practical purposes, 1976 was the last year until 2000 that Ohio Republicans had a say in their party's nominating process, because over the next two decades the GOP contest was usually over before the state voted. Ronald Reagan in 1980 and 1984, and George Bush in 1988 and 1992, each took more than 80 percent of the Ohio GOP primary vote. Dole won almost as easily in 1996.

Pat Buchanan was a distant second in both the 1992 and 1996 primaries, and failed to carry even one of Ohio's 88 counties. The best Buchanan could do was to take slightly more than one-third of the vote in 1996 in a trio of counties in the industrial Youngstown area.

George W. Bush's victory in the 2000 Republican primary was not so one-sided. John McCain carried congressional districts that included Akron and the majority-black east side of Cleveland. But Bush won decisively in the rest of Ohio, denying McCain a victory in a major heartland state that might have kept his upstart challenge alive.

As it was, the Bush-McCain contest was a hit at the ballot box. It drew nearly 1.4 million voters–a record for a Republican presidential primary in Ohio.

OHIO DEMOCRATIC PRIMARY

2000

County	Total Vote	Bradley	Gore	LaRouche	Winner	Percentage of Total Vote		
						Bradley	Gore	LaRouche
ADAMS	1,948	461	1,422	65	Gore	23.7%	73.0%	3.3%
ALLEN	6,272	1,667	4,484	121	Gore	26.6%	71.5%	1.9%
ASHLAND	2,926	732	2,102	92	Gore	25.0%	71.8%	3.1%
ASHTABULA	10,200	2,157	7,794	249	Gore	21.1%	76.4%	2.4%
ATHENS	6,468	2,287	4,012	169	Gore	35.4%	62.0%	2.6%
AUGLAIZE	2,527	660	1,802	65	Gore	26.1%	71.3%	2.6%
BELMONT	13,791	4,969	8,347	475	Gore	36.0%	60.5%	3.4%
BROWN	4,041	1,257	2,670	114	Gore	31.1%	66.1%	2.8%
BUTLER	13,949	3,152	10,646	151	Gore	22.6%	76.3%	1.1%
CARROLL	2,575	646	1,860	69	Gore	25.1%	72.2%	2.7%
CHAMPAIGN	2,355	554	1,763	38	Gore	23.5%	74.9%	1.6%
CLARK	12,527	2,770	9,601	156	Gore	22.1%	76.6%	1.2%
CLERMONT	5,931	1,402	4,449	80	Gore	23.6%	75.0%	1.3%
CLINTON	1,552	370	1,156	26	Gore	23.8%	74.5%	1.7%
COLUMBIANA	13,333	3,648	9,309	376	Gore	27.4%	69.8%	2.8%
COSHOCTON	2,209	558	1,610	41	Gore	25.3%	72.9%	1.9%
CRAWFORD	3,744	1,010	2,650	84	Gore	27.0%	70.8%	2.2%
CUYAHOGA	165,795	35,065	128,925	1,805	Gore	21.1%	77.8%	1.1%
DARKE	3,811	917	2,799	95	Gore	24.1%	73.4%	2.5%
DEFIANCE	2,123	566	1,510	47	Gore	26.7%	71.1%	2.2%
DELAWARE	5,181	1,460	3,654	67	Gore	28.2%	70.5%	1.3%
ERIE	8,881	2,093	6,638	150	Gore	23.6%	74.7%	1.7%
FAIRFIELD	7,668	1,966	5,570	132	Gore	25.6%	72.6%	1.7%
FAYETTE	1,093	221	856	16	Gore	20.2%	78.3%	1.5%
FRANKLIN	61,632	14,782	46,315	535	Gore	24.0%	75.1%	0.9%
FULTON	1,955	434	1,498	23	Gore	22.2%	76.6%	1.2%
GALLIA	2,276	603	1,624	49	Gore	26.5%	71.4%	2.2%
GEAUGA	6,410	1,764	4,543	103	Gore	27.5%	70.9%	1.6%
GREENE	8,508	2,046	6,359	103	Gore	24.0%	74.7%	1.2%
GUERNSEY	3,171	834	2,239	98	Gore	26.3%	70.6%	3.1%
HAMILTON	52,606	12,142	39,870	594	Gore	23.1%	75.8%	1.1%
HANCOCK	2,629	710	1,871	48	Gore	27.0%	71.2%	1.8%
HARDIN	1,701	430	1,247	24	Gore	25.3%	73.3%	1.4%
HARRISON	3,567	1,219	2,230	118	Gore	34.2%	62.5%	3.3%
HENRY	1,345	330	998	17	Gore	24.5%	74.2%	1.3%
HIGHLAND	1,959	430	1,493	36	Gore	21.9%	76.2%	1.8%
HOCKING	2,158	545	1,544	69	Gore	25.3%	71.5%	3.2%
HOLMES	1,287	396	855	36	Gore	30.8%	66.4%	2.8%
HURON	3,231	861	2,307	63	Gore	26.6%	71.4%	1.9%
JACKSON	1,658	342	1,276	40	Gore	20.6%	77.0%	2.4%
JEFFERSON	14,511	5,527	8,541	443	Gore	38.1%	58.9%	3.1%
KNOX	2,950	771	2,134	45	Gore	26.1%	72.3%	1.5%
LAKE	17,734	4,207	13,246	281	Gore	23.7%	74.7%	1.6%
LAWRENCE	5,189	1,095	3,990	104	Gore	21.1%	76.9%	2.0%
LICKING	10,440	2,560	7,679	201	Gore	24.5%	73.6%	1.9%

OHIO DEMOCRATIC PRIMARY

2000

County	Total Vote	Bradley	Gore	LaRouche	Winner	Percentage of Total Vote		
						Bradley	Gore	LaRouche
LOGAN	1,835	420	1,371	44	Gore	22.9%	74.7%	2.4%
LORAIN	29,421	7,668	21,266	487	Gore	26.1%	72.3%	1.7%
LUCAS	38,977	7,761	30,882	334	Gore	19.9%	79.2%	0.9%
MADISON	1,789	390	1,375	24	Gore	21.8%	76.9%	1.3%
MAHONING	58,751	16,568	40,992	1,191	Gore	28.2%	69.8%	2.0%
MARION	5,619	1,501	4,002	116	Gore	26.7%	71.2%	2.1%
MEDINA	10,010	2,521	7,358	131	Gore	25.2%	73.5%	1.3%
MEIGS	2,035	497	1,470	68	Gore	24.4%	72.2%	3.3%
MERCER	3,582	905	2,158	519	Gore	25.3%	60.2%	14.5%
MIAMI	5,720	1,276	4,340	104	Gore	22.3%	75.9%	1.8%
MONROE	3,681	1,321	2,195	165	Gore	35.9%	59.6%	4.5%
MONTGOMERY	45,827	8,621	36,702	504	Gore	18.8%	80.1%	1.1%
MORGAN	927	218	690	19	Gore	23.5%	74.4%	2.0%
MORROW	2,099	526	1,494	79	Gore	25.1%	71.2%	3.8%
MUSKINGUM	4,641	1,071	3,476	94	Gore	23.1%	74.9%	2.0%
NOBLE	1,904	611	1,219	74	Gore	32.1%	64.0%	3.9%
OTTAWA	3,351	760	2,552	39	Gore	22.7%	76.2%	1.2%
PAULDING	1,527	424	1,057	46	Gore	27.8%	69.2%	3.0%
PERRY	2,846	666	2,112	68	Gore	23.4%	74.2%	2.4%
PICKAWAY	2,739	660	2,043	36	Gore	24.1%	74.6%	1.3%
PIKE	2,613	557	2,006	50	Gore	21.3%	76.8%	1.9%
PORTAGE	13,854	4,183	9,434	237	Gore	30.2%	68.1%	1.7%
PREBLE	2,295	462	1,782	51	Gore	20.1%	77.6%	2.2%
PUTNAM	3,443	1,205	2,124	114	Gore	35.0%	61.7%	3.3%
RICHLAND	9,187	2,379	6,632	176	Gore	25.9%	72.2%	1.9%
ROSS	4,884	1,049	3,784	51	Gore	21.5%	77.5%	1.0%
SANDUSKY	4,430	985	3,380	65	Gore	22.2%	76.3%	1.5%
SCIOTO	6,717	1,499	5,091	127	Gore	22.3%	75.8%	1.9%
SENECA	4,534	1,308	3,125	101	Gore	28.8%	68.9%	2.2%
SHELBY	5,984	2,030	3,791	163	Gore	33.9%	63.4%	2.7%
STARK	42,245	10,052	31,348	845	Gore	23.8%	74.2%	2.0%
SUMMIT	51,830	13,986	37,167	677	Gore	27.0%	71.7%	1.3%
TRUMBULL	45,687	12,535	32,100	1,052	Gore	27.4%	70.3%	2.3%
TUSCARAWAS	12,550	4,075	8,097	378	Gore	32.5%	64.5%	3.0%
UNION	1,715	422	1,264	29	Gore	24.6%	73.7%	1.7%
VAN WERT	1,929	501	1,382	46	Gore	26.0%	71.6%	2.4%
VINTON	1,551	355	1,152	44	Gore	22.9%	74.3%	2.8%
WARREN	5,624	1,283	4,266	75	Gore	22.8%	75.9%	1.3%
WASHINGTON	4,824	1,219	3,510	95	Gore	25.3%	72.8%	2.0%
WAYNE	6,116	1,718	4,271	127	Gore	28.1%	69.8%	2.1%
WILLIAMS	1,486	369	1,090	27	Gore	24.8%	73.4%	1.8%
WOOD	8,439	2,109	6,235	95	Gore	25.0%	73.9%	1.1%
WYANDOT	1,477	406	1,038	33	Gore	27.5%	70.3%	2.2%
TOTAL	978,512	241,688	720,311	16,513	Gore	24.7%	73.6%	1.7%

Note: Ohio election officials did not compile statewide totals for the Democratic presidential primary in 2000. This table is based on the aggregate vote for each candidate's congressional district delegate slates.

OHIO REPUBLICAN PRIMARY

2000

County	Total Vote	G.W. Bush	McCain	Other	Winner	Percentage of Total Vote G.W. Bush	McCain	Other
ADAMS	4,104	2,786	1,099	219	G.W. Bush	67.9%	26.8%	5.3%
ALLEN	18,552	13,463	3,872	1,217	G.W. Bush	72.6%	20.9%	6.6%
ASHLAND	8,912	5,511	2,820	581	G.W. Bush	61.8%	31.6%	6.5%
ASHTABULA	11,049	6,324	3,890	835	G.W. Bush	57.2%	35.2%	7.6%
ATHENS	5,014	2,777	1,963	274	G.W. Bush	55.4%	39.2%	5.5%
AUGLAIZE	7,593	5,107	2,030	456	G.W. Bush	67.3%	26.7%	6.0%
BELMONT	5,051	3,015	1,696	340	G.W. Bush	59.7%	33.6%	6.7%
BROWN	4,533	2,923	1,418	192	G.W. Bush	64.5%	31.3%	4.2%
BUTLER	46,442	28,495	16,044	1,903	G.W. Bush	61.4%	34.5%	4.1%
CARROLL	4,259	2,451	1,506	302	G.W. Bush	57.5%	35.4%	7.1%
CHAMPAIGN	7,400	4,355	2,670	375	G.W. Bush	58.9%	36.1%	5.1%
CLARK	18,651	10,800	6,881	970	G.W. Bush	57.9%	36.9%	5.2%
CLERMONT	25,240	15,141	9,165	934	G.W. Bush	60.0%	36.3%	3.7%
CLINTON	7,460	4,090	3,073	297	G.W. Bush	54.8%	41.2%	4.0%
COLUMBIANA	13,360	7,983	4,602	775	G.W. Bush	59.8%	34.4%	5.8%
COSHOCTON	6,249	3,678	2,242	329	G.W. Bush	58.9%	35.9%	5.3%
CRAWFORD	6,556	4,174	1,950	432	G.W. Bush	63.7%	29.7%	6.6%
CUYAHOGA	115,860	56,928	53,317	5,615	G.W. Bush	49.1%	46.0%	4.8%
DARKE	9,969	6,191	3,250	528	G.W. Bush	62.1%	32.6%	5.3%
DEFIANCE	5,444	3,393	1,774	277	G.W. Bush	62.3%	32.6%	5.1%
DELAWARE	21,933	13,243	7,704	986	G.W. Bush	60.4%	35.1%	4.5%
ERIE	10,690	5,945	4,119	626	G.W. Bush	55.6%	38.5%	5.9%
FAIRFIELD	24,974	15,135	8,686	1,153	G.W. Bush	60.6%	34.8%	4.6%
FAYETTE	4,419	2,649	1,611	159	G.W. Bush	59.9%	36.5%	3.6%
FRANKLIN	114,798	67,844	41,805	5,149	G.W. Bush	59.1%	36.4%	4.5%
FULTON	7,653	4,861	2,431	361	G.W. Bush	63.5%	31.8%	4.7%
GALLIA	4,983	3,288	1,423	272	G.W. Bush	66.0%	28.6%	5.5%
GEAUGA	16,232	8,629	6,710	893	G.W. Bush	53.2%	41.3%	5.5%
GREENE	24,589	14,066	9,352	1,171	G.W. Bush	57.2%	38.0%	4.8%
GUERNSEY	4,972	2,979	1,696	297	G.W. Bush	59.9%	34.1%	6.0%
HAMILTON	113,472	65,370	43,562	4,540	G.W. Bush	57.6%	38.4%	4.0%
HANCOCK	14,567	9,653	4,144	770	G.W. Bush	66.3%	28.4%	5.3%
HARDIN	4,910	3,164	1,428	318	G.W. Bush	64.4%	29.1%	6.5%
HARRISON	1,852	1,144	578	130	G.W. Bush	61.8%	31.2%	7.0%
HENRY	4,667	2,939	1,524	204	G.W. Bush	63.0%	32.7%	4.4%
HIGHLAND	6,136	3,718	2,178	240	G.W. Bush	60.6%	35.5%	3.9%
HOCKING	2,842	1,693	983	166	G.W. Bush	59.6%	34.6%	5.8%
HOLMES	4,037	2,766	994	277	G.W. Bush	68.5%	24.6%	6.9%
HURON	6,294	3,781	2,131	382	G.W. Bush	60.1%	33.9%	6.1%
JACKSON	6,608	3,795	2,546	267	G.W. Bush	57.4%	38.5%	4.0%
JEFFERSON	6,270	3,498	1,886	886	G.W. Bush	55.8%	30.1%	14.1%
KNOX	9,234	5,684	3,039	511	G.W. Bush	61.6%	32.9%	5.5%
LAKE	27,266	14,322	11,119	1,825	G.W. Bush	52.5%	40.8%	6.7%
LAWRENCE	7,438	4,962	2,122	354	G.W. Bush	66.7%	28.5%	4.8%
LICKING	24,094	14,478	8,496	1,120	G.W. Bush	60.1%	35.3%	4.6%

OHIO REPUBLICAN PRIMARY

2000

County	Total Vote	G.W. Bush	McCain	Other	Winner	Percentage of Total Vote		
						G.W. Bush	McCain	Other
LOGAN	8,630	5,304	2,892	434	G.W. Bush	61.5%	33.5%	5.0%
LORAIN	25,924	14,106	10,610	1,208	G.W. Bush	54.4%	40.9%	4.7%
LUCAS	40,337	24,051	14,316	1,970	G.W. Bush	59.6%	35.5%	4.9%
MADISON	5,916	3,613	2,028	275	G.W. Bush	61.1%	34.3%	4.6%
MAHONING	17,549	10,041	6,574	934	G.W. Bush	57.2%	37.5%	5.3%
MARION	9,062	5,615	3,006	441	G.W. Bush	62.0%	33.2%	4.9%
MEDINA	22,775	11,775	9,731	1,269	G.W. Bush	51.7%	42.7%	5.6%
MEIGS	4,702	2,921	1,556	225	G.W. Bush	62.1%	33.1%	4.8%
MERCER	6,655	4,245	2,039	371	G.W. Bush	63.8%	30.6%	5.6%
MIAMI	17,495	10,226	6,449	820	G.W. Bush	58.5%	36.9%	4.7%
MONROE	1,224	768	360	96	G.W. Bush	62.7%	29.4%	7.8%
MONTGOMERY	66,687	38,515	25,137	3,035	G.W. Bush	57.8%	37.7%	4.6%
MORGAN	3,739	2,146	1,368	225	G.W. Bush	57.4%	36.6%	6.0%
MORROW	5,286	3,365	1,645	276	G.W. Bush	63.7%	31.1%	5.2%
MUSKINGUM	10,538	6,343	3,705	490	G.W. Bush	60.2%	35.2%	4.6%
NOBLE	2,216	1,385	698	133	G.W. Bush	62.5%	31.5%	6.0%
OTTAWA	4,984	2,953	1,853	178	G.W. Bush	59.2%	37.2%	3.6%
PAULDING	2,719	1,807	747	165	G.W. Bush	66.5%	27.5%	6.1%
PERRY	4,042	2,462	1,411	169	G.W. Bush	60.9%	34.9%	4.2%
PICKAWAY	5,667	3,655	1,777	235	G.W. Bush	64.5%	31.4%	4.1%
PIKE	2,038	1,347	599	92	G.W. Bush	66.1%	29.4%	4.5%
PORTAGE	15,477	7,564	7,101	812	G.W. Bush	48.9%	45.9%	5.2%
PREBLE	7,547	4,568	2,613	366	G.W. Bush	60.5%	34.6%	4.8%
PUTNAM	6,375	4,608	1,372	395	G.W. Bush	72.3%	21.5%	6.2%
RICHLAND	16,391	10,656	4,644	1,091	G.W. Bush	65.0%	28.3%	6.7%
ROSS	7,741	4,727	2,661	353	G.W. Bush	61.1%	34.4%	4.6%
SANDUSKY	8,523	5,081	3,068	374	G.W. Bush	59.6%	36.0%	4.4%
SCIOTO	7,540	4,881	2,263	396	G.W. Bush	64.7%	30.0%	5.3%
SENECA	8,442	5,190	2,848	404	G.W. Bush	61.5%	33.7%	4.8%
SHELBY	6,867	4,292	2,196	379	G.W. Bush	62.5%	32.0%	5.5%
STARK	53,884	29,235	21,232	3,417	G.W. Bush	54.3%	39.4%	6.3%
SUMMIT	61,173	29,064	28,775	3,334	G.W. Bush	47.5%	47.0%	5.5%
TRUMBULL	17,132	9,585	6,515	1,032	G.W. Bush	55.9%	38.0%	6.0%
TUSCARAWAS	7,949	4,784	2,650	515	G.W. Bush	60.2%	33.3%	6.5%
UNION	7,637	4,874	2,429	334	G.W. Bush	63.8%	31.8%	4.4%
VAN WERT	5,958	3,988	1,655	315	G.W. Bush	66.9%	27.8%	5.3%
VINTON	1,892	1,203	604	85	G.W. Bush	63.6%	31.9%	4.5%
WARREN	27,615	17,019	9,458	1,138	G.W. Bush	61.6%	34.2%	4.1%
WASHINGTON	10,067	6,344	3,203	520	G.W. Bush	63.0%	31.8%	5.2%
WAYNE	15,612	9,482	5,255	875	G.W. Bush	60.7%	33.7%	5.6%
WILLIAMS	8,174	4,775	2,996	403	G.W. Bush	58.4%	36.7%	4.9%
WOOD	16,758	10,182	5,893	683	G.W. Bush	60.8%	35.2%	4.1%
WYANDOT	3,961	2,433	1,329	199	G.W. Bush	61.4%	33.6%	5.0%
TOTAL	1,397,528	810,369	516,790	70,369	G.W. Bush	58.0%	37.0%	5.0%

Note: Other vote was 55,266 Alan Keyes; 8,934 Steve Forbes; 6,169 Gary Bauer.

OHIO DEMOCRATIC PRIMARY

2004

County	Total Vote	Edwards	Kerry	Kucinich	Other	Winner	Percentage of Total Vote			
							Edwards	Kerry	Kucinich	Other
ADAMS	1,842	684	983	28	147	Kerry	37.1%	53.4%	1.5%	8.0%
ALLEN	8,729	2,641	5,120	226	742	Kerry	30.3%	58.7%	2.6%	8.5%
ASHLAND	4,281	1,474	2,217	378	212	Kerry	34.4%	51.8%	8.8%	5.0%
ASHTABULA	11,138	3,769	5,605	1,269	495	Kerry	33.8%	50.3%	11.4%	4.4%
ATHENS	8,897	3,013	4,233	1,108	543	Kerry	33.9%	47.6%	12.5%	6.1%
AUGLAIZE	3,536	1,315	1,819	81	321	Kerry	37.2%	51.4%	2.3%	9.1%
BELMONT	14,678	5,320	7,342	480	1,536	Kerry	36.2%	50.0%	3.3%	10.5%
BROWN	3,702	1,439	1,900	41	322	Kerry	38.9%	51.3%	1.1%	8.7%
BUTLER	20,717	7,896	11,116	508	1,197	Kerry	38.1%	53.7%	2.5%	5.8%
CARROLL	3,378	1,223	1,696	240	219	Kerry	36.2%	50.2%	7.1%	6.5%
CHAMPAIGN	3,013	1,290	1,481	72	170	Kerry	42.8%	49.2%	2.4%	5.6%
CLARK	15,907	6,116	8,645	324	822	Kerry	38.4%	54.3%	2.0%	5.2%
CLERMONT	9,659	3,991	4,795	201	672	Kerry	41.3%	49.6%	2.1%	7.0%
CLINTON	1,864	727	965	51	121	Kerry	39.0%	51.8%	2.7%	6.5%
COLUMBIANA	11,049	4,685	5,249	461	654	Kerry	42.4%	47.5%	4.2%	5.9%
COSHOCTON	4,134	1,436	2,310	122	266	Kerry	34.7%	55.9%	3.0%	6.4%
CRAWFORD	4,389	1,655	2,224	198	312	Kerry	37.7%	50.7%	4.5%	7.1%
CUYAHOGA	208,613	50,270	101,153	49,761	7,429	Kerry	24.1%	48.5%	23.9%	3.6%
DARKE	4,379	1,871	2,157	76	275	Kerry	42.7%	49.3%	1.7%	6.3%
DEFIANCE	2,743	1,085	1,415	70	173	Kerry	39.6%	51.6%	2.6%	6.3%
DELAWARE	10,953	4,307	5,811	388	447	Kerry	39.3%	53.1%	3.5%	4.1%
ERIE	13,023	4,656	6,320	1,260	787	Kerry	35.8%	48.5%	9.7%	6.0%
FAIRFIELD	11,642	4,893	5,858	300	591	Kerry	42.0%	50.3%	2.6%	5.1%
FAYETTE	1,343	576	669	22	76	Kerry	42.9%	49.8%	1.6%	5.7%
FRANKLIN	101,106	34,133	57,454	4,841	4,678	Kerry	33.8%	56.8%	4.8%	4.6%
FULTON	3,594	1,428	1,911	75	180	Kerry	39.7%	53.2%	2.1%	5.0%
GALLIA	2,464	770	1,431	51	212	Kerry	31.3%	58.1%	2.1%	8.6%
GEAUGA	9,391	3,041	4,646	1,348	356	Kerry	32.4%	49.5%	14.4%	3.8%
GREENE	14,879	5,593	7,686	728	872	Kerry	37.6%	51.7%	4.9%	5.9%
GUERNSEY	3,165	1,111	1,680	149	225	Kerry	35.1%	53.1%	4.7%	7.1%
HAMILTON	56,284	17,579	32,981	2,186	3,538	Kerry	31.2%	58.6%	3.9%	6.3%
HANCOCK	3,557	1,498	1,788	94	177	Kerry	42.1%	50.3%	2.6%	5.0%
HARDIN	2,435	881	1,321	50	183	Kerry	36.2%	54.3%	2.1%	7.5%
HARRISON	3,172	1,102	1,636	114	320	Kerry	34.7%	51.6%	3.6%	10.1%
HENRY	2,647	1,101	1,374	44	128	Kerry	41.6%	51.9%	1.7%	4.8%
HIGHLAND	2,146	865	1,093	40	148	Kerry	40.3%	50.9%	1.9%	6.9%
HOCKING	2,882	1,287	1,364	90	141	Kerry	44.7%	47.3%	3.1%	4.9%
HOLMES	1,481	502	757	136	86	Kerry	33.9%	51.1%	9.2%	5.8%
HURON	4,583	1,718	2,258	364	243	Kerry	37.5%	49.3%	7.9%	5.3%
JACKSON	2,032	572	1,298	39	123	Kerry	28.1%	63.9%	1.9%	6.1%
JEFFERSON	14,666	5,277	7,331	480	1,578	Kerry	36.0%	50.0%	3.3%	10.8%
KNOX	4,168	1,674	2,106	159	229	Kerry	40.2%	50.5%	3.8%	5.5%
LAKE	29,431	9,308	15,033	3,998	1,092	Kerry	31.6%	51.1%	13.6%	3.7%
LAWRENCE	5,571	1,724	3,299	73	475	Kerry	30.9%	59.2%	1.3%	8.5%
LICKING	12,597	5,091	6,593	360	553	Kerry	40.4%	52.3%	2.9%	4.4%

OHIO DEMOCRATIC PRIMARY

2004

County	Total Vote	Edwards	Kerry	Kucinich	Other	Winner	Percentage of Total Vote			
							Edwards	Kerry	Kucinich	Other
LOGAN	3,071	1,235	1,526	95	215	Kerry	40.2%	49.7%	3.1%	7.0%
LORAIN	37,661	11,513	18,659	6,005	1,484	Kerry	30.6%	49.5%	15.9%	3.9%
LUCAS	40,325	13,905	24,035	1,082	1,303	Kerry	34.5%	59.6%	2.7%	3.2%
MADISON	2,670	1,110	1,356	62	142	Kerry	41.6%	50.8%	2.3%	5.3%
MAHONING	53,481	21,930	25,583	2,956	3,012	Kerry	41.0%	47.8%	5.5%	5.6%
MARION	7,540	3,057	3,695	240	548	Kerry	40.5%	49.0%	3.2%	7.3%
MEDINA	15,799	5,434	7,502	2,230	633	Kerry	34.4%	47.5%	14.1%	4.0%
MEIGS	2,014	551	1,193	89	181	Kerry	27.4%	59.2%	4.4%	9.0%
MERCER	4,402	1,623	2,324	115	340	Kerry	36.9%	52.8%	2.6%	7.7%
MIAMI	6,813	2,883	3,452	151	327	Kerry	42.3%	50.7%	2.2%	4.8%
MONROE	4,335	1,411	2,224	126	574	Kerry	32.5%	51.3%	2.9%	13.2%
MONTGOMERY	53,409	18,517	31,188	1,255	2,449	Kerry	34.7%	58.4%	2.3%	4.6%
MORGAN	1,423	457	798	56	112	Kerry	32.1%	56.1%	3.9%	7.9%
MORROW	3,035	1,211	1,537	94	193	Kerry	39.9%	50.6%	3.1%	6.4%
MUSKINGUM	6,146	1,987	3,526	169	464	Kerry	32.3%	57.4%	2.7%	7.5%
NOBLE	1,830	606	978	56	190	Kerry	33.1%	53.4%	3.1%	10.4%
OTTAWA	5,017	2,129	2,535	144	209	Kerry	42.4%	50.5%	2.9%	4.2%
PAULDING	2,174	746	1,176	41	211	Kerry	34.3%	54.1%	1.9%	9.7%
PERRY	3,592	1,355	1,936	77	224	Kerry	37.7%	53.9%	2.1%	6.2%
PICKAWAY	5,031	2,182	2,388	125	336	Kerry	43.4%	47.5%	2.5%	6.7%
PIKE	2,752	1,033	1,510	48	161	Kerry	37.5%	54.9%	1.7%	5.9%
PORTAGE	21,889	7,795	10,384	2,560	1,150	Kerry	35.6%	47.4%	11.7%	5.3%
PREBLE	3,520	1,481	1,723	47	269	Kerry	42.1%	48.9%	1.3%	7.6%
PUTNAM	4,106	1,608	1,938	98	462	Kerry	39.2%	47.2%	2.4%	11.3%
RICHLAND	14,004	4,636	7,336	1,097	935	Kerry	33.1%	52.4%	7.8%	6.7%
ROSS	6,442	2,554	3,353	156	379	Kerry	39.6%	52.0%	2.4%	5.9%
SANDUSKY	5,770	2,253	3,115	154	248	Kerry	39.0%	54.0%	2.7%	4.3%
SCIOTO	8,670	2,995	4,806	154	715	Kerry	34.5%	55.4%	1.8%	8.2%
SENECA	6,088	2,544	2,960	204	380	Kerry	41.8%	48.6%	3.4%	6.2%
SHELBY	3,824	1,645	1,910	58	211	Kerry	43.0%	49.9%	1.5%	5.5%
STARK	47,602	16,552	24,825	4,146	2,079	Kerry	34.8%	52.2%	8.7%	4.4%
SUMMIT	67,261	22,056	34,895	7,861	2,449	Kerry	32.8%	51.9%	11.7%	3.6%
TRUMBULL	47,047	21,270	20,644	2,684	2,449	Edwards	45.2%	43.9%	5.7%	5.2%
TUSCARAWAS	10,584	3,925	5,392	714	553	Kerry	37.1%	50.9%	6.7%	5.2%
UNION	2,639	1,156	1,296	53	134	Kerry	43.8%	49.1%	2.0%	5.1%
VAN WERT	1,980	694	1,084	40	162	Kerry	35.1%	54.7%	2.0%	8.2%
VINTON	1,253	381	734	39	99	Kerry	30.4%	58.6%	3.1%	7.9%
WARREN	9,312	3,819	4,819	153	521	Kerry	41.0%	51.8%	1.6%	5.6%
WASHINGTON	6,259	2,074	3,574	148	463	Kerry	33.1%	57.1%	2.4%	7.4%
WAYNE	9,505	3,422	4,695	909	479	Kerry	36.0%	49.4%	9.6%	5.0%
WILLIAMS	2,320	842	1,269	46	163	Kerry	36.3%	54.7%	2.0%	7.0%
WOOD	10,855	4,259	5,737	398	461	Kerry	39.2%	52.9%	3.7%	4.2%
WYANDOT	1,716	683	866	48	119	Kerry	39.8%	50.5%	2.8%	6.9%
TOTAL	1,221,026	416,106	632,599	110,067	62,254	Kerry	34.1%	51.8%	9.0%	5.1%

Note: Ohio election officials did not compile statewide totals for the Democratic presidential primary in 2004. This table is based on the aggregate vote for each candidate's congressional district delegate slates. Other vote was 30,983 Howard Dean; 14,676 Joseph I. Lieberman; 12,577 Wesley Clark; 4,018 Lyndon H. LaRouche Jr.

OKLAHOMA

Oklahoma is rock-ribbed Republican in presidential voting, firmly in the GOP column in every election since 1964. But the state's Democratic presidential primary in early 2004 was arguably the most competitive and one of the most meaningful of the entire primary season. Voting with a half dozen other states on the first Tuesday in February, Oklahoma offered Wesley Clark, John Edwards, and John Kerry a chance for a meaningful victory. Ultimately, Clark defeated Edwards by barely 1,200 votes out of more than 300,000 cast, providing the former general with his lone win in the 2004 primaries and critically delaying Edwards' bid to emerge as the sole alternative to Kerry.

All three Democrats found a toehold in Oklahoma. Clark carried much of the western half of the state, which faces the Southwest. Edwards won most of the eastern half, a portion of which bears the name "Little Dixie." Kerry swept the major population centers, Oklahoma (Oklahoma City) and Tulsa counties, as well as Cleveland County, the home of the University of Oklahoma at Norman. Kerry's strong urban showing helped him finish a close third in the primary, less than 10,000 votes behind Clark.

Oklahoma's first presidential primary was in 1988, as the Sooner State helped anchor the western flank of that year's huge, Southern-oriented primary dubbed Super Tuesday. Oklahoma Republicans staged one of the closest and most evenly contested votes of the truncated GOP primary season, the only other presidential primary in the state's history that has been very meaningful for either party. George Bush beat Bob Dole in the Sooner State that year, as he did in every primary on Super Tuesday. But in Oklahoma, as almost nowhere else, the outcome was in doubt until the next day.

It was a border war—Bush from Texas, Dole from Kansas. And in the end, Bush won Oklahoma by barely 5,000 votes out of more than 200,000 cast, with his winning 37 percent vote share by far his lowest in the vast array of primaries held in 1988 on Super Tuesday.

Dole swept much of the Republican-oriented farm and ranch country in the northern part of the state that abuts Kansas. But Bush capitalized on the urban orientation of the Oklahoma GOP to narrowly prevail. More than half the vote was cast in Oklahoma, Tulsa, and Cleveland counties, and Bush won all three.

Recent Oklahoma Primary Results

Oklahoma held its first presidential primary in 1988.

| Year | DEMOCRATS | | | REPUBLICANS | | |
	Turnout	Candidates	%	Turnout	Candidates	%
2004 (Feb. 3)	302,285	WESLEY CLARK	30	66,198	GEORGE W. BUSH*	90
		John Edwards	30		Bill Wyatt	10
		John Kerry	27			
		Joe Lieberman	7			
2000 (March 14)	134,850	AL GORE	69	124,809	GEORGE W. BUSH	79
		Bill Bradley	25		John McCain	10
		Lyndon LaRouche	6		Alan Keyes	9
1996 (March 12)	366,604	BILL CLINTON*	76	264,542	BOB DOLE	59
		Lyndon LaRouche	13		Pat Buchanan	22
		Elvena Lloyd-Duffie	11		Steve Forbes	14
1992 (March 10)	416,129	BILL CLINTON	70	217,721	GEORGE BUSH*	70
		Jerry Brown	17		Pat Buchanan	27
1988 (March 8)	392,727	AL GORE	41	208,938	GEORGE BUSH	37
		Richard Gephardt	21		Bob Dole	35
		Michael Dukakis	17		Pat Robertson	21
		Jesse Jackson	13		Jack Kemp	5

Note: All candidates are listed that drew at least 5 percent of their party's primary vote. The names of winning candidates are capitalized. An asterisk (*) indicates an incumbent president.

Evangelist Pat Robertson ran a strong third in Oklahoma with 21 percent of the vote, his best showing in any 1988 primary. Robertson ran particularly well in the rural counties of southern Oklahoma, carrying nine and finishing second in roughly a dozen others.

Oklahoma's Republican presidential primaries since then have been less competitive. Bush won big in 1992; so did Dole in 1996; as did George W. Bush in both 2000 and 2004. Pat Buchanan was a distant runner-up in 1992 and 1996, carrying none of Oklahoma's 77 counties in 1992, and only one (McCurtain) in 1996.

The younger Bush rolled up nearly 80 percent of the Republican primary vote in 2000 as Oklahoma voted after he had clinched the nomination. He did even better in 2004, taking 90 percent against a political unknown named Bill Wyatt, who was essentially a human "none of the above" option. Wyatt did, though, reach double digits percentagewise in more than 30 counties.

Oklahoma's Democratic primary has given a boost to the ambitions of candidates from Dixie—Al Gore in 1988, Bill Clinton in the 1990s, Gore again in 2000, and Clark (who was raised in neighboring Arkansas) in 2004.

Gore won the first time by taking advantage of his Southern roots, his relatively conservative image and his support from an array of big-name Oklahoma Democrats, featuring Sen. David L. Boren. Gore rolled up his highest percentages in the rural counties of south-central Oklahoma, including historically Democratic "Little Dixie." But like Bush in the Republican primary voting in 1988, Gore also carried Oklahoma's major population centers. The only three counties not carried by Gore in 1988 were won by Richard Gephardt, the most populous being Ottawa in the northeast corner of the state adjacent to Gephardt's native Missouri.

Clinton easily won Oklahoma's Democratic primary in the 1990s. His 70 percent share was one of his highest of the 1992 primary season. But his 76 percent share in 1996 was his lowest of the year, as Clinton lost nearly one-quarter of the primary vote in the process of running essentially unopposed for renomination. Gore's primary victory in 2000 came after he had driven his principal rival, Bill Bradley, from the race. Still, Bradley carried two of the three counties in the Oklahoma panhandle, Beaver and Cimarron.

OKLAHOMA DEMOCRATIC PRIMARY

2000

County	Total Vote	Bradley	Gore	LaRouche	Winner	Percentage of Total Vote Bradley	Gore	LaRouche
ADAIR	588	127	419	42	Gore	21.6%	71.3%	7.1%
ALFALFA	306	78	205	23	Gore	25.5%	67.0%	7.5%
ATOKA	615	154	406	55	Gore	25.0%	66.0%	8.9%
BEAVER	201	93	86	22	Bradley	46.3%	42.8%	10.9%
BECKHAM	797	168	568	61	Gore	21.1%	71.3%	7.7%
BLAINE	421	118	277	26	Gore	28.0%	65.8%	6.2%
BRYAN	1,209	291	847	71	Gore	24.1%	70.1%	5.9%
CADDO	1,217	306	840	71	Gore	25.1%	69.0%	5.8%
CANADIAN	2,382	743	1,448	191	Gore	31.2%	60.8%	8.0%
CARTER	1,634	437	1,088	109	Gore	26.7%	66.6%	6.7%
CHEROKEE	1,161	251	849	61	Gore	21.6%	73.1%	5.3%
CHOCTAW	1,445	325	998	122	Gore	22.5%	69.1%	8.4%
CIMARRON	258	119	111	28	Bradley	46.1%	43.0%	10.9%
CLEVELAND	5,428	1,585	3,480	363	Gore	29.2%	64.1%	6.7%
COAL	388	89	264	35	Gore	22.9%	68.0%	9.0%
COMANCHE	4,544	1,132	3,149	263	Gore	24.9%	69.3%	5.8%
COTTON	431	114	291	26	Gore	26.5%	67.5%	6.0%
CRAIG	651	144	475	32	Gore	22.1%	73.0%	4.9%
CREEK	3,172	810	2,198	164	Gore	25.5%	69.3%	5.2%
CUSTER	974	256	639	79	Gore	26.3%	65.6%	8.1%
DELAWARE	2,704	763	1,756	185	Gore	28.2%	64.9%	6.8%
DEWEY	386	134	222	30	Gore	34.7%	57.5%	7.8%
ELLIS	241	71	149	21	Gore	29.5%	61.8%	8.7%
GARFIELD	1,322	305	964	53	Gore	23.1%	72.9%	4.0%
GARVIN	1,385	337	946	102	Gore	24.3%	68.3%	7.4%
GRADY	1,883	561	1,204	118	Gore	29.8%	63.9%	6.3%
GRANT	301	75	202	24	Gore	24.9%	67.1%	8.0%
GREER	395	138	230	27	Gore	34.9%	58.2%	6.8%
HARMON	248	60	177	11	Gore	24.2%	71.4%	4.4%
HARPER	236	72	148	16	Gore	30.5%	62.7%	6.8%
HASKELL	508	105	374	29	Gore	20.7%	73.6%	5.7%
HUGHES	651	135	477	39	Gore	20.7%	73.3%	6.0%
JACKSON	1,191	338	754	99	Gore	28.4%	63.3%	8.3%
JEFFERSON	477	135	318	24	Gore	28.3%	66.7%	5.0%
JOHNSTON	640	175	414	51	Gore	27.3%	64.7%	8.0%
KAY	1,866	462	1,307	97	Gore	24.8%	70.0%	5.2%
KINGFISHER	482	136	310	36	Gore	28.2%	64.3%	7.5%
KIOWA	625	199	380	46	Gore	31.8%	60.8%	7.4%
LATIMER	590	127	430	33	Gore	21.5%	72.9%	5.6%
LE FLORE	1,799	421	1,252	126	Gore	23.4%	69.6%	7.0%
LINCOLN	1,165	285	791	89	Gore	24.5%	67.9%	7.6%
LOGAN	1,069	262	740	67	Gore	24.5%	69.2%	6.3%
LOVE	459	111	318	30	Gore	24.2%	69.3%	6.5%
MCCLAIN	942	262	595	85	Gore	27.8%	63.2%	9.0%
MCCURTAIN	904	296	491	117	Gore	32.7%	54.3%	12.9%

OKLAHOMA DEMOCRATIC PRIMARY

2000

County	Total Vote	Bradley	Gore	LaRouche	Winner	Percentage of Total Vote		
						Bradley	Gore	LaRouche
MCINTOSH	1,097	244	811	42	Gore	22.2%	73.9%	3.8%
MAJOR	270	72	181	17	Gore	26.7%	67.0%	6.3%
MARSHALL	828	244	544	40	Gore	29.5%	65.7%	4.8%
MAYES	1,851	413	1,341	97	Gore	22.3%	72.4%	5.2%
MURRAY	740	198	487	55	Gore	26.8%	65.8%	7.4%
MUSKOGEE	2,879	577	2,164	138	Gore	20.0%	75.2%	4.8%
NOBLE	483	126	318	39	Gore	26.1%	65.8%	8.1%
NOWATA	495	108	358	29	Gore	21.8%	72.3%	5.9%
OKFUSKEE	612	133	438	41	Gore	21.7%	71.6%	6.7%
OKLAHOMA	24,180	6,483	16,347	1,350	Gore	26.8%	67.6%	5.6%
OKMULGEE	1,749	366	1,311	72	Gore	20.9%	75.0%	4.1%
OSAGE	2,201	454	1,656	91	Gore	20.6%	75.2%	4.1%
OTTAWA	1,144	225	860	59	Gore	19.7%	75.2%	5.2%
PAWNEE	602	136	441	25	Gore	22.6%	73.3%	4.2%
PAYNE	3,320	947	2,210	163	Gore	28.5%	66.6%	4.9%
PITTSBURG	4,565	1,220	2,989	356	Gore	26.7%	65.5%	7.8%
PONTOTOC	1,313	331	886	96	Gore	25.2%	67.5%	7.3%
POTTAWATOMIE	2,248	617	1,478	153	Gore	27.4%	65.7%	6.8%
PUSHMATAHA	787	230	468	89	Gore	29.2%	59.5%	11.3%
ROGER MILLS	279	99	152	28	Gore	35.5%	54.5%	10.0%
ROGERS	2,694	712	1,827	155	Gore	26.4%	67.8%	5.8%
SEMINOLE	845	207	581	57	Gore	24.5%	68.8%	6.7%
SEQUOYAH	1,493	359	1,032	102	Gore	24.0%	69.1%	6.8%
STEPHENS	2,051	529	1,384	138	Gore	25.8%	67.5%	6.7%
TEXAS	591	222	320	49	Gore	37.6%	54.1%	8.3%
TILLMAN	487	135	320	32	Gore	27.7%	65.7%	6.6%
TULSA	19,713	4,321	14,723	669	Gore	21.9%	74.7%	3.4%
WAGONER	1,659	420	1,136	103	Gore	25.3%	68.5%	6.2%
WASHINGTON	1,448	334	1,035	79	Gore	23.1%	71.5%	5.5%
WASHITA	922	302	548	72	Gore	32.8%	59.4%	7.8%
WOODS	411	91	298	22	Gore	22.1%	72.5%	5.4%
WOODWARD	602	151	423	28	Gore	25.1%	70.3%	4.7%
TOTAL	134,850	34,311	92,654	7,885	Gore	25.4%	68.7%	5.8%

OKLAHOMA REPUBLICAN PRIMARY

2000

County	Total Vote	G.W. Bush	Keyes	McCain	Other	Winner	Percentage of Total Vote			
							G.W. Bush	Keyes	McCain	Other
ADAIR	384	323	31	28	2	G.W. Bush	84.1%	8.1%	7.3%	0.5%
ALFALFA	506	416	33	52	5	G.W. Bush	82.2%	6.5%	10.3%	1.0%
ATOKA	131	109	12	10	0	G.W. Bush	83.2%	9.2%	7.6%	0.0%
BEAVER	401	337	31	29	4	G.W. Bush	84.0%	7.7%	7.2%	1.0%
BECKHAM	351	273	44	30	4	G.W. Bush	77.8%	12.5%	8.5%	1.1%
BLAINE	522	427	31	56	8	G.W. Bush	81.8%	5.9%	10.7%	1.5%
BRYAN	306	239	36	25	6	G.W. Bush	78.1%	11.8%	8.2%	2.0%
CADDO	424	336	37	40	11	G.W. Bush	79.2%	8.7%	9.4%	2.6%
CANADIAN	3,986	3,248	372	329	37	G.W. Bush	81.5%	9.3%	8.3%	0.9%
CARTER	788	665	61	54	8	G.W. Bush	84.4%	7.7%	6.9%	1.0%
CHEROKEE	694	533	62	92	7	G.W. Bush	76.8%	8.9%	13.3%	1.0%
CHOCTAW	140	127	5	6	2	G.W. Bush	90.7%	3.6%	4.3%	1.4%
CIMARRON	300	249	35	12	4	G.W. Bush	83.0%	11.7%	4.0%	1.3%
CLEVELAND	7,796	6,041	987	701	67	G.W. Bush	77.5%	12.7%	9.0%	0.9%
COAL	72	59	7	6	0	G.W. Bush	81.9%	9.7%	8.3%	0.0%
COMANCHE	2,308	1,841	145	297	25	G.W. Bush	79.8%	6.3%	12.9%	1.1%
COTTON	66	52	5	8	1	G.W. Bush	78.8%	7.6%	12.1%	1.5%
CRAIG	293	231	25	30	7	G.W. Bush	78.8%	8.5%	10.2%	2.4%
CREEK	2,495	1,962	210	278	45	G.W. Bush	78.6%	8.4%	11.1%	1.8%
CUSTER	678	555	57	56	10	G.W. Bush	81.9%	8.4%	8.3%	1.5%
DELAWARE	1,765	1,408	83	249	25	G.W. Bush	79.8%	4.7%	14.1%	1.4%
DEWEY	254	220	14	14	6	G.W. Bush	86.6%	5.5%	5.5%	2.4%
ELLIS	311	271	12	24	4	G.W. Bush	87.1%	3.9%	7.7%	1.3%
GARFIELD	2,849	2,362	188	263	36	G.W. Bush	82.9%	6.6%	9.2%	1.3%
GARVIN	438	366	40	27	5	G.W. Bush	83.6%	9.1%	6.2%	1.1%
GRADY	1,201	964	115	98	24	G.W. Bush	80.3%	9.6%	8.2%	2.0%
GRANT	319	249	33	33	4	G.W. Bush	78.1%	10.3%	10.3%	1.3%
GREER	84	72	4	7	1	G.W. Bush	85.7%	4.8%	8.3%	1.2%
HARMON	18	17	1	0	0	G.W. Bush	94.4%	5.6%	0.0%	0.0%
HARPER	255	215	14	22	4	G.W. Bush	84.3%	5.5%	8.6%	1.6%
HASKELL	95	68	8	17	2	G.W. Bush	71.6%	8.4%	17.9%	2.1%
HUGHES	133	111	8	12	2	G.W. Bush	83.5%	6.0%	9.0%	1.5%
JACKSON	614	516	40	51	7	G.W. Bush	84.0%	6.5%	8.3%	1.1%
JEFFERSON	66	57	4	5	0	G.W. Bush	86.4%	6.1%	7.6%	0.0%
JOHNSTON	112	90	6	14	2	G.W. Bush	80.4%	5.4%	12.5%	1.8%
KAY	2,735	2,099	204	367	65	G.W. Bush	76.7%	7.5%	13.4%	2.4%
KINGFISHER	947	812	57	67	11	G.W. Bush	85.7%	6.0%	7.1%	1.2%
KIOWA	177	147	7	22	1	G.W. Bush	83.1%	4.0%	12.4%	0.6%
LATIMER	68	48	9	10	1	G.W. Bush	70.6%	13.2%	14.7%	1.5%
LE FLORE	516	432	47	34	3	G.W. Bush	83.7%	9.1%	6.6%	0.6%
LINCOLN	1,044	854	79	98	13	G.W. Bush	81.8%	7.6%	9.4%	1.2%
LOGAN	1,534	1,241	164	118	11	G.W. Bush	80.9%	10.7%	7.7%	0.7%
LOVE	134	122	6	6	0	G.W. Bush	91.0%	4.5%	4.5%	0.0%
MCCLAIN	682	553	90	33	6	G.W. Bush	81.1%	13.2%	4.8%	0.9%
MCCURTAIN	164	127	22	15	0	G.W. Bush	77.4%	13.4%	9.1%	0.0%

OKLAHOMA REPUBLICAN PRIMARY

2000

County	Total Vote	G.W. Bush	Keyes	McCain	Other	Winner	Percentage of Total Vote			
							G.W. Bush	Keyes	McCain	Other
MCINTOSH	261	199	27	32	3	G.W. Bush	76.2%	10.3%	12.3%	1.1%
MAJOR	641	547	29	56	9	G.W. Bush	85.3%	4.5%	8.7%	1.4%
MARSHALL	185	160	11	13	1	G.W. Bush	86.5%	5.9%	7.0%	0.5%
MAYES	961	746	84	118	13	G.W. Bush	77.6%	8.7%	12.3%	1.4%
MURRAY	188	146	25	17	0	G.W. Bush	77.7%	13.3%	9.0%	0.0%
MUSKOGEE	1,092	818	144	120	10	G.W. Bush	74.9%	13.2%	11.0%	0.9%
NOBLE	516	413	36	59	8	G.W. Bush	80.0%	7.0%	11.4%	1.6%
NOWATA	271	212	23	33	3	G.W. Bush	78.2%	8.5%	12.2%	1.1%
OKFUSKEE	148	119	13	14	2	G.W. Bush	80.4%	8.8%	9.5%	1.4%
OKLAHOMA	31,667	25,452	3,240	2,651	324	G.W. Bush	80.4%	10.2%	8.4%	1.0%
OKMULGEE	616	499	54	56	7	G.W. Bush	81.0%	8.8%	9.1%	1.1%
OSAGE	1,146	887	94	152	13	G.W. Bush	77.4%	8.2%	13.3%	1.1%
OTTAWA	485	403	26	54	2	G.W. Bush	83.1%	5.4%	11.1%	0.4%
PAWNEE	492	388	44	54	6	G.W. Bush	78.9%	8.9%	11.0%	1.2%
PAYNE	2,996	2,300	232	415	49	G.W. Bush	76.8%	7.7%	13.9%	1.6%
PITTSBURG	771	596	83	79	13	G.W. Bush	77.3%	10.8%	10.2%	1.7%
PONTOTOC	492	395	51	43	3	G.W. Bush	80.3%	10.4%	8.7%	0.6%
POTTAWATOMIE	1,409	1,067	205	118	19	G.W. Bush	75.7%	14.5%	8.4%	1.3%
PUSHMATAHA	71	62	5	4	0	G.W. Bush	87.3%	7.0%	5.6%	0.0%
ROGER MILLS	116	91	11	10	4	G.W. Bush	78.4%	9.5%	8.6%	3.4%
ROGERS	2,674	2,017	288	339	30	G.W. Bush	75.4%	10.8%	12.7%	1.1%
SEMINOLE	285	232	28	20	5	G.W. Bush	81.4%	9.8%	7.0%	1.8%
SEQUOYAH	404	336	24	39	5	G.W. Bush	83.2%	5.9%	9.7%	1.2%
STEPHENS	1,012	849	84	69	10	G.W. Bush	83.9%	8.3%	6.8%	1.0%
TEXAS	810	712	54	37	7	G.W. Bush	87.9%	6.7%	4.6%	0.9%
TILLMAN	84	73	7	4	0	G.W. Bush	86.9%	8.3%	4.8%	0.0%
TULSA	29,317	22,412	2,634	3,931	340	G.W. Bush	76.4%	9.0%	13.4%	1.2%
WAGONER	1,665	1,325	175	146	19	G.W. Bush	79.6%	10.5%	8.8%	1.1%
WASHINGTON	3,202	2,504	251	399	48	G.W. Bush	78.2%	7.8%	12.5%	1.5%
WASHITA	280	221	33	22	4	G.W. Bush	78.9%	11.8%	7.9%	1.4%
WOODS	527	429	37	57	4	G.W. Bush	81.4%	7.0%	10.8%	0.8%
WOODWARD	869	727	62	67	13	G.W. Bush	83.7%	7.1%	7.7%	1.5%
TOTAL	124,809	98,781	11,595	12,973	1,460	G.W. Bush	79.1%	9.3%	10.4%	1.2%

Note: Other vote was 1,066 Steve Forbes; 394 Gary Bauer.

OKLAHOMA DEMOCRATIC PRIMARY

2004

County	Total Vote	Clark	Edwards	Kerry	Lieberman	Other	Winner	Percentage of Total Vote				
								Clark	Edwards	Kerry	Lieberman	Other
ADAIR	1,546	494	539	363	82	68	Edwards	32.0%	34.9%	23.5%	5.3%	4.4%
ALFALFA	516	175	147	129	33	32	Clark	33.9%	28.5%	25.0%	6.4%	6.2%
ATOKA	1,477	358	708	251	84	76	Edwards	24.2%	47.9%	17.0%	5.7%	5.1%
BEAVER	276	62	66	90	23	35	Kerry	22.5%	23.9%	32.6%	8.3%	12.7%
BECKHAM	1,818	564	547	488	114	105	Clark	31.0%	30.1%	26.8%	6.3%	5.8%
BLAINE	980	322	280	283	48	47	Clark	32.9%	28.6%	28.9%	4.9%	4.8%
BRYAN	3,991	885	2,184	594	207	121	Edwards	22.2%	54.7%	14.9%	5.2%	3.0%
CADDO	3,193	1,153	963	740	167	170	Clark	36.1%	30.2%	23.2%	5.2%	5.3%
CANADIAN	5,964	1,735	1,785	1,637	438	369	Edwards	29.1%	29.9%	27.4%	7.3%	6.2%
CARTER	4,096	1,171	1,498	875	307	245	Edwards	28.6%	36.6%	21.4%	7.5%	6.0%
CHEROKEE	4,898	1,691	1,511	1,171	238	287	Clark	34.5%	30.8%	23.9%	4.9%	5.9%
CHOCTAW	1,773	338	857	362	109	107	Edwards	19.1%	48.3%	20.4%	6.1%	6.0%
CIMARRON	239	41	60	76	20	42	Kerry	17.2%	25.1%	31.8%	8.4%	17.6%
CLEVELAND	17,074	4,746	4,491	4,997	1,139	1,701	Kerry	27.8%	26.3%	29.3%	6.7%	10.0%
COAL	957	249	472	132	57	47	Edwards	26.0%	49.3%	13.8%	6.0%	4.9%
COMANCHE	7,223	3,262	1,120	1,780	531	530	Clark	45.2%	15.5%	24.6%	7.4%	7.3%
COTTON	729	347	129	171	37	45	Clark	47.6%	17.7%	23.5%	5.1%	6.2%
CRAIG	1,874	580	587	469	116	122	Edwards	30.9%	31.3%	25.0%	6.2%	6.5%
CREEK	6,339	1,790	2,122	1,694	356	377	Edwards	28.2%	33.5%	26.7%	5.6%	5.9%
CUSTER	2,297	681	718	583	145	170	Edwards	29.6%	31.3%	25.4%	6.3%	7.4%
DELAWARE	3,598	1,048	1,207	949	183	211	Edwards	29.1%	33.5%	26.4%	5.1%	5.9%
DEWEY	637	208	185	151	50	43	Clark	32.7%	29.0%	23.7%	7.8%	6.8%
ELLIS	439	159	108	105	34	33	Clark	36.2%	24.6%	23.9%	7.7%	7.5%
GARFIELD	3,491	1,189	830	1,058	225	189	Clark	34.1%	23.8%	30.3%	6.4%	5.4%
GARVIN	3,395	1,098	1,097	770	238	192	Clark	32.3%	32.3%	22.7%	7.0%	5.7%
GRADY	4,441	1,380	1,502	1,059	281	219	Edwards	31.1%	33.8%	23.8%	6.3%	4.9%
GRANT	527	201	146	124	34	22	Clark	38.1%	27.7%	23.5%	6.5%	4.2%
GREER	731	238	187	207	57	42	Clark	32.6%	25.6%	28.3%	7.8%	5.7%
HARMON	383	104	120	95	37	27	Edwards	27.2%	31.3%	24.8%	9.7%	7.0%
HARPER	360	100	122	77	29	32	Edwards	27.8%	33.9%	21.4%	8.1%	8.9%
HASKELL	1,735	582	599	395	84	75	Edwards	33.5%	34.5%	22.8%	4.8%	4.3%
HUGHES	1,934	624	668	454	109	79	Edwards	32.3%	34.5%	23.5%	5.6%	4.1%
JACKSON	1,826	670	446	459	129	122	Clark	36.7%	24.4%	25.1%	7.1%	6.7%
JEFFERSON	821	344	150	218	51	58	Clark	41.9%	18.3%	26.6%	6.2%	7.1%
JOHNSTON	1,332	355	645	201	63	68	Edwards	26.7%	48.4%	15.1%	4.7%	5.1%
KAY	3,420	998	972	1,089	152	209	Kerry	29.2%	28.4%	31.8%	4.4%	6.1%
KINGFISHER	928	293	246	264	79	46	Clark	31.6%	26.5%	28.4%	8.5%	5.0%
KIOWA	1,378	519	383	327	75	74	Clark	37.7%	27.8%	23.7%	5.4%	5.4%
LATIMER	1,644	526	572	343	102	101	Edwards	32.0%	34.8%	20.9%	6.2%	6.1%
LE FLORE	4,416	1,229	1,575	1,051	249	312	Edwards	27.8%	35.7%	23.8%	5.6%	7.1%
LINCOLN	3,233	978	993	825	238	199	Edwards	30.3%	30.7%	25.5%	7.4%	6.2%
LOGAN	2,542	768	666	703	180	225	Clark	30.2%	26.2%	27.7%	7.1%	8.9%
LOVE	1,007	268	385	217	65	72	Edwards	26.6%	38.2%	21.5%	6.5%	7.1%
MCCLAIN	2,959	867	942	734	235	181	Edwards	29.3%	31.8%	24.8%	7.9%	6.1%
MCCURTAIN	2,893	481	1,373	617	190	232	Edwards	16.6%	47.5%	21.3%	6.6%	8.0%

OKLAHOMA DEMOCRATIC PRIMARY

2004

County	Total Vote	Clark	Edwards	Kerry	Lieberman	Other	Winner	Clark	Edwards	Kerry	Lieberman	Other
								Percentage of Total Vote				
MCINTOSH	3,307	1,039	1,136	790	182	160	Edwards	31.4%	34.4%	23.9%	5.5%	4.8%
MAJOR	467	136	150	123	35	23	Edwards	29.1%	32.1%	26.3%	7.5%	4.9%
MARSHALL	1,573	385	737	289	79	83	Edwards	24.5%	46.9%	18.4%	5.0%	5.3%
MAYES	4,893	1,295	1,951	1,176	237	234	Edwards	26.5%	39.9%	24.0%	4.8%	4.8%
MURRAY	1,809	509	652	410	132	106	Edwards	28.1%	36.0%	22.7%	7.3%	5.9%
MUSKOGEE	8,434	2,673	2,724	2,005	531	501	Edwards	31.7%	32.3%	23.8%	6.3%	5.9%
NOBLE	1,112	344	332	281	97	58	Clark	30.9%	29.9%	25.3%	8.7%	5.2%
NOWATA	1,151	383	327	315	55	71	Clark	33.3%	28.4%	27.4%	4.8%	6.2%
OKFUSKEE	1,567	422	583	373	106	83	Edwards	26.9%	37.2%	23.8%	6.8%	5.3%
OKLAHOMA	45,903	13,360	10,524	14,079	3,473	4,467	Kerry	29.1%	22.9%	30.7%	7.6%	9.7%
OKMULGEE	4,807	1,438	1,547	1,257	284	281	Edwards	29.9%	32.2%	26.1%	5.9%	5.8%
OSAGE	5,218	1,466	1,601	1,442	277	432	Edwards	28.1%	30.7%	27.6%	5.3%	8.3%
OTTAWA	3,210	757	849	1,217	178	209	Kerry	23.6%	26.4%	37.9%	5.5%	6.5%
PAWNEE	1,740	539	516	469	132	84	Clark	31.0%	29.7%	27.0%	7.6%	4.8%
PAYNE	5,791	1,694	1,489	1,598	375	635	Clark	29.3%	25.7%	27.6%	6.5%	11.0%
PITTSBURG	6,688	2,245	2,292	1,351	483	317	Edwards	33.6%	34.3%	20.2%	7.2%	4.7%
PONTOTOC	3,941	1,192	1,242	984	311	212	Edwards	30.2%	31.5%	25.0%	7.9%	5.4%
POTTAWATOMIE	6,370	1,918	1,974	1,680	505	293	Edwards	30.1%	31.0%	26.4%	7.9%	4.6%
PUSHMATAHA	1,521	394	678	277	79	93	Edwards	25.9%	44.6%	18.2%	5.2%	6.1%
ROGER MILLS	465	149	136	101	45	34	Clark	32.0%	29.2%	21.7%	9.7%	7.3%
ROGERS	7,325	2,116	2,393	1,942	440	434	Edwards	28.9%	32.7%	26.5%	6.0%	5.9%
SEMINOLE	2,837	817	941	697	219	163	Edwards	28.8%	33.2%	24.6%	7.7%	5.7%
SEQUOYAH	3,559	1,020	1,295	837	189	218	Edwards	28.7%	36.4%	23.5%	5.3%	6.1%
STEPHENS	4,648	1,861	1,028	1,218	268	273	Clark	40.0%	22.1%	26.2%	5.8%	5.9%
TEXAS	749	148	175	271	56	99	Kerry	19.8%	23.4%	36.2%	7.5%	13.2%
TILLMAN	994	417	205	256	54	62	Clark	42.0%	20.6%	25.8%	5.4%	6.2%
TULSA	42,133	12,201	10,832	12,735	2,722	3,643	Kerry	29.0%	25.7%	30.2%	6.5%	8.6%
WAGONER	5,470	1,573	1,852	1,465	283	297	Edwards	28.8%	33.9%	26.8%	5.2%	5.4%
WASHINGTON	3,828	1,110	1,147	1,122	206	243	Edwards	29.0%	30.0%	29.3%	5.4%	6.3%
WASHITA	1,489	414	535	339	103	98	Edwards	27.8%	35.9%	22.8%	6.9%	6.6%
WOODS	753	234	187	235	40	57	Kerry	31.1%	24.8%	31.2%	5.3%	7.6%
WOODWARD	1,303	406	377	362	84	74	Clark	31.2%	28.9%	27.8%	6.4%	5.7%
TOTAL	302,385	90,526	89,310	81,073	19,680	21,796	Clark	29.9%	29.5%	26.8%	6.5%	7.2%

Note: Other vote was 12,734 Howard Dean; 3,939 Al Sharpton; 2,544 Dennis J. Kucinich; 1,890 Richard A. Gephardt; 689 Lyndon H. LaRouche Jr.

OKLAHOMA REPUBLICAN PRIMARY

2004

County	Total Vote	G.W. Bush	Wyatt	Winner	Percentage of Total Vote	
					G.W. Bush	Wyatt
ADAIR	213	192	21	G.W. Bush	90.1%	9.9%
ALFALFA	370	338	32	G.W. Bush	91.4%	8.6%
ATOKA	68	66	2	G.W. Bush	97.1%	2.9%
BEAVER	160	153	7	G.W. Bush	95.6%	4.4%
BECKHAM	251	233	18	G.W. Bush	92.8%	7.2%
BLAINE	389	348	41	G.W. Bush	89.5%	10.5%
BRYAN	155	146	9	G.W. Bush	94.2%	5.8%
CADDO	316	278	38	G.W. Bush	88.0%	12.0%
CANADIAN	2,226	2,059	167	G.W. Bush	92.5%	7.5%
CARTER	369	345	24	G.W. Bush	93.5%	6.5%
CHEROKEE	483	432	51	G.W. Bush	89.4%	10.6%
CHOCTAW	64	61	3	G.W. Bush	95.3%	4.7%
CIMARRON	188	182	6	G.W. Bush	96.8%	3.2%
CLEVELAND	3,767	3,406	361	G.W. Bush	90.4%	9.6%
COAL	47	44	3	G.W. Bush	93.6%	6.4%
COMANCHE	1,295	1,168	127	G.W. Bush	90.2%	9.8%
COTTON	41	39	2	G.W. Bush	95.1%	4.9%
CRAIG	241	215	26	G.W. Bush	89.2%	10.8%
CREEK	1,028	864	164	G.W. Bush	84.0%	16.0%
CUSTER	410	381	29	G.W. Bush	92.9%	7.1%
DELAWARE	627	545	82	G.W. Bush	86.9%	13.1%
DEWEY	186	174	12	G.W. Bush	93.5%	6.5%
ELLIS	211	200	11	G.W. Bush	94.8%	5.2%
GARFIELD	2,018	1,845	173	G.W. Bush	91.4%	8.6%
GARVIN	299	263	36	G.W. Bush	88.0%	12.0%
GRADY	673	610	63	G.W. Bush	90.6%	9.4%
GRANT	239	216	23	G.W. Bush	90.4%	9.6%
GREER	64	55	9	G.W. Bush	85.9%	14.1%
HARMON	20	18	2	G.W. Bush	90.0%	10.0%
HARPER	152	145	7	G.W. Bush	95.4%	4.6%
HASKELL	65	58	7	G.W. Bush	89.2%	10.8%
HUGHES	94	85	9	G.W. Bush	90.4%	9.6%
JACKSON	289	270	19	G.W. Bush	93.4%	6.6%
JEFFERSON	32	29	3	G.W. Bush	90.6%	9.4%
JOHNSTON	62	62	0	G.W. Bush	100.0%	0.0%
KAY	1,320	1,156	164	G.W. Bush	87.6%	12.4%
KINGFISHER	614	578	36	G.W. Bush	94.1%	5.9%
KIOWA	125	114	11	G.W. Bush	91.2%	8.8%
LATIMER	43	39	4	G.W. Bush	90.7%	9.3%
LE FLORE	224	201	23	G.W. Bush	89.7%	10.3%
LINCOLN	689	614	75	G.W. Bush	89.1%	10.9%
LOGAN	846	745	101	G.W. Bush	88.1%	11.9%
LOVE	76	65	11	G.W. Bush	85.5%	14.5%
MCCLAIN	494	467	27	G.W. Bush	94.5%	5.5%
MCCURTAIN	137	132	5	G.W. Bush	96.4%	3.6%

OKLAHOMA REPUBLICAN PRIMARY

2004

| County | Total Vote | G.W. Bush | Wyatt | Winner | Percentage of Total Vote | |
					G.W. Bush	Wyatt
MCINTOSH	157	141	16	G.W. Bush	89.8%	10.2%
MAJOR	405	383	22	G.W. Bush	94.6%	5.4%
MARSHALL	80	77	3	G.W. Bush	96.3%	3.8%
MAYES	543	456	87	G.W. Bush	84.0%	16.0%
MURRAY	103	89	14	G.W. Bush	86.4%	13.6%
MUSKOGEE	536	488	48	G.W. Bush	91.0%	9.0%
NOBLE	371	331	40	G.W. Bush	89.2%	10.8%
NOWATA	188	151	37	G.W. Bush	80.3%	19.7%
OKFUSKEE	128	118	10	G.W. Bush	92.2%	7.8%
OKLAHOMA	12,220	11,215	1,005	G.W. Bush	91.8%	8.2%
OKMULGEE	400	344	56	G.W. Bush	86.0%	14.0%
OSAGE	777	683	94	G.W. Bush	87.9%	12.1%
OTTAWA	266	235	31	G.W. Bush	88.3%	11.7%
PAWNEE	351	304	47	G.W. Bush	86.6%	13.4%
PAYNE	1,337	1,200	137	G.W. Bush	89.8%	10.2%
PITTSBURG	437	409	28	G.W. Bush	93.6%	6.4%
PONTOTOC	432	403	29	G.W. Bush	93.3%	6.7%
POTTAWATOMIE	783	709	74	G.W. Bush	90.5%	9.5%
PUSHMATAHA	49	47	2	G.W. Bush	95.9%	4.1%
ROGER MILLS	71	68	3	G.W. Bush	95.8%	4.2%
ROGERS	1,336	1,159	177	G.W. Bush	86.8%	13.2%
SEMINOLE	283	251	32	G.W. Bush	88.7%	11.3%
SEQUOYAH	215	192	23	G.W. Bush	89.3%	10.7%
STEPHENS	780	731	49	G.W. Bush	93.7%	6.3%
TEXAS	359	342	17	G.W. Bush	95.3%	4.7%
TILLMAN	85	82	3	G.W. Bush	96.5%	3.5%
TULSA	18,187	16,099	2,088	G.W. Bush	88.5%	11.5%
WAGONER	1,024	887	137	G.W. Bush	86.6%	13.4%
WASHINGTON	1,611	1,421	190	G.W. Bush	88.2%	11.8%
WASHITA	182	157	25	G.W. Bush	86.3%	13.7%
WOODS	322	296	26	G.W. Bush	91.9%	8.1%
WOODWARD	500	473	27	G.W. Bush	94.6%	5.4%
TOTAL	66,198	59,577	6,621	G.W. Bush	90.0%	10.0%

OREGON

Oregon made history in 1996 by being the first state to hold its presidential primary by mail. It was hoped that the innovation would decrease election costs and increase voter participation, and the experiment proved successful enough to make balloting by mail a permanent fixture on the Oregon political scene.

That Oregon would be the first to try a ballot-by-mail primary (beating Nevada to that distinction, as it turns out, by two weeks) is not surprising. Oregon has been in the forefront of

creative election procedures, from the establishment of one of the first presidential primaries early this century to widespread use of absentee ballots in recent years.

But that creativity has not been able to keep the state's presidential primary relevant on its traditional May date. In 2004, the Democratic primary offered Oregon voters a choice between nominee in waiting John Kerry and Dennis Kucinich, whose low budget candidacy kept on going after those of better-heeled rivals had ended. Kucinich saw Oregon as favorable

Recent Oregon Primary Results

Oregon held its first presidential primary in 1912.

Year	DEMOCRATS			REPUBLICANS		
	Turnout	Candidates	%	Turnout	Candidates	%
2004 (May 18)	368,544	JOHN KERRY	79	309,506	GEORGE W. BUSH*	95
		Dennis Kucinich	16			
2000 (May 16)	354,594	AL GORE	85	349,831	GEORGE W. BUSH	84
		Lyndon LaRouche	11		Alan Keyes	13
1996 (March 12)	369,178	BILL CLINTON*	95	407,514	BOB DOLE	51
					Pat Buchanan	21
					Steve Forbes	13
					Lamar Alexander	7
1992 (May 19)	354,332	BILL CLINTON	45	304,159	GEORGE BUSH*	67
		Jerry Brown	31		Pat Buchanan	19
		Paul Tsongas	10			
1988 (May 17)	388,932	MICHAEL DUKAKIS	57	274,486	GEORGE BUSH	73
		Jesse Jackson	38		Bob Dole	18
					Pat Robertson	8
1984 (May 15)	399,679	GARY HART	58	243,346	RONALD REAGAN*	98
		Walter Mondale	28			
		Jesse Jackson	9			
1980 (May 20)	368,322	JIMMY CARTER*	57	315,366	RONALD REAGAN	54
		Edward Kennedy	31		George Bush	35
		Jerry Brown	9		John Anderson	10
1976 (May 25)	432,632	FRANK CHURCH	34	298,535	GERALD FORD*	50
		Jimmy Carter	27		Ronald Reagan	46
		Jerry Brown#	25			
		Hubert Humphrey	5			
1972 (May 23)	408,644	GEORGE McGOVERN	50	282,010	RICHARD NIXON*	82
		George Wallace	20		Paul McCloskey	10
		Hubert Humphrey	13		John Ashbrook	6
		Henry Jackson	5			
1968 (May 28)	373,070	EUGENE McCARTHY	44	312,159	RICHARD NIXON	65
		Robert Kennedy	38		Ronald Reagan	20
		Lyndon Johnson*	12		Nelson Rockefeller#	12

Note: All candidates are listed that drew at least 5 percent of their party's primary vote. The names of winning candidates are capitalized. An asterisk (*) indicates an incumbent president. A pound sign (#) indicates a write-in candidate.

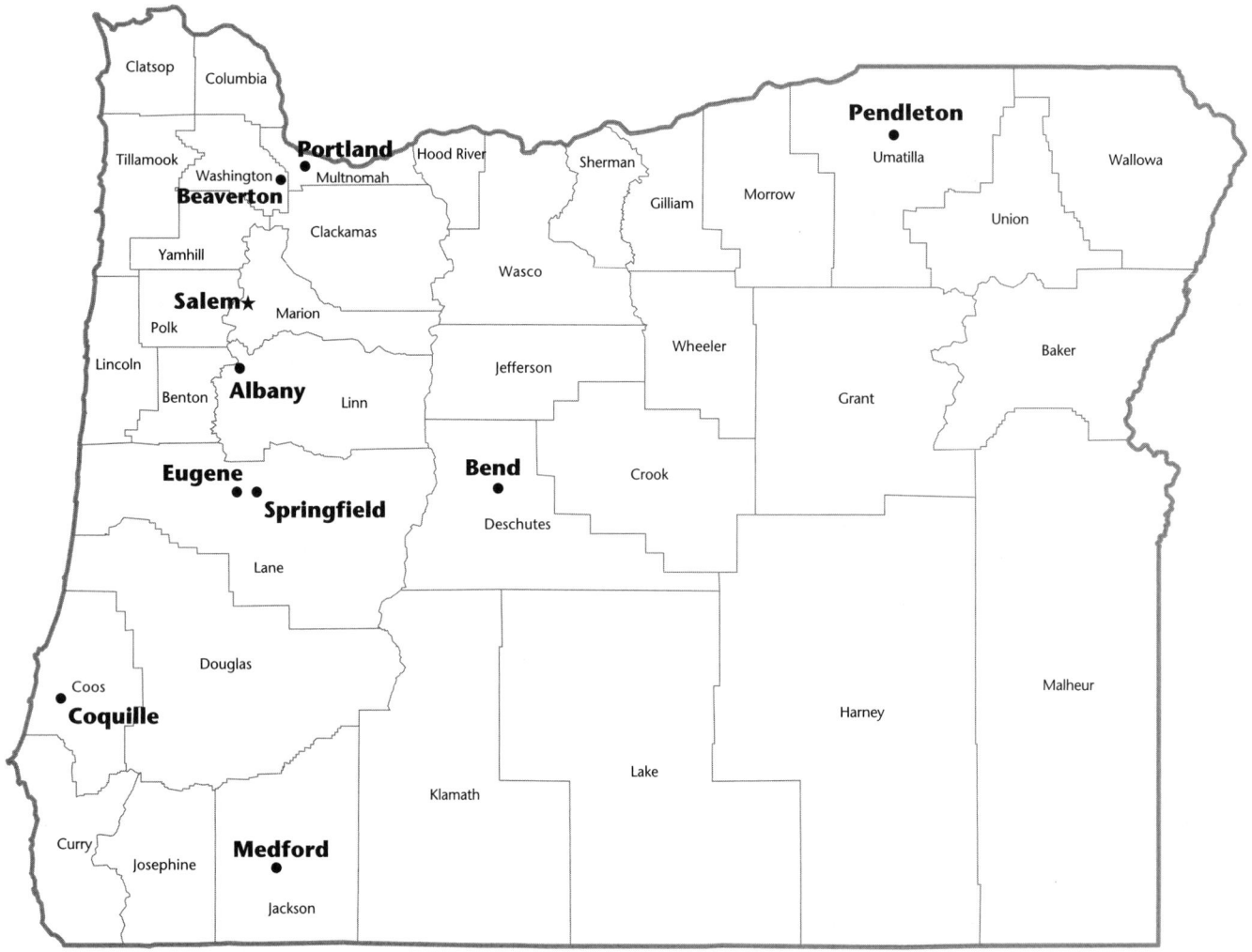

terrain for his anti–Iraq war candidacy, and netted 16 percent of the vote, his best showing of the primary season. However, the Ohio congressman did not come close to beating Kerry in a single county, topping out at 30 percent in Benton County, the home of Oregon State University at Corvallis.

Oregon's primary voters have often supported the presidential candidate who "cares enough to come" to this part of the Pacific Northwest. Nelson Rockefeller used that slogan in upsetting Barry Goldwater in the 1964 Republican primary. Four years later, Eugene McCarthy gave the Kennedy family its first electoral defeat in a quarter century, defeating Robert Kennedy in the Democratic balloting.

On the whole, Oregon voters have tended to support moderate Republicans and fairly liberal Democrats in its presidential primary. Twice before he won the Republican nomination in 1980, Ronald Reagan was on the Oregon GOP primary ballot—in 1968 and 1976—and lost both times. Democratic primary winners have included George McGovern, Frank Church, and

Gary Hart. In 1988, Jesse Jackson drew 38 percent of the Democratic vote, his best showing that year in any of the 16 primary states that voted after Super Tuesday—including New York, Illinois, and California.

Jackson's performance was built around victories in the two academic-oriented counties, Benton and Lane (Eugene), the latter the home of the University of Oregon, as well as a decent showing in the trio of counties that make up metropolitan Portland—Multnomah, Clackamas, and Washington. About 45 percent of the statewide Democratic primary vote of late has been cast in the Portland area, while the comparable number for the Republicans is roughly one-third.

The Oregon GOP has grown more conservative in the last few decades. But in the most memorable of the state's Republican primaries, the more moderate entries ran quite well. A dozen years after Rockefeller's victory, President Gerald Ford narrowly beat Reagan in Oregon, Reagan's only loss that year in a primary west of the Mississippi River. In 1980, George

Bush and John Anderson together collected nearly half the primary vote, even as Reagan was moving at full gallop toward the Republican nomination.

A generation ago, Oregon held the penultimate primary, with its May contest setting the stage for the make-or-break vote in early June in California. But none of the recent contests in its corner of the Pacific Northwest have drawn much attention.

Oregon moved its primary to the second Tuesday in March in 1996 in an attempt to return the state to the front ranks of presidential primaries. With both the ease and novelty of balloting by mail, combined turnout in the Democratic and Republican presidential primaries was up by more than 100,000 from 1992. But the vote was still held too late to have much impact on the nominating contest, and the primary was moved back to May in 2000.

OREGON DEMOCRATIC PRIMARY

2000

County	Total Vote	Gore	LaRouche	Other	Winner	Percentage of Total Vote		
						Gore	LaRouche	Other
BAKER	1,608	1,061	405	142	Gore	66.0%	25.2%	8.8%
BENTON	8,619	7,548	575	496	Gore	87.6%	6.7%	5.8%
CLACKAMAS	33,157	29,154	3,696	307	Gore	87.9%	11.1%	0.9%
CLATSOP	4,554	3,923	397	234	Gore	86.1%	8.7%	5.1%
COLUMBIA	6,159	4,978	842	339	Gore	80.8%	13.7%	5.5%
COOS	8,547	6,332	1,388	827	Gore	74.1%	16.2%	9.7%
CROOK	1,926	1,381	361	184	Gore	71.7%	18.7%	9.6%
CURRY	2,803	2,147	375	281	Gore	76.6%	13.4%	10.0%
DESCHUTES	9,933	8,144	1,130	659	Gore	82.0%	11.4%	6.6%
DOUGLAS	10,400	7,378	2,147	875	Gore	70.9%	20.6%	8.4%
GILLIAM	259	203	31	25	Gore	78.4%	12.0%	9.7%
GRANT	838	371	228	239	Gore	44.3%	27.2%	28.5%
HARNEY	859	469	175	215	Gore	54.6%	20.4%	25.0%
HOOD RIVER	2,312	1,998	234	80	Gore	86.4%	10.1%	3.5%
JACKSON	18,106	15,223	1,688	1,195	Gore	84.1%	9.3%	6.6%
JEFFERSON	1,670	1,357	217	96	Gore	81.3%	13.0%	5.7%
JOSEPHINE	7,522	5,746	1,047	729	Gore	76.4%	13.9%	9.7%
KLAMATH	5,921	4,212	1,225	484	Gore	71.1%	20.7%	8.2%
LAKE	738	431	307	0	Gore	58.4%	41.6%	0.0%
LANE	40,608	35,071	4,833	704	Gore	86.4%	11.9%	1.7%
LINCOLN	5,992	5,166	552	274	Gore	86.2%	9.2%	4.6%
LINN	9,591	7,601	1,827	163	Gore	79.3%	19.0%	1.7%
MALHEUR	1,654	1,122	354	178	Gore	67.8%	21.4%	10.8%
MARION	24,082	20,430	2,372	1,280	Gore	84.8%	9.8%	5.3%
MORROW	563	450	113	0	Gore	79.9%	20.1%	0.0%
MULTNOMAH	86,394	78,053	4,612	3,729	Gore	90.3%	5.3%	4.3%
POLK	5,098	4,437	590	71	Gore	87.0%	11.6%	1.4%
SHERMAN	253	189	49	15	Gore	74.7%	19.4%	5.9%
TILLAMOOK	3,708	3,070	442	196	Gore	82.8%	11.9%	5.3%
UMATILLA	3,896	3,159	729	8	Gore	81.1%	18.7%	0.2%
UNION	2,577	1,833	614	130	Gore	71.1%	23.8%	5.0%
WALLOWA	715	402	167	146	Gore	56.2%	23.4%	20.4%
WASCO	3,121	2,581	399	141	Gore	82.7%	12.8%	4.5%
WASHINGTON	33,253	29,394	3,540	319	Gore	88.4%	10.6%	1.0%
WHEELER	188	115	53	20	Gore	61.2%	28.2%	10.6%
YAMHILL	6,970	5,793	807	370	Gore	83.1%	11.6%	5.3%
TOTAL	354,594	300,922	38,521	15,151	Gore	84.9%	10.9%	4.3%

Note: Other vote was 15,151 write-in.

OREGON REPUBLICAN PRIMARY

2000

County	Total Vote	G.W. Bush	Keyes	Other	Winner	Percentage of Total Vote		
						G.W. Bush	Keyes	Other
BAKER	2,383	2,013	315	55	G.W. Bush	84.5%	13.2%	2.3%
BENTON	7,972	6,482	1,106	384	G.W. Bush	81.3%	13.9%	4.8%
CLACKAMAS	36,230	30,889	4,879	462	G.W. Bush	85.3%	13.5%	1.3%
CLATSOP	3,551	2,889	524	138	G.W. Bush	81.4%	14.8%	3.9%
COLUMBIA	4,072	3,264	643	165	G.W. Bush	80.2%	15.8%	4.1%
COOS	7,172	5,963	874	335	G.W. Bush	83.1%	12.2%	4.7%
CROOK	2,428	2,095	242	91	G.W. Bush	86.3%	10.0%	3.7%
CURRY	3,516	2,822	510	184	G.W. Bush	80.3%	14.5%	5.2%
DESCHUTES	14,253	12,255	1,345	653	G.W. Bush	86.0%	9.4%	4.6%
DOUGLAS	14,500	12,332	1,757	411	G.W. Bush	85.0%	12.1%	2.8%
GILLIAM	289	252	29	8	G.W. Bush	87.2%	10.0%	2.8%
GRANT	1,373	1,204	146	23	G.W. Bush	87.7%	10.6%	1.7%
HARNEY	1,485	1,306	146	33	G.W. Bush	87.9%	9.8%	2.2%
HOOD RIVER	2,240	1,840	315	85	G.W. Bush	82.1%	14.1%	3.8%
JACKSON	23,628	19,587	3,095	946	G.W. Bush	82.9%	13.1%	4.0%
JEFFERSON	2,080	1,827	191	62	G.W. Bush	87.8%	9.2%	3.0%
JOSEPHINE	12,916	10,348	1,984	584	G.W. Bush	80.1%	15.4%	4.5%
KLAMATH	9,467	8,166	1,029	272	G.W. Bush	86.3%	10.9%	2.9%
LAKE	1,464	1,296	168	0	G.W. Bush	88.5%	11.5%	0.0%
LANE	31,399	26,057	4,784	558	G.W. Bush	83.0%	15.2%	1.8%
LINCOLN	4,668	3,724	690	254	G.W. Bush	79.8%	14.8%	5.4%
LINN	11,057	9,473	1,485	99	G.W. Bush	85.7%	13.4%	0.9%
MALHEUR	3,747	3,220	459	68	G.W. Bush	85.9%	12.2%	1.8%
MARION	29,752	24,837	3,907	1,008	G.W. Bush	83.5%	13.1%	3.4%
MORROW	725	634	91	0	G.W. Bush	87.4%	12.6%	0.0%
MULTNOMAH	43,811	35,255	6,201	2,355	G.W. Bush	80.5%	14.2%	5.4%
POLK	7,150	6,072	969	109	G.W. Bush	84.9%	13.6%	1.5%
SHERMAN	317	271	37	9	G.W. Bush	85.5%	11.7%	2.8%
TILLAMOOK	3,170	2,600	439	131	G.W. Bush	82.0%	13.8%	4.1%
UMATILLA	5,164	4,533	601	30	G.W. Bush	87.8%	11.6%	0.6%
UNION	3,416	2,922	434	60	G.W. Bush	85.5%	12.7%	1.8%
WALLOWA	1,184	1,028	123	33	G.W. Bush	86.8%	10.4%	2.8%
WASCO	2,901	2,440	358	103	G.W. Bush	84.1%	12.3%	3.6%
WASHINGTON	40,670	34,518	5,629	523	G.W. Bush	84.9%	13.8%	1.3%
WHEELER	268	232	26	10	G.W. Bush	86.6%	9.7%	3.7%
YAMHILL	9,413	7,876	1,233	304	G.W. Bush	83.7%	13.1%	3.2%
TOTAL	349,831	292,522	46,764	10,545	G.W. Bush	83.6%	13.4%	3.0%

Note: Other vote was 10,545 write-in.

OREGON DEMOCRATIC PRIMARY

2004

County	Total Vote	Kerry	Kucinich	Other	Winner	Percentage of Total Vote		
						Kerry	Kucinich	Other
BAKER	1,766	1,296	260	210	Kerry	73.4%	14.7%	11.9%
BENTON	9,857	6,680	2,925	252	Kerry	67.8%	29.7%	2.6%
CLACKAMAS	35,364	29,751	3,925	1,688	Kerry	84.1%	11.1%	4.8%
CLATSOP	4,372	3,631	511	230	Kerry	83.1%	11.7%	5.3%
COLUMBIA	6,125	5,052	671	402	Kerry	82.5%	11.0%	6.6%
COOS	8,268	6,236	1,239	793	Kerry	75.4%	15.0%	9.6%
CROOK	1,629	1,244	195	190	Kerry	76.4%	12.0%	11.7%
CURRY	2,589	2,058	319	212	Kerry	79.5%	12.3%	8.2%
DESCHUTES	13,188	10,226	2,080	882	Kerry	77.5%	15.8%	6.7%
DOUGLAS	9,156	6,669	1,720	767	Kerry	72.8%	18.8%	8.4%
GILLIAM	240	198	20	22	Kerry	82.5%	8.3%	9.2%
GRANT	618	386	85	147	Kerry	62.5%	13.8%	23.8%
HARNEY	674	442	110	122	Kerry	65.6%	16.3%	18.1%
HOOD RIVER	2,525	1,937	481	107	Kerry	76.7%	19.0%	4.2%
JACKSON	17,655	12,790	4,015	850	Kerry	72.4%	22.7%	4.8%
JEFFERSON	1,404	1,094	209	101	Kerry	77.9%	14.9%	7.2%
JOSEPHINE	6,858	5,010	1,298	550	Kerry	73.1%	18.9%	8.0%
KLAMATH	4,708	3,272	838	598	Kerry	69.5%	17.8%	12.7%
LAKE	490	324	76	90	Kerry	66.1%	15.5%	18.4%
LANE	43,730	33,165	8,805	1,760	Kerry	75.8%	20.1%	4.0%
LINCOLN	6,257	4,781	1,224	252	Kerry	76.4%	19.6%	4.0%
LINN	8,007	6,305	1,109	593	Kerry	78.7%	13.9%	7.4%
MALHEUR	1,553	1,164	182	207	Kerry	75.0%	11.7%	13.3%
MARION	24,069	19,309	3,272	1,488	Kerry	80.2%	13.6%	6.2%
MORROW	674	546	59	69	Kerry	81.0%	8.8%	10.2%
MULTNOMAH	93,234	73,888	16,429	2,917	Kerry	79.3%	17.6%	3.1%
POLK	5,593	4,485	848	260	Kerry	80.2%	15.2%	4.6%
SHERMAN	194	156	21	17	Kerry	80.4%	10.8%	8.8%
TILLAMOOK	3,465	2,702	593	170	Kerry	78.0%	17.1%	4.9%
UMATILLA	4,058	3,234	479	345	Kerry	79.7%	11.8%	8.5%
UNION	2,605	1,907	406	292	Kerry	73.2%	15.6%	11.2%
WALLOWA	722	513	90	119	Kerry	71.1%	12.5%	16.5%
WASCO	2,541	2,006	369	166	Kerry	78.9%	14.5%	6.5%
WASHINGTON	37,269	31,728	4,146	1,395	Kerry	85.1%	11.1%	3.7%
WHEELER	176	118	26	32	Kerry	67.0%	14.8%	18.2%
YAMHILL	6,911	5,501	984	426	Kerry	79.6%	14.2%	6.2%
TOTAL	368,544	289,804	60,019	18,721	Kerry	78.6%	16.3%	5.1%

Note: Other vote was 8,571 Lyndon H. LaRouche Jr.; 10,150 write-in.

OREGON REPUBLICAN PRIMARY

2004

County	Total Vote	G.W. Bush	Other	Winner	Percentage of Total Vote	
					G.W. Bush	Other
BAKER	2,818	2,716	102	G.W. Bush	96.4%	3.6%
BENTON	6,018	5,650	368	G.W. Bush	93.9%	6.1%
CLACKAMAS	33,829	32,380	1,449	G.W. Bush	95.7%	4.3%
CLATSOP	2,844	2,653	191	G.W. Bush	93.3%	6.7%
COLUMBIA	3,933	3,694	239	G.W. Bush	93.9%	6.1%
COOS	6,888	6,556	332	G.W. Bush	95.2%	4.8%
CROOK	2,234	2,146	88	G.W. Bush	96.1%	3.9%
CURRY	2,996	2,841	155	G.W. Bush	94.8%	5.2%
DESCHUTES	17,380	16,694	686	G.W. Bush	96.1%	3.9%
DOUGLAS	13,364	12,876	488	G.W. Bush	96.3%	3.7%
GILLIAM	284	277	7	G.W. Bush	97.5%	2.5%
GRANT	1,229	1,197	32	G.W. Bush	97.4%	2.6%
HARNEY	1,457	1,420	37	G.W. Bush	97.5%	2.5%
HOOD RIVER	1,890	1,773	117	G.W. Bush	93.8%	6.2%
JACKSON	17,658	16,860	798	G.W. Bush	95.5%	4.5%
JEFFERSON	1,934	1,833	101	G.W. Bush	94.8%	5.2%
JOSEPHINE	10,685	10,174	511	G.W. Bush	95.2%	4.8%
KLAMATH	9,420	9,232	188	G.W. Bush	98.0%	2.0%
LAKE	1,443	1,421	22	G.W. Bush	98.5%	1.5%
LANE	26,459	24,864	1,595	G.W. Bush	94.0%	6.0%
LINCOLN	3,940	3,677	263	G.W. Bush	93.3%	6.7%
LINN	8,953	8,670	283	G.W. Bush	96.8%	3.2%
MALHEUR	3,670	3,601	69	G.W. Bush	98.1%	1.9%
MARION	27,139	25,855	1,284	G.W. Bush	95.3%	4.7%
MORROW	857	827	30	G.W. Bush	96.5%	3.5%
MULTNOMAH	33,518	30,517	3,001	G.W. Bush	91.0%	9.0%
POLK	7,111	6,813	298	G.W. Bush	95.8%	4.2%
SHERMAN	274	264	10	G.W. Bush	96.4%	3.6%
TILLAMOOK	2,520	2,378	142	G.W. Bush	94.4%	5.6%
UMATILLA	5,365	5,210	155	G.W. Bush	97.1%	2.9%
UNION	3,465	3,327	138	G.W. Bush	96.0%	4.0%
WALLOWA	1,528	1,468	60	G.W. Bush	96.1%	3.9%
WASCO	2,194	2,069	125	G.W. Bush	94.3%	5.7%
WASHINGTON	35,544	33,594	1,950	G.W. Bush	94.5%	5.5%
WHEELER	226	217	9	G.W. Bush	96.0%	4.0%
YAMHILL	8,439	8,062	377	G.W. Bush	95.5%	4.5%
TOTAL	309,506	293,806	15,700	G.W. Bush	94.9%	5.1%

Note: Other vote was 15,700 write-in.

PENNSYLVANIA

Pennsylvania held its first presidential primary on April 13, 1912—just hours before the Titanic encountered the iceberg. But the heyday of the Keystone State primary came more than a half century later, when candidates who fashioned themselves as champions of the lunch-bucket crowd first had to prove themselves in Pennsylvania.

Hubert Humphrey in 1972, Edward Kennedy in 1980, and Walter Mondale in 1984 all scored key victories in Democratic primary voting in Pennsylvania that advanced their candidacies. Henry Jackson lost the Pennsylvania primary decisively to Jimmy Carter in 1976, and folded his campaign shortly thereafter.

The state's electorate is less trendy and liberal than some of its Eastern neighbors. Rather, it has earned a reputation as the quintessential Frost Belt industrial state. Long dependent on coal and steel, it has a strong union tradition, a rich variety

Recent Pennsylvania Primary Results

Pennsylvania held its first presidential primary in 1912.

Year	DEMOCRATS Turnout	Candidates	%	REPUBLICANS Turnout	Candidates	%
2004 (April 27)	789,882	JOHN KERRY	74	861,555	GEORGE W. BUSH*	100
		Howard Dean	10			
		John Edwards	10			
2000 (April 4)	707,990	AL GORE	74	651,809	GEORGE W. BUSH	72
		Bill Bradley	21		John McCain	22
1996 (April 23)	724,069	BILL CLINTON*	92	684,204	BOB DOLE	64
		Lyndon LaRouche	8		Pat Buchanan	18
					Steve Forbes	8
					Alan Keyes	6
1992 (April 28)	1,265,495	BILL CLINTON	57	1,008,777	GEORGE BUSH*	77
		Jerry Brown	26		Pat Buchanan	23
		Paul Tsongas	13			
1988 (April 26)	1,507,690	MICHAEL DUKAKIS	66	870,549	GEORGE BUSH	79
		Jesse Jackson	27		Bob Dole	12
					Pat Robertson	9
1984 (April 10)	1,656,294	WALTER MONDALE	45	621,206	RONALD REAGAN*	99
		Gary Hart	33			
		Jesse Jackson	16			
1980 (April 22)	1,613,551	EDWARD KENNEDY	46	1,241,411	GEORGE BUSH	50
		Jimmy Carter*	45		Ronald Reagan	43
		No Preference	6			
1976 (April 27)	1,385,042	JIMMY CARTER	37	796,660	GERALD FORD*	92
		Henry Jackson	25		Ronald Reagan#	5
		Morris Udall	19			
		George Wallace	11			
1972 (April 25)	1,374,839	HUBERT HUMPHREY	35	184,801	RICHARD NIXON*#	83
		George Wallace	21		George Wallace#	11
		George McGovern	20			
		Edmund Muskie	20			
1968 (April 23)	597,089	EUGENE McCARTHY	72	287,573	RICHARD NIXON#	60
		Robert Kennedy#	11		Nelson Rockefeller#	18
		Hubert Humphrey#	9		Eugene McCarthy (D)#	7

Note: All candidates are listed that drew at least 5 percent of their party's primary vote. The names of winning candidates are capitalized. An asterisk (*) indicates an incumbent president. A pound sign (#) indicates a write-in candidate.

of ethnic groups, and fairly potent party organizations in the major population centers.

Pennsylvania's blue-collar Democrats have looked with suspicion on some of the party's more liberal presidential aspirants. George McGovern in 1972 and Morris Udall in 1976 both ran a poor third in the primary. Gary Hart fared little better in 1984, running nearly 200,000 votes behind Mondale. Of Pennsylvania's 67 counties, the only one to vote for McGovern, Udall, and Hart was Centre County (which includes Penn State University).

Candidates, though, do not spend much time around Penn State in bucolic central Pennsylvania. The greatest concentration of votes is at opposite ends of the state, which frequently leads to intense regional competition. The Philadelphia area is an integral part of the Eastern megalopolis that spreads from Washington, D.C., to Boston. Western Pennsylvania, anchored by Allegheny County (Pittsburgh), faces the industrial Midwest. It tends to vote more like the adjacent "smokestack" region of Ohio than more cosmopolitan Philadelphia 300 miles away.

The regional rivalry can be quite sharp in Democratic contests. When Kennedy beat President Carter in 1980 by barely 4,000 votes, Kennedy won decisively in the Philadelphia area and carried several other industrial counties in eastern Pennsylvania. But west of the Susquehanna River, Kennedy could carry just one county.

The Democratic primary was not close at all in 1984, since Mondale was able to win both ends of the state. And it has not been particularly relevant since then, with the April voting coming too late to affect the nominating contests. Jesse Jackson could carry little more than Philadelphia in 1988 against Michael Dukakis. Four years later against Bill Clinton, Jerry Brown won only Luzerne (Wilkes-Barre) and Lackawanna (Scranton) counties, the home base of the state's anti-abortion Democratic governor, Robert P. Casey.

While Democratic strength in Pennsylvania is concentrated in the major cities—with Allegheny and Philadelphia alone casting one-third of the Democratic presidential primary vote in 2004—Republican strength is concentrated in two other areas, the Philadelphia suburbs and a part of the state known as the Republican "T." The latter is the predominantly rural central portion of the state that extends northward from the Pennsylvania Dutch country through the Susquehanna River Valley to the forested northern tier of counties along the New York border.

Philadelphia is only a small part of the Republican equation in Pennsylvania. The "city of brotherly love" cast less than 20,000 votes in the 2000 GOP presidential primary, a total exceeded by nine other counties across the state. Actually, nearly twice as many Republican primary ballots were cast in both Lancaster and York counties in the 2000 primary, which together boast barely half the population of Philadelphia.

The last contested Republican presidential primary in Pennsylvania came in 1980, when George Bush took advantage of the moderate tone of the state GOP, particularly among its leadership, to defeat Ronald Reagan. Even though Bush's campaign was on the verge of collapse at the time of the primary, he defeated Reagan in the Keystone State by nearly 100,000 votes. Bush built up a lead in the Philadelphia suburbs and western Pennsylvania that Reagan could not overcome in the Republican "T" and Philadelphia, where Reagan had the backing of the city's GOP leadership.

While Bush's victory in Pennsylvania in 1980 came too late to slow Reagan's bid for the GOP nomination, it did embellish Bush's credentials as a potential running mate for Reagan, an eventuality that came to pass several months later.

PENNSYLVANIA DEMOCRATIC PRIMARY

2000

County	Total Vote	Bradley	Gore	Other	Winner	Percentage of Total Vote		
						Bradley	Gore	Other
ADAMS	3,327	788	2,482	57	Gore	23.7%	74.6%	1.7%
ALLEGHENY	135,104	29,814	99,585	5,705	Gore	22.1%	73.7%	4.2%
ARMSTRONG	5,714	1,294	4,128	292	Gore	22.6%	72.2%	5.1%
BEAVER	20,919	3,500	16,662	757	Gore	16.7%	79.7%	3.6%
BEDFORD	1,983	433	1,486	64	Gore	21.8%	74.9%	3.2%
BERKS	13,948	3,901	9,436	611	Gore	28.0%	67.7%	4.4%
BLAIR	4,248	930	3,156	162	Gore	21.9%	74.3%	3.8%
BRADFORD	1,557	340	1,177	40	Gore	21.8%	75.6%	2.6%
BUCKS	19,599	5,112	13,484	1,003	Gore	26.1%	68.8%	5.1%
BUTLER	8,640	2,136	6,037	467	Gore	24.7%	69.9%	5.4%
CAMBRIA	13,453	3,047	9,844	562	Gore	22.6%	73.2%	4.2%
CAMERON	312	64	236	12	Gore	20.5%	75.6%	3.8%
CARBON	3,142	737	2,276	129	Gore	23.5%	72.4%	4.1%
CENTRE	5,228	1,398	3,696	134	Gore	26.7%	70.7%	2.6%
CHESTER	9,303	2,487	6,663	153	Gore	26.7%	71.6%	1.6%
CLARION	2,396	526	1,794	76	Gore	22.0%	74.9%	3.2%
CLEARFIELD	5,203	1,108	3,906	189	Gore	21.3%	75.1%	3.6%
CLINTON	1,642	294	1,291	57	Gore	17.9%	78.6%	3.5%
COLUMBIA	3,128	730	2,281	117	Gore	23.3%	72.9%	3.7%
CRAWFORD	3,572	701	2,667	204	Gore	19.6%	74.7%	5.7%
CUMBERLAND	8,373	1,974	6,219	180	Gore	23.6%	74.3%	2.1%
DAUPHIN	10,207	2,020	7,920	267	Gore	19.8%	77.6%	2.6%
DELAWARE	15,315	3,416	11,003	896	Gore	22.3%	71.8%	5.9%
ELK	2,784	682	1,997	105	Gore	24.5%	71.7%	3.8%
ERIE	17,629	3,281	13,756	592	Gore	18.6%	78.0%	3.4%
FAYETTE	12,821	2,526	9,792	503	Gore	19.7%	76.4%	3.9%
FOREST	288	61	219	8	Gore	21.2%	76.0%	2.8%
FRANKLIN	2,987	605	2,308	74	Gore	20.3%	77.3%	2.5%
FULTON	576	136	426	14	Gore	23.6%	74.0%	2.4%
GREENE	3,771	647	2,936	188	Gore	17.2%	77.9%	5.0%
HUNTINGDON	1,677	355	1,275	47	Gore	21.2%	76.0%	2.8%
INDIANA	6,024	1,176	4,649	199	Gore	19.5%	77.2%	3.3%
JEFFERSON	2,506	531	1,877	98	Gore	21.2%	74.9%	3.9%
JUNIATA	1,219	240	941	38	Gore	19.7%	77.2%	3.1%
LACKAWANNA	19,242	3,927	14,524	791	Gore	20.4%	75.5%	4.1%
LANCASTER	8,496	1,988	6,094	414	Gore	23.4%	71.7%	4.9%
LAWRENCE	9,585	1,487	7,854	244	Gore	15.5%	81.9%	2.5%
LEBANON	2,901	689	2,080	132	Gore	23.8%	71.7%	4.6%
LEHIGH	13,704	3,822	9,261	621	Gore	27.9%	67.6%	4.5%
LUZERNE	18,676	4,055	13,584	1,037	Gore	21.7%	72.7%	5.6%
LYCOMING	3,944	1,008	2,802	134	Gore	25.6%	71.0%	3.4%
MCKEAN	1,068	232	782	54	Gore	21.7%	73.2%	5.1%
MERCER	6,470	1,085	5,050	335	Gore	16.8%	78.1%	5.2%
MIFFLIN	1,813	382	1,306	125	Gore	21.1%	72.0%	6.9%
MONROE	3,873	971	2,715	187	Gore	25.1%	70.1%	4.8%

PENNSYLVANIA DEMOCRATIC PRIMARY

2000

County	Total Vote	Bradley	Gore	Other	Winner	Percentage of Total Vote		
						Bradley	Gore	Other
MONTGOMERY	26,388	6,296	19,733	359	Gore	23.9%	74.8%	1.4%
MONTOUR	737	202	512	23	Gore	27.4%	69.5%	3.1%
NORTHAMPTON	12,488	3,622	8,376	490	Gore	29.0%	67.1%	3.9%
NORTHUMBERLAND	4,581	1,161	3,238	182	Gore	25.3%	70.7%	4.0%
PERRY	1,386	316	1,016	54	Gore	22.8%	73.3%	3.9%
PHILADELPHIA	121,753	17,147	96,673	7,933	Gore	14.1%	79.4%	6.5%
PIKE	716	188	483	45	Gore	26.3%	67.5%	6.3%
POTTER	581	134	426	21	Gore	23.1%	73.3%	3.6%
SCHUYLKILL	6,926	1,411	5,251	264	Gore	20.4%	75.8%	3.8%
SNYDER	840	170	647	23	Gore	20.2%	77.0%	2.7%
SOMERSET	4,816	936	3,741	139	Gore	19.4%	77.7%	2.9%
SULLIVAN	423	100	306	17	Gore	23.6%	72.3%	4.0%
SUSQUEHANNA	1,546	324	1,172	50	Gore	21.0%	75.8%	3.2%
TIOGA	1,184	247	900	37	Gore	20.9%	76.0%	3.1%
UNION	1,061	317	714	30	Gore	29.9%	67.3%	2.8%
VENANGO	2,047	381	1,572	94	Gore	18.6%	76.8%	4.6%
WARREN	1,556	344	1,155	57	Gore	22.1%	74.2%	3.7%
WASHINGTON	22,252	4,428	16,780	1,044	Gore	19.9%	75.4%	4.7%
WAYNE	1,244	308	878	58	Gore	24.8%	70.6%	4.7%
WESTMORELAND	37,629	8,668	27,230	1,731	Gore	23.0%	72.4%	4.6%
WYOMING	1,028	190	800	38	Gore	18.5%	77.8%	3.7%
YORK	14,601	3,271	10,046	1,284	Gore	22.4%	68.8%	8.8%
TOTAL	707,990	146,797	525,306	35,887	Gore	20.7%	74.2%	5.1%

Note: Other vote was 32,047 Lyndon H. LaRouche Jr.; 688 Alan Keyes (write-in); 3,172 scattered write-in. The statewide "Total Vote" and "Other" vote totals include write-in votes, but not the county-by-county entries.

PENNSYLVANIA REPUBLICAN PRIMARY

2000

County	Total Vote	G.W. Bush	McCain	Other	Winner	Percentage of Total Vote		
						G.W. Bush	McCain	Other
ADAMS	7,931	6,196	1,526	209	G.W. Bush	78.1%	19.2%	2.6%
ALLEGHENY	48,881	35,932	10,659	2,290	G.W. Bush	73.5%	21.8%	4.7%
ARMSTRONG	5,725	4,460	1,041	224	G.W. Bush	77.9%	18.2%	3.9%
BEAVER	7,167	5,725	1,184	258	G.W. Bush	79.9%	16.5%	3.6%
BEDFORD	3,434	2,820	532	82	G.W. Bush	82.1%	15.5%	2.4%
BERKS	13,584	10,516	2,577	491	G.W. Bush	77.4%	19.0%	3.6%
BLAIR	8,286	6,456	1,569	261	G.W. Bush	77.9%	18.9%	3.1%
BRADFORD	5,100	3,546	1,379	175	G.W. Bush	69.5%	27.0%	3.4%
BUCKS	33,674	23,021	9,143	1,510	G.W. Bush	68.4%	27.2%	4.5%
BUTLER	10,660	8,021	2,074	565	G.W. Bush	75.2%	19.5%	5.3%
CAMBRIA	6,219	4,525	1,443	251	G.W. Bush	72.8%	23.2%	4.0%
CAMERON	445	316	117	12	G.W. Bush	71.0%	26.3%	2.7%
CARBON	2,279	1,670	534	75	G.W. Bush	73.3%	23.4%	3.3%
CENTRE	7,638	5,340	2,069	229	G.W. Bush	69.9%	27.1%	3.0%
CHESTER	24,559	16,606	6,898	1,055	G.W. Bush	67.6%	28.1%	4.3%
CLARION	3,100	2,403	575	122	G.W. Bush	77.5%	18.5%	3.9%
CLEARFIELD	5,357	4,075	1,097	185	G.W. Bush	76.1%	20.5%	3.5%
CLINTON	1,707	1,254	390	63	G.W. Bush	73.5%	22.8%	3.7%
COLUMBIA	2,921	2,155	666	100	G.W. Bush	73.8%	22.8%	3.4%
CRAWFORD	6,583	4,783	1,516	284	G.W. Bush	72.7%	23.0%	4.3%
CUMBERLAND	24,134	18,551	5,019	564	G.W. Bush	76.9%	20.8%	2.3%
DAUPHIN	20,493	15,510	4,390	593	G.W. Bush	75.7%	21.4%	2.9%
DELAWARE	45,685	29,512	14,141	2,032	G.W. Bush	64.6%	31.0%	4.4%
ELK	1,837	1,250	509	78	G.W. Bush	68.0%	27.7%	4.2%
ERIE	14,758	10,032	4,103	623	G.W. Bush	68.0%	27.8%	4.2%
FAYETTE	3,253	2,623	483	147	G.W. Bush	80.6%	14.8%	4.5%
FOREST	524	365	144	15	G.W. Bush	69.7%	27.5%	2.9%
FRANKLIN	7,361	5,829	1,384	148	G.W. Bush	79.2%	18.8%	2.0%
FULTON	874	694	156	24	G.W. Bush	79.4%	17.8%	2.7%
GREENE	1,208	970	188	50	G.W. Bush	80.3%	15.6%	4.1%
HUNTINGDON	3,481	2,720	654	107	G.W. Bush	78.1%	18.8%	3.1%
INDIANA	6,390	4,897	1,264	229	G.W. Bush	76.6%	19.8%	3.6%
JEFFERSON	3,654	2,798	721	135	G.W. Bush	76.6%	19.7%	3.7%
JUNIATA	2,274	1,844	362	68	G.W. Bush	81.1%	15.9%	3.0%
LACKAWANNA	10,407	7,486	2,539	382	G.W. Bush	71.9%	24.4%	3.7%
LANCASTER	35,991	28,613	6,118	1,260	G.W. Bush	79.5%	17.0%	3.5%
LAWRENCE	5,370	4,105	1,065	200	G.W. Bush	76.4%	19.8%	3.7%
LEBANON	8,501	6,483	1,736	282	G.W. Bush	76.3%	20.4%	3.3%
LEHIGH	13,902	9,851	3,477	574	G.W. Bush	70.9%	25.0%	4.1%
LUZERNE	11,704	8,348	2,900	456	G.W. Bush	71.3%	24.8%	3.9%
LYCOMING	7,598	5,990	1,358	250	G.W. Bush	78.8%	17.9%	3.3%
MCKEAN	3,041	2,237	677	127	G.W. Bush	73.6%	22.3%	4.2%
MERCER	7,490	5,663	1,508	319	G.W. Bush	75.6%	20.1%	4.3%
MIFFLIN	3,288	2,586	604	98	G.W. Bush	78.6%	18.4%	3.0%
MONROE	4,742	3,349	1,205	188	G.W. Bush	70.6%	25.4%	4.0%

PENNSYLVANIA REPUBLICAN PRIMARY

2000

County	Total Vote	G.W. Bush	McCain	Other	Winner	Percentage of Total Vote		
						G.W. Bush	McCain	Other
MONTGOMERY	47,931	33,468	12,959	1,504	G.W. Bush	69.8%	27.0%	3.1%
MONTOUR	939	672	239	28	G.W. Bush	71.6%	25.5%	3.0%
NORTHAMPTON	9,434	7,055	2,015	364	G.W. Bush	74.8%	21.4%	3.9%
NORTHUMBERLAND	4,851	3,597	1,047	207	G.W. Bush	74.1%	21.6%	4.3%
PERRY	3,961	3,103	730	128	G.W. Bush	78.3%	18.4%	3.2%
PHILADELPHIA	19,836	13,917	4,786	1,133	G.W. Bush	70.2%	24.1%	5.7%
PIKE	1,652	1,156	412	84	G.W. Bush	70.0%	24.9%	5.1%
POTTER	1,411	1,093	270	48	G.W. Bush	77.5%	19.1%	3.4%
SCHUYLKILL	8,847	6,335	2,174	338	G.W. Bush	71.6%	24.6%	3.8%
SNYDER	3,036	2,382	522	132	G.W. Bush	78.5%	17.2%	4.3%
SOMERSET	5,857	4,723	951	183	G.W. Bush	80.6%	16.2%	3.1%
SULLIVAN	632	469	142	21	G.W. Bush	74.2%	22.5%	3.3%
SUSQUEHANNA	3,700	2,664	919	117	G.W. Bush	72.0%	24.8%	3.2%
TIOGA	3,572	2,672	777	123	G.W. Bush	74.8%	21.8%	3.4%
UNION	2,750	2,146	506	98	G.W. Bush	78.0%	18.4%	3.6%
VENANGO	3,624	2,662	803	159	G.W. Bush	73.5%	22.2%	4.4%
WARREN	3,103	1,883	981	239	G.W. Bush	60.7%	31.6%	7.7%
WASHINGTON	7,402	5,591	1,451	360	G.W. Bush	75.5%	19.6%	4.9%
WAYNE	3,769	2,464	915	390	G.W. Bush	65.4%	24.3%	10.3%
WESTMORELAND	16,146	12,634	2,642	870	G.W. Bush	78.2%	16.4%	5.4%
WYOMING	2,829	2,024	711	94	G.W. Bush	71.5%	25.1%	3.3%
YORK	34,593	27,562	6,073	958	G.W. Bush	79.7%	17.6%	2.8%
TOTAL	651,809	472,398	145,719	33,692	G.W. Bush	72.5%	22.4%	5.2%

Note: Other vote was 16,162 Steve Forbes; 8,806 Gary Bauer; 7,100 Alan Keyes (write-in); 1,624 scattered write-in. The statewide "Total Vote" and "Other" vote totals include write-in votes, but not the county-by-county entries.

PENNSYLVANIA DEMOCRATIC PRIMARY

2004

County	Total Vote	Dean	Edwards	Kerry	Other	Winner	Percentage of Total Vote			
							Dean	Edwards	Kerry	Other
ADAMS	3,271	322	430	2,407	112	Kerry	9.8%	13.1%	73.6%	3.4%
ALLEGHENY	130,904	9,791	10,000	102,311	8,802	Kerry	7.5%	7.6%	78.2%	6.7%
ARMSTRONG	5,929	527	672	4,422	308	Kerry	8.9%	11.3%	74.6%	5.2%
BEAVER	18,986	897	1,618	14,794	1,677	Kerry	4.7%	8.5%	77.9%	8.8%
BEDFORD	2,753	248	362	2,027	116	Kerry	9.0%	13.1%	73.6%	4.2%
BERKS	16,722	2,111	2,181	11,502	928	Kerry	12.6%	13.0%	68.8%	5.5%
BLAIR	6,291	536	843	4,686	226	Kerry	8.5%	13.4%	74.5%	3.6%
BRADFORD	1,695	115	193	1,327	60	Kerry	6.8%	11.4%	78.3%	3.5%
BUCKS	30,981	4,290	2,657	22,512	1,522	Kerry	13.8%	8.6%	72.7%	4.9%
BUTLER	10,133	887	1,209	7,407	630	Kerry	8.8%	11.9%	73.1%	6.2%
CAMBRIA	18,965	1,572	2,407	14,082	904	Kerry	8.3%	12.7%	74.3%	4.8%
CAMERON	323	27	44	240	12	Kerry	8.4%	13.6%	74.3%	3.7%
CARBON	3,789	402	375	2,829	183	Kerry	10.6%	9.9%	74.7%	4.8%
CENTRE	6,981	555	857	5,076	493	Kerry	8.0%	12.3%	72.7%	7.1%
CHESTER	13,197	1,088	1,078	10,357	674	Kerry	8.2%	8.2%	78.5%	5.1%
CLARION	2,669	197	339	2,019	114	Kerry	7.4%	12.7%	75.6%	4.3%
CLEARFIELD	7,130	515	959	5,424	232	Kerry	7.2%	13.5%	76.1%	3.3%
CLINTON	2,083	225	261	1,518	79	Kerry	10.8%	12.5%	72.9%	3.8%
COLUMBIA	4,139	445	632	2,896	166	Kerry	10.8%	15.3%	70.0%	4.0%
CRAWFORD	4,607	582	543	3,214	268	Kerry	12.6%	11.8%	69.8%	5.8%
CUMBERLAND	10,040	824	1,135	7,686	395	Kerry	8.2%	11.3%	76.6%	3.9%
DAUPHIN	13,364	1,192	1,233	10,344	595	Kerry	8.9%	9.2%	77.4%	4.5%
DELAWARE	19,362	2,852	1,122	14,213	1,175	Kerry	14.7%	5.8%	73.4%	6.1%
ELK	3,177	255	408	2,401	113	Kerry	8.0%	12.8%	75.6%	3.6%
ERIE	22,225	1,943	2,984	15,402	1,896	Kerry	8.7%	13.4%	69.3%	8.5%
FAYETTE	14,088	1,358	1,584	10,184	962	Kerry	9.6%	11.2%	72.3%	6.8%
FOREST	389	40	40	298	11	Kerry	10.3%	10.3%	76.6%	2.8%
FRANKLIN	4,494	342	573	3,446	133	Kerry	7.6%	12.8%	76.7%	3.0%
FULTON	634	44	90	480	20	Kerry	6.9%	14.2%	75.7%	3.2%
GREENE	4,024	287	437	3,110	190	Kerry	7.1%	10.9%	77.3%	4.7%
HUNTINGDON	2,257	170	354	1,675	58	Kerry	7.5%	15.7%	74.2%	2.6%
INDIANA	5,723	400	635	4,471	217	Kerry	7.0%	11.1%	78.1%	3.8%
JEFFERSON	2,513	236	313	1,843	121	Kerry	9.4%	12.5%	73.3%	4.8%
JUNIATA	1,385	143	191	1,006	45	Kerry	10.3%	13.8%	72.6%	3.2%
LACKAWANNA	17,621	1,596	1,689	13,575	761	Kerry	9.1%	9.6%	77.0%	4.3%
LANCASTER	10,669	1,180	968	8,016	505	Kerry	11.1%	9.1%	75.1%	4.7%
LAWRENCE	8,172	381	802	6,492	497	Kerry	4.7%	9.8%	79.4%	6.1%
LEBANON	3,891	496	656	2,449	290	Kerry	12.7%	16.9%	62.9%	7.5%
LEHIGH	17,495	1,903	1,848	12,714	1,030	Kerry	10.9%	10.6%	72.7%	5.9%
LUZERNE	19,632	2,309	2,753	13,031	1,539	Kerry	11.8%	14.0%	66.4%	7.8%
LYCOMING	4,391	637	803	2,581	370	Kerry	14.5%	18.3%	58.8%	8.4%
MCKEAN	1,417	233	169	962	53	Kerry	16.4%	11.9%	67.9%	3.7%
MERCER	6,484	334	728	5,084	338	Kerry	5.2%	11.2%	78.4%	5.2%
MIFFLIN	1,962	226	267	1,387	82	Kerry	11.5%	13.6%	70.7%	4.2%
MONROE	4,839	531	462	3,555	291	Kerry	11.0%	9.5%	73.5%	6.0%

PENNSYLVANIA DEMOCRATIC PRIMARY

2004

County	Total Vote	Dean	Edwards	Kerry	Other	Winner	Percentage of Total Vote			
							Dean	Edwards	Kerry	Other
MONTGOMERY	41,552	2,993	2,319	34,515	1,725	Kerry	7.2%	5.6%	83.1%	4.2%
MONTOUR	915	129	134	614	38	Kerry	14.1%	14.6%	67.1%	4.2%
NORTHAMPTON	16,426	1,629	1,540	12,515	742	Kerry	9.9%	9.4%	76.2%	4.5%
NORTHUMBERLAND	5,257	576	677	3,818	186	Kerry	11.0%	12.9%	72.6%	3.5%
PERRY	1,763	202	243	1,257	61	Kerry	11.5%	13.8%	71.3%	3.5%
PHILADELPHIA	133,361	20,317	9,917	94,072	9,055	Kerry	15.2%	7.4%	70.5%	6.8%
PIKE	868	105	84	638	41	Kerry	12.1%	9.7%	73.5%	4.7%
POTTER	706	77	89	518	22	Kerry	10.9%	12.6%	73.4%	3.1%
SCHUYLKILL	8,456	741	937	6,490	288	Kerry	8.8%	11.1%	76.8%	3.4%
SNYDER	977	69	154	713	41	Kerry	7.1%	15.8%	73.0%	4.2%
SOMERSET	6,593	473	870	5,007	243	Kerry	7.2%	13.2%	75.9%	3.7%
SULLIVAN	484	34	81	343	26	Kerry	7.0%	16.7%	70.9%	5.4%
SUSQUEHANNA	1,748	127	178	1,372	71	Kerry	7.3%	10.2%	78.5%	4.1%
TIOGA	1,295	102	164	975	54	Kerry	7.9%	12.7%	75.3%	4.2%
UNION	1,103	114	120	802	67	Kerry	10.3%	10.9%	72.7%	6.1%
VENANGO	2,503	189	315	1,869	130	Kerry	7.6%	12.6%	74.7%	5.2%
WARREN	1,912	216	221	1,389	86	Kerry	11.3%	11.6%	72.6%	4.5%
WASHINGTON	21,273	1,421	2,146	16,577	1,129	Kerry	6.7%	10.1%	77.9%	5.3%
WAYNE	1,512	192	171	1,072	77	Kerry	12.7%	11.3%	70.9%	5.1%
WESTMORELAND	33,924	2,936	4,489	22,747	3,752	Kerry	8.7%	13.2%	67.1%	11.1%
WYOMING	1,215	118	149	907	41	Kerry	9.7%	12.3%	74.7%	3.4%
YORK	14,243	1,795	1,860	10,018	570	Kerry	12.6%	13.1%	70.3%	4.0%
TOTAL	789,882	79,799	76,762	585,683	47,638	Kerry	10.1%	9.7%	74.1%	6.0%

Note: Other vote was 30,110 Dennis J. Kucinich; 17,528 Lyndon H. LaRouche Jr.

RHODE ISLAND

Rhode Island is heavily Catholic, urban, and ethnic, and one of the most Democratic states in the country. In the first two decades after the inception of the Rhode Island presidential primary in 1972, Democrats often took the opportunity to rebuke their party's eventual nominee. An "Uncommitted" slate adopted by Jerry Brown beat Jimmy Carter in 1976; Edward Kennedy routed Carter in 1980; Gary Hart defeated Walter Mondale in 1984; and Paul Tsongas overwhelmed Bill Clinton in 1992.

An exception to this trend was apparent in 2000, when Al Gore defeated Bill Bradley. Still, while Gore tended to dominate the vote in the industrial northern half of the state, Bradley carried nearly a dozen communities, many around

the Narragansett Bay. He also won two of Rhode Island's five counties, bay-oriented Bristol and Washington. In 2004, the front-runner won again, as John Kerry trounced runner-up John Edwards by more than 50 percentage points.

These anomalous results have been partly attributable to low turnout, which have allowed relatively small numbers of voters to tip the results. Even though Rhode Island independents are permitted to vote in either the Democratic or Republican primary, as they are in much of New England, that allure has failed to produce high turnouts. Since the state's first presidential primary was held in 1972, no more than 85,000 of its more than half-million voters have cast ballots in the major-party primaries in any given year.

Recent Rhode Island Primary Results

Rhode Island held its first presidential primary in 1972.

Year	Turnout	DEMOCRATS Candidates	%	Turnout	REPUBLICANS Candidates	%
2004 (March 2)	35,759	JOHN KERRY / John Edwards	71 / 19	2,535	GEORGE W. BUSH* / Uncommitted	85 / 12
2000 (March 7)	47,084	AL GORE / Bill Bradley	57 / 40	36,137	JOHN McCAIN / George W. Bush	60 / 36
1996 (March 5)	8,780	BILL CLINTON* / Uncommitted	89 / 6	15,009	BOB DOLE / Lamar Alexander / Uncommitted	64 / 19 / 8
1992 (March 10)	50,709	PAUL TSONGAS / Bill Clinton / Jerry Brown	53 / 21 / 19	15,636	GEORGE BUSH* / Pat Buchanan	63 / 32
1988 (March 8)	49,029	MICHAEL DUKAKIS / Jesse Jackson	70 / 15	16,035	GEORGE BUSH / Bob Dole / Pat Robertson	65 / 23 / 6
1984 (March 13)	44,511	GARY HART / Walter Mondale / Jesse Jackson / John Glenn	45 / 34 / 9 / 5	2,235	RONALD REAGAN* / Uncommitted	91 / 9
1980 (June 3)	38,327	EDWARD KENNEDY / Jimmy Carter*	68 / 26	5,335	RONALD REAGAN / George Bush / Uncommitted	72 / 19 / 7
1976 (June 1)	60,348	UNCOMMITTED / Jimmy Carter / Frank Church	32 / 30 / 27	14,352	GERALD FORD* / Ronald Reagan	65 / 31
1972 (May 23)	37,864	GEORGE McGOVERN / Edmund Muskie / Hubert Humphrey / George Wallace	41 / 21 / 20 / 15	5,611	RICHARD NIXON* / Paul McCloskey	88 / 6

Note: All candidates are listed that drew at least 5 percent of their party's primary vote. The names of winning candidates are capitalized. An asterisk (*) indicates an incumbent president.

Woonsocket

Providence

Pawtucket

Providence ★

Cranston ●

Warwick

Kent

Bristol

Bristol

Washington

Newport

Newport

With such a limited turnout, liberal activists have often tended to have the upper hand in Democratic primary voting in spite of Rhode Island's heritage as a heavily unionized state with conservative social values.

But geography also has driven the vote in a number of Democratic primaries. In 2004, Kerry continued Rhode Island's tradition of supporting candidates from neighboring Massachusetts.

Both Kennedy in 1980 and Michael Dukakis in 1988 took more than two-thirds of the primary ballots in Rhode Island, besting their showings in their home state. Paul Tsongas won Rhode Island easily in 1992 with 53 percent of the vote, his best showing in a primary outside Massachusetts. Clinton finished a distant second statewide. In 2004, Kerry topped 70 percent, also his best showing in a primary outside Massachusetts in the competitive stage of the Democratic nominating fight that year (which ended on the first Tuesday in March).

While Democratic interest in the presidential primary has never been high, the GOP turnout has been downright minuscule, surpassing 20,000 only once (in 2000). Most Rhode Islanders who cast Republican primary ballots seem satisfied with moderates of the Gerald Ford–George Bush stripe.

Conservative Republicans, even well-known ones, have had trouble reaching one-third of the vote in competitive GOP presidential primaries in Rhode Island. Ronald Reagan drew only 31 percent against Ford in 1976. Pat Buchanan garnered only 32 percent against Bush in 1992. And George W. Bush, brandishing his "compassionate" brand of conservatism, could muster only 36 percent against John McCain in 2000. McCain's victory over the future president was broad based, as he carried all 39 Rhode Island cities and towns. In all but one (the town of Johnston), McCain trounced Bush by at least 15 percentage points.

RHODE ISLAND DEMOCRATIC PRIMARY

2000

County	Total Vote	Bradley	Gore	Other	Winner	Percentage of Total Vote		
						Bradley	Gore	Other
BRISTOL	2,257	1,154	1,073	30	Bradley	51.1%	47.5%	1.3%
KENT	7,594	3,071	4,346	177	Gore	40.4%	57.2%	2.3%
NEWPORT	3,942	1,829	2,042	71	Gore	46.4%	51.8%	1.8%
PROVIDENCE	27,085	9,998	16,454	633	Gore	36.9%	60.7%	2.3%
WASHINGTON	4,868	2,594	2,195	79	Bradley	53.3%	45.1%	1.6%
Machine Total	45,746	18,646	26,110	990	Gore	40.8%	57.1%	2.2%
Mail Ballots	1,098	354	691	53	Gore	32.2%	62.9%	4.8%
TOTAL	47,084	19,000	26,801	1,283	Gore	40.4%	56.9%	2.7%
City/Town								
BARRINGTON	1,044	669	365	10	Bradley	64.1%	35.0%	1.0%
BRISTOL	795	321	464	10	Gore	40.4%	58.4%	1.3%
BURRILLVILLE	461	157	289	15	Gore	34.1%	62.7%	3.3%
CENTRAL FALLS	833	156	645	32	Gore	18.7%	77.4%	3.8%
CHARLESTOWN	235	128	102	5	Bradley	54.5%	43.4%	2.1%
COVENTRY	1,036	390	625	21	Gore	37.6%	60.3%	2.0%
CRANSTON	3,092	1,129	1,907	56	Gore	36.5%	61.7%	1.8%
CUMBERLAND	2,008	879	1,072	57	Gore	43.8%	53.4%	2.8%
EAST GREENWICH	533	330	191	12	Bradley	61.9%	35.8%	2.3%
EAST PROVIDENCE	2,310	825	1,426	59	Gore	35.7%	61.7%	2.6%
EXETER	152	63	85	4	Gore	41.4%	55.9%	2.6%
FOSTER	107	65	41	1	Bradley	60.7%	38.3%	0.9%
GLOCESTER	271	124	141	6	Gore	45.8%	52.0%	2.2%
HOPKINTON	169	81	84	4	Gore	47.9%	49.7%	2.4%
JAMESTOWN	458	261	189	8	Bradley	57.0%	41.3%	1.7%
JOHNSTON	1,204	387	782	35	Gore	32.1%	65.0%	2.9%
LINCOLN	740	272	453	15	Gore	36.8%	61.2%	2.0%
LITTLE COMPTON	220	125	92	3	Bradley	56.8%	41.8%	1.4%
MIDDLETOWN	525	227	287	11	Gore	43.2%	54.7%	2.1%
NARRAGANSETT	953	502	440	11	Bradley	52.7%	46.2%	1.2%
NEWPORT	1,283	605	653	25	Gore	47.2%	50.9%	1.9%
NEW SHOREHAM	150	98	50	2	Bradley	65.3%	33.3%	1.3%
NORTH KINGSTOWN	1,155	654	482	19	Bradley	56.6%	41.7%	1.6%
NORTH PROVIDENCE	1,781	613	1,133	35	Gore	34.4%	63.6%	2.0%
NORTH SMITHFIELD	498	173	304	21	Gore	34.7%	61.0%	4.2%
PAWTUCKET	3,882	1,244	2,530	108	Gore	32.0%	65.2%	2.8%
PORTSMOUTH	750	359	379	12	Gore	47.9%	50.5%	1.6%
PROVIDENCE	7,574	3,187	4,259	128	Gore	42.1%	56.2%	1.7%
RICHMOND	166	71	91	4	Gore	42.8%	54.8%	2.4%
SCITUATE	226	121	101	4	Bradley	53.5%	44.7%	1.8%
SMITHFIELD	643	283	345	15	Gore	44.0%	53.7%	2.3%
SOUTH KINGSTOWN	1,241	724	497	20	Bradley	58.3%	40.0%	1.6%
TIVERTON	706	252	442	12	Gore	35.7%	62.6%	1.7%
WARREN	418	164	244	10	Gore	39.2%	58.4%	2.4%
WARWICK	5,171	2,045	3,000	126	Gore	39.5%	58.0%	2.4%

RHODE ISLAND DEMOCRATIC PRIMARY

2000

County	Total Vote	Bradley	Gore	Other	Winner	Percentage of Total Vote		
						Bradley	Gore	Other
WESTERLY	647	273	364	10	Gore	42.2%	56.3%	1.5%
WEST GREENWICH	115	53	62	0	Gore	46.1%	53.9%	0.0%
WEST WARWICK	739	253	468	18	Gore	34.2%	63.3%	2.4%
WOONSOCKET	1,455	383	1,026	46	Gore	26.3%	70.5%	3.2%
Machine Total	45,746	18,646	26,110	990	Gore	40.8%	57.1%	2.2%
Mail Ballots	1,098	354	691	53	Gore	32.2%	62.9%	4.8%
TOTAL	47,084	19,000	26,801	1,283	Gore	40.4%	56.9%	2.7%

Note: Other vote was 844 Uncommitted; 199 Lyndon H. LaRouche Jr.; 240 write-in. Only the ballots cast by machine were readily broken down by community. Mail ballots and write-in votes were not.

RHODE ISLAND REPUBLICAN PRIMARY

2000

County	Total Vote	G.W. Bush	McCain	Other	Winner	Percentage of Total Vote		
						G.W. Bush	McCain	Other
BRISTOL	2,732	1,005	1,666	61	McCain	36.8%	61.0%	2.2%
KENT	7,166	2,609	4,356	201	McCain	36.4%	60.8%	2.8%
NEWPORT	5,045	1,813	3,102	130	McCain	35.9%	61.5%	2.6%
PROVIDENCE	13,895	5,166	8,163	566	McCain	37.2%	58.7%	4.1%
WASHINGTON	6,697	2,302	4,179	216	McCain	34.4%	62.4%	3.2%
Machine Total	35,535	12,895	21,466	1,174	McCain	36.3%	60.4%	3.3%
Mail Ballots	585	275	288	22	McCain	47.0%	49.2%	3.8%
TOTAL	36,137	13,170	21,754	1,213	McCain	36.4%	60.2%	3.4%
City/Town								
BARRINGTON	1,459	564	874	21	McCain	38.7%	59.9%	1.4%
BRISTOL	874	315	535	24	McCain	36.0%	61.2%	2.7%
BURRILLVILLE	445	181	249	15	McCain	40.7%	56.0%	3.4%
CENTRAL FALLS	125	49	70	6	McCain	39.2%	56.0%	4.8%
CHARLESTOWN	547	196	342	9	McCain	35.8%	62.5%	1.6%
COVENTRY	1,288	431	808	49	McCain	33.5%	62.7%	3.8%
CRANSTON	2,555	1,025	1,446	84	McCain	40.1%	56.6%	3.3%
CUMBERLAND	1,151	412	701	38	McCain	35.8%	60.9%	3.3%
EAST GREENWICH	1,082	337	723	22	McCain	31.1%	66.8%	2.0%
EAST PROVIDENCE	1,233	474	711	48	McCain	38.4%	57.7%	3.9%
EXETER	317	126	186	5	McCain	39.7%	58.7%	1.6%
FOSTER	249	89	154	6	McCain	35.7%	61.8%	2.4%
GLOCESTER	460	148	278	34	McCain	32.2%	60.4%	7.4%
HOPKINTON	314	101	200	13	McCain	32.2%	63.7%	4.1%
JAMESTOWN	560	156	390	14	McCain	27.9%	69.6%	2.5%

RHODE ISLAND REPUBLICAN PRIMARY

2000

County	Total Vote	G.W. Bush	McCain	Other	Winner	Percentage of Total Vote		
						G.W. Bush	McCain	Other
JOHNSTON	400	173	212	15	McCain	43.3%	53.0%	3.8%
LINCOLN	969	350	591	28	McCain	36.1%	61.0%	2.9%
LITTLE COMPTON	381	153	217	11	McCain	40.2%	57.0%	2.9%
MIDDLETOWN	877	315	542	20	McCain	35.9%	61.8%	2.3%
NARRAGANSETT	770	262	483	25	McCain	34.0%	62.7%	3.2%
NEWPORT	1,186	415	737	34	McCain	35.0%	62.1%	2.9%
NEW SHOREHAM	131	39	90	2	McCain	29.8%	68.7%	1.5%
NORTH KINGSTOWN	1,917	659	1,206	52	McCain	34.4%	62.9%	2.7%
NORTH PROVIDENCE	589	213	352	24	McCain	36.2%	59.8%	4.1%
NORTH SMITHFIELD	563	194	358	11	McCain	34.5%	63.6%	2.0%
PAWTUCKET	1,171	439	672	60	McCain	37.5%	57.4%	5.1%
PORTSMOUTH	1,306	481	794	31	McCain	36.8%	60.8%	2.4%
PROVIDENCE	1,780	590	1,082	108	McCain	33.1%	60.8%	6.1%
RICHMOND	360	121	223	16	McCain	33.6%	61.9%	4.4%
SCITUATE	673	268	377	28	McCain	39.8%	56.0%	4.2%
SMITHFIELD	749	270	455	24	McCain	36.0%	60.7%	3.2%
SOUTH KINGSTOWN	1,361	461	858	42	McCain	33.9%	63.0%	3.1%
TIVERTON	735	293	422	20	McCain	39.9%	57.4%	2.7%
WARREN	399	126	257	16	McCain	31.6%	64.4%	4.0%
WARWICK	3,705	1,412	2,196	97	McCain	38.1%	59.3%	2.6%
WESTERLY	980	337	591	52	McCain	34.4%	60.3%	5.3%
WEST GREENWICH	325	118	200	7	McCain	36.3%	61.5%	2.2%
WEST WARWICK	766	311	429	26	McCain	40.6%	56.0%	3.4%
WOONSOCKET	783	291	455	37	McCain	37.2%	58.1%	4.7%
Machine Total	35,535	12,895	21,466	1,174	McCain	36.3%	60.4%	3.3%
Mail Ballots	585	275	288	22	McCain	47.0%	49.2%	3.8%
TOTAL	36,137	13,170	21,754	1,213	McCain	36.4%	60.2%	3.4%

Note: Other vote was 923 Alan Keyes; 114 Uncommitted; 89 Steve Forbes; 35 Gary Bauer; 35 Orrin G. Hatch; 17 write-in. Only the ballots cast by machine were readily broken down by community. Mail ballots and write-in votes were not.

RHODE ISLAND DEMOCRATIC PRIMARY

2004

County	Total Vote	Edwards	Kerry	Other	Winner	Percentage of Total Vote		
						Edwards	Kerry	Other
BRISTOL	2,229	400	1,647	182	Kerry	17.9%	73.9%	8.2%
KENT	5,409	1,150	3,844	415	Kerry	21.3%	71.1%	7.7%
NEWPORT	3,606	652	2,561	393	Kerry	18.1%	71.0%	10.9%
PROVIDENCE	18,445	3,282	13,327	1,836	Kerry	17.8%	72.3%	10.0%
WASHINGTON	4,339	969	2,909	461	Kerry	22.3%	67.0%	10.6%
Machine Total	34,028	6,453	24,288	3,287	Kerry	19.0%	71.4%	9.7%
Mail Ballots	1,570	182	1,178	210	Kerry	11.6%	75.0%	13.4%
TOTAL	35,759	6,635	25,466	3,658	Kerry	18.6%	71.2%	10.2%
City/Town								
BARRINGTON	869	149	636	84	Kerry	17.1%	73.2%	9.7%
BRISTOL	958	186	698	74	Kerry	19.4%	72.9%	7.7%
BURRILLVILLE	401	77	292	32	Kerry	19.2%	72.8%	8.0%
CENTRAL FALLS	545	67	439	39	Kerry	12.3%	80.6%	7.2%
CHARLESTOWN	259	66	163	30	Kerry	25.5%	62.9%	11.6%
COVENTRY	763	182	519	62	Kerry	23.9%	68.0%	8.1%
CRANSTON	2,015	417	1,402	196	Kerry	20.7%	69.6%	9.7%
CUMBERLAND	1,150	230	834	86	Kerry	20.0%	72.5%	7.5%
EAST GREENWICH	476	121	300	55	Kerry	25.4%	63.0%	11.6%
EAST PROVIDENCE	1,550	282	1,166	102	Kerry	18.2%	75.2%	6.6%
EXETER	172	46	115	11	Kerry	26.7%	66.9%	6.4%
FOSTER	120	29	77	14	Kerry	24.2%	64.2%	11.7%
GLOCESTER	222	41	164	17	Kerry	18.5%	73.9%	7.7%
HOPKINTON	167	30	117	20	Kerry	18.0%	70.1%	12.0%
JAMESTOWN	432	76	312	44	Kerry	17.6%	72.2%	10.2%
JOHNSTON	680	130	502	48	Kerry	19.1%	73.8%	7.1%
LINCOLN	518	109	361	48	Kerry	21.0%	69.7%	9.3%
LITTLE COMPTON	207	39	131	37	Kerry	18.8%	63.3%	17.9%
MIDDLETOWN	514	93	339	82	Kerry	18.1%	66.0%	16.0%
NARRAGANSETT	618	139	444	35	Kerry	22.5%	71.8%	5.7%
NEWPORT	1,062	190	762	110	Kerry	17.9%	71.8%	10.4%
NEW SHOREHAM	139	30	93	16	Kerry	21.6%	66.9%	11.5%
NORTH KINGSTOWN	1,033	245	673	115	Kerry	23.7%	65.2%	11.1%
NORTH PROVIDENCE	1,103	201	830	72	Kerry	18.2%	75.2%	6.5%
NORTH SMITHFIELD	301	47	238	16	Kerry	15.6%	79.1%	5.3%
PAWTUCKET	2,514	395	1,910	209	Kerry	15.7%	76.0%	8.3%
PORTSMOUTH	767	152	556	59	Kerry	19.8%	72.5%	7.7%
PROVIDENCE	5,548	941	3,780	827	Kerry	17.0%	68.1%	14.9%
RICHMOND	191	37	121	33	Kerry	19.4%	63.4%	17.3%
SCITUATE	197	50	126	21	Kerry	25.4%	64.0%	10.7%
SMITHFIELD	503	105	357	41	Kerry	20.9%	71.0%	8.2%
SOUTH KINGSTOWN	1,181	263	756	162	Kerry	22.3%	64.0%	13.7%
TIVERTON	624	102	461	61	Kerry	16.3%	73.9%	9.8%
WARREN	402	65	313	24	Kerry	16.2%	77.9%	6.0%
WARWICK	3,341	692	2,405	244	Kerry	20.7%	72.0%	7.3%

RHODE ISLAND DEMOCRATIC PRIMARY

2004

County	Total Vote	Edwards	Kerry	Other	Winner	Percentage of Total Vote		
						Edwards	Kerry	Other
WESTERLY	579	113	427	39	Kerry	19.5%	73.7%	6.7%
WEST GREENWICH	117	22	85	10	Kerry	18.8%	72.6%	8.5%
WEST WARWICK	712	133	535	44	Kerry	18.7%	75.1%	6.2%
WOONSOCKET	1,078	161	849	68	Kerry	14.9%	78.8%	6.3%
Machine Total	34,028	6,453	24,288	3,287	Kerry	19.0%	71.4%	9.7%
Mail Ballots	1,570	182	1,178	210	Kerry	11.6%	75.0%	13.4%
TOTAL	35,759	6,635	25,466	3,658	Kerry	18.6%	71.2%	10.2%

Note: Other vote was 1,425 Howard Dean; 1,054 Dennis J. Kucinich; 415 Uncommitted; 303 Joseph I. Lieberman; 237 Wesley Clark; 63 Lyndon H. LaRouche Jr.; 38 Al Sharpton (write-in); 123 scattered write-in. Only the ballots cast by machine were readily broken down by community. Mail ballots and write-in votes were not.

RHODE ISLAND REPUBLICAN PRIMARY

2004

County	Total Vote	G.W. Bush	Other	Winner	Percentage of Total Vote	
					G.W. Bush	Other
BRISTOL	234	209	25	G.W. Bush	89.3%	10.7%
KENT	335	294	41	G.W. Bush	87.8%	12.2%
NEWPORT	467	408	59	G.W. Bush	87.4%	12.6%
PROVIDENCE	786	692	94	G.W. Bush	88.0%	12.0%
WASHINGTON	412	344	68	G.W. Bush	83.5%	16.5%
Machine Total	2,234	1,947	287	G.W. Bush	87.2%	12.8%
Mail Ballots	232	205	27	G.W. Bush	88.4%	11.6%
TOTAL	2,535	2,152	383	G.W. Bush	84.9%	15.1%
City/Town						
BARRINGTON	115	100	15	G.W. Bush	87.0%	13.0%
BRISTOL	95	85	10	G.W. Bush	89.5%	10.5%
BURRILLVILLE	20	17	3	G.W. Bush	85.0%	15.0%
CENTRAL FALLS	11	9	2	G.W. Bush	81.8%	18.2%
CHARLESTOWN	42	36	6	G.W. Bush	85.7%	14.3%
COVENTRY	45	37	8	G.W. Bush	82.2%	17.8%
CRANSTON	139	119	20	G.W. Bush	85.6%	14.4%
CUMBERLAND	46	44	2	G.W. Bush	95.7%	4.3%
EAST GREENWICH	60	52	8	G.W. Bush	86.7%	13.3%
EAST PROVIDENCE	63	56	7	G.W. Bush	88.9%	11.1%
EXETER	15	14	1	G.W. Bush	93.3%	6.7%
FOSTER	15	14	1	G.W. Bush	93.3%	6.7%
GLOCESTER	18	14	4	G.W. Bush	77.8%	22.2%
HOPKINTON	25	22	3	G.W. Bush	88.0%	12.0%
JAMESTOWN	54	45	9	G.W. Bush	83.3%	16.7%

RHODE ISLAND REPUBLICAN PRIMARY

2004

County	Total Vote	G.W. Bush	Other	Winner	Percentage of Total Vote G.W. Bush	Other
JOHNSTON	17	17	0	G.W. Bush	100.0%	0.0%
LINCOLN	73	67	6	G.W. Bush	91.8%	8.2%
LITTLE COMPTON	35	32	3	G.W. Bush	91.4%	8.6%
MIDDLETOWN	81	70	11	G.W. Bush	86.4%	13.6%
NARRAGANSETT	50	42	8	G.W. Bush	84.0%	16.0%
NEWPORT	120	110	10	G.W. Bush	91.7%	8.3%
NEW SHOREHAM	10	8	2	G.W. Bush	80.0%	20.0%
NORTH KINGSTOWN	96	82	14	G.W. Bush	85.4%	14.6%
NORTH PROVIDENCE	13	12	1	G.W. Bush	92.3%	7.7%
NORTH SMITHFIELD	37	32	5	G.W. Bush	86.5%	13.5%
PAWTUCKET	86	75	11	G.W. Bush	87.2%	12.8%
PORTSMOUTH	123	105	18	G.W. Bush	85.4%	14.6%
PROVIDENCE	106	88	18	G.W. Bush	83.0%	17.0%
RICHMOND	16	12	4	G.W. Bush	75.0%	25.0%
SCITUATE	66	62	4	G.W. Bush	93.9%	6.1%
SMITHFIELD	33	28	5	G.W. Bush	84.8%	15.2%
SOUTH KINGSTOWN	55	42	13	G.W. Bush	76.4%	23.6%
TIVERTON	54	46	8	G.W. Bush	85.2%	14.8%
WARREN	24	24	0	G.W. Bush	100.0%	0.0%
WARWICK	176	157	19	G.W. Bush	89.2%	10.8%
WESTERLY	103	86	17	G.W. Bush	83.5%	16.5%
WEST GREENWICH	14	11	3	G.W. Bush	78.6%	21.4%
WEST WARWICK	40	37	3	G.W. Bush	92.5%	7.5%
WOONSOCKET	43	38	5	G.W. Bush	88.4%	11.6%
Machine Total	2,234	1,947	287	G.W. Bush	87.2%	12.8%
Mail Ballots	232	205	27	G.W. Bush	88.4%	11.6%
TOTAL	2,535	2,152	383	G.W. Bush	84.9%	15.1%

Note: Other vote was 314 Uncommitted; 69 write-in. Only the ballots cast by machine were readily broken down by community. Mail ballots and write-in votes were not.

SOUTH CAROLINA

After years of watching the quadrennial trek of Republican presidential candidates to South Carolina, the state's Democrats responded in 2004 with an early primary of their own. The vote had an impact, giving South Carolina native and North Carolina senator John Edwards his lone primary victory and helping to establish him as a solid number two to John Kerry in that year's Democratic nominating contest. But the contest was not as influential as many of those held over the years by their GOP counterparts, who had made their primary a major event in Republican presidential politics.

During the 1980s and 1990s, South Carolina was the gateway to the South for Republican candidates—a New Hampshire below the Mason-Dixon line. But in 2000, it was more than that. South Carolina was the place where George W. Bush stopped John McCain and put his badly dented candidacy back on track toward the Republican nomination.

Bush campaigned in South Carolina with a gusto he had not shown in New Hampshire, where he lost badly to McCain.

Attempting to mute McCain's reform image, the Texas governor campaigned across the Palmetto State as a "reformer with results." But his prime focus was on South Carolina's large conservative Republican base, which he successfully courted with a hard-hitting campaign.

Bush won the primary by nearly a dozen percentage points. But he won by twice that margin in Greenville County, the leading source of GOP primary votes in the state and the home of Bob Jones University, where Bush made a well-publicized visit before the primary. Meanwhile, McCain carried only eight of South Carolina's 46 counties, four of them along the Atlantic coast where there is a large number of veterans and newcomers from other parts of the country.

The state's presidential primary is a legacy of Lee Atwater, a native South Carolinian who worked the state for Ronald Reagan and then George Bush as he earned his spurs as one of the GOP's premier political strategists. Atwater encouraged South Carolina Republicans to hold a primary at least a few

Recent South Carolina Primary Results

South Carolina Republicans held their first presidential primary in 1980; South Carolina Democrats in 1992.

Year	DEMOCRATS			REPUBLICANS		
	Turnout	Candidates	%	Turnout	Candidates	%
2004 (Feb. 3)	293,843	JOHN EDWARDS	45	—	No Primary	
		John Kerry	30			
		Al Sharpton	10			
		Wesley Clark	7			
2000 (Feb. 19)	—	No Primary		573,101	GEORGE W. BUSH	53
					John McCain	42
1996 (March 2)	—	No Primary		276,741	BOB DOLE	45
					Pat Buchanan	29
					Steve Forbes	13
					Lamar Alexander	10
1992 (March 7)	116,414	BILL CLINTON	63	148,840	GEORGE BUSH*	67
		Paul Tsongas	18		Pat Buchanan	26
		Tom Harkin	7		David Duke	7
		Jerry Brown	6			
1988 (March 5)	—	No Primary		195,292	GEORGE BUSH	49
					Bob Dole	21
					Pat Robertson	19
					Jack Kemp	11
1984	—	No Primary		—	No Primary	
1980 (March 8)	—	No Primary		145,501	RONALD REAGAN	55
					John Connally	30
					George Bush	15

Note: All candidates are listed that drew at least 5 percent of their party's primary vote. The names of winning candidates are capitalized. An asterisk (*) indicates an incumbent president.

days before the early March Super Tuesday vote to dominate the news leading up to what was then a far-flung Dixie-oriented event.

The presidential primary proved an effective party-building tool for South Carolina Republicans. Before its creation, turnout for statewide GOP primaries rarely exceeded the 35,000 voters that turned out for the party's gubernatorial contest in 1974, when the featured candidate was retired general William C. Westmoreland.

But the party's first presidential primary in 1980 drew nearly 150,000 voters. The second in 1988 attracted almost 200,000, and turnout for the GOP presidential primary in 2000 surpassed 570,000. In the process, the South Carolina GOP has expanded beyond white-collar professionals and well-heeled retirees to include Christian conservatives and converts from the Democratic Party.

While the state's presidential primary has often been crucial, placing or confirming its winner on the path to nomination, it has never been particularly close. In 1980, Reagan beat runner-up John Connally by a margin of nearly 2 to 1. Connally carried only a handful of counties, including Beaufort (with the coastal resort of Hilton Head).

The elder Bush made a belated effort in the 1980 primary but finished a distant third. His leading backer in the state, former Nixon White House aide Harry Dent, sought to win votes for Bush by promoting him as "a good ol' Southern boy from Texas."

As a sitting vice president, Bush did better in 1988, sweeping every county in the state and winning almost as many votes as his rivals combined. Televangelist Pat Robertson had hoped to tap the state's large cadre of fundamentalist voters. According to exit polls, one-third of the Republican primary voters in South Carolina were born-again Christians. But Bush did nearly as well among these voters as Robertson.

In 1996, it was Dole who harnessed the momentum from victory in South Carolina, with a decisive triumph that covered all but three small counties in the northwest part of the state, which he lost to Pat Buchanan. Dole had lost three of the first five presidential primaries before the South Carolina contest in early March. After South Carolina, he was not to lose again.

The Democrats have been slower to embrace a presidential primary. Their first in 1992 was a little-noticed event, won easily by the region's native son, Bill Clinton. With South Carolina Republicans holding a competitive contest the same day, turnout for the Democratic primary barely exceeded 100,000 votes.

There was an interlude of a dozen years before Democrats held their second presidential primary, which was conducted under more favorable circumstances. The state party picked the earliest date it could–the first Tuesday in February–which made South Carolina the first truly Southern state to vote in 2004. Primary sponsors advertised the state's racial diversity–nearly 30 percent African-American according to the 2000 Census, with the percentage higher than that for the Democratic primary. And with no contest for the Republican nomination in 2004, there was no competition with the GOP for primary voters as there had been in 1992. (South Carolina is one of nearly two dozen states without party registration, giving voters a freedom of movement in terms of primary participation.)

Still, the Democratic primary in 2004 was at best a mixed success. Candidates descended on the state, as party leaders had hoped. And South Carolina voters gave a solid 15 percentage point victory to native son, John Edwards, who defeated Kerry in all but five counties. But the turnout was less than 300,000– much higher than 1992, yet barely half the number that Republicans attracted for the Bush-McCain contest in 2000.

SOUTH CAROLINA REPUBLICAN PRIMARY

2000

County	Total Vote	G.W. Bush	McCain	Other	Winner	Percentage of Total Vote		
						G.W. Bush	McCain	Other
ABBEVILLE	3,129	1,440	1,496	193	McCain	46.0%	47.8%	6.2%
AIKEN	23,701	13,188	9,281	1,232	G.W. Bush	55.6%	39.2%	5.2%
ALLENDALE	633	346	268	19	G.W. Bush	54.7%	42.3%	3.0%
ANDERSON	26,748	13,560	11,868	1,320	G.W. Bush	50.7%	44.4%	4.9%
BAMBERG	1,319	710	556	53	G.W. Bush	53.8%	42.2%	4.0%
BARNWELL	2,728	1,639	1,003	86	G.W. Bush	60.1%	36.8%	3.2%
BEAUFORT	21,212	9,329	11,276	607	McCain	44.0%	53.2%	2.9%
BERKELEY	17,059	8,747	7,719	593	G.W. Bush	51.3%	45.2%	3.5%
CALHOUN	2,119	1,345	677	97	G.W. Bush	63.5%	31.9%	4.6%
CHARLESTON	47,269	22,380	23,516	1,373	McCain	47.3%	49.7%	2.9%
CHEROKEE	5,792	3,477	2,116	199	G.W. Bush	60.0%	36.5%	3.4%
CHESTER	2,863	1,379	1,390	94	McCain	48.2%	48.6%	3.3%
CHESTERFIELD	2,788	1,469	1,231	88	G.W. Bush	52.7%	44.2%	3.2%
CLARENDON	3,327	2,050	1,163	114	G.W. Bush	61.6%	35.0%	3.4%
COLLETON	4,297	2,217	1,957	123	G.W. Bush	51.6%	45.5%	2.9%
DARLINGTON	6,892	4,216	2,456	220	G.W. Bush	61.2%	35.6%	3.2%
DILLON	2,374	1,192	1,127	55	G.W. Bush	50.2%	47.5%	2.3%
DORCHESTER	14,796	7,616	6,665	515	G.W. Bush	51.5%	45.0%	3.5%
EDGEFIELD	2,883	1,716	1,050	117	G.W. Bush	59.5%	36.4%	4.1%
FAIRFIELD	2,110	1,157	817	136	G.W. Bush	54.8%	38.7%	6.4%
FLORENCE	15,222	9,737	5,023	462	G.W. Bush	64.0%	33.0%	3.0%
GEORGETOWN	7,458	3,633	3,705	120	McCain	48.7%	49.7%	1.6%
GREENVILLE	73,281	42,846	25,553	4,882	G.W. Bush	58.5%	34.9%	6.7%
GREENWOOD	8,854	4,561	3,918	375	G.W. Bush	51.5%	44.3%	4.2%
HAMPTON	1,209	622	551	36	G.W. Bush	51.4%	45.6%	3.0%
HORRY	27,735	12,309	14,763	663	McCain	44.4%	53.2%	2.4%
JASPER	1,250	630	585	35	G.W. Bush	50.4%	46.8%	2.8%
KERSHAW	8,981	4,854	3,736	391	G.W. Bush	54.0%	41.6%	4.4%
LANCASTER	6,122	3,349	2,576	197	G.W. Bush	54.7%	42.1%	3.2%
LAURENS	8,245	4,165	3,709	371	G.W. Bush	50.5%	45.0%	4.5%
LEE	1,668	1,052	557	59	G.W. Bush	63.1%	33.4%	3.5%
LEXINGTON	45,277	25,990	16,250	3,037	G.W. Bush	57.4%	35.9%	6.7%
MCCORMICK	1,386	688	661	37	G.W. Bush	49.6%	47.7%	2.7%
MARION	2,509	1,599	858	52	G.W. Bush	63.7%	34.2%	2.1%
MARLBORO	1,413	666	715	32	McCain	47.1%	50.6%	2.3%
NEWBERRY	5,758	3,186	2,305	267	G.W. Bush	55.3%	40.0%	4.6%
OCONEE	12,262	5,066	6,697	499	McCain	41.3%	54.6%	4.1%
ORANGEBURG	9,096	5,379	3,358	359	G.W. Bush	59.1%	36.9%	3.9%
PICKENS	17,733	9,797	7,012	924	G.W. Bush	55.2%	39.5%	5.2%
RICHLAND	44,811	21,955	19,534	3,322	G.W. Bush	49.0%	43.6%	7.4%
SALUDA	3,101	1,642	1,342	117	G.W. Bush	53.0%	43.3%	3.8%
SPARTANBURG	37,159	21,736	13,334	2,089	G.W. Bush	58.5%	35.9%	5.6%
SUMTER	11,461	6,937	4,009	515	G.W. Bush	60.5%	35.0%	4.5%
UNION	3,385	1,882	1,409	94	G.W. Bush	55.6%	41.6%	2.8%
WILLIAMSBURG	2,544	1,648	840	56	G.W. Bush	64.8%	33.0%	2.2%
YORK	21,142	10,896	9,332	914	G.W. Bush	51.5%	44.1%	4.3%
TOTAL	573,101	305,998	239,964	27,139	G.W. Bush	53.4%	41.9%	4.7%

Note: Other vote was 25,996 Alan Keyes; 618 Gary Bauer; 449 Steve Forbes; 76 Orrin G. Hatch.

SOUTH CAROLINA DEMOCRATIC PRIMARY

2004

County	Total Vote	Clark	Edwards	Kerry	Sharpton	Other	Winner	Percentage of Total Vote				
								Clark	Edwards	Kerry	Sharpton	Other
ABBEVILLE	2,183	152	1,099	607	191	134	Edwards	7.0%	50.3%	27.8%	8.7%	6.1%
AIKEN	7,846	660	2,633	2,822	1,010	721	Kerry	8.4%	33.6%	36.0%	12.9%	9.2%
ALLENDALE	849	88	313	277	102	69	Edwards	10.4%	36.9%	32.6%	12.0%	8.1%
ANDERSON	9,700	566	5,416	2,539	487	692	Edwards	5.8%	55.8%	26.2%	5.0%	7.1%
BAMBERG	1,566	114	509	536	185	222	Kerry	7.3%	32.5%	34.2%	11.8%	14.2%
BARNWELL	1,361	116	591	450	113	91	Edwards	8.5%	43.4%	33.1%	8.3%	6.7%
BEAUFORT	9,644	850	2,604	3,690	1,537	963	Kerry	8.8%	27.0%	38.3%	15.9%	10.0%
BERKELEY	8,130	587	3,683	2,531	821	508	Edwards	7.2%	45.3%	31.1%	10.1%	6.2%
CALHOUN	1,319	125	571	412	135	76	Edwards	9.5%	43.3%	31.2%	10.2%	5.8%
CHARLESTON	27,251	1,968	11,212	8,497	2,916	2,658	Edwards	7.2%	41.1%	31.2%	10.7%	9.8%
CHEROKEE	2,517	217	1,367	643	143	147	Edwards	8.6%	54.3%	25.5%	5.7%	5.8%
CHESTER	2,060	111	1,047	623	169	110	Edwards	5.4%	50.8%	30.2%	8.2%	5.3%
CHESTERFIELD	3,984	255	2,514	724	205	286	Edwards	6.4%	63.1%	18.2%	5.1%	7.2%
CLARENDON	3,528	208	1,788	1,054	278	200	Edwards	5.9%	50.7%	29.9%	7.9%	5.7%
COLLETON	2,877	165	1,398	812	301	201	Edwards	5.7%	48.6%	28.2%	10.5%	7.0%
DARLINGTON	4,857	328	2,389	1,338	548	254	Edwards	6.8%	49.2%	27.5%	11.3%	5.2%
DILLON	2,113	164	1,266	453	118	112	Edwards	7.8%	59.9%	21.4%	5.6%	5.3%
DORCHESTER	6,127	427	2,889	1,746	646	419	Edwards	7.0%	47.2%	28.5%	10.5%	6.8%
EDGEFIELD	1,328	71	587	487	118	65	Edwards	5.3%	44.2%	36.7%	8.9%	4.9%
FAIRFIELD	2,766	178	1,121	1,042	272	153	Edwards	6.4%	40.5%	37.7%	9.8%	5.5%
FLORENCE	9,826	667	4,059	3,087	1,262	751	Edwards	6.8%	41.3%	31.4%	12.8%	7.6%
GEORGETOWN	5,561	332	2,509	1,636	584	500	Edwards	6.0%	45.1%	29.4%	10.5%	9.0%
GREENVILLE	25,221	1,578	11,618	6,782	2,499	2,744	Edwards	6.3%	46.1%	26.9%	9.9%	10.9%
GREENWOOD	3,482	226	1,557	1,096	341	262	Edwards	6.5%	44.7%	31.5%	9.8%	7.5%
HAMPTON	1,645	176	685	445	223	116	Edwards	10.7%	41.6%	27.1%	13.6%	7.1%
HORRY	13,140	927	6,757	3,795	712	949	Edwards	7.1%	51.4%	28.9%	5.4%	7.2%
JASPER	1,658	110	600	402	433	113	Edwards	6.6%	36.2%	24.2%	26.1%	6.8%
KERSHAW	6,102	428	2,777	1,955	377	565	Edwards	7.0%	45.5%	32.0%	6.2%	9.3%
LANCASTER	3,896	275	2,222	938	251	210	Edwards	7.1%	57.0%	24.1%	6.4%	5.4%
LAURENS	4,369	299	2,101	1,177	415	377	Edwards	6.8%	48.1%	26.9%	9.5%	8.6%
LEE	2,259	133	892	793	301	140	Edwards	5.9%	39.5%	35.1%	13.3%	6.2%
LEXINGTON	12,617	999	6,144	3,429	898	1,147	Edwards	7.9%	48.7%	27.2%	7.1%	9.1%
MCCORMICK	981	71	310	424	90	86	Kerry	7.2%	31.6%	43.2%	9.2%	8.8%
MARION	3,246	182	1,587	776	495	206	Edwards	5.6%	48.9%	23.9%	15.2%	6.3%
MARLBORO	2,410	158	1,547	386	194	125	Edwards	6.6%	64.2%	16.0%	8.0%	5.2%
NEWBERRY	2,796	231	1,425	776	191	173	Edwards	8.3%	51.0%	27.8%	6.8%	6.2%
OCONEE	5,355	257	3,685	917	107	389	Edwards	4.8%	68.8%	17.1%	2.0%	7.3%
ORANGEBURG	10,977	809	4,569	3,172	1,315	1,112	Edwards	7.4%	41.6%	28.9%	12.0%	10.1%
PICKENS	5,390	375	2,994	1,272	233	516	Edwards	7.0%	55.5%	23.6%	4.3%	9.6%
RICHLAND	35,161	3,048	13,129	11,793	4,454	2,737	Edwards	8.7%	37.3%	33.5%	12.7%	7.8%
SALUDA	1,454	83	698	464	107	102	Edwards	5.7%	48.0%	31.9%	7.4%	7.0%
SPARTANBURG	11,930	805	5,989	3,400	747	989	Edwards	6.7%	50.2%	28.5%	6.3%	8.3%
SUMTER	7,955	524	2,924	3,111	940	456	Kerry	6.6%	36.8%	39.1%	11.8%	5.7%
UNION	2,163	139	1,208	578	123	115	Edwards	6.4%	55.8%	26.7%	5.7%	5.3%
WILLIAMSBURG	4,204	357	1,702	1,441	475	229	Edwards	8.5%	40.5%	34.3%	11.3%	5.4%
YORK	8,039	679	3,975	2,292	433	660	Edwards	8.4%	49.4%	28.5%	5.4%	8.2%
TOTAL	293,843	21,218	132,660	87,620	28,495	23,850	Edwards	7.2%	45.1%	29.8%	9.7%	8.1%

Note: Other vote was 13,984 Howard Dean; 7,101 Joseph I. Lieberman; 1,344 Dennis J. Kucinich; 828 Richard A. Gephardt; 593 Carol Moseley Braun.

SOUTH DAKOTA

South Dakota is a small state, with a long presidential primary tradition that dates back to 1912. But unlike New Hampshire, it has struggled to find a niche on the primary calendar–bouncing back and forth in recent years between dates in February and June. It stayed with a spring date in both 2000 and 2004.

Candidates that have made it to South Dakota find a state that straddles two regions. On the east side of the Missouri River is the relatively sedate farm land of the agrarian Midwest; on the other side is the wide-open ranch land of the West.

Most voters live in the eastern half, which adjoins the Corn Belt territory of Iowa and Minnesota. Democrats have

Recent South Dakota Primary Results

South Dakota held its first presidential primary in 1912.

Year	DEMOCRATS			REPUBLICANS		
	Turnout	Candidates	%	Turnout	Candidates	%
2004 (June 1)	84,405	JOHN KERRY	82	—	No Primary	
		Uncommitted	6			
		Howard Dean	6			
2000 (June 6)	—	No Primary		45,279	GEORGE W. BUSH	78
					John McCain	14
					Alan Keyes	8
1996 (Feb. 27)	—	No Primary		69,170	BOB DOLE	45
					Pat Buchanan	29
					Steve Forbes	13
					Lamar Alexander	9
1992 (Feb. 25)	59,503	BOB KERREY	40	44,671	GEORGE BUSH*	69
		Tom Harkin	25		Uncommitted	31
		Bill Clinton	19			
		Paul Tsongas	10			
1988 (Feb. 23)	71,606	RICHARD GEPHARDT	44	93,405	BOB DOLE	55
		Michael Dukakis	31		Pat Robertson	20
		Al Gore	8		George Bush	19
		Paul Simon	6			
		Gary Hart	5			
		Jesse Jackson	5			
1984 (June 5)	52,561	GARY HART	51	—	No Primary	
		Walter Mondale	39			
		Jesse Jackson	5			
1980 (June 3)	68,763	EDWARD KENNEDY	49	82,905	RONALD REAGAN	82
		Jimmy Carter*	45		No Preference	6
		Uncommitted	6			
1976 (June 1)	58,671	JIMMY CARTER	41	84,077	RONALD REAGAN	51
		Morris Udall	33		Gerald Ford*	44
		"None"	13			
		Ellen McCormack	8			
1972 (June 6)	28,017	GEORGE McGOVERN	100	52,820	RICHARD NIXON*	100
1968 (June 4)	64,287	ROBERT KENNEDY	50	68,113	RICHARD NIXON	100
		Lyndon Johnson*	30			
		Eugene McCarthy	20			

Note: All candidates are listed that drew at least 5 percent of their party's primary vote. The names of winning candidates are capitalized. An asterisk (*) indicates an incumbent president.

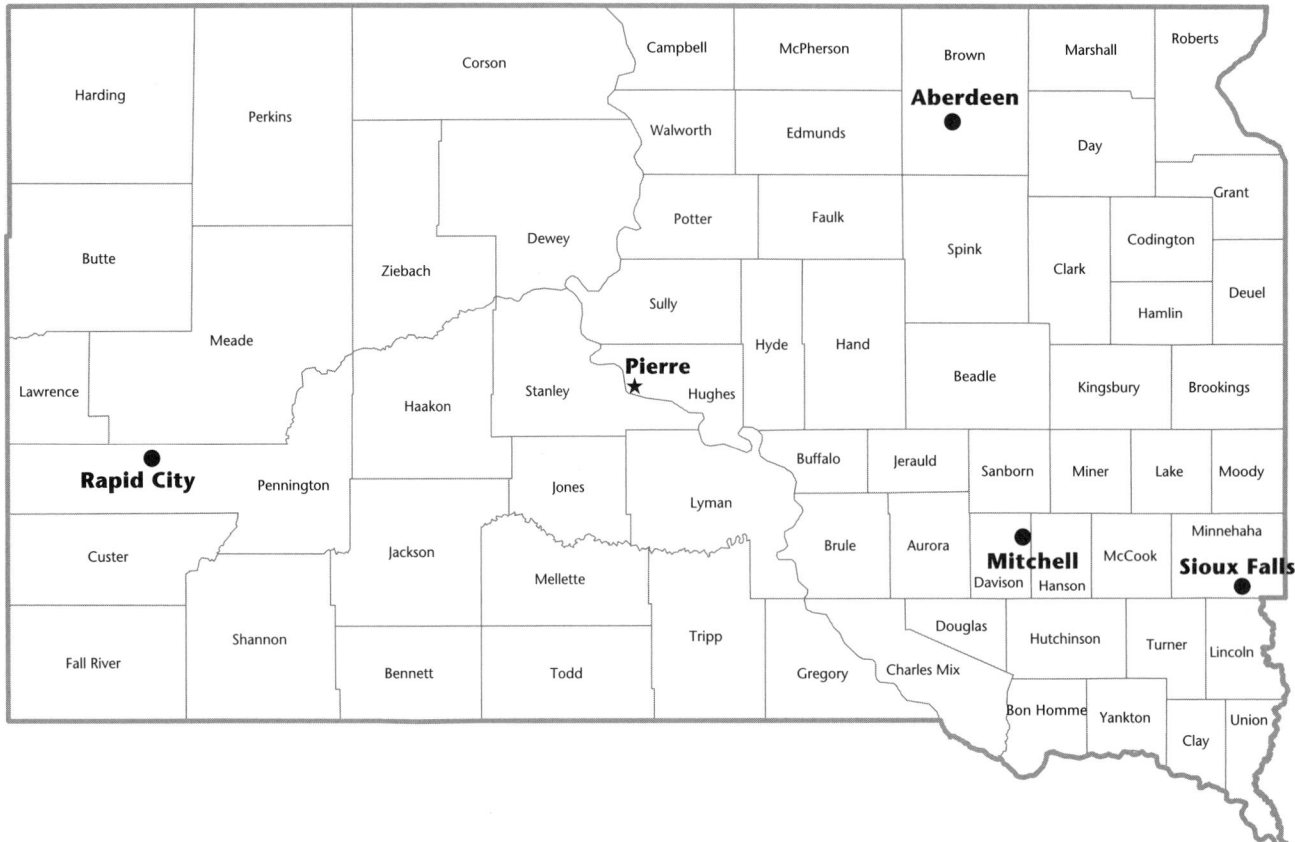

a registration advantage in roughly a dozen counties in eastern South Dakota.

The western side of the state is strongly Republican, with plenty of frontier individualists eager for government to let them alone. The Democratic presence west of the Missouri does not extend much beyond the scattered Native American reservations.

The east-west variation was illustrated in the 1976 Republican primary between President Gerald Ford and Ronald Reagan. Ford carried seven of the eight counties on the eastern border, including the state's leading population center, Minnehaha County (Sioux Falls). Reagan swept all six counties on the western border, including South Dakota's second-most populous county, Pennington (Rapid City). Reagan won the primary by also carrying nearly all the counties between Rapid City and Sioux Falls.

The effects of geography can sometimes be felt in the Democratic primary as well. South Dakota provided a farm-state showdown in 1992 between Sens. Bob Kerrey of Nebraska and Tom Harkin of Iowa. Harkin won nearly a dozen counties in the eastern part of the state. But Kerrey won the primary handily by sweeping the western half, rolling up some of his largest margins in the state's two most heavily Indian counties, Shannon and Todd, where Kerrey was the only one of the major Democratic candidates to spend much time campaigning.

Good times or bad, there has always been a strong strain of agrarian populism among South Dakota Democrats. They cast their primary ballots for Robert Kennedy in 1968 and for his brother, Edward, in 1980. But the party's presidential primary has rarely been very predictive. Before John Kerry's primary victory in 2004, it was last won by the eventual Democratic nominee in 1976, when Jimmy Carter defeated Morris Udall.

Nor has the primary always been that predictive on the Republican side. In 1988, it was the only primary that George Bush lost (or for that matter, Bob Dole won). South Dakota had never seemed to offer much of a payday for Bush, who as vice president was at a disadvantage defending the Reagan administration's farm policy. After his loss in neighboring Iowa, Bush pulled out of South Dakota to focus on New Hampshire and other, more promising, terrain.

Dole won the South Dakota primary again in 1996, in a contest that was closer but far more helpful to his nomination chances than eight years earlier. His winning percentage was down 10 points from 1988, and after sweeping every county his first try, Dole lost four counties to Pat Buchanan in 1996. But Dole's South Dakota victory, along with one the same late February day in North Dakota, stabilized his campaign after a rough start and set the stage for a whirlwind of primary victories in March.

South Dakota has held its presidential primary in early June since then, making it no more than an afterthought in the nominating process. Nonetheless, the Democratic contest in 2004 drew nearly 85,000 voters, a record turnout for a Democratic presidential primary in South Dakota. To be sure, it was not the presidential contest that drew voters–Kerry won with 82 percent of the vote–but a closely fought special congressional election that was on the South Dakota ballot the same day.

SOUTH DAKOTA REPUBLICAN PRIMARY

2000

County	Total Vote	G.W. Bush	Keyes	McCain	Other	Winner	Percentage of Total Vote			
							G.W. Bush	Keyes	McCain	Other
AURORA	165	134	12	18	1	G.W. Bush	81.2%	7.3%	10.9%	0.6%
BEADLE	659	520	38	99	2	G.W. Bush	78.9%	5.8%	15.0%	0.3%
BENNETT	258	211	16	31	0	G.W. Bush	81.8%	6.2%	12.0%	0.0%
BON HOMME	490	391	40	59	0	G.W. Bush	79.8%	8.2%	12.0%	0.0%
BROOKINGS	688	502	83	100	3	G.W. Bush	73.0%	12.1%	14.5%	0.4%
BROWN	2,276	1,842	112	320	2	G.W. Bush	80.9%	4.9%	14.1%	0.1%
BRULE	83	65	7	11	0	G.W. Bush	78.3%	8.4%	13.3%	0.0%
BUFFALO	34	22	9	3	0	G.W. Bush	64.7%	26.5%	8.8%	0.0%
BUTTE	840	640	83	114	3	G.W. Bush	76.2%	9.9%	13.6%	0.4%
CAMPBELL	136	127	4	5	0	G.W. Bush	93.4%	2.9%	3.7%	0.0%
CHARLES MIX	249	202	18	27	2	G.W. Bush	81.1%	7.2%	10.8%	0.8%
CLARK	240	193	10	33	4	G.W. Bush	80.4%	4.2%	13.8%	1.7%
CLAY	206	163	16	26	1	G.W. Bush	79.1%	7.8%	12.6%	0.5%
CODINGTON	729	579	52	94	4	G.W. Bush	79.4%	7.1%	12.9%	0.5%
CORSON	221	177	12	30	2	G.W. Bush	80.1%	5.4%	13.6%	0.9%
CUSTER	592	404	105	83	0	G.W. Bush	68.2%	17.7%	14.0%	0.0%
DAVISON	726	589	41	95	1	G.W. Bush	81.1%	5.6%	13.1%	0.1%
DAY	232	196	14	21	1	G.W. Bush	84.5%	6.0%	9.1%	0.4%
DEUEL	303	238	24	40	1	G.W. Bush	78.5%	7.9%	13.2%	0.3%
DEWEY	157	138	3	16	0	G.W. Bush	87.9%	1.9%	10.2%	0.0%
DOUGLAS	667	537	29	100	1	G.W. Bush	80.5%	4.3%	15.0%	0.1%
EDMUNDS	227	187	11	27	2	G.W. Bush	82.4%	4.8%	11.9%	0.9%
FALL RIVER	1,201	864	134	201	2	G.W. Bush	71.9%	11.2%	16.7%	0.2%
FAULK	427	343	12	69	3	G.W. Bush	80.3%	2.8%	16.2%	0.7%
GRANT	1,202	945	60	194	3	G.W. Bush	78.6%	5.0%	16.1%	0.2%
GREGORY	187	161	7	18	1	G.W. Bush	86.1%	3.7%	9.6%	0.5%
HAAKON	357	297	26	34	0	G.W. Bush	83.2%	7.3%	9.5%	0.0%
HAMLIN	386	328	19	37	2	G.W. Bush	85.0%	4.9%	9.6%	0.5%
HAND	220	185	13	21	1	G.W. Bush	84.1%	5.9%	9.5%	0.5%
HANSON	127	101	13	12	1	G.W. Bush	79.5%	10.2%	9.4%	0.8%
HARDING	206	160	27	18	1	G.W. Bush	77.7%	13.1%	8.7%	0.5%
HUGHES	3,138	2,493	157	470	18	G.W. Bush	79.4%	5.0%	15.0%	0.6%
HUTCHINSON	750	597	48	101	4	G.W. Bush	79.6%	6.4%	13.5%	0.5%
HYDE	114	89	10	15	0	G.W. Bush	78.1%	8.8%	13.2%	0.0%
JACKSON	320	261	22	37	0	G.W. Bush	81.6%	6.9%	11.6%	0.0%
JERAULD	125	102	6	17	0	G.W. Bush	81.6%	4.8%	13.6%	0.0%
JONES	375	317	23	34	1	G.W. Bush	84.5%	6.1%	9.1%	0.3%
KINGSBURY	319	230	46	37	6	G.W. Bush	72.1%	14.4%	11.6%	1.9%
LAKE	1,128	846	24	255	3	G.W. Bush	75.0%	2.1%	22.6%	0.3%
LAWRENCE	2,697	1,935	209	537	16	G.W. Bush	71.7%	7.7%	19.9%	0.6%
LINCOLN	754	604	54	96	0	G.W. Bush	80.1%	7.2%	12.7%	0.0%
LYMAN	265	220	9	35	1	G.W. Bush	83.0%	3.4%	13.2%	0.4%
MCCOOK	167	132	11	24	0	G.W. Bush	79.0%	6.6%	14.4%	0.0%
MCPHERSON	553	477	22	52	2	G.W. Bush	86.3%	4.0%	9.4%	0.4%
MARSHALL	154	133	7	14	0	G.W. Bush	86.4%	4.5%	9.1%	0.0%

SOUTH DAKOTA REPUBLICAN PRIMARY

2000

County	Total Vote	G.W. Bush	Keyes	McCain	Other	Winner	Percentage of Total Vote			
							G.W. Bush	Keyes	McCain	Other
MEADE	2,193	1,650	210	328	5	G.W. Bush	75.2%	9.6%	15.0%	0.2%
MELLETTE	230	192	18	20	0	G.W. Bush	83.5%	7.8%	8.7%	0.0%
MINER	83	62	4	17	0	G.W. Bush	74.7%	4.8%	20.5%	0.0%
MINNEHAHA	5,020	3,938	411	655	16	G.W. Bush	78.4%	8.2%	13.0%	0.3%
MOODY	110	94	11	5	0	G.W. Bush	85.5%	10.0%	4.5%	0.0%
PENNINGTON	6,002	4,605	682	703	12	G.W. Bush	76.7%	11.4%	11.7%	0.2%
PERKINS	292	221	42	29	0	G.W. Bush	75.7%	14.4%	9.9%	0.0%
POTTER	631	546	35	49	1	G.W. Bush	86.5%	5.5%	7.8%	0.2%
ROBERTS	540	439	35	64	2	G.W. Bush	81.3%	6.5%	11.9%	0.4%
SANBORN	183	143	10	29	1	G.W. Bush	78.1%	5.5%	15.8%	0.5%
SHANNON	0	0	0	0	0					
SPINK	251	189	27	34	1	G.W. Bush	75.3%	10.8%	13.5%	0.4%
STANLEY	352	280	13	56	3	G.W. Bush	79.5%	3.7%	15.9%	0.9%
SULLY	216	177	13	24	2	G.W. Bush	81.9%	6.0%	11.1%	0.9%
TODD	96	65	13	18	0	G.W. Bush	67.7%	13.5%	18.8%	0.0%
TRIPP	783	666	42	72	3	G.W. Bush	85.1%	5.4%	9.2%	0.4%
TURNER	310	254	19	35	2	G.W. Bush	81.9%	6.1%	11.3%	0.6%
UNION	440	348	31	59	2	G.W. Bush	79.1%	7.0%	13.4%	0.5%
WALWORTH	575	454	39	76	6	G.W. Bush	79.0%	6.8%	13.2%	1.0%
YANKTON	1,563	1,168	123	268	4	G.W. Bush	74.7%	7.9%	17.1%	0.3%
ZIEBACH	59	50	2	7	0	G.W. Bush	84.7%	3.4%	11.9%	0.0%
TOTAL	45,279	35,418	3,478	6,228	155	G.W. Bush	78.2%	7.7%	13.8%	0.3%

Note: Other vote was 155 James Attia. No vote reported from Shannon County.

SOUTH DAKOTA DEMOCRATIC PRIMARY

2004

County	Total Vote	Dean	Kerry	Uncommitted	Other	Winner	Percentage of Total Vote			
							Dean	Kerry	Uncommitted	Other
AURORA	582	56	418	46	62	Kerry	9.6%	71.8%	7.9%	10.7%
BEADLE	2,285	137	1,874	172	102	Kerry	6.0%	82.0%	7.5%	4.5%
BENNETT	450	32	328	34	56	Kerry	7.1%	72.9%	7.6%	12.4%
BON HOMME	792	49	638	43	62	Kerry	6.2%	80.6%	5.4%	7.8%
BROOKINGS	2,834	189	2,315	153	177	Kerry	6.7%	81.7%	5.4%	6.2%
BROWN	5,476	267	4,701	233	275	Kerry	4.9%	85.8%	4.3%	5.0%
BRULE	770	61	588	76	45	Kerry	7.9%	76.4%	9.9%	5.8%
BUFFALO	372	19	273	26	54	Kerry	5.1%	73.4%	7.0%	14.5%
BUTTE	487	38	367	46	36	Kerry	7.8%	75.4%	9.4%	7.4%
CAMPBELL	97	6	76	8	7	Kerry	6.2%	78.4%	8.2%	7.2%
CHARLES MIX	1,511	92	1,217	86	116	Kerry	6.1%	80.5%	5.7%	7.7%
CLARK	610	46	504	38	22	Kerry	7.5%	82.6%	6.2%	3.6%
CLAY	1,662	96	1,409	67	90	Kerry	5.8%	84.8%	4.0%	5.4%
CODINGTON	3,030	214	2,455	231	130	Kerry	7.1%	81.0%	7.6%	4.3%
CORSON	482	35	377	18	52	Kerry	7.3%	78.2%	3.7%	10.8%
CUSTER	609	34	476	52	47	Kerry	5.6%	78.2%	8.5%	7.7%
DAVISON	1,993	112	1,665	114	102	Kerry	5.6%	83.5%	5.7%	5.1%
DAY	1,356	85	1,125	91	55	Kerry	6.3%	83.0%	6.7%	4.1%
DEUEL	629	38	519	44	28	Kerry	6.0%	82.5%	7.0%	4.5%
DEWEY	972	50	811	45	66	Kerry	5.1%	83.4%	4.6%	6.8%
DOUGLAS	262	21	182	28	31	Kerry	8.0%	69.5%	10.7%	11.8%
EDMUNDS	574	35	460	37	42	Kerry	6.1%	80.1%	6.4%	7.3%
FALL RIVER	594	41	464	35	54	Kerry	6.9%	78.1%	5.9%	9.1%
FAULK	379	25	276	42	36	Kerry	6.6%	72.8%	11.1%	9.5%
GRANT	1,019	68	839	49	63	Kerry	6.7%	82.3%	4.8%	6.2%
GREGORY	651	38	496	56	61	Kerry	5.8%	76.2%	8.6%	9.4%
HAAKON	175	23	111	21	20	Kerry	13.1%	63.4%	12.0%	11.4%
HAMLIN	667	49	542	51	25	Kerry	7.3%	81.3%	7.6%	3.7%
HAND	605	58	436	70	41	Kerry	9.6%	72.1%	11.6%	6.8%
HANSON	396	27	321	27	21	Kerry	6.8%	81.1%	6.8%	5.3%
HARDING	83	14	60	6	3	Kerry	16.9%	72.3%	7.2%	3.6%
HUGHES	1,300	75	1,084	76	65	Kerry	5.8%	83.4%	5.8%	5.0%
HUTCHINSON	620	27	511	32	50	Kerry	4.4%	82.4%	5.2%	8.1%
HYDE	210	24	153	22	11	Kerry	11.4%	72.9%	10.5%	5.2%
JACKSON	254	11	201	13	29	Kerry	4.3%	79.1%	5.1%	11.4%
JERAULD	374	36	313	9	16	Kerry	9.6%	83.7%	2.4%	4.3%
JONES	118	14	90	5	9	Kerry	11.9%	76.3%	4.2%	7.6%
KINGSBURY	678	48	546	42	42	Kerry	7.1%	80.5%	6.2%	6.2%
LAKE	1,465	76	1,225	92	72	Kerry	5.2%	83.6%	6.3%	4.9%
LAWRENCE	1,674	98	1,353	124	99	Kerry	5.9%	80.8%	7.4%	5.9%
LINCOLN	2,847	159	2,407	173	108	Kerry	5.6%	84.5%	6.1%	3.8%
LYMAN	500	38	394	25	43	Kerry	7.6%	78.8%	5.0%	8.6%
MCCOOK	948	59	763	64	62	Kerry	6.2%	80.5%	6.8%	6.5%
MCPHERSON	187	17	145	10	15	Kerry	9.1%	77.5%	5.3%	8.0%
MARSHALL	883	51	766	30	36	Kerry	5.8%	86.7%	3.4%	4.1%

SOUTH DAKOTA DEMOCRATIC PRIMARY

2004

County	Total Vote	Dean	Kerry	Uncommitted	Other	Winner	Percentage of Total Vote			
							Dean	Kerry	Uncommitted	Other
MEADE	1,565	83	1,266	114	102	Kerry	5.3%	80.9%	7.3%	6.5%
MELLETTE	233	12	171	17	33	Kerry	5.2%	73.4%	7.3%	14.2%
MINER	473	35	376	37	25	Kerry	7.4%	79.5%	7.8%	5.3%
MINNEHAHA	17,388	788	14,899	952	749	Kerry	4.5%	85.7%	5.5%	4.3%
MOODY	937	46	766	53	72	Kerry	4.9%	81.8%	5.7%	7.7%
PENNINGTON	6,527	305	5,311	440	471	Kerry	4.7%	81.4%	6.7%	7.2%
PERKINS	257	24	195	29	9	Kerry	9.3%	75.9%	11.3%	3.5%
POTTER	330	21	264	25	20	Kerry	6.4%	80.0%	7.6%	6.1%
ROBERTS	1,454	102	1,173	84	95	Kerry	7.0%	80.7%	5.8%	6.5%
SANBORN	419	35	321	35	28	Kerry	8.4%	76.6%	8.4%	6.7%
SHANNON	1,463	53	1,170	60	180	Kerry	3.6%	80.0%	4.1%	12.3%
SPINK	1,076	65	897	53	61	Kerry	6.0%	83.4%	4.9%	5.7%
STANLEY	324	15	258	28	23	Kerry	4.6%	79.6%	8.6%	7.1%
SULLY	187	16	144	16	11	Kerry	8.6%	77.0%	8.6%	5.9%
TODD	1,225	57	968	57	143	Kerry	4.7%	79.0%	4.7%	11.7%
TRIPP	712	53	572	33	54	Kerry	7.4%	80.3%	4.6%	7.6%
TURNER	902	55	737	55	55	Kerry	6.1%	81.7%	6.1%	6.1%
UNION	1,254	72	1,061	75	46	Kerry	5.7%	84.6%	6.0%	3.7%
WALWORTH	528	47	412	34	35	Kerry	8.9%	78.0%	6.4%	6.6%
YANKTON	2,338	133	1,965	131	109	Kerry	5.7%	84.0%	5.6%	4.7%
ZIEBACH	351	33	273	15	30	Kerry	9.4%	77.8%	4.3%	8.5%
TOTAL	84,405	4,838	69,473	5,105	4,989	Kerry	5.7%	82.3%	6.0%	5.9%

Note: Other vote was 2,943 Lyndon H. LaRouche Jr.; 2,046 Dennis J. Kucinich.

TENNESSEE

Tennessee has fielded a number of presidential candidates since World War II–Republicans Howard Baker and Lamar Alexander on one side, Democrats Estes Kefauver and Al Gore on the other. But Gore was the only one to make it to Tennessee's presidential primary as an active candidate, both in 1988 and 2000.

The state did not have a primary when Kefauver ran for president in the 1950s, and Baker (in 1980) and Alexander (in 1996) both had withdrawn from the race before the Volunteer State voted.

But Gore showed what Tennessee would do for a popular native son, taking 72 percent of the 1988 Democratic primary

vote–a higher percentage than any of the other major contenders won in their home states that year. In 2000, Tennessee gave Gore, then the sitting vice president, an even higher percentage.

That year, though, Tennessee voted in March after the nominations in each party had been settled. Seeking a more influential spot on the calendar, Tennessee moved its primary forward a month in 2004 to the second Tuesday in February. The move did offer favorable terrain to the Southern candidates in the race, as John Edwards of North Carolina and Wesley Clark of Arkansas together split 50 percent of the Democratic primary vote. Still, John Kerry of Massachusetts was able to score a comfortable

Recent Tennessee Primary Results

Tennessee held its first presidential primary in 1972.

Year	DEMOCRATS Turnout	Candidates	%	REPUBLICANS Turnout	Candidates	%
2004 (Feb. 10)	369,385	JOHN KERRY John Edwards Wesley Clark	41 27 23	99,061	GEORGE W. BUSH*	95
2000 (March 14)	215,203	AL GORE Bill Bradley	92 5	250,791	GEORGE W. BUSH John McCain Alan Keyes	77 15 7
1996 (March 12)	137,797	BILL CLINTON* Uncommitted	89 11	289,386	BOB DOLE Pat Buchanan Lamar Alexander Steve Forbes	51 25 11 8
1992 (March 10)	318,482	BILL CLINTON Paul Tsongas Jerry Brown	67 19 8	245,653	GEORGE BUSH* Pat Buchanan	73 22
1988 (March 8)	576,314	AL GORE Jesse Jackson	72 21	254,252	GEORGE BUSH Bob Dole Pat Robertson	60 22 13
1984 (May 1)	322,063	WALTER MONDALE Gary Hart Jesse Jackson	41 29 25	82,921	RONALD REAGAN* Uncommitted	91 9
1980 (May 6)	294,680	JIMMY CARTER* Edward Kennedy	75 18	195,210	RONALD REAGAN George Bush	74 18
1976 (May 25)	334,078	JIMMY CARTER George Wallace	78 11	242,535	GERALD FORD* Ronald Reagan	50 49
1972 (May 4)	492,721	GEORGE WALLACE Hubert Humphrey George McGovern	68 16 7	114,489	RICHARD NIXON*	96

Note: All candidates are listed that drew at least 5 percent of their party's primary vote. The names of winning candidates are capitalized. An asterisk (*) indicates an incumbent president.

plurality victory, which combined with a one-sided primary win in Virginia the same day, added to the momentum that his front-running campaign had already generated.

Edwards did carry Gore's home county, Smith (Carthage). But it was one of only four counties in the state that Kerry did not win in the primary. The loss in Tennessee effectively ended Clark's campaign. Edwards labored on for three more weeks.

With little action on the Republican side in 2004, turnout for the Democratic primary approached 370,000, the highest in Tennessee since 1988. That year, despite Gore's dominance, Jesse Jackson was able to establish a toehold in southwest Tennessee. Jackson carried three counties, including vote-rich Shelby (Memphis), which has a population roughly 50 percent black. But Jackson had done better than that in the 1984 primary, when he ran against Walter Mondale and Gary Hart. In that earlier race, Jackson was also able to win populous Davidson (Nashville) and Hamilton (Chattanooga) counties. Running against Gore, Jackson was trampled everywhere outside the Memphis area.

One reason was that Gore's presence on the 1988 ballot nearly doubled the Democratic primary turnout from what it had been four years earlier. Fewer than 325,000 voted in 1984, while more than 575,000 did so in 1988. It was a record high for a Democratic or Republican presidential primary in Tennessee.

With the active support of then-governor Ned McWherter, a skilled political operator with strong links to the rural courthouse crowd, Gore outpolled Jackson by a margin of at least 10 to 1 in many counties. In a few rural ones around Gore's home base of Carthage in middle Tennessee, the margins approached 100 to 1.

Bill Clinton swept Tennessee's Democratic primary in 1992 with two-thirds of the vote. He boasted endorsements from much of the state party leadership, but not Gore, who was never especially close to Clinton before being tapped as his running mate in 1992. As Arkansas governor, Clinton had made no secret of his preference for Dukakis over Gore in the 1988 primaries.

The classic Republican presidential primary in Tennessee took place in 1976 between President Gerald Ford and Ronald Reagan, which pitted the two major power centers of Tennessee Republicanism against each other. Reagan swept the western half of the state, anchored by the burgeoning conservative suburbs around Memphis. Ford swept nearly all of the eastern half of the state, anchored by mountain counties that had been a bastion of racially moderate Republicanism since the Civil War. Nearly a quarter-million votes were cast and Ford won by less than 2,000.

GOP contests since then have been much more one-sided. Reagan beat George Bush in all of Tennessee's 95 counties in 1980. Bush came back to win all 95 in 1988. Bush's dominance was a bit surprising in that former senator William Brock, originally from the Chattanooga area, was the national chairman of Bob Dole's campaign.

Bush easily won the Tennessee primary again in 1992, even though Pat Buchanan sought to identify with the local economy by campaigning in a Saturn, a Tennessee-built car. Buchanan did not peak in Tennessee until his second try, when he took 25 percent of the GOP primary vote. But that was still less than half of the winning share in 1996 for Dole, who also ran better in Tennessee on his second try.

TENNESSEE DEMOCRATIC PRIMARY

2000

County	Total Vote	Bradley	Gore	Other	Winner	Percentage of Total Vote		
						Bradley	Gore	Other
ANDERSON	3,093	168	2,863	62	Gore	5.4%	92.6%	2.0%
BEDFORD	4,762	571	3,769	422	Gore	12.0%	79.1%	8.9%
BENTON	1,527	72	1,409	46	Gore	4.7%	92.3%	3.0%
BLEDSOE	479	17	454	8	Gore	3.5%	94.8%	1.7%
BLOUNT	2,325	113	2,174	38	Gore	4.9%	93.5%	1.6%
BRADLEY	1,621	101	1,480	40	Gore	6.2%	91.3%	2.5%
CAMPBELL	1,182	40	1,127	15	Gore	3.4%	95.3%	1.3%
CANNON	837	22	801	14	Gore	2.6%	95.7%	1.7%
CARROLL	1,028	26	991	11	Gore	2.5%	96.4%	1.1%
CARTER	627	24	589	14	Gore	3.8%	93.9%	2.2%
CHEATHAM	1,155	42	1,100	13	Gore	3.6%	95.2%	1.1%
CHESTER	450	12	437	1	Gore	2.7%	97.1%	0.2%
CLAIBORNE	532	32	493	7	Gore	6.0%	92.7%	1.3%
CLAY	403	7	389	7	Gore	1.7%	96.5%	1.7%
COCKE	355	17	328	10	Gore	4.8%	92.4%	2.8%
COFFEE	2,330	114	2,168	48	Gore	4.9%	93.0%	2.1%
CROCKETT	480	17	458	5	Gore	3.5%	95.4%	1.0%
CUMBERLAND	1,813	102	1,666	45	Gore	5.6%	91.9%	2.5%
DAVIDSON	25,793	1,093	24,421	279	Gore	4.2%	94.7%	1.1%
DECATUR	583	16	565	2	Gore	2.7%	96.9%	0.3%
DE KALB	1,826	137	1,621	68	Gore	7.5%	88.8%	3.7%
DICKSON	1,672	45	1,600	27	Gore	2.7%	95.7%	1.6%
DYER	936	48	871	17	Gore	5.1%	93.1%	1.8%
FAYETTE	807	24	773	10	Gore	3.0%	95.8%	1.2%
FENTRESS	428	12	410	6	Gore	2.8%	95.8%	1.4%
FRANKLIN	3,048	304	2,604	140	Gore	10.0%	85.4%	4.6%
GIBSON	2,100	80	1,975	45	Gore	3.8%	94.0%	2.1%
GILES	1,032	32	990	10	Gore	3.1%	95.9%	1.0%
GRAINGER	458	17	435	6	Gore	3.7%	95.0%	1.3%
GREENE	2,200	122	2,012	66	Gore	5.5%	91.5%	3.0%
GRUNDY	2,470	213	1,969	288	Gore	8.6%	79.7%	11.7%
HAMBLEN	953	54	881	18	Gore	5.7%	92.4%	1.9%
HAMILTON	15,333	820	13,988	525	Gore	5.3%	91.2%	3.4%
HANCOCK	114	2	112	0	Gore	1.8%	98.2%	0.0%
HARDEMAN	1,096	63	999	34	Gore	5.7%	91.1%	3.1%
HARDIN	699	9	683	7	Gore	1.3%	97.7%	1.0%
HAWKINS	1,326	62	1,239	25	Gore	4.7%	93.4%	1.9%
HAYWOOD	728	24	694	10	Gore	3.3%	95.3%	1.4%
HENDERSON	350	10	340	0	Gore	2.9%	97.1%	0.0%
HENRY	1,471	56	1,371	44	Gore	3.8%	93.2%	3.0%
HICKMAN	1,171	39	1,113	19	Gore	3.3%	95.0%	1.6%
HOUSTON	484	23	456	5	Gore	4.8%	94.2%	1.0%
HUMPHREYS	1,139	34	1,084	21	Gore	3.0%	95.2%	1.8%
JACKSON	1,283	50	1,203	30	Gore	3.9%	93.8%	2.3%
JEFFERSON	732	22	696	14	Gore	3.0%	95.1%	1.9%
JOHNSON	336	15	314	7	Gore	4.5%	93.5%	2.1%
KNOX	12,863	756	11,865	242	Gore	5.9%	92.2%	1.9%
LAKE	228	13	212	3	Gore	5.7%	93.0%	1.3%
LAUDERDALE	636	24	598	14	Gore	3.8%	94.0%	2.2%
LAWRENCE	3,144	372	2,628	144	Gore	11.8%	83.6%	4.6%

TENNESSEE DEMOCRATIC PRIMARY

2000

County	Total Vote	Bradley	Gore	Other	Winner	Percentage of Total Vote		
						Bradley	Gore	Other
LEWIS	543	18	521	4	Gore	3.3%	95.9%	0.7%
LINCOLN	927	43	866	18	Gore	4.6%	93.4%	1.9%
LOUDON	820	40	775	5	Gore	4.9%	94.5%	0.6%
MCMINN	1,326	66	1,228	32	Gore	5.0%	92.6%	2.4%
MCNAIRY	678	19	656	3	Gore	2.8%	96.8%	0.4%
MACON	669	18	640	11	Gore	2.7%	95.7%	1.6%
MADISON	2,501	69	2,412	20	Gore	2.8%	96.4%	0.8%
MARION	2,160	160	1,870	130	Gore	7.4%	86.6%	6.0%
MARSHALL	731	27	697	7	Gore	3.7%	95.3%	1.0%
MAURY	1,882	75	1,776	31	Gore	4.0%	94.4%	1.6%
MEIGS	353	18	331	4	Gore	5.1%	93.8%	1.1%
MONROE	963	28	921	14	Gore	2.9%	95.6%	1.5%
MONTGOMERY	8,195	552	7,440	203	Gore	6.7%	90.8%	2.5%
MOORE	243	8	231	4	Gore	3.3%	95.1%	1.6%
MORGAN	611	14	589	8	Gore	2.3%	96.4%	1.3%
OBION	1,982	141	1,732	109	Gore	7.1%	87.4%	5.5%
OVERTON	2,255	101	2,055	99	Gore	4.5%	91.1%	4.4%
PERRY	717	48	627	42	Gore	6.7%	87.4%	5.9%
PICKETT	195	1	192	2	Gore	0.5%	98.5%	1.0%
POLK	1,941	209	1,561	171	Gore	10.8%	80.4%	8.8%
PUTNAM	6,416	766	5,232	418	Gore	11.9%	81.5%	6.5%
RHEA	870	48	793	29	Gore	5.5%	91.1%	3.3%
ROANE	1,768	78	1,663	27	Gore	4.4%	94.1%	1.5%
ROBERTSON	2,077	87	1,946	44	Gore	4.2%	93.7%	2.1%
RUTHERFORD	5,920	252	5,513	155	Gore	4.3%	93.1%	2.6%
SCOTT	417	12	393	12	Gore	2.9%	94.2%	2.9%
SEQUATCHIE	400	28	363	9	Gore	7.0%	90.8%	2.3%
SEVIER	1,178	65	1,093	20	Gore	5.5%	92.8%	1.7%
SHELBY	25,782	950	24,530	302	Gore	3.7%	95.1%	1.2%
SMITH	2,844	120	2,668	56	Gore	4.2%	93.8%	2.0%
STEWART	773	31	729	13	Gore	4.0%	94.3%	1.7%
SULLIVAN	2,420	138	2,226	56	Gore	5.7%	92.0%	2.3%
SUMNER	4,225	114	4,069	42	Gore	2.7%	96.3%	1.0%
TIPTON	976	42	916	18	Gore	4.3%	93.9%	1.8%
TROUSDALE	439	14	423	2	Gore	3.2%	96.4%	0.5%
UNICOI	229	9	210	10	Gore	3.9%	91.7%	4.4%
UNION	422	16	404	2	Gore	3.8%	95.7%	0.5%
VAN BUREN	456	13	436	7	Gore	2.9%	95.6%	1.5%
WARREN	2,939	132	2,742	65	Gore	4.5%	93.3%	2.2%
WASHINGTON	1,648	79	1,540	29	Gore	4.8%	93.4%	1.8%
WAYNE	301	3	295	3	Gore	1.0%	98.0%	1.0%
WEAKLEY	1,770	119	1,548	103	Gore	6.7%	87.5%	5.8%
WHITE	2,776	255	2,240	281	Gore	9.2%	80.7%	10.1%
WILLIAMSON	2,311	98	2,193	20	Gore	4.2%	94.9%	0.9%
WILSON	3,716	111	3,561	44	Gore	3.0%	95.8%	1.2%
TOTAL	215,203	11,323	198,264	5,616	Gore	5.3%	92.1%	2.6%

Note: Other vote was 4,407 Uncommitted; 1,031 Lyndon H. LaRouche Jr.; 178 write-in.

TENNESSEE REPUBLICAN PRIMARY

2000

County	Total Vote	G.W. Bush	Keyes	McCain	Other	Winner	G.W. Bush	Keyes	McCain	Other
							Percentage of Total Vote			
ANDERSON	3,256	2,426	286	512	32	G.W. Bush	74.5%	8.8%	15.7%	1.0%
BEDFORD	505	369	44	78	14	G.W. Bush	73.1%	8.7%	15.4%	2.8%
BENTON	632	466	38	119	9	G.W. Bush	73.7%	6.0%	18.8%	1.4%
BLEDSOE	537	462	30	35	10	G.W. Bush	86.0%	5.6%	6.5%	1.9%
BLOUNT	9,051	6,911	518	1,412	210	G.W. Bush	76.4%	5.7%	15.6%	2.3%
BRADLEY	4,618	3,533	315	715	55	G.W. Bush	76.5%	6.8%	15.5%	1.2%
CAMPBELL	1,185	970	49	137	29	G.W. Bush	81.9%	4.1%	11.6%	2.4%
CANNON	330	246	25	56	3	G.W. Bush	74.5%	7.6%	17.0%	0.9%
CARROLL	891	739	34	108	10	G.W. Bush	82.9%	3.8%	12.1%	1.1%
CARTER	3,132	2,323	198	537	74	G.W. Bush	74.2%	6.3%	17.1%	2.4%
CHEATHAM	1,115	802	145	154	14	G.W. Bush	71.9%	13.0%	13.8%	1.3%
CHESTER	490	436	6	37	11	G.W. Bush	89.0%	1.2%	7.6%	2.2%
CLAIBORNE	861	740	36	70	15	G.W. Bush	85.9%	4.2%	8.1%	1.7%
CLAY	200	163	6	22	9	G.W. Bush	81.5%	3.0%	11.0%	4.5%
COCKE	2,176	1,749	51	304	72	G.W. Bush	80.4%	2.3%	14.0%	3.3%
COFFEE	1,647	1,112	116	402	17	G.W. Bush	67.5%	7.0%	24.4%	1.0%
CROCKETT	370	325	12	27	6	G.W. Bush	87.8%	3.2%	7.3%	1.6%
CUMBERLAND	3,013	2,335	114	507	57	G.W. Bush	77.5%	3.8%	16.8%	1.9%
DAVIDSON	15,582	11,187	1,897	2,289	209	G.W. Bush	71.8%	12.2%	14.7%	1.3%
DECATUR	348	313	14	20	1	G.W. Bush	89.9%	4.0%	5.7%	0.3%
DE KALB	331	256	30	43	2	G.W. Bush	77.3%	9.1%	13.0%	0.6%
DICKSON	1,167	845	126	178	18	G.W. Bush	72.4%	10.8%	15.3%	1.5%
DYER	954	784	49	112	9	G.W. Bush	82.2%	5.1%	11.7%	0.9%
FAYETTE	954	779	58	96	21	G.W. Bush	81.7%	6.1%	10.1%	2.2%
FENTRESS	490	416	20	47	7	G.W. Bush	84.9%	4.1%	9.6%	1.4%
FRANKLIN	819	594	46	159	20	G.W. Bush	72.5%	5.6%	19.4%	2.4%
GIBSON	1,216	1,045	48	108	15	G.W. Bush	85.9%	3.9%	8.9%	1.2%
GILES	644	517	46	75	6	G.W. Bush	80.3%	7.1%	11.6%	0.9%
GRAINGER	1,670	1,439	37	160	34	G.W. Bush	86.2%	2.2%	9.6%	2.0%
GREENE	4,886	3,836	281	660	109	G.W. Bush	78.5%	5.8%	13.5%	2.2%
GRUNDY	125	101	7	14	3	G.W. Bush	80.8%	5.6%	11.2%	2.4%
HAMBLEN	4,832	3,765	186	743	138	G.W. Bush	77.9%	3.8%	15.4%	2.9%
HAMILTON	30,015	23,702	1,838	4,095	380	G.W. Bush	79.0%	6.1%	13.6%	1.3%
HANCOCK	378	333	10	30	5	G.W. Bush	88.1%	2.6%	7.9%	1.3%
HARDEMAN	919	754	33	116	16	G.W. Bush	82.0%	3.6%	12.6%	1.7%
HARDIN	749	636	37	72	4	G.W. Bush	84.9%	4.9%	9.6%	0.5%
HAWKINS	3,310	2,623	116	515	56	G.W. Bush	79.2%	3.5%	15.6%	1.7%
HAYWOOD	415	359	17	35	4	G.W. Bush	86.5%	4.1%	8.4%	1.0%
HENDERSON	980	825	21	114	20	G.W. Bush	84.2%	2.1%	11.6%	2.0%
HENRY	788	589	37	152	10	G.W. Bush	74.7%	4.7%	19.3%	1.3%
HICKMAN	554	393	43	113	5	G.W. Bush	70.9%	7.8%	20.4%	0.9%
HOUSTON	211	140	21	49	1	G.W. Bush	66.4%	10.0%	23.2%	0.5%
HUMPHREYS	543	402	42	95	4	G.W. Bush	74.0%	7.7%	17.5%	0.7%
JACKSON	363	285	8	62	8	G.W. Bush	78.5%	2.2%	17.1%	2.2%
JEFFERSON	2,863	2,307	136	345	75	G.W. Bush	80.6%	4.8%	12.1%	2.6%
JOHNSON	960	774	38	134	14	G.W. Bush	80.6%	4.0%	14.0%	1.5%
KNOX	26,124	19,956	1,824	3,805	539	G.W. Bush	76.4%	7.0%	14.6%	2.1%
LAKE	126	111	8	6	1	G.W. Bush	88.1%	6.3%	4.8%	0.8%
LAUDERDALE	418	333	30	51	4	G.W. Bush	79.7%	7.2%	12.2%	1.0%
LAWRENCE	689	568	35	76	10	G.W. Bush	82.4%	5.1%	11.0%	1.5%

TENNESSEE REPUBLICAN PRIMARY

2000

County	Total Vote	G.W. Bush	Keyes	McCain	Other	Winner	Percentage of Total Vote			
							G.W. Bush	Keyes	McCain	Other
LEWIS	350	235	35	72	8	G.W. Bush	67.1%	10.0%	20.6%	2.3%
LINCOLN	786	608	63	108	7	G.W. Bush	77.4%	8.0%	13.7%	0.9%
LOUDON	2,276	1,879	107	255	35	G.W. Bush	82.6%	4.7%	11.2%	1.5%
MCMINN	3,020	2,409	185	374	52	G.W. Bush	79.8%	6.1%	12.4%	1.7%
MCNAIRY	702	602	30	63	7	G.W. Bush	85.8%	4.3%	9.0%	1.0%
MACON	767	612	30	112	13	G.W. Bush	79.8%	3.9%	14.6%	1.7%
MADISON	2,963	2,388	149	394	32	G.W. Bush	80.6%	5.0%	13.3%	1.1%
MARION	1,017	824	48	122	23	G.W. Bush	81.0%	4.7%	12.0%	2.3%
MARSHALL	491	353	40	89	9	G.W. Bush	71.9%	8.1%	18.1%	1.8%
MAURY	1,994	1,490	140	353	11	G.W. Bush	74.7%	7.0%	17.7%	0.6%
MEIGS	492	393	18	70	11	G.W. Bush	79.9%	3.7%	14.2%	2.2%
MONROE	2,572	2,142	101	251	78	G.W. Bush	83.3%	3.9%	9.8%	3.0%
MONTGOMERY	8,466	5,612	439	2,252	163	G.W. Bush	66.3%	5.2%	26.6%	1.9%
MOORE	189	151	6	27	5	G.W. Bush	79.9%	3.2%	14.3%	2.6%
MORGAN	562	405	31	53	73	G.W. Bush	72.1%	5.5%	9.4%	13.0%
OBION	1,231	1,032	62	122	15	G.W. Bush	83.8%	5.0%	9.9%	1.2%
OVERTON	454	369	19	51	15	G.W. Bush	81.3%	4.2%	11.2%	3.3%
PERRY	135	98	11	25	1	G.W. Bush	72.6%	8.1%	18.5%	0.7%
PICKETT	860	704	24	92	40	G.W. Bush	81.9%	2.8%	10.7%	4.7%
POLK	446	382	21	36	7	G.W. Bush	85.7%	4.7%	8.1%	1.6%
PUTNAM	1,575	1,168	120	272	15	G.W. Bush	74.2%	7.6%	17.3%	1.0%
RHEA	1,314	1,032	92	175	15	G.W. Bush	78.5%	7.0%	13.3%	1.1%
ROANE	2,346	1,809	176	319	42	G.W. Bush	77.1%	7.5%	13.6%	1.8%
ROBERTSON	1,585	1,175	171	223	16	G.W. Bush	74.1%	10.8%	14.1%	1.0%
RUTHERFORD	6,155	4,281	687	1,083	104	G.W. Bush	69.6%	11.2%	17.6%	1.7%
SCOTT	540	441	29	63	7	G.W. Bush	81.7%	5.4%	11.7%	1.3%
SEQUATCHIE	442	327	26	78	11	G.W. Bush	74.0%	5.9%	17.6%	2.5%
SEVIER	4,131	3,329	233	485	84	G.W. Bush	80.6%	5.6%	11.7%	2.0%
SHELBY	28,735	23,180	1,534	3,598	423	G.W. Bush	80.7%	5.3%	12.5%	1.5%
SMITH	929	719	51	142	17	G.W. Bush	77.4%	5.5%	15.3%	1.8%
STEWART	437	273	26	129	9	G.W. Bush	62.5%	5.9%	29.5%	2.1%
SULLIVAN	5,477	4,171	496	747	63	G.W. Bush	76.2%	9.1%	13.6%	1.2%
SUMNER	5,207	3,903	558	673	73	G.W. Bush	75.0%	10.7%	12.9%	1.4%
TIPTON	1,517	1,222	93	179	23	G.W. Bush	80.6%	6.1%	11.8%	1.5%
TROUSDALE	187	132	21	29	5	G.W. Bush	70.6%	11.2%	15.5%	2.7%
UNICOI	1,680	1,200	65	353	62	G.W. Bush	71.4%	3.9%	21.0%	3.7%
UNION	637	550	28	53	6	G.W. Bush	86.3%	4.4%	8.3%	0.9%
VAN BUREN	221	182	5	29	5	G.W. Bush	82.4%	2.3%	13.1%	2.3%
WARREN	1,313	1,020	79	192	22	G.W. Bush	77.7%	6.0%	14.6%	1.7%
WASHINGTON	6,682	4,799	406	1,336	141	G.W. Bush	71.8%	6.1%	20.0%	2.1%
WAYNE	412	344	31	28	9	G.W. Bush	83.5%	7.5%	6.8%	2.2%
WEAKLEY	968	827	45	93	3	G.W. Bush	85.4%	4.6%	9.6%	0.3%
WHITE	423	308	52	54	9	G.W. Bush	72.8%	12.3%	12.8%	2.1%
WILLIAMSON	6,349	4,640	715	919	75	G.W. Bush	73.1%	11.3%	14.5%	1.2%
WILSON	3,324	2,372	456	462	34	G.W. Bush	71.4%	13.7%	13.9%	1.0%
TOTAL	250,791	193,166	16,916	36,436	4,273	G.W. Bush	77.0%	6.7%	14.5%	1.7%

Note: Other vote was 1,623 Uncommitted; 1,305 Gary Bauer; 1,018 Steve Forbes; 252 Orrin G. Hatch; 75 write-in.

TENNESSEE DEMOCRATIC PRIMARY

2004

County	Total Vote	Clark	Edwards	Kerry	Other	Winner	Percentage of Total Vote			
							Clark	Edwards	Kerry	Other
ANDERSON	5,430	1,375	1,528	2,092	435	Kerry	25.3%	28.1%	38.5%	8.0%
BEDFORD	2,483	699	768	845	171	Kerry	28.2%	30.9%	34.0%	6.9%
BENTON	3,249	851	857	1,112	429	Kerry	26.2%	26.4%	34.2%	13.2%
BLEDSOE	781	162	165	414	40	Kerry	20.7%	21.1%	53.0%	5.1%
BLOUNT	5,021	1,239	1,304	2,163	315	Kerry	24.7%	26.0%	43.1%	6.3%
BRADLEY	2,816	684	736	1,189	207	Kerry	24.3%	26.1%	42.2%	7.4%
CAMPBELL	1,821	390	530	813	88	Kerry	21.4%	29.1%	44.6%	4.8%
CANNON	1,249	239	462	472	76	Kerry	19.1%	37.0%	37.8%	6.1%
CARROLL	1,777	273	569	789	146	Kerry	15.4%	32.0%	44.4%	8.2%
CARTER	2,626	186	1,030	1,199	211	Kerry	7.1%	39.2%	45.7%	8.0%
CHEATHAM	2,505	669	780	872	184	Kerry	26.7%	31.1%	34.8%	7.3%
CHESTER	594	98	190	261	45	Kerry	16.5%	32.0%	43.9%	7.6%
CLAIBORNE	1,182	196	414	490	82	Kerry	16.6%	35.0%	41.5%	6.9%
CLAY	505	105	167	205	28	Kerry	20.8%	33.1%	40.6%	5.5%
COCKE	2,108	449	583	923	153	Kerry	21.3%	27.7%	43.8%	7.3%
COFFEE	5,327	1,311	1,591	1,836	589	Kerry	24.6%	29.9%	34.5%	11.1%
CROCKETT	1,469	299	542	450	178	Edwards	20.4%	36.9%	30.6%	12.1%
CUMBERLAND	4,468	856	1,260	1,821	531	Kerry	19.2%	28.2%	40.8%	11.9%
DAVIDSON	52,888	12,358	13,665	20,269	6,596	Kerry	23.4%	25.8%	38.3%	12.5%
DECATUR	910	168	306	404	32	Kerry	18.5%	33.6%	44.4%	3.5%
DE KALB	2,165	412	768	762	223	Edwards	19.0%	35.5%	35.2%	10.3%
DICKSON	3,462	893	1,011	1,343	215	Kerry	25.8%	29.2%	38.8%	6.2%
DYER	1,516	355	413	627	121	Kerry	23.4%	27.2%	41.4%	8.0%
FAYETTE	1,335	286	237	714	98	Kerry	21.4%	17.8%	53.5%	7.3%
FENTRESS	748	187	207	296	58	Kerry	25.0%	27.7%	39.6%	7.8%
FRANKLIN	4,216	870	1,269	1,640	437	Kerry	20.6%	30.1%	38.9%	10.4%
GIBSON	3,070	593	1,014	1,251	212	Kerry	19.3%	33.0%	40.7%	6.9%
GILES	1,648	413	457	667	111	Kerry	25.1%	27.7%	40.5%	6.7%
GRAINGER	1,172	236	391	479	66	Kerry	20.1%	33.4%	40.9%	5.6%
GREENE	3,656	393	1,382	1,570	311	Kerry	10.7%	37.8%	42.9%	8.5%
GRUNDY	1,874	370	460	845	199	Kerry	19.7%	24.5%	45.1%	10.6%
HAMBLEN	2,563	514	853	1,009	187	Kerry	20.1%	33.3%	39.4%	7.3%
HAMILTON	20,075	5,661	3,885	8,704	1,825	Kerry	28.2%	19.4%	43.4%	9.1%
HANCOCK	191	25	54	95	17	Kerry	13.1%	28.3%	49.7%	8.9%
HARDEMAN	1,500	365	353	638	144	Kerry	24.3%	23.5%	42.5%	9.6%
HARDIN	1,276	183	472	554	67	Kerry	14.3%	37.0%	43.4%	5.3%
HAWKINS	2,302	209	834	1,131	128	Kerry	9.1%	36.2%	49.1%	5.6%
HAYWOOD	1,078	249	206	557	66	Kerry	23.1%	19.1%	51.7%	6.1%
HENDERSON	677	92	231	307	47	Kerry	13.6%	34.1%	45.3%	6.9%
HENRY	2,395	524	721	980	170	Kerry	21.9%	30.1%	40.9%	7.1%
HICKMAN	1,667	439	510	611	107	Kerry	26.3%	30.6%	36.7%	6.4%
HOUSTON	815	180	286	308	41	Kerry	22.1%	35.1%	37.8%	5.0%
HUMPHREYS	1,889	503	496	787	103	Kerry	26.6%	26.3%	41.7%	5.5%
JACKSON	1,065	208	356	440	61	Kerry	19.5%	33.4%	41.3%	5.7%
JEFFERSON	2,165	468	664	891	142	Kerry	21.6%	30.7%	41.2%	6.6%
JOHNSON	550	44	213	247	46	Kerry	8.0%	38.7%	44.9%	8.4%
KNOX	23,718	6,592	5,816	9,100	2,210	Kerry	27.8%	24.5%	38.4%	9.3%
LAKE	299	45	68	155	31	Kerry	15.1%	22.7%	51.8%	10.4%
LAUDERDALE	1,168	285	282	485	116	Kerry	24.4%	24.1%	41.5%	9.9%
LAWRENCE	3,103	603	1,023	1,249	228	Kerry	19.4%	33.0%	40.3%	7.3%

TENNESSEE DEMOCRATIC PRIMARY

2004

County	Total Vote	Clark	Edwards	Kerry	Other	Winner	Percentage of Total Vote			
							Clark	Edwards	Kerry	Other
LEWIS	876	205	240	315	116	Kerry	23.4%	27.4%	36.0%	13.2%
LINCOLN	1,644	213	472	823	136	Kerry	13.0%	28.7%	50.1%	8.3%
LOUDON	1,991	514	530	824	123	Kerry	25.8%	26.6%	41.4%	6.2%
MCMINN	2,200	497	581	995	127	Kerry	22.6%	26.4%	45.2%	5.8%
MCNAIRY	1,428	214	510	626	78	Kerry	15.0%	35.7%	43.8%	5.5%
MACON	646	172	218	222	34	Kerry	26.6%	33.7%	34.4%	5.3%
MADISON	4,333	847	1,373	1,694	419	Kerry	19.5%	31.7%	39.1%	9.7%
MARION	4,304	1,074	1,030	1,620	580	Kerry	25.0%	23.9%	37.6%	13.5%
MARSHALL	1,536	365	496	584	91	Kerry	23.8%	32.3%	38.0%	5.9%
MAURY	3,628	833	1,045	1,498	252	Kerry	23.0%	28.8%	41.3%	6.9%
MEIGS	636	164	128	314	30	Kerry	25.8%	20.1%	49.4%	4.7%
MONROE	1,850	393	500	839	118	Kerry	21.2%	27.0%	45.4%	6.4%
MONTGOMERY	6,446	2,055	1,478	2,372	541	Kerry	31.9%	22.9%	36.8%	8.4%
MOORE	383	93	129	134	27	Kerry	24.3%	33.7%	35.0%	7.0%
MORGAN	1,157	243	334	505	75	Kerry	21.0%	28.9%	43.6%	6.5%
OBION	1,716	224	552	785	155	Kerry	13.1%	32.2%	45.7%	9.0%
OVERTON	3,133	706	994	1,163	270	Kerry	22.5%	31.7%	37.1%	8.6%
PERRY	676	136	244	251	45	Kerry	20.1%	36.1%	37.1%	6.7%
PICKETT	354	65	132	145	12	Kerry	18.4%	37.3%	41.0%	3.4%
POLK	2,539	536	656	981	366	Kerry	21.1%	25.8%	38.6%	14.4%
PUTNAM	6,513	1,576	2,162	2,064	711	Edwards	24.2%	33.2%	31.7%	10.9%
RHEA	1,636	379	430	716	111	Kerry	23.2%	26.3%	43.8%	6.8%
ROANE	3,532	909	1,026	1,367	230	Kerry	25.7%	29.0%	38.7%	6.5%
ROBERTSON	3,492	939	1,109	1,226	218	Kerry	26.9%	31.8%	35.1%	6.2%
RUTHERFORD	12,381	3,018	3,703	4,356	1,304	Kerry	24.4%	29.9%	35.2%	10.5%
SCOTT	737	180	190	314	53	Kerry	24.4%	25.8%	42.6%	7.2%
SEQUATCHIE	709	193	187	297	32	Kerry	27.2%	26.4%	41.9%	4.5%
SEVIER	2,949	642	880	1,220	207	Kerry	21.8%	29.8%	41.4%	7.0%
SHELBY	51,665	12,954	7,037	25,913	5,761	Kerry	25.1%	13.6%	50.2%	11.2%
SMITH	1,363	343	474	455	91	Edwards	25.2%	34.8%	33.4%	6.7%
STEWART	1,302	303	412	514	73	Kerry	23.3%	31.6%	39.5%	5.6%
SULLIVAN	6,515	479	2,739	2,890	407	Kerry	7.4%	42.0%	44.4%	6.2%
SUMNER	7,332	1,735	2,379	2,786	432	Kerry	23.7%	32.4%	38.0%	5.9%
TIPTON	2,001	448	491	884	178	Kerry	22.4%	24.5%	44.2%	8.9%
TROUSDALE	570	171	172	186	41	Kerry	30.0%	30.2%	32.6%	7.2%
UNICOI	667	53	237	310	67	Kerry	7.9%	35.5%	46.5%	10.0%
UNION	838	204	239	340	55	Kerry	24.3%	28.5%	40.6%	6.6%
VAN BUREN	800	206	219	324	51	Kerry	25.8%	27.4%	40.5%	6.4%
WARREN	4,376	1,253	1,335	1,429	359	Kerry	28.6%	30.5%	32.7%	8.2%
WASHINGTON	6,383	510	2,504	2,827	542	Kerry	8.0%	39.2%	44.3%	8.5%
WAYNE	598	84	192	285	37	Kerry	14.0%	32.1%	47.7%	6.2%
WEAKLEY	2,710	284	937	1,105	384	Kerry	10.5%	34.6%	40.8%	14.2%
WHITE	3,089	735	878	1,049	427	Kerry	23.8%	28.4%	34.0%	13.8%
WILLIAMSON	7,588	1,749	2,291	2,955	593	Kerry	23.0%	30.2%	38.9%	7.8%
WILSON	5,596	1,615	1,670	1,964	347	Kerry	28.9%	29.8%	35.1%	6.2%
TOTAL	369,385	85,315	97,914	151,527	34,629	Kerry	23.1%	26.5%	41.0%	9.4%

Note: Other vote was 16,128 Howard Dean; 6,107 Al Sharpton; 3,213 Joseph I. Lieberman; 2,727 Uncommitted; 2,490 Carol Moseley Braun; 2,279 Dennis J. Kucinich; 1,402 Richard A. Gephardt; 283 Lyndon H. LaRouche Jr.

TENNESSEE REPUBLICAN PRIMARY

2004

County	Total Vote	G.W. Bush	Uncommitted	Winner	Percentage of Total Vote G.W. Bush	Uncommitted
ANDERSON	623	601	22	G.W. Bush	96.5%	3.5%
BEDFORD	191	189	2	G.W. Bush	99.0%	1.0%
BENTON	221	205	16	G.W. Bush	92.8%	7.2%
BLEDSOE	189	179	10	G.W. Bush	94.7%	5.3%
BLOUNT	2,031	1,950	81	G.W. Bush	96.0%	4.0%
BRADLEY	1,217	1,188	29	G.W. Bush	97.6%	2.4%
CAMPBELL	348	337	11	G.W. Bush	96.8%	3.2%
CANNON	102	101	1	G.W. Bush	99.0%	1.0%
CARROLL	287	274	13	G.W. Bush	95.5%	4.5%
CARTER	4,028	3,725	303	G.W. Bush	92.5%	7.5%
CHEATHAM	507	484	23	G.W. Bush	95.5%	4.5%
CHESTER	145	144	1	G.W. Bush	99.3%	0.7%
CLAIBORNE	241	235	6	G.W. Bush	97.5%	2.5%
CLAY	41	41	0	G.W. Bush	100.0%	0.0%
COCKE	2,316	2,197	119	G.W. Bush	94.9%	5.1%
COFFEE	635	619	16	G.W. Bush	97.5%	2.5%
CROCKETT	56	55	1	G.W. Bush	98.2%	1.8%
CUMBERLAND	1,440	1,417	23	G.W. Bush	98.4%	1.6%
DAVIDSON	5,517	5,308	209	G.W. Bush	96.2%	3.8%
DECATUR	106	99	7	G.W. Bush	93.4%	6.6%
DE KALB	98	93	5	G.W. Bush	94.9%	5.1%
DICKSON	417	404	13	G.W. Bush	96.9%	3.1%
DYER	344	336	8	G.W. Bush	97.7%	2.3%
FAYETTE	286	280	6	G.W. Bush	97.9%	2.1%
FENTRESS	158	157	1	G.W. Bush	99.4%	0.6%
FRANKLIN	311	306	5	G.W. Bush	98.4%	1.6%
GIBSON	327	320	7	G.W. Bush	97.9%	2.1%
GILES	187	180	7	G.W. Bush	96.3%	3.7%
GRAINGER	936	905	31	G.W. Bush	96.7%	3.3%
GREENE	4,345	4,028	317	G.W. Bush	92.7%	7.3%
GRUNDY	98	95	3	G.W. Bush	96.9%	3.1%
HAMBLEN	2,409	2,270	139	G.W. Bush	94.2%	5.8%
HAMILTON	6,890	6,646	244	G.W. Bush	96.5%	3.5%
HANCOCK	609	562	47	G.W. Bush	92.3%	7.7%
HARDEMAN	133	127	6	G.W. Bush	95.5%	4.5%
HARDIN	288	280	8	G.W. Bush	97.2%	2.8%
HAWKINS	1,773	1,688	85	G.W. Bush	95.2%	4.8%
HAYWOOD	83	79	4	G.W. Bush	95.2%	4.8%
HENDERSON	1,275	1,146	129	G.W. Bush	89.9%	10.1%
HENRY	186	181	5	G.W. Bush	97.3%	2.7%
HICKMAN	172	165	7	G.W. Bush	95.9%	4.1%
HOUSTON	80	77	3	G.W. Bush	96.3%	3.8%
HUMPHREYS	152	149	3	G.W. Bush	98.0%	2.0%
JACKSON	98	92	6	G.W. Bush	93.9%	6.1%
JEFFERSON	1,355	1,292	63	G.W. Bush	95.4%	4.6%
JOHNSON	290	268	22	G.W. Bush	92.4%	7.6%
KNOX	10,338	9,885	453	G.W. Bush	95.6%	4.4%
LAKE	37	37	0	G.W. Bush	100.0%	0.0%
LAUDERDALE	181	177	4	G.W. Bush	97.8%	2.2%
LAWRENCE	210	197	13	G.W. Bush	93.8%	6.2%

TENNESSEE REPUBLICAN PRIMARY

2004

County	Total Vote	G.W. Bush	Uncommitted	Winner	Percentage of Total Vote	
					G.W. Bush	Uncommitted
LEWIS	82	75	7	G.W. Bush	91.5%	8.5%
LINCOLN	333	327	6	G.W. Bush	98.2%	1.8%
LOUDON	595	579	16	G.W. Bush	97.3%	2.7%
MCMINN	888	845	43	G.W. Bush	95.2%	4.8%
MCNAIRY	327	317	10	G.W. Bush	96.9%	3.1%
MACON	993	884	109	G.W. Bush	89.0%	11.0%
MADISON	1,735	1,636	99	G.W. Bush	94.3%	5.7%
MARION	438	406	32	G.W. Bush	92.7%	7.3%
MARSHALL	109	106	3	G.W. Bush	97.2%	2.8%
MAURY	604	592	12	G.W. Bush	98.0%	2.0%
MEIGS	232	232	0	G.W. Bush	100.0%	0.0%
MONROE	683	667	16	G.W. Bush	97.7%	2.3%
MONTGOMERY	1,267	1,219	48	G.W. Bush	96.2%	3.8%
MOORE	70	69	1	G.W. Bush	98.6%	1.4%
MORGAN	164	159	5	G.W. Bush	97.0%	3.0%
OBION	137	131	6	G.W. Bush	95.6%	4.4%
OVERTON	270	262	8	G.W. Bush	97.0%	3.0%
PERRY	40	38	2	G.W. Bush	95.0%	5.0%
PICKETT	432	385	47	G.W. Bush	89.1%	10.9%
POLK	244	232	12	G.W. Bush	95.1%	4.9%
PUTNAM	543	524	19	G.W. Bush	96.5%	3.5%
RHEA	801	768	33	G.W. Bush	95.9%	4.1%
ROANE	544	534	10	G.W. Bush	98.2%	1.8%
ROBERTSON	359	349	10	G.W. Bush	97.2%	2.8%
RUTHERFORD	3,673	3,483	190	G.W. Bush	94.8%	5.2%
SCOTT	153	149	4	G.W. Bush	97.4%	2.6%
SEQUATCHIE	83	80	3	G.W. Bush	96.4%	3.6%
SEVIER	2,418	2,297	121	G.W. Bush	95.0%	5.0%
SHELBY	12,198	11,792	406	G.W. Bush	96.7%	3.3%
SMITH	100	99	1	G.W. Bush	99.0%	1.0%
STEWART	207	204	3	G.W. Bush	98.6%	1.4%
SULLIVAN	1,306	1,261	45	G.W. Bush	96.6%	3.4%
SUMNER	1,088	1,064	24	G.W. Bush	97.8%	2.2%
TIPTON	548	531	17	G.W. Bush	96.9%	3.1%
TROUSDALE	38	37	1	G.W. Bush	97.4%	2.6%
UNICOI	2,022	1,778	244	G.W. Bush	87.9%	12.1%
UNION	212	199	13	G.W. Bush	93.9%	6.1%
VAN BUREN	124	123	1	G.W. Bush	99.2%	0.8%
WARREN	423	409	14	G.W. Bush	96.7%	3.3%
WASHINGTON	4,520	4,337	183	G.W. Bush	96.0%	4.0%
WAYNE	259	254	5	G.W. Bush	98.1%	1.9%
WEAKLEY	231	224	7	G.W. Bush	97.0%	3.0%
WHITE	156	144	12	G.W. Bush	92.3%	7.7%
WILLIAMSON	2,317	2,222	95	G.W. Bush	95.9%	4.1%
WILSON	788	764	24	G.W. Bush	97.0%	3.0%
TOTAL	99,061	94,557	4,504	G.W. Bush	95.5%	4.5%

TEXAS

Texas is the most populous state in the South, the second-most populous in the nation, and has been the anchor of the early March Southern voting since 1988. Of late, that has been a dubious honor, as much of the rest of the country has voted earlier and earlier in the election year.

George W. Bush did not need the support of his home state in his pursuit of the Republican presidential nomination in 2000. His last major rival, John McCain, had already quit the race before the Texas primary was held. As it was, Bush drew in the vicinity of 90 percent of the vote in the Texas GOP primary in 2000 and again in 2004, although in the latter year at least 10 percent of Republican primary voters in more than two dozen Texas counties deserted Bush in favor of an "Uncommitted" line on the ballot.

Befitting a state so large, Texas has a variety of racial and ideological divisions. But these are most apparent among the once-dominant Democrats. Within the fast-growing Republi-can Party, there is little evidence of a moderate wing; rather, there are gradations of conservatism.

That has been plainly visible since the Texas GOP's first presi-dential primary in 1964 produced 104,137 votes for Barry Gold-water and 6,207 for Nelson Rockefeller. Faced with a choice in 1976 between Ronald Reagan and President Gerald Ford, Texas Republicans spurned Ford and elected that year's entire com-plement of 100 delegates for Reagan.

Reagan won again in 1980, but his margin over George Bush in the primary was less than 20,000 votes out of more than 500,000 cast. Reagan swept most of the state, but Bush ran close by winning his home base of Harris County (Houston) with 63 percent of the vote.

In 1988 and 1992, Texas formed the cornerstone of a Bush sweep of the Super Tuesday South. It was not the "kinder, gen-tler" Bush that dominated the Texas primary both years, but the Bush with the ten-gallon hat and the oilman's swagger.

Recent Texas Primary Results

Texas Republicans held a presidential primary in 1964. The first year both parties held a presidential primary with a direct vote for candidates was in 1980.

	DEMOCRATS			REPUBLICANS		
Year	Turnout	Candidates	%	Turnout	Candidates	%
2004 (March 9)	839,231	JOHN KERRY John Edwards	67 14	687,615	GEORGE W. BUSH* Uncommitted	92 8
2000 (March 14)	786,890	AL GORE Bill Bradley	80 16	1,126,757	GEORGE W. BUSH John McCain	88 7
1996 (March 12)	921,256	BILL CLINTON*	86	1,019,803	BOB DOLE Pat Buchanan Steve Forbes	56 21 13
1992 (March 10)	1,482,975	BILL CLINTON Paul Tsongas Jerry Brown	66 19 8	797,146	GEORGE BUSH* Pat Buchanan	70 24
1988 (March 8)	1,767,045	MICHAEL DUKAKIS Jesse Jackson Al Gore Richard Gephardt	33 25 20 14	1,014,956	GEORGE BUSH Pat Robertson Bob Dole Jack Kemp	64 15 14 5
1984 (May 5)	—	No Primary		319,839	RONALD REAGAN*	97
1980 (May 3)	1,377,354	JIMMY CARTER* Edward Kennedy Uncommitted	56 23 19	526,769	RONALD REAGAN George Bush	51 47

Note: All candidates are listed that drew at least 5 percent of their party's primary vote. The names of winning candidates are capitalized. An asterisk (*) indicates an incumbent president.

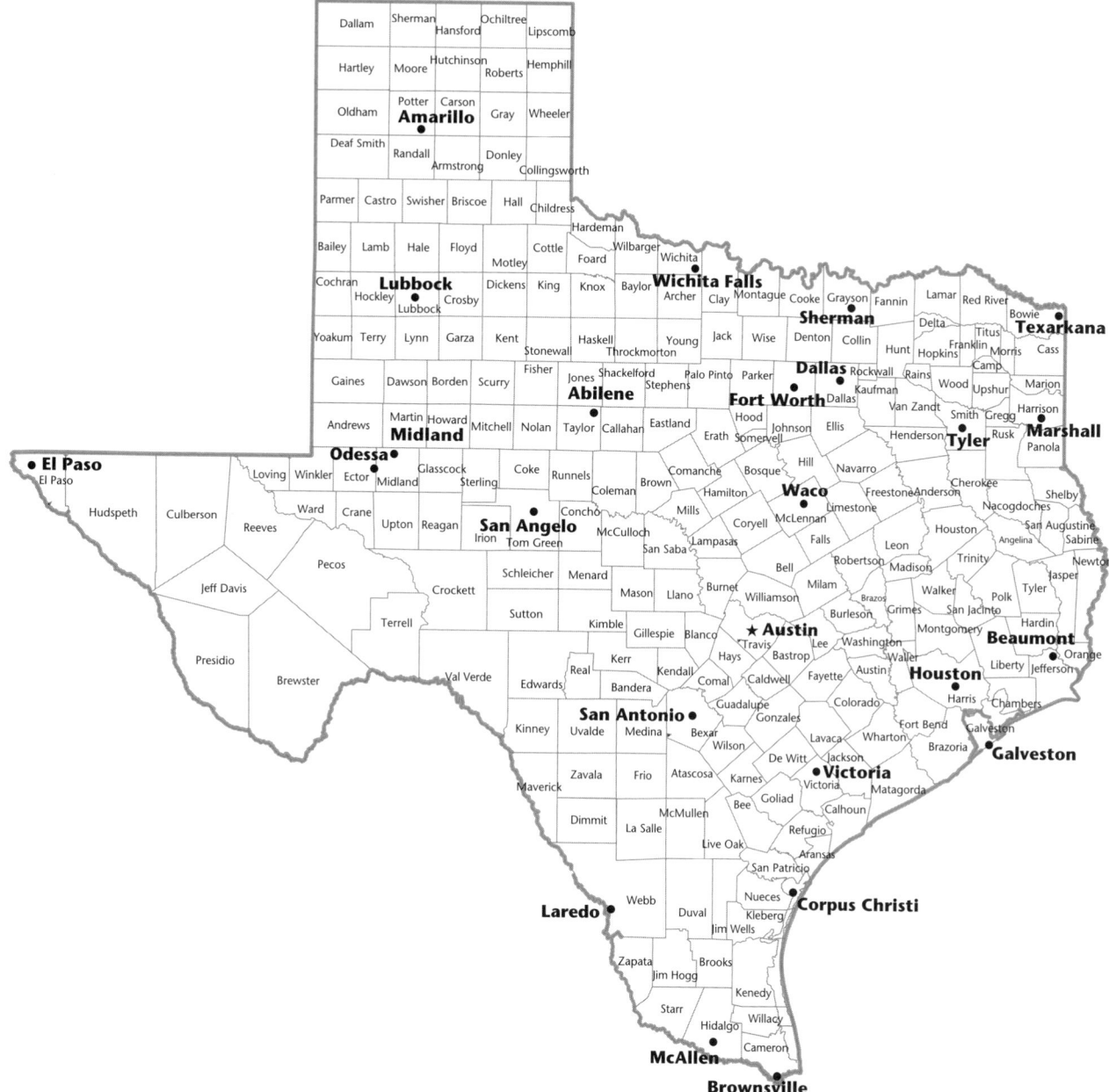

Both times Bush won his adopted home state with roughly two-thirds of the vote. That left little room for Bob Dole, who finished a poor third in Texas in 1988 behind Pat Robertson. Dole ran a distant second in most of the urban areas, but Robertson ran better in rural Texas, where he won a handful of counties out of the state's total complement of 254 (far more than any other state in the country).

Pat Buchanan did not find a much better toehold in the 1992 primary. He taunted the New England-born Bush as an "inauthentic" Texan and conservative. But Buchanan spent little time in the state and carried only two west Texas counties where the total vote was in the dozens. Buchanan carried a few more

small counties in 1996, but he ran only slightly closer to Dole in the statewide tally than he had to Bush four years earlier.

The bigger story in 1996 was the turnout in the GOP presidential primary; it exceeded the Democrats for the first time ever. And it was more than just the absence of competition on the Democratic side that produced it, since the ballots of both parties also featured contests for the Senate and House. Still, the Democratic constituency remains more disparate–a coalition of south Texas Hispanics, east Texas "Bubbas," urban blacks, and Austin liberals.

The Democratic mosaic was vividly on display in the party's 1988 presidential primary, which Michael Dukakis won with just one-third of the vote. Dukakis, who could speak fluent Spanish, won south Texas and the western panhandle, Bexar (San Antonio) and Travis (Austin) counties, and many of the suburbs around the major population centers.

Jesse Jackson won most of the other big population centers–Harris, Dallas, and Tarrant (Fort Worth) counties–all with significant minority populations. Al Gore and Richard Gephardt split much of the heavily white eastern, central, and northern portions of the state.

In the 1992 Democratic primary, Bill Clinton swept everything, but the turnout was down nearly 300,000 from 1988. It was one of many signs that the broad base of "yellow dog" Democrats across Texas (those who would vote Democratic even if it meant voting for a yellow dog) was eroding. However, the diversity within the Texas Democratic Party is still there, evident in the fact that Bill Bradley in 2000 and John Edwards in 2004 each carried a handful of Texas counties even though they had quit the race before the Lone Star state voted.

TEXAS DEMOCRATIC PRIMARY

2000

County	Total Vote	Bradley	Gore	LaRouche	Winner	Percentage of Total Vote		
						Bradley	Gore	LaRouche
ANDERSON	3,196	596	2,472	128	Gore	18.6%	77.3%	4.0%
ANDREWS	1,582	653	773	156	Gore	41.3%	48.9%	9.9%
ANGELINA	7,619	2,107	5,084	428	Gore	27.7%	66.7%	5.6%
ARANSAS	698	114	566	18	Gore	16.3%	81.1%	2.6%
ARCHER	718	190	494	34	Gore	26.5%	68.8%	4.7%
ARMSTRONG	66	14	45	7	Gore	21.2%	68.2%	10.6%
ATASCOSA	1,937	354	1,458	125	Gore	18.3%	75.3%	6.5%
AUSTIN	592	59	529	4	Gore	10.0%	89.4%	0.7%
BAILEY	503	190	279	34	Gore	37.8%	55.5%	6.8%
BANDERA	325	54	260	11	Gore	16.6%	80.0%	3.4%
BASTROP	2,690	550	2,046	94	Gore	20.4%	76.1%	3.5%
BAYLOR	276	67	203	6	Gore	24.3%	73.6%	2.2%
BEE	1,757	258	1,431	68	Gore	14.7%	81.4%	3.9%
BELL	3,726	338	3,213	175	Gore	9.1%	86.2%	4.7%
BEXAR	44,556	4,148	39,670	738	Gore	9.3%	89.0%	1.7%
BLANCO	142	10	131	1	Gore	7.0%	92.3%	0.7%
BORDEN	182	82	82	18		45.1%	45.1%	9.9%
BOSQUE	2,430	710	1,522	198	Gore	29.2%	62.6%	8.1%
BOWIE	10,772	2,534	7,664	574	Gore	23.5%	71.1%	5.3%
BRAZORIA	3,874	386	3,405	83	Gore	10.0%	87.9%	2.1%
BRAZOS	1,885	270	1,599	16	Gore	14.3%	84.8%	0.8%
BREWSTER	1,131	343	720	68	Gore	30.3%	63.7%	6.0%
BRISCOE	226	70	135	21	Gore	31.0%	59.7%	9.3%
BROOKS	3,094	438	2,490	166	Gore	14.2%	80.5%	5.4%
BROWN	1,376	297	1,024	55	Gore	21.6%	74.4%	4.0%
BURLESON	1,088	169	885	34	Gore	15.5%	81.3%	3.1%
BURNET	1,332	240	1,051	41	Gore	18.0%	78.9%	3.1%
CALDWELL	2,481	647	1,720	114	Gore	26.1%	69.3%	4.6%
CALHOUN	1,682	387	1,214	81	Gore	23.0%	72.2%	4.8%
CALLAHAN	899	275	556	68	Gore	30.6%	61.8%	7.6%
CAMERON	19,681	2,576	16,347	758	Gore	13.1%	83.1%	3.9%
CAMP	1,697	444	1,179	74	Gore	26.2%	69.5%	4.4%
CARSON	225	60	157	8	Gore	26.7%	69.8%	3.6%
CASS	4,738	1,114	3,306	318	Gore	23.5%	69.8%	6.7%
CASTRO	1,125	364	690	71	Gore	32.4%	61.3%	6.3%
CHAMBERS	2,340	627	1,578	135	Gore	26.8%	67.4%	5.8%
CHEROKEE	4,895	1,272	3,323	300	Gore	26.0%	67.9%	6.1%
CHILDRESS	321	81	224	16	Gore	25.2%	69.8%	5.0%
CLAY	1,524	448	995	81	Gore	29.4%	65.3%	5.3%
COCHRAN	212	74	125	13	Gore	34.9%	59.0%	6.1%
COKE	273	105	154	14	Gore	38.5%	56.4%	5.1%
COLEMAN	963	350	547	66	Gore	36.3%	56.8%	6.9%
COLLIN	3,644	420	3,188	36	Gore	11.5%	87.5%	1.0%
COLLINGSWORTH	753	283	426	44	Gore	37.6%	56.6%	5.8%
COLORADO	1,960	460	1,404	96	Gore	23.5%	71.6%	4.9%

TEXAS DEMOCRATIC PRIMARY

2000

County	Total Vote	Bradley	Gore	LaRouche	Winner	Percentage of Total Vote		
						Bradley	Gore	LaRouche
COMAL	1,511	161	1,323	27	Gore	10.7%	87.6%	1.8%
COMANCHE	2,119	612	1,368	139	Gore	28.9%	64.6%	6.6%
CONCHO	316	114	186	16	Gore	36.1%	58.9%	5.1%
COOKE	675	101	560	14	Gore	15.0%	83.0%	2.1%
CORYELL	1,850	435	1,325	90	Gore	23.5%	71.6%	4.9%
COTTLE	407	115	270	22	Gore	28.3%	66.3%	5.4%
CRANE	581	254	283	44	Gore	43.7%	48.7%	7.6%
CROCKETT	1,042	349	636	57	Gore	33.5%	61.0%	5.5%
CROSBY	362	79	267	16	Gore	21.8%	73.8%	4.4%
CULBERSON	629	131	456	42	Gore	20.8%	72.5%	6.7%
DALLAM	251	74	171	6	Gore	29.5%	68.1%	2.4%
DALLAS	46,105	2,907	42,795	403	Gore	6.3%	92.8%	0.9%
DAWSON	583	148	409	26	Gore	25.4%	70.2%	4.5%
DEAF SMITH	619	144	445	30	Gore	23.3%	71.9%	4.8%
DELTA	774	171	556	47	Gore	22.1%	71.8%	6.1%
DENTON	3,491	398	3,067	26	Gore	11.4%	87.9%	0.7%
DE WITT	396	49	345	2	Gore	12.4%	87.1%	0.5%
DICKENS	201	42	150	9	Gore	20.9%	74.6%	4.5%
DIMMIT	3,189	491	2,555	143	Gore	15.4%	80.1%	4.5%
DONLEY	320	84	218	18	Gore	26.3%	68.1%	5.6%
DUVAL	4,455	277	4,088	90	Gore	6.2%	91.8%	2.0%
EASTLAND	1,117	243	826	48	Gore	21.8%	73.9%	4.3%
ECTOR	3,409	481	2,835	93	Gore	14.1%	83.2%	2.7%
EDWARDS	182	44	129	9	Gore	24.2%	70.9%	4.9%
ELLIS	2,221	240	1,944	37	Gore	10.8%	87.5%	1.7%
EL PASO	23,462	2,804	19,995	663	Gore	12.0%	85.2%	2.8%
ERATH	1,241	269	930	42	Gore	21.7%	74.9%	3.4%
FALLS	3,280	840	2,255	185	Gore	25.6%	68.8%	5.6%
FANNIN	3,145	677	2,330	138	Gore	21.5%	74.1%	4.4%
FAYETTE	1,594	310	1,226	58	Gore	19.4%	76.9%	3.6%
FISHER	1,272	276	944	52	Gore	21.7%	74.2%	4.1%
FLOYD	442	132	284	26	Gore	29.9%	64.3%	5.9%
FOARD	337	67	256	14	Gore	19.9%	76.0%	4.2%
FORT BEND	6,318	444	5,836	38	Gore	7.0%	92.4%	0.6%
FRANKLIN	957	234	685	38	Gore	24.5%	71.6%	4.0%
FREESTONE	2,597	752	1,679	166	Gore	29.0%	64.7%	6.4%
FRIO	3,141	565	2,404	172	Gore	18.0%	76.5%	5.5%
GAINES	553	163	356	34	Gore	29.5%	64.4%	6.1%
GALVESTON	12,655	1,776	10,542	337	Gore	14.0%	83.3%	2.7%
GARZA	827	270	436	121	Gore	32.6%	52.7%	14.6%
GILLESPIE	190	29	159	2	Gore	15.3%	83.7%	1.1%
GLASSCOCK	12	4	8	0	Gore	33.3%	66.7%	0.0%
GOLIAD	1,366	363	901	102	Gore	26.6%	66.0%	7.5%
GONZALES	696	151	529	16	Gore	21.7%	76.0%	2.3%
GRAY	323	43	262	18	Gore	13.3%	81.1%	5.6%

TEXAS DEMOCRATIC PRIMARY

2000

County	Total Vote	Bradley	Gore	LaRouche	Winner	Percentage of Total Vote		
						Bradley	Gore	LaRouche
GRAYSON	2,710	298	2,362	50	Gore	11.0%	87.2%	1.8%
GREGG	1,781	149	1,620	12	Gore	8.4%	91.0%	0.7%
GRIMES	1,537	303	1,159	75	Gore	19.7%	75.4%	4.9%
GUADALUPE	1,323	120	1,183	20	Gore	9.1%	89.4%	1.5%
HALE	530	115	395	20	Gore	21.7%	74.5%	3.8%
HALL	497	145	323	29	Gore	29.2%	65.0%	5.8%
HAMILTON	342	70	254	18	Gore	20.5%	74.3%	5.3%
HANSFORD	0	0	0	0				
HARDEMAN	358	85	255	18	Gore	23.7%	71.2%	5.0%
HARDIN	4,949	1,240	3,402	307	Gore	25.1%	68.7%	6.2%
HARRIS	52,196	3,251	48,336	609	Gore	6.2%	92.6%	1.2%
HARRISON	6,791	1,578	4,866	347	Gore	23.2%	71.7%	5.1%
HARTLEY	190	58	126	6	Gore	30.5%	66.3%	3.2%
HASKELL	1,668	445	1,160	63	Gore	26.7%	69.5%	3.8%
HAYS	2,797	436	2,311	50	Gore	15.6%	82.6%	1.8%
HEMPHILL	89	21	66	2	Gore	23.6%	74.2%	2.2%
HENDERSON	4,624	883	3,505	236	Gore	19.1%	75.8%	5.1%
HIDALGO	41,085	4,484	34,749	1,852	Gore	10.9%	84.6%	4.5%
HILL	1,595	323	1,220	52	Gore	20.3%	76.5%	3.3%
HOCKLEY	914	280	584	50	Gore	30.6%	63.9%	5.5%
HOOD	962	102	839	21	Gore	10.6%	87.2%	2.2%
HOPKINS	3,577	885	2,497	195	Gore	24.7%	69.8%	5.5%
HOUSTON	1,993	556	1,314	123	Gore	27.9%	65.9%	6.2%
HOWARD	677	102	542	33	Gore	15.1%	80.1%	4.9%
HUDSPETH	563	162	349	52	Gore	28.8%	62.0%	9.2%
HUNT	2,242	319	1,857	66	Gore	14.2%	82.8%	2.9%
HUTCHINSON	387	58	312	17	Gore	15.0%	80.6%	4.4%
IRION	121	43	75	3	Gore	35.5%	62.0%	2.5%
JACK	883	281	550	52	Gore	31.8%	62.3%	5.9%
JACKSON	1,116	294	769	53	Gore	26.3%	68.9%	4.7%
JASPER	4,253	1,240	2,756	257	Gore	29.2%	64.8%	6.0%
JEFF DAVIS	374	140	205	29	Gore	37.4%	54.8%	7.8%
JEFFERSON	13,677	1,882	11,493	302	Gore	13.8%	84.0%	2.2%
JIM HOGG	2,121	317	1,721	83	Gore	14.9%	81.1%	3.9%
JIM WELLS	7,486	1,254	5,974	258	Gore	16.8%	79.8%	3.4%
JOHNSON	1,555	152	1,380	23	Gore	9.8%	88.7%	1.5%
JONES	2,539	761	1,631	147	Gore	30.0%	64.2%	5.8%
KARNES	1,983	516	1,304	163	Gore	26.0%	65.8%	8.2%
KAUFMAN	2,048	212	1,809	27	Gore	10.4%	88.3%	1.3%
KENDALL	233	26	205	2	Gore	11.2%	88.0%	0.9%
KENEDY	157	38	112	7	Gore	24.2%	71.3%	4.5%
KENT	355	127	209	19	Gore	35.8%	58.9%	5.4%
KERR	689	89	597	3	Gore	12.9%	86.6%	0.4%
KIMBLE	215	90	118	7	Gore	41.9%	54.9%	3.3%
KING	79	27	46	6	Gore	34.2%	58.2%	7.6%

TEXAS DEMOCRATIC PRIMARY

2000

County	Total Vote	Bradley	Gore	LaRouche	Winner	Percentage of Total Vote		
						Bradley	Gore	LaRouche
KINNEY	707	180	477	50	Gore	25.5%	67.5%	7.1%
KLEBERG	3,241	504	2,614	123	Gore	15.6%	80.7%	3.8%
KNOX	593	135	421	37	Gore	22.8%	71.0%	6.2%
LAMAR	5,382	1,424	3,681	277	Gore	26.5%	68.4%	5.1%
LAMB	1,384	537	748	99	Gore	38.8%	54.0%	7.2%
LAMPASAS	454	82	356	16	Gore	18.1%	78.4%	3.5%
LA SALLE	1,564	202	1,293	69	Gore	12.9%	82.7%	4.4%
LAVACA	2,190	524	1,546	120	Gore	23.9%	70.6%	5.5%
LEE	1,155	312	779	64	Gore	27.0%	67.4%	5.5%
LEON	1,677	429	1,139	109	Gore	25.6%	67.9%	6.5%
LIBERTY	5,462	1,207	3,980	275	Gore	22.1%	72.9%	5.0%
LIMESTONE	3,383	932	2,263	188	Gore	27.5%	66.9%	5.6%
LIPSCOMB	443	185	224	34	Gore	41.8%	50.6%	7.7%
LIVE OAK	719	178	487	54	Gore	24.8%	67.7%	7.5%
LLANO	617	72	530	15	Gore	11.7%	85.9%	2.4%
LOVING	39	21	16	2	Bradley	53.8%	41.0%	5.1%
LUBBOCK	4,049	529	3,440	80	Gore	13.1%	85.0%	2.0%
LYNN	800	307	425	68	Gore	38.4%	53.1%	8.5%
MCCULLOCH	369	97	260	12	Gore	26.3%	70.5%	3.3%
MCLENNAN	8,540	1,232	7,122	186	Gore	14.4%	83.4%	2.2%
MCMULLEN	245	96	120	29	Gore	39.2%	49.0%	11.8%
MADISON	552	99	437	16	Gore	17.9%	79.2%	2.9%
MARION	976	377	488	111	Gore	38.6%	50.0%	11.4%
MARTIN	694	273	380	41	Gore	39.3%	54.8%	5.9%
MASON	531	183	290	58	Gore	34.5%	54.6%	10.9%
MATAGORDA	3,669	971	2,499	199	Gore	26.5%	68.1%	5.4%
MAVERICK	5,190	641	4,379	170	Gore	12.4%	84.4%	3.3%
MEDINA	1,887	390	1,398	99	Gore	20.7%	74.1%	5.2%
MENARD	218	61	149	8	Gore	28.0%	68.3%	3.7%
MIDLAND	1,936	197	1,703	36	Gore	10.2%	88.0%	1.9%
MILAM	3,896	1,032	2,654	210	Gore	26.5%	68.1%	5.4%
MILLS	979	343	563	73	Gore	35.0%	57.5%	7.5%
MITCHELL	548	132	404	12	Gore	24.1%	73.7%	2.2%
MONTAGUE	1,261	323	854	84	Gore	25.6%	67.7%	6.7%
MONTGOMERY	2,895	303	2,548	44	Gore	10.5%	88.0%	1.5%
MOORE	278	31	238	9	Gore	11.2%	85.6%	3.2%
MORRIS	1,796	389	1,322	85	Gore	21.7%	73.6%	4.7%
MOTLEY	240	104	105	31	Gore	43.3%	43.8%	12.9%
NACOGDOCHES	2,371	387	1,922	62	Gore	16.3%	81.1%	2.6%
NAVARRO	4,256	1,019	3,048	189	Gore	23.9%	71.6%	4.4%
NEWTON	2,081	470	1,516	95	Gore	22.6%	72.8%	4.6%
NOLAN	2,611	856	1,565	190	Gore	32.8%	59.9%	7.3%
NUECES	18,411	2,707	15,230	474	Gore	14.7%	82.7%	2.6%
OCHILTREE	51	11	40	0	Gore	21.6%	78.4%	0.0%
OLDHAM	176	63	95	18	Gore	35.8%	54.0%	10.2%

TEXAS DEMOCRATIC PRIMARY

2000

County	Total Vote	Bradley	Gore	LaRouche	Winner	Percentage of Total Vote		
						Bradley	Gore	LaRouche
ORANGE	9,412	2,347	6,639	426	Gore	24.9%	70.5%	4.5%
PALO PINTO	2,972	719	2,065	188	Gore	24.2%	69.5%	6.3%
PANOLA	1,678	391	1,163	124	Gore	23.3%	69.3%	7.4%
PARKER	2,031	230	1,750	51	Gore	11.3%	86.2%	2.5%
PARMER	386	130	227	29	Gore	33.7%	58.8%	7.5%
PECOS	2,244	646	1,460	138	Gore	28.8%	65.1%	6.1%
POLK	4,133	1,005	2,930	198	Gore	24.3%	70.9%	4.8%
POTTER	1,704	169	1,500	35	Gore	9.9%	88.0%	2.1%
PRESIDIO	1,250	248	924	78	Gore	19.8%	73.9%	6.2%
RAINS	1,041	253	733	55	Gore	24.3%	70.4%	5.3%
RANDALL	1,286	184	1,084	18	Gore	14.3%	84.3%	1.4%
REAGAN	37	8	29	0	Gore	21.6%	78.4%	0.0%
REAL	88	19	66	3	Gore	21.6%	75.0%	3.4%
RED RIVER	2,237	597	1,509	131	Gore	26.7%	67.5%	5.9%
REEVES	2,694	610	1,935	149	Gore	22.6%	71.8%	5.5%
REFUGIO	850	220	591	39	Gore	25.9%	69.5%	4.6%
ROBERTS	21	6	15	0	Gore	28.6%	71.4%	0.0%
ROBERTSON	2,653	495	2,158	0	Gore	18.7%	81.3%	0.0%
ROCKWALL	437	51	381	5	Gore	11.7%	87.2%	1.1%
RUNNELS	1,184	458	642	84	Gore	38.7%	54.2%	7.1%
RUSK	2,882	717	2,007	158	Gore	24.9%	69.6%	5.5%
SABINE	1,995	569	1,301	125	Gore	28.5%	65.2%	6.3%
SAN AUGUSTINE	2,031	578	1,297	156	Gore	28.5%	63.9%	7.7%
SAN JACINTO	3,089	822	2,084	183	Gore	26.6%	67.5%	5.9%
SAN PATRICIO	3,436	583	2,705	148	Gore	17.0%	78.7%	4.3%
SAN SABA	305	61	236	8	Gore	20.0%	77.4%	2.6%
SCHLEICHER	148	38	100	10	Gore	25.7%	67.6%	6.8%
SCURRY	649	152	471	26	Gore	23.4%	72.6%	4.0%
SHACKELFORD	300	108	175	17	Gore	36.0%	58.3%	5.7%
SHELBY	4,067	1,261	2,519	287	Gore	31.0%	61.9%	7.1%
SHERMAN	159	77	66	16	Bradley	48.4%	41.5%	10.1%
SMITH	3,017	241	2,741	35	Gore	8.0%	90.9%	1.2%
SOMERVELL	1,214	385	733	96	Gore	31.7%	60.4%	7.9%
STARR	10,076	914	8,916	246	Gore	9.1%	88.5%	2.4%
STEPHENS	854	304	509	41	Gore	35.6%	59.6%	4.8%
STERLING	61	22	33	6	Gore	36.1%	54.1%	9.8%
STONEWALL	573	171	368	34	Gore	29.8%	64.2%	5.9%
SUTTON	278	106	154	18	Gore	38.1%	55.4%	6.5%
SWISHER	725	226	449	50	Gore	31.2%	61.9%	6.9%
TARRANT	26,758	2,163	24,370	225	Gore	8.1%	91.1%	0.8%
TAYLOR	2,214	282	1,904	28	Gore	12.7%	86.0%	1.3%
TERRELL	371	102	249	20	Gore	27.5%	67.1%	5.4%
TERRY	788	235	507	46	Gore	29.8%	64.3%	5.8%
THROCKMORTON	420	125	266	29	Gore	29.8%	63.3%	6.9%
TITUS	3,297	913	2,248	136	Gore	27.7%	68.2%	4.1%

TEXAS DEMOCRATIC PRIMARY

2000

County	Total Vote	Bradley	Gore	LaRouche	Winner	Percentage of Total Vote Bradley	Gore	LaRouche
TOM GREEN	2,220	263	1,922	35	Gore	11.8%	86.6%	1.6%
TRAVIS	34,186	5,962	27,858	366	Gore	17.4%	81.5%	1.1%
TRINITY	2,514	695	1,678	141	Gore	27.6%	66.7%	5.6%
TYLER	3,616	946	2,479	191	Gore	26.2%	68.6%	5.3%
UPSHUR	4,161	1,116	2,797	248	Gore	26.8%	67.2%	6.0%
UPTON	869	350	445	74	Gore	40.3%	51.2%	8.5%
UVALDE	2,837	838	1,754	245	Gore	29.5%	61.8%	8.6%
VAL VERDE	4,281	785	3,305	191	Gore	18.3%	77.2%	4.5%
VAN ZANDT	2,962	597	2,204	161	Gore	20.2%	74.4%	5.4%
VICTORIA	2,251	333	1,868	50	Gore	14.8%	83.0%	2.2%
WALKER	1,139	149	954	36	Gore	13.1%	83.8%	3.2%
WALLER	1,156	127	1,002	27	Gore	11.0%	86.7%	2.3%
WARD	2,268	739	1,358	171	Gore	32.6%	59.9%	7.5%
WASHINGTON	1,297	181	1,079	37	Gore	14.0%	83.2%	2.9%
WEBB	22,229	3,074	18,291	864	Gore	13.8%	82.3%	3.9%
WHARTON	1,491	196	1,259	36	Gore	13.1%	84.4%	2.4%
WHEELER	1,143	429	635	79	Gore	37.5%	55.6%	6.9%
WICHITA	2,505	281	2,183	41	Gore	11.2%	87.1%	1.6%
WILBARGER	857	281	553	23	Gore	32.8%	64.5%	2.7%
WILLACY	3,341	596	2,573	172	Gore	17.8%	77.0%	5.1%
WILLIAMSON	3,812	504	3,266	42	Gore	13.2%	85.7%	1.1%
WILSON	1,516	211	1,245	60	Gore	13.9%	82.1%	4.0%
WINKLER	179	41	135	3	Gore	22.9%	75.4%	1.7%
WISE	1,715	318	1,333	64	Gore	18.5%	77.7%	3.7%
WOOD	1,890	368	1,432	90	Gore	19.5%	75.8%	4.8%
YOAKUM	709	246	409	54	Gore	34.7%	57.7%	7.6%
YOUNG	1,195	322	808	65	Gore	26.9%	67.6%	5.4%
ZAPATA	2,472	266	2,126	80	Gore	10.8%	86.0%	3.2%
ZAVALA	2,858	364	2,392	102	Gore	12.7%	83.7%	3.6%
TOTAL	786,890	128,564	631,428	26,898	Gore	16.3%	80.2%	3.4%

Note: No vote reported from Hansford County.

TEXAS REPUBLICAN PRIMARY

2000

County	Total Vote	G.W. Bush	McCain	Other	Winner	Percentage of Total Vote		
						G.W. Bush	McCain	Other
ANDERSON	3,680	3,274	208	198	G.W. Bush	89.0%	5.7%	5.4%
ANDREWS	503	453	13	37	G.W. Bush	90.1%	2.6%	7.4%
ANGELINA	3,340	2,995	191	154	G.W. Bush	89.7%	5.7%	4.6%
ARANSAS	2,802	2,377	344	81	G.W. Bush	84.8%	12.3%	2.9%
ARCHER	469	443	12	14	G.W. Bush	94.5%	2.6%	3.0%
ARMSTRONG	529	456	36	37	G.W. Bush	86.2%	6.8%	7.0%
ATASCOSA	1,106	986	46	74	G.W. Bush	89.2%	4.2%	6.7%
AUSTIN	3,014	2,726	151	137	G.W. Bush	90.4%	5.0%	4.5%
BAILEY	179	168	0	11	G.W. Bush	93.9%	0.0%	6.1%
BANDERA	3,444	2,879	277	288	G.W. Bush	83.6%	8.0%	8.4%
BASTROP	3,222	2,827	206	189	G.W. Bush	87.7%	6.4%	5.9%
BAYLOR	150	133	11	6	G.W. Bush	88.7%	7.3%	4.0%
BEE	1,233	1,129	70	34	G.W. Bush	91.6%	5.7%	2.8%
BELL	16,187	14,073	1,113	1,001	G.W. Bush	86.9%	6.9%	6.2%
BEXAR	64,688	54,676	5,463	4,549	G.W. Bush	84.5%	8.4%	7.0%
BLANCO	1,590	1,378	123	89	G.W. Bush	86.7%	7.7%	5.6%
BORDEN	22	19	0	3	G.W. Bush	86.4%	0.0%	13.6%
BOSQUE	815	757	29	29	G.W. Bush	92.9%	3.6%	3.6%
BOWIE	2,871	2,616	111	144	G.W. Bush	91.1%	3.9%	5.0%
BRAZORIA	19,333	16,887	1,588	858	G.W. Bush	87.3%	8.2%	4.4%
BRAZOS	11,635	10,013	907	715	G.W. Bush	86.1%	7.8%	6.1%
BREWSTER	439	346	68	25	G.W. Bush	78.8%	15.5%	5.7%
BRISCOE	105	97	2	6	G.W. Bush	92.4%	1.9%	5.7%
BROOKS	6	5	0	1	G.W. Bush	83.3%	0.0%	16.7%
BROWN	2,078	1,947	72	59	G.W. Bush	93.7%	3.5%	2.8%
BURLESON	1,194	1,108	37	49	G.W. Bush	92.8%	3.1%	4.1%
BURNET	3,551	3,182	222	147	G.W. Bush	89.6%	6.3%	4.1%
CALDWELL	1,167	1,037	52	78	G.W. Bush	88.9%	4.5%	6.7%
CALHOUN	663	611	30	22	G.W. Bush	92.2%	4.5%	3.3%
CALLAHAN	664	615	28	21	G.W. Bush	92.6%	4.2%	3.2%
CAMERON	6,105	5,568	344	193	G.W. Bush	91.2%	5.6%	3.2%
CAMP	263	242	9	12	G.W. Bush	92.0%	3.4%	4.6%
CARSON	695	642	17	36	G.W. Bush	92.4%	2.4%	5.2%
CASS	487	453	16	18	G.W. Bush	93.0%	3.3%	3.7%
CASTRO	199	173	5	21	G.W. Bush	86.9%	2.5%	10.6%
CHAMBERS	1,615	1,491	64	60	G.W. Bush	92.3%	4.0%	3.7%
CHEROKEE	2,077	1,888	96	93	G.W. Bush	90.9%	4.6%	4.5%
CHILDRESS	287	260	10	17	G.W. Bush	90.6%	3.5%	5.9%
CLAY	336	305	10	21	G.W. Bush	90.8%	3.0%	6.3%
COCHRAN	156	151	2	3	G.W. Bush	96.8%	1.3%	1.9%
COKE	135	118	5	12	G.W. Bush	87.4%	3.7%	8.9%
COLEMAN	296	280	10	6	G.W. Bush	94.6%	3.4%	2.0%
COLLIN	31,353	27,081	2,288	1,984	G.W. Bush	86.4%	7.3%	6.3%
COLLINGSWORTH	68	62	2	4	G.W. Bush	91.2%	2.9%	5.9%
COLORADO	927	874	28	25	G.W. Bush	94.3%	3.0%	2.7%

TEXAS REPUBLICAN PRIMARY

2000

County	Total Vote	G.W. Bush	McCain	Other	Winner	Percentage of Total Vote		
						G.W. Bush	McCain	Other
COMAL	9,168	7,779	677	712	G.W. Bush	84.8%	7.4%	7.8%
COMANCHE	344	314	4	26	G.W. Bush	91.3%	1.2%	7.6%
CONCHO	127	114	9	4	G.W. Bush	89.8%	7.1%	3.1%
COOKE	2,977	2,750	124	103	G.W. Bush	92.4%	4.2%	3.5%
CORYELL	2,576	2,252	203	121	G.W. Bush	87.4%	7.9%	4.7%
COTTLE	7	5	1	1	G.W. Bush	71.4%	14.3%	14.3%
CRANE	300	270	12	18	G.W. Bush	90.0%	4.0%	6.0%
CROCKETT	12	10	0	2	G.W. Bush	83.3%	0.0%	16.7%
CROSBY	186	174	3	9	G.W. Bush	93.5%	1.6%	4.8%
CULBERSON	0	0	0	0				
DALLAM	538	485	23	30	G.W. Bush	90.1%	4.3%	5.6%
DALLAS	91,139	79,314	6,220	5,605	G.W. Bush	87.0%	6.8%	6.1%
DAWSON	935	868	27	40	G.W. Bush	92.8%	2.9%	4.3%
DEAF SMITH	1,762	1,602	76	84	G.W. Bush	90.9%	4.3%	4.8%
DELTA	81	71	1	9	G.W. Bush	87.7%	1.2%	11.1%
DENTON	26,109	22,014	2,152	1,943	G.W. Bush	84.3%	8.2%	7.4%
DE WITT	1,220	1,133	44	43	G.W. Bush	92.9%	3.6%	3.5%
DICKENS	86	83	3	0	G.W. Bush	96.5%	3.5%	0.0%
DIMMIT	12	8	2	2	G.W. Bush	66.7%	16.7%	16.7%
DONLEY	365	345	7	13	G.W. Bush	94.5%	1.9%	3.6%
DUVAL	0	0	0	0				
EASTLAND	1,233	1,124	52	57	G.W. Bush	91.2%	4.2%	4.6%
ECTOR	12,095	10,593	850	652	G.W. Bush	87.6%	7.0%	5.4%
EDWARDS	209	191	5	13	G.W. Bush	91.4%	2.4%	6.2%
ELLIS	7,364	6,649	330	385	G.W. Bush	90.3%	4.5%	5.2%
EL PASO	14,110	11,904	1,521	685	G.W. Bush	84.4%	10.8%	4.9%
ERATH	1,944	1,791	77	76	G.W. Bush	92.1%	4.0%	3.9%
FALLS	158	149	5	4	G.W. Bush	94.3%	3.2%	2.5%
FANNIN	1,059	964	40	55	G.W. Bush	91.0%	3.8%	5.2%
FAYETTE	1,905	1,781	59	65	G.W. Bush	93.5%	3.1%	3.4%
FISHER	26	22	3	1	G.W. Bush	84.6%	11.5%	3.8%
FLOYD	340	322	5	13	G.W. Bush	94.7%	1.5%	3.8%
FOARD	0	0	0	0				
FORT BEND	23,086	20,530	1,650	906	G.W. Bush	88.9%	7.1%	3.9%
FRANKLIN	423	388	15	20	G.W. Bush	91.7%	3.5%	4.7%
FREESTONE	725	681	21	23	G.W. Bush	93.9%	2.9%	3.2%
FRIO	152	145	2	5	G.W. Bush	95.4%	1.3%	3.3%
GAINES	483	452	17	14	G.W. Bush	93.6%	3.5%	2.9%
GALVESTON	10,921	9,786	654	481	G.W. Bush	89.6%	6.0%	4.4%
GARZA	151	76	4	71	G.W. Bush	50.3%	2.6%	47.0%
GILLESPIE	5,142	4,512	388	242	G.W. Bush	87.7%	7.5%	4.7%
GLASSCOCK	294	278	9	7	G.W. Bush	94.6%	3.1%	2.4%
GOLIAD	380	352	12	16	G.W. Bush	92.6%	3.2%	4.2%
GONZALES	1,212	1,132	37	43	G.W. Bush	93.4%	3.1%	3.5%
GRAY	3,681	3,330	176	175	G.W. Bush	90.5%	4.8%	4.8%

TEXAS REPUBLICAN PRIMARY

2000

County	Total Vote	G.W. Bush	McCain	Other	Winner	Percentage of Total Vote G.W. Bush	McCain	Other
GRAYSON	7,353	6,565	415	373	G.W. Bush	89.3%	5.6%	5.1%
GREGG	11,439	10,203	674	562	G.W. Bush	89.2%	5.9%	4.9%
GRIMES	1,261	1,155	61	45	G.W. Bush	91.6%	4.8%	3.6%
GUADALUPE	10,051	8,540	811	700	G.W. Bush	85.0%	8.1%	7.0%
HALE	1,477	1,376	34	67	G.W. Bush	93.2%	2.3%	4.5%
HALL	88	88	0	0	G.W. Bush	100.0%	0.0%	0.0%
HAMILTON	490	439	25	26	G.W. Bush	89.6%	5.1%	5.3%
HANSFORD	1,030	956	38	36	G.W. Bush	92.8%	3.7%	3.5%
HARDEMAN	81	79	0	2	G.W. Bush	97.5%	0.0%	2.5%
HARDIN	1,717	1,545	49	123	G.W. Bush	90.0%	2.9%	7.2%
HARRIS	160,624	140,889	12,351	7,384	G.W. Bush	87.7%	7.7%	4.6%
HARRISON	3,044	2,794	127	123	G.W. Bush	91.8%	4.2%	4.0%
HARTLEY	655	599	30	26	G.W. Bush	91.5%	4.6%	4.0%
HASKELL	45	41	0	4	G.W. Bush	91.1%	0.0%	8.9%
HAYS	6,447	5,383	603	461	G.W. Bush	83.5%	9.4%	7.2%
HEMPHILL	710	648	42	20	G.W. Bush	91.3%	5.9%	2.8%
HENDERSON	4,099	3,823	123	153	G.W. Bush	93.3%	3.0%	3.7%
HIDALGO	5,739	5,048	430	261	G.W. Bush	88.0%	7.5%	4.5%
HILL	1,556	1,468	46	42	G.W. Bush	94.3%	3.0%	2.7%
HOCKLEY	1,557	1,452	10	95	G.W. Bush	93.3%	0.6%	6.1%
HOOD	6,532	5,513	626	393	G.W. Bush	84.4%	9.6%	6.0%
HOPKINS	939	877	28	34	G.W. Bush	93.4%	3.0%	3.6%
HOUSTON	945	883	32	30	G.W. Bush	93.4%	3.4%	3.2%
HOWARD	2,678	2,357	196	125	G.W. Bush	88.0%	7.3%	4.7%
HUDSPETH	37	29	1	7	G.W. Bush	78.4%	2.7%	18.9%
HUNT	4,823	4,335	202	286	G.W. Bush	89.9%	4.2%	5.9%
HUTCHINSON	3,705	3,236	260	209	G.W. Bush	87.3%	7.0%	5.6%
IRION	148	144	1	3	G.W. Bush	97.3%	0.7%	2.0%
JACK	223	209	8	6	G.W. Bush	93.7%	3.6%	2.7%
JACKSON	625	584	23	18	G.W. Bush	93.4%	3.7%	2.9%
JASPER	706	659	22	25	G.W. Bush	93.3%	3.1%	3.5%
JEFF DAVIS	148	118	18	12	G.W. Bush	79.7%	12.2%	8.1%
JEFFERSON	8,901	7,959	565	377	G.W. Bush	89.4%	6.3%	4.2%
JIM HOGG	15	14	0	1	G.W. Bush	93.3%	0.0%	6.7%
JIM WELLS	368	345	10	13	G.W. Bush	93.8%	2.7%	3.5%
JOHNSON	8,098	7,156	473	469	G.W. Bush	88.4%	5.8%	5.8%
JONES	295	277	8	10	G.W. Bush	93.9%	2.7%	3.4%
KARNES	219	197	6	16	G.W. Bush	90.0%	2.7%	7.3%
KAUFMAN	5,393	4,886	283	224	G.W. Bush	90.6%	5.2%	4.2%
KENDALL	4,889	4,083	391	415	G.W. Bush	83.5%	8.0%	8.5%
KENEDY	2	2	0	0	G.W. Bush	100.0%	0.0%	0.0%
KENT	7	7	0	0	G.W. Bush	100.0%	0.0%	0.0%
KERR	8,543	7,190	862	491	G.W. Bush	84.2%	10.1%	5.7%
KIMBLE	310	292	8	10	G.W. Bush	94.2%	2.6%	3.2%
KING	12	6	0	6		50.0%	0.0%	50.0%

TEXAS REPUBLICAN PRIMARY

2000

County	Total Vote	G.W. Bush	McCain	Other	Winner	Percentage of Total Vote		
						G.W. Bush	McCain	Other
KINNEY	150	134	10	6	G.W. Bush	89.3%	6.7%	4.0%
KLEBERG	891	788	61	42	G.W. Bush	88.4%	6.8%	4.7%
KNOX	75	70	2	3	G.W. Bush	93.3%	2.7%	4.0%
LAMAR	1,823	1,693	54	76	G.W. Bush	92.9%	3.0%	4.2%
LAMB	338	318	10	10	G.W. Bush	94.1%	3.0%	3.0%
LAMPASAS	1,566	1,394	103	69	G.W. Bush	89.0%	6.6%	4.4%
LA SALLE	0	0	0	0				
LAVACA	757	688	19	50	G.W. Bush	90.9%	2.5%	6.6%
LEE	686	655	16	15	G.W. Bush	95.5%	2.3%	2.2%
LEON	1,214	1,146	30	38	G.W. Bush	94.4%	2.5%	3.1%
LIBERTY	2,588	2,349	110	129	G.W. Bush	90.8%	4.3%	5.0%
LIMESTONE	578	534	17	27	G.W. Bush	92.4%	2.9%	4.7%
LIPSCOMB	240	218	6	16	G.W. Bush	90.8%	2.5%	6.7%
LIVE OAK	566	533	10	23	G.W. Bush	94.2%	1.8%	4.1%
LLANO	2,584	2,371	143	70	G.W. Bush	91.8%	5.5%	2.7%
LOVING	0	0	0	0				
LUBBOCK	23,537	21,140	1,306	1,091	G.W. Bush	89.8%	5.5%	4.6%
LYNN	109	98	0	11	G.W. Bush	89.9%	0.0%	10.1%
MCCULLOCH	451	434	11	6	G.W. Bush	96.2%	2.4%	1.3%
MCLENNAN	15,720	14,288	791	641	G.W. Bush	90.9%	5.0%	4.1%
MCMULLEN	13	13	0	0	G.W. Bush	100.0%	0.0%	0.0%
MADISON	631	577	17	37	G.W. Bush	91.4%	2.7%	5.9%
MARION	146	135	4	7	G.W. Bush	92.5%	2.7%	4.8%
MARTIN	172	152	6	14	G.W. Bush	88.4%	3.5%	8.1%
MASON	284	256	9	19	G.W. Bush	90.1%	3.2%	6.7%
MATAGORDA	1,426	1,288	66	72	G.W. Bush	90.3%	4.6%	5.0%
MAVERICK	86	81	0	5	G.W. Bush	94.2%	0.0%	5.8%
MEDINA	2,739	2,485	93	161	G.W. Bush	90.7%	3.4%	5.9%
MENARD	246	220	19	7	G.W. Bush	89.4%	7.7%	2.8%
MIDLAND	18,120	15,540	1,418	1,162	G.W. Bush	85.8%	7.8%	6.4%
MILAM	743	686	26	31	G.W. Bush	92.3%	3.5%	4.2%
MILLS	111	104	2	5	G.W. Bush	93.7%	1.8%	4.5%
MITCHELL	285	257	10	18	G.W. Bush	90.2%	3.5%	6.3%
MONTAGUE	736	702	12	22	G.W. Bush	95.4%	1.6%	3.0%
MONTGOMERY	27,944	24,416	2,011	1,517	G.W. Bush	87.4%	7.2%	5.4%
MOORE	1,239	1,151	40	48	G.W. Bush	92.9%	3.2%	3.9%
MORRIS	217	201	10	6	G.W. Bush	92.6%	4.6%	2.8%
MOTLEY	56	53	1	2	G.W. Bush	94.6%	1.8%	3.6%
NACOGDOCHES	8,225	7,029	784	412	G.W. Bush	85.5%	9.5%	5.0%
NAVARRO	1,562	1,454	39	69	G.W. Bush	93.1%	2.5%	4.4%
NEWTON	203	183	9	11	G.W. Bush	90.1%	4.4%	5.4%
NOLAN	190	174	9	7	G.W. Bush	91.6%	4.7%	3.7%
NUECES	12,044	10,670	835	539	G.W. Bush	88.6%	6.9%	4.5%
OCHILTREE	1,236	1,150	47	39	G.W. Bush	93.0%	3.8%	3.2%
OLDHAM	92	86	3	3	G.W. Bush	93.5%	3.3%	3.3%

TEXAS REPUBLICAN PRIMARY

2000

County	Total Vote	G.W. Bush	McCain	Other	Winner	Percentage of Total Vote		
						G.W. Bush	McCain	Other
ORANGE	2,291	2,032	114	145	G.W. Bush	88.7%	5.0%	6.3%
PALO PINTO	810	747	26	37	G.W. Bush	92.2%	3.2%	4.6%
PANOLA	753	710	13	30	G.W. Bush	94.3%	1.7%	4.0%
PARKER	9,412	8,137	751	524	G.W. Bush	86.5%	8.0%	5.6%
PARMER	1,174	1,092	44	38	G.W. Bush	93.0%	3.7%	3.2%
PECOS	541	490	21	30	G.W. Bush	90.6%	3.9%	5.5%
POLK	2,947	2,398	454	95	G.W. Bush	81.4%	15.4%	3.2%
POTTER	8,956	7,675	653	628	G.W. Bush	85.7%	7.3%	7.0%
PRESIDIO	32	24	7	1	G.W. Bush	75.0%	21.9%	3.1%
RAINS	290	268	11	11	G.W. Bush	92.4%	3.8%	3.8%
RANDALL	15,124	13,318	928	878	G.W. Bush	88.1%	6.1%	5.8%
REAGAN	974	851	70	53	G.W. Bush	87.4%	7.2%	5.4%
REAL	544	479	39	26	G.W. Bush	88.1%	7.2%	4.8%
RED RIVER	149	139	3	7	G.W. Bush	93.3%	2.0%	4.7%
REEVES	22	19	1	2	G.W. Bush	86.4%	4.5%	9.1%
REFUGIO	188	183	3	2	G.W. Bush	97.3%	1.6%	1.1%
ROBERTS	385	339	28	18	G.W. Bush	88.1%	7.3%	4.7%
ROBERTSON	496	453	22	21	G.W. Bush	91.3%	4.4%	4.2%
ROCKWALL	6,459	5,554	528	377	G.W. Bush	86.0%	8.2%	5.8%
RUNNELS	298	273	16	9	G.W. Bush	91.6%	5.4%	3.0%
RUSK	2,930	2,728	103	99	G.W. Bush	93.1%	3.5%	3.4%
SABINE	329	300	20	9	G.W. Bush	91.2%	6.1%	2.7%
SAN AUGUSTINE	87	75	5	7	G.W. Bush	86.2%	5.7%	8.0%
SAN JACINTO	979	874	60	45	G.W. Bush	89.3%	6.1%	4.6%
SAN PATRICIO	1,699	1,546	76	77	G.W. Bush	91.0%	4.5%	4.5%
SAN SABA	456	426	18	12	G.W. Bush	93.4%	3.9%	2.6%
SCHLEICHER	229	221	5	3	G.W. Bush	96.5%	2.2%	1.3%
SCURRY	1,504	1,360	89	55	G.W. Bush	90.4%	5.9%	3.7%
SHACKELFORD	129	121	7	1	G.W. Bush	93.8%	5.4%	0.8%
SHELBY	911	858	25	28	G.W. Bush	94.2%	2.7%	3.1%
SHERMAN	202	194	5	3	G.W. Bush	96.0%	2.5%	1.5%
SMITH	14,805	13,539	598	668	G.W. Bush	91.4%	4.0%	4.5%
SOMERVELL	298	275	7	16	G.W. Bush	92.3%	2.3%	5.4%
STARR	56	48	5	3	G.W. Bush	85.7%	8.9%	5.4%
STEPHENS	297	271	13	13	G.W. Bush	91.2%	4.4%	4.4%
STERLING	222	210	6	6	G.W. Bush	94.6%	2.7%	2.7%
STONEWALL	13	12	0	1	G.W. Bush	92.3%	0.0%	7.7%
SUTTON	236	225	6	5	G.W. Bush	95.3%	2.5%	2.1%
SWISHER	149	134	5	10	G.W. Bush	89.9%	3.4%	6.7%
TARRANT	83,656	72,557	6,410	4,689	G.W. Bush	86.7%	7.7%	5.6%
TAYLOR	9,768	8,730	587	451	G.W. Bush	89.4%	6.0%	4.6%
TERRELL	9	9	0	0	G.W. Bush	100.0%	0.0%	0.0%
TERRY	535	524	0	11	G.W. Bush	97.9%	0.0%	2.1%
THROCKMORTON	19	19	0	0	G.W. Bush	100.0%	0.0%	0.0%
TITUS	633	585	18	30	G.W. Bush	92.4%	2.8%	4.7%

TEXAS REPUBLICAN PRIMARY

2000

County	Total Vote	G.W. Bush	McCain	Other	Winner	Percentage of Total Vote		
						G.W. Bush	McCain	Other
TOM GREEN	10,556	9,295	807	454	G.W. Bush	88.1%	7.6%	4.3%
TRAVIS	47,157	39,128	5,237	2,792	G.W. Bush	83.0%	11.1%	5.9%
TRINITY	405	366	25	14	G.W. Bush	90.4%	6.2%	3.5%
TYLER	419	381	18	20	G.W. Bush	90.9%	4.3%	4.8%
UPSHUR	1,370	1,282	32	56	G.W. Bush	93.6%	2.3%	4.1%
UPTON	0	0	0	0				
UVALDE	703	620	25	58	G.W. Bush	88.2%	3.6%	8.3%
VAL VERDE	948	812	71	65	G.W. Bush	85.7%	7.5%	6.9%
VAN ZANDT	3,155	2,934	84	137	G.W. Bush	93.0%	2.7%	4.3%
VICTORIA	4,700	4,261	202	237	G.W. Bush	90.7%	4.3%	5.0%
WALKER	3,043	2,626	248	169	G.W. Bush	86.3%	8.1%	5.6%
WALLER	1,431	1,331	39	61	G.W. Bush	93.0%	2.7%	4.3%
WARD	129	110	5	14	G.W. Bush	85.3%	3.9%	10.9%
WASHINGTON	4,250	3,963	144	143	G.W. Bush	93.2%	3.4%	3.4%
WEBB	1,301	1,157	104	40	G.W. Bush	88.9%	8.0%	3.1%
WHARTON	4,231	3,745	297	189	G.W. Bush	88.5%	7.0%	4.5%
WHEELER	305	277	3	25	G.W. Bush	90.8%	1.0%	8.2%
WICHITA	6,158	5,534	369	255	G.W. Bush	89.9%	6.0%	4.1%
WILBARGER	654	613	27	14	G.W. Bush	93.7%	4.1%	2.1%
WILLACY	54	46	6	2	G.W. Bush	85.2%	11.1%	3.7%
WILLIAMSON	22,124	18,694	2,165	1,265	G.W. Bush	84.5%	9.8%	5.7%
WILSON	1,701	1,549	61	91	G.W. Bush	91.1%	3.6%	5.3%
WINKLER	1,032	851	100	81	G.W. Bush	82.5%	9.7%	7.8%
WISE	2,558	2,334	111	113	G.W. Bush	91.2%	4.3%	4.4%
WOOD	3,166	2,912	132	122	G.W. Bush	92.0%	4.2%	3.9%
YOAKUM	655	594	26	35	G.W. Bush	90.7%	4.0%	5.3%
YOUNG	1,039	935	35	69	G.W. Bush	90.0%	3.4%	6.6%
ZAPATA	102	88	10	4	G.W. Bush	86.3%	9.8%	3.9%
ZAVALA	57	49	2	6	G.W. Bush	86.0%	3.5%	10.5%
TOTAL	1,126,757	986,416	80,082	60,259	G.W. Bush	87.5%	7.1%	5.3%

Note: Other vote was 43,518 Alan Keyes; 9,570 Uncommitted; 2,865 Steve Forbes; 2,189 Gary Bauer; 1,324 Orrin G. Hatch; 793 Charles Bass Urban. No vote was reported in six counties.

TEXAS DEMOCRATIC PRIMARY

2004

County	Total Vote	Edwards	Kerry	Other	Winner	Percentage of Total Vote		
						Edwards	Kerry	Other
ANDERSON	2,294	424	1,446	424	Kerry	18.5%	63.0%	18.5%
ANDREWS	1,245	483	466	296	Edwards	38.8%	37.4%	23.8%
ANGELINA	4,727	1,016	3,074	637	Kerry	21.5%	65.0%	13.5%
ARANSAS	673	82	523	68	Kerry	12.2%	77.7%	10.1%
ARCHER	888	166	495	227	Kerry	18.7%	55.7%	25.6%
ARMSTRONG	44	8	31	5	Kerry	18.2%	70.5%	11.4%
ATASCOSA	2,735	366	1,867	502	Kerry	13.4%	68.3%	18.4%
AUSTIN	499	53	376	70	Kerry	10.6%	75.4%	14.0%
BAILEY	272	51	163	58	Kerry	18.8%	59.9%	21.3%
BANDERA	279	37	215	27	Kerry	13.3%	77.1%	9.7%
BASTROP	4,598	688	3,021	889	Kerry	15.0%	65.7%	19.3%
BAYLOR	402	108	195	99	Kerry	26.9%	48.5%	24.6%
BEE	3,437	505	2,127	805	Kerry	14.7%	61.9%	23.4%
BELL	3,229	400	2,460	369	Kerry	12.4%	76.2%	11.4%
BEXAR	48,808	4,326	38,059	6,423	Kerry	8.9%	78.0%	13.2%
BLANCO	340	48	241	51	Kerry	14.1%	70.9%	15.0%
BORDEN	167	46	63	58	Kerry	27.5%	37.7%	34.7%
BOSQUE	1,753	417	999	337	Kerry	23.8%	57.0%	19.2%
BOWIE	8,785	1,628	5,250	1,907	Kerry	18.5%	59.8%	21.7%
BRAZORIA	3,972	529	2,921	522	Kerry	13.3%	73.5%	13.1%
BRAZOS	2,059	232	1,518	309	Kerry	11.3%	73.7%	15.0%
BREWSTER	1,373	287	747	339	Kerry	20.9%	54.4%	24.7%
BRISCOE	75	14	47	14	Kerry	18.7%	62.7%	18.7%
BROOKS	2,627	323	1,613	691	Kerry	12.3%	61.4%	26.3%
BROWN	850	169	586	95	Kerry	19.9%	68.9%	11.2%
BURLESON	1,241	159	908	174	Kerry	12.8%	73.2%	14.0%
BURNET	1,305	179	1,013	113	Kerry	13.7%	77.6%	8.7%
CALDWELL	2,609	406	1,672	531	Kerry	15.6%	64.1%	20.4%
CALHOUN	2,055	412	1,231	412	Kerry	20.0%	59.9%	20.0%
CALLAHAN	259	65	159	35	Kerry	25.1%	61.4%	13.5%
CAMERON	22,761	3,868	14,117	4,776	Kerry	17.0%	62.0%	21.0%
CAMP	1,204	225	777	202	Kerry	18.7%	64.5%	16.8%
CARSON	221	47	149	25	Kerry	21.3%	67.4%	11.3%
CASS	2,843	512	1,802	529	Kerry	18.0%	63.4%	18.6%
CASTRO	428	68	269	91	Kerry	15.9%	62.9%	21.3%
CHAMBERS	968	142	620	206	Kerry	14.7%	64.0%	21.3%
CHEROKEE	2,669	507	1,541	621	Kerry	19.0%	57.7%	23.3%
CHILDRESS	187	47	118	22	Kerry	25.1%	63.1%	11.8%
CLAY	1,488	330	825	333	Kerry	22.2%	55.4%	22.4%
COCHRAN	160	39	93	28	Kerry	24.4%	58.1%	17.5%
COKE	590	173	250	167	Kerry	29.3%	42.4%	28.3%
COLEMAN	415	88	232	95	Kerry	21.2%	55.9%	22.9%
COLLIN	6,503	1,041	4,665	797	Kerry	16.0%	71.7%	12.3%
COLLINGSWORTH	499	149	242	108	Kerry	29.9%	48.5%	21.6%
COLORADO	859	122	567	170	Kerry	14.2%	66.0%	19.8%

TEXAS DEMOCRATIC PRIMARY

2004

County	Total Vote	Edwards	Kerry	Other	Winner	Percentage of Total Vote Edwards	Kerry	Other
COMAL	2,295	248	1,778	269	Kerry	10.8%	77.5%	11.7%
COMANCHE	1,183	227	707	249	Kerry	19.2%	59.8%	21.0%
CONCHO	497	120	226	151	Kerry	24.1%	45.5%	30.4%
COOKE	481	76	362	43	Kerry	15.8%	75.3%	8.9%
CORYELL	1,055	220	735	100	Kerry	20.9%	69.7%	9.5%
COTTLE	307	75	169	63	Kerry	24.4%	55.0%	20.5%
CRANE	972	385	298	289	Edwards	39.6%	30.7%	29.7%
CROCKETT	482	69	268	145	Kerry	14.3%	55.6%	30.1%
CROSBY	216	29	129	58	Kerry	13.4%	59.7%	26.9%
CULBERSON	640	106	404	130	Kerry	16.6%	63.1%	20.3%
DALLAM	70	11	48	11	Kerry	15.7%	68.6%	15.7%
DALLAS	51,775	4,201	39,374	8,200	Kerry	8.1%	76.0%	15.8%
DAWSON	465	111	263	91	Kerry	23.9%	56.6%	19.6%
DEAF SMITH	183	36	119	28	Kerry	19.7%	65.0%	15.3%
DELTA	785	167	422	196	Kerry	21.3%	53.8%	25.0%
DENTON	4,679	700	3,264	715	Kerry	15.0%	69.8%	15.3%
DE WITT	503	64	385	54	Kerry	12.7%	76.5%	10.7%
DICKENS	356	97	174	85	Kerry	27.2%	48.9%	23.9%
DIMMIT	2,468	311	1,654	503	Kerry	12.6%	67.0%	20.4%
DONLEY	164	23	123	18	Kerry	14.0%	75.0%	11.0%
DUVAL	3,844	251	3,233	360	Kerry	6.5%	84.1%	9.4%
EASTLAND	745	136	505	104	Kerry	18.3%	67.8%	14.0%
ECTOR	1,744	416	1,157	171	Kerry	23.9%	66.3%	9.8%
EDWARDS	122	29	67	26	Kerry	23.8%	54.9%	21.3%
ELLIS	1,634	208	1,233	193	Kerry	12.7%	75.5%	11.8%
EL PASO	33,396	4,307	23,109	5,980	Kerry	12.9%	69.2%	17.9%
ERATH	792	140	574	78	Kerry	17.7%	72.5%	9.8%
FALLS	1,580	293	959	328	Kerry	18.5%	60.7%	20.8%
FANNIN	1,725	338	1,169	218	Kerry	19.6%	67.8%	12.6%
FAYETTE	2,263	305	1,474	484	Kerry	13.5%	65.1%	21.4%
FISHER	824	162	503	159	Kerry	19.7%	61.0%	19.3%
FLOYD	185	36	107	42	Kerry	19.5%	57.8%	22.7%
FOARD	376	56	222	98	Kerry	14.9%	59.0%	26.1%
FORT BEND	10,343	749	7,557	2,037	Kerry	7.2%	73.1%	19.7%
FRANKLIN	620	119	399	102	Kerry	19.2%	64.4%	16.5%
FREESTONE	1,565	378	794	393	Kerry	24.2%	50.7%	25.1%
FRIO	3,103	402	2,001	700	Kerry	13.0%	64.5%	22.6%
GAINES	900	271	389	240	Kerry	30.1%	43.2%	26.7%
GALVESTON	9,812	1,203	6,914	1,695	Kerry	12.3%	70.5%	17.3%
GARZA	448	81	234	133	Kerry	18.1%	52.2%	29.7%
GILLESPIE	458	48	379	31	Kerry	10.5%	82.8%	6.8%
GLASSCOCK	0	0	0	0				
GOLIAD	1,010	102	665	243	Kerry	10.1%	65.8%	24.1%
GONZALES	1,056	192	653	211	Kerry	18.2%	61.8%	20.0%
GRAY	169	18	139	12	Kerry	10.7%	82.2%	7.1%

TEXAS DEMOCRATIC PRIMARY

2004

County	Total Vote	Edwards	Kerry	Other	Winner	Percentage of Total Vote		
						Edwards	Kerry	Other
GRAYSON	2,680	503	1,891	286	Kerry	18.8%	70.6%	10.7%
GREGG	2,019	217	1,552	250	Kerry	10.7%	76.9%	12.4%
GRIMES	866	125	585	156	Kerry	14.4%	67.6%	18.0%
GUADALUPE	2,176	228	1,739	209	Kerry	10.5%	79.9%	9.6%
HALE	464	81	344	39	Kerry	17.5%	74.1%	8.4%
HALL	486	78	288	120	Kerry	16.0%	59.3%	24.7%
HAMILTON	324	67	214	43	Kerry	20.7%	66.0%	13.3%
HANSFORD	0	0	0	0				
HARDEMAN	508	100	248	160	Kerry	19.7%	48.8%	31.5%
HARDIN	4,960	990	2,730	1,240	Kerry	20.0%	55.0%	25.0%
HARRIS	73,747	8,668	53,034	12,045	Kerry	11.8%	71.9%	16.3%
HARRISON	4,028	889	2,550	589	Kerry	22.1%	63.3%	14.6%
HARTLEY	76	19	51	6	Kerry	25.0%	67.1%	7.9%
HASKELL	969	161	655	153	Kerry	16.6%	67.6%	15.8%
HAYS	4,531	664	3,014	853	Kerry	14.7%	66.5%	18.8%
HEMPHILL	32	10	17	5	Kerry	31.3%	53.1%	15.6%
HENDERSON	2,292	225	1,795	272	Kerry	9.8%	78.3%	11.9%
HIDALGO	40,261	4,579	26,294	9,388	Kerry	11.4%	65.3%	23.3%
HILL	1,395	263	984	148	Kerry	18.9%	70.5%	10.6%
HOCKLEY	303	63	203	37	Kerry	20.8%	67.0%	12.2%
HOOD	959	197	686	76	Kerry	20.5%	71.5%	7.9%
HOPKINS	2,274	474	1,301	499	Kerry	20.8%	57.2%	21.9%
HOUSTON	2,594	497	1,367	730	Kerry	19.2%	52.7%	28.1%
HOWARD	1,454	290	896	268	Kerry	19.9%	61.6%	18.4%
HUDSPETH	446	50	240	156	Kerry	11.2%	53.8%	35.0%
HUNT	2,130	355	1,498	277	Kerry	16.7%	70.3%	13.0%
HUTCHINSON	255	31	210	14	Kerry	12.2%	82.4%	5.5%
IRION	147	34	67	46	Kerry	23.1%	45.6%	31.3%
JACK	474	102	261	111	Kerry	21.5%	55.1%	23.4%
JACKSON	1,981	315	1,062	604	Kerry	15.9%	53.6%	30.5%
JASPER	4,450	864	2,406	1,180	Kerry	19.4%	54.1%	26.5%
JEFF DAVIS	508	147	221	140	Kerry	28.9%	43.5%	27.6%
JEFFERSON	21,789	3,361	13,814	4,614	Kerry	15.4%	63.4%	21.2%
JIM HOGG	2,183	190	1,613	380	Kerry	8.7%	73.9%	17.4%
JIM WELLS	7,559	1,000	4,996	1,563	Kerry	13.2%	66.1%	20.7%
JOHNSON	2,330	312	1,788	230	Kerry	13.4%	76.7%	9.9%
JONES	551	102	382	67	Kerry	18.5%	69.3%	12.2%
KARNES	2,279	364	1,315	600	Kerry	16.0%	57.7%	26.3%
KAUFMAN	2,151	213	1,632	306	Kerry	9.9%	75.9%	14.2%
KENDALL	416	58	306	52	Kerry	13.9%	73.6%	12.5%
KENEDY	103	18	54	31	Kerry	17.5%	52.4%	30.1%
KENT	326	76	149	101	Kerry	23.3%	45.7%	31.0%
KERR	1,034	155	775	104	Kerry	15.0%	75.0%	10.1%
KIMBLE	136	22	94	20	Kerry	16.2%	69.1%	14.7%
KING	57	21	18	18	Edwards	36.8%	31.6%	31.6%

TEXAS DEMOCRATIC PRIMARY

2004

County	Total Vote	Edwards	Kerry	Other	Winner	Percentage of Total Vote Edwards	Kerry	Other
KINNEY	445	100	220	125	Kerry	22.5%	49.4%	28.1%
KLEBERG	4,235	619	2,696	920	Kerry	14.6%	63.7%	21.7%
KNOX	679	118	406	155	Kerry	17.4%	59.8%	22.8%
LAMAR	5,420	1,240	2,876	1,304	Kerry	22.9%	53.1%	24.1%
LAMB	919	255	460	204	Kerry	27.7%	50.1%	22.2%
LAMPASAS	407	79	282	46	Kerry	19.4%	69.3%	11.3%
LA SALLE	1,466	141	977	348	Kerry	9.6%	66.6%	23.7%
LAVACA	3,086	542	1,726	818	Kerry	17.6%	55.9%	26.5%
LEE	1,994	484	1,093	417	Kerry	24.3%	54.8%	20.9%
LEON	549	96	417	36	Kerry	17.5%	76.0%	6.6%
LIBERTY	4,251	819	2,395	1,037	Kerry	19.3%	56.3%	24.4%
LIMESTONE	2,371	514	1,347	510	Kerry	21.7%	56.8%	21.5%
LIPSCOMB	95	20	63	12	Kerry	21.1%	66.3%	12.6%
LIVE OAK	949	160	538	251	Kerry	16.9%	56.7%	26.4%
LLANO	777	71	644	62	Kerry	9.1%	82.9%	8.0%
LOVING	52	11	17	24	Kerry	21.2%	32.7%	46.2%
LUBBOCK	4,747	674	3,413	660	Kerry	14.2%	71.9%	13.9%
LYNN	777	176	378	223	Kerry	22.7%	48.6%	28.7%
MCCULLOCH	579	109	347	123	Kerry	18.8%	59.9%	21.2%
MCLENNAN	5,196	705	3,949	542	Kerry	13.6%	76.0%	10.4%
MCMULLEN	85	18	36	31	Kerry	21.2%	42.4%	36.5%
MADISON	725	143	424	158	Kerry	19.7%	58.5%	21.8%
MARION	1,806	362	1,038	406	Kerry	20.0%	57.5%	22.5%
MARTIN	61	16	34	11	Kerry	26.2%	55.7%	18.0%
MASON	87	20	59	8	Kerry	23.0%	67.8%	9.2%
MATAGORDA	1,485	263	949	273	Kerry	17.7%	63.9%	18.4%
MAVERICK	6,529	820	4,012	1,697	Kerry	12.6%	61.4%	26.0%
MEDINA	2,096	337	1,292	467	Kerry	16.1%	61.6%	22.3%
MENARD	286	51	170	65	Kerry	17.8%	59.4%	22.7%
MIDLAND	1,616	291	1,080	245	Kerry	18.0%	66.8%	15.2%
MILAM	2,496	501	1,514	481	Kerry	20.1%	60.7%	19.3%
MILLS	622	180	275	167	Kerry	28.9%	44.2%	26.8%
MITCHELL	378	132	193	53	Kerry	34.9%	51.1%	14.0%
MONTAGUE	1,774	305	1,052	417	Kerry	17.2%	59.3%	23.5%
MONTGOMERY	3,336	473	2,491	372	Kerry	14.2%	74.7%	11.2%
MOORE	142	26	97	19	Kerry	18.3%	68.3%	13.4%
MORRIS	2,616	482	1,573	561	Kerry	18.4%	60.1%	21.4%
MOTLEY	92	19	54	19	Kerry	20.7%	58.7%	20.7%
NACOGDOCHES	1,931	225	1,492	214	Kerry	11.7%	77.3%	11.1%
NAVARRO	1,782	365	1,202	215	Kerry	20.5%	67.5%	12.1%
NEWTON	2,845	553	1,626	666	Kerry	19.4%	57.2%	23.4%
NOLAN	907	244	467	196	Kerry	26.9%	51.5%	21.6%
NUECES	24,331	3,428	16,373	4,530	Kerry	14.1%	67.3%	18.6%
OCHILTREE	0	0	0	0				
OLDHAM	210	58	97	55	Kerry	27.6%	46.2%	26.2%

TEXAS DEMOCRATIC PRIMARY

2004

County	Total Vote	Edwards	Kerry	Other	Winner	Percentage of Total Vote		
						Edwards	Kerry	Other
ORANGE	8,250	2,050	4,746	1,454	Kerry	24.8%	57.5%	17.6%
PALO PINTO	2,323	400	1,380	543	Kerry	17.2%	59.4%	23.4%
PANOLA	2,090	439	1,158	493	Kerry	21.0%	55.4%	23.6%
PARKER	1,723	234	1,310	179	Kerry	13.6%	76.0%	10.4%
PARMER	190	38	114	38	Kerry	20.0%	60.0%	20.0%
PECOS	2,059	574	944	541	Kerry	27.9%	45.8%	26.3%
POLK	3,097	678	1,876	543	Kerry	21.9%	60.6%	17.5%
POTTER	1,419	164	1,103	152	Kerry	11.6%	77.7%	10.7%
PRESIDIO	1,341	264	794	283	Kerry	19.7%	59.2%	21.1%
RAINS	1,355	202	775	378	Kerry	14.9%	57.2%	27.9%
RANDALL	1,170	189	894	87	Kerry	16.2%	76.4%	7.4%
REAGAN	16	2	13	1	Kerry	12.5%	81.3%	6.3%
REAL	52	8	36	8	Kerry	15.4%	69.2%	15.4%
RED RIVER	2,173	450	1,157	566	Kerry	20.7%	53.2%	26.0%
REEVES	2,499	630	1,264	605	Kerry	25.2%	50.6%	24.2%
REFUGIO	1,452	238	801	413	Kerry	16.4%	55.2%	28.4%
ROBERTS	0	0	0	0				
ROBERTSON	2,275	448	1,375	452	Kerry	19.7%	60.4%	19.9%
ROCKWALL	734	116	470	148	Kerry	15.8%	64.0%	20.2%
RUNNELS	760	189	376	195	Kerry	24.9%	49.5%	25.7%
RUSK	1,991	428	1,241	322	Kerry	21.5%	62.3%	16.2%
SABINE	1,584	320	886	378	Kerry	20.2%	55.9%	23.9%
SAN AUGUSTINE	1,728	333	902	493	Kerry	19.3%	52.2%	28.5%
SAN JACINTO	2,056	433	1,333	290	Kerry	21.1%	64.8%	14.1%
SAN PATRICIO	3,950	547	2,686	717	Kerry	13.8%	68.0%	18.2%
SAN SABA	139	22	104	13	Kerry	15.8%	74.8%	9.4%
SCHLEICHER	397	89	187	121	Kerry	22.4%	47.1%	30.5%
SCURRY	297	41	224	32	Kerry	13.8%	75.4%	10.8%
SHACKELFORD	91	21	55	15	Kerry	23.1%	60.4%	16.5%
SHELBY	3,052	629	1,699	724	Kerry	20.6%	55.7%	23.7%
SHERMAN	77	22	36	19	Kerry	28.6%	46.8%	24.7%
SMITH	2,995	336	2,257	402	Kerry	11.2%	75.4%	13.4%
SOMERVELL	324	54	219	51	Kerry	16.7%	67.6%	15.7%
STARR	6,401	479	4,540	1,382	Kerry	7.5%	70.9%	21.6%
STEPHENS	718	219	353	146	Kerry	30.5%	49.2%	20.3%
STERLING	32	4	22	6	Kerry	12.5%	68.8%	18.8%
STONEWALL	230	44	146	40	Kerry	19.1%	63.5%	17.4%
SUTTON	153	23	100	30	Kerry	15.0%	65.4%	19.6%
SWISHER	364	69	232	63	Kerry	19.0%	63.7%	17.3%
TARRANT	30,372	3,229	22,998	4,145	Kerry	10.6%	75.7%	13.6%
TAYLOR	2,197	427	1,488	282	Kerry	19.4%	67.7%	12.8%
TERRELL	296	67	167	62	Kerry	22.6%	56.4%	20.9%
TERRY	1,355	324	615	416	Kerry	23.9%	45.4%	30.7%
THROCKMORTON	190	41	113	36	Kerry	21.6%	59.5%	18.9%
TITUS	2,296	497	1,391	408	Kerry	21.6%	60.6%	17.8%

TEXAS DEMOCRATIC PRIMARY

2004

County	Total Vote	Edwards	Kerry	Other	Winner	Percentage of Total Vote		
						Edwards	Kerry	Other
TOM GREEN	2,096	355	1,542	199	Kerry	16.9%	73.6%	9.5%
TRAVIS	63,964	9,225	41,732	13,007	Kerry	14.4%	65.2%	20.3%
TRINITY	3,023	655	1,538	830	Kerry	21.7%	50.9%	27.5%
TYLER	4,063	788	2,218	1,057	Kerry	19.4%	54.6%	26.0%
UPSHUR	2,869	500	1,762	607	Kerry	17.4%	61.4%	21.2%
UPTON	478	141	176	161	Kerry	29.5%	36.8%	33.7%
UVALDE	3,760	608	2,161	991	Kerry	16.2%	57.5%	26.4%
VAL VERDE	1,814	160	1,412	242	Kerry	8.8%	77.8%	13.3%
VAN ZANDT	1,880	315	1,293	272	Kerry	16.8%	68.8%	14.5%
VICTORIA	3,790	500	2,479	811	Kerry	13.2%	65.4%	21.4%
WALKER	2,145	359	1,492	294	Kerry	16.7%	69.6%	13.7%
WALLER	1,357	112	885	360	Kerry	8.3%	65.2%	26.5%
WARD	1,505	422	653	430	Kerry	28.0%	43.4%	28.6%
WASHINGTON	1,023	110	748	165	Kerry	10.8%	73.1%	16.1%
WEBB	27,120	3,847	17,086	6,187	Kerry	14.2%	63.0%	22.8%
WHARTON	997	119	722	156	Kerry	11.9%	72.4%	15.6%
WHEELER	730	180	327	223	Kerry	24.7%	44.8%	30.5%
WICHITA	2,523	374	1,838	311	Kerry	14.8%	72.8%	12.3%
WILBARGER	1,212	243	638	331	Kerry	20.0%	52.6%	27.3%
WILLACY	2,968	394	1,852	722	Kerry	13.3%	62.4%	24.3%
WILLIAMSON	8,078	1,369	5,632	1,077	Kerry	16.9%	69.7%	13.3%
WILSON	3,376	436	2,390	550	Kerry	12.9%	70.8%	16.3%
WINKLER	144	30	95	19	Kerry	20.8%	66.0%	13.2%
WISE	1,846	313	1,270	263	Kerry	17.0%	68.8%	14.2%
WOOD	2,134	371	1,339	424	Kerry	17.4%	62.7%	19.9%
YOAKUM	265	61	159	45	Kerry	23.0%	60.0%	17.0%
YOUNG	605	113	425	67	Kerry	18.7%	70.2%	11.1%
ZAPATA	2,194	253	1,473	468	Kerry	11.5%	67.1%	21.3%
ZAVALA	1,389	125	1,046	218	Kerry	9.0%	75.3%	15.7%
TOTAL	839,231	120,413	563,237	155,581	Kerry	14.3%	67.1%	18.5%

Note: Other vote was 40,035 Howard Dean; 31,020 Al Sharpton; 25,245 Joseph I. Lieberman; 18,437 Wesley Clark; 15,475 Dennis J. Kucinich; 12,160 Richard A. Gephardt; 6,871 Lyndon H. LaRouche Jr.; 6,338 Randy Crow. No vote was reported in four counties.

TEXAS REPUBLICAN PRIMARY

2004

| County | Total Vote | G.W. Bush | Uncommitted | Winner | Percentage of Total Vote | |
					G.W. Bush	Uncommitted
ANDERSON	3,425	3,069	356	G.W. Bush	89.6%	10.4%
ANDREWS	316	307	9	G.W. Bush	97.2%	2.8%
ANGELINA	2,980	2,859	121	G.W. Bush	95.9%	4.1%
ARANSAS	2,535	2,272	263	G.W. Bush	89.6%	10.4%
ARCHER	167	160	7	G.W. Bush	95.8%	4.2%
ARMSTRONG	399	348	51	G.W. Bush	87.2%	12.8%
ATASCOSA	527	507	20	G.W. Bush	96.2%	3.8%
AUSTIN	2,600	2,384	216	G.W. Bush	91.7%	8.3%
BAILEY	701	654	47	G.W. Bush	93.3%	6.7%
BANDERA	3,360	2,920	440	G.W. Bush	86.9%	13.1%
BASTROP	2,883	2,681	202	G.W. Bush	93.0%	7.0%
BAYLOR	33	31	2	G.W. Bush	93.9%	6.1%
BEE	754	702	52	G.W. Bush	93.1%	6.9%
BELL	8,314	7,913	401	G.W. Bush	95.2%	4.8%
BEXAR	21,507	20,340	1,167	G.W. Bush	94.6%	5.4%
BLANCO	900	835	65	G.W. Bush	92.8%	7.2%
BORDEN	6	6	0	G.W. Bush	100.0%	0.0%
BOSQUE	1,001	961	40	G.W. Bush	96.0%	4.0%
BOWIE	3,731	3,556	175	G.W. Bush	95.3%	4.7%
BRAZORIA	12,119	10,796	1,323	G.W. Bush	89.1%	10.9%
BRAZOS	8,648	7,870	778	G.W. Bush	91.0%	9.0%
BREWSTER	273	260	13	G.W. Bush	95.2%	4.8%
BRISCOE	93	92	1	G.W. Bush	98.9%	1.1%
BROOKS	0	0	0			
BROWN	3,629	3,413	216	G.W. Bush	94.0%	6.0%
BURLESON	1,115	1,066	49	G.W. Bush	95.6%	4.4%
BURNET	3,729	3,376	353	G.W. Bush	90.5%	9.5%
CALDWELL	1,166	1,103	63	G.W. Bush	94.6%	5.4%
CALHOUN	268	254	14	G.W. Bush	94.8%	5.2%
CALLAHAN	534	498	36	G.W. Bush	93.3%	6.7%
CAMERON	2,479	2,359	120	G.W. Bush	95.2%	4.8%
CAMP	91	88	3	G.W. Bush	96.7%	3.3%
CARSON	587	554	33	G.W. Bush	94.4%	5.6%
CASS	458	452	6	G.W. Bush	98.7%	1.3%
CASTRO	213	193	20	G.W. Bush	90.6%	9.4%
CHAMBERS	1,879	1,723	156	G.W. Bush	91.7%	8.3%
CHEROKEE	840	828	12	G.W. Bush	98.6%	1.4%
CHILDRESS	73	73	0	G.W. Bush	100.0%	0.0%
CLAY	172	166	6	G.W. Bush	96.5%	3.5%
COCHRAN	60	60	0	G.W. Bush	100.0%	0.0%
COKE	60	58	2	G.W. Bush	96.7%	3.3%
COLEMAN	278	270	8	G.W. Bush	97.1%	2.9%
COLLIN	16,374	15,038	1,336	G.W. Bush	91.8%	8.2%
COLLINGSWORTH	102	97	5	G.W. Bush	95.1%	4.9%
COLORADO	708	675	33	G.W. Bush	95.3%	4.7%

TEXAS REPUBLICAN PRIMARY

2004

County	Total Vote	G.W. Bush	Uncommitted	Winner	Percentage of Total Vote G.W. Bush	Uncommitted
COMAL	5,657	5,205	452	G.W. Bush	92.0%	8.0%
COMANCHE	332	326	6	G.W. Bush	98.2%	1.8%
CONCHO	106	102	4	G.W. Bush	96.2%	3.8%
COOKE	4,942	4,284	658	G.W. Bush	86.7%	13.3%
CORYELL	3,093	2,847	246	G.W. Bush	92.0%	8.0%
COTTLE	0	0	0			
CRANE	114	114	0	G.W. Bush	100.0%	0.0%
CROCKETT	0	0	0			
CROSBY	0	0	0			
CULBERSON	7	7	0	G.W. Bush	100.0%	0.0%
DALLAM	358	341	17	G.W. Bush	95.3%	4.7%
DALLAS	30,038	28,076	1,962	G.W. Bush	93.5%	6.5%
DAWSON	324	316	8	G.W. Bush	97.5%	2.5%
DEAF SMITH	1,216	1,132	84	G.W. Bush	93.1%	6.9%
DELTA	40	40	0	G.W. Bush	100.0%	0.0%
DENTON	14,922	13,201	1,721	G.W. Bush	88.5%	11.5%
DE WITT	1,566	1,442	124	G.W. Bush	92.1%	7.9%
DICKENS	9	9	0	G.W. Bush	100.0%	0.0%
DIMMIT	3	3	0	G.W. Bush	100.0%	0.0%
DONLEY	153	150	3	G.W. Bush	98.0%	2.0%
DUVAL	0	0	0			
EASTLAND	1,018	950	68	G.W. Bush	93.3%	6.7%
ECTOR	11,386	10,701	685	G.W. Bush	94.0%	6.0%
EDWARDS	95	95	0	G.W. Bush	100.0%	0.0%
ELLIS	4,252	3,920	332	G.W. Bush	92.2%	7.8%
EL PASO	8,229	7,776	453	G.W. Bush	94.5%	5.5%
ERATH	978	949	29	G.W. Bush	97.0%	3.0%
FALLS	191	187	4	G.W. Bush	97.9%	2.1%
FANNIN	1,150	1,081	69	G.W. Bush	94.0%	6.0%
FAYETTE	2,193	2,063	130	G.W. Bush	94.1%	5.9%
FISHER	9	9	0	G.W. Bush	100.0%	0.0%
FLOYD	252	245	7	G.W. Bush	97.2%	2.8%
FOARD	0	0	0			
FORT BEND	13,338	12,311	1,027	G.W. Bush	92.3%	7.7%
FRANKLIN	653	628	25	G.W. Bush	96.2%	3.8%
FREESTONE	319	314	5	G.W. Bush	98.4%	1.6%
FRIO	17	16	1	G.W. Bush	94.1%	5.9%
GAINES	381	375	6	G.W. Bush	98.4%	1.6%
GALVESTON	4,820	4,556	264	G.W. Bush	94.5%	5.5%
GARZA	103	103	0	G.W. Bush	100.0%	0.0%
GILLESPIE	3,626	3,285	341	G.W. Bush	90.6%	9.4%
GLASSCOCK	355	331	24	G.W. Bush	93.2%	6.8%
GOLIAD	378	354	24	G.W. Bush	93.7%	6.3%
GONZALES	792	717	75	G.W. Bush	90.5%	9.5%
GRAY	1,182	1,117	65	G.W. Bush	94.5%	5.5%

TEXAS REPUBLICAN PRIMARY

2004

County	Total Vote	G.W. Bush	Uncommitted	Winner	Percentage of Total Vote G.W. Bush	Uncommitted
GRAYSON	8,222	7,324	898	G.W. Bush	89.1%	10.9%
GREGG	8,813	8,313	500	G.W. Bush	94.3%	5.7%
GRIMES	1,271	1,152	119	G.W. Bush	90.6%	9.4%
GUADALUPE	6,074	5,496	578	G.W. Bush	90.5%	9.5%
HALE	2,515	2,303	212	G.W. Bush	91.6%	8.4%
HALL	24	24	0	G.W. Bush	100.0%	0.0%
HAMILTON	418	400	18	G.W. Bush	95.7%	4.3%
HANSFORD	1,833	1,607	226	G.W. Bush	87.7%	12.3%
HARDEMAN	19	18	1	G.W. Bush	94.7%	5.3%
HARDIN	1,021	990	31	G.W. Bush	97.0%	3.0%
HARRIS	78,898	73,845	5,053	G.W. Bush	93.6%	6.4%
HARRISON	2,723	2,608	115	G.W. Bush	95.8%	4.2%
HARTLEY	943	865	78	G.W. Bush	91.7%	8.3%
HASKELL	41	41	0	G.W. Bush	100.0%	0.0%
HAYS	4,363	4,109	254	G.W. Bush	94.2%	5.8%
HEMPHILL	1,017	909	108	G.W. Bush	89.4%	10.6%
HENDERSON	4,241	3,836	405	G.W. Bush	90.5%	9.5%
HIDALGO	2,307	2,205	102	G.W. Bush	95.6%	4.4%
HILL	1,273	1,230	43	G.W. Bush	96.6%	3.4%
HOCKLEY	2,336	2,151	185	G.W. Bush	92.1%	7.9%
HOOD	4,968	4,415	553	G.W. Bush	88.9%	11.1%
HOPKINS	538	528	10	G.W. Bush	98.1%	1.9%
HOUSTON	545	532	13	G.W. Bush	97.6%	2.4%
HOWARD	1,433	1,364	69	G.W. Bush	95.2%	4.8%
HUDSPETH	5	5	0	G.W. Bush	100.0%	0.0%
HUNT	3,603	3,331	272	G.W. Bush	92.5%	7.5%
HUTCHINSON	4,275	3,798	477	G.W. Bush	88.8%	11.2%
IRION	121	118	3	G.W. Bush	97.5%	2.5%
JACK	97	96	1	G.W. Bush	99.0%	1.0%
JACKSON	232	228	4	G.W. Bush	98.3%	1.7%
JASPER	322	319	3	G.W. Bush	99.1%	0.9%
JEFF DAVIS	135	125	10	G.W. Bush	92.6%	7.4%
JEFFERSON	4,517	4,370	147	G.W. Bush	96.7%	3.3%
JIM HOGG	9	9	0	G.W. Bush	100.0%	0.0%
JIM WELLS	430	409	21	G.W. Bush	95.1%	4.9%
JOHNSON	7,509	6,913	596	G.W. Bush	92.1%	7.9%
JONES	216	202	14	G.W. Bush	93.5%	6.5%
KARNES	105	98	7	G.W. Bush	93.3%	6.7%
KAUFMAN	2,965	2,736	229	G.W. Bush	92.3%	7.7%
KENDALL	3,818	3,405	413	G.W. Bush	89.2%	10.8%
KENEDY	11	11	0	G.W. Bush	100.0%	0.0%
KENT	4	4	0	G.W. Bush	100.0%	0.0%
KERR	6,402	5,751	651	G.W. Bush	89.8%	10.2%
KIMBLE	652	603	49	G.W. Bush	92.5%	7.5%
KING	42	42	0	G.W. Bush	100.0%	0.0%

TEXAS REPUBLICAN PRIMARY

2004

County	Total Vote	G.W. Bush	Uncommitted	Winner	Percentage of Total Vote G.W. Bush	Uncommitted
KINNEY	0	0	0			
KLEBERG	240	226	14	G.W. Bush	94.2%	5.8%
KNOX	35	35	0	G.W. Bush	100.0%	0.0%
LAMAR	1,312	1,282	30	G.W. Bush	97.7%	2.3%
LAMB	134	132	2	G.W. Bush	98.5%	1.5%
LAMPASAS	1,007	930	77	G.W. Bush	92.4%	7.6%
LA SALLE	1	1	0	G.W. Bush	100.0%	0.0%
LAVACA	394	375	19	G.W. Bush	95.2%	4.8%
LEE	437	424	13	G.W. Bush	97.0%	3.0%
LEON	1,084	1,014	70	G.W. Bush	93.5%	6.5%
LIBERTY	1,107	1,069	38	G.W. Bush	96.6%	3.4%
LIMESTONE	468	458	10	G.W. Bush	97.9%	2.1%
LIPSCOMB	588	554	34	G.W. Bush	94.2%	5.8%
LIVE OAK	325	314	11	G.W. Bush	96.6%	3.4%
LLANO	2,206	2,079	127	G.W. Bush	94.2%	5.8%
LOVING	0	0	0			
LUBBOCK	10,772	10,301	471	G.W. Bush	95.6%	4.4%
LYNN	17	17	0	G.W. Bush	100.0%	0.0%
MCCULLOCH	445	435	10	G.W. Bush	97.8%	2.2%
MCLENNAN	11,874	11,265	609	G.W. Bush	94.9%	5.1%
MCMULLEN	80	73	7	G.W. Bush	91.3%	8.8%
MADISON	384	372	12	G.W. Bush	96.9%	3.1%
MARION	68	68	0	G.W. Bush	100.0%	0.0%
MARTIN	730	671	59	G.W. Bush	91.9%	8.1%
MASON	977	855	122	G.W. Bush	87.5%	12.5%
MATAGORDA	763	700	63	G.W. Bush	91.7%	8.3%
MAVERICK	10	10	0	G.W. Bush	100.0%	0.0%
MEDINA	2,029	1,869	160	G.W. Bush	92.1%	7.9%
MENARD	311	278	33	G.W. Bush	89.4%	10.6%
MIDLAND	11,186	10,502	684	G.W. Bush	93.9%	6.1%
MILAM	376	366	10	G.W. Bush	97.3%	2.7%
MILLS	100	100	0	G.W. Bush	100.0%	0.0%
MITCHELL	230	215	15	G.W. Bush	93.5%	6.5%
MONTAGUE	548	494	54	G.W. Bush	90.1%	9.9%
MONTGOMERY	23,099	20,768	2,331	G.W. Bush	89.9%	10.1%
MOORE	2,484	2,207	277	G.W. Bush	88.8%	11.2%
MORRIS	101	96	5	G.W. Bush	95.0%	5.0%
MOTLEY	53	50	3	G.W. Bush	94.3%	5.7%
NACOGDOCHES	4,467	4,164	303	G.W. Bush	93.2%	6.8%
NAVARRO	1,144	1,104	40	G.W. Bush	96.5%	3.5%
NEWTON	122	121	1	G.W. Bush	99.2%	0.8%
NOLAN	145	144	1	G.W. Bush	99.3%	0.7%
NUECES	6,157	5,923	234	G.W. Bush	96.2%	3.8%
OCHILTREE	1,278	1,187	91	G.W. Bush	92.9%	7.1%
OLDHAM	88	83	5	G.W. Bush	94.3%	5.7%

TEXAS REPUBLICAN PRIMARY

2004

| County | Total Vote | G.W. Bush | Uncommitted | Winner | Percentage of Total Vote | |
					G.W. Bush	Uncommitted
ORANGE	1,109	1,070	39	G.W. Bush	96.5%	3.5%
PALO PINTO	341	332	9	G.W. Bush	97.4%	2.6%
PANOLA	444	433	11	G.W. Bush	97.5%	2.5%
PARKER	6,842	6,115	727	G.W. Bush	89.4%	10.6%
PARMER	803	756	47	G.W. Bush	94.1%	5.9%
PECOS	153	153	0	G.W. Bush	100.0%	0.0%
POLK	1,501	1,413	88	G.W. Bush	94.1%	5.9%
POTTER	8,160	7,231	929	G.W. Bush	88.6%	11.4%
PRESIDIO	14	14	0	G.W. Bush	100.0%	0.0%
RAINS	209	200	9	G.W. Bush	95.7%	4.3%
RANDALL	15,883	14,561	1,322	G.W. Bush	91.7%	8.3%
REAGAN	980	845	135	G.W. Bush	86.2%	13.8%
REAL	717	626	91	G.W. Bush	87.3%	12.7%
RED RIVER	77	75	2	G.W. Bush	97.4%	2.6%
REEVES	0	0	0			
REFUGIO	107	106	1	G.W. Bush	99.1%	0.9%
ROBERTS	173	158	15	G.W. Bush	91.3%	8.7%
ROBERTSON	479	465	14	G.W. Bush	97.1%	2.9%
ROCKWALL	4,674	4,321	353	G.W. Bush	92.4%	7.6%
RUNNELS	267	258	9	G.W. Bush	96.6%	3.4%
RUSK	3,885	3,627	258	G.W. Bush	93.4%	6.6%
SABINE	359	343	16	G.W. Bush	95.5%	4.5%
SAN AUGUSTINE	119	117	2	G.W. Bush	98.3%	1.7%
SAN JACINTO	692	667	25	G.W. Bush	96.4%	3.6%
SAN PATRICIO	924	891	33	G.W. Bush	96.4%	3.6%
SAN SABA	1,020	913	107	G.W. Bush	89.5%	10.5%
SCHLEICHER	103	99	4	G.W. Bush	96.1%	3.9%
SCURRY	1,070	1,019	51	G.W. Bush	95.2%	4.8%
SHACKELFORD	56	55	1	G.W. Bush	98.2%	1.8%
SHELBY	1,386	1,289	97	G.W. Bush	93.0%	7.0%
SHERMAN	241	225	16	G.W. Bush	93.4%	6.6%
SMITH	18,118	16,815	1,303	G.W. Bush	92.8%	7.2%
SOMERVELL	349	332	17	G.W. Bush	95.1%	4.9%
STARR	18	18	0	G.W. Bush	100.0%	0.0%
STEPHENS	82	78	4	G.W. Bush	95.1%	4.9%
STERLING	345	331	14	G.W. Bush	95.9%	4.1%
STONEWALL	19	19	0	G.W. Bush	100.0%	0.0%
SUTTON	122	119	3	G.W. Bush	97.5%	2.5%
SWISHER	302	262	40	G.W. Bush	86.8%	13.2%
TARRANT	25,033	23,601	1,432	G.W. Bush	94.3%	5.7%
TAYLOR	7,028	6,521	507	G.W. Bush	92.8%	7.2%
TERRELL	4	4	0	G.W. Bush	100.0%	0.0%
TERRY	125	122	3	G.W. Bush	97.6%	2.4%
THROCKMORTON	17	17	0	G.W. Bush	100.0%	0.0%
TITUS	561	549	12	G.W. Bush	97.9%	2.1%

TEXAS REPUBLICAN PRIMARY

2004

County	Total Vote	G.W. Bush	Uncommitted	Winner	Percentage of Total Vote	
					G.W. Bush	Uncommitted
TOM GREEN	7,485	6,998	487	G.W. Bush	93.5%	6.5%
TRAVIS	28,159	26,093	2,066	G.W. Bush	92.7%	7.3%
TRINITY	83	82	1	G.W. Bush	98.8%	1.2%
TYLER	134	134	0	G.W. Bush	100.0%	0.0%
UPSHUR	1,721	1,638	83	G.W. Bush	95.2%	4.8%
UPTON	0	0	0			
UVALDE	192	182	10	G.W. Bush	94.8%	5.2%
VAL VERDE	648	612	36	G.W. Bush	94.4%	5.6%
VAN ZANDT	1,446	1,376	70	G.W. Bush	95.2%	4.8%
VICTORIA	2,712	2,600	112	G.W. Bush	95.9%	4.1%
WALKER	3,347	3,039	308	G.W. Bush	90.8%	9.2%
WALLER	2,945	2,426	519	G.W. Bush	82.4%	17.6%
WARD	48	48	0	G.W. Bush	100.0%	0.0%
WASHINGTON	2,936	2,746	190	G.W. Bush	93.5%	6.5%
WEBB	846	788	58	G.W. Bush	93.1%	6.9%
WHARTON	2,514	2,306	208	G.W. Bush	91.7%	8.3%
WHEELER	242	233	9	G.W. Bush	96.3%	3.7%
WICHITA	2,086	2,016	70	G.W. Bush	96.6%	3.4%
WILBARGER	119	115	4	G.W. Bush	96.6%	3.4%
WILLACY	28	28	0	G.W. Bush	100.0%	0.0%
WILLIAMSON	23,998	20,637	3,361	G.W. Bush	86.0%	14.0%
WILSON	689	656	33	G.W. Bush	95.2%	4.8%
WINKLER	946	834	112	G.W. Bush	88.2%	11.8%
WISE	3,076	2,804	272	G.W. Bush	91.2%	8.8%
WOOD	3,290	3,121	169	G.W. Bush	94.9%	5.1%
YOAKUM	758	711	47	G.W. Bush	93.8%	6.2%
YOUNG	855	811	44	G.W. Bush	94.9%	5.1%
ZAPATA	21	21	0	G.W. Bush	100.0%	0.0%
ZAVALA	14	14	0	G.W. Bush	100.0%	0.0%
TOTAL	687,615	635,948	51,667	G.W. Bush	92.5%	7.5%

Note: No vote was reported in ten counties.

UTAH

Utah's first presidential primary in 2000 was something of a dud. The competitive stage of the nominating process was already over in both parties when the primary was held in March. And voters could not even cast a complimentary vote for the state's senior senator, Orrin G. Hatch, who had quit the Republican race several weeks earlier.

As it was, probably the most noteworthy element of the GOP primary was Alan Keyes' solid second-place finish. He won 30 percent of the vote in Utah County (Provo), where he personally campaigned, and took 21 percent of the vote statewide–Keyes' best showing in the 2000 primary season.

The state did not fund a presidential primary in 2004. But Utah Democrats held one of their own, using more than 100 libraries around the state as polling places. While the turnout of 35,000 was less than half the number that cast ballots in the Republican primary four years earlier, it was more than double the number that had participated in the 2000 Democratic primary. The state party had to print several thousand extra ballots to handle the unexpected turnout.

Much of the increased interest was due to the earlier date (the last Tuesday in February), when the Democratic nomination was still being contested. John Edwards, still alive in his challenge to John Kerry, did carry two rural counties. But Kerry won the statewide vote handily with a 2-to-1 margin over Edwards in populous Salt Lake County (Salt Lake City), where more than half the Democratic primary ballots were cast.

Kerry's winter-time victory in Utah, though, portended nothing for the fall. Democrats have not elected a governor in Utah since 1980, a U.S. senator since 1970, or carried the state in a presidential election since 1964. In six of the last eight presidential elections (including 2004), Utah has given the Republican candidate a higher share of the vote than any other state.

With its Mormon heritage, Utah is distinctive, although the concentration of its population mirrors Colorado's Front Range. More than three-fourths of Utah's residents live in a four-country strip along the Wasatch Range, from Weber County (Ogden) on the north to Utah County on the south. Forty percent live in Salt Lake County alone.

Despite its large membership, the Utah Republican Party has often been of one mind when selecting a presidential nominee. In the party's great moderate-conservative nominating contests since World War II, Utah consistently cast its vote for the conservative–from Robert A. Taft in 1952 to Barry Goldwater in 1964 to Ronald Reagan in 1976.

Utah's smaller cadre of Democrats have been more eclectic in their tastes. In 1984, the party's caucus attendees favored Gary Hart of neighboring Colorado. But in 1988 and 1992, Utah Democrats went for two Massachusetts natives, Michael Dukakis and Paul Tsongas, respectively. In 1992, Tsongas swept the populous four-county "Front Range" and took 33 percent of the 31,638 caucus votes cast statewide to defeat Jerry Brown (28 percent) and Bill Clinton (18 percent) in the early March balloting.

Yet over the years, Utah has rarely been more than a blip on the radar screen during the nominating season. In 1988, Utah's GOP caucuses were conducted so late in the process that the party ended up holding a straw vote to gauge preferences for vice president rather than for president.

Recent Utah Primary Results

Utah held its first presidential primary in 2000.

	DEMOCRATS			REPUBLICANS		
Year	Turnout	Candidates	%	Turnout	Candidates	%
2004 (Feb. 24)	34,854	JOHN KERRY	55	—	No Primary	
		John Edwards	30			
		Dennis Kucinich	7			
2000 (March 10)	15,687	AL GORE	80	91,053	GEORGE W. BUSH	63
		Bill Bradley	20		Alan Keyes	21
					John McCain	14

Note: All candidates are listed that drew at least 5 percent of their party's primary vote. The names of winning candidates are capitalized.

UTAH DEMOCRATIC PRIMARY

2000

| County | Total Vote | Bradley | Gore | Winner | Percentage of Total Vote | |
					Bradley	Gore
BEAVER	82	32	50	Gore	39.0%	61.0%
BOX ELDER	275	63	212	Gore	22.9%	77.1%
CACHE	430	116	314	Gore	27.0%	73.0%
CARBON	348	66	282	Gore	19.0%	81.0%
DAGGETT	16	5	11	Gore	31.3%	68.8%
DAVIS	1,117	226	891	Gore	20.2%	79.8%
DUCHESNE	107	17	90	Gore	15.9%	84.1%
EMERY	144	41	103	Gore	28.5%	71.5%
GARFIELD	46	12	34	Gore	26.1%	73.9%
GRAND	121	25	96	Gore	20.7%	79.3%
IRON	218	57	161	Gore	26.1%	73.9%
JUAB	88	21	67	Gore	23.9%	76.1%
KANE	70	16	54	Gore	22.9%	77.1%
MILLARD	128	49	79	Gore	38.3%	61.7%
MORGAN	30	5	25	Gore	16.7%	83.3%
PIUTE	36	15	21	Gore	41.7%	58.3%
RICH	25	6	19	Gore	24.0%	76.0%
SALT LAKE	7,015	1,327	5,688	Gore	18.9%	81.1%
SAN JUAN	390	113	277	Gore	29.0%	71.0%
SANPETE	166	49	117	Gore	29.5%	70.5%
SEVIER	133	30	103	Gore	22.6%	77.4%
SUMMIT	202	69	133	Gore	34.2%	65.8%
TOOELE	368	66	302	Gore	17.9%	82.1%
UINTAH	149	36	113	Gore	24.2%	75.8%
UTAH	1,260	260	1,000	Gore	20.6%	79.4%
WASATCH	75	15	60	Gore	20.0%	80.0%
WASHINGTON	624	107	517	Gore	17.1%	82.9%
WAYNE	19	8	11	Gore	42.1%	57.9%
WEBER	2,005	308	1,697	Gore	15.4%	84.6%
TOTAL	15,687	3,160	12,527	Gore	20.1%	79.9%

UTAH REPUBLICAN PRIMARY

2000

County	Total Vote	G.W. Bush	Keyes	McCain	Other	Winner	Percentage of Total Vote			
							G.W. Bush	Keyes	McCain	Other
BEAVER	264	210	17	36	1	G.W. Bush	79.5%	6.4%	13.6%	0.4%
BOX ELDER	2,189	1,461	348	348	32	G.W. Bush	66.7%	15.9%	15.9%	1.5%
CACHE	3,461	2,397	615	404	45	G.W. Bush	69.3%	17.8%	11.7%	1.3%
CARBON	427	292	49	75	11	G.W. Bush	68.4%	11.5%	17.6%	2.6%
DAGGETT	85	58	5	22	0	G.W. Bush	68.2%	5.9%	25.9%	0.0%
DAVIS	10,606	6,978	1,957	1,523	148	G.W. Bush	65.8%	18.5%	14.4%	1.4%
DUCHESNE	725	501	95	119	10	G.W. Bush	69.1%	13.1%	16.4%	1.4%
EMERY	626	461	49	107	9	G.W. Bush	73.6%	7.8%	17.1%	1.4%
GARFIELD	554	408	64	70	12	G.W. Bush	73.6%	11.6%	12.6%	2.2%
GRAND	445	260	99	79	7	G.W. Bush	58.4%	22.2%	17.8%	1.6%
IRON	1,959	1,271	406	249	33	G.W. Bush	64.9%	20.7%	12.7%	1.7%
JUAB	367	204	80	73	10	G.W. Bush	55.6%	21.8%	19.9%	2.7%
KANE	822	555	115	140	12	G.W. Bush	67.5%	14.0%	17.0%	1.5%
MILLARD	945	612	121	193	19	G.W. Bush	64.8%	12.8%	20.4%	2.0%
MORGAN	403	254	62	81	6	G.W. Bush	63.0%	15.4%	20.1%	1.5%
PIUTE	212	156	17	37	2	G.W. Bush	73.6%	8.0%	17.5%	0.9%
RICH	202	149	17	33	3	G.W. Bush	73.8%	8.4%	16.3%	1.5%
SALT LAKE	28,439	17,730	5,649	4,630	430	G.W. Bush	62.3%	19.9%	16.3%	1.5%
SAN JUAN	678	428	102	132	16	G.W. Bush	63.1%	15.0%	19.5%	2.4%
SANPETE	1,079	727	206	129	17	G.W. Bush	67.4%	19.1%	12.0%	1.6%
SEVIER	1,310	997	139	154	20	G.W. Bush	76.1%	10.6%	11.8%	1.5%
SUMMIT	682	378	123	172	9	G.W. Bush	55.4%	18.0%	25.2%	1.3%
TOOELE	1,229	762	249	200	18	G.W. Bush	62.0%	20.3%	16.3%	1.5%
UINTAH	1,257	963	135	138	21	G.W. Bush	76.6%	10.7%	11.0%	1.7%
UTAH	17,908	10,619	5,425	1,676	188	G.W. Bush	59.3%	30.3%	9.4%	1.0%
WASATCH	452	280	100	70	2	G.W. Bush	61.9%	22.1%	15.5%	0.4%
WASHINGTON	6,180	3,684	1,792	625	79	G.W. Bush	59.6%	29.0%	10.1%	1.3%
WAYNE	188	151	17	19	1	G.W. Bush	80.3%	9.0%	10.1%	0.5%
WEBER	7,359	4,671	1,314	1,250	124	G.W. Bush	63.5%	17.9%	17.0%	1.7%
TOTAL	91,053	57,617	19,367	12,784	1,285	G.W. Bush	63.3%	21.3%	14.0%	1.4%

Note: Other vote was 859 Steve Forbes; 426 Gary Bauer.

UTAH DEMOCRATIC PIMARY

2004

County	Total Vote	Edwards	Kerry	Kucinich	Other	Winner	Percentage of Total Vote			
							Edwards	Kerry	Kucinich	Other
BEAVER	95	33	48	2	12	Kerry	34.7%	50.5%	2.1%	12.6%
BOX ELDER	253	95	114	21	23	Kerry	37.5%	45.1%	8.3%	9.1%
CACHE	1,293	440	623	126	104	Kerry	34.0%	48.2%	9.7%	8.0%
CARBON	956	267	579	25	85	Kerry	27.9%	60.6%	2.6%	8.9%
DAGGETT										
DAVIS	2,435	799	1,360	119	157	Kerry	32.8%	55.9%	4.9%	6.4%
DUCHESNE	145	48	78	8	11	Kerry	33.1%	53.8%	5.5%	7.6%
EMERY	252	70	147	9	26	Kerry	27.8%	58.3%	3.6%	10.3%
GARFIELD	15	8	7	0	0	Edwards	53.3%	46.7%	0.0%	0.0%
GRAND	420	86	200	92	42	Kerry	20.5%	47.6%	21.9%	10.0%
IRON	534	189	294	18	33	Kerry	35.4%	55.1%	3.4%	6.2%
JUAB	67	27	32	1	7	Kerry	40.3%	47.8%	1.5%	10.4%
KANE	152	39	89	21	3	Kerry	25.7%	58.6%	13.8%	2.0%
MILLARD	116	33	64	1	18	Kerry	28.4%	55.2%	0.9%	15.5%
MORGAN	88	37	32	2	17	Edwards	42.0%	36.4%	2.3%	19.3%
PIUTE										
RICH										
SALT LAKE	18,688	5,168	10,457	1,640	1,423	Kerry	27.7%	56.0%	8.8%	7.6%
SAN JUAN	107	15	64	16	12	Kerry	14.0%	59.8%	15.0%	11.2%
SANPETE	222	63	113	11	35	Kerry	28.4%	50.9%	5.0%	15.8%
SEVIER	158	41	96	10	11	Kerry	25.9%	60.8%	6.3%	7.0%
SUMMIT	1,038	264	633	73	68	Kerry	25.4%	61.0%	7.0%	6.6%
TOOELE	523	154	307	33	29	Kerry	29.4%	58.7%	6.3%	5.5%
UINTAH	138	55	75	1	7	Kerry	39.9%	54.3%	0.7%	5.1%
UTAH	2,672	1,031	1,280	147	214	Kerry	38.6%	47.9%	5.5%	8.0%
WASATCH	245	82	124	15	24	Kerry	33.5%	50.6%	6.1%	9.8%
WASHINGTON	1,472	477	885	53	57	Kerry	32.4%	60.1%	3.6%	3.9%
WAYNE	62	17	37	3	5	Kerry	27.4%	59.7%	4.8%	8.1%
WEBER	2,263	722	1,250	111	180	Kerry	31.9%	55.2%	4.9%	8.0%
Absentee	401	89	237	32	43	Kerry	22.2%	59.1%	8.0%	10.7%
TOTAL	34,810	10,349	19,225	2,590	2,646	Kerry	29.7%	55.2%	7.4%	7.6%
Published Totals	34,854	10,384	19,232	2,590	2,648	Kerry	29.8%	55.2%	7.4%	7.6%

Note: Other vote as compiled by the Utah Democratic Party was 1,335 Howard Dean; 489 Wesley Clark; 402 Joseph I. Lieberman; 298 Uncommitted; 124 Richard A. Gephardt. The votes from Daggett, Rich and Piute counties were cast by mail and not tallied separately. Their votes were included in the tally of absentee ballots.

VERMONT

Vermont has undergone a metamorphosis in recent years. Long associated with the flinty Yankee Republicanism of Calvin Coolidge, it is now as apt to be identified in the public mind with its socially conscious ice cream makers, Ben & Jerry.

But voting in the wake of neighboring New Hampshire, its presidential primary has been strongly affected by geography and momentum. Ever since Vermont reinstituted its primary in 1976 after a 60-year hiatus, its winners have been the same as in the Granite State. That is, with two exceptions. In 1996, Pat Buchanan won New Hampshire; Bob Dole won Vermont, as the momentum in the Republican race shifted sharply in the two-week interval between the two contests.

In 2004, John Kerry won New Hampshire, but former Vermont governor Howard Dean carried the Democratic vote in his home state five weeks later. Kerry was well on his way to wrapping up the nomination when Vermont voted in early March and Dean had already taken a seat on the sidelines. But Democrats in the Green Mountain State gave their former governor a strong complimentary vote.

Dean swept 12 of Vermont's 14 counties, and took more than 60 percent of the vote in Burlington, Brattleboro, and the state capital of Montpelier. He even received a significant share of the vote in several upstate New York counties on the western side of Lake Champlain, including Clinton (Plattsburgh), where he drew nearly one-third of the Democratic primary vote, and

Recent Vermont Primary Results

Vermont held its first presidential primary in 1916, but none between 1920 and 1976.

		DEMOCRATS			REPUBLICANS	
Year	Turnout	Candidates	%	Turnout	Candidates	%
2004 (March 2)	82,881	HOWARD DEAN	54	26,289	GEORGE W. BUSH*	97
		John Kerry	32			
		John Edwards#	6			
2000 (March 7)	49,283	AL GORE	54	81,355	JOHN McCAIN	60
		Bill Bradley	44		George W. Bush	35
1996 (March 5)	30,838	BILL CLINTON*	97	58,113	BOB DOLE	40
					Pat Buchanan	17
					Steve Forbes	16
					Richard Lugar	14
					Lamar Alexander	11
1992	—	No Primary		—	No Primary	
1988 (March 1)	50,791	MICHAEL DUKAKIS	56	47,832	GEORGE BUSH	49
		Jesse Jackson	26		Bob Dole	39
		Richard Gephardt	8		Pat Robertson	5
		Paul Simon	5			
1984 (March 6)	74,059	Gary Hart	70	33,643	RONALD REAGAN*	99
		Walter Mondale	20			
		Jesse Jackson	8			
1980 (March 4)	39,703	JIMMY CARTER*	73	65,611	RONALD REAGAN	30
		Edward Kennedy	26		John Anderson	29
					George Bush	22
					Howard Baker	12
1976 (March 2)	38,714	JIMMY CARTER	42	32,157	GERALD FORD*	84
		Sargent Shriver	28		Ronald Reagan#	15
		Fred Harris	13			
		Ellen McCormack	9			

Note: All candidates are listed that drew at least 5 percent of their party's primary vote. The names of winning candidates are capitalized. An asterisk (*) indicates an incumbent president. A pound sign (#) indicates a write-in candidate.

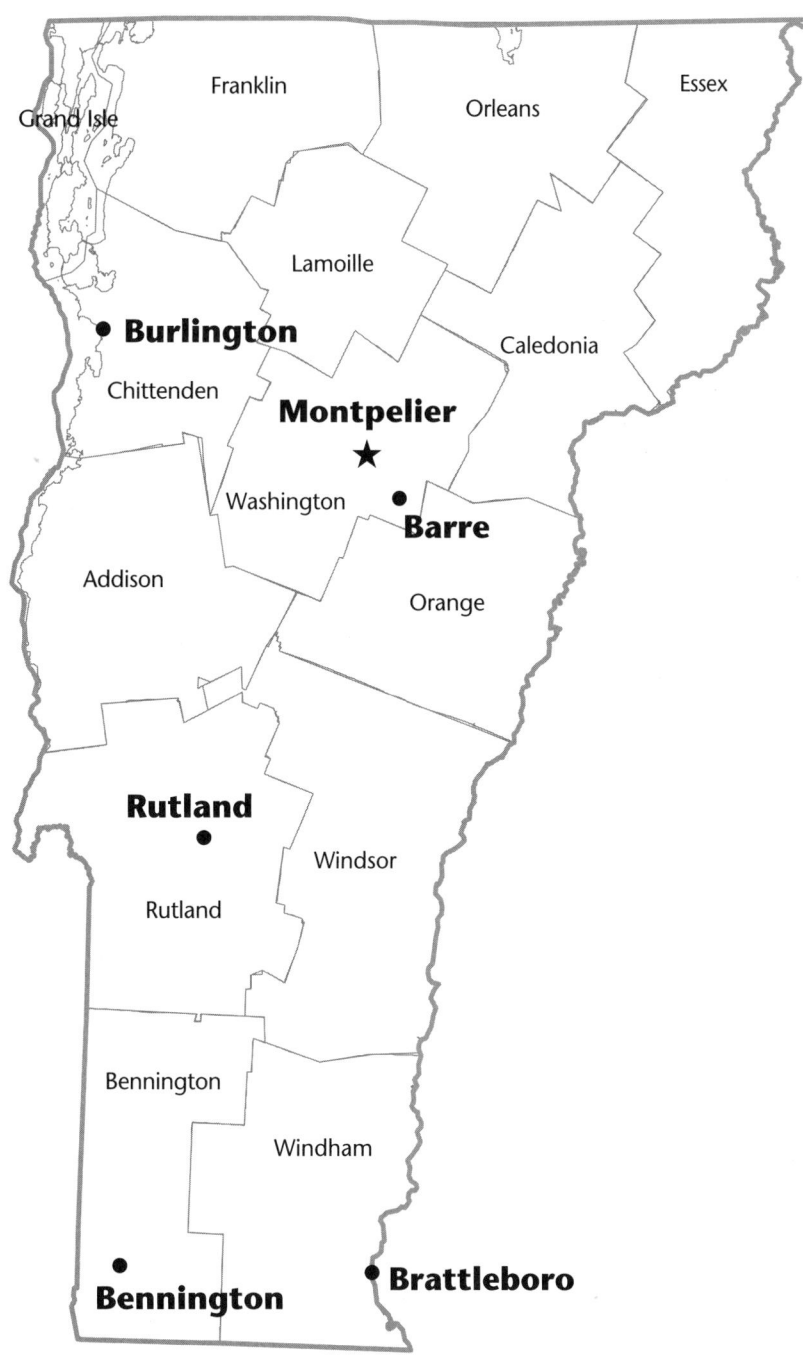

Essex (Lake Placid), where he pulled almost one-quarter. (By comparison, Dean drew less than 5 percent statewide in the New York primary that was held in 2004 on the same day that Vermont voted.)

Dean's victory is the latest example of the liberal nature of Vermont's activist Democrats. In 2000, Bill Bradley took 44 percent in Vermont, his best showing after the leadoff primary in New Hampshire. For nearly a quarter century before

that, Vermont Democrats often held a nonbinding primary but elected delegates through a separate caucus process. For years, the two systems produced different winners, with the comparatively small cadre of caucus voters (around 6,000 in many years) regularly opting for the more liberal alternative.

In 1980, for instance, President Jimmy Carter easily won the primary, but Edward Kennedy prevailed in the Democratic caucuses. In 1988, Michael Dukakis was the primary winner, while Jesse Jackson won the caucuses. In 1992, when there was no presidential primary, Jerry Brown won his highest share of the vote—primary or caucus—in Vermont. By winning nearly half of the state convention delegates, he finished a solid first in the first-round Democratic caucus voting, with Uncommitted next. Bill Clinton ran third, even though Clinton boasted an endorsement from Dean, who was then governor.

Dean, though, did endorse the Vermont Democratic primary winner in 2000, Al Gore. The latter returned the favor in late 2003, just as Dean's own campaign had reached its apex.

By and large, moderate Republicans tend to run better in Vermont than in neighboring New Hampshire. In 1980, John Anderson barely got on the radar screen in New Hampshire, but nearly won the GOP primary in Vermont. In 1996, Richard Lugar pulled barely 5 percent of the primary vote in New Hampshire, but rose to 14 percent in Vermont, where he chose to make his last stand.

On the other hand, conservative Republicans have not run that well in Vermont's presidential primary. Ronald Reagan won it in 1980 with only 30 percent of the vote. Buchanan drew less than 20 percent in 1996, just two weeks removed from his New Hampshire triumph. George W. Bush lost Vermont by 25 percentage points to John McCain in 2000, with the Arizona senator handily sweeping every county in the state.

For both parties, the more conservative voters are generally found in the northern part of the state, where there is a large concentration of French Canadians and rural Republicans. Both Reagan and Buchanan ran best in northern Vermont, each posting his highest percentage in Essex County in the farthest reaches of the sparsely populated and long-isolated "Northeast Kingdom."

To the south and west, voters generally tend to be more moderate. Anderson carried four counties in his 1980 primary run, including Vermont's most populous, Chittenden, which features several colleges and some high-tech industry around Burlington. Just to the south is Addison County, the home of Middlebury College, where Lugar made his best showing in 1996 (20 percent of the vote). Anderson also carried Addison, as did Dole in his 1988 primary challenge to George Bush. It was the only Vermont county that Dole won that year.

Meanwhile, Bennington County, in Vermont's southwest corner, was the only county to back the elder Bush in the closely fought 1980 primary. It is an area of settled wealth where Republicans have been described as "moderate but not daring."

VERMONT DEMOCRATIC PRIMARY

2000

County	Total Vote	Bradley	Gore	Other	Winner	Percentage of Total Vote		
						Bradley	Gore	Other
ADDISON	3,317	1,585	1,686	46	Gore	47.8%	50.8%	1.4%
BENNINGTON	2,750	1,153	1,561	36	Gore	41.9%	56.8%	1.3%
CALEDONIA	1,512	611	871	30	Gore	40.4%	57.6%	2.0%
CHITTENDEN	13,394	6,381	6,854	159	Gore	47.6%	51.2%	1.2%
ESSEX	388	107	269	12	Gore	27.6%	69.3%	3.1%
FRANKLIN	2,532	896	1,568	68	Gore	35.4%	61.9%	2.7%
GRAND ISLE	584	216	360	8	Gore	37.0%	61.6%	1.4%
LAMOILLE	1,498	680	795	23	Gore	45.4%	53.1%	1.5%
ORANGE	2,022	974	1,004	44	Gore	48.2%	49.7%	2.2%
ORLEANS	1,297	469	790	38	Gore	36.2%	60.9%	2.9%
RUTLAND	4,746	1,700	2,969	77	Gore	35.8%	62.6%	1.6%
WASHINGTON	5,526	2,490	2,941	95	Gore	45.1%	53.2%	1.7%
WINDHAM	4,417	2,103	2,196	118	Gore	47.6%	49.7%	2.7%
WINDSOR	5,300	2,264	2,910	126	Gore	42.7%	54.9%	2.4%
TOTAL	49,283	21,629	26,774	880	Gore	43.9%	54.3%	1.8%

Note: Other vote was 355 Lyndon H. LaRouche Jr.; 525 write-in.

City/Town								
BARRE CITY	556	156	390	10	Gore	28.1%	70.1%	1.8%
BARRE TOWN	493	162	324	7	Gore	32.9%	65.7%	1.4%
BENNINGTON	1,010	372	626	12	Gore	36.8%	62.0%	1.2%
BRATTLEBORO	1,273	641	609	23	Bradley	50.4%	47.8%	1.8%
BURLINGTON	4,749	2,229	2,457	63	Gore	46.9%	51.7%	1.3%
COLCHESTER	1,167	472	689	6	Gore	40.4%	59.0%	0.5%
DERBY	234	82	149	3	Gore	35.0%	63.7%	1.3%
ESSEX	975	482	486	7	Gore	49.4%	49.8%	0.7%
HARTFORD	675	279	381	15	Gore	41.3%	56.4%	2.2%
JERICHO	482	227	247	8	Gore	47.1%	51.2%	1.7%
LYNDON	153	55	94	4	Gore	35.9%	61.4%	2.6%
MANCHESTER	310	165	140	5	Bradley	53.2%	45.2%	1.6%
MIDDLEBURY	699	379	316	4	Bradley	54.2%	45.2%	0.6%
MILTON	244	98	138	8	Gore	40.2%	56.6%	3.3%
MONTPELIER	1,369	669	673	27	Gore	48.9%	49.2%	2.0%
MORRISTOWN	230	108	119	3	Gore	47.0%	51.7%	1.3%
NORTHFIELD	398	144	245	9	Gore	36.2%	61.6%	2.3%
RANDOLPH	371	160	197	14	Gore	43.1%	53.1%	3.8%
RICHMOND	536	265	264	7	Bradley	49.4%	49.3%	1.3%
ROCKINGHAM	598	201	362	35	Gore	33.6%	60.5%	5.9%
RUTLAND CITY	1,336	460	856	20	Gore	34.4%	64.1%	1.5%
RUTLAND TOWN	372	131	237	4	Gore	35.2%	63.7%	1.1%
SHELBURNE	840	447	387	6	Bradley	53.2%	46.1%	0.7%
SOUTH BURLINGTON	1,103	594	504	5	Bradley	53.9%	45.7%	0.5%
SPRINGFIELD	836	267	537	32	Gore	31.9%	64.2%	3.8%

VERMONT DEMOCRATIC PRIMARY

2000

County	Total Vote	Bradley	Gore	Other	Winner	Percentage of Total Vote		
						Bradley	Gore	Other
ST. ALBANS CITY	394	138	247	9	Gore	35.0%	62.7%	2.3%
ST. ALBANS TOWN	455	144	294	17	Gore	31.6%	64.6%	3.7%
ST. JOHNSBURY	377	141	224	12	Gore	37.4%	59.4%	3.2%
STOWE	404	221	177	6	Bradley	54.7%	43.8%	1.5%
SWANTON	351	102	242	7	Gore	29.1%	68.9%	2.0%
WATERBURY	386	160	216	10	Gore	41.5%	56.0%	2.6%
WILLISTON	773	352	416	5	Gore	45.5%	53.8%	0.6%
WINOOSKI	602	226	365	11	Gore	37.5%	60.6%	1.8%
WOODSTOCK	354	159	192	3	Gore	44.9%	54.2%	0.8%

Note: The cities and towns included are basically those with a population of at least 5,000 in the 2000 Census plus a few other selected communities.

VERMONT REPUBLICAN PRIMARY

2000

County	Total Vote	G.W. Bush	McCain	Other	Winner	Percentage of Total Vote		
						G.W. Bush	McCain	Other
ADDISON	4,916	1,999	2,729	188	McCain	40.7%	55.5%	3.8%
BENNINGTON	5,215	1,957	3,059	199	McCain	37.5%	58.7%	3.8%
CALEDONIA	3,642	1,334	2,078	230	McCain	36.6%	57.1%	6.3%
CHITTENDEN	18,000	6,362	11,023	615	McCain	35.3%	61.2%	3.4%
ESSEX	1,000	383	570	47	McCain	38.3%	57.0%	4.7%
FRANKLIN	4,486	1,642	2,664	180	McCain	36.6%	59.4%	4.0%
GRAND ISLE	1,065	365	674	26	McCain	34.3%	63.3%	2.4%
LAMOILLE	2,878	1,044	1,747	87	McCain	36.3%	60.7%	3.0%
ORANGE	3,739	1,171	2,361	207	McCain	31.3%	63.1%	5.5%
ORLEANS	2,731	1,058	1,539	134	McCain	38.7%	56.4%	4.9%
RUTLAND	10,502	4,297	5,762	443	McCain	40.9%	54.9%	4.2%
WASHINGTON	7,633	2,745	4,560	328	McCain	36.0%	59.7%	4.3%
WINDHAM	6,075	1,755	3,995	325	McCain	28.9%	65.8%	5.3%
WINDSOR	9,473	2,629	6,284	560	McCain	27.8%	66.3%	5.9%
TOTAL	81,355	28,741	49,045	3,569	McCain	35.3%	60.3%	4.4%

Note: Other vote was 2,164 Alan Keyes; 616 Steve Forbes; 293 Gary Bauer; 496 write-in.

VERMONT REPUBLICAN PRIMARY

2000

City/Town	Total Vote	G.W. Bush	McCain	Other	Winner	Percentage of Total Vote		
						G.W. Bush	McCain	Other
BARRE CITY	980	410	532	38	McCain	41.8%	54.3%	3.9%
BARRE TOWN	1,120	486	590	44	McCain	43.4%	52.7%	3.9%
BENNINGTON	1,499	510	929	60	McCain	34.0%	62.0%	4.0%
BRATTLEBORO	1,401	395	965	41	McCain	28.2%	68.9%	2.9%
BURLINGTON	3,995	1,222	2,625	148	McCain	30.6%	65.7%	3.7%
COLCHESTER	2,001	704	1,228	69	McCain	35.2%	61.4%	3.4%
DERBY	533	202	301	30	McCain	37.9%	56.5%	5.6%
ESSEX	2,323	893	1,352	78	McCain	38.4%	58.2%	3.4%
HARTFORD	1,342	351	922	69	McCain	26.2%	68.7%	5.1%
JERICHO	828	337	461	30	McCain	40.7%	55.7%	3.6%
LYNDON	472	187	247	38	McCain	39.6%	52.3%	8.1%
MANCHESTER	719	274	424	21	McCain	38.1%	59.0%	2.9%
MIDDLEBURY	737	309	405	23	McCain	41.9%	55.0%	3.1%
MILTON	745	302	413	30	McCain	40.5%	55.4%	4.0%
MONTPELIER	1,294	415	830	49	McCain	32.1%	64.1%	3.8%
MORRISTOWN	463	178	273	12	McCain	38.4%	59.0%	2.6%
NORTHFIELD	758	287	436	35	McCain	37.9%	57.5%	4.6%
RANDOLPH	651	201	398	52	McCain	30.9%	61.1%	8.0%
RICHMOND	749	277	450	22	McCain	37.0%	60.1%	2.9%
ROCKINGHAM	683	153	455	75	McCain	22.4%	66.6%	11.0%
RUTLAND CITY	2,442	955	1,401	86	McCain	39.1%	57.4%	3.5%
RUTLAND TOWN	1,162	487	633	42	McCain	41.9%	54.5%	3.6%
SHELBURNE	1,281	503	751	27	McCain	39.3%	58.6%	2.1%
SOUTH BURLINGTON	1,726	608	1,062	56	McCain	35.2%	61.5%	3.2%
SPRINGFIELD	1,635	435	1,047	153	McCain	26.6%	64.0%	9.4%
ST. ALBANS CITY	660	198	426	36	McCain	30.0%	64.5%	5.5%
ST. ALBANS TOWN	707	255	426	26	McCain	36.1%	60.3%	3.7%
ST. JOHNSBURY	1,058	396	555	107	McCain	37.4%	52.5%	10.1%
STOWE	926	284	615	27	McCain	30.7%	66.4%	2.9%
SWANTON	610	224	365	21	McCain	36.7%	59.8%	3.4%
WATERBURY	652	182	402	68	McCain	27.9%	61.7%	10.4%
WILLISTON	1,412	509	850	53	McCain	36.0%	60.2%	3.8%
WINOOSKI	565	203	340	22	McCain	35.9%	60.2%	3.9%
WOODSTOCK	715	239	415	61	McCain	33.4%	58.0%	8.5%

Note: The cities and towns included are basically those with a population of at least 5,000 in the 2000 Census plus a few other selected communities.

VERMONT DEMOCRATIC PRIMARY

2004

County	Total Vote	Dean	Edwards	Kerry	Other	Winner	Percentage of Total Vote Dean	Edwards	Kerry	Other
ADDISON	5,740	3,223	296	1,628	593	Dean	56.1%	5.2%	28.4%	10.3%
BENNINGTON	4,658	1,700	360	2,251	347	Kerry	36.5%	7.7%	48.3%	7.4%
CALEDONIA	2,562	1,409	184	743	226	Dean	55.0%	7.2%	29.0%	8.8%
CHITTENDEN	21,768	13,286	1,211	5,536	1,735	Dean	61.0%	5.6%	25.4%	8.0%
ESSEX	709	221	67	345	76	Kerry	31.2%	9.4%	48.7%	10.7%
FRANKLIN	5,016	2,260	413	1,920	423	Dean	45.1%	8.2%	38.3%	8.4%
GRAND ISLE	1,164	568	73	431	92	Dean	48.8%	6.3%	37.0%	7.9%
LAMOILLE	2,563	1,490	153	759	161	Dean	58.1%	6.0%	29.6%	6.3%
ORANGE	3,424	1,898	237	1,005	284	Dean	55.4%	6.9%	29.4%	8.3%
ORLEANS	2,232	1,018	137	883	194	Dean	45.6%	6.1%	39.6%	8.7%
RUTLAND	7,338	3,553	496	2,722	567	Dean	48.4%	6.8%	37.1%	7.7%
WASHINGTON	9,742	5,684	487	2,555	1,016	Dean	58.3%	5.0%	26.2%	10.4%
WINDHAM	7,232	3,862	427	2,185	758	Dean	53.4%	5.9%	30.2%	10.5%
WINDSOR	8,733	4,221	572	3,208	732	Dean	48.3%	6.5%	36.7%	8.4%
TOTAL	82,881	44,393	5,113	26,171	7,204	Dean	53.6%	6.2%	31.6%	8.7%

Note: Other vote was 3,396 Dennis J. Kucinich; 2,749 Wesley Clark; 386 Lyndon H. LaRouche Jr.; 673 scattered write-in. The votes cast for Edwards were write-ins.

City/Town	Total Vote	Dean	Edwards	Kerry	Other	Winner	Dean	Edwards	Kerry	Other
BARRE CITY	998	504	64	342	88	Dean	50.5%	6.4%	34.3%	8.8%
BARRE TOWN	779	418	46	252	63	Dean	53.7%	5.9%	32.3%	8.1%
BENNINGTON	1,666	713	94	746	113	Kerry	42.8%	5.6%	44.8%	6.8%
BRATTLEBORO	2,229	1376	100	517	236	Dean	61.7%	4.5%	23.2%	10.6%
BURLINGTON	6,758	4,237	299	1,595	627	Dean	62.7%	4.4%	23.6%	9.3%
COLCHESTER	1,903	1,046	114	565	178	Dean	55.0%	6.0%	29.7%	9.4%
DERBY	445	203	25	182	35	Dean	45.6%	5.6%	40.9%	7.9%
ESSEX	1,918	1,146	148	475	149	Dean	59.7%	7.7%	24.8%	7.8%
HARTFORD	1,035	455	82	398	100	Dean	44.0%	7.9%	38.5%	9.7%
JERICHO	879	556	47	216	60	Dean	63.3%	5.3%	24.6%	6.8%
LYNDON	292	147	25	92	28	Dean	50.3%	8.6%	31.5%	9.6%
MANCHESTER	378	123	37	194	24	Kerry	32.5%	9.8%	51.3%	6.3%
MIDDLEBURY	1,012	608	66	263	75	Dean	60.1%	6.5%	26.0%	7.4%
MILTON	928	469	79	301	79	Dean	50.5%	8.5%	32.4%	8.5%
MONTPELIER	2,325	1,490	107	468	260	Dean	64.1%	4.6%	20.1%	11.2%
MORRISTOWN	627	383	41	169	34	Dean	61.1%	6.5%	27.0%	5.4%
NORTHFIELD	750	398	39	251	62	Dean	53.1%	5.2%	33.5%	8.3%
RANDOLPH	579	326	46	159	48	Dean	56.3%	7.9%	27.5%	8.3%
RICHMOND	757	486	36	174	61	Dean	64.2%	4.8%	23.0%	8.1%
ROCKINGHAM	837	439	47	282	69	Dean	52.4%	5.6%	33.7%	8.2%
RUTLAND CITY	1,662	903	101	558	100	Dean	54.3%	6.1%	33.6%	6.0%
RUTLAND TOWN	571	240	42	237	52	Dean	42.0%	7.4%	41.5%	9.1%
SHELBURNE	1,567	968	80	430	89	Dean	61.8%	5.1%	27.4%	5.7%
SOUTH BURLINGTON	1,722	1,090	125	394	113	Dean	63.3%	7.3%	22.9%	6.6%
SPRINGFIELD	1,267	647	88	442	90	Dean	51.1%	6.9%	34.9%	7.1%

VERMONT DEMOCRATIC PRIMARY

2004

County	Total Vote	Dean	Edwards	Kerry	Other	Winner	Percentage of Total Vote			
							Dean	Edwards	Kerry	Other
ST. ALBANS CITY	926	459	73	325	69	Dean	49.6%	7.9%	35.1%	7.5%
ST. ALBANS TOWN	747	328	61	302	56	Dean	43.9%	8.2%	40.4%	7.5%
ST. JOHNSBURY	541	285	39	173	44	Dean	52.7%	7.2%	32.0%	8.1%
STOWE	819	431	44	294	50	Dean	52.6%	5.4%	35.9%	6.1%
SWANTON	643	257	58	269	59	Kerry	40.0%	9.0%	41.8%	9.2%
WATERBURY	700	440	0	183	77	Dean	62.9%	0.0%	26.1%	11.0%
WILLISTON	1,537	913	90	440	94	Dean	59.4%	5.9%	28.6%	6.1%
WINOOSKI	602	336	19	195	52	Dean	55.8%	3.2%	32.4%	8.6%
WOODSTOCK	622	288	56	233	45	Dean	46.3%	9.0%	37.5%	7.2%

Note: The cities and towns included are basically those with a population of at least 5,000 in the 2000 Census plus a few other selected communities.

VERMONT REPUBLICAN PRIMARY

2004

County	Total Vote	G.W. Bush	Other	Winner	Percentage of Total Vote	
					G.W. Bush	Other
ADDISON	1,937	1,881	56	G.W. Bush	97.1%	2.9%
BENNINGTON	1,404	1,349	55	G.W. Bush	96.1%	3.9%
CALEDONIA	1,111	1,074	37	G.W. Bush	96.7%	3.3%
CHITTENDEN	5,243	5,080	163	G.W. Bush	96.9%	3.1%
ESSEX	465	449	16	G.W. Bush	96.6%	3.4%
FRANKLIN	1,907	1,855	52	G.W. Bush	97.3%	2.7%
GRAND ISLE	464	454	10	G.W. Bush	97.8%	2.2%
LAMOILLE	843	813	30	G.W. Bush	96.4%	3.6%
ORANGE	1,117	1,068	49	G.W. Bush	95.6%	4.4%
ORLEANS	898	848	50	G.W. Bush	94.4%	5.6%
RUTLAND	3,693	3,615	78	G.W. Bush	97.9%	2.1%
WASHINGTON	2,794	2,695	99	G.W. Bush	96.5%	3.5%
WINDHAM	1,787	1,710	77	G.W. Bush	95.7%	4.3%
WINDSOR	2,626	2,524	102	G.W. Bush	96.1%	3.9%
TOTAL	26,289	25,415	874	G.W. Bush	96.7%	3.3%

Note: Other vote was 874 write-in.

VERMONT REPUBLICAN PRIMARY

2004

| City/Town | Total Vote | G.W. Bush | Other | Winner | Percentage of Total Vote | |
					G.W. Bush	Other
BARRE CITY	440	428	12	G.W. Bush	97.3%	2.7%
BARRE TOWN	408	401	7	G.W. Bush	98.3%	1.7%
BENNINGTON	283	268	15	G.W. Bush	94.7%	5.3%
BRATTLEBORO	371	353	18	G.W. Bush	95.1%	4.9%
BURLINGTON	1,039	976	63	G.W. Bush	93.9%	6.1%
COLCHESTER	703	682	21	G.W. Bush	97.0%	3.0%
DERBY	215	202	13	G.W. Bush	94.0%	6.0%
ESSEX	622	602	20	G.W. Bush	96.8%	3.2%
HARTFORD	305	297	8	G.W. Bush	97.4%	2.6%
JERICHO	253	249	4	G.W. Bush	98.4%	1.6%
LYNDON	166	163	3	G.W. Bush	98.2%	1.8%
MANCHESTER	118	114	4	G.W. Bush	96.6%	3.4%
MIDDLEBURY	217	205	12	G.W. Bush	94.5%	5.5%
MILTON	471	465	6	G.W. Bush	98.7%	1.3%
MONTPELIER	459	439	20	G.W. Bush	95.6%	4.4%
MORRISTOWN	194	188	6	G.W. Bush	96.9%	3.1%
NORTHFIELD	287	277	10	G.W. Bush	96.5%	3.5%
RANDOLPH	186	179	7	G.W. Bush	96.2%	3.8%
RICHMOND	181	175	6	G.W. Bush	96.7%	3.3%
ROCKINGHAM	155	151	4	G.W. Bush	97.4%	2.6%
RUTLAND CITY	672	652	20	G.W. Bush	97.0%	3.0%
RUTLAND TOWN	455	446	9	G.W. Bush	98.0%	2.0%
SHELBURNE	388	374	14	G.W. Bush	96.4%	3.6%
SOUTH BURLINGTON	335	328	7	G.W. Bush	97.9%	2.1%
SPRINGFIELD	411	398	13	G.W. Bush	96.8%	3.2%
ST. ALBANS CITY	265	260	5	G.W. Bush	98.1%	1.9%
ST. ALBANS TOWN	358	349	9	G.W. Bush	97.5%	2.5%
ST. JOHNSBURY	254	244	10	G.W. Bush	96.1%	3.9%
STOWE	322	311	11	G.W. Bush	96.6%	3.4%
SWANTON	291	288	3	G.W. Bush	99.0%	1.0%
WATERBURY	156	152	4	G.W. Bush	97.4%	2.6%
WILLISTON	460	451	9	G.W. Bush	98.0%	2.0%
WINOOSKI	111	111	0	G.W. Bush	100.0%	0.0%
WOODSTOCK	217	208	9	G.W. Bush	95.9%	4.1%

Note: The cities and towns included are basically those with a population of at least 5,000 in the 2000 Census plus a few other selected communities.

VIRGINIA

Primaries are not a regular part of the political scene in Virginia. They have only been employed three times at the presidential level–in 1988 by both parties, in 2000 by the Republicans, and in 2004 by the Democrats.

The 2000 Republican vote arguably gave George W. Bush his second most important victory of the Republican primary season, ranking just behind his critical triumph 10 days earlier in South Carolina. For Bush's victory in Virginia, along with his win the same day in Washington, blunted the momentum that John McCain had gained the previous week with primary successes in Michigan and his home state of Arizona.

Virginia's primary was open like the one in Michigan–allowing independents and Democrats to participate in the Republican balloting. But Virginia was never considered very friendly terrain for McCain. As in many other states, the party establishment–led by GOP governor James S. Gilmore III–was lined up behind Bush. And McCain made himself an object of controversy by attacking two Virginia-based pillars of the Christian Right, televangelists Pat Robertson and Jerry Falwell, as "agents of intolerance."

With the sparks flying, voter turnout for the primary surpassed 660,000, more than the combined number that participated in the Democratic and Republican primaries in 1988. Bush prevailed by a margin of nearly 10 percentage points, as McCain was successful only on the fringes of the state. The former Naval Academy graduate carried Norfolk and Virginia Beach, with their strong Navy presence, and the suburbs of Northern Virginia closest to Washington, D.C., including Fairfax County, the most populous jurisdiction in the state. But Bush dominated primary balloting in the rest of the Old Dominion.

The Democratic primary four years later was much less compelling and drew less than 400,000 voters to the polls. John Kerry used a victory in Virginia and on the same early February day in Tennessee to advertise his vote-getting appeal in the South. But Kerry was barely tested in swamping runner-up John Edwards by a margin of nearly 2 to 1. Edwards ran best in the mountainous panhandle of southwest Virginia, where he won a handful of counties. But he was swamped by Kerry in other parts of the state.

That Virginia instituted a presidential primary at all is in large part a tribute to Charles S. Robb. A former Virginia governor and senator, Robb was instrumental in the creation of the Democratic Leadership Council in the 1980s as a counterweight to party liberals, and he pushed the Southern regional primary in 1988 (commonly known as Super Tuesday) as a means toward nominating a Southern-oriented candidate for president. The event, though, proved to be a disappointment for its sponsors, both in Virginia and across the region.

Recent Virginia Primary Results

Virginia held its first presidential primary in 1988.

| Year | DEMOCRATS | | | REPUBLICANS | | |
	Turnout	Candidates	%	Turnout	Candidates	%
2004 (Feb. 10)	396,223	JOHN KERRY	52	—	No Primary	
		John Edwards	27			
		Wesley Clark	9			
		Howard Dean	7			
2000 (Feb. 29)	—	No Primary		664,093	GEORGE W. BUSH	53
					John McCain	44
1996	—	No Primary		—	No Primary	
1992	—	No Primary		—	No Primary	
1988 (March 8)	364,899	JESSE JACKSON	45	234,142	GEORGE BUSH	53
		Al Gore	22		Bob Dole	26
		Michael Dukakis	22		Pat Robertson	14

Note: All candidates are listed who drew at least 5 percent of their party's primary vote. The names of winning candidates are capitalized.

Michael Dukakis and Jesse Jackson both won chunks of the South away from Al Gore, the favorite of many Democratic leaders across Dixie. And in Virginia, Jackson was an easy winner.

The Democratic vote, though, did highlight the demographic diversity of the state. Dukakis won the Northern Virginia suburbs outside Washington, D.C. (the southern fringe of the megalopolis that extends from Boston to Washington). Gore won the rural white counties west of the Blue Ridge Mountains, rolling up his best numbers in the Virginia panhandle, which borders Gore's home state of Tennessee. Jackson won almost everywhere else, from the old plantation country of the Piedmont to the bustling cities of the Tidewater, where a heavy military presence mingles with a large African American population.

Jackson carried some of the prime symbols of the old Confederacy in 1988, including Richmond, which has a black majority, and Lexington, a small college town in the Shenandoah

Valley that is the burial place of Robert E. Lee. Virginia handed Jackson the highest vote share he received in any primary in 1988, even though it had the smallest black population of any primary state that he carried.

Jackson's primary victory proved to be a harbinger of sorts. A year later, Democrat L. Douglas Wilder won the gubernatorial election in Virginia and became the nation's first elected African American governor.

On the Republican side, the 1988 presidential primary spurred limited interest because it was a "beauty contest" that bound no delegates. George Bush dominated both the primary and the later caucuses that actually chose the delegates.

Probably the chief casualty of Bush's easy win was Pat Robertson. The son of a Virginia senator, Robertson had based his nationwide television ministry in Virginia Beach. But Bush swept all of the state's 95 counties and total that year of 41 independent cities; Robertson could run no better than third, even in Virginia Beach.

VIRGINIA REPUBLICAN PRIMARY

2000

County	Total Vote	Bush	McCain	Other	Winner	Percentage of Total Vote		
						Bush	McCain	Other
ACCOMACK	2,890	1,436	1,348	106	Bush	49.7%	46.6%	3.7%
ALBEMARLE	9,881	5,077	4,488	316	Bush	51.4%	45.4%	3.2%
ALLEGHANY	809	477	306	26	Bush	59.0%	37.8%	3.2%
AMELIA	886	660	209	17	Bush	74.5%	23.6%	1.9%
AMHERST	2,040	1,299	667	74	Bush	63.7%	32.7%	3.6%
APPOMATTOX	1,056	758	272	26	Bush	71.8%	25.8%	2.5%
ARLINGTON	23,313	8,467	14,258	588	McCain	36.3%	61.2%	2.5%
AUGUSTA	5,691	3,611	1,781	299	Bush	63.5%	31.3%	5.3%
BATH	422	221	182	19	Bush	52.4%	43.1%	4.5%
BEDFORD COUNTY	6,438	4,074	2,145	219	Bush	63.3%	33.3%	3.4%
BLAND	416	296	102	18	Bush	71.2%	24.5%	4.3%
BOTETOURT	3,650	2,459	1,066	125	Bush	67.4%	29.2%	3.4%
BRUNSWICK	733	523	190	20	Bush	71.4%	25.9%	2.7%
BUCHANAN	686	512	152	22	Bush	74.6%	22.2%	3.2%
BUCKINGHAM	808	535	246	27	Bush	66.2%	30.4%	3.3%
CAMPBELL	4,405	3,079	1,183	143	Bush	69.9%	26.9%	3.2%
CAROLINE	1,344	819	491	34	Bush	60.9%	36.5%	2.5%
CARROLL	2,381	1,664	649	68	Bush	69.9%	27.3%	2.9%
CHARLES CITY	311	211	89	11	Bush	67.8%	28.6%	3.5%
CHARLOTTE	947	697	219	31	Bush	73.6%	23.1%	3.3%
CHESTERFIELD	28,192	18,381	8,976	835	Bush	65.2%	31.8%	3.0%
CLARKE	1,435	672	698	65	McCain	46.8%	48.6%	4.5%
CRAIG	437	296	127	14	Bush	67.7%	29.1%	3.2%
CULPEPER	3,242	1,859	1,259	124	Bush	57.3%	38.8%	3.8%
CUMBERLAND	721	471	232	18	Bush	65.3%	32.2%	2.5%
DICKENSON	601	456	134	11	Bush	75.9%	22.3%	1.8%
DINWIDDIE	1,454	1,041	370	43	Bush	71.6%	25.4%	3.0%
ESSEX	706	457	232	17	Bush	64.7%	32.9%	2.4%
FAIRFAX COUNTY	126,234	56,141	66,599	3,494	McCain	44.5%	52.8%	2.8%
FAUQUIER	7,750	3,990	3,483	277	Bush	51.5%	44.9%	3.6%
FLOYD	1,120	762	325	33	Bush	68.0%	29.0%	2.9%
FLUVANNA	2,015	1,158	804	53	Bush	57.5%	39.9%	2.6%
FRANKLIN COUNTY	3,747	2,411	1,236	100	Bush	64.3%	33.0%	2.7%
FREDERICK	5,481	3,140	2,092	249	Bush	57.3%	38.2%	4.5%
GILES	995	610	356	29	Bush	61.3%	35.8%	2.9%
GLOUCESTER	3,268	1,606	1,533	129	Bush	49.1%	46.9%	3.9%
GOOCHLAND	2,190	1,418	723	49	Bush	64.7%	33.0%	2.2%
GRAYSON	1,032	675	328	29	Bush	65.4%	31.8%	2.8%
GREENE	1,211	731	425	55	Bush	60.4%	35.1%	4.5%
GREENSVILLE	368	285	76	7	Bush	77.4%	20.7%	1.9%
HALIFAX	2,229	1,751	419	59	Bush	78.6%	18.8%	2.6%
HANOVER	10,979	7,327	3,377	275	Bush	66.7%	30.8%	2.5%
HENRICO	29,558	18,491	10,347	720	Bush	62.6%	35.0%	2.4%
HENRY	2,821	1,827	950	44	Bush	64.8%	33.7%	1.6%
HIGHLAND	402	222	148	32	Bush	55.2%	36.8%	8.0%

VIRGINIA REPUBLICAN PRIMARY

2000

County	Total Vote	Bush	McCain	Other	Winner	Percentage of Total Vote		
						Bush	McCain	Other
ISLE OF WIGHT	2,740	1,579	1,064	97	Bush	57.6%	38.8%	3.5%
JAMES CITY	8,303	3,789	4,238	276	McCain	45.6%	51.0%	3.3%
KING AND QUEEN	397	254	131	12	Bush	64.0%	33.0%	3.0%
KING GEORGE	1,593	710	762	121	McCain	44.6%	47.8%	7.6%
KING WILLIAM	1,043	693	318	32	Bush	66.4%	30.5%	3.1%
LANCASTER	2,028	1,179	799	50	Bush	58.1%	39.4%	2.5%
LEE	842	631	179	32	Bush	74.9%	21.3%	3.8%
LOUDOUN	20,005	9,725	9,564	716	Bush	48.6%	47.8%	3.6%
LOUISA	1,876	1,160	656	60	Bush	61.8%	35.0%	3.2%
LUNENBURG	808	577	217	14	Bush	71.4%	26.9%	1.7%
MADISON	1,320	826	445	49	Bush	62.6%	33.7%	3.7%
MATHEWS	1,129	581	516	32	Bush	51.5%	45.7%	2.8%
MECKLENBURG	1,710	1,127	538	45	Bush	65.9%	31.5%	2.6%
MIDDLESEX	1,183	645	493	45	Bush	54.5%	41.7%	3.8%
MONTGOMERY	5,600	3,012	2,417	171	Bush	53.8%	43.2%	3.1%
NELSON	1,025	521	477	27	Bush	50.8%	46.5%	2.6%
NEW KENT	1,385	865	481	39	Bush	62.5%	34.7%	2.8%
NORTHAMPTON	1,087	508	552	27	McCain	46.7%	50.8%	2.5%
NORTHUMBERLAND	1,848	1,062	732	54	Bush	57.5%	39.6%	2.9%
NOTTOWAY	941	646	273	22	Bush	68.7%	29.0%	2.3%
ORANGE	2,928	1,553	1,269	106	Bush	53.0%	43.3%	3.6%
PAGE	1,385	883	454	48	Bush	63.8%	32.8%	3.5%
PATRICK	1,170	761	384	25	Bush	65.0%	32.8%	2.1%
PITTSYLVANIA	4,528	3,503	946	79	Bush	77.4%	20.9%	1.7%
POWHATAN	2,358	1,669	621	68	Bush	70.8%	26.3%	2.9%
PRINCE EDWARD	1,295	836	431	28	Bush	64.6%	33.3%	2.2%
PRINCE GEORGE	2,242	1,549	633	60	Bush	69.1%	28.2%	2.7%
PRINCE WILLIAM	25,821	12,755	11,689	1,377	Bush	49.4%	45.3%	5.3%
PULASKI	1,991	1,338	609	44	Bush	67.2%	30.6%	2.2%
RAPPAHANNOCK	969	471	452	46	Bush	48.6%	46.6%	4.7%
RICHMOND COUNTY	615	424	177	14	Bush	68.9%	28.8%	2.3%
ROANOKE COUNTY	10,523	6,880	3,354	289	Bush	65.4%	31.9%	2.7%
ROCKBRIDGE	1,837	978	805	54	Bush	53.2%	43.8%	2.9%
ROCKINGHAM	5,380	3,517	1,587	276	Bush	65.4%	29.5%	5.1%
RUSSELL	748	572	148	28	Bush	76.5%	19.8%	3.7%
SCOTT	1,490	1,108	339	43	Bush	74.4%	22.8%	2.9%
SHENANDOAH	3,574	2,159	1,262	153	Bush	60.4%	35.3%	4.3%
SMYTH	1,474	1,003	418	53	Bush	68.0%	28.4%	3.6%
SOUTHAMPTON	1,101	641	438	22	Bush	58.2%	39.8%	2.0%
SPOTSYLVANIA	7,246	3,762	3,102	382	Bush	51.9%	42.8%	5.3%
STAFFORD	8,597	4,269	3,942	386	Bush	49.7%	45.9%	4.5%
SURRY	472	294	157	21	Bush	62.3%	33.3%	4.4%
SUSSEX	599	438	148	13	Bush	73.1%	24.7%	2.2%
TAZEWELL	1,826	1,285	491	50	Bush	70.4%	26.9%	2.7%
WARREN	2,766	1,380	1,097	289	Bush	49.9%	39.7%	10.4%

VIRGINIA REPUBLICAN PRIMARY

2000

County	Total Vote	Bush	McCain	Other	Winner	Percentage of Total Vote		
						Bush	McCain	Other
WASHINGTON	2,817	1,835	847	135	Bush	65.1%	30.1%	4.8%
WESTMORELAND	1,264	670	542	52	Bush	53.0%	42.9%	4.1%
WISE	1,108	659	389	60	Bush	59.5%	35.1%	5.4%
WYTHE	1,613	1,139	434	40	Bush	70.6%	26.9%	2.5%
YORK	7,751	3,705	3,763	283	McCain	47.8%	48.5%	3.7%
City								
ALEXANDRIA	14,453	5,516	8,552	385	McCain	38.2%	59.2%	2.7%
BEDFORD CITY	541	296	227	18	Bush	54.7%	42.0%	3.3%
BRISTOL	1,101	688	353	60	Bush	62.5%	32.1%	5.4%
BUENA VISTA	312	180	120	12	Bush	57.7%	38.5%	3.8%
CHARLOTTESVILLE	2,768	1,175	1,504	89	McCain	42.4%	54.3%	3.2%
CHESAPEAKE	17,095	9,073	7,286	736	Bush	53.1%	42.6%	4.3%
CLIFTON FORGE	263	128	131	4	McCain	48.7%	49.8%	1.5%
COLONIAL HEIGHTS	2,089	1,474	545	70	Bush	70.6%	26.1%	3.4%
COVINGTON	333	189	125	19	Bush	56.8%	37.5%	5.7%
DANVILLE	3,820	2,826	927	67	Bush	74.0%	24.3%	1.8%
EMPORIA	363	268	91	4	Bush	73.8%	25.1%	1.1%
FAIRFAX CITY	3,185	1,484	1,590	111	McCain	46.6%	49.9%	3.5%
FALLS CHURCH	1,722	686	995	41	McCain	39.8%	57.8%	2.4%
FRANKLIN CITY	617	317	283	17	Bush	51.4%	45.9%	2.8%
FREDERICKSBURG	1,416	605	743	68	McCain	42.7%	52.5%	4.8%
GALAX	379	210	158	11	Bush	55.4%	41.7%	2.9%
HAMPTON	9,903	5,059	4,405	439	Bush	51.1%	44.5%	4.4%
HARRISONBURG	2,087	1,208	763	116	Bush	57.9%	36.6%	5.6%
HOPEWELL	1,351	970	342	39	Bush	71.8%	25.3%	2.9%
LEXINGTON	636	259	363	14	McCain	40.7%	57.1%	2.2%
LYNCHBURG	6,034	3,715	2,104	215	Bush	61.6%	34.9%	3.6%
MANASSAS	3,149	1,644	1,301	204	Bush	52.2%	41.3%	6.5%
MANASSAS PARK	569	297	233	39	Bush	52.2%	40.9%	6.9%
MARTINSVILLE	914	594	288	32	Bush	65.0%	31.5%	3.5%
NEWPORT NEWS	13,684	7,074	6,122	488	Bush	51.7%	44.7%	3.6%
NORFOLK	14,177	5,645	8,033	499	McCain	39.8%	56.7%	3.5%
NORTON	163	73	83	7	McCain	44.8%	50.9%	4.3%
PETERSBURG	1,160	653	459	48	Bush	56.3%	39.6%	4.1%
POQUOSON	1,882	1,055	768	59	Bush	56.1%	40.8%	3.1%
PORTSMOUTH	6,088	2,949	2,922	217	Bush	48.4%	48.0%	3.6%
RADFORD	839	456	364	19	Bush	54.4%	43.4%	2.3%
RICHMOND CITY	13,500	6,802	6,358	340	Bush	50.4%	47.1%	2.5%
ROANOKE CITY	6,856	4,183	2,461	212	Bush	61.0%	35.9%	3.1%
SALEM	2,603	1,665	853	85	Bush	64.0%	32.8%	3.3%
STAUNTON	2,030	1,169	774	87	Bush	57.6%	38.1%	4.3%
SUFFOLK	4,999	2,938	1,893	168	Bush	58.8%	37.9%	3.4%
VIRGINIA BEACH	44,217	19,242	23,605	1,370	McCain	43.5%	53.4%	3.1%
WAYNESBORO	1,796	1,045	663	88	Bush	58.2%	36.9%	4.9%
WILLIAMSBURG	1,286	509	720	57	McCain	39.6%	56.0%	4.4%
WINCHESTER	2,067	1,090	909	68	Bush	52.7%	44.0%	3.3%
TOTAL	664,093	350,588	291,488	22,017	Bush	52.8%	43.9%	3.3%

Note: Other vote was 20,356 Alan Keyes; 852 Gary Bauer; 809 Steve Forbes.

VIRGINIA DEMOCRATIC PRIMARY

2004

County	Total Vote	Clark	Dean	Edwards	Kerry	Other	Winner	Percentage of Total Vote Clark	Dean	Edwards	Kerry	Other
ACCOMACK	1,659	134	122	424	880	99	Kerry	8.1%	7.4%	25.6%	53.0%	6.0%
ALBEMARLE	7,232	573	840	1,510	3,996	313	Kerry	7.9%	11.6%	20.9%	55.3%	4.3%
ALLEGHANY	971	115	22	276	516	42	Kerry	11.8%	2.3%	28.4%	53.1%	4.3%
AMELIA	528	34	18	98	334	44	Kerry	6.4%	3.4%	18.6%	63.3%	8.3%
AMHERST	1,182	152	46	318	614	52	Kerry	12.9%	3.9%	26.9%	51.9%	4.4%
APPOMATTOX	633	68	11	203	326	25	Kerry	10.7%	1.7%	32.1%	51.5%	3.9%
ARLINGTON	24,316	2,123	2,931	6,033	12,338	891	Kerry	8.7%	12.1%	24.8%	50.7%	3.7%
AUGUSTA	1,719	147	109	536	851	76	Kerry	8.6%	6.3%	31.2%	49.5%	4.4%
BATH	250	38	7	71	122	12	Kerry	15.2%	2.8%	28.4%	48.8%	4.8%
BEDFORD COUNTY	2,706	310	132	982	1,193	89	Kerry	11.5%	4.9%	36.3%	44.1%	3.3%
BLAND	244	18	7	109	104	6	Edwards	7.4%	2.9%	44.7%	42.6%	2.5%
BOTETOURT	1,389	136	71	510	632	40	Kerry	9.8%	5.1%	36.7%	45.5%	2.9%
BRUNSWICK	699	56	30	124	424	65	Kerry	8.0%	4.3%	17.7%	60.7%	9.3%
BUCHANAN	988	40	27	305	599	17	Kerry	4.0%	2.7%	30.9%	60.6%	1.7%
BUCKINGHAM	711	56	30	169	393	63	Kerry	7.9%	4.2%	23.8%	55.3%	8.9%
CAMPBELL	1,815	253	60	595	834	73	Kerry	13.9%	3.3%	32.8%	46.0%	4.0%
CAROLINE	1,025	87	50	238	574	76	Kerry	8.5%	4.9%	23.2%	56.0%	7.4%
CARROLL	1,171	66	18	653	413	21	Edwards	5.6%	1.5%	55.8%	35.3%	1.8%
CHARLES CITY	448	35	17	76	261	59	Kerry	7.8%	3.8%	17.0%	58.3%	13.2%
CHARLOTTE	613	68	19	151	336	39	Kerry	11.1%	3.1%	24.6%	54.8%	6.4%
CHESTERFIELD	12,078	1,380	733	3,367	5,497	1,101	Kerry	11.4%	6.1%	27.9%	45.5%	9.1%
CLARKE	780	62	62	197	412	47	Kerry	7.9%	7.9%	25.3%	52.8%	6.0%
CRAIG	299	22	17	128	124	8	Edwards	7.4%	5.7%	42.8%	41.5%	2.7%
CULPEPER	1,461	86	117	379	812	67	Kerry	5.9%	8.0%	25.9%	55.6%	4.6%
CUMBERLAND	357	33	21	103	173	27	Kerry	9.2%	5.9%	28.9%	48.5%	7.6%
DICKENSON	742	46	21	253	407	15	Kerry	6.2%	2.8%	34.1%	54.9%	2.0%
DINWIDDIE	965	68	51	232	529	85	Kerry	7.0%	5.3%	24.0%	54.8%	8.8%
ESSEX	356	33	14	71	219	19	Kerry	9.3%	3.9%	19.9%	61.5%	5.3%
FAIRFAX COUNTY	69,704	5,476	6,726	16,076	38,761	2,665	Kerry	7.9%	9.6%	23.1%	55.6%	3.8%
FAUQUIER	3,026	222	213	825	1,627	139	Kerry	7.3%	7.0%	27.3%	53.8%	4.6%
FLOYD	750	64	52	285	298	51	Kerry	8.5%	6.9%	38.0%	39.7%	6.8%
FLUVANNA	1,112	121	79	233	633	46	Kerry	10.9%	7.1%	21.0%	56.9%	4.1%
FRANKLIN COUNTY	2,345	195	72	894	1,070	114	Kerry	8.3%	3.1%	38.1%	45.6%	4.9%
FREDERICK	2,236	150	157	696	1,094	139	Kerry	6.7%	7.0%	31.1%	48.9%	6.2%
GILES	855	111	32	269	418	25	Kerry	13.0%	3.7%	31.5%	48.9%	2.9%
GLOUCESTER	1,622	184	73	506	770	89	Kerry	11.3%	4.5%	31.2%	47.5%	5.5%
GOOCHLAND	1,004	93	50	247	537	77	Kerry	9.3%	5.0%	24.6%	53.5%	7.7%
GRAYSON	787	68	16	379	308	16	Edwards	8.6%	2.0%	48.2%	39.1%	2.0%
GREENE	589	65	66	144	283	31	Kerry	11.0%	11.2%	24.4%	48.0%	5.3%
GREENSVILLE	449	24	7	89	287	42	Kerry	5.3%	1.6%	19.8%	63.9%	9.4%
HALIFAX	1,622	143	60	457	842	120	Kerry	8.8%	3.7%	28.2%	51.9%	7.4%
HANOVER	3,994	424	222	1,271	1,798	279	Kerry	10.6%	5.6%	31.8%	45.0%	7.0%
HENRICO	15,449	1,544	853	4,022	7,543	1,487	Kerry	10.0%	5.5%	26.0%	48.8%	9.6%
HENRY	2,256	154	61	900	1,054	87	Kerry	6.8%	2.7%	39.9%	46.7%	3.9%
HIGHLAND	188	13	5	53	108	9	Kerry	6.9%	2.7%	28.2%	57.4%	4.8%

VIRGINIA DEMOCRATIC PRIMARY

2004

County	Total Vote	Clark	Dean	Edwards	Kerry	Other	Winner	Percentage of Total Vote				
								Clark	Dean	Edwards	Kerry	Other
ISLE OF WIGHT	1,467	133	44	565	653	72	Kerry	9.1%	3.0%	38.5%	44.5%	4.9%
JAMES CITY	4,449	481	252	1,335	2,204	177	Kerry	10.8%	5.7%	30.0%	49.5%	4.0%
KING AND QUEEN	325	18	27	73	180	27	Kerry	5.5%	8.3%	22.5%	55.4%	8.3%
KING GEORGE	735	69	47	222	347	50	Kerry	9.4%	6.4%	30.2%	47.2%	6.8%
KING WILLIAM	529	56	20	137	279	37	Kerry	10.6%	3.8%	25.9%	52.7%	7.0%
LANCASTER	923	73	75	244	471	60	Kerry	7.9%	8.1%	26.4%	51.0%	6.5%
LEE	835	52	22	231	511	19	Kerry	6.2%	2.6%	27.7%	61.2%	2.3%
LOUDOUN	9,398	720	893	2,181	5,138	466	Kerry	7.7%	9.5%	23.2%	54.7%	5.0%
LOUISA	1,318	130	70	298	720	100	Kerry	9.9%	5.3%	22.6%	54.6%	7.6%
LUNENBURG	607	54	18	162	322	51	Kerry	8.9%	3.0%	26.7%	53.0%	8.4%
MADISON	599	42	49	161	307	40	Kerry	7.0%	8.2%	26.9%	51.3%	6.7%
MATHEWS	624	59	37	195	308	25	Kerry	9.5%	5.9%	31.3%	49.4%	4.0%
MECKLENBURG	1,165	67	25	571	415	87	Edwards	5.8%	2.1%	49.0%	35.6%	7.5%
MIDDLESEX	665	51	25	197	338	54	Kerry	7.7%	3.8%	29.6%	50.8%	8.1%
MONTGOMERY	4,284	443	363	1,377	1,738	363	Kerry	10.3%	8.5%	32.1%	40.6%	8.5%
NELSON	1,080	121	89	258	546	66	Kerry	11.2%	8.2%	23.9%	50.6%	6.1%
NEW KENT	688	50	32	216	333	57	Kerry	7.3%	4.7%	31.4%	48.4%	8.3%
NORTHAMPTON	743	69	32	184	415	43	Kerry	9.3%	4.3%	24.8%	55.9%	5.8%
NORTHUMBERLAND	917	71	53	261	489	43	Kerry	7.7%	5.8%	28.5%	53.3%	4.7%
NOTTOWAY	641	62	30	129	379	41	Kerry	9.7%	4.7%	20.1%	59.1%	6.4%
ORANGE	1,336	95	102	397	685	57	Kerry	7.1%	7.6%	29.7%	51.3%	4.3%
PAGE	586	39	33	168	336	10	Kerry	6.7%	5.6%	28.7%	57.3%	1.7%
PATRICK	896	41	30	495	302	28	Edwards	4.6%	3.3%	55.2%	33.7%	3.1%
PITTSYLVANIA	2,146	218	60	683	1,067	118	Kerry	10.2%	2.8%	31.8%	49.7%	5.5%
POWHATAN	690	76	30	197	345	42	Kerry	11.0%	4.3%	28.6%	50.0%	6.1%
PRINCE EDWARD	907	69	43	198	529	68	Kerry	7.6%	4.7%	21.8%	58.3%	7.5%
PRINCE GEORGE	1,211	131	32	296	647	105	Kerry	10.8%	2.6%	24.4%	53.4%	8.7%
PRINCE WILLIAM	11,382	958	836	2,698	6,203	687	Kerry	8.4%	7.3%	23.7%	54.5%	6.0%
PULASKI	1,351	106	32	591	583	39	Edwards	7.8%	2.4%	43.7%	43.2%	2.9%
RAPPAHANNOCK	654	69	68	128	356	33	Kerry	10.6%	10.4%	19.6%	54.4%	5.0%
RICHMOND COUNTY	331	28	9	103	173	18	Kerry	8.5%	2.7%	31.1%	52.3%	5.4%
ROANOKE COUNTY	4,680	483	203	1,769	2,092	133	Kerry	10.3%	4.3%	37.8%	44.7%	2.8%
ROCKBRIDGE	1,393	129	107	453	634	70	Kerry	9.3%	7.7%	32.5%	45.5%	5.0%
ROCKINGHAM	1,834	130	160	567	911	66	Kerry	7.1%	8.7%	30.9%	49.7%	3.6%
RUSSELL	964	46	11	328	566	13	Kerry	4.8%	1.1%	34.0%	58.7%	1.3%
SCOTT	647	37	27	243	328	12	Kerry	5.7%	4.2%	37.6%	50.7%	1.9%
SHENANDOAH	1,317	105	99	376	688	49	Kerry	8.0%	7.5%	28.5%	52.2%	3.7%
SMYTH	1,026	78	28	423	478	19	Kerry	7.6%	2.7%	41.2%	46.6%	1.9%
SOUTHAMPTON	1,123	108	34	382	539	60	Kerry	9.6%	3.0%	34.0%	48.0%	5.3%
SPOTSYLVANIA	3,632	276	187	1,073	1,927	169	Kerry	7.6%	5.1%	29.5%	53.1%	4.7%
STAFFORD	3,874	365	244	1,182	1,904	179	Kerry	9.4%	6.3%	30.5%	49.1%	4.6%
SURRY	498	37	13	132	275	41	Kerry	7.4%	2.6%	26.5%	55.2%	8.2%
SUSSEX	565	54	11	100	355	45	Kerry	9.6%	1.9%	17.7%	62.8%	8.0%
TAZEWELL	1,526	101	46	485	862	32	Kerry	6.6%	3.0%	31.8%	56.5%	2.1%
WARREN	1,191	103	85	308	653	42	Kerry	8.6%	7.1%	25.9%	54.8%	3.5%

VIRGINIA DEMOCRATIC PRIMARY

2004

County	Total Vote	Clark	Dean	Edwards	Kerry	Other	Winner	Percentage of Total Vote				
								Clark	Dean	Edwards	Kerry	Other
WASHINGTON	1,681	129	52	630	817	53	Kerry	7.7%	3.1%	37.5%	48.6%	3.2%
WESTMORELAND	753	54	39	171	459	30	Kerry	7.2%	5.2%	22.7%	61.0%	4.0%
WISE	1,048	63	27	307	633	18	Kerry	6.0%	2.6%	29.3%	60.4%	1.7%
WYTHE	1,043	67	34	603	325	14	Edwards	6.4%	3.3%	57.8%	31.2%	1.3%
YORK	3,742	431	226	1,217	1,669	199	Kerry	11.5%	6.0%	32.5%	44.6%	5.3%
City												
ALEXANDRIA	13,720	1,120	1,526	3,164	7,303	607	Kerry	8.2%	11.1%	23.1%	53.2%	4.4%
BEDFORD CITY	328	29	10	98	182	9	Kerry	8.8%	3.0%	29.9%	55.5%	2.7%
BRISTOL	718	56	20	280	350	12	Kerry	7.8%	2.8%	39.0%	48.7%	1.7%
BUENA VISTA	306	27	5	107	160	7	Kerry	8.8%	1.6%	35.0%	52.3%	2.3%
CHARLOTTESVILLE	3,918	334	568	773	1,938	305	Kerry	8.5%	14.5%	19.7%	49.5%	7.8%
CHESAPEAKE	10,350	1,005	354	2,651	5,603	737	Kerry	9.7%	3.4%	25.6%	54.1%	7.1%
COLONIAL HEIGHTS	620	78	25	190	291	36	Kerry	12.6%	4.0%	30.6%	46.9%	5.8%
COVINGTON	405	47	10	119	214	15	Kerry	11.6%	2.5%	29.4%	52.8%	3.7%
DANVILLE	2,349	385	72	578	1,145	169	Kerry	16.4%	3.1%	24.6%	48.7%	7.2%
EMPORIA	234	14	9	63	118	30	Kerry	6.0%	3.8%	26.9%	50.4%	12.8%
FAIRFAX CITY	1,770	149	182	420	948	71	Kerry	8.4%	10.3%	23.7%	53.6%	4.0%
FALLS CHURCH	1,723	122	290	373	875	63	Kerry	7.1%	16.8%	21.6%	50.8%	3.7%
FRANKLIN CITY	503	36	13	150	263	41	Kerry	7.2%	2.6%	29.8%	52.3%	8.2%
FREDERICKSBURG	1,218	108	101	343	607	59	Kerry	8.9%	8.3%	28.2%	49.8%	4.8%
GALAX	329	23	4	142	153	7	Kerry	7.0%	1.2%	43.2%	46.5%	2.1%
HAMPTON	8,915	969	349	2,422	4,517	658	Kerry	10.9%	3.9%	27.2%	50.7%	7.4%
HARRISONBURG	1,091	119	114	270	516	72	Kerry	10.9%	10.4%	24.7%	47.3%	6.6%
HOPEWELL	738	90	35	171	389	53	Kerry	12.2%	4.7%	23.2%	52.7%	7.2%
LEXINGTON	616	76	37	174	306	23	Kerry	12.3%	6.0%	28.2%	49.7%	3.7%
LYNCHBURG	3,545	841	175	809	1,574	146	Kerry	23.7%	4.9%	22.8%	44.4%	4.1%
MANASSAS	1,275	102	128	347	628	70	Kerry	8.0%	10.0%	27.2%	49.3%	5.5%
MANASSAS PARK	213	20	22	63	99	9	Kerry	9.4%	10.3%	29.6%	46.5%	4.2%
MARTINSVILLE	724	40	17	253	377	37	Kerry	5.5%	2.3%	34.9%	52.1%	5.1%
NEWPORT NEWS	9,162	1,002	468	2,541	4,506	645	Kerry	10.9%	5.1%	27.7%	49.2%	7.0%
NORFOLK	12,020	1,224	614	2,774	6,507	901	Kerry	10.2%	5.1%	23.1%	54.1%	7.5%
NORTON	156	10	3	42	97	4	Kerry	6.4%	1.9%	26.9%	62.2%	2.6%
PETERSBURG	1,976	133	45	228	1,300	270	Kerry	6.7%	2.3%	11.5%	65.8%	13.7%
POQUOSON	657	98	35	235	251	38	Kerry	14.9%	5.3%	35.8%	38.2%	5.8%
PORTSMOUTH	6,424	625	239	1,531	3,617	412	Kerry	9.7%	3.7%	23.8%	56.3%	6.4%
RADFORD	588	71	23	200	256	38	Kerry	12.1%	3.9%	34.0%	43.5%	6.5%
RICHMOND CITY	14,976	1,371	939	3,282	7,704	1,680	Kerry	9.2%	6.3%	21.9%	51.4%	11.2%
ROANOKE CITY	4,916	436	249	1,594	2,419	218	Kerry	8.9%	5.1%	32.4%	49.2%	4.4%
SALEM	1,244	132	48	460	563	41	Kerry	10.6%	3.9%	37.0%	45.3%	3.3%
STAUNTON	930	89	75	235	483	48	Kerry	9.6%	8.1%	25.3%	51.9%	5.2%
SUFFOLK	3,459	283	138	909	1,869	260	Kerry	8.2%	4.0%	26.3%	54.0%	7.5%
VIRGINIA BEACH	19,870	2,329	1,021	5,526	9,766	1,228	Kerry	11.7%	5.1%	27.8%	49.1%	6.2%
WAYNESBORO	783	73	38	251	383	38	Kerry	9.3%	4.9%	32.1%	48.9%	4.9%
WILLIAMSBURG	1,011	99	99	283	485	45	Kerry	9.8%	9.8%	28.0%	48.0%	4.5%
WINCHESTER	1,099	70	79	296	602	52	Kerry	6.4%	7.2%	26.9%	54.8%	4.7%
TOTAL	396,223	36,572	27,637	105,504	204,142	22,368	Kerry	9.2%	7.0%	26.6%	51.5%	5.6%

Note: Other vote was 12,864 Al Sharpton; 5,016 Dennis J. Kucinich; 2,866 Joseph I. Lieberman; 1,042 Lyndon H. LaRouche Jr.; 580 Richard A. Gephardt.

WASHINGTON

Washington held a unique presidential primary in 2000. It included a contest for Republican voters that George W. Bush won easily, a tally for Democratic voters that Al Gore swept handily, and an "Unaffiliated" ballot for other voters featuring all the Democratic and Republican candidates that John McCain won decisively. In the combined tally of all three votes, Bush finished narrowly ahead of McCain, 402,287 to 399,980. Bush won a majority of Washington's 39 counties in this overall popularity test, but McCain carried the state's most populous county, King (Seattle).

The only real casualty of the late February votefest was Democrat Bill Bradley, who spent nearly a week of valuable campaign time in the Evergreen State in a bid to jumpstart his lagging candidacy. He failed, taking less than one-third of the Democratic primary ballots and carrying just one county (San Juan), which is essentially a cluster of islands northeast of the Olympic Peninsula near the Canadian border.

If a bit confusing in operation—only the Republican primary elected delegates—the whole affair was a hit at the ballot box, attracting more than 1.3 million Washington voters. But the presidential primary is not deeply rooted in Washington's political tradition. And in 2004, the primary was abandoned with Democrats attracting roughly 100,000 voters to their first-round caucus action in early February.

At one point, Washington looked like highly favorable terrain for Howard Dean. Even in the course of his post-Iowa fade, he still captured 30 percent of the caucus tally, his best showing in any primary or caucus state outside Vermont. But he badly trailed Kerry, who took 48 percent. Dean ended up carrying only one of Washington's nine congressional districts, a Seattle constituency represented by liberal Democrat Jim McDermott, a Dean supporter.

As it is, the state's flirtation with a presidential primary has been brief, but the event has often been noteworthy.

Before the first primary in May 1992, the Ross Perot phenomenon was plainly visible in the polls. In Washington, Perot's clout began to be felt at the ballot box, as he drew nearly 20 percent of the vote on write-ins in both the Democratic and Republican primaries and carried San Juan County in each. The strong vote for Perot overshadowed primary victories by President George Bush and Democrat Bill Clinton.

In 1996, the Washington primary went more to form. Bob Dole was the easy winner on the Republican side; Clinton was virtually unopposed on the Democratic. But two-thirds of the

Recent Washington Primary Results

Washington held its first presidential primary in 1992.

	DEMOCRATS			**REPUBLICANS**		
Year	Turnout	Candidates	%	Turnout	Candidates	%
2004	—	No Primary		—	No Primary	
2000 (Feb. 29)	297,001	AL GORE	68	491,148	GEORGE W. BUSH	58
		Bill Bradley	31		John McCain	39
1996 (March 26)	98,946	BILL CLINTON*	99	120,684	BOB DOLE	63
					Pat Buchanan	21
					Steve Forbes	9
1992 (May 19)	147,981	BILL CLINTON	42	129,655	GEORGE BUSH*	67
		Jerry Brown	23		Ross Perot#	20
		Ross Perot#	19		Pat Buchanan	10
		Paul Tsongas	13			

Note: All candidates are listed that drew at least 5 percent of their party's primary vote. The names of winning candidates are capitalized. An asterisk (*) indicates an incumbent president. A pound sign (#) indicates a write-in candidate. In 1996, there was also an "Unaffiliated" ballot that listed candidates from both parties. A total of 444,619 votes were cast in this Unaffiliated primary, led by Democrat Bill Clinton with 51 percent, Republican Bob Dole with 28 percent, Republican Pat Buchanan with 10 percent, and Republican Steve Forbes with 6 percent. A similar Unaffiliated vote was held in 2000 with 521,218 ballots cast. Republican John McCain was the favorite of 40 percent, followed by Republican George W. Bush with 23 percent, Democrat Al Gore with 21 percent, and Democrat Bill Bradley with 13 percent. A combined total of 1,309,367 votes were cast in the Democratic, Republican and Unaffiliated balloting in 2000, according to Washington state election officials, with Bush winning 30.7 percent of the overall all-party vote, followed by McCain with 30.5 percent, Gore with 24 percent, and Bradley with 12 percent.

primary voters cast a third ballot that listed both Democratic and Republican candidates. The results of this unique balloting had nothing to do with the delegate-selection process but did prove prescient. Clinton won the all-party primary with 51 percent of the vote. In the general election, his winning share in Washington was 50 percent.

Conservative Republicans have long enjoyed the upper hand in the state's GOP caucus process. Barry Goldwater swept nearly all the Washington delegates in his successful 1964 insurgency. So did Ronald Reagan in his 1976 challenge to President Gerald Ford.

But neither result was as traumatic as Pat Robertson's caucus victory in 1988, providing the elder Bush with his lone defeat in that year's myriad Super Tuesday contests. Robertson took about 40 percent of the vote in a statewide straw vote held in conjunction with the early March caucuses–a success based in part on his ability to organize many precincts that had been neglected by party regulars in the past. It was not long after Robertson's triumph that the call for a presidential primary in Washington gained momentum.

WASHINGTON DEMOCRATIC PRIMARY

2000

County	Total Vote	Bradley	Gore	LaRouche	Winner	Percentage of Total Vote		
--------	-----------:	--------:	-----:	---------:	--------	Bradley	Gore	LaRouche
						Bradley	Gore	LaRouche
ADAMS	361	95	260	6	Gore	26.3%	72.0%	1.7%
ASOTIN	584	188	391	5	Gore	32.2%	67.0%	0.9%
BENTON	5,805	1,534	4,214	57	Gore	26.4%	72.6%	1.0%
CHELAN	2,094	632	1,449	13	Gore	30.2%	69.2%	0.6%
CLALLAM	3,883	1,174	2,681	28	Gore	30.2%	69.0%	0.7%
CLARK	16,690	4,648	11,956	86	Gore	27.8%	71.6%	0.5%
COLUMBIA	199	57	134	8	Gore	28.6%	67.3%	4.0%
COWLITZ	5,776	1,364	4,381	31	Gore	23.6%	75.8%	0.5%
DOUGLAS	735	188	541	6	Gore	25.6%	73.6%	0.8%
FERRY	294	94	199	1	Gore	32.0%	67.7%	0.3%
FRANKLIN	1,211	236	967	8	Gore	19.5%	79.9%	0.7%
GARFIELD	120	51	69	0	Gore	42.5%	57.5%	0.0%
GRANT	1,970	498	1,452	20	Gore	25.3%	73.7%	1.0%
GRAYS HARBOR	4,762	1,253	3,481	28	Gore	26.3%	73.1%	0.6%
ISLAND	3,822	1,254	2,549	19	Gore	32.8%	66.7%	0.5%
JEFFERSON	2,381	920	1,450	11	Gore	38.6%	60.9%	0.5%
KING	113,912	41,373	72,315	224	Gore	36.3%	63.5%	0.2%
KITSAP	12,180	3,894	8,254	32	Gore	32.0%	67.8%	0.3%
KITTITAS	1,238	376	854	8	Gore	30.4%	69.0%	0.6%
KLICKITAT	737	236	489	12	Gore	32.0%	66.4%	1.6%
LEWIS	3,036	809	2,194	33	Gore	26.6%	72.3%	1.1%
LINCOLN	406	97	304	5	Gore	23.9%	74.9%	1.2%
MASON	3,002	748	2,226	28	Gore	24.9%	74.2%	0.9%
OKANOGAN	1,341	495	818	28	Gore	36.9%	61.0%	2.1%
PACIFIC	1,703	436	1,244	23	Gore	25.6%	73.0%	1.4%
PEND OREILLE	654	175	473	6	Gore	26.8%	72.3%	0.9%
PIERCE	30,761	6,974	23,688	99	Gore	22.7%	77.0%	0.3%
SAN JUAN	1,111	560	548	3	Bradley	50.4%	49.3%	0.3%
SKAGIT	4,320	1,432	2,869	19	Gore	33.1%	66.4%	0.4%
SKAMANIA	524	164	348	12	Gore	31.3%	66.4%	2.3%
SNOHOMISH	24,950	6,900	17,968	82	Gore	27.7%	72.0%	0.3%
SPOKANE	15,399	5,072	10,249	78	Gore	32.9%	66.6%	0.5%
STEVENS	1,205	405	781	19	Gore	33.6%	64.8%	1.6%
THURSTON	13,682	4,059	9,567	56	Gore	29.7%	69.9%	0.4%
WAHKIAKUM	256	78	175	3	Gore	30.5%	68.4%	1.2%
WALLA WALLA	2,114	619	1,489	6	Gore	29.3%	70.4%	0.3%
WHATCOM	6,844	2,695	4,132	17	Gore	39.4%	60.4%	0.2%
WHITMAN	1,761	642	1,109	10	Gore	36.5%	63.0%	0.6%
YAKIMA	5,178	950	4,188	40	Gore	18.3%	80.9%	0.8%
TOTAL	297,001	93,375	202,456	1,170	Gore	31.4%	68.2%	0.4%

WASHINGTON REPUBLICAN PRIMARY

2000

County	Total Vote	G.W. Bush	McCain	Other	Winner	Percentage of Total Vote		
						G.W. Bush	McCain	Other
ADAMS	1,347	930	359	58	G.W. Bush	69.0%	26.7%	4.3%
ASOTIN	1,564	927	595	42	G.W. Bush	59.3%	38.0%	2.7%
BENTON	18,502	12,723	5,181	598	G.W. Bush	68.8%	28.0%	3.2%
CHELAN	7,714	5,285	2,196	233	G.W. Bush	68.5%	28.5%	3.0%
CLALLAM	7,305	3,870	3,067	368	G.W. Bush	53.0%	42.0%	5.0%
CLARK	29,106	17,115	10,571	1,420	G.W. Bush	58.8%	36.3%	4.9%
COLUMBIA	679	505	160	14	G.W. Bush	74.4%	23.6%	2.1%
COWLITZ	6,322	3,701	2,317	304	G.W. Bush	58.5%	36.6%	4.8%
DOUGLAS	2,794	2,063	663	68	G.W. Bush	73.8%	23.7%	2.4%
FERRY	630	323	266	41	G.W. Bush	51.3%	42.2%	6.5%
FRANKLIN	3,225	2,336	771	118	G.W. Bush	72.4%	23.9%	3.7%
GARFIELD	374	258	104	12	G.W. Bush	69.0%	27.8%	3.2%
GRANT	6,536	4,546	1,753	237	G.W. Bush	69.6%	26.8%	3.6%
GRAYS HARBOR	4,421	2,532	1,737	152	G.W. Bush	57.3%	39.3%	3.4%
ISLAND	8,447	4,328	3,867	252	G.W. Bush	51.2%	45.8%	3.0%
JEFFERSON	3,340	1,596	1,647	97	McCain	47.8%	49.3%	2.9%
KING	141,589	76,384	61,989	3,216	G.W. Bush	53.9%	43.8%	2.3%
KITSAP	20,834	11,160	9,015	659	G.W. Bush	53.6%	43.3%	3.2%
KITTITAS	3,132	1,897	1,138	97	G.W. Bush	60.6%	36.3%	3.1%
KLICKITAT	1,603	865	645	93	G.W. Bush	54.0%	40.2%	5.8%
LEWIS	7,677	5,190	2,153	334	G.W. Bush	67.6%	28.0%	4.4%
LINCOLN	1,528	981	487	60	G.W. Bush	64.2%	31.9%	3.9%
MASON	4,507	2,554	1,805	148	G.W. Bush	56.7%	40.0%	3.3%
OKANOGAN	3,735	2,261	1,306	168	G.W. Bush	60.5%	35.0%	4.5%
PACIFIC	1,537	847	626	64	G.W. Bush	55.1%	40.7%	4.2%
PEND OREILLE	1,295	684	544	67	G.W. Bush	52.8%	42.0%	5.2%
PIERCE	47,796	29,346	17,122	1,328	G.W. Bush	61.4%	35.8%	2.8%
SAN JUAN	1,652	702	874	76	McCain	42.5%	52.9%	4.6%
SKAGIT	8,557	4,970	3,291	296	G.W. Bush	58.1%	38.5%	3.5%
SKAMANIA	866	480	331	55	G.W. Bush	55.4%	38.2%	6.4%
SNOHOMISH	41,911	25,087	15,385	1,439	G.W. Bush	59.9%	36.7%	3.4%
SPOKANE	41,684	21,098	19,035	1,551	G.W. Bush	50.6%	45.7%	3.7%
STEVENS	4,765	2,480	2,008	277	G.W. Bush	52.0%	42.1%	5.8%
THURSTON	16,974	10,007	6,439	528	G.W. Bush	59.0%	37.9%	3.1%
WAHKIAKUM	311	167	129	15	G.W. Bush	53.7%	41.5%	4.8%
WALLA WALLA	6,075	4,060	1,820	195	G.W. Bush	66.8%	30.0%	3.2%
WHATCOM	11,218	6,773	3,904	541	G.W. Bush	60.4%	34.8%	4.8%
WHITMAN	4,286	2,655	1,463	168	G.W. Bush	61.9%	34.1%	3.9%
YAKIMA	15,310	10,367	4,338	605	G.W. Bush	67.7%	28.3%	4.0%
TOTAL	491,148	284,053	191,101	15,994	G.W. Bush	57.8%	38.9%	3.3%

Note: Other vote was 11,753 Alan Keyes; 1,749 Steve Forbes; 1,469 Gary Bauer; 1,023 Orrin G. Hatch.

WASHINGTON ALL-PARTY PRIMARY

2000

County	Total Vote	Bradley	G.W. Bush	Gore	McCain	Other	Winner	Percentage of Total Vote				
								Bradley	G.W. Bush	Gore	McCain	Other
ADAMS	3,484	214	1,694	492	949	135	G.W. Bush	6.1%	48.6%	14.1%	27.2%	3.9%
ASOTIN	3,212	281	1,194	486	1,157	94	G.W. Bush	8.7%	37.2%	15.1%	36.0%	2.9%
BENTON	35,464	2,440	16,708	5,694	9,515	1,107	G.W. Bush	6.9%	47.1%	16.1%	26.8%	3.1%
CHELAN	15,908	1,250	7,366	2,318	4,532	442	G.W. Bush	7.9%	46.3%	14.6%	28.5%	2.8%
CLALLAM	21,899	2,447	6,555	4,654	7,374	869	McCain	11.2%	29.9%	21.3%	33.7%	4.0%
CLARK	67,256	7,462	21,667	16,178	19,509	2,440	G.W. Bush	11.1%	32.2%	24.1%	29.0%	3.6%
COLUMBIA	1,622	119	822	224	410	47	G.W. Bush	7.3%	50.7%	13.8%	25.3%	2.9%
COWLITZ	21,804	2,457	6,007	6,532	6,013	795	Gore	11.3%	27.5%	30.0%	27.6%	3.6%
DOUGLAS	7,152	506	3,457	1,050	1,956	183	G.W. Bush	7.1%	48.3%	14.7%	27.3%	2.6%
FERRY	2,217	215	707	353	809	133	McCain	9.7%	31.9%	15.9%	36.5%	6.0%
FRANKLIN	8,785	535	4,158	1,731	2,079	282	G.W. Bush	6.1%	47.3%	19.7%	23.7%	3.2%
GARFIELD	1,008	98	467	111	309	23	G.W. Bush	9.7%	46.3%	11.0%	30.7%	2.3%
GRANT	14,729	991	6,790	2,310	4,115	523	G.W. Bush	6.7%	46.1%	15.7%	27.9%	3.6%
GRAYS HARBOR	17,417	2,248	4,454	5,118	5,099	498	Gore	12.9%	25.6%	29.4%	29.3%	2.9%
ISLAND	18,775	2,185	5,445	3,668	6,977	500	McCain	11.6%	29.0%	19.5%	37.2%	2.7%
JEFFERSON	9,316	1,431	2,206	2,170	3,302	207	McCain	15.4%	23.7%	23.3%	35.4%	2.2%
KING	381,615	65,855	94,459	99,042	116,024	6,235	McCain	17.3%	24.8%	26.0%	30.4%	1.6%
KITSAP	64,920	7,629	18,459	14,959	22,238	1,635	McCain	11.8%	28.4%	23.0%	34.3%	2.5%
KITTITAS	6,917	669	2,548	1,241	2,265	194	G.W. Bush	9.7%	36.8%	17.9%	32.7%	2.8%
KLICKITAT	3,832	373	1,242	700	1,331	186	McCain	9.7%	32.4%	18.3%	34.7%	4.9%
LEWIS	19,314	1,687	8,076	3,558	5,225	768	G.W. Bush	8.7%	41.8%	18.4%	27.1%	4.0%
LINCOLN	3,372	208	1,469	477	1,081	137	G.W. Bush	6.2%	43.6%	14.1%	32.1%	4.1%
MASON	13,261	1,400	3,797	3,350	4,362	352	G.W. Bush	10.6%	28.6%	25.3%	32.9%	2.7%
OKANOGAN	9,704	980	3,718	1,290	3,308	408	G.W. Bush	10.1%	38.3%	13.3%	34.1%	4.2%
PACIFIC	6,455	879	1,520	1,882	1,961	213	McCain	13.6%	23.5%	29.2%	30.4%	3.3%
PEND OREILLE	3,404	296	1,045	639	1,270	154	McCain	8.7%	30.7%	18.8%	37.3%	4.5%
PIERCE	147,108	14,263	45,760	41,348	42,101	3,636	G.W. Bush	9.7%	31.1%	28.1%	28.6%	2.5%
SAN JUAN	4,650	955	950	879	1,725	141	McCain	20.5%	20.4%	18.9%	37.1%	3.0%
SKAGIT	21,547	2,605	6,976	4,456	6,939	571	G.W. Bush	12.1%	32.4%	20.7%	32.2%	2.7%
SKAMANIA	2,522	295	752	551	795	129	McCain	11.7%	29.8%	21.8%	31.5%	5.1%
SNOHOMISH	119,857	13,824	36,580	31,043	35,250	3,160	G.W. Bush	11.5%	30.5%	25.9%	29.4%	2.6%
SPOKANE	78,185	7,446	25,665	13,542	29,127	2,405	McCain	9.5%	32.8%	17.3%	37.3%	3.1%
STEVENS	8,836	643	3,306	1,043	3,357	487	McCain	7.3%	37.4%	11.8%	38.0%	5.5%
THURSTON	62,331	8,212	17,123	17,426	18,009	1,561	McCain	13.2%	27.5%	28.0%	28.9%	2.5%
WAHKIAKUM	1,252	149	364	293	396	50	McCain	11.9%	29.1%	23.4%	31.6%	4.0%
WALLA WALLA	12,913	1,013	5,659	2,148	3,722	371	G.W. Bush	7.8%	43.8%	16.6%	28.8%	2.9%
WHATCOM	36,157	5,144	11,689	7,657	10,474	1,193	G.W. Bush	14.2%	32.3%	21.2%	29.0%	3.3%
WHITMAN	9,721	1,047	3,755	1,656	2,972	291	G.W. Bush	10.8%	38.6%	17.0%	30.6%	3.0%
YAKIMA	41,446	2,276	17,678	8,137	11,943	1,412	G.W. Bush	5.5%	42.7%	19.6%	28.8%	3.4%
TOTAL	1,309,367	162,727	402,287	310,406	399,980	33,967	G.W. Bush	12.4%	30.7%	23.7%	30.5%	2.6%

Note: The nonbinding all-party primary results represent an aggregation of the vote in the Democratic, Republican and "Unaffiliated" primaries as compiled by Washington state election officials. Other vote in this overall tally was 21,122 Alan Keyes; 5,136 Steve Forbes; 2,870 Gary Bauer; 2,576 Lyndon H. LaRouche Jr.; 2,263 Orrin G. Hatch. The 2000 Democratic and Republican primary results are featured in separate tables. Washington voters that did not want to participate in either the Democratic or Republican primary could cast an Unaffiliated ballot that included the names of candidates from both parties. The results of the Unaffiliated balloting were as follows: 208,879 John McCain (R); 118,234 George W. Bush (R); 107,950 Al Gore (D); 69,352 Bill Bradley (D); 9,369 Alan Keyes (R); 3,387 Steve Forbes (R); 1,406 Lyndon H. LaRouche Jr. (D); 1,401 Gary Bauer (R); 1,240 Orrin G. Hatch (R).

WEST VIRGINIA

West Virginia's presidential primary assured itself a place in American political lore in 1960, when John F. Kennedy chose it as the place to test whether an urban Catholic could win in a rural Protestant environment. After an expensive and closely watched campaign that has earned its place in the "Camelot" saga, Kennedy defeated Hubert Humphrey, 61 to 39 percent. The result knocked Humphrey from the race and moved Kennedy's own candidacy a big step closer to the Democratic nomination.

No presidential primary in West Virginia before or since has had such an impact on the nominating process. In recent years, it has taken second billing on the May primary ballot to party gubernatorial contests that are decided at the same time. So much so that in 2004, more votes were cast in both the Democratic and Republican primaries for governor than for president; on the Democratic side, it was better than 30,000 votes more.

Presidential candidates that do come to West Virginia find a state that is poor, proud, and patriotic. Although won by Republican George W. Bush in the 2000 and 2004 presidential elections, West Virginia still boasts a hefty Democratic registration advantage.

The backdrop has long made the state fertile ground for Democratic candidates willing to proclaim a love of country and embrace New Deal-style programs that are out of vogue in much of the rest of the nation. Humphrey avenged his loss to Kennedy by swamping George Wallace by a margin of better than 2 to 1 in the 1972 primary. Twelve years later, Humphrey's

Recent West Virginia Primary Results

West Virginia held its first presidential primary in 1916.

Year	DEMOCRATS			REPUBLICANS		
	Turnout	Candidates	%	Turnout	Candidates	%
2004 (May 11)	252,839	JOHN KERRY	69	111,109	GEORGE W. BUSH*	100
		John Edwards	13			
		Joe Lieberman	5			
2000 (May 9)	253,310	AL GORE	72	109,404	GEORGE W. BUSH	80
		Bill Bradley	18		John McCain	13
		Angus McDonald	8			
1996 (May 14)	297,121	BILL CLINTON*	87	127,454	BOB DOLE	69
		Lyndon LaRouche	13		Pat Buchanan	16
1992 (May 12)	306,866	BILL CLINTON	74	124,157	GEORGE BUSH*	81
		Jerry Brown	12		Pat Buchanan	15
		Paul Tsongas	7			
1988 (May 10)	340,097	MICHAEL DUKAKIS	75	143,140	GEORGE BUSH	77
		Jesse Jackson	13		Bob Dole	11
					Pat Robertson	7
1984 (June 5)	369,245	WALTER MONDALE	54	136,996	RONALD REAGAN*	92
		Gary Hart	37		Harold Stassen	8
		Jesse Jackson	7			
1980 (June 3)	317,934	JIMMY CARTER*	62	138,016	RONALD REAGAN	84
		Edward Kennedy	38		George Bush	14
1976 (May 11)	372,577	ROBERT BYRD	89	155,692	GERALD FORD*	57
		George Wallace	11		Ronald Reagan	43
1972 (May 9)	368,484	HUBERT HUMPHREY	67	95,813	UNPLEDGED	100
		George Wallace	33			
1968 (May 14)	149,282	UNPLEDGED	100	81,039	UNPLEDGED	100

Note: All candidates are listed that drew at least 5 percent of their party's primary vote. The names of winning candidates are capitalized. An asterisk (*) indicates an incumbent president.

protégé, Walter Mondale, took a majority of the Democratic vote. West Virginia was the only primary state that Mondale carried in 1984 with more than 50 percent.

Edward Kennedy sought to duplicate his brother's success in West Virginia in 1980, but fell short. Forced to choose between nostalgia and loyalty, West Virginia Democrats chose to be loyal. The United Mine Workers and much of the state party hierarchy lined up behind President Jimmy Carter, who carried all but one county.

Bill Clinton was an easy winner in the West Virginia primary the two times he ran, although in 1996 he lost 13 percent of the vote to Lyndon LaRouche. It was the largest share of the vote that LaRouche won that year in any primary where he went head-to-head with Clinton.

No recent Republican primaries have been very compelling. The closest was in 1976 between President Gerald Ford and Ronald Reagan. But with the backing of the state's most powerful Republican at the time, Gov. Arch Moore, Ford swept all but three of West Virginia's 55 counties. Wood County (Parkersburg) was the largest that voted for Reagan.

WEST VIRGINIA DEMOCRATIC PRIMARY

2000

County	Total Vote	Bradley	Gore	LaRouche	McDonald	Winner	Percentage of Total Vote			
							Bradley	Gore	LaRouche	McDonald
BARBOUR	2,280	416	1,662	36	166	Gore	18.2%	72.9%	1.6%	7.3%
BERKELEY	4,687	931	3,211	123	422	Gore	19.9%	68.5%	2.6%	9.0%
BOONE	5,744	979	4,233	97	435	Gore	17.0%	73.7%	1.7%	7.6%
BRAXTON	3,325	528	2,338	69	390	Gore	15.9%	70.3%	2.1%	11.7%
BROOKE	4,233	1,049	2,705	96	383	Gore	24.8%	63.9%	2.3%	9.0%
CABELL	10,603	1,729	8,168	170	536	Gore	16.3%	77.0%	1.6%	5.1%
CALHOUN	1,191	195	859	19	118	Gore	16.4%	72.1%	1.6%	9.9%
CLAY	2,246	347	1,624	56	219	Gore	15.4%	72.3%	2.5%	9.8%
DODDRIDGE	461	82	318	2	59	Gore	17.8%	69.0%	0.4%	12.8%
FAYETTE	7,970	1,456	5,723	184	607	Gore	18.3%	71.8%	2.3%	7.6%
GILMER	1,771	387	1,163	41	180	Gore	21.9%	65.7%	2.3%	10.2%
GRANT	318	64	224	10	20	Gore	20.1%	70.4%	3.1%	6.3%
GREENBRIER	5,101	982	3,488	115	516	Gore	19.3%	68.4%	2.3%	10.1%
HAMPSHIRE	2,058	391	1,386	61	220	Gore	19.0%	67.3%	3.0%	10.7%
HANCOCK	6,400	1,755	4,075	164	406	Gore	27.4%	63.7%	2.6%	6.3%
HARDY	1,819	355	1,233	72	159	Gore	19.5%	67.8%	4.0%	8.7%
HARRISON	12,459	2,189	9,247	145	878	Gore	17.6%	74.2%	1.2%	7.0%
JACKSON	3,635	524	2,849	41	221	Gore	14.4%	78.4%	1.1%	6.1%
JEFFERSON	3,504	586	2,409	39	470	Gore	16.7%	68.8%	1.1%	13.4%
KANAWHA	28,110	5,019	21,253	400	1,438	Gore	17.9%	75.6%	1.4%	5.1%
LEWIS	1,996	379	1,408	51	158	Gore	19.0%	70.5%	2.6%	7.9%
LINCOLN	3,809	410	3,025	65	309	Gore	10.8%	79.4%	1.7%	8.1%
LOGAN	7,785	1,221	5,917	115	532	Gore	15.7%	76.0%	1.5%	6.8%
MCDOWELL	4,944	685	3,793	92	374	Gore	13.9%	76.7%	1.9%	7.6%
MARION	12,394	2,187	9,059	211	937	Gore	17.6%	73.1%	1.7%	7.6%
MARSHALL	4,909	1,248	3,015	135	511	Gore	25.4%	61.4%	2.8%	10.4%
MASON	4,715	838	3,404	72	401	Gore	17.8%	72.2%	1.5%	8.5%
MERCER	8,292	1,518	5,894	205	675	Gore	18.3%	71.1%	2.5%	8.1%
MINERAL	2,286	421	1,617	43	205	Gore	18.4%	70.7%	1.9%	9.0%
MINGO	7,173	903	5,798	93	379	Gore	12.6%	80.8%	1.3%	5.3%
MONONGALIA	9,113	1,790	6,451	163	709	Gore	19.6%	70.8%	1.8%	7.8%
MONROE	2,052	330	1,511	57	154	Gore	16.1%	73.6%	2.8%	7.5%
MORGAN	1,125	191	845	7	82	Gore	17.0%	75.1%	0.6%	7.3%
NICHOLAS	2,740	804	1,389	88	459	Gore	29.3%	50.7%	3.2%	16.8%
OHIO	6,939	1,835	4,569	164	371	Gore	26.4%	65.8%	2.4%	5.3%
PENDLETON	1,271	219	907	27	118	Gore	17.2%	71.4%	2.1%	9.3%
PLEASANTS	1,208	245	847	25	91	Gore	20.3%	70.1%	2.1%	7.5%
POCAHONTAS	1,529	284	1,091	34	120	Gore	18.6%	71.4%	2.2%	7.8%
PRESTON	3,133	523	2,162	89	359	Gore	16.7%	69.0%	2.8%	11.5%
PUTNAM	6,119	1,117	4,490	107	405	Gore	18.3%	73.4%	1.7%	6.6%
RALEIGH	9,280	1,904	6,519	211	646	Gore	20.5%	70.2%	2.3%	7.0%
RANDOLPH	4,866	970	3,365	105	426	Gore	19.9%	69.2%	2.2%	8.8%
RITCHIE	725	114	529	15	67	Gore	15.7%	73.0%	2.1%	9.2%
ROANE	1,999	327	1,505	33	134	Gore	16.4%	75.3%	1.7%	6.7%
SUMMERS	2,854	456	2,105	64	229	Gore	16.0%	73.8%	2.2%	8.0%

WEST VIRGINIA DEMOCRATIC PRIMARY

2000

County	Total Vote	Bradley	Gore	LaRouche	McDonald	Winner	Percentage of Total Vote			
							Bradley	Gore	LaRouche	McDonald
TAYLOR	2,528	483	1,838	32	175	Gore	19.1%	72.7%	1.3%	6.9%
TUCKER	1,546	326	1,021	31	168	Gore	21.1%	66.0%	2.0%	10.9%
TYLER	783	166	513	19	85	Gore	21.2%	65.5%	2.4%	10.9%
UPSHUR	1,783	363	1,281	30	109	Gore	20.4%	71.8%	1.7%	6.1%
WAYNE	7,565	1,163	5,671	128	603	Gore	15.4%	75.0%	1.7%	8.0%
WEBSTER	2,546	369	1,818	51	308	Gore	14.5%	71.4%	2.0%	12.1%
WETZEL	3,171	739	2,066	86	280	Gore	23.3%	65.2%	2.7%	8.8%
WIRT	936	185	625	23	103	Gore	19.8%	66.8%	2.5%	11.0%
WOOD	6,902	1,353	4,981	141	427	Gore	19.6%	72.2%	2.0%	6.2%
WYOMING	4,379	680	3,206	71	422	Gore	15.5%	73.2%	1.6%	9.6%
TOTAL	253,310	46,710	182,403	4,823	19,374	Gore	18.4%	72.0%	1.9%	7.6%

WEST VIRGINIA REPUBLICAN PRIMARY

2000

County	Total Vote	G.W. Bush	McCain	Other	Winner	Percentage of Total Vote		
						G.W. Bush	McCain	Other
BARBOUR	1,444	1,188	146	110	G.W. Bush	82.3%	10.1%	7.6%
BERKELEY	3,782	2,949	556	277	G.W. Bush	78.0%	14.7%	7.3%
BOONE	585	504	38	43	G.W. Bush	86.2%	6.5%	7.4%
BRAXTON	572	464	73	35	G.W. Bush	81.1%	12.8%	6.1%
BROOKE	958	701	157	100	G.W. Bush	73.2%	16.4%	10.4%
CABELL	5,971	4,721	759	491	G.W. Bush	79.1%	12.7%	8.2%
CALHOUN	417	362	35	20	G.W. Bush	86.8%	8.4%	4.8%
CLAY	483	388	57	38	G.W. Bush	80.3%	11.8%	7.9%
DODDRIDGE	1,334	1,044	199	91	G.W. Bush	78.3%	14.9%	6.8%
FAYETTE	1,097	842	146	109	G.W. Bush	76.8%	13.3%	9.9%
GILMER	466	371	63	32	G.W. Bush	79.6%	13.5%	6.9%
GRANT	2,494	2,061	302	131	G.W. Bush	82.6%	12.1%	5.3%
GREENBRIER	1,420	1,154	166	100	G.W. Bush	81.3%	11.7%	7.0%
HAMPSHIRE	859	697	105	57	G.W. Bush	81.1%	12.2%	6.6%
HANCOCK	1,687	1,262	224	201	G.W. Bush	74.8%	13.3%	11.9%
HARDY	537	446	60	31	G.W. Bush	83.1%	11.2%	5.8%
HARRISON	3,710	2,876	536	298	G.W. Bush	77.5%	14.4%	8.0%
JACKSON	3,437	2,843	400	194	G.W. Bush	82.7%	11.6%	5.6%
JEFFERSON	1,613	1,184	274	155	G.W. Bush	73.4%	17.0%	9.6%
KANAWHA	13,568	10,556	1,936	1,076	G.W. Bush	77.8%	14.3%	7.9%

WEST VIRGINIA REPUBLICAN PRIMARY

2000

County	Total Vote	G.W. Bush	McCain	Other	Winner	Percentage of Total Vote		
						G.W. Bush	McCain	Other
LEWIS	1,404	1,094	201	109	G.W. Bush	77.9%	14.3%	7.8%
LINCOLN	753	658	54	41	G.W. Bush	87.4%	7.2%	5.4%
LOGAN	413	332	28	53	G.W. Bush	80.4%	6.8%	12.8%
MCDOWELL	270	223	30	17	G.W. Bush	82.6%	11.1%	6.3%
MARION	2,903	2,248	425	230	G.W. Bush	77.4%	14.6%	7.9%
MARSHALL	2,474	1,790	438	246	G.W. Bush	72.4%	17.7%	9.9%
MASON	2,987	2,428	390	169	G.W. Bush	81.3%	13.1%	5.7%
MERCER	2,189	1,810	233	146	G.W. Bush	82.7%	10.6%	6.7%
MINERAL	2,468	1,980	320	168	G.W. Bush	80.2%	13.0%	6.8%
MINGO	364	311	30	23	G.W. Bush	85.4%	8.2%	6.3%
MONONGALIA	3,588	2,685	537	366	G.W. Bush	74.8%	15.0%	10.2%
MONROE	917	806	65	46	G.W. Bush	87.9%	7.1%	5.0%
MORGAN	1,652	1,274	256	122	G.W. Bush	77.1%	15.5%	7.4%
NICHOLAS	1,088	890	131	67	G.W. Bush	81.8%	12.0%	6.2%
OHIO	3,932	3,029	547	356	G.W. Bush	77.0%	13.9%	9.1%
PENDLETON	570	490	48	32	G.W. Bush	86.0%	8.4%	5.6%
PLEASANTS	813	673	87	53	G.W. Bush	82.8%	10.7%	6.5%
POCAHONTAS	818	638	116	64	G.W. Bush	78.0%	14.2%	7.8%
PRESTON	3,607	2,832	461	314	G.W. Bush	78.5%	12.8%	8.7%
PUTNAM	4,303	3,515	488	300	G.W. Bush	81.7%	11.3%	7.0%
RALEIGH	2,240	1,820	250	170	G.W. Bush	81.3%	11.2%	7.6%
RANDOLPH	1,063	864	138	61	G.W. Bush	81.3%	13.0%	5.7%
RITCHIE	1,712	1,400	212	100	G.W. Bush	81.8%	12.4%	5.8%
ROANE	1,528	1,277	174	77	G.W. Bush	83.6%	11.4%	5.0%
SUMMERS	467	379	45	43	G.W. Bush	81.2%	9.6%	9.2%
TAYLOR	1,141	899	181	61	G.W. Bush	78.8%	15.9%	5.3%
TUCKER	728	604	68	56	G.W. Bush	83.0%	9.3%	7.7%
TYLER	1,730	1,370	253	107	G.W. Bush	79.2%	14.6%	6.2%
UPSHUR	2,745	2,146	394	205	G.W. Bush	78.2%	14.4%	7.5%
WAYNE	2,137	1,794	189	154	G.W. Bush	83.9%	8.8%	7.2%
WEBSTER	194	157	22	15	G.W. Bush	80.9%	11.3%	7.7%
WETZEL	904	697	113	94	G.W. Bush	77.1%	12.5%	10.4%
WIRT	617	506	62	49	G.W. Bush	82.0%	10.0%	7.9%
WOOD	7,493	6,144	848	501	G.W. Bush	82.0%	11.3%	6.7%
WYOMING	758	674	55	29	G.W. Bush	88.9%	7.3%	3.8%
TOTAL	109,404	87,050	14,121	8,233	G.W. Bush	79.6%	12.9%	7.5%

Note: Other vote was 5,210 Alan Keyes; 1,733 Steve Forbes; 1,290 Gary Bauer.

WEST VIRGINIA DEMOCRATIC PRIMARY

2004

County	Total Vote	Edwards	Kerry	Lieberman	Other	Winner	Percentage of Total Vote			
							Edwards	Kerry	Lieberman	Other
BARBOUR	2,246	259	1,585	122	280	Kerry	11.5%	70.6%	5.4%	12.5%
BERKELEY	4,441	579	2,981	247	634	Kerry	13.0%	67.1%	5.6%	14.3%
BOONE	5,982	764	4,491	223	504	Kerry	12.8%	75.1%	3.7%	8.4%
BRAXTON	3,251	464	2,215	142	430	Kerry	14.3%	68.1%	4.4%	13.2%
BROOKE	4,497	512	3,174	258	553	Kerry	11.4%	70.6%	5.7%	12.3%
CABELL	12,892	2,080	8,941	753	1,118	Kerry	16.1%	69.4%	5.8%	8.7%
CALHOUN	1,293	192	841	53	207	Kerry	14.8%	65.0%	4.1%	16.0%
CLAY	2,213	288	1,467	110	348	Kerry	13.0%	66.3%	5.0%	15.7%
DODDRIDGE	527	56	363	22	86	Kerry	10.6%	68.9%	4.2%	16.3%
FAYETTE	7,042	987	4,865	322	868	Kerry	14.0%	69.1%	4.6%	12.3%
GILMER	1,496	220	937	82	257	Kerry	14.7%	62.6%	5.5%	17.2%
GRANT	331	49	232	12	38	Kerry	14.8%	70.1%	3.6%	11.5%
GREENBRIER	5,333	878	3,470	274	711	Kerry	16.5%	65.1%	5.1%	13.3%
HAMPSHIRE	2,178	318	1,387	139	334	Kerry	14.6%	63.7%	6.4%	15.3%
HANCOCK	5,640	657	3,955	333	695	Kerry	11.6%	70.1%	5.9%	12.3%
HARDY	1,709	273	1,066	101	269	Kerry	16.0%	62.4%	5.9%	15.7%
HARRISON	11,703	1,411	8,120	892	1,280	Kerry	12.1%	69.4%	7.6%	10.9%
JACKSON	3,576	408	2,732	131	305	Kerry	11.4%	76.4%	3.7%	8.5%
JEFFERSON	4,371	393	3,310	201	467	Kerry	9.0%	75.7%	4.6%	10.7%
KANAWHA	27,784	3,999	19,675	1,345	2,765	Kerry	14.4%	70.8%	4.8%	10.0%
LEWIS	2,402	355	1,540	151	356	Kerry	14.8%	64.1%	6.3%	14.8%
LINCOLN	4,313	456	3,290	125	442	Kerry	10.6%	76.3%	2.9%	10.2%
LOGAN	6,806	611	5,093	284	818	Kerry	9.0%	74.8%	4.2%	12.0%
MCDOWELL	4,641	668	3,309	168	496	Kerry	14.4%	71.3%	3.6%	10.7%
MARION	11,555	1,381	8,215	736	1,223	Kerry	12.0%	71.1%	6.4%	10.6%
MARSHALL	5,410	748	3,719	299	644	Kerry	13.8%	68.7%	5.5%	11.9%
MASON	4,142	415	3,112	158	457	Kerry	10.0%	75.1%	3.8%	11.0%
MERCER	7,626	1,519	4,640	559	908	Kerry	19.9%	60.8%	7.3%	11.9%
MINERAL	2,613	312	1,738	156	407	Kerry	11.9%	66.5%	6.0%	15.6%
MINGO	6,642	605	5,004	241	792	Kerry	9.1%	75.3%	3.6%	11.9%
MONONGALIA	9,129	989	6,093	773	1,274	Kerry	10.8%	66.7%	8.5%	14.0%
MONROE	1,882	351	1,232	87	212	Kerry	18.7%	65.5%	4.6%	11.3%
MORGAN	932	121	656	46	109	Kerry	13.0%	70.4%	4.9%	11.7%
NICHOLAS	4,445	619	3,064	275	487	Kerry	13.9%	68.9%	6.2%	11.0%
OHIO	6,199	738	4,238	506	717	Kerry	11.9%	68.4%	8.2%	11.6%
PENDLETON	1,428	178	1,010	51	189	Kerry	12.5%	70.7%	3.6%	13.2%
PLEASANTS	1,199	202	810	67	120	Kerry	16.8%	67.6%	5.6%	10.0%
POCAHONTAS	1,407	169	950	64	224	Kerry	12.0%	67.5%	4.5%	15.9%
PRESTON	2,776	336	1,836	177	427	Kerry	12.1%	66.1%	6.4%	15.4%
PUTNAM	6,549	863	4,596	286	804	Kerry	13.2%	70.2%	4.4%	12.3%
RALEIGH	9,339	1,668	5,853	607	1,211	Kerry	17.9%	62.7%	6.5%	13.0%
RANDOLPH	5,022	698	3,223	284	817	Kerry	13.9%	64.2%	5.7%	16.3%
RITCHIE	668	96	451	28	93	Kerry	14.4%	67.5%	4.2%	13.9%
ROANE	1,840	207	1,367	49	217	Kerry	11.3%	74.3%	2.7%	11.8%
SUMMERS	2,419	434	1,560	128	297	Kerry	17.9%	64.5%	5.3%	12.3%

WEST VIRGINIA DEMOCRATIC PRIMARY

2004

County	Total Vote	Edwards	Kerry	Lieberman	Other	Winner	Percentage of Total Vote			
							Edwards	Kerry	Lieberman	Other
TAYLOR	2,359	320	1,589	132	318	Kerry	13.6%	67.4%	5.6%	13.5%
TUCKER	1,370	228	887	71	184	Kerry	16.6%	64.7%	5.2%	13.4%
TYLER	872	105	592	58	117	Kerry	12.0%	67.9%	6.7%	13.4%
UPSHUR	1,981	245	1,396	74	266	Kerry	12.4%	70.5%	3.7%	13.4%
WAYNE	7,649	921	5,517	385	826	Kerry	12.0%	72.1%	5.0%	10.8%
WEBSTER	2,474	342	1,715	98	319	Kerry	13.8%	69.3%	4.0%	12.9%
WETZEL	3,447	563	2,259	200	425	Kerry	16.3%	65.5%	5.8%	12.3%
WIRT	930	113	638	56	123	Kerry	12.2%	68.6%	6.0%	13.2%
WOOD	7,842	977	5,333	496	1,036	Kerry	12.5%	68.0%	6.3%	13.2%
WYOMING	4,026	610	2,733	244	439	Kerry	15.2%	67.9%	6.1%	10.9%
TOTAL	252,839	33,950	175,065	13,881	29,943	Kerry	13.4%	69.2%	5.5%	11.8%

Note: Other vote was 10,576 Howard Dean; 9,170 Wesley Clark; 6,114 Dennis J. Kucinich; 4,083 Lyndon H. LaRouche Jr.

WISCONSIN

If Virginia can claim to be the "mother of presidents," then Wisconsin could boast that it is the "mother of presidential primaries." It was from the progressive agenda of Wisconsin's legendary Robert M. La Follette that presidential primaries got a major boost, and Wisconsin initiated one of the first in 1912.

Few states have as rich a primary heritage as Wisconsin or as distinctive a voting process—the state's long-standing open primary rules make it effortless for voters to participate in either party's contest.

For more than a half-century after the primary's inception, Wisconsin was a necessary stop for candidates traveling the primary route to their party's nomination. But the recent proliferation of primaries, especially early ones, has forced Wisconsin to scramble to retain much of its luster.

Recent Wisconsin Primary Results

Wisconsin held its first presidential primary in 1912.

Year	DEMOCRATS Turnout	DEMOCRATS Candidates	%	REPUBLICANS Turnout	REPUBLICANS Candidates	%
2004 (Feb. 17)	828,364	JOHN KERRY	40	160,428	GEORGE W. BUSH*	99
		John Edwards	34			
		Howard Dean	18			
2000 (April 4)	371,196	AL GORE	89	495,769	GEORGE W. BUSH	69
		Bill Bradley	9		John McCain	18
					Alan Keyes	10
1996 (March 19)	356,168	BILL CLINTON*	98	576,575	BOB DOLE	52
					Pat Buchanan	34
					Steve Forbes	6
1992 (April 7)	772,596	BILL CLINTON	37	482,248	GEORGE BUSH*	76
		Jerry Brown	34		Pat Buchanan	16
		Paul Tsongas	22			
1988 (April 5)	1,014,782	MICHAEL DUKAKIS	48	359,294	GEORGE BUSH	82
		Jesse Jackson	28		Bob Dole	8
		Al Gore	17		Pat Robertson	7
1984 (April 3)	635,768	GARY HART	44	294,813	RONALD REAGAN*	95
		Walter Mondale	41			
		Jesse Jackson	10			
1980 (April 1)	629,619	JIMMY CARTER*	56	907,853	RONALD REAGAN	40
		Edward Kennedy	30		George Bush	30
		Jerry Brown	12		John Anderson	27
1976 (April 6)	740,528	JIMMY CARTER	37	591,812	GERALD FORD*	55
		Morris Udall	36		Ronald Reagan	44
		George Wallace	12			
		Henry Jackson	6			
1972 (April 4)	1,128,584	GEORGE McGOVERN	30	286,444	RICHARD NIXON*	97
		George Wallace	22			
		Hubert Humphrey	21			
		Edmund Muskie	10			
		Henry Jackson	8			
		John Lindsay	7			
1968 (April 2)	733,002	EUGENE McCARTHY	56	489,853	RICHARD NIXON	80
		Lyndon Johnson*	35		Ronald Reagan	10
		Robert Kennedy#	6		Harold Stassen	6

Note: All candidates are listed that drew at least 5 percent of their party's primary vote. The names of winning candidates are capitalized. An asterisk (*) indicates an incumbent president. A pound sign (#) indicates a write-in candidate.

In 1968, Wisconsin voted second after New Hampshire. But in 2000, more than two dozen states held primaries in between the two. Reflecting the old saying, "if you can't beat them, join them," Wisconsin moved its traditional early spring primary forward in 2004 to mid-February.

The move paid off, as Wisconsin emerged as a key stop on the Democratic campaign trail. Howard Dean picked the state to make his last stand. And John Edwards came close to scoring an upset. But the winner was the front-running John Kerry, who showed the same broad-based vote-getting ability in Wisconsin that was evident in most of his other early primary and caucus triumphs. Kerry swept the vast majority of Wisconsin's 72 counties, including nine of the 10 most populous. And he carried the two large Democratic strongholds of Milwaukee and Dane (Madison) counties.

Edwards capitalized on the wide open nature of the primary by carrying many of the more Republican areas of the state, from the suburbs of Milwaukee to the county (Fond du Lac) which contains the small town of Ripon, the widely acknowledged birthplace of the Republican Party.

As for Dean, he had hoped that Wisconsin's progressive heritage would revive his flagging candidacy, but he failed to carry a single county. Even in Dane, home to the University of Wisconsin and a legion of liberal activists, Dean drew only 21 percent of the vote and finished third.

Wisconsin has gained an image as an outpost of Midwestern liberalism. But that is based largely on just two Democratic primaries—Eugene McCarthy's victory in 1968 and George McGovern's in 1972. Both were fueled by opposition to the Vietnam War.

The list is longer of liberal contenders who needed a breakthrough win in Wisconsin, and failed to get it. Democrats Morris Udall in 1976, Jerry Brown in 1980, Jesse Jackson in 1988, and Dean in 2004, as well as Republican John Anderson in 1980, all made Wisconsin either the cornerstone of their campaigns or viewed it as a major target of opportunity. Yet all five lost the Wisconsin primary.

It would be closer to the mark to say that Wisconsin has a soft spot for outsiders. George Wallace bolted onto the national scene in 1964 by taking one-third of the Democratic primary vote in Wisconsin after campaigning against the pending civil rights bill. Jimmy Carter's dark-horse candidacy also was pushed along by a Wisconsin victory in 1976 (over Udall). Gary Hart edged Walter Mondale in the 1984 Democratic primary (a nonbinding vote that year by national party fiat). And Brown nearly beat Bill Clinton in the state in 1992.

Brown had focused on Wisconsin early, knowing its terrain and proclivities well from his 1980 run. He carried a swath of counties on the eastern side of the state, from Racine through the Milwaukee suburbs north to Brown County (Green Bay). But Brown was hurt badly by his inability to win decisively in Dane County. McCarthy, McGovern, and Udall had all carried Dane by more than 20,000 votes; Brown won it by barely 2,000.

That enabled Clinton to win with a coalition of city and countryside. He carried Milwaukee County, source of nearly one-quarter of the Democratic primary vote, and swept the vast majority of counties in rural Wisconsin.

Clinton's winning 37 percent share of the primary vote was more than double the total that his fellow Southerner, Al Gore, had drawn in Wisconsin four years earlier. Looking for a post-Super Tuesday toehold in the Frost Belt, Gore came to Wisconsin calling for higher dairy price supports. He finished third statewide, although he did leapfrog Jesse Jackson for second place in a number of rural counties.

Wisconsin's Democratic primary is usually where the action has been over the years. Only three times since 1956—in 1980, 1996, and 2000—have more votes been cast on the Republican side of the ballot.

In 2000, both party's nominations had been settled weeks before Wisconsin voted, although the residue of the lively Republican contest between George W. Bush and John McCain still attracted voters to the polls.

In 1996, there was no contest in the Democratic primary. Pat Buchanan took advantage of the situation to win his second-highest vote share of the primary season (33.8 percent—just one-tenth of a percentage point behind his showing the same day in Michigan). But Buchanan could carry only one small county in Wisconsin, and was unable to crack 40 percent of the vote in any of the more populous ones.

The more compelling Republican primary was in 1980. Stakes were high for John Anderson, who had lost the primary in his home state of Illinois two weeks earlier. But Ronald Reagan won the Wisconsin vote comfortably, giving Anderson a final nudge out of the GOP race and reducing George Bush's already slim prospects for the Republican nomination that year.

Bush ran virtually even with Reagan in the Milwaukee area and in prosperous Republican farm country in the south-central part of Wisconsin. But Reagan won almost everywhere else, including most of the smaller industrial centers. Anderson carried only three counties, all containing a branch of the University of Wisconsin.

WISCONSIN DEMOCRATIC PRIMARY

2000

County	Total Vote	Bradley	Gore	Other	Winner	Percentage of Total Vote		
						Bradley	Gore	Other
ADAMS	1,481	84	1,368	29	Gore	5.7%	92.4%	2.0%
ASHLAND	1,103	104	966	33	Gore	9.4%	87.6%	3.0%
BARRON	2,741	226	2,455	60	Gore	8.2%	89.6%	2.2%
BAYFIELD	1,340	155	1,131	54	Gore	11.6%	84.4%	4.0%
BROWN	15,816	891	14,671	254	Gore	5.6%	92.8%	1.6%
BUFFALO	760	54	678	28	Gore	7.1%	89.2%	3.7%
BURNETT	1,053	102	923	28	Gore	9.7%	87.7%	2.7%
CALUMET	2,178	177	1,959	42	Gore	8.1%	89.9%	1.9%
CHIPPEWA	4,042	257	3,677	108	Gore	6.4%	91.0%	2.7%
CLARK	2,730	164	2,505	61	Gore	6.0%	91.8%	2.2%
COLUMBIA	2,755	217	2,473	65	Gore	7.9%	89.8%	2.4%
CRAWFORD	1,384	106	1,238	40	Gore	7.7%	89.5%	2.9%
DANE	38,452	5,938	30,971	1,543	Gore	15.4%	80.5%	4.0%
DODGE	3,738	287	3,353	98	Gore	7.7%	89.7%	2.6%
DOOR	3,167	280	2,794	93	Gore	8.8%	88.2%	2.9%
DOUGLAS	4,049	343	3,620	86	Gore	8.5%	89.4%	2.1%
DUNN	2,535	242	2,237	56	Gore	9.5%	88.2%	2.2%
EAU CLAIRE	6,923	495	6,259	169	Gore	7.2%	90.4%	2.4%
FLORENCE	191	17	169	5	Gore	8.9%	88.5%	2.6%
FOND DU LAC	4,746	376	4,257	113	Gore	7.9%	89.7%	2.4%
FOREST	656	36	607	13	Gore	5.5%	92.5%	2.0%
GRANT	2,769	279	2,436	54	Gore	10.1%	88.0%	2.0%
GREEN	1,612	116	1,468	28	Gore	7.2%	91.1%	1.7%
GREEN LAKE	787	63	703	21	Gore	8.0%	89.3%	2.7%
IOWA	1,711	143	1,517	51	Gore	8.4%	88.7%	3.0%
IRON	884	77	774	33	Gore	8.7%	87.6%	3.7%
JACKSON	1,492	95	1,354	43	Gore	6.4%	90.8%	2.9%
JEFFERSON	4,170	365	3,676	129	Gore	8.8%	88.2%	3.1%
JUNEAU	1,643	96	1,504	43	Gore	5.8%	91.5%	2.6%
KENOSHA	7,490	605	6,676	209	Gore	8.1%	89.1%	2.8%
KEWAUNEE	2,168	98	2,031	39	Gore	4.5%	93.7%	1.8%
LA CROSSE	5,440	462	4,844	134	Gore	8.5%	89.0%	2.5%
LAFAYETTE	1,553	113	1,408	32	Gore	7.3%	90.7%	2.1%
LANGLADE	1,247	104	1,116	27	Gore	8.3%	89.5%	2.2%
LINCOLN	3,220	216	2,932	72	Gore	6.7%	91.1%	2.2%
MANITOWOC	6,496	415	5,919	162	Gore	6.4%	91.1%	2.5%
MARATHON	8,505	594	7,729	182	Gore	7.0%	90.9%	2.1%
MARINETTE	2,111	110	1,954	47	Gore	5.2%	92.6%	2.2%
MARQUETTE	820	58	744	18	Gore	7.1%	90.7%	2.2%
MENOMINEE	147	9	135	3	Gore	6.1%	91.8%	2.0%
MILWAUKEE	92,124	7,784	81,967	2,373	Gore	8.4%	89.0%	2.6%
MONROE	2,616	177	2,380	59	Gore	6.8%	91.0%	2.3%
OCONTO	2,922	135	2,741	46	Gore	4.6%	93.8%	1.6%
ONEIDA	3,106	253	2,773	80	Gore	8.1%	89.3%	2.6%
OUTAGAMIE	8,155	654	7,347	154	Gore	8.0%	90.1%	1.9%

WISCONSIN DEMOCRATIC PRIMARY

2000

County	Total Vote	Bradley	Gore	Other	Winner	Percentage of Total Vote		
						Bradley	Gore	Other
OZAUKEE	3,942	407	3,416	119	Gore	10.3%	86.7%	3.0%
PEPIN	612	44	549	19	Gore	7.2%	89.7%	3.1%
PIERCE	2,245	245	1,937	63	Gore	10.9%	86.3%	2.8%
POLK	2,055	231	1,748	76	Gore	11.2%	85.1%	3.7%
PORTAGE	4,626	376	4,131	119	Gore	8.1%	89.3%	2.6%
PRICE	1,693	135	1,516	42	Gore	8.0%	89.5%	2.5%
RACINE	11,568	915	10,342	311	Gore	7.9%	89.4%	2.7%
RICHLAND	1,168	68	1,076	24	Gore	5.8%	92.1%	2.1%
ROCK	8,869	721	7,922	226	Gore	8.1%	89.3%	2.5%
RUSK	1,041	82	927	32	Gore	7.9%	89.0%	3.1%
ST. CROIX	2,613	242	2,291	80	Gore	9.3%	87.7%	3.1%
SAUK	3,655	314	3,246	95	Gore	8.6%	88.8%	2.6%
SAWYER	1,044	85	910	49	Gore	8.1%	87.2%	4.7%
SHAWANO	1,951	110	1,793	48	Gore	5.6%	91.9%	2.5%
SHEBOYGAN	6,933	534	6,281	118	Gore	7.7%	90.6%	1.7%
TAYLOR	1,212	86	1,098	28	Gore	7.1%	90.6%	2.3%
TREMPEALEAU	1,877	118	1,696	63	Gore	6.3%	90.4%	3.4%
VERNON	2,074	126	1,879	69	Gore	6.1%	90.6%	3.3%
VILAS	1,608	154	1,394	60	Gore	9.6%	86.7%	3.7%
WALWORTH	4,632	408	4,079	145	Gore	8.8%	88.1%	3.1%
WASHBURN	1,171	105	1,014	52	Gore	9.0%	86.6%	4.4%
WASHINGTON	4,680	460	4,044	176	Gore	9.8%	86.4%	3.8%
WAUKESHA	17,266	1,683	15,086	497	Gore	9.7%	87.4%	2.9%
WAUPACA	3,485	241	3,167	77	Gore	6.9%	90.9%	2.2%
WAUSHARA	1,022	73	908	41	Gore	7.1%	88.8%	4.0%
WINNEBAGO	7,546	637	6,705	204	Gore	8.4%	88.9%	2.7%
WOOD	5,580	388	5,088	104	Gore	7.0%	91.2%	1.9%
TOTAL	371,196	32,560	328,682	9,954	Gore	8.8%	88.5%	2.7%

Note: Other vote was 4,105 Uninstructed Delegation; 3,743 Lyndon H. LaRouche Jr.; 2,106 write-in.

WISCONSIN REPUBLICAN PRIMARY

2000

County	Total Vote	G.W. Bush	Keyes	McCain	Other	Winner	Percentage of Total Vote			
							G.W. Bush	Keyes	McCain	Other
ADAMS	1,827	1,167	130	468	62	G.W. Bush	63.9%	7.1%	25.6%	3.4%
ASHLAND	1,041	693	67	237	44	G.W. Bush	66.6%	6.4%	22.8%	4.2%
BARRON	3,527	2,461	297	675	94	G.W. Bush	69.8%	8.4%	19.1%	2.7%
BAYFIELD	1,328	843	87	317	81	G.W. Bush	63.5%	6.6%	23.9%	6.1%
BROWN	23,539	16,843	2,663	3,590	443	G.W. Bush	71.6%	11.3%	15.3%	1.9%
BUFFALO	1,004	710	57	205	32	G.W. Bush	70.7%	5.7%	20.4%	3.2%
BURNETT	1,393	951	114	277	51	G.W. Bush	68.3%	8.2%	19.9%	3.7%
CALUMET	3,882	2,662	429	686	105	G.W. Bush	68.6%	11.1%	17.7%	2.7%
CHIPPEWA	5,375	3,582	613	1,018	162	G.W. Bush	66.6%	11.4%	18.9%	3.0%
CLARK	4,077	2,912	303	720	142	G.W. Bush	71.4%	7.4%	17.7%	3.5%
COLUMBIA	4,011	2,828	288	798	97	G.W. Bush	70.5%	7.2%	19.9%	2.4%
CRAWFORD	1,637	968	317	282	70	G.W. Bush	59.1%	19.4%	17.2%	4.3%
DANE	32,867	19,722	2,292	9,909	944	G.W. Bush	60.0%	7.0%	30.1%	2.9%
DODGE	7,191	5,392	595	1,003	201	G.W. Bush	75.0%	8.3%	13.9%	2.8%
DOOR	4,908	3,396	431	905	176	G.W. Bush	69.2%	8.8%	18.4%	3.6%
DOUGLAS	3,045	1,964	271	668	142	G.W. Bush	64.5%	8.9%	21.9%	4.7%
DUNN	3,009	1,995	309	609	96	G.W. Bush	66.3%	10.3%	20.2%	3.2%
EAU CLAIRE	8,360	5,534	1,033	1,594	199	G.W. Bush	66.2%	12.4%	19.1%	2.4%
FLORENCE	462	332	31	89	10	G.W. Bush	71.9%	6.7%	19.3%	2.2%
FOND DU LAC	9,584	7,024	811	1,517	232	G.W. Bush	73.3%	8.5%	15.8%	2.4%
FOREST	1,033	770	53	191	19	G.W. Bush	74.5%	5.1%	18.5%	1.8%
GRANT	3,669	2,478	363	607	221	G.W. Bush	67.5%	9.9%	16.5%	6.0%
GREEN	2,235	1,590	134	447	64	G.W. Bush	71.1%	6.0%	20.0%	2.9%
GREEN LAKE	1,701	1,204	124	332	41	G.W. Bush	70.8%	7.3%	19.5%	2.4%
IOWA	1,948	1,344	126	406	72	G.W. Bush	69.0%	6.5%	20.8%	3.7%
IRON	961	706	44	184	27	G.W. Bush	73.5%	4.6%	19.1%	2.8%
JACKSON	1,729	1,170	148	356	55	G.W. Bush	67.7%	8.6%	20.6%	3.2%
JEFFERSON	7,167	5,210	574	1,204	179	G.W. Bush	72.7%	8.0%	16.8%	2.5%
JUNEAU	2,612	1,697	332	501	82	G.W. Bush	65.0%	12.7%	19.2%	3.1%
KENOSHA	8,624	5,675	1,042	1,635	272	G.W. Bush	65.8%	12.1%	19.0%	3.2%
KEWAUNEE	2,599	1,852	271	412	64	G.W. Bush	71.3%	10.4%	15.9%	2.5%
LA CROSSE	7,272	4,569	990	1,492	221	G.W. Bush	62.8%	13.6%	20.5%	3.0%
LAFAYETTE	1,845	1,360	102	292	91	G.W. Bush	73.7%	5.5%	15.8%	4.9%
LANGLADE	1,688	1,187	134	310	57	G.W. Bush	70.3%	7.9%	18.4%	3.4%
LINCOLN	3,762	2,688	197	766	111	G.W. Bush	71.5%	5.2%	20.4%	3.0%
MANITOWOC	8,169	5,791	730	1,383	265	G.W. Bush	70.9%	8.9%	16.9%	3.2%
MARATHON	10,527	7,595	867	1,745	320	G.W. Bush	72.1%	8.2%	16.6%	3.0%
MARINETTE	3,526	2,461	405	581	79	G.W. Bush	69.8%	11.5%	16.5%	2.2%
MARQUETTE	1,322	919	101	269	33	G.W. Bush	69.5%	7.6%	20.3%	2.5%
MENOMINEE	88	64	10	12	2	G.W. Bush	72.7%	11.4%	13.6%	2.3%
MILWAUKEE	83,142	57,701	9,171	13,928	2,342	G.W. Bush	69.4%	11.0%	16.8%	2.8%
MONROE	3,891	2,469	481	823	118	G.W. Bush	63.5%	12.4%	21.2%	3.0%
OCONTO	4,013	3,040	304	567	102	G.W. Bush	75.8%	7.6%	14.1%	2.5%
ONEIDA	4,221	2,905	252	934	130	G.W. Bush	68.8%	6.0%	22.1%	3.1%
OUTAGAMIE	14,338	9,013	2,120	2,819	386	G.W. Bush	62.9%	14.8%	19.7%	2.7%

WISCONSIN REPUBLICAN PRIMARY

2000

County	Total Vote	G.W. Bush	Keyes	McCain	Other	Winner	Percentage of Total Vote			
							G.W. Bush	Keyes	McCain	Other
OZAUKEE	11,514	8,733	896	1,647	238	G.W. Bush	75.8%	7.8%	14.3%	2.1%
PEPIN	689	443	68	146	32	G.W. Bush	64.3%	9.9%	21.2%	4.6%
PIERCE	2,439	1,571	224	532	112	G.W. Bush	64.4%	9.2%	21.8%	4.6%
POLK	2,471	1,613	236	497	125	G.W. Bush	65.3%	9.6%	20.1%	5.1%
PORTAGE	4,279	2,644	524	976	135	G.W. Bush	61.8%	12.2%	22.8%	3.2%
PRICE	2,280	1,507	186	482	105	G.W. Bush	66.1%	8.2%	21.1%	4.6%
RACINE	16,563	11,918	1,883	2,335	427	G.W. Bush	72.0%	11.4%	14.1%	2.6%
RICHLAND	1,786	1,008	462	266	50	G.W. Bush	56.4%	25.9%	14.9%	2.8%
ROCK	10,207	6,778	842	2,264	323	G.W. Bush	66.4%	8.2%	22.2%	3.2%
RUSK	1,499	942	199	313	45	G.W. Bush	62.8%	13.3%	20.9%	3.0%
ST. CROIX	3,477	2,126	501	708	142	G.W. Bush	61.1%	14.4%	20.4%	4.1%
SAUK	4,877	3,384	352	1,003	138	G.W. Bush	69.4%	7.2%	20.6%	2.8%
SAWYER	1,686	1,138	127	371	50	G.W. Bush	67.5%	7.5%	22.0%	3.0%
SHAWANO	3,797	2,732	360	602	103	G.W. Bush	72.0%	9.5%	15.9%	2.7%
SHEBOYGAN	11,600	8,493	1,109	1,734	264	G.W. Bush	73.2%	9.6%	14.9%	2.3%
TAYLOR	2,035	1,482	163	343	47	G.W. Bush	72.8%	8.0%	16.9%	2.3%
TREMPEALEAU	2,008	1,282	223	433	70	G.W. Bush	63.8%	11.1%	21.6%	3.5%
VERNON	2,650	1,580	441	540	89	G.W. Bush	59.6%	16.6%	20.4%	3.4%
VILAS	3,234	2,186	209	735	104	G.W. Bush	67.6%	6.5%	22.7%	3.2%
WALWORTH	9,296	6,696	744	1,573	283	G.W. Bush	72.0%	8.0%	16.9%	3.0%
WASHBURN	1,598	1,123	96	323	56	G.W. Bush	70.3%	6.0%	20.2%	3.5%
WASHINGTON	12,893	9,757	1,209	1,599	328	G.W. Bush	75.7%	9.4%	12.4%	2.5%
WAUKESHA	46,854	35,527	4,530	5,825	972	G.W. Bush	75.8%	9.7%	12.4%	2.1%
WAUPACA	7,182	5,129	656	1,202	195	G.W. Bush	71.4%	9.1%	16.7%	2.7%
WAUSHARA	2,081	1,456	186	376	63	G.W. Bush	70.0%	8.9%	18.1%	3.0%
WINNEBAGO	14,097	9,095	1,586	3,007	409	G.W. Bush	64.5%	11.3%	21.3%	2.9%
WOOD	8,528	5,512	694	2,089	233	G.W. Bush	64.6%	8.1%	24.5%	2.7%
TOTAL	495,769	343,292	48,919	89,684	13,874	G.W. Bush	69.2%	9.9%	18.1%	2.8%

Note: Other vote was 5,505 Steve Forbes; 3,452 Uninstructed Delegation; 1,813 Gary Bauer; 1,712 Orrin G. Hatch; 1,392 write-in.

WISCONSIN DEMOCRATIC PRIMARY

2004

County	Total Vote	Dean	Edwards	Kerry	Other	Winner	Percentage of Total Vote			
							Dean	Edwards	Kerry	Other
ADAMS	2,994	354	1,089	1,392	159	Kerry	11.8%	36.4%	46.5%	5.3%
ASHLAND	2,400	368	424	1,254	354	Kerry	15.3%	17.7%	52.3%	14.8%
BARRON	4,067	577	1,162	2,061	267	Kerry	14.2%	28.6%	50.7%	6.6%
BAYFIELD	2,869	512	562	1,421	374	Kerry	17.8%	19.6%	49.5%	13.0%
BROWN	26,542	4,742	9,490	10,501	1,809	Kerry	17.9%	35.8%	39.6%	6.8%
BUFFALO	1,518	276	483	674	85	Kerry	18.2%	31.8%	44.4%	5.6%
BURNETT	1,845	328	413	1,011	93	Kerry	17.8%	22.4%	54.8%	5.0%
CALUMET	4,811	747	1,902	1,873	289	Edwards	15.5%	39.5%	38.9%	6.0%
CHIPPEWA	6,134	1,000	2,542	2,276	316	Edwards	16.3%	41.4%	37.1%	5.2%
CLARK	3,713	648	1,420	1,420	225		17.5%	38.2%	38.2%	6.1%
COLUMBIA	8,060	1,325	3,011	3,206	518	Kerry	16.4%	37.4%	39.8%	6.4%
CRAWFORD	2,600	332	780	1,264	224	Kerry	12.8%	30.0%	48.6%	8.6%
DANE	125,363	25,978	41,560	45,777	12,048	Kerry	20.7%	33.2%	36.5%	9.6%
DODGE	8,824	1,561	3,366	3,368	529	Kerry	17.7%	38.1%	38.2%	6.0%
DOOR	4,808	767	1,611	2,016	414	Kerry	16.0%	33.5%	41.9%	8.6%
DOUGLAS	5,830	1,484	890	3,089	367	Kerry	25.5%	15.3%	53.0%	6.3%
DUNN	4,106	842	1,148	1,754	362	Kerry	20.5%	28.0%	42.7%	8.8%
EAU CLAIRE	13,197	2,718	4,474	5,082	923	Kerry	20.6%	33.9%	38.5%	7.0%
FLORENCE	366	43	91	212	20	Kerry	11.7%	24.9%	57.9%	5.5%
FOND DU LAC	9,949	1,669	4,055	3,678	547	Edwards	16.8%	40.8%	37.0%	5.5%
FOREST	1,052	118	373	514	47	Kerry	11.2%	35.5%	48.9%	4.5%
GRANT	5,396	742	1,829	2,549	276	Kerry	13.8%	33.9%	47.2%	5.1%
GREEN	4,130	628	1,627	1,634	241	Kerry	15.2%	39.4%	39.6%	5.8%
GREEN LAKE	1,826	246	732	699	149	Edwards	13.5%	40.1%	38.3%	8.2%
IOWA	3,489	536	1,230	1,464	259	Kerry	15.4%	35.3%	42.0%	7.4%
IRON	1,027	134	243	587	63	Kerry	13.0%	23.7%	57.2%	6.1%
JACKSON	3,374	506	1,262	1,406	200	Kerry	15.0%	37.4%	41.7%	5.9%
JEFFERSON	8,997	1,597	3,572	3,244	584	Edwards	17.8%	39.7%	36.1%	6.5%
JUNEAU	2,955	396	1,063	1,329	167	Kerry	13.4%	36.0%	45.0%	5.7%
KENOSHA	17,783	3,217	5,655	7,701	1,210	Kerry	18.1%	31.8%	43.3%	6.8%
KEWAUNEE	2,521	445	1,003	920	153	Edwards	17.7%	39.8%	36.5%	6.1%
LA CROSSE	14,554	2,477	5,792	5,007	1,278	Edwards	17.0%	39.8%	34.4%	8.8%
LAFAYETTE	2,114	297	787	920	110	Kerry	14.0%	37.2%	43.5%	5.2%
LANGLADE	2,457	399	800	1,113	145	Kerry	16.2%	32.6%	45.3%	5.9%
LINCOLN	4,761	814	1,583	2,094	270	Kerry	17.1%	33.2%	44.0%	5.7%
MANITOWOC	13,420	2,175	5,133	5,298	814	Kerry	16.2%	38.2%	39.5%	6.1%
MARATHON	17,195	3,694	5,529	7,113	859	Kerry	21.5%	32.2%	41.4%	5.0%
MARINETTE	4,327	592	1,499	2,020	216	Kerry	13.7%	34.6%	46.7%	5.0%
MARQUETTE	2,015	310	711	896	98	Kerry	15.4%	35.3%	44.5%	4.9%
MENOMINEE	303	42	55	188	18	Kerry	13.9%	18.2%	62.0%	5.9%
MILWAUKEE	189,135	34,016	58,384	76,901	19,834	Kerry	18.0%	30.9%	40.7%	10.5%
MONROE	3,937	636	1,551	1,514	236	Edwards	16.2%	39.4%	38.5%	6.0%
OCONTO	4,022	607	1,457	1,718	240	Kerry	15.1%	36.2%	42.7%	6.0%
ONEIDA	5,118	714	1,778	2,315	311	Kerry	14.0%	34.7%	45.2%	6.1%
OUTAGAMIE	19,022	2,985	7,240	7,648	1,149	Kerry	15.7%	38.1%	40.2%	6.0%

WISCONSIN DEMOCRATIC PRIMARY

2004

County	Total Vote	Dean	Edwards	Kerry	Other	Winner	Percentage of Total Vote			
							Dean	Edwards	Kerry	Other
OZAUKEE	11,752	2,415	4,593	4,000	744	Edwards	20.5%	39.1%	34.0%	6.3%
PEPIN	825	152	237	384	52	Kerry	18.4%	28.7%	46.5%	6.3%
PIERCE	3,687	696	852	1,875	264	Kerry	18.9%	23.1%	50.9%	7.2%
POLK	3,611	543	839	2,019	210	Kerry	15.0%	23.2%	55.9%	5.8%
PORTAGE	10,935	2,657	3,139	4,374	765	Kerry	24.3%	28.7%	40.0%	7.0%
PRICE	2,214	330	699	1,056	129	Kerry	14.9%	31.6%	47.7%	5.8%
RACINE	27,248	5,187	9,708	10,338	2,015	Kerry	19.0%	35.6%	37.9%	7.4%
RICHLAND	2,406	335	872	1,027	172	Kerry	13.9%	36.2%	42.7%	7.1%
ROCK	24,600	3,421	9,235	10,552	1,392	Kerry	13.9%	37.5%	42.9%	5.7%
RUSK	2,170	352	759	877	182	Kerry	16.2%	35.0%	40.4%	8.4%
ST. CROIX	5,659	1,044	1,318	2,939	358	Kerry	18.4%	23.3%	51.9%	6.3%
SAUK	8,711	1,327	3,164	3,568	652	Kerry	15.2%	36.3%	41.0%	7.5%
SAWYER	2,128	290	632	1,006	200	Kerry	13.6%	29.7%	47.3%	9.4%
SHAWANO	4,107	630	1,494	1,718	265	Kerry	15.3%	36.4%	41.8%	6.5%
SHEBOYGAN	16,013	2,848	6,339	5,896	930	Edwards	17.8%	39.6%	36.8%	5.8%
TAYLOR	2,342	396	899	908	139	Kerry	16.9%	38.4%	38.8%	5.9%
TREMPEALEAU	3,358	462	1,206	1,461	229	Kerry	13.8%	35.9%	43.5%	6.8%
VERNON	3,730	522	1,354	1,463	391	Kerry	14.0%	36.3%	39.2%	10.5%
VILAS	5,565	933	1,873	2,379	380	Kerry	16.8%	33.7%	42.7%	6.8%
WALWORTH	8,756	1,614	3,113	3,422	607	Kerry	18.4%	35.6%	39.1%	6.9%
WASHBURN	2,249	342	587	1,168	152	Kerry	15.2%	26.1%	51.9%	6.8%
WASHINGTON	13,222	2,635	5,480	4,433	674	Edwards	19.9%	41.4%	33.5%	5.1%
WAUKESHA	51,286	10,645	21,409	16,270	2,962	Edwards	20.8%	41.7%	31.7%	5.8%
WAUPACA	5,111	797	1,790	2,175	349	Kerry	15.6%	35.0%	42.6%	6.8%
WAUSHARA	2,346	349	872	977	148	Kerry	14.9%	37.2%	41.6%	6.3%
WINNEBAGO	19,673	3,614	6,773	7,980	1,306	Kerry	18.4%	34.4%	40.6%	6.6%
WOOD	9,734	1,715	3,566	3,972	481	Kerry	17.6%	36.6%	40.8%	4.9%
TOTAL	828,364	150,845	284,163	328,358	64,998	Kerry	18.2%	34.3%	39.6%	7.8%

Note: Other vote was 27,353 Dennis J. Kucinich; 14,701 Al Sharpton; 12,713 Wesley Clark; 3,929 Joseph I. Lieberman; 1,637 Lyndon H. LaRouche Jr.; 1,590 Carol Moseley Braun; 1,263 Richard A. Gephardt; 1,146 Uninstructed Delegation; 666 write-in.

WISCONSIN REPUBLICAN PRIMARY

2004

County	Total Vote	G.W. Bush	Other	Winner	Percentage of Total Vote G.W. Bush	Other
ADAMS	535	530	5	G.W. Bush	99.1%	0.9%
ASHLAND	366	348	18	G.W. Bush	95.1%	4.9%
BARRON	582	576	6	G.W. Bush	99.0%	1.0%
BAYFIELD	364	361	3	G.W. Bush	99.2%	0.8%
BROWN	5,797	5,752	45	G.W. Bush	99.2%	0.8%
BUFFALO	212	208	4	G.W. Bush	98.1%	1.9%
BURNETT	599	593	6	G.W. Bush	99.0%	1.0%
CALUMET	991	983	8	G.W. Bush	99.2%	0.8%
CHIPPEWA	656	650	6	G.W. Bush	99.1%	0.9%
CLARK	527	520	7	G.W. Bush	98.7%	1.3%
COLUMBIA	1,563	1,552	11	G.W. Bush	99.3%	0.7%
CRAWFORD	418	411	7	G.W. Bush	98.3%	1.7%
DANE	19,395	19,179	216	G.W. Bush	98.9%	1.1%
DODGE	1,942	1,926	16	G.W. Bush	99.2%	0.8%
DOOR	1,342	1,333	9	G.W. Bush	99.3%	0.7%
DOUGLAS	429	422	7	G.W. Bush	98.4%	1.6%
DUNN	516	510	6	G.W. Bush	98.8%	1.2%
EAU CLAIRE	1,752	1,741	11	G.W. Bush	99.4%	0.6%
FLORENCE	92	90	2	G.W. Bush	97.8%	2.2%
FOND DU LAC	2,457	2,442	15	G.W. Bush	99.4%	0.6%
FOREST	190	190	0	G.W. Bush	100.0%	0.0%
GRANT	903	895	8	G.W. Bush	99.1%	0.9%
GREEN	476	474	2	G.W. Bush	99.6%	0.4%
GREEN LAKE	414	412	2	G.W. Bush	99.5%	0.5%
IOWA	460	455	5	G.W. Bush	98.9%	1.1%
IRON	226	220	6	G.W. Bush	97.3%	2.7%
JACKSON	633	628	5	G.W. Bush	99.2%	0.8%
JEFFERSON	1,611	1,595	16	G.W. Bush	99.0%	1.0%
JUNEAU	643	637	6	G.W. Bush	99.1%	0.9%
KENOSHA	3,223	3,185	38	G.W. Bush	98.8%	1.2%
KEWAUNEE	533	530	3	G.W. Bush	99.4%	0.6%
LA CROSSE	2,105	2,090	15	G.W. Bush	99.3%	0.7%
LAFAYETTE	356	353	3	G.W. Bush	99.2%	0.8%
LANGLADE	471	465	6	G.W. Bush	98.7%	1.3%
LINCOLN	1,162	1,156	6	G.W. Bush	99.5%	0.5%
MANITOWOC	2,825	2,799	26	G.W. Bush	99.1%	0.9%
MARATHON	3,622	3,583	39	G.W. Bush	98.9%	1.1%
MARINETTE	716	709	7	G.W. Bush	99.0%	1.0%
MARQUETTE	383	382	1	G.W. Bush	99.7%	0.3%
MENOMINEE	15	14	1	G.W. Bush	93.3%	6.7%
MILWAUKEE	35,519	35,206	313	G.W. Bush	99.1%	0.9%
MONROE	535	529	6	G.W. Bush	98.9%	1.1%
OCONTO	817	813	4	G.W. Bush	99.5%	0.5%
ONEIDA	774	757	17	G.W. Bush	97.8%	2.2%
OUTAGAMIE	4,239	4,205	34	G.W. Bush	99.2%	0.8%

WISCONSIN REPUBLICAN PRIMARY

2004

County	Total Vote	G.W. Bush	Other	Winner	Percentage of Total Vote	
					G.W. Bush	Other
OZAUKEE	2,553	2,531	22	G.W. Bush	99.1%	0.9%
PEPIN	150	149	1	G.W. Bush	99.3%	0.7%
PIERCE	753	743	10	G.W. Bush	98.7%	1.3%
POLK	656	644	12	G.W. Bush	98.2%	1.8%
PORTAGE	1,067	1,043	24	G.W. Bush	97.8%	2.2%
PRICE	342	339	3	G.W. Bush	99.1%	0.9%
RACINE	6,478	6,412	66	G.W. Bush	99.0%	1.0%
RICHLAND	434	422	12	G.W. Bush	97.2%	2.8%
ROCK	4,899	4,849	50	G.W. Bush	99.0%	1.0%
RUSK	330	323	7	G.W. Bush	97.9%	2.1%
ST. CROIX	1,448	1,436	12	G.W. Bush	99.2%	0.8%
SAUK	1,563	1,541	22	G.W. Bush	98.6%	1.4%
SAWYER	612	606	6	G.W. Bush	99.0%	1.0%
SHAWANO	1,035	1,023	12	G.W. Bush	98.8%	1.2%
SHEBOYGAN	3,337	3,330	7	G.W. Bush	99.8%	0.2%
TAYLOR	480	473	7	G.W. Bush	98.5%	1.5%
TREMPEALEAU	393	392	1	G.W. Bush	99.7%	0.3%
VERNON	565	561	4	G.W. Bush	99.3%	0.7%
VILAS	2,994	2,966	28	G.W. Bush	99.1%	0.9%
WALWORTH	1,874	1,849	25	G.W. Bush	98.7%	1.3%
WASHBURN	464	461	3	G.W. Bush	99.4%	0.6%
WASHINGTON	3,588	3,563	25	G.W. Bush	99.3%	0.7%
WAUKESHA	13,582	13,503	79	G.W. Bush	99.4%	0.6%
WAUPACA	1,342	1,329	13	G.W. Bush	99.0%	1.0%
WAUSHARA	486	481	5	G.W. Bush	99.0%	1.0%
WINNEBAGO	4,072	4,024	48	G.W. Bush	98.8%	1.2%
WOOD	1,545	1,531	14	G.W. Bush	99.1%	0.9%
TOTAL	160,428	158,933	1,495	G.W. Bush	99.1%	0.9%

Note: Other vote was 1,184 Uninstructed Delegation; 311 write-in.

WYOMING

Although presidential primaries are much in vogue in the rest of the country, they have not caught on in Wyoming. But in a sense, the traditional caucus fits the old-fashioned style of the state's politics. There is no major media market and Wyoming has been likened to one town "spread over miles and miles."

Neither party's caucuses draw more than several thousand voters statewide. But while GOP voters in the heavily Republican state can be found all over, Democrats have long been concentrated in the southern tier. More than a century ago, immigrant laborers came to southern Wyoming to build the Union Pacific rail line; the state's first coal miners followed. Like their counterparts in other states, most of these working men were drawn to the Democratic Party.

But the hearty band of Wyoming Democrats is hardly a liberal club. Democratic caucus-goers provided Bill Clinton with his first win outside the South in 1992 and gave Al Gore his initial victory anywhere in 1988. Four years earlier, Wyoming Democrats voted overwhelmingly for regional favorite son, Gary Hart of Colorado.

For a time, Wyoming's Democratic caucuses were held in early March on the eve of Super Tuesday. In 1988, the result was something of a split decision. Michael Dukakis ran ahead in the head count of caucus participants, but in the vote that mattered most—the election of delegates to the state convention—Al Gore won by a narrow margin. Gore thus gained a measure of momentum going into the Super Tuesday events, which would be the high-water mark of his candidacy that year.

In Wyoming two factors worked in Gore's favor. He was seen as a moderate Democrat, and he had the support of popular former Democratic governor Ed Herschler. Gore carried Natrona County (Casper), the second most populous in the state, as well as much of rural Wyoming.

Of late, Wyoming has been about as much of an afterthought in the nominating process as a state can be—a caucus state voting after the nominations had been settled. In 2000, the Democratic and Republican caucuses each drew less than 1,000 voters as did the Democratic caucuses in 2004 (according to unofficial tallies by the state parties).

Republicans in the Cowboy State are as conservative as their GOP brethren in other Rocky Mountain states, but they do not always move in lockstep with them.

In 1952, the Wyoming delegation divided evenly between Dwight Eisenhower and Robert Taft when most other states in the region were overwhelmingly for Taft. In 1976, though a majority of Wyoming's delegation was for Ronald Reagan, President Gerald Ford won more delegates in Wyoming than any other Rocky Mountain state.

Still, one thing has remained constant about Wyoming and that is its bit role in the presidential nominating process. The last time that Wyoming took center stage was at the 1960 Democratic convention. With John Kennedy on the verge of victory, Wyoming's divided delegation regrouped to vote as a bloc and dramatically put Kennedy over the top near the end of the first roll call.

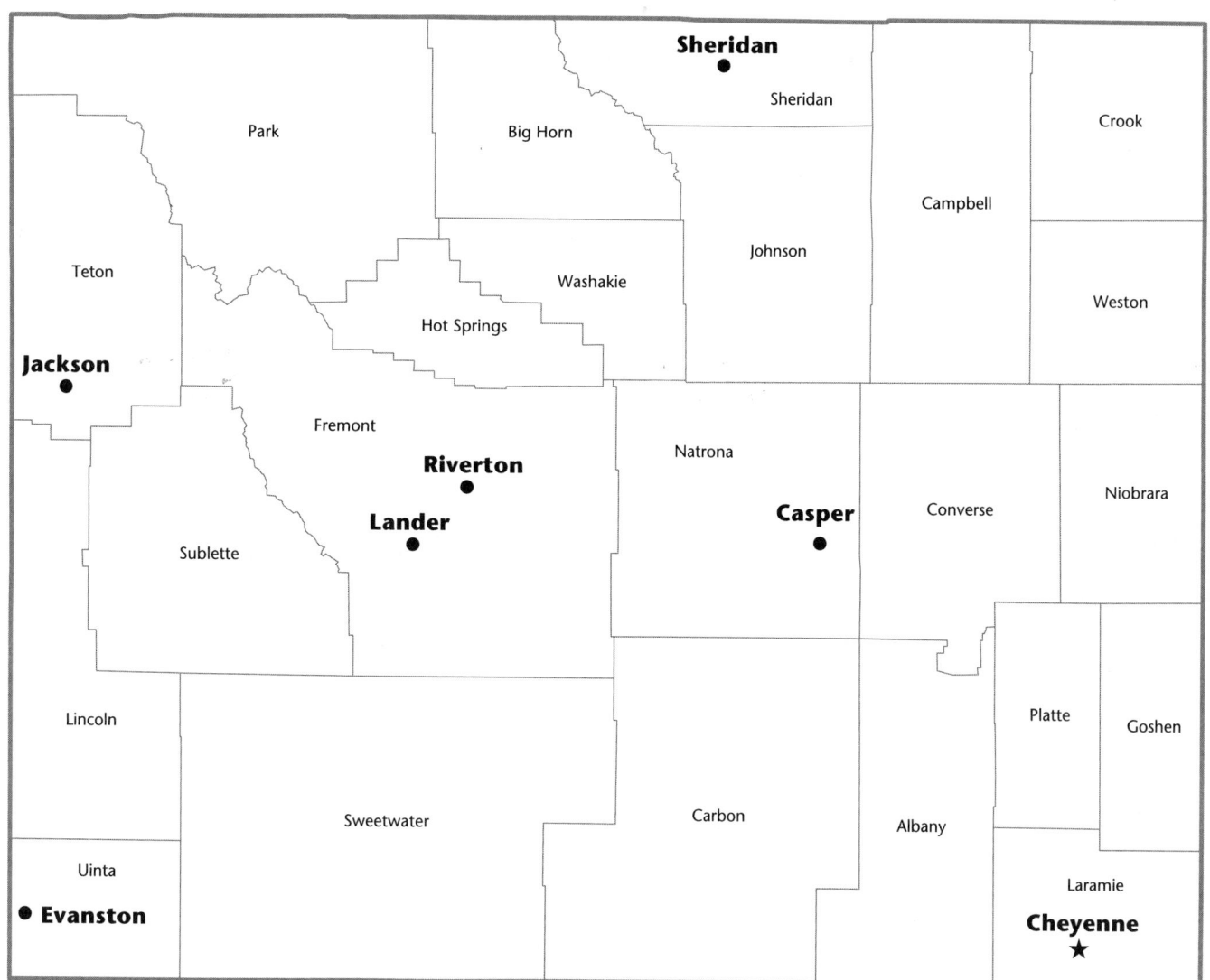

DISTRICT OF COLUMBIA

District of Columbia officials made a bold play for national attention in 2004, as they moved the city's presidential primary forward to a mid-January spot at the start of the primary calendar. But their hopes to make a big splash were not realized, as the Democratic National Committee refused to recognize the event and most major candidates avoided it in deference to the two "kingmakers," Iowa and New Hampshire.

The front-runner at the time, Howard Dean, made a modest effort and won the District primary with 43 percent of the votes cast. The two African-American candidates, Al Sharpton and Carol Moseley Braun, followed with 34 percent and 12 percent, respectively.

No delegates were at stake, though, in the primary. And the early vote did little to advance the District's protest of its lack of voting representation in Congress. Delegates were awarded to reflect the result of a separate low-profile caucus vote held in mid-February, an event that John Kerry won with 47 percent of the vote. Sharpton ran second in this "official" vote with 20 percent. Dean slipped to third place with 17 percent. However, the turnout of barely 9,000 District Democrats for the

Recent District of Columbia Primary Results

The District of Columbia held its first presidential primary in 1952.

	DEMOCRATS			REPUBLICANS		
Year	Turnout	Candidates	%	Turnout	Candidates	%
2004 (Jan. 13)	42,516	HOWARD DEAN	43	—	No Primary	
		Al Sharpton	34			
		Carol Moseley Braun	12			
		Dennis Kucinich	8			
2000 (May 2)	19,417	AL GORE	96	2,433	GEORGE W. BUSH	73
					John McCain	24
1996 (May 7)	20,959	BILL CLINTON*	98	2,987	BOB DOLE	76
					Uncommitted	13
					Pat Buchanan	9
1992 (May 5)	61,904	BILL CLINTON	74	5,235	GEORGE BUSH*	81
		Paul Tsongas	10		Pat Buchanan	19
		Uncommitted	9			
		Jerry Brown	7			
1988 (May 3)	86,052	JESSE JACKSON	80	6,720	GEORGE BUSH	88
		Michael Dukakis	18		Bob Dole	7
1984 (May 1)	102,731	JESSE JACKSON	67	5,692	RONALD REAGAN*	100
		Walter Mondale	26			
		Gary Hart	7			
1980 (May 6)	64,150	EDWARD KENNEDY	62	7,529	GEORGE BUSH	66
		Jimmy Carter*	37		John Anderson	27
1976 (May 4)	33,291	JIMMY CARTER	32	—	No Primary	
		Walter Fauntroy	30			
		Morris Udall	21			
		Walter Washington	16			
1972 (May 2)	29,560	WALTER FAUNTROY	72	—	No Primary	
		Uncommitted	28			
1968 (May 7)	92,114	ROBERT KENNEDY	62	13,430	NIXON-ROCKEFELLER	90
		Hubert Humphrey	35		Uncommitted	10

Note: All candidates are listed that drew at least 5 percent of their party's primary vote. The names of winning candidates are capitalized. An asterisk (*) indicates an incumbent president. The remainder of the vote in the 1968 Democratic primary was cast for an independent Humphrey slate. The 1968 Republican primary was won by a joint slate pledged to Richard Nixon and Nelson Rockefeller; they divided the delegates.

caucuses was a fraction of the more than 40,000 that had participated in the party's nonbinding presidential primary.

Voter interest in the city's presidential primary reached its apex in 1984, when Jesse Jackson made his first run for the Democratic presidential nomination. Turnout that year surpassed 100,000, with Jackson the choice of two-thirds of the voters. Although participation declined in 1988, he fared even better with those who turned out–winning 80 percent of the vote. In both 1984 and 1988, Jackson won all but affluent northwest Washington. Bill Clinton swept all the city's wards in the 1992 primary, but barely 60,000 Democrats voted.

Since 1968, victories in the District's Democratic presidential primary have often come in pairs. Jackson won twice. So did Clinton. Together, the Kennedy brothers also won a pair–

Robert in 1968, Edward in 1980; each with 62 percent of the District's primary vote.

The nation's capital is heavily black and overwhelmingly Democratic. District Republicans, by and large, are a very small and moderate lot. George Bush won the city's GOP primary in 1980, 1988, and 1992. Bob Dole won handily in 1996. John McCain drew nearly 25 percent of the vote in 2000, even though he had quit the race nearly two months earlier.

With few exceptions, conservative GOP candidates have either fared poorly or have not even tried to win delegates from the District. Ronald Reagan bypassed the Republican primary in both 1976 and 1980. And in spite of his roots in the Washington area, Pat Buchanan could not crack 20 percent in either of his runs for the GOP presidential nomination in the 1990s.